JUSTICE ADMINISTRATION

THE CRIMINAL

FELONIES

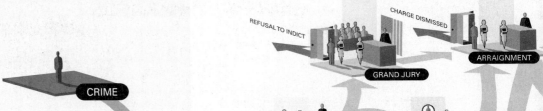

REFUSAL TO INDICT

CHARGE DISMISSED

GRAND JURY

ARRAIGNMENT

CRIME

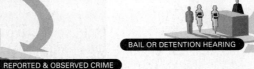

911

REPORTED & OBSERVED CRIME

BAIL OR DETENTION HEARING

REDUCTION OF CHARGE

INFORMATION

UNRESOLVED OR NOT ARRESTED

INVESTIGATION

CHARGES DROPPED OR DISMISSED

PRELIMINARY HEARING

MISDEMEANORS

CHARGES DISMISSED

ARRAIGNMENT

RELEASED WITHOUT PROSECUTION

ARREST

CHARGES DROPPED OR DISMISSED

INITIAL APPEARANCE

INFORMATION

RELEASED WITHOUT PROSECUTION

CHARGES FILED

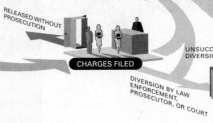

UNSUCCESSFUL DIVERSION

OUT OF SYSTEM

DIVERSION BY LAW ENFORCEMENT, PROSECUTOR, OR COURT

JUSTICE SYSTEM

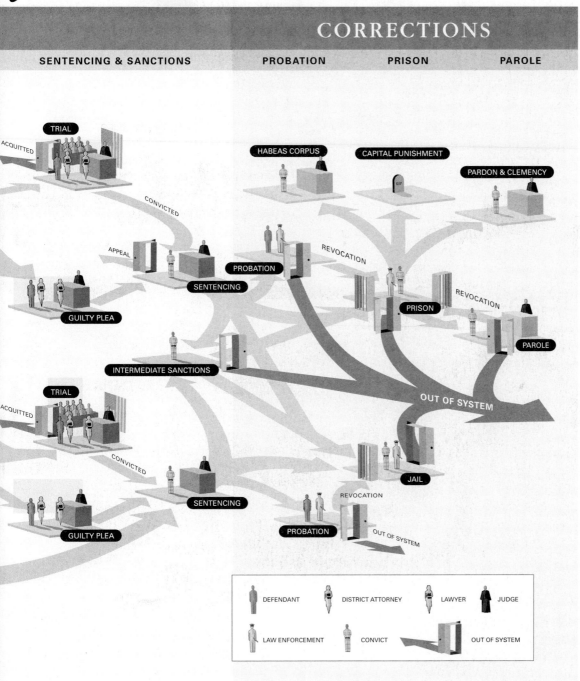

CORRECTIONS

| SENTENCING & SANCTIONS | PROBATION | PRISON | PAROLE |

TRIAL
ACQUITTED
CONVICTED
APPEAL

HABEAS CORPUS
CAPITAL PUNISHMENT
PARDON & CLEMENCY

GUILTY PLEA
PROBATION
SENTENCING
REVOCATION
PRISON
REVOCATION
PAROLE

INTERMEDIATE SANCTIONS
OUT OF SYSTEM

TRIAL
ACQUITTED
CONVICTED
SENTENCING
GUILTY PLEA

JAIL
REVOCATION
PROBATION
OUT OF SYSTEM

DEFENDANT   DISTRICT ATTORNEY   LAWYER   JUDGE

LAW ENFORCEMENT   CONVICT   OUT OF SYSTEM

Seventh Edition

Justice Administration
Police, Courts, and Corrections Management

Kenneth J. Peak
University of Nevada, Reno

Boston   Columbus   Indianapolis   New York   San Francisco   Upper Saddle River
Amsterdam   Cape Town   Dubai   London   Madrid   Milan   Munich   Paris   Montreal   Toronto
Delhi   Mexico City   São Paulo   Sydney   Hong Kong   Seoul   Singapore   Taipei   Tokyo

Vice President and Executive Publisher: Vernon Anthony
Senior Acquisitions Editor: Eric Krassow
Assistant Editor: Tiffany Bitzel
Editorial Assistant: Lynda Cramer
Media Project Manager: Karen Bretz
Director of Marketing: David Gesell
Marketing Manager: Cyndi Eller
Senior Marketing Coordinator: Alicia Wozniak
Production Manager: Holly Shufeldt
Creative Director: Jayne Conte
Cover Designer: Suzanne Behnke
Cover Illustration/Photo: Fotolia
Full-Service Project Management/Composition: Nitin Agarwal/Aptara®, Inc.
Printer/Binder: Courier

Credits and acknowledgments borrowed from other sources and reproduced, with permission, in this textbook appear on appropriate page within text.

Shutterstock, pp. 2, 19, 56, 103, 136, 175, 296, 386; Courtesy of Washoe County Sheriff's Office, pp. 77, 156, 231, 249; Dreamstime LLC -Royalty Free, pp. 200, 274, 356; Spencer Grant/ PhotoEdit Inc., p. 320.

Pearson Education Ltd.
Pearson Education Australia PTY, Ltd.
Pearson Education Singapore, Pte. Ltd.
Pearson Education North Asia Ltd.
Pearson Education, Canada, Ltd.
Pearson Educación de Mexico, S.A. de C.V.
Pearson Education–Japan
Pearson Education Malaysia, Pte. Ltd.

Library of Congress Cataloging-in-Publication Data

Peak, Kenneth J.,
    Justice administration / Kenneth J. Peak. — 7th ed.
        p. cm.
    Rev. ed. of: Justice administration : police, courts, and corrections
management. 6th ed.
    ISBN-13: 978-0-13-270899-9
    ISBN-10: 0-13-270899-X
    1.   Criminal justice, Administration of—United States.   2.   Law
enforcement—United States.   3.   Prison administration—United States.
I.   Title.
    HV9950.P43   2012
    364.973—dc23   2011031845

10 9 8 7 6 5 4 3 2 1

ISBN-10:   0-13-270899-X
ISBN-13: 978-0-13-270899-9

Dedication

"Novus ordo seclorum"

This Latin phrase—meaning "a new order for the ages"—is the motto inscribed below the pyramid on a US one-dollar bill. It was approved by the Congress in 1782 to signify "the beginning of the new American Era," which commenced in 1776.

In keeping with that theme, this seventh edition is dedicated to all criminal justice administrators, practitioners, academics, and students. May they always aspire to provide innovative and more efficacious means—novus ordo seclorum— toward achieving justice in our communities.

BRIEF CONTENTS

CONTENTS

NEW TOPICS IN THIS SEVENTH EDITION

In addition to the general updated information given throughout the book, as well as dozens of new examples of what criminal justice administrators are doing to address crime and to improve the administration of justice, following are other substantively new additions to this revised seventh edition:

Chapter 1:   "Learn by Doing" exercises

Chapter 2:   "Learn by Doing" exercises

Chapter 3:   The influence on COPPS of Harvard/NIJ Executive Sessions; "Learn by Doing" exercises

Chapter 4:   Innovative techniques for recruiting the best police officers; "good politics, bad politics"; using social networking sites for background checks; "Learn by Doing" exercises

Chapter 5:   Intelligence-led policing; predictive policing; fusion centers; police reorganization since 9/11; federalization and militarization of police; legal and psychological aspects of police uniforms and dress codes; "Learn by Doing" exercises (also, note that terrorism is included, being located in Chapter 6 in the previous edition)

Chapter 6:   An "insider's view" of a lower court; the legal culture of trial courts; "Learn by Doing" exercises

Chapter 7:   Judges' use of social networking sites; "Learn by Doing" exercises

Chapter 8:   The "CSI Effect"; courthouse shootings; veterans' courts; research concerning mental health courts; methods of disposing of cases in timely manner; "Learn by Doing" exercises

Chapter 9:   Supermax prisons and public safety; podular/direct supervision jails; roles of local jails in preparing inmates for reentry; jail administrators' functions; "Learn by Doing" exercises

Chapter 10: Managing corruption; jail administrators' duties; motivating and retaining personnel; "Learn by Doing" exercises

Chapter 11: Constitutionality of juveniles serving life-without-parole sentences; research concerning sexual and physical violence in prisons; outcomes of the Prison Rape Elimination Act of 2003; proliferation and inmate use of cell phones in prisons; evaluations of private prisons; offenders' perceptions of electronic monitoring/house arrest; benefits of day reporting centers; evaluations of intermediate sanctions; amendments to "three-strikes" laws; "Learn by Doing" exercises

Chapter 12: Ethics training for federal judges; "Learn by Doing" exercises

Chapter 13: First Amendment challenges concerning religious expression; religious expression and personal appearance (uniforms, beards); federal, state, and local Hatch Acts; amendments to the Family Medical Leave Act; sexual harassment of males; "Learn by Doing" exercises

Chapter 14: Recent political battles over collective bargaining; the labor-management relationship (or "navigating the waters of unionization"); "Learn by Doing" exercises

Chapter 15: Effects of the recent financial crisis on police, courts, and corrections agencies' operations; "Learn by Doing" exercises

Chapter 16: Developments with less-lethal technologies, license plate recognition systems, "smart cams" for predicting crimes; Interactive Crime Mapping on the Internet (ARJIS), strategic planning for technologies in courts, using Wi-Fi to enhance jury pools; use of heat waves to control jail inmates, and the use of GPS bracelets to track both adult and juvenile offenders; "Learn by Doing" exercises (CompStat moved to this chapter)

PREFACE

This seventh edition of *Justice Administration: Police, Courts, and Corrections Management* continues its examination of all facets of the criminal justice system as well as several related matters of interest to prospective and current administrators. The author has held several administrative and academic positions in a criminal justice career spanning more than 35 years; thus, this book's 16 chapters contain a palpable real-world flavor not found in most textbooks.

The author is particularly pleased with this edition's new "Learn by Doing" features, intended to further enhance the text's applied nature as well as the reader's practical application of information provided in the chapters. Beginning in the early 1900s, famed educator John Dewey promulgated the "learning by doing" approach to education or problem-based learning. This approach also comports with the popular learning method espoused by Benjamin Bloom in 1956, known as Bloom's Taxonomy, in which he called for "higher-order thinking skills"—critical and creative thinking that involves analysis, synthesis, and evaluation. These new chapter scenarios and activities place the reader in hypothetical situations, shifting attention away from textbook-centered instructions and moving the emphasis to student-centered projects. These activities also create opportunities to practice skills in communication and self-management, problem solving, and learning about and addressing current community issues. Hopefully, readers will be inspired to become engaged in some or all of these scenarios and activities.

In addition to the chapters concerning police, courts, and corrections administration, the book includes chapters on personnel and financial administration, rights of criminal justice employees, technologies, discipline and liability, and ethics. A practice continued in this edition is the listing of key terms and concepts and chapter learning objectives, which appear at the beginning of each chapter. At the end of each chapter is a list of related web sites and listservs.

Note that there are two appendices at the book's end. The first appendix includes a total of 28 case studies that apply to most of the book's chapters; they are listed by the number of chapter to which they apply. They allow the reader to experience some of the real-world problems confronted daily by justice administrators; with a fundamental knowledge of the system and a reading of the appropriate chapters, readers should be in a position to arrive at several feasible solutions to each problem that is presented. Appendix II provides some writings of three noted early philosophers: Confucius, Machiavelli, and Lao-Tzu.

Criminal justice is a people business. This book reflects that fact as it looks at human foibles and some of the problems of personnel and policy in justice administration. Thanks to many innovators in the field, a number of exciting and positive changes are occurring. The general goal of the book is to inform the reader of the primary people, practices, and terms that are utilized in justice administration.

I would also like to explain briefly why a future development's component is included in several chapters. Justice administration exists in a dynamic world where society and its problems and challenges are constantly evolving. As a result, our lives will be drastically altered as the world continues to change. Our choice is either to ignore the future until it is upon us or to try to anticipate what the future holds and gear our resources to cope with it. Not predicting the future would be akin to driving a car without looking out the windshield—and who can afford to drive into the twenty-first century with their eyes fixed firmly on the rear-view mirror? Criminal justice administrators must anticipate what the future holds so that they can bring appropriate resources and methods to bear on the problems ahead.

Finally, there may well be activities, policies, actions, and my own views with which the reader will disagree. This is not at all bad because in the management of people and agencies, there are few absolutes, only ideas and endeavors to make the system better. From the beginning to the end of the book, the reader is provided with a comprehensive and penetrating view of what is certainly one of the most difficult and challenging positions that one can occupy in the USA: the administration of a criminal justice agency. I solicit your input concerning any facet of this textbook; feel free to contact me if you have ideas for improving it.

SUPPLEMENTS

To access supplementary materials online, instructors need to request an instructor access code. Go to **www.pearsonhighered.com/irc**, where you can register for an instructor access code. Within 48 hours after registering, you will receive a confirming e-mail, including an instructor access code. Once you have received your code, go to the site and log on for full instructions on downloading the materials you wish to use.

ACKNOWLEDGMENTS

This edition, like its six predecessors, is the result of the professional assistance of several people. First, I continue to benefit by the guidance of the staff at Prentice Hall. This effort involved: Eric Krassow, Senior Acquisitions Editor, as well as Tiffany Bitzel, Assistant Editor. Copyediting was masterfully accomplished by Dr Anupam Raina and Ms Sudipti Walia. I also wish to acknowledge the invaluable assistance of William Kelly, Auburn University, whose reviews of this edition resulted in many beneficial additions and modifications.

Ken Peak
peak_k@unr.edu

ABOUT THE AUTHOR

Kenneth J. Peak is a full professor and former Chairman of the Department of Criminal Justice, University of Nevada, Reno, where he was named "Teacher of the Year" by the university's Honor Society. He has served as the Chairman of the Police Section of the Academy of Criminal Justice Sciences, as well as the President of the Western Association of Criminal Justice. He entered municipal policing in Kansas in 1970 and subsequently held positions as a nine-county criminal justice planner for southeast Kansas, Director of a four-state Technical Assistance Institute for the Law Enforcement Assistance Administration, Director of University Police at Pittsburg State University, and Assistant Professor of Criminal Justice at Wichita State University. He has authored or coauthored 24 textbooks and two historical books on bootlegging and temperance. His other recent books include *Policing America: Methods, Issues, Challenges*, 7th ed.; *Community Policing and Problem Solving: Strategies and Practices*, 6th ed. (with R. W. Glensor); *Police Supervision and Management*, 3rd ed. (with L. K. Gaines and R. W. Glensor); and *Women in Law Enforcement Careers* (with V. B. Lord). He has also published more than 60 monographs, journal articles, and invited chapters on a variety of policing topics. His teaching interests include policing, planned change, administration, victimology, and comparative justice systems. He holds a doctorate from the University of Kansas.

PART 1

Justice Administration
An Introduction

This part, consisting of two chapters, sets the stage for the later analysis of criminal justice agencies and their issues, problems, functions, and challenges in Parts II through V. Chapter 1 examines the scope of justice administration and why we study it. Chapter 2 discusses organization and administration in general, looking at both how organizations are managed and how people are motivated. The introductory section of each chapter previews the specific chapter content.

The Study and Scope of Justice Administration

KEY TERMS AND CONCEPTS

Administration

Conflict model

Consensus model

Criminal justice network

Criminal justice nonsystem

Criminal justice process

Due process

Force-field analysis

Manager

Planned change

Policymaking

Social contract

Supervisor

System fragmentation

LEARNING OBJECTIVES

After reading this chapter, the student will:

- learn the concepts of *administration*, *manager*, and *supervisor*
- understand and be able to distinguish among criminal justice process, network, and nonsystem
- understand system fragmentation and how it affects the amount and type of crime
- be familiar with consensus and conflict theorists and their theories
- understand the two goals of U.S. criminal justice system (CJS)
- be able to distinguish between extrinsic and intrinsic rewards and how they relate to the CJS

The true administration of justice is the firmest pillar of good government.
—Inscription on the New York State
Supreme Courthouse, Foley Square,
Manhattan, New York

Fiat justitia; ruat caelum
("Let justice be done, though heaven may fall.")
—A Maxim Meaning That Justice Must Be Achieved,
Regardless of Consequences; Author Unknown

WHY STUDY JUSTICE ADMINISTRATION?

The new millennium began by putting many corporate administrators on the defensive or in a negative (even criminal) light. The lengthening list of disgraced and prosecuted chief executive officers (CEOs) brought a crisis of corporate leadership that affected all executives, as the average citizens began paying attention to the litany of CEOs who failed in corporate governance and indicated their disgust through actions that dramatically affected the stock markets. Administration has never been easy, and in the face of this public outrage against executives in the private sector, criminal justice administrators in the public sector must wonder whether they, too, will be pressured to put stricter controls in place and to bring greater accountability to their own organizations.

Many of us may find it difficult when we are young to imagine ourselves assuming a leadership role in later life. As one person quipped, we may even have difficulty envisioning ourselves serving as captain of our neighborhood block watch program. The fact is, however, that the organizations increasingly seek people with a high level of education and experience as prospective administrators. The college experience, in addition to transmitting knowledge, is believed to make people more tolerant and secure and less susceptible to debilitating stress and anxiety than those who do not have this experience. We also assume that administration is a science that can be taught; it is not a talent that one must be born with. Unfortunately, however, administrative skills are often learnt through on-the-job training; many of us who have worked for a boss with inadequate administrative skills can attest to the inadequacy of this training.

Purpose of the Book and Key Terms

This book alone, as is true for any other single work on the subject of administration, cannot instantly transform the reader into a bona fide expert in organizational behavior and administrative techniques. It alone cannot prepare someone to accept the reins of administration, supervision, or leadership; formal education, training, and experience are also necessary for such undertakings.

Many good basic books about administration exist; they discuss general aspects of leadership, the use of power and authority, and a number of specialized subjects that are beyond the reach of this book. Instead, here I simply consider some of the major theories, aspects, and issues of administration, laying the foundation for the reader's future study and experience.

Many textbooks have been written about *police* administration; a few have addressed administering courts and corrections agencies. Even fewer have analyzed justice administration from a *systems* perspective, considering all of the components of the justice system and their administration, issues, and practices. This book takes that perspective. Furthermore, most books on administration are immersed in pure administrative theory and concepts; in this way, the *practical* criminal justice perspective is often lost on many college and university students. Conversely, many books dwell on minute concepts, thereby obscuring the administrative principles involved. This book, which necessarily delves into some theory and specialized subject matter, focuses on the practical aspects of justice administration.

Justice Administration is not written as a guidebook for a major sweeping reform of the U.S. justice system. Rather, its primary intent is to familiarize the reader with the methods and challenges of criminal justice administrators. It also challenges the reader, however, to consider what reform is desirable or even necessary and to be open-minded and visualize where changes might be implemented.

Although the terms *administration*, *manager*, and *supervisor* are often used synonymously, each is a unique concept that is related to the others. **Administration** encompasses both management and supervision; it is the process by which a group of people is organized and directed toward achieving the group's objective. The exact nature of the organization will vary among the different types and sizes of agencies, but the general principles and the form of administration are similar. Administration focuses on the overall organization, its mission, and its relationship with other organizations and groups external to it.

Managers, who are a part of administration, are most closely associated with the day-to-day operations of the various elements within the organization. **Supervisors** are involved in the direction of staff members in their daily activities, often on a one-to-one basis. Confusion may arise because a chief administrator may act in all three capacities. Perhaps the most useful and easiest description is to define top-level personnel as administrators, mid-level personnel as managers, and those who oversee the work as it is being done as supervisors.[1] In policing, for example, although we tend to think of the chief executive as the administrator, the bureau chiefs or commanders (e.g., captains and lieutenants) as managers, and the sergeants as supervisors, it is important to note that on occasion all three of these roles are required of one administrator; such may be the case when a critical situation occurs, such as a hostage or barricaded-subject incident, and a single person is responsible for all of these levels of decision making.

The terms *police* and *law enforcement* are generally used interchangeably. Many people in the police field believe, however, that the police do more than merely enforce laws; they prefer to use the term *police*.

Organization of the Book

To understand the challenges that administrators of justice organizations face, we first need to place justice administration within the big picture. Thus, in Part I, Justice Administration: An Introduction, I discuss the organization, administration, and general nature of the U.S. justice system; the state of our country with respect to crime and government control; and the evolution of justice administration in all of its three components: police, courts, and corrections.

Parts II, III, and IV, which discuss contemporary police, courts, and corrections administration, respectively, follow the same organization: The first chapter of each part deals with the *organization and operation* of the component, followed in the next chapter by an examination of the component's *personnel roles and functions*, and in the third chapter by a discussion of *issues and practices* (including future considerations).

Part V examines administrative problems and factors that influence the entire justice system, including the rights of criminal justice employees, financial administration, and technology for today and the future.

This initial chapter sets the stage for later discussions of the CJS and its administration. I first consider whether the justice system comprises a process, a network, a nonsystem, or a true system. A discussion of the legal and historical bases for justice and administration follows (an examination of what some great thinkers have said about governance in general is provided at the end of the book, in Appendix II). The differences between public- and private-sector administration are reviewed next, and the chapter concludes with a discussion of policymaking in justice administration. After completing this chapter, the reader will have a better grasp of the structure, purpose, and foundation of our CJS.

A TRUE *SYSTEM* OF JUSTICE?

What do justice administrators—police, courts, and corrections officials—actually *administer*? Do they provide leadership over a system that has succeeded in accomplishing its mission? Do individuals within the system work amiably and communicate well with one another? Do they all share the same goals? Do their efforts result in crime reduction? In short, do they compose a *system*? I now turn to these questions, taking a fundamental yet expansive view of justice administration.

The U.S. CJS attempts to decrease criminal behavior through a wide variety of uncoordinated and sometimes uncomplementary efforts. Each system component—police, courts, and corrections—has varying degrees of responsibility and discretion for dealing with crime. Each system component fails, however, to engage in any coordinated planning effort; hence, relations among and between these components are often characterized by friction, conflict, and deficient communication. Role conflicts also serve to ensure that planning and communication are stifled.

For example, one role of the police is to arrest suspected offenders. Police typically are not judged by the public on the quality (e.g., having probable cause) of arrests but on their number. Prosecutors often complain that police provide case reports of poor quality. Prosecutors, for their part, are partially judged by their success in obtaining convictions; a public defender or defense attorney is judged by success in getting suspected offenders' charges dropped. The courts are very independent in their operation, largely sentencing offenders as they see fit. Corrections agencies are torn between the philosophies of punishment and rehabilitation and, in the view of many, wind up performing neither function with a large degree of success. These agencies are further burdened with overcrowded conditions, high caseloads, and antiquated facilities.[2] Unfortunately, this situation has existed for several decades and continues today.

This criticism of the justice system or process—that it is fragmented and rife with role conflicts and other problems—is a common refrain. Following are several views of the CJS as it currently operates: the process, network, and nonsystem points of view. Following the discussion of those three points of view, I consider whether criminal justice truly represents a system.

A Criminal Justice Process?

What is readily seen in the foregoing discussion is that our CJS may not be a system at all. Given its current operation and fragmentation, it might be better described as a **criminal justice process**. As a process, it involves the decisions and actions taken by an institution, offender, victim, or society that influence the offender's movement into, through, or out of the justice system.[3] In its purest form, the criminal justice process occurs as shown in Figure 1.1. Note that the horizontal effects result from factors, such as the amount of crime, the number of prosecutions, and the type of court disposition affecting the population in correctional facilities and rehabilitative programs. Vertical effects represent the primary system steps or procedures.[4]

At one end of this process are the police, who understandably may view their primary role as getting lawbreakers off the street. At the other end of the process are the corrections officials, who may see their role as being primarily custodial in nature. Somewhere in between are the courts, which try to ensure a fair application of the law to each case coming to the bar.

As a process, the justice system cannot reduce crime by itself nor can any of the component parts afford to be insensitive to the needs and problems of the other parts. In criminal justice planning jargon, "You can't rock one end of the boat." In other words, every action has a reaction, especially in the justice process. If, say, a bond issue for funds to provide 10 percent more police officers on the streets is passed in a community, the additional arrests made by those added police personnel will have a decided impact on the courts and correction components. Obviously, although each component operates largely on its own, the actions and reactions of each with respect to crime will send ripples throughout the process.

Much of the failure to deal effectively with crime may be attributed to organizational and administrative fragmentation of the justice process. Fragmentation exists among the components of the process, within the individual components, among political jurisdictions, and among persons.

A Criminal Justice Network?

Other observers contend that U.S. justice systems constitute a **criminal justice network**.[5] According to Steven Cox and John Wade, the justice system functions much like a television or radio network whose stations share many programs but in which each station also presents programs that the network does not air on other stations. The network appears as a three-dimensional model in which the public, legislators, police, prosecutors, judges, and correctional officials interact with one another and with others who are outside the traditionally conceived CJS.[6]

Furthermore, the criminal justice network is said to be based on several key yet erroneous assumptions, including the following:

1. The components of the network cooperate and share similar goals.
2. The network operates according to a set of formal procedural rules to ensure uniform treatment of all persons, the outcome of which constitutes justice.
3. Each person accused of a crime receives due process and is presumed innocent until proven guilty.

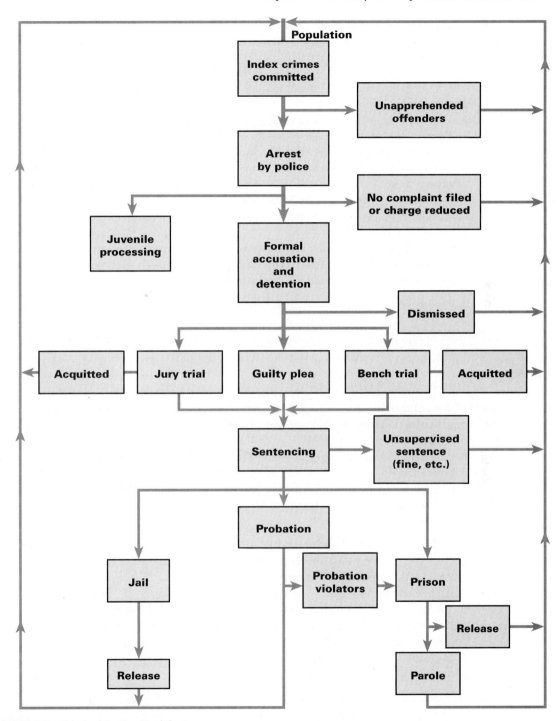

FIGURE 1.1 Criminal Justice Model

Source: Adapted from the President's Commission on Law Enforcement and Administration of Justice, *The Challenge of Crime in a Free Society* (Washington, DC: U.S. Government Printing Office, 1967), pp. 262–263.

4. Each person receives a speedy public trial before an impartial jury of his or her peers and is represented by competent legal counsel.[7]

Cox and Wade asserted that these key assumptions are erroneous for the following reasons:

1. The three components have incompatible goals and are continually competing with one another for budgetary dollars.
2. Evidence indicates that blacks and whites, male and female individuals, and middle-class and lower-class citizens receive differential treatment in the criminal justice network.
3. Some persons are prosecuted, some are not; some are involved in plea bargaining, others are not; some are convicted and sent to prison, whereas others convicted of the same type of offense are not. A great deal of the plea negotiation process remains largely invisible, such as "unofficial probation" with juveniles. In addition, Cox and Wade argued, considerable evidence points to the fact that criminal justice employees do not presume their clients or arrestees to be innocent.
4. Finally, these proponents of a network view of the justice process argued that the current backlog of cases does not ensure a speedy trial, even though a vast majority (at least 90 percent) of all arrestees plead guilty prior to trial.[8]

Adherents of this position, therefore, believe that our CJS is probably not a just network in the eyes of the poor, minority groups, or individual victims. Citizens, they also assert, may not know what to expect from such a network. Some believe that the system does not work as a network at all and that this conception is not worth their support.[9]

A Criminal Justice Nonsystem?

Many observers argue that the three components of the criminal justice system actually comprise a **criminal justice nonsystem**. They maintain that the three segments of the U.S. criminal justice system that deal with criminal behavior do not always function in harmony and that the system is neither efficient enough to create a credible fear of punishment nor fair enough to command respect for its values.

Indeed, these theorists are given considerable support by the President's Commission on Law Enforcement and the Administration of Justice (commonly known as the *Crime Commission*), which made the following comment:

> The system of criminal justice used in America to deal with those crimes it cannot prevent and those criminals it cannot deter is not a monolithic, or even a consistent, system. It was not designed or built in one piece at one time. Its philosophic core is that a person may be punished by the Government, if, and only if, it has been proven by an impartial and deliberate process that he has violated a specific law. Around that core, layer upon layer of institutions and procedures, some carefully constructed and some improvised, some inspired by principle and some by expediency, have accumulated. Parts of the system—magistrates, courts, trial by jury, bail—are of great antiquity. Other parts—juvenile courts, probation and parole, professional policemen—are relatively new. Every village, town, county, city, and State has its own criminal justice system, and there is a Federal one as well. All of them operate somewhat alike, no two of them operate precisely alike.[10]

Alfred Cohn and Roy Udolf stated that criminal justice "is not a system, and it has little to do with justice as that term is ordinarily understood."[11] Also, in this school of thought are

Burton Wright and Vernon Fox, who asserted that "the criminal justice system—is frequently criticized because it is not a coordinated structure—not really a system. In many ways this is true."[12]

These writers would probably agree that little has changed since 1971, when *Newsweek* stated in a special report entitled "Justice on Trial" that

> America's system of criminal justice is too swamped to deliver more than the roughest justice—and too ragged really to be called a system. "What we have," says one former government hand, "is a non-system in which the police don't catch criminals, the courts don't try them, and the prisons don't reform them. The system, in a word, is in trouble. The trouble has been neglect. The paralysis of the civil courts, where it takes five years to get a judgment in a damage suit—the courts—badly managed, woefully undermanned and so inundated with cases that they have to run fast just to stand still."[13]

Unfortunately, in many jurisdictions, those words still ring true. Too often, today's justice administrators cannot be innovators or reformers but rather simply "make do." As one law professor stated, "Oliver Wendell Holmes could not survive in our criminal court. How can you be an eminent jurist when you have to deal with this mess?"[14]

Those who hold that the justice system is in reality no system at all can also point to the fact that many practitioners in the field (police, judges, prosecutors, correctional workers, and private attorneys) and academicians concede that the entire justice system is in crisis, even rapidly approaching a major breakdown. They can cite problems everywhere—large numbers of police calls for service, overcrowded court dockets, and increasing prison populations. In short, they contend that the system is in a state of dysfunction, largely as a result of its fragmentation and lack of cohesion.[15]

System fragmentation is largely believed to directly affect the amount and type of crime that exists. Contributing to this fragmentation are the wide discretionary powers possessed by actors in the justice system. For example, police officers (primarily those having the least experience, education, and training) have great discretion over whom they arrest and are effectively able to dictate policy as they go about performing their duties. Here again, the Crime Commission was moved to comment as follows, realizing that how the police officer moves around his or her territory depends largely on this discretion:

> Crime does not look the same on the street as it does in a legislative chamber. How much noise or profanity makes conduct "disorderly" within the meaning of the law? When must a quarrel be treated as a criminal assault: at the first threat, or at the first shove, or at the first blow, or after blood is drawn, or when a serious injury is inflicted? How suspicious must conduct be before there is "probable cause," the constitutional basis for an arrest? Every [officer], however sketchy or incomplete his education, is an interpreter of the law.[16]

Judicial officers also possess great discretionary latitude. State statutes require judges to provide deterrence, retribution, rehabilitation, and incapacitation—all in the same sentence. Well-publicized studies of the sentencing tendencies of judges—in which participants were given identical facts in cases and were to impose sentences based on the offender's violation of the law—have demonstrated considerable discretion and unevenness in the judges' sentences. The nonsystem advocates believe this to be further evidence that a basic inequality exists—an inequality in justice that is communicated to the offender.[17]

Finally, fragmentation also occurs in corrections—the part of the criminal justice process that the U.S. public sees the least of and knows the least about. Indeed, as the Crime Commission noted, the federal government, all 50 states, the District of Columbia, and most of the country's 3,047 counties now engage in correctional activities of some form. Each level of government acts independently of the others and responsibility for the administration of corrections is divided within given jurisdictions as well.[18]

With this fragmentation comes polarity in identifying and establishing the primary goals of the system. The police, enforcing the laws, emphasize community protection; the courts weigh both sides of the issue—individual rights and community needs; and corrections facilities work with the individual. Each of these groups has its own perception of the offender, creating goal conflict, that is, the goal of the police and the prosecutor is to get the transgressor off the street, which is antithetical to the caretaker role of the corrections worker, who often wants to rehabilitate and return the offender to the community. The criminal justice process does not allow many alternative means of dealing with offenders. The nonsystem adherent believes that eventually the offender will become a mere statistic, more important on paper than as a human being.[19]

Because the justice process lacks sufficient program and procedural flexibility, these adherents argue, its workers either can circumvent policies, rules, and regulations or adhere to organizational practices they know are, at times, dysfunctional. (As evidence of the former, they point to instances of *informal* treatment of criminal cases; e.g., a police officer "bends" someone's constitutional rights in order to return stolen property to its rightful owner; or a juvenile probation officer, without a solid case but with strong suspicion, warns a youth that any further infractions will result in formal court-involved proceedings.)

Or, Is It a True Criminal Justice System?

That all of the foregoing perspectives on the justice system are grounded in truth is probably evident by now. In many ways, the police, courts, and corrections components work and interact to function like a process, a network, or even a nonsystem. However, the justice system may still constitute a true system. As Willa Dawson stated, "Administration of justice can be regarded as a system by most standards. It may be a poorly functioning system but it does meet the criteria nonetheless. The systems approach is still in its infancy."[20] J. W. La Patra added that "I do believe that a criminal justice system [CJS] does exist, but that it functions very poorly. The CJS is a loosely connected, nonharmonious, group of social entities."[21]

To be fair, however, perhaps this method of dealing with offenders is best after all; it may be that having a well-oiled machine—in which all activities are coordinated, goals and objectives are unified, and communication between participants is maximized, all serving to grind out justice in a highly efficacious manner—may not be what we truly want or need in a democracy.

I hope that I have not belabored the subject; however, it is important to establish early in this book the type of system and the components that you, as a potential criminal justice administrator, may encounter. You can reconcile for yourself the differences of opinion described earlier. In this book, I adhere to the notion that even with all of its disunity and lack of fluidity, what criminal justice officials administer in the United States is a system. Nonetheless, it is good to look at its operation and shortcomings and, as stated earlier, confront the CJS's problems and possible areas for improvement.

Now that we have a systemic view of what it is that criminal justice managers actually administer, it would be good to look briefly at how they go about doing it. I first consider the legal and historical bases that created the United States as a democracy regulated by a government and by a system of justice; I include the consensus–conflict continuum, with the social contract on one end and the maintenance of the status quo/repression on the other. Next, I distinguish between administration and work in the public and private sectors because the styles, incentives, and rewards of each are, by their very nature, quite different. This provides the foundation for the final point of discussion, a brief look at the policymaking process in criminal justice agencies.

THE FOUNDATIONS OF JUSTICE AND ADMINISTRATION: LEGAL AND HISTORICAL BASES

Given that our system of justice is founded on a large, powerful system of government, the following questions must be addressed: From where is that power derived? How can governments presume to maintain a system of laws that effectively governs its people and, furthermore, a legal system that exists to punish persons who willfully suborn those laws? We now consider the answers to those questions.

The Consensus-versus-Conflict Debate

U.S. society has innumerable lawbreakers. Most of them are easily handled by the police and do not challenge the legitimacy of the law while being arrested and incarcerated for violating it. Nor do they challenge the system of government that enacts the laws or the justice agencies that carry them out. The stability of our government for more than 200 years is a testimony to the existence of a fair degree of consensus as to its legitimacy.[22] Thomas Jefferson's statements in the *Declaration of Independence* are as true today as the day when he wrote them and are accepted as common sense:

> We hold these truths to be self-evident, that all men are created equal, that they are endowed by their Creator with certain inalienable Rights, that among these are Life, Liberty, and the pursuit of Happiness—That to secure these rights, Governments are instituted among Men, deriving their just powers from the consent of the governed. That whenever any Form of Government becomes destructive of these ends, it is the Right of the People to alter or abolish it

The principles of the Declaration are almost a paraphrase of John Locke's *Second Treatise on Civil Government*, which justifies the acts of government on the basis of Locke's theory of social contract. In the state of nature, people, according to Locke, were created by God to be free, equal, independent, and with inherent inalienable rights to life, liberty, and property. Each person had the right of self-protection against those who would infringe on these liberties. In Locke's view, although most people were good, some would be likely to prey on their fellows, who in turn would constantly have to be on guard against such evildoers. To avoid this brutish existence, people joined together, forming governments to which they surrendered their right of self-protection. In return, they received governmental protection of their lives, property, and liberty. As with any contract, each side has benefits and considerations; people give up their right to protect themselves and receive protection in return. Governments give protection and receive loyalty and obedience in return.[23]

Locke believed that the chief purpose of government was the protection of property. Properties would be joined together to form the commonwealth. Once the people unite into a commonwealth, they cannot withdraw from it nor can their lands be removed from it. Property holders become members of that commonwealth only with their express consent to submit to the government of the commonwealth. This is Locke's famous theory of *tacit consent*: "Every Man—doth hereby give his *tacit Consent*, and is as far forth obliged to Obedience to the Laws of the Government."[24] Locke's theory essentially describes an association of landowners.[25]

Another theorist connected with the **social contract** theory is Thomas Hobbes, who argued that all people were essentially irrational and selfish. He maintained that people had just enough rationality to recognize their situation and to come together to form governments for self-protection, agreeing "amongst themselves to submit to some Man, or Assembly of men, voluntarily, on confidence to be protected by him against all others."[26] Therefore, they existed in a state of consensus with their governments.

Jean-Jacques Rousseau, a conflict theorist, differed substantively from both Hobbes and Locke, arguing that "Man is born free, but everywhere he is in chains."[27] Like Plato, Rousseau associated the loss of freedom and the creation of conflict in modern societies with the development of private property and the unequal distribution of resources. Rousseau described conflict between the ruling group and the other groups in society, whereas Locke described consensus within the ruling group and the need to use force and other means to ensure the compliance of the other groups.[28]

Thus, the primary difference between the consensus and conflict theorists with respect to their view of government vis-à-vis the governed concerns their evaluation of the legitimacy of the actions of ruling groups in contemporary societies. Locke saw those actions as consistent with natural law, describing societies as consensual and arguing that any conflict was illegitimate and could be repressed by force and other means. Rousseau evaluated the actions of ruling groups as irrational and selfish, creating conflicts among the various groups in society.[29]

This debate is important because it plays out the competing views of humankind toward its ruling group; it also has relevance with respect to the kind of justice system (or process) we have. The system's model has been criticized for implying a greater level of organization and cooperation among the various agencies of justice than actually exists. The word *system* conjures an idea of machinelike precision in which wasted effort, redundancy, and conflicting actions are nearly nonexistent; our current justice system does not possess such a level of perfection. As mentioned earlier, conflicts among and within agencies are rife, goals are not shared by the system's three components, and the system may move in different directions. Therefore, the systems approach is part of the **consensus model** point of view, which assumes that all parts of the system work toward a common goal.[30] The **conflict model**, holding that agency interests tend to make actors within the system self-serving, provides the other approach. This view notes the pressures for success, promotion, and general accountability, which together result in fragmented efforts of the system as a whole, leading to a criminal justice nonsystem.[31]

This debate also has relevance for criminal justice administrators. Assume a consensus–conflict continuum, with social contract (the people totally allow government to use its means to protect them) on one end and class repression on the other. That our administrators *not* allow their agencies to drift too far to one end of the continuum or the other is of paramount importance. Americans cannot allow the compliance or conflict that would result at either end; the safer point is toward the middle of the continuum, where people are not totally dependent on their government for protection and maintain enough control to prevent totalitarianism.

Crime Control through Due Process

Both the systems and nonsystems models of criminal justice provide a view of agency relationships. Another way to view the U.S. criminal justice system is in terms of its goals. Two primary goals are as follows: (1) the need to enforce the law and maintain social order and (2) the need to protect people from injustice.[32] The first, often referred to as the *crime control model*, values the arrest and conviction of criminal offenders. The second, because of its emphasis on individual rights, is commonly known as the *due process model*. **Due process**—found in the Bill of Rights, particularly in the Fourteenth Amendment—is a central and necessary part of our system. It requires a careful and informed consideration of the facts of each individual case. Due process seeks to ensure that innocent people are not convicted of crimes.

The dual goals of crime control and due process are often suggested to be in constant and unavoidable opposition to each other. Many critics of criminal justice, as it exists in the United States, argue that our attempt to achieve justice for offenders too often occurs at the expense of due process. Other more conservative observers believe that our system is too lenient with its clients, coddling offenders rather than protecting the innocent.

We are never going to be in a position to avoid ideological conflicts such as these. However, some observers, such as Frank Schmalleger, believe it is realistic to think of the U.S. system of justice as representative of *crime control through due process*.[33] This model of crime control is infused with the recognition of individual rights, which provides the conceptual framework for this book.

PUBLIC- VERSUS PRIVATE-SECTOR ADMINISTRATION

The fact that people derive positive personal experiences from their work has long been recognized.[34] Because work is a vital part of our lives and carries tremendous meaning in terms of our personal identity and happiness, the right match of person to job has long been recognized as a determinant of job satisfaction.[35] Factors such as job importance, accomplishment, challenge, teamwork, management fairness, and rewards become very important.

People in both the public (i.e., government) and private (e.g., retail business) sectors derive personal satisfactions from their work. The means by which they arrive at those positive feelings and are rewarded for their efforts, however, are often quite different. Basically, whereas private businesses and corporations can use a panoply of *extrinsic* (external) rewards to motivate and reward their employees, people working in the public sector must achieve job satisfaction primarily through *intrinsic* (internal) rewards.

Extrinsic rewards include perquisites such as financial compensation (salary and a benefits package), a private office, a key to the executive washroom, bonuses, trips, a company car, awards (including designations such as the employee of the month or the insurance industry's "million-dollar roundtable"), an expense account, membership in country clubs and organizations, and a prestigious job title. The title assigned to a job can affect one's general perceptions of the job regardless of the actual job content. For example, the role once known disparagingly as "grease monkey" in a gasoline service station has commonly become known as "lubrication technician," garbage collectors have become "sanitation engineers," and so on. Enhancement of job titles is done to add job satisfaction and extrinsic rewards to what may often be lackluster positions.

Corporations often devote tremendous amounts of time and money to bestowing extrinsic rewards, incentives, and job titles on employees to enhance their job satisfaction. These rewards, of course, cannot and do not exist in the public sector anywhere near the extent that they do in the private sector.

As indicated earlier, public-sector workers must seek and obtain job satisfaction primarily from within—through intrinsic means. These workers, unable to become wealthy through their salaries and to be in a position that is filled with perks, need jobs that are gratifying and that intrinsically make them feel good about themselves and what they accomplish. Practitioners often characterize criminal justice work as intrinsically rewarding, providing a sense of worth in making the world a little better place in which to live. These employees also seek appreciation from their supervisors and co-workers and generally enjoy challenges.

To be successful, administrators should attempt to understand the personalities, needs, and motivations of their employees and attempt to meet those needs and provide motivation to the extent possible. The late Sam Walton, the multibillionaire founder of Wal-Mart stores, provided a unique example of the attempt to do this. One night, Walton could not sleep, so he went to a nearby all-night bakery in Bentonville, Arkansas, bought four dozen doughnuts, and took them to a distribution center where he chatted with graveyard-shift Wal-Mart employees. From that chat, he discovered that two more shower stalls were needed at that location.[36] Walton obviously solicited—and valued—employees' input and was concerned about their morale and working conditions. Although Walton was known to be unique in his business sense, these are elements of administration that can be applied by all public administrators.

PLANNED CHANGE AND POLICYMAKING IN JUSTICE ADMINISTRATION

Planning Interventions

In past decades and simpler times, change in criminal justice agencies typically occurred slowly and incrementally. Continuous change is now a constant rather than an exception, however, and the pace and frequency of change have increased. While change is not bad in itself, if unplanned, programs will often fail and even result in negative consequences in the workplace—absences, tardiness, medical or stress leaves, high turnover rates, and even sabotage. Remember, too, that a major change occurring in one component of the justice system can have severe repercussions on the others if not anticipated and planned for. Often times, major changes are enacted without due consideration given to planning, design, implementation, and evaluation; a good example is the initial "three-strikes" laws, initiated in California in 1994, which had a very different structure and outcome than originally intended.

Obviously, then, change in criminal justice should not and typically does not occur accidentally or haphazardly. Justice administrators must know how to plan, implement, and evaluate interventions that address problems in their organizations and systems while taking into account components such as time frame, target population, outcomes, and normative values—guiding assumptions about how the CJS *ought* to function. **Planned change** therefore, involves problem analysis, setting goals and objectives, program and policy design, developing an action plan, and monitoring and evaluation.

As examples, specific programs and policies have been developed to address domestic violence; prostitution; drug abuse; gang activities; repeat offenders; the availability of handguns; prison overcrowding; and the efficacy of statutory enactments such as the "three-strikes" law.

The most complex and comprehensive approach to effecting planned change in criminal justice is to create a *policy*. Policies vary in the complexity of the rule or guidelines being implemented and the amount of discretion given to those who apply them. For example, police officers are required to read *Miranda* warnings to suspects before they begin questioning them if the information might later be used in court against the defendant. This is an example where discretion is relatively constrained, although the Supreme Court has formulated specific exceptions to the rule. Sometimes policies are more complex, such as "the social policy" of President Lyndon Johnson's War on Poverty in the 1960s. Organizations, too, create policies specifying how they are going to accomplish their mission, expend their resources, and so on.[37]

Imagine the following scenario. Someone in criminal justice operations (e.g., a city, or county manager, or a municipal, or criminal justice planner) is charged with formulating an omnibus policy with respect to crime reduction. He or she might begin by trying to list all the related variables that contribute to the crime problem: poverty; employment; demographics of people residing within the jurisdiction; environmental conditions (such as housing density and conditions and slum areas); mortality, morbidity, and suicide rates; educational levels of the populace; and so on.

The administrator would request more specific information from each justice administrator within the jurisdiction to determine where problems might exist in the practitioners' view of the police, courts, and corrections subsystems. For example, a police executive would contribute information concerning calls for service, arrests, and crime data (including offender information and crime information—time of day, day of week, methods, locations, targets, and so on). The status of existing programs, such as community policing and crime prevention, would also be provided. From the courts, information would be sought concerning the sizes of civil and criminal court dockets and backlogs ("justice delayed is justice denied"). Included in this report would be input from the prosecutor's office concerning the quality and quantity of police reports and arrests, as well as data on case dismissals and conviction rates at trial. From corrections administrators would come the average officer caseload and the recidivism and revocation rates. Budgetary information would certainly be solicited from all subsystems, as well as miscellaneous data regarding personnel levels, training levels, and so on. Finally, the administrator would attempt to formulate a crime policy, setting forth goals and objectives for addressing the jurisdiction's needs.

As an alternative, the policymaker could approach this task in a far less complex manner, simply setting, either explicitly or without conscious thought, the relatively simple goal of "keeping crime down." This goal might be compromised or complicated by other factors, such as a bullish economy. This administrator could in fact disregard most of the other variables discussed earlier as being beyond his or her current needs and interest and would not even attempt to consider them as immediately relevant. The criminal justice practitioners would not be pressed to attempt to provide information and critical analyses. If pressed for time (as is often the case in these real-life scenarios), the planner would readily admit that these variables were being ignored.[38]

Because executives and planners of the alternative approach expect to achieve their goals only partially, they anticipate repeating endlessly the sequence just described as conditions and aspirations change and as accuracy of prediction improves. Realistically, however, the first of these two approaches assumes intellectual capacities and sources of information that people often do not possess; furthermore, the time and money that can be allocated to a policy problem are limited. Public agencies are in effect usually too hamstrung to practice the first method; it is the second method that is followed. Curiously, however, the literature on decision making, planning, policy formulation, and public administration formalizes and preaches the first approach.[39] The second method is much neglected in this literature.

In the United States, probably no part of government has attempted a comprehensive analysis and overview of policy on crime (the first method just described). Thus, making crime policy is at best a rough process. Without a more comprehensive process, we cannot possibly understand, for example, how a variety of problems—education, housing, recreation, employment, race, and policing methods—might encourage or discourage juvenile delinquency. What we normally engage in is a comparative analysis of the results of similar past policy decisions. This explains why justice administrators often believe that outside experts or academics are not helpful to them—why it is safer to "fly by the seat of one's pants." Theorists often urge the administrator to go the long way to the solution of his or her problems, following the scientific method, when the administrator knows that the best available theory will not work. Theorists, for their part, do not realize that the administrator is often in fact practicing a systematic method.[40] So, what may appear to be mere muddling through is both highly praised as a sophisticated form of policymaking and decision making and soundly denounced as no method at all. What society needs to bear in mind is that justice administrators possess an intimate knowledge of past consequences of actions that outsiders do not. Although seemingly less effective and rational, this method, according to policymaking experts, has merit. Indeed, this method is commonly used for problem solving in which the means and ends are often impossible to separate, aspirations or objectives undergo constant development, and drastic simplification of the complexity of the real world is urgent if problems are to be solved in reasonable periods of time.[41]

Force-Field Analysis

There will always be barriers and resistance to change in criminal justice organizations. Such barriers may be physical, social, financial, legal, political, and/or technological in nature. One useful technique for identifying sources of resistance (and support) is called **force-field analysis**. This technique, developed by Kurt Lewin, is based on an analogy to physics: A body will remain at rest when the sum of forces operating on it is zero. When the forces pushing or pulling it in one direction exceed the forces pushing or pulling it in the opposite one, the body will move in the direction of the greater forces. (Note, however, that in criminal justice administration, change involves *social* forces rather than *physical* ones.) Generally, we focus on reducing rather than overcoming resistance.

Three steps are involved in a force-field analysis:

1. Identifying driving forces (those supporting change) and restraining forces (those resisting change);
2. Analyzing the forces identified in Step 1; and
3. Identifying alternative strategies for changing each force identified in Step 1; focus on reducing forces of resistance.[42]

Take, for example, the forces at work concerning whether or not one will attend a university that is some distance away. Forces favoring the decision might be parents' and friends' encouragement to attend; the opportunity to meet new people and to experience new places and cultures; the prospect of attaining a desirable career with higher income; and the acquisition of far greater knowledge. Forces in opposition might be the costs of tuition, books, and living expenses; the financial loss while attending school and not working; unexceptional high school grades; the number of years required to graduate; and perhaps going to a strange locale and leaving friends, family, and other support groups behind. To reduce the opposing pressures, the student might obtain financial aid or scholarships; plan to call family and friends often; visit the school and community first to try to become more comfortable with them; and so on.

Summary

This chapter presented the foundation for the study of justice administration. It also established the legal existence of governments, laws, and the justice agencies that administer them. It demonstrated that the three components of the justice system are independent and fragmented and often work at odds with one another toward the accomplishment of the system's overall mission.

Questions for Review

1. Do the three justice components (police, courts, and corrections) constitute a true system or are they more appropriately described as a process or a true nonsystem? Defend your response.
2. What are the legal and historical bases for a justice system and its administration in the United States? Why is the conflict-versus-consensus debate important?
3. What are some of the substantive ways in which public- and private-sector administration are similar? How are they dissimilar?
4. What elements of planned change must the justice administrator be familiar with in order to ensure that change is effected rationally and successfully?
5. Which method, a rational process or just muddling through, appears to be used in criminal justice policy-making today? Which method is probably best, given real-world realities? Explain your response.

Learn by Doing

1. Your criminal justice professor asks you to consider the CJS flow chart displayed on the inside cover of the text. Then, after reading this chapter, you are asked to prepare a paper concerning how this chart both implies that criminal justice agencies constitute a *system* as well as a *non*system. What will be your response? Alternatively, do you believe that the CJS most closely resembles a *network* or *process*? Explain.
2. It is announced that because of financial shortfalls, your local police department must eliminate 10 percent of its officer positions through layoffs and retirements.
   a. Given the criminal justice planning adage that "you cannot rock one end of the boat," what might be the effects of such position reductions on your local criminal justice system?
   b. Assume instead that local revenues have *increased* in your jurisdiction, and your local police department is told it can add 10 percent more officers' positions. What possible impacts on your local CJS might result?
3. Your criminal justice professor is working on a journal article concerning the social compact or contract theory of the origin of government. As her research assistant, you are assigned to summarize John Locke's theory of same, including its significance and application to the U.S. CJS. What will be contained in your report?
4. The head of your state department of corrections wants to close the state's oldest prison, now located in the state capitol; constructed in the 1920s, it is now extremely dangerous as well as very expensive to operate. Although the new location would be in a community that is 50 miles away, the new location would be nearer the state capitol and offer a considerably larger labor pool of prospective prison employees as well as a much better public transportation system. Being politically astute, the director asks you and several of your fellow staff members to conduct a force-field analysis, looking at *both* communities to determine opposition and support for the move. Identify at least three forces or factors that are likely to *support* the decision to relocate the prison and three that are likely to *oppose* it.

Related Websites

360 Degrees: Perspectives on the Criminal Justice System
   http://www.360degrees.org
British Journal of Criminology—Crime Control and Due Process
   http://bjc.oxfordjournals.org/cgi/content/abstract/38/4/611
Crime Spider—A Crime and Justice Search Engine
   http://crimespider.com
Crime Theory
   http://crimetheory.com
Justice Administration Commission
   http://www.justiceadmin.org

MegaLinks in Criminal Justice
   http://faculty.ncwc.edu/toconnor
National Criminal Justice Reference Service (NCJRS)
   http://www.ncjrs.org
Office for Victims of Crime
   http://ojp.usdoj.gov/ovc
Talk Justice
   http://talkjustice.com
Uniform Crime Reports (UCR)
   http://fbi.gov/ucr/ucr.htm
U.S. Department of Justice
   http://www.usdoj.gov

Notes

1. For a more thorough explication of these terms and roles, particularly as applied in policing, see Richard N. Holden, *Modern Police Management* (Upper Saddle River, NJ: Prentice Hall, 1986).
2. Michael E. O'Neill, Ronald F. Bykowski, and Robert S. Blair, *Criminal Justice Planning: A Practical Approach* (San Jose, CA: Justice Systems Development, 1976), p. 5.
3. Ibid., p. 12.
4. Ibid.
5. Steven M. Cox and John E. Wade, *The Criminal Justice Network: An Introduction,* 2nd ed. (Dubuque, IA: Wm. C. Brown, 1989), p. 1.
6. Ibid., p. 4.
7. Ibid., p. 12.
8. Ibid., pp. 13–14.
9. Philip H. Ennis, "Crime, Victims, and the Police," *Transaction* 4 (1967):36–44.
10. The President's Commission on Law Enforcement and the Administration of Justice, *The Challenge of Crime in a Free Society* (Washington, DC: U.S. Government Printing Office, 1967), p. 7.
11. Alfred Cohn and Roy Udolf, *The Criminal Justice System and Its Psychology* (New York: Van Nostrand Reinhold, 1979), p. 152.
12. Burton Wright and Vernon Fox, *Criminal Justice and the Social Sciences* (Philadelphia, PA: W. B. Saunders, 1978).
13. "Justice on Trial: A Special Report," *Newsweek* (March 8, 1971):16.
14. Ibid., p. 18.
15. Alan R. Coffey and Edward Eldefonso, *Process and Impact of Justice* (Beverly Hills, CA: Glencoe Press, 1975), p. 32.
16. The President's Commission, *Challenge of Crime in a Free Society,* p. 5.
17. Alan R. Coffey and Edward Eldefonso, *Process and Impact of Justice,* p. 35.
18. Ibid., p. 39.
19. Ibid., p. 41.
20. Willa Dawson, "The Need for a System Approach to Criminal Justice," in Donald T. Shanahan (ed.), *The Administration of Justice System—An Introduction* (Boston, MA: Holbrook, 1977), p. 141.
21. J. W. La Patra, *Analyzing the Criminal Justice System* (Lexington, MA: Lexington Books, 1978), p. 75.
22. Alexander B. Smith and Harriet Pollack, *Criminal Justice: An Overview* (New York: Holt, Rinehart and Winston, 1980), p. 9.
23. Ibid., p. 10.
24. Ibid., p. 366.
25. Thomas J. Bernard, *The Consensus–Conflict Debate: Form and Content in Social Theories* (New York: Columbia University Press, 1983), p. 78.
26. Thomas Hobbes, *Leviathan* (New York: E. P. Dutton, 1950), pp. 290–291.
27. Jean-Jacques Rousseau, "A Discourse on the Origin of Inequality," in G. D. H. Cole (ed.), *The Social Contract and Discourses* (New York: E. P. Dutton, 1946), p. 240.
28. Bernard, *Consensus–Conflict Debate,* pp. 83, 85.
29. Ibid., p. 86.
30. Frank Schmalleger, *Criminal Justice Today,* 10th ed. (Upper Saddle River, NJ: Prentice Hall, 2009), pp. 16–17.
31. One of the first publications to express the nonsystems approach was the American Bar Association, *New Perspective on Urban Crime* (Washington, DC: ABA Special Committee on Crime Prevention and Control, 1972).
32. Schmalleger, *Criminal Justice Today,* pp. 23–24.
33. Ibid.
34. Fernando Bartolome and Paul A. Lee Evans, "Professional Lives versus Private Lives: Shifting Patterns of Managerial Commitment," *Organizational Dynamics* 7 (1982):2–29; Ronald C. Kessler and James A. McRae, Jr., "The Effect of Wives' Employment on the Mental Health of Married Men and Women," *American Sociological Review* 47 (1979): 216–227.
35. Robert V. Presthus, *The Organizational Society* (New York: Alfred A. Knopf, 1962).
36. Joseph A. Petrick and George E. Manning, "How to Manage Morale," *Personnel Journal* 69 (1990):87.
37. Wayne N. Welsh and Philip W. Harris, *Criminal Justice Policy and Planning,* 2nd ed. (Cincinnati, OH: LexisNexis Anderson, 2004), p. 5.
38. This scenario is modeled on one set out by Harvard economist Charles E. Lindblom, "The Science of 'Muddling Through,'" *Public Administration Review* 19 (Spring 1959):79–89.
39. Ibid., p. 80.
40. Ibid., p. 87.
41. Ibid., p. 88.
42. Kurt Lewin, *Field Theory in Social Science* (New York: Harper and Row, 1951).

2

Organization and Administration
Principles and Practices

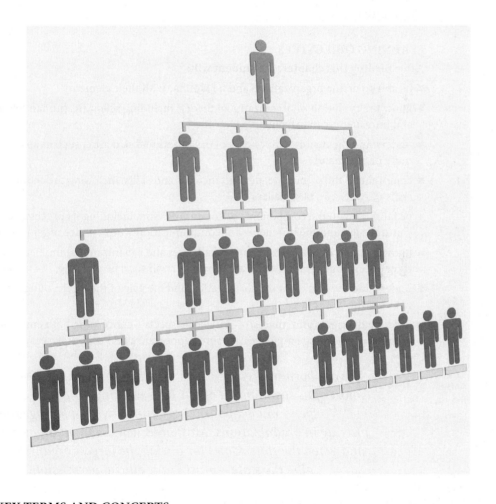

KEY TERMS AND CONCEPTS

Autocratic leader

Bureaucracy

Communication

Democratic leader

Digital gaming and tattooing

Generations X, Y, and Next

Grapevine

Hawthorne effect

Humanistic school

Inputs/outputs

Laissez-faire leader

Leadership

Maintenance and hygiene factors

McGregor's Theory X/Theory Y

Motivational factors

Organization

Organizational theory

POSDCORB

Relatively identifiable boundary

Scientific management

Social entity

Span of control

Style theory

Trait theory

Unity of command

LEARNING OBJECTIVES

After reading this chapter, the student will:

- be able to define organizations and be familiar with their elements
- know the evolution of organizational theory, including scientific, human relations, systems, and bureaucratic management
- understand the major components of organizational structure, such as span of control and unity of command
- comprehend the primary leadership theories and skills, including the characteristics and skills of America's best leaders
- be familiar with the components of communication, including its process, barriers, role, cultural cues, and the uniqueness of communication within police organizations
- know the kind of world and related challenges and organizational implications of persons of three younger generations who are now in, or will soon be entering, the workplace
- understand the impact of the socialization and lifestyle of the three younger generations now entering the workplace
- describe the rights and interests—and legal aspects—concerning both employees and employers regarding employees' personal appearance at the workplace

We are born in organizations, educated by organizations, and most of us spend much of our lives working for organizations. We spend much of our leisure time paying, playing, and praying in organizations. Most of us will die in an organization, and when the time comes for burial, the largest organization of all—the state—must grant official permission.

—AMITAI ETZIONI

Omnes aequo animo parent ubi digni imperant.
[All men cheerfully obey where worthy men rule.]

—PUBLILIUS SYRUS

INTRODUCTION

It is no surprise that *Dilbert*—one of today's most popular cartoon strips and television programs—portrays downtrodden workers, inconsiderate bosses, and dysfunctional organizations. Scott Adams's cartoon "hero," a mouthless engineer with a perpetually bent necktie, is believed by many Americans to be representative of today's workers. Although a sizable majority of U.S. workers routinely indicate that their workplace is a pleasant environment, more than 70 percent also experience stress at work because of red tape, unnecessary rules, poor communication with management, and other causes. Indeed, what gives Adams grist for the Dilbert mill is the way managers mishandle their employees and carry out downsizing.[1] But, as we will see, it does not have to be so.

This chapter—one of the lengthiest in this book and certainly one of the most essential chapters in terms of providing the foundation of administration—examines organizations and the employees within them and how they should be managed and motivated. The chapter offers a general discussion of organizations, focusing on their definition, theory and function, and structure. Included are several approaches to managing and communicating within organizations.

Also, as indicated in Chapter 1, the initial chapters of Parts II, III, and IV of this book discuss the organization and operation of police, courts, and corrections agencies, respectively. Similarly, countless books and articles have been written about organization and administration in general (many of them in the business and human resources disciplines); therefore, in this chapter, I will attempt to discuss the major elements of organization and administration that apply to the field of criminal justice administration. Then, we review the evolution of organizational theory, including scientific, human relations, systems, and bureacratic management.

Next, we consider the structure of organizations (including concepts such as span of control and unity of command). We then focus on one of the most important aspects of organizations: communications; after defining what constitutes communication, we consider its process, barriers, role, some cultural cues, and the uniqueness of communication within police organizations. Next is leadership and primary theories of how to lead the organization; included is an overview of the characteristics and skills of America's best leaders.

Following is a discussion of several classical motivational techniques that are used with employees; here, we include major theorists in the field such as McGregor, Maslow, Katz, and Herzberg.

Then, I look at some of the unique challenges posed by younger (so-called Generations X, Y, and Next) employees who are entering the workplace—including the world into which they were born, the influences of television and **digital gaming** on their worldview, their non-traditional lifestyle and penchant for bodily adornment, and the implications for the criminal justice workplace.

DEFINING ORGANIZATIONS

Like *supervision* and *management,* the word *organization* has a number of meanings and interpretations that have evolved over the years. We think of organizations as entities of two or more people who cooperate to achieve an objective(s). In that sense, certainly, the concept of organization is not new. Undoubtedly, the first organizations were primitive hunting parties. Organization and a high degree of coordination were required to bring down huge animals, as revealed in fossils from as early as 40,000 years ago.[2]

An **organization** may be formally defined as "a consciously coordinated social entity, with a relative identifiable boundary, that functions on a relatively continuous basis to achieve a common goal or set of goals."[3] The term consciously coordinated implies management. **Social entity** refers to the fact that organizations are composed of people who interact with one another and with people in other organizations. **Relatively identifiable boundary** alludes to the organization's goals and the public served.[4] Using this definition, we can consider many types of formal groups as full-blown organizations. Four different types of formal organizations have been identified by asking the question "Who benefits?" Answers include (1) mutual benefit associations, such as police labor unions; (2) business concerns, such as General Motors; (3) service organizations, such as community mental health centers, where the client group is the prime beneficiary; and (4) commonweal (e.g., those that exist for the public good or welfare) organizations, such as the Department of Defense and criminal justice agencies, where the beneficiaries are the public at large.[5] The following analogy is designed to help the reader to understand organizations.

An organization corresponds to the bones that structure or give form to the body. Imagine that the hand is a single mass of bone rather than four separate fingers and a thumb made up of bones joined by cartilage to be flexible. The single mass of bones could not, due to its structure, play musical instruments, hold a pencil, or grip a baseball bat. A criminal justice organization is analogous. It must be structured properly if it is to be effective in fulfilling its many diverse goals.[6]

It is important to note that no two organizations are structured or function exactly alike, nor is there one best way to run an organization.

THE EVOLUTION OF ORGANIZATIONAL THEORY

Next, we discuss the evolution of **organizational theory**, which is the study of organizational designs and structures, the relationship of organizations with their external environment, and the behavior of administrators and managers within organizations.

According to Ronald Lynch,[7] the history of management can be divided into three approaches and time periods: (1) scientific management (1900–1940), (2) human relations management (1930–1970), and (3) systems management (1965–present). To this, I would add another important element to the concept of organizations: bureaucratic management, which is also discussed in this section.

Scientific Management

Frederick W. Taylor, who first emphasized time and motion studies, is known today as the father of **scientific management**. Spending his early years in the steel mills of Pennsylvania, Taylor became chief engineer and later discovered a new method of making steel; this allowed him to retire at the age of 45 years to write and lecture. He became interested in methods for getting greater productivity from workers and was hired in 1898 by Bethlehem Steel, where he measured the time it took workers to shovel and carry pig iron. Taylor recommended giving workers hourly breaks and going to a piecework system, among other adjustments. Worker productivity soared; the total number of shovelers needed dropped from about 600 to 140, and worker earnings increased from $1.15 to $1.88 per day. The average cost of handling a long ton (2,240 pounds) dropped from $0.072 to $0.033.[8]

PLANNING: working out in broad outline what needs to be done and the methods for doing it to accomplish the purpose set for the enterprise

ORGANIZING: the establishment of a formal structure of authority through which work subdivisions are arranged, defined, and coordinated for the defined objective

STAFFING: the whole personnel function of bringing in and training the staff and maintaining favorable conditions of work

DIRECTING: the continuous task of making decisions, embodying them in specific and general orders and instructions, and serving as the leader of the enterprise

COORDINATING: the all-important duty of interrelating the various parts of the organization

REPORTING: informing the executive and his or her assistants as to what is going on, through records, research, and inspection

BUDGETING: all that is related to budgeting in the form of fiscal planning, accounting, and control

FIGURE 2.1 Gulick's POSDCORB

Source: Luther Gulick and Lyndall Urwick, *Papers on the Science of Administration* (New York: Institute of Public Administration, 1937).

Taylor, who was highly criticized by unions for his management-oriented views, proved that administrators must know their employees. He published a book, *The Principles of Scientific Management,* in 1911. His views caught on, and soon emphasis was placed entirely on the formal administrative structure; terms such as *authority, chain of command, span of control,* and *division of labor* were coined.

In 1935, Luther Gulick formulated the theory of **POSDCORB**, an acronym for planning, organizing, staffing, directing, coordinating, reporting, and budgeting (Figure 2.1); this philosophy was emphasized in police management for many years. Gulick stressed the technical and engineering side of management, virtually ignoring the human side.

The application of scientific management to criminal justice agencies was heavily criticized. It viewed employees as passive instruments whose feelings were completely disregarded. In addition, employees were considered to be motivated by money alone.

Human Relations Management

Beginning in 1930s, people began to realize the negative effects of scientific management on the worker. A view arose in policing that management should instill pride and dignity in officers. The movement toward human relations management began with the famous studies conducted during the late 1920s through the mid-1930s by the Harvard Business School at the Hawthorne plant of the Western Electric Company.[9] These studies, which are discussed in more detail later in this chapter, found that worker productivity is more closely related to *social* capacity than to physical capacity, that noneconomic rewards play a prominent part in motivating and satisfying employees, and that employees do not react to management and its rewards as individuals but as members of groups.[10]

In the 1940s and 1950s, police departments began to recognize the strong effect of the informal structure on the organization; agencies began using techniques such as job enlargement and job enrichment to generate interest in policing as a career. Studies indicated that the supervisor who was "employee centered" was more effective than one who was "production centered." Democratic or participatory management began to appear in police agencies. The human relations approach had its limitations, however. With the emphasis placed on the employee, the role of the organizational structure became secondary; the primary goal seemed to many to be social rewards, with little attention given to task accomplishment. Many police managers saw this trend as unrealistic. Employees began to give less and expect more in return.[11]

Systems Management

In the mid-1960s, features of the human relations and scientific management approaches were combined in the *systems management* approach. Designed to bring the individual and the organization together, it attempted to help managers use employees to reach desired production goals. The systems approach recognized that it was still necessary to have some hierarchical arrangement to bring about coordination, that authority and responsibility were essential, and that overall organization was required.

The systems management approach combined the work of Abraham Maslow,[12] who developed a hierarchy of needs; Douglas McGregor,[13] who stressed the general theory of human motivation; and Robert Blake and Jane Mouton,[14] who developed the "managerial grid," which emphasized two concerns—for task and for people—that managers must have. In effect, the systems management approach holds that to be effective, and the manager must be interdependent with other individuals and groups and have the ability to recognize and deal with conflict and change. More than mere technical skills are required; managers require knowledge of several major resources: people, money, time, and equipment.[15] Team cooperation is required to achieve organizational goals.

Several theories of leadership and means of motivating employees have also evolved over the past several decades; we discuss several of them below.

Bureaucratic Management

Criminal justice agencies certainly fit the description of an organization. First, they are managed by being organized into a number of specialized units. Administrators, managers, and supervisors exist to ensure that these units work together toward a common goal (each unit working independently would lead to fragmentation, conflict, and competition). Second, these agencies consist of people who interact within the organization and with external organizations, and they exist to serve the public. Through a mission statement, policies and procedures, a proper management style, and direction, criminal justice administrators attempt to ensure that the organization maintains its overall goals of crime treatment and suppression, and that it works amicably with other organizations and people. As the organization becomes larger, the need becomes greater for people to cooperate to achieve organizational goals.

Criminal justice organizations are *bureaucracies,* as are virtually all large organizations in modern society. The idea of a pure bureaucracy was developed by Max Weber, the German sociologist and the "father of sociology," who argued that if a bureaucratic structure is to function efficiently, it must have the following elements:

1. *Rulification and routinization.* Organizations stress continuity. Rules save effort by eliminating the need for deriving a new solution for every problem. They also facilitate standard and equal treatment of similar situations.
2. *Division of labor.* This involves the performance of functions by various parts of an organization along with providing the necessary authority to carry out these functions.
3. *Hierarchy of authority.* Each lower office is under the control and supervision of a higher one.
4. *Expertise.* Specialized training is necessary. Only a person who has demonstrated adequate technical training is qualified to be a member of the administrative staff.
5. *Written rules.* Administrative acts, decisions, and rules are formulated and recorded in writing.[16]

Today, many people view bureaucracies in negative terms, believing that all too often, officials tell clients "That's not my job," or appear to be "going by the book"—relying heavily on rules and regulations, and policies and procedures ("red tape"). Second, they are said to stifle the individual freedom, spontaneity, and self-realization of their employees.[17] James Q. Wilson referred to this widespread discontent with modern organizations as the "bureaucracy problem," where the key issue is "getting the frontline worker . . . to do 'the right thing.'"[18]

Weber's ideal bureaucracy, however, as described earlier, was designed to eliminate inefficiency and waste in organizations. As shown for each of the earlier principles, many of the characteristics that he proposed many years ago are found in today's criminal justice agencies as well as in other bureaucracies (e.g., political parties, churches, educational institutions, and private businesses).

The administration of most police and prison organizations is based on the traditional, pyramidal, quasimilitary organizational structure containing the elements of a **bureaucracy**: specialized functions, adherence to fixed rules, and a hierarchy of authority. (This pyramidal organizational environment is undergoing increasing challenges, especially as a result of departments implementing community policing, as will be seen in Chapter 3.)

Organizational Inputs/Outputs

Another way to view organizations is as systems that take **inputs**, process them, and thus produce **outputs**. These outputs are then sold in the marketplace or given free to citizens in the form of a service. A police agency, for example, processes reports of criminal activity and, like other systems, attempts to satisfy the customer (crime victim). Figure 2.2 demonstrates the input/output model for the police and private business. There are other types of inputs by police agencies; for example, a robbery problem might result in an input of newly created robbery surveillance teams, the processing would be their stakeouts, and the output would be the number of subsequent arrests by the team. Feedback would occur in the form of conviction rates at trial.

ORGANIZATIONAL STRUCTURE

Primary Principles

All organizations have an organizational structure or table of organization, be it written or unwritten, very basic or highly complex. An experienced manager uses this organizational chart

BUSINESS ORGANIZATION

Inputs	**Processes**	**Outputs**
Customer takes photos to shop to be developed.	Photos are developed and packaged for customer to pick up.	Customer picks up photos and pays for them.

Feedback
Analysis is made of expenses/revenues and customer satisfaction.

LAW ENFORCEMENT AGENCY

Inputs	**Processes**	**Outputs**
A crime prevention unit is initiated.	Citizens contact unit for advice.	Police provide spot checks and lectures.

Feedback
Target hardening results; property crimes decrease.

COURT

Inputs	**Processes**	**Outputs**
A house arrest program is initiated.	Certain people in pre- and post-trial status are screened and offered the option.	Decrease in number of people in jail, speeding up court process.

Feedback
Violation rates are analyzed for success; some offenders are mainstreamed back into the community more smoothly.

FIGURE 2.2 The Organization as an Input–Output Model

PROBATION/PAROLE AGENCIES

Inputs	**Processes**	**Outputs**
Parole guidelines are changed to shorten length of incarceration and reduce overcrowding.	Qualified inmates are contacted by parole agency and given new parole dates.	A higher number of inmates are paroled into the community.

Feedback
Parole officer's caseload and revocation rates might increase; less time to devote per case.

CORRECTIONAL INSTITUTION

Inputs	**Processes**	**Outputs**
Person is incarcerated for felony offense(s).	Prison incapacitates and often provides counseling, GED or higher; job skills; other treatment or programming.	Person is released—generally supervised—to maintain a noncriminal lifestyle.

Feedback
Does inmate recidivate (return to the institution for committing new crimes or for violating parole conditions)?

FIGURE 2.2 *(continued)*

or table as a blueprint for action. The size of the organization depends on the demands placed on it and the resources available to it. Growth precipitates the need for more personnel, greater division of labor, specialization, written rules, and other such elements.

In building the organizational structure, the following principles should be kept in mind:

1. *Principle of the objective.* Every part of every organization must be an expression of the purpose of the undertaking. You cannot organize in a vacuum; you must organize for something.
2. *Principle of specialization.* The activities of every member of any organized group should be confined, as far as possible, to the performance of a single function.
3. *Principle of authority.* In every organized group, the supreme authority must rest somewhere. There should be a clear line of authority to every person in the group.

4. ***Principle of responsibility.*** The responsibility of the superior for the acts of his or her subordinates is absolute.
5. ***Principle of definition.*** The content of each position, the duties involved, the authority and responsibility contemplated, and the relationships with other positions should be clearly defined in writing and published for all concerned.
6. ***Principle of correspondence.*** In every position, the responsibility and the authority to carry out the responsibility should correspond.
7. ***Span of control.*** No person should supervise more than six direct subordinates whose work interlocks.[19]

Span of Control and Unity of Command

The last concept in the preceding list, **span of control**, has recently been revisited in the literature and deserves additional commentary. How many subordinates can a chief executive, manager, or supervisor in a criminal justice organization effectively supervise? The answer will depend on factors such as the capacity of the leader and the persons supervised, the type of work performed, the complexity of the work, the area covered, distances between elements, the time needed to perform the tasks, and the types of persons served. Normally, a police patrol sergeant will supervise 6–10 officers, while a patrol lieutenant may have four or five sergeants reporting to him or her.[20]

Several authors now argue for even higher spans of control, however, to afford reductions in the distortion of information as it flows through the organization; less slow, ineffective decision making and action; fewer functional roadblocks and "turf protection"; greater emphasis on controlling the bureaucracy rather than on customer service; and reduced costs because of the lower number of managers and management support staff. Some also argue that rank-and-file employees favor high spans of control because they receive less detailed and micromanaged supervision, greater responsibility, and a higher level of trust by their supervisors.[21]

A related, major principle of hierarchy of authority is **unity of command**, which refers to placing one and only one superior officer in command or in control of every situation and employee. When a critical situation occurs, it is imperative that someone should be responsible and in charge. The unity-of-command principle ensures, for example, that multiple and/or conflicting orders are not issued to the same police officers by several superior officers. For example, a patrol sergeant might arrive at a hostage situation, deploy personnel, and give all appropriate orders, only to have a shift lieutenant or captain come to the scene and countermand the sergeant's orders with his or her own orders. This type of situation would obviously be counterproductive for all concerned. All officers must know and follow the chain of command at such incidents. Every person in the organization should report to one and only one superior officer. When the unity-of-command principle is followed, everyone involved is aware of the actions initiated by superiors and subordinates. A simple structure indicating the direct line of authority in a chain of command is shown in Figure 2.3.

An organization should be developed through careful evaluation of its responsibilities; otherwise, the agency may become unable to respond efficiently to clients' needs. For example, the implementation of too many specialized units in a police department (e.g., community relations, crime analysis, media relations) may obligate too many personnel to these functions and result in too few patrol officers. Today, 56 to 90 percent of all sworn personnel are assigned to patrol.[22]

The classic pyramidal design is shown in Figure 2.4. The pyramidal structure has the following characteristics:

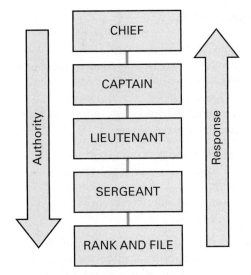

FIGURE 2.3   Chain of Command

1. Nearly all contacts take the form of orders going *down* and reports of results going *up* the pyramid.
2. Each subordinate must receive instructions and orders from only one boss.
3. Important decisions are made at the top of the pyramid.
4. Superiors have a specific span of control, supervising only a limited number of people.
5. Personnel at all levels, except at the top and bottom, have contact only with their boss above them and their subordinates below them.[23]

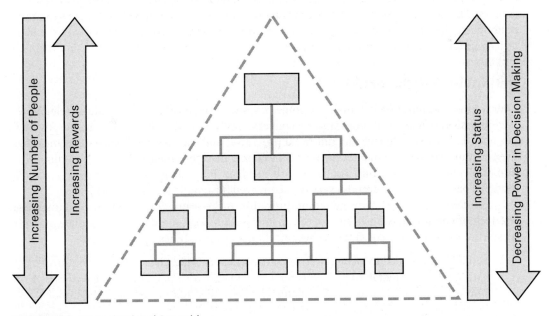

FIGURE 2.4   Organizational Pyramid

Source: Adapted from Leonard R. Sayles and George Strauss, *Human Behavior in Organizations,* p. 349. © 1966. Reproduced by permission of Pearson Education, Inc., Upper Saddle River, New Jersey.

COMMUNICATION WITHIN THE ORGANIZATION

Import and Consequence

Communication is obviously important in every segment of our society. As Mark Twain put it, "The difference between the right word and the almost right word is the difference between lightning and lightning bug."[24]

And to that we might add one more quote, by the noted Italian-American linguist Mario Pei,[25] who wrote about the essential nature of proper communication in general:

> Rightly or wrongly, most people consider language as an index of culture, breeding, upbringing, personality, sometimes even of intelligence, decency, and integrity. Under the circumstances, it is unwise, not to say harmful, to pay no heed to your language. Ignorance or improper use of language can easily interfere with your success and advancement. It can take money out of your pocket.

Certainly there is no discipline where communication is more important than that of criminal justice, where people communicate in and through offense reports; in affidavits; via general orders, policies, procedures, rules, and regulations; on the courtroom witness stand; and in competency, parole, or probation hearings. Indeed, it might be fairly said that communication is the foundation of criminal justice organization and administration.

Communication also becomes exceedingly important and sensitive in criminal justice organizations because of the nature of information that is processed by practitioners—particularly police officers, who often see people at their worst and when they are in the most embarrassing and compromising situations. To communicate what is known about these kinds of behaviors could be devastating to the parties concerned. A former Detroit police chief lamented several decades ago that "many police officers, without realizing they carry such authority, do pass on rumors. The average police officer doesn't stop to weigh what he says."[26] Certainly the same holds true today and extends to courts and corrections personnel, especially in view of the high-tech communications equipment now in use.

Definition and Characteristics

Today, we communicate via e-mail, facsimile machines, video camcorders, cellular telephones, satellite dishes, and many other forms. We converse orally, in written letters and memos, through our body language, via television and radio programs, and through newspapers and meetings. Even private thoughts—which occur four times faster than the spoken word—are communication. Every waking hour, our minds are full of ideas. Psychologists say that nearly 100,000 thoughts pass through our minds every day, conveyed by a multitude of media.[27]

Studies have long shown that communication is the primary problem in administration and lack of communication is employees' primary complaint about their immediate supervisors.[28] Indeed, managers are in the communications business. It has been said that

> [o]f all skills needed to be an effective manager/leader/supervisor, skill in communicating is *the* most vital. In fact, research has shown that 93 percent of police work is one-on-one communication. Estimates vary, but all studies emphasize the importance of communications in everyday law enforcement operations.[29]

Several elements compose the communication process: encoding, transmission, medium, reception, decoding, and feedback.[30]

Encoding. To convey an experience or idea, we translate, or encode, that experience into symbols. We use words or other verbal behaviors or nonverbal behaviors such as gestures to convey the experience or idea.

Transmission. This element involves the translation of the encoded symbols into some behavior that another person can observe. The actual articulation (moving our lips, tongue, and so on) of the symbol into verbal or nonverbal observable behavior is transmission.

Medium. Communication must be conveyed through some channel or medium. Media for communication include sight, hearing, taste, touch, and smell. Some other media are television, telephone, paper and pencil, and radio. The choice of the medium is important. For example, a message that is transmitted via a formal letter from the CEO will carry more weight than the same message conveyed via a secretary's memo.

Reception. The stimuli, the verbal and nonverbal symbols, reach the senses of the receiver and are conveyed to the brain for interpretation.

Decoding. The individual who receives the stimuli develops some meaning for the verbal and nonverbal symbols and decodes the stimuli. These symbols are translated into some concept or experience for the receiver. Whether or not the receiver is familiar with the symbols, or whether or not interference such as noise or a physiological problem occurs, determines how closely the message that the receiver has decoded approximates the message that the sender has encoded.

Feedback. After decoding the transmitted symbols, the receiver usually provides some response or feedback to the sender. If someone appears puzzled, we repeat the message or we encode the concept differently and transmit some different symbols to express that concept. Feedback that we receive acts as a guide or steering device and lets us know whether the receiver has interpreted our symbols as we intended. Feedback is obviously a crucial element in guaranteeing that the sender's intended meaning was in fact conveyed to the receiver.

An organization's systems of communication are usually created by establishing formal areas of responsibility and explicit delegations of duties, including statements of the nature, content, and direction of the communications that are necessary for the group's performance. Most criminal justice administrators prefer a formal system, regardless of how cumbersome it may be, because they can control it and because it tends to create a record for future reference. Several human factors, however, affect the flow of communication. Employees typically communicate with those persons who can help them to achieve their aims; they avoid communicating with those who do not assist, or may retard, their accomplishing those goals; and they tend to avoid communicating with people who threaten them and make them feel anxious.[31] Other barriers to effective communication are discussed later.

Communication within a criminal justice organization may be downward, upward, or horizontal. There are five types of downward communication within a criminal justice organization:

1. *Job instruction.* Communication relating to the performance of a certain task
2. *Job rationale.* Communication relating a certain task to organizational tasks
3. *Procedures and practice.* Communication about organizational policies, procedures, rules, and regulations (discussed in Chapter 3)
4. *Feedback.* Communication appraising how an individual performs the assigned task
5. *Indoctrination.* Communication designed to motivate the employee[32]

Other reasons for communicating downward—implicit in this list—are opportunities for administrators to spell out objectives, to change attitudes and mold opinions, to prevent misunderstandings from lack of information, and to prepare employees for change.[33]

Upward communication in a criminal justice organization may be likened to a trout trying to swim upstream: With its many currents of resistance, it is a much harder task than to float downstream. Several deterrents restrict upward communication. The physical distance between superior and subordinate impedes upward communication. Communication is often difficult and infrequent when superiors are isolated and seldom seen or spoken to. In large criminal justice organizations, administrators may be located in headquarters that are removed from the operations personnel. The complexity of the organization may also cause prolonged delays of communication. For example, if a corrections officer or a patrol officer observes a problem that needs to be taken to the highest level, normally this information must first be taken to the sergeant, then to the lieutenant, captain, deputy warden or chief, and so on. At each level, these higher-level individuals will reflect on the problem, put their own interpretation on it (possibly including how the problem might affect them professionally or even personally), and possibly even dilute or distort the problem. Thus, delays in communication are inherent in a bureaucracy. Delays could mean that problems are not brought to the attention of the CEO for a long time. The more levels the communication passes through, the more it is filtered and diluted in its accuracy.

There is also the danger that administrators have a "no news is good news" or "slay the messenger" attitude, thereby discouraging the reception of information. Unless the superior does in fact maintain an open-door atmosphere, subordinates are often reluctant to bring, or will temper, bad news, unfavorable opinions, and mistakes or failures to the superior.[34] Administrators may also believe that they know and understand what their subordinates want and think, and that complaints from subordinates are an indication of disloyalty.

For all of these reasons, administrators may fail to take action on undesirable conditions brought to their attention; this will cause subordinates to lose faith in their leaders. Many time-consuming problems could be minimized or eliminated if superiors took the time to listen to their employees.

Horizontal communication thrives in an organization when formal communication channels are not open.[35] The disadvantage of horizontal communication is that it is much easier and more natural to achieve than vertical communication and therefore it often replaces vertical channels. The horizontal channels are usually informal in nature and include the grapevine, discussed next. The advantage is that horizontal communication is essential if the subsystems within a criminal justice organization are to function in an effective and coordinated manner. Horizontal communication among peers may also provide emotional and social bonds that build morale and feelings of teamwork among employees.

Communicating in Police Organizations: Consequence, Jargon, and the Grapevine

As noted earlier, communication skills in policing are of vital importance. Officers must possess the ability to communicate internally and externally regarding policies and procedures that affect daily operations. The ability of police to communicate effectively using both oral and written means is also paramount because of the damage that can be done by, say, not completing an offense report properly or failing to convey accurately to one's supervisors, to the district attorney, or in court what actually happened in a criminal matter. Officers must also be prepared to converse with highly educated people in their day-to-day work.

Like people in other occupations and the professions, the police have their own jargon, dialect, and/or slang that they use on a daily basis. To the police, an offender might be a "perp" (perpetrator); a "subject" is simply someone of interest whom they are talking with, while a "suspect" is someone suspected of having committed a crime. In an "interview," the officer attempts to obtain basic information about a person (name, address, date of birth, and so forth), while an "interrogation" involves questioning an individual about his or her knowledge of, or involvement in, a crime. Such jargon and slang help officers to communicate among themselves.

The police also communicate with one another by listening and talking on the squad car radio. Agencies generally have detailed instructions and do's and don'ts in their policies and procedures regarding the use of radio. Supervisors must ensure that officers' radio transmissions are as concise, complete, and accurate as possible; officers are to refrain from making unprofessional, rude, sarcastic, or unnecessary remarks while on their radio; and those who fail to abide by these rules will quickly be admonished or even disciplined.

Police communicate on their radios using codes and have done so since the 1920s. The codes that are actually used may vary somewhat from agency to agency, but a fairly common listing of codes is provided in Table 2.1.

The police also communicate with the use of a phonetic alphabet, which was designed to avoid confusion between letters that sound alike, say, when radioing in the name of a person or a license plate number to the dispatcher. For example, a *d* might easily be confused with a *b* or an *m* with an *n*. So, if radioing in a license plate number that is "DOM-123," the officer would say "David Ocean Mary 1-2-3." This eliminates any possible confusion on the receiver's part. Table 2.2 shows the standard police and military phonetic alphabets.[36]

In addition to the several barriers to effective communication just discussed, the so-called **grapevine**—so called because it zigzags back and forth across organizations—can also hinder communication. Communication includes rumors, and probably *no* type of organization in our society has more grapevine "scuttlebutt" than police agencies. Departments even establish *rumor control* centers during major crisis situations. Increasing the usual barriers to communication is the fact that policing, prisons, and jails are 24-hour, 7-day operations, so that rumors are easily carried from one shift to the next.

The grapevine's most effective characteristics are that it is fast, it operates mostly at the place of work, and it supplements regular, formal communication. On the positive side, it can be a tool for management to gauge employees' attitudes, to spread useful information, and to help employees vent their frustrations. However, the grapevine can also carry untruths and be malicious. Without a doubt, the grapevine is a force for administrators to reckon with on a daily basis.

Oral and Written Communication

Our society tends to place considerable confidence in the written word within complex organizations. Writing establishes a permanent record, but transmitting information this way does not necessarily ensure that the message will be clear to the receiver. Often, in spite of the writer's best efforts, information is not conveyed clearly. This may be due in large measure to shortcomings with the writer's skills. Nonetheless, criminal justice organizations seem to rely increasingly on written communication, as evidenced by the proliferation of written directives found in most agencies.

This tendency for organizations to promulgate written rules, policies, and procedures has been caused by three contemporary developments. First is the *requirement for administrative*

TABLE 2.1	Partial List of Standard Radio Codes Used by Many Agencies

10-1 Signal weak

10-2 Signal good

10-3 Stop transmitting

10-4 Message received

10-5 Relay

10-6 Busy

10-7 Out of service

10-8 In service

10-9 Repeat

10-10 Fight in progress

10-11 Animal problem

10-12 Stand by

10-13 Report conditions

10-14 Prowler report

10-15 Civil disturbance

10-16 Domestic problem

10-17 Meet complainant

10-18 Urgent

10-19 Go to station

10-20 Location

10-21 Phone

10-22 Disregard

10-23 Arrived at scene

10-24 Assignment complete

10-25 Report to—

10-26 Detaining suspect

10-27 Driver's license information

10-28 Vehicle registration information

10-29 Check for wants/warrants

10-30 Unauthorized use of radio

10-31 Crime in progress

10-32 Person with gun

10-33 Emergency, stand by

10-34 Riot

10-35 Major crime alert

10-36 Correct time

10-37 Investigate suspicious vehicle

10-38 Stop suspicious vehicle

10-39 Use lights and siren

10-40 Respond quickly

10-41 Beginning shift

10-42 Ending shift

10-43 Information

10-44 Permission to leave

10-45 Dead animal

10-46 Assist motorist

10-47 Emergency road repair

10-48 Traffic control

10-49 Traffic signal out

10-50 Traffic accident

10-51 Request tow truck

10-52 Request ambulance

10-54 Livestock on roadway

10-55 Intoxicated driver

10-56 Intoxicated pedestrian

10-57 Hit-and-run accident

10-58 Direct traffic

10-59 Escort

10-60 Squad in vicinity

10-61 Personnel in vicinity

10-62 Reply to message

10-63 Prepare to copy

10-64 Local message

10-65 Network message

10-66 Cancel message

10-67 Clear for network message

10-68 Dispatch information

10-69 Message received

10-70 Fire alarm

10-71 Advise of nature of fire

10-72 Report progress of fire

10-73 Smoke report

10-74 Negative

10-75 In contact with—

10-76 En route to—

10-77 E.T.A.

10-78 Request assistance

10-79 Notify coroner

TABLE 2.1	(continued)		
10-80 Pursuit in progress		10-90 Bank alarm	
10-81 Breathalyzer report		10-91 Pick up subject	
10-82 Reserve lodgings		10-92 Illegally parked vehicle	
10-83 School crossing detai		10-93 Blockage	
10-84 E.T.A.		10-94 Drag racing	
10-85 Arrival delayed		10-95 Subject in custody	
10-86 Operator on duty		10-96 Detain subject	
10-87 Pick up		10-97 Test signa	
10-88 Advise of telephone number		10-98 Escaped prisoner	
10-89 Bomb threat		10-99 Wanted	

Source: From Michael Birzer and Cliff Roberson, *Police Field Operations: Theory Meets Practice,* p. 406. © 2008. Reproduced by permission of Pearson Education, Inc., Upper Saddle River, New Jersey.

due process in employee disciplinary matters, encouraged by federal court rulings, police officer bill of rights legislation, and labor contracts. Another development is *civil liability*. Lawsuits against local governments and their criminal justice agencies and administrators have become commonplace; written agency guidelines prohibiting certain acts provide a hedge against successful civil litigation.[37] Written communication is preferred as a medium for dealing with citizens or groups outside the criminal justice agency. This means of communication provides the greatest protection against the growing number of legal actions taken against agencies by activists, citizens, and interest groups.

Finally, a third stimulus is the *accreditation movement*. Agencies that are either pursuing accreditation or have become accredited must possess a wealth of written policies and procedures.[38]

In recent years, electronic mail (e-mail) has proliferated as a communication medium in criminal justice organizations. E-mail provides easy-to-use and almost instantaneous communication with anyone possessing a personal computer—in upward, downward, or horizontal directions. For all their advantages, however, e-mail messages can lack security and can be ambiguous—not only with respect to content meaning but also with regard to what they represent. Are such messages, in fact, mail, to be given the full weight of an office letter or memo, or should they be treated more as offhand comments?[39]

Other Barriers to Effective Communication

In addition to the barriers just discussed, several other potential barriers to effective communication exist. Some people, for example, are not good listeners. Unfortunately, listening is one of the most neglected and the least understood of the communication arts.[40] We allow other things to obstruct our communication, including time constraints, inadequate or excessive information, the tendency to say what we think others want to hear, failure to select the best word, prejudices, and strained sender–receiver relationships.[41] In addition, subordinates do not always have the same "big picture" viewpoint that superiors possess and do not always communicate well with someone in a higher position who is perhaps more fluent and persuasive than they are.

TABLE 2.2	Phonetic Alphabet

Two general phonetic alphabets are used in the United States. Law enforcement agencies generally use the one on the top, while fire agencies primarily use the one on the bottom.

LAW ENFORCEMENT

A	Adam	N	Nora
B	Boy	O	Ocean
C	Charlie	P	Pau
D	David	Q	Queen
E	Edward	R	Robert
F	Frank	S	Sam
G	George	T	Tom
H	Henry	U	Union
I	Ida	V	Victor
J	John	W	William
K	King	X	X-ray
L	Lincoln	Y	Young
M	Mary	Z	Zebra

FIRE AND MILITARY

A	Alpha	N	November
B	Bravo	O	Oscar
C	Charlie	P	Papa
D	Delta	Q	Quebec
E	Echo	R	Romeo
F	Foxtrot	S	Sierra
G	Golf	T	Tango
H	Hotel	U	Uniform
I	India	V	Victor
J	Juliet	W	Whiskey
K	Kilo	X	X-ray
L	Lima	Y	Yankee
M	Mike	Z	Zulu

Source: From Michael Birzer and Cliff Roberson, *Police Field Operations: Theory Meets Practice,* p. 406. © 2008. Reproduced by permission of Pearson Education, Inc., Upper Saddle River, New Jersey.

Cultural Cues

It is important to note that at least 90 percent of communication is *nonverbal* in nature, involving posture, facial expressions, gestures, tone of voice ("it's not what you say but how you say it"), and so on.[42] People learn to interpret these nonverbal messages by growing up in a particular culture, but not every culture interprets nonverbal cues in the same way.

For example, in some cultures, avoiding eye contact by looking at the ground is meant to convey respect and humility. Making what to some people are exaggerated hand gestures may be a normal means of communication in some cultures, and social distance for conversation in some societies may be much closer than it is in the United States. Someone from Nigeria, for example, may stand less than 15 inches from someone while conversing, whereas about 2 feet is a comfortable conversation zone for Americans. These few examples demonstrate why criminal justice practitioners must possess cultural empathy and understand the cultural cues of citizens from other nations.

Over 20 years ago, Peter Drucker, often referred to as the *business guru*,[43] conducted a study of the Los Angeles Police Department; among Drucker's findings was: "You police are so concerned with doing things right that you fail to do the right things." Drucker added that "Managers do things right; leaders do the right thing." Another leadership guru, Warren Bennis, has said essentially the same thing. In other words, administrators cannot be so concerned with managing that they fail to lead.[44]

We now look at theories underlying leadership and what leaders can do to motivate their subordinates.

PRIMARY LEADERSHIP THEORIES

What Is Leadership?

Probably since the dawn of time, when cave dwellers clustered into hunting groups and some particularly dominant person assumed a leadership role over the party, administrators have received advice on how to do their jobs from those around them. Even today, manuals for leaders and upwardly mobile executives abound, offering quick studies in how to govern others. Although many have doubtlessly been profitable for their authors, most of these how-to primers on leading others enjoy only a brief, ephemeral existence.

To understand **leadership**, we must first define the term. This is an important and fairly complex undertaking, however. Perhaps the simplest definition is to say that leading is "getting things done through people." In general, it may be said that a manager operates in the status quo, but a leader takes risks. Managers are conformers; leaders are reformers. Managers control; leaders empower. Managers supervise; leaders coach. Managers are efficient; leaders are effective. Managers are position oriented; leaders are people oriented. In sum, police administrators must be both skilled managers and effective leaders.[45]

Other definitions of leadership include the following:

- "The process of influencing the activities of an individual or a group in efforts toward goal achievement in a given situation"[46]
- "Working with and through individuals and groups to accomplish organizational goals"[47]
- "The activity of influencing people to strive willingly for group objectives"[48]
- "The exercise of influence"[49]

Conversely, it has been said that the manager may be viewed as a team captain, parent, steward, battle commander, fountain of wisdom, poker player, group spokesperson, gatekeeper, minister, drill instructor, facilitator, initiator, mediator, navigator, candy-store keeper, linchpin, umbrella-holder, and everything else between nurse and Attila-the-Hun.[50]

In criminal justice organizations, leaders take the macro view; their role might best be defined as "the process of influencing organizational members to use their energies willingly and appropriately to facilitate the achievement of the [agency's] goals."[51] I discuss leaders and managers in greater length later in this chapter and in Chapter 4 (the Mintzberg model of CEOs).

Next, we discuss what kinds of activities and philosophies constitute leadership. One would also do well to consider the views of Lawrence B. Kokkelenberg, in Exhibit 2.1.

EXHIBIT 2.1

Leadership's Bond of Trust

By Lawrence B. Kokkelenberg

The old military dogma, one also quite familiar to many areas of the private sector, was "I am the boss you are the subordinate, just do what I tell you to do. Just follow orders." Many old adages support this paradigm: "A manager's job is to manage, not run a popularity contest." "When I tell you to jump, just go up, I'll tell you when to come down."

This autocratic approach worked well for America for 200 years, but that was back in the days when life was simple. Back then if you did not work, you did not eat. Today if you don't work, you can make a pretty good living. We are not economically or financially bound by a job today as we were then. Back then, having a job was only a means to an end (providing for your family). Today, having a meaningful career is an important end in itself. Back then, we worked for someone; today we want to work with someone.

People today are more sophisticated and more mature than the workers of 50 years ago. In fact, the entire culture has changed, and if leadership does not change its style then it is the leadership that is out of sync with the culture and the desires of the American work force.

More than ever before in the history of American management, values are critical. A leader's values color the entire organization or country. Values drive the behavior and therefore the culture of an organization. All organizations have values, whether they know it or not. Simply watch how people are treated in any organization and you'll see their informal values. Trust is one of those critical values.

Why is trust important? Because all good sustained relationships require trust. Think about this: Would you voluntarily follow anyone you did not trust? We learned this lesson in Vietnam about not trusting our military leaders. Look what happened to those individuals.

So the question to ask yourself is why in the world would anyone choose to voluntarily follow you? What traits or characteristics do you possess that would encourage people to say, "I'll go with you anywhere"? Here is the acid test. If you left your current department or agency and went to another, would you have people who would want to transfer with you, or would the remaining staff now have a party because you're gone?

Certainly one of the key characteristics of an effective leader is that followers trust him or her. Have you ever worked for someone you did not trust? What was the atmosphere like? How would you characterize your relationship with him or her? What were some of the qualities or traits of this boss? Contrast this with someone you did trust. What was this atmosphere like? How would you characterize this trusting relationship? What were some of the qualities or traits of this boss?

Leadership is not about position, title, or rank; it is about developing, possessing or acquiring the necessary traits to encourage people to voluntarily follow us. We tend to trust those individuals who have integrity, solid values, and a strong character ethic. We tend not to trust those individuals who are duplicitous, upholding the law for others while violating it themselves. How many officers speed on their way to and from work every day, and then write tickets for citizens who do the same?

If you want to be a trusted leader, work on your character, and be trustworthy. Over time, establish yourself as an individual of great character and moral strength, walk the talk, have integrity, be honest and fair, do the right things, and you will be a trusted leader.

Source: Reprinted with permission from *Law Enforcement News,* May 15, 2001, pp. 9, 10. John Jay College of Criminal Justice (CCNY), 555 West 57th St., New York, NY 10019.

Trait Theory

Trait theory was popular until the 1950s. This theory was based on the contention that good leaders possessed certain character traits that poor leaders did not. Those who developed this theory, Stogdill and Goode, believed that a leader could be identified through a two-step process. The first step involved studying leaders and comparing them to nonleaders to determine which traits only the leaders possessed. The second step sought people who possessed these traits to be promoted to managerial positions.[52]

A study of 468 administrators in 13 companies found certain traits in successful administrators. They were more intelligent and better educated; had a stronger need for power; preferred independent activity, intense thought, and some risk; enjoyed relationships with people; and disliked detail work more than their subordinates.[53] Figure 2.5 shows traits and skills commonly associated with leader effectiveness, according to Gary Yuki. Following this study, a review of the literature on trait theory revealed the traits most identified with leadership ability: intelligence, initiative, extroversion, a sense of humor, enthusiasm, fairness, sympathy, and self-confidence.[54]

Trait theory has lost much of its support since the 1950s, partly because of the basic assumption of the theory that leadership cannot be taught. A more important reason, however, is simply the growth of new, more sophisticated approaches to the study of leadership. Quantifiable means to test trait theory were limited. What does it mean to say that a leader must be intelligent? By whose standards? Compared with persons within the organization or within society? How can traits such as a sense of humor, enthusiasm, fairness, and the others listed earlier be measured or tested? The inability to measure these factors was the real flaw in and the reason for the decline of trait theory.

Traits	Skills
Adaptable to situations	Clever (intelligent)
Alert to social environment	Conceptually skilled
Ambitious and achievement oriented	Creative
Assertive	Diplomatic and tactful
Cooperative	Fluent in speaking
Decisive	Knowledgeable about group task
Dependable	Organized (administrative ability)
Dominant (desire to influence others)	Persuasive
Energetic (high activity level)	Socially skilled
Persistent	
Self-confident	
Tolerant of stress	
Willing to assume responsibility	

FIGURE 2.5 Traits and Skills Commonly Associated with Leader Effectiveness

Source: Adapted from Gary A. Yukl, Leadership in Organizations, pp. 70, 121–125, Table 3-6. © 1981. Reproduced by permission of Pearson Education, Inc., Upper Saddle River, New Jersey.

Initiating structure

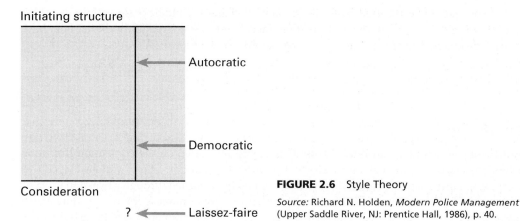

Consideration

FIGURE 2.6   Style Theory

Source: Richard N. Holden, *Modern Police Management* (Upper Saddle River, NJ: Prentice Hall, 1986), p. 40.

Style Theory

A study at Michigan State University investigated how leaders motivated individuals or groups to achieve organizational goals. The study determined that leaders must have a sense of the task to be accomplished as well as the environment in which their subordinates work. Three principles of leadership behavior emerged from the Michigan study:

1. Leaders must give task direction to their followers.
2. Closeness of supervision directly affects employee production. High-producing units had less direct supervision; highly supervised units had lower production. Conclusion: Employees need some area of freedom to make choices. Given this, they produce at a higher rate.
3. Leaders must be employee oriented. It is the leader's responsibility to facilitate employees' accomplishment of goals.[55]

In the 1950s, Edwin Fleishman began studies of leadership at Ohio State University. After focusing on leader behavior rather than personality traits, he identified two dimensions or basic principles of leadership that could be taught: *initiating structure* and *consideration* (Figure 2.6).[56] Initiating structure referred to supervisory behavior that focused on the achievement of organizational goals, and consideration was directed toward a supervisor's openness to subordinates' ideas and respect for their feelings as persons. High consideration and moderate initiating structure were assumed to yield higher job satisfaction and productivity than high initiating structure and low consideration.[57]

The major focus of **style theory** is the adoption of a single managerial style by a manager based on his or her position in regard to initiating structure and consideration. Three pure leadership styles were thought to be the basis for all managers: autocratic, democratic, and laissez-faire.

Autocratic leaders are leader centered and have a high initiating structure. They are primarily authoritarian in nature and prefer to give orders rather than invite group participation. They have a tendency to be personal in their criticism. This style works best in emergency situations in which strict control and rapid decision making are needed. The problem with autocratic leadership is the organization's inability to function when the leader is absent. It also stifles individual development and initiative because subordinates are rarely allowed to make an independent decision.[58]

The **democratic leader** tends to focus on working within the group and strives to attain cooperation from group members by eliciting their ideas and support. Democratic managers tend to be viewed as consideration oriented and strive to attain mutual respect with subordinates.

These leaders operate within an atmosphere of trust and delegate much authority. The democratic style is useful in organizations in which the course of action is uncertain and problems are relatively unstructured. It often taps the decision-making ability of subordinates. In emergency situations requiring a highly structured response, however, democratic leadership may prove too time-consuming and awkward to be effective. Thus, although the worker may appreciate the strengths of this style, its weaknesses must be recognized as well.[59]

The third leadership style, the **laissez-faire leader**, is a hands-off approach in which the leader is actually a nonleader. The organization in effect runs itself, with no input or control from the manager. This style has no positive aspects, as the entire organization is soon placed in jeopardy. In truth, this may not be a leadership style at all; instead, it may be an abdication of administrative duties.

CHARACTERISTICS AND SKILLS OF AMERICA'S BEST LEADERS

"Good in Their Skin"

Given today's deep-seated skepticism and distrust of leaders—often justified by public- and private-sector leaders' ethical violations, fraud, and cover-ups—it may seem that there is a complete dearth of leadership. To assess that view, recently, a weekly news magazine, *U.S. News & World Report*, teamed with Harvard University's Center for Public Leadership to identify leaders who are making a difference. A national panel sifted through nominations and agreed on a small group of men and women who embody the more important traits of leadership. The survey determined that there is not a lack of leadership, but rather a "wrong-headed notion of what a leader is," causing leaders to be hired for their style rather than substance and their image instead of integrity. It was also learned that there is no shortage of people with the capacity to lead who are just waiting for the opportunity.[60]

The survey found that twenty-first-century authentic leaders know who they are; they are "good in their skin," so they do not feel a need to impress or please others. They inspire those around them and bring people together around a shared purpose and a common set of values. They know the "true north" of their moral compass and are prepared to stay the course despite challenges and disappointments. They are more concerned about serving others than about their own success or recognition. By acknowledging their weaknesses, failings, and errors, they connect with people and empower them to take risks. Usually authentic leaders demonstrate the following five traits: pursuing their purpose with passion; practicing solid values; leading with their hearts as well as their heads; establishing connected relationships; and demonstrating self-discipline.[61]

For a less contemporary, classical view of what skills leaders need to possess, we consider the views of Robert Katz.

Katz's Three Skills

Robert Katz, in 1975, identified three essential skills that leaders should possess: technical, human, and conceptual. Katz defined a *skill* as the capacity to translate knowledge into action in such a way that a task is accomplished successfully.[62] Each of these skills (when performed effectively) results in the achievement of objectives and goals, which is the primary task of management.

Technical skills are those a manager needs to ensure that specific tasks are performed correctly. They are based on proven knowledge, procedures, or techniques. A police detective, a court administrator, and a probation officer have all developed technical skills directly related to the work they perform. Katz wrote that a technical skill "involves specialized knowledge, analytical ability within that specialty, and facility in the use of the tools and techniques of the specific discipline."[63] This is the skill most easily trained for. A court administrator, for example, has to be knowledgeable in areas such as computer applications, budgeting, caseload management, space utilization, public relations, and personnel administration; a police detective must possess technical skills in interviewing, fingerprinting, and surveillance techniques.[64]

Human skills involve working with people, including being thoroughly familiar with what motivates employees and how to utilize group processes. Katz visualized human skills as including "the executive's ability to work effectively as a group member and to build cooperative effort within the team he leads."[65] Katz added that the human relations skill involves tolerance of ambiguity and empathy. *Tolerance of ambiguity* means that the manager is able to handle problems when insufficient information precludes making a totally informed decision. *Empathy* is the ability to put oneself in another's place. An awareness of human skills allows a manager to provide the necessary leadership and direction, ensuring that tasks are accomplished in a timely fashion and with the least expenditure of resources.[66]

Conceptual skills, Katz said, involve "coordinating and integrating all the activities and interests of the organization toward a common objective."[67] Katz considered such skills to include "an ability to translate knowledge into action." For example, in a criminal justice setting, a court decision concerning the admissibility of evidence would need to be examined in terms of how it affects detectives, other court cases, the forensic laboratory, the property room, and the work of the street officer.

Katz emphasized that these skills can be taught to actual and prospective administrators; thus, good administrators are not simply born but can be trained in the classroom. Furthermore, all three of these skills are present in varying degrees at each management level. As one moves up the hierarchy, conceptual skills become more important and technical skills less important. The common denominator for all levels of management is *human* skills. In today's litigious environment, it is inconceivable that a manager could neglect the human skills.

MOTIVATING EMPLOYEES

One of the most fascinating subjects throughout history has been how to motivate people. Some have sought to do so through justice (Plato), others through psychoanalysis (Freud), some through conditioning (Pavlov), some through incentives (Taylor), and still others through fear (any number of dictators and despots). From the Industrial Revolution to the present, managers have been trying to get a full day's work from their subordinates. The controversy in the early 1990s caused by Japanese businessmen who stated that American workers were lazy certainly raised our collective ire; many U.S. businesspeople and managers would probably agree that better worker motivation is needed. As Donald Favreau and Joseph Gillespie stated, "Getting people to work, the way you want them to work, when you want them to work, is indeed a challenge."[68]

Many theories have attempted to explain motivation. Some of the best known are those resulting from the Hawthorne studies and those developed by Abraham Maslow, Douglas McGregor, and Frederick Herzberg, all of which are discussed here along with the expectancy and contingency theories.

The Hawthorne Studies

Another important theory that criminal justice leaders must comprehend is that of the **Hawthorne effect**, which essentially means that employees' behavior may be altered if they know they are being studied—and that management *cares*; this was demonstrated in the following research project.

As mentioned earlier, one of the most important studies of worker motivation and behavior, launching intense interest and research in those areas, was the Western Electric Company's study in the 1920s. In 1927, engineers at the Hawthorne plant of Western Electric near Chicago conducted an experiment with several groups of workers to determine the effect of illumination on production. The engineers found that when illumination was increased in stages, production increased. To verify their finding, they reduced illumination to its previous level; again, production increased. Confused by their findings, they contacted Elton Mayo and his colleague Fritz Roethlisberger from Harvard to investigate.[69] First, the researchers selected several experienced female assemblers for an experiment. Management removed the women from their formal group and isolated them in a room. The women were compensated on the basis of the output of their group. Next, researchers began a series of environmental changes, each discussed with the women in advance of its implementation. For example, breaks were introduced and light refreshments were served. The normal 6-day workweek was reduced to 5 days and the workday was cut by 1 hour. *Each* of these changes resulted in increased output.[70] To verify these findings, researchers returned the women to their original working conditions; breaks were eliminated, the 6-day workweek was reinstituted, and all other work conditions were reinstated. The results were that production again increased!

Mayo and his team then performed a second study at the Hawthorne plant. A new group of 14 workers—all men who performed simple, repetitive telephone coil-winding tasks—were given variations in rest periods and workweeks.[71] The men were also put on a reasonable piece rate—that is, the more they produced, the more money they would earn. The assumption was that the workers would strive to produce more because it was in their own economic interest to do so.

The workers soon split into two informal groups on their own, each group setting its own standards of output and conduct. The workers' output did not increase. Neither too little nor too much production was permitted, and peers exerted pressure to keep members in line. The values of the informal group appeared to be more powerful than the allure of bigger incomes:

1. Don't be a "rate buster" and produce too much work.
2. If you turn out too little work, you are a "chiseler."
3. Don't be a "squealer" to supervisors.
4. Don't be officious; if you aren't a supervisor, don't act like one.[72]

Taken together, the Hawthorne studies revealed that people work for a variety of reasons, not just for money and subsistence. They seek satisfaction for more than their physical needs at work and from their coworkers. For the first time, clear evidence was gathered to support workers' social and esteem needs. As a result, this collision between the human relations school, begun in the Hawthorne studies, and traditional organizational theory sent researchers and theorists off in new and different directions. At least three major new areas of inquiry evolved: (1) what motivates workers (leading to the work of Maslow and Herzberg), (2) leadership (discussed earlier), and (3) organizations as behavioral systems.

Maslow's Hierarchy of Needs

Abraham H. Maslow (1908–1970), founder of the **humanistic school** of psychology, conducted research on human behavior at the Air University, Maxwell Air Force Base, Alabama, during the 1940s. His approach to motivation was unique in that the behavior patterns analyzed were those of motivated, happy, and production-oriented people—achievers, not underachievers. He studied biographies of historical and public figures, including Abraham Lincoln, Albert Einstein, and Eleanor Roosevelt; he also observed and interviewed some of his contemporaries—all of whom showed no psychological problems or signs of neurotic behavior.

Maslow hypothesized that if he could understand what made these people function, it would be possible to apply the same techniques to others, thus achieving a high state of motivation. His observations were coalesced into a *hierarchy of needs*.[73]

Maslow concluded that because human beings are part of the animal kingdom, their basic and primary needs or drives are physiological: air, food, water, sex, and shelter. These needs are related to survival. Next in order of importance are needs related to safety or security; protection against danger: murder, criminal assault, threat, deprivation, and tyranny. At the middle of the hierarchy is belonging, or social needs: being accepted by one's peers and associating with members of groups. At the next level of the hierarchy are the needs or drives related to ego: self-esteem, self-respect, power, prestige, recognition, and status. At the top of the hierarchy is self-realization or actualization: self-fulfillment, creativity, becoming all that one is capable of becoming.[74] Figure 2.7 depicts this hierarchy.

Unlike the lower needs, the higher needs are rarely satisfied. Maslow suggested that to prevent frustration, needs should be filled in sequential order. A satisfied need is no longer a motivator. Maslow's research also indicated that once a person reaches a high state of motivation (i.e., esteem or self-realization levels), he or she will remain highly motivated, will have a positive attitude toward the organization, and will adopt a "pitch in and help" philosophy.

McGregor's Theory X/Theory Y

Douglas **McGregor** (1906–1967), who served as president of Antioch College and then on the faculty of the Massachusetts Institute of Technology, was one of the great advocates of humane and democratic management. At Antioch, McGregor tested his theories of democratic management. He noted that behind every managerial decision or action are assumptions about human behavior. He chose the simplest terms possible with which to express them, designating one set of assumptions as **Theory X** and the other as **Theory Y**.[75]

Theory X managers hold traditional views of direction and control, such as the following:

- The average human being has an inherent dislike of work and will avoid it if possible. This assumption has deep roots, beginning with the punishment of Adam and Eve and their banishment into a world where they had to work for a living. Management's use of negative reinforcement and the emphasis on "a fair day's work" reflect an underlying belief that management must counter an inherent dislike for work.[76]
- Because of their dislike of work, most people must be coerced, controlled, directed, or threatened with punishment to get them to put forth adequate effort to achieve organizational objectives. Their dislike of work is so strong that even the promise of rewards is not generally enough to overcome it. People will accept the rewards and demand greater ones. Only the threat of punishment will work.[77]
- The average human being prefers to be directed, wishes to avoid responsibility, has relatively little ambition, and wants security above all. This assumption of the "mediocrity of the masses" is rarely expressed so bluntly. Although much lip service is paid to the "sanctity" of the worker and of human beings in general, many managers reflect this assumption in practice and policy.

Self-Realization Needs	Job-Related Satisfiers
Reaching Your Potential Independence Creativity Self-Expression	Involvement in Planning Your Work Freedom to Make Decisions Affecting Work Creative Work to Perform Opportunities for Growth and Development

Esteem Needs	Job-Related Satisfiers
Responsibility Self-Respect Recognition Sense of Accomplishment Sense of Competence	Status Symbols Merit Awards Challenging Work Sharing in Decisions Opportunity for Advancement

Social Needs	Job-Related Satisfiers
Companionship Acceptance Love and Affection Group Membership	Opportunities for Interaction with Others Team Spirit Friendly Co-workers

Safety Needs	Job-Related Satisfiers
Security for Self and Possessions Avoidance of Risks Avoidance of Harm Avoidance of Pain	Safe Working Conditions Seniority Fringe Benefits Proper Supervision Sound Company Policies, Programs, and Practices

Physical Needs	Job-Related Satisfiers
Food Clothing Shelter Comfort Self-Preservation	Pleasant Working Conditions Adequate Wage or Salary Rest Periods Labor-Saving Devices Efficient Work Methods

FIGURE 2.7   Maslow's Hierarchy of Human Needs

Source: A. H. Maslow, *Motivation and Personality,* 2nd ed. (New York: Harper & Row, 1970).

Theory Y managers take the opposite view of the worker:

- The expenditure of physical and mental effort in work is as natural as play or rest. The average human being does not inherently dislike work; it may even be a source of satisfaction, to be performed voluntarily.
- External control and the threat of punishment are not the only means for producing effort to achieve organizational objectives.
- Commitment to objectives is a function of the rewards associated with their achievement. The most significant rewards—satisfaction of ego and self-actualization needs—can be direct products of effort directed to organizational objectives.
- Under proper conditions, the average human being learns not only to accept but also to seek responsibility. In this view, the avoidance of responsibility, lack of ambition, and emphasis on security are general consequences of experience, not inherent human characteristics.
- The capacity to exercise a high degree of imagination, ingenuity, and creativity in the solution of organizational problems is widely, not narrowly, distributed in the population.
- Under the conditions of modern industrial life, the intellectual potential of the average human being is only partially utilized.

Herzberg's Motivation-Hygiene Theory

During the 1950s, Frederick Herzberg conducted a series of studies in which he asked workers, primarily engineers, to describe the times when they felt particularly good and particularly bad about their jobs. The respondents identified several sources of satisfaction and dissatisfaction in their work. Then, from these findings, Herzberg isolated two vital factors found in all jobs: maintenance or hygiene factors and motivational factors.

Maintenance or hygiene factors are those elements in the work environment that meet an employee's hedonistic need to avoid pain. These factors include the necessities of any job (e.g., adequate pay, benefits, job security, decent working conditions, supervision, interpersonal relations). Hygiene factors do not satisfy or motivate; they set the stage for motivation. They are, however, a major source of dissatisfaction when they are inadequate.[78]

Motivational factors are those psychosocial factors that provide intrinsic satisfaction and serve as an incentive for people to invest more of their time, talent, energy, and expertise in productive behavior. Examples include achievement, recognition, responsibility, the work itself, advancement, and potential for growth. The absence of motivators does not necessarily produce job dissatisfaction.[79]

Although these needs are obviously related, they represent totally different dimensions of satisfaction.

Expectancy and Contingency Theories

In the 1960s, *expectancy theory* was developed, focusing on certain beliefs that can influence effort and performance. As examples, if an employee believes that his or her efforts will result in a certain level of performance leading to a desired reward, then that employee will likely take action accordingly. Of course, the opposite is true as well: If an employee perceives a low correlation between effort or performance and reward, then the result may well be inaction. Essentially, expectancy theory holds that employees will do what their managers or organizations want them to do if the following are true:

1. The task appears to be possible (employees believe they possess the necessary competence).
2. The reward (outcome) offered is seen as desirable by the employees (intrinsic rewards come from the job itself; extrinsic rewards are supplied by others).

3. Employees believe that performing the required behavior or task will bring the desired outcome.
4. There is a good chance that better performance will bring greater rewards.[80]

Expectancy theory will work for an organization that specifies what behaviors it expects from people and what the rewards or outcomes will be for those who exhibit such behaviors. Rewards may be pay increases, time off, chances for advancement, a sense of achievement, or other benefits. Managers and organizations can find out what their employees want and see to it that they are provided with the rewards they seek. Walter Newsom[81] said that the reality of the expectancy theory can be summarized by the "nine C's": (1) capability (does a person have the capability to perform well?), (2) confidence (does a person believe that he or she can perform the job well?), (3) challenge (does a person have to work hard to perform the job well?), (4) criteria (does a person know the difference between good and poor performance?), (5) credibility (does a person believe the manager will deliver on promises?), (6) consistency (do subordinates believe that all employees receive similar preferred outcomes for good performance, and vice versa?), (7) compensation (do the outcomes associated with good performance reward the employee with money and other types of rewards?), (8) cost (what does it cost a person, in effort and outcomes foregone, to perform well?), and (9) communication (does the manager communicate with the subordinate?).

Later, in the 1970s, Morse and Lorsch built on McGregor's and Herzberg's theories with their theory of motivation called *contingency theory.* This theory sought to determine the fit between the organization's characteristics and its tasks and the motivations of individuals. The basic components of the contingency theory are that (1) among people's needs is a central need to achieve a sense of competence, (2) the ways in which people fulfill this need will vary from person to person, (3) competence motivation is most likely to be achieved when there is a fit between task and organization, and (4) a sense of competence continues to motivate people even after competence is achieved. In essence, we all want to be competent in our work. Contingency theory contends that people performing highly structured and organized tasks perform better in Theory X organizations and that those who perform unstructured and uncertain tasks perform better under a Theory Y approach. This theory tells managers to tailor jobs to fit people or to give people the skills, knowledge, and attitudes they will need to become competent.[82]

GAMERS, TATTOOS, AND ATTITUDES: GENERATIONS X, Y, AND NEXT EMPLOYEES

Born in a Different World

Although not a subject of major theory, many articles and books[83] are being written about understanding and motivating those persons of four younger generations who are now entering or will soon enter the workplace: the first, termed **Generation X**, includes those persons born between 1965 and 1975; **Generation Y** was born between 1976 and 1980.[84] Those who were born between 1990 and 1995 are being labeled the **Next generation**.[85] Finally, some attention is now being given to the *Millennials,* also termed by some *Generation 2.0*—those 20—some things who are extremely tech-savvy and digitally literate and who are preparing to enter the workplace.

From the Gen Xers on, these generations grew up very quickly amid rising crime rates and violence as hostage crises and major disasters unfolded around them; their youthful years included a national fear of AIDS; and they entered the job market only to be confronted with new terms like *downsizing*.[86] They grew up in a world where terrorism is a fact of life; with scheduled, structured lives; with a multicultural society; and with a resurgence of the "American hero": police officers and firefighters who commonly are in the news. As a result, they have an emerging sense of patriotism and political interest, and regard themselves as special, connected, confident, hopeful, goal and achievement oriented, and inclusive.[87]

Almost 90 percent of the X, Y, Next, and Millennial generations have used or will use the Internet; more than half send text messages daily and use social networking sites, have gotten a tattoo or had a body piercing, or have dyed their hair a nontraditional color.[88] Their television viewing habits are unique as well. For those who grew up on a steady diet of television in the 1960s and 1970s, consider the evolution in television programming using the following examples: *Dragnet* versus *CSI* or *NYPD Blue*; *Marcus Welby, M.D.* versus *ER*; *Starsky and Hutch* versus *24*; and *Three's Company* versus *The Simpsons*. Certainly today's programs are more complex; that complexity, along with the impact of video gaming, has created a culture that is more intellectually demanding.[89]

Those who are now in their twenties have never known a world without digital gaming—indeed, the digital gaming industry has sold more than 100 million units, and 70 percent of children under 18 live in households where there is a game console. An entire generation grew up in a game world—where reward is everywhere. Gaming taps into the brain's natural reward circuitry; it offers everyone the opportunity to be in charge, succeed, and be a star; be bosses and experts in their gaming environments; experience thrills, crashes, and deaths without getting hurt; and be in a world where anything is possible, and trial and error is the best way to find an answer.[90]

With respect to tattooing, almost one-half of all Americans between the ages of 18 and 29 have either a tattoo or a piercing other than pierced ears according to the *Journal of the American Academy of Dermatology*.[91] While a member of these younger generations might not look twice at exposed ink or metal, an administrator of the baby boomer generation might find it offensive. Others in public and private organizations often find themselves caught in the middle, trying to be more flexible with their dress codes while projecting a professional image.[92]

The restricting of tattoos and body piercings is discussed further.

Implications for the Criminal Justice Workplace

Many veterans in today's workplace already view Gen X workers as slackers and malign them as being unreliable, unwilling to work long hours, thinking in terms of a job rather than a career, and having unrealistic expectations about raises and promotions.[93] The Y Generation, or echo boomers, and the Millennials, are viewed by some as coddled and confident, technologically savvy, and with the attitude that "I'm here to make a difference."[94] These complaints, of course, are nothing new; even in the time of Aristotle, adults condemned the younger generation's lack of motivation and believed that they would fail in their work from a lack of loyalty.[95]

Considering the earlier and the possible impact of these generations entering criminal justice with an interactive, self-reliant, wired upbringing and a reliance on the strategy of trial and error, how might criminal justice integrate such individuals into a work environment with a strong hierarchy and no reset button? First, the task ahead for aging baby boomers is to adapt the wisdom of their years to the habits of gamers and millennials as they welcome these newcomers into entry-level roles. They will be adept at probing, participatory thinking, and adapting to changing circumstances.[96]

The American workplace will increasingly become a playing field of competing viewpoints and values, and young adults from the three aforementioned generations share, or will soon share, the same workspace and attempt to navigate unknown cultural territory.[97] The implications for criminal justice administrators are several. First, they should think of ways in which they can take advantage of the motivations of these younger generations as they enter the field: They desire to work in teams, perform work of significance, engage in activities consistent with heroism, and have flexibility in their daily environment.

It is also recommended that these leaders attempt to understand that the younger employee's preferred work environment is more casual and friendly, technologically up-to-date, neat and orderly, collegial and a place to learn, and includes a high level of freedom. Furthermore, such leaders should avoid judging those whose work ethic is slightly different from theirs; accommodate individual needs whenever possible; forgive impatience (if individuals are anxious for raises and promotions); and, when possible, allow room for mistakes and for the youthful workers to correct the mistakes themselves and to learn from them.[98]

Finally, regarding tattooing, administrators can legally restrict tattoos, body piercings, and body art with dress codes or uniform requirements unless their state has additional legislation granting protection. Some agencies, like the Houston, Texas, police department, have implemented new policies; they require all tattoo-bearing officers to cover their ink with their uniforms or plain clothes (no bandages or sweatbands allowed) or have them removed by laser or other treatment (officers working undercover are exempt from the rule, but bike police, who might generally wear shorts, are required to wear long pants if they have leg tattoos).[99]

Attempts to restrict such bodily adornments, however, have met with lawsuits and discrimination allegations filed with the Equal Employment Opportunity Commission (some employees have even sued, claiming membership in the Church of Body Modification). As more body art discrimination cases go to court, organizations and companies need to develop dress code policies that are applied consistently and equally.[100]

In a related vein, criminal justice administrators are given some control over their employees' appearance—and may find guidance in that arena—in a 1976 U.S. Supreme Court decision, *Kelley v. Johnson*.[101] There, a police agency restricted the personal appearance of male members of the department by providing that officers "shall be neat and clean at all times while on duty"; placing specific restrictions on hair length and grooming, sideburns, mustaches, and the wearing of wigs; and prohibiting beards and goatees. The Court's analysis began with the presumption that such regulations are valid and placed the burden of proof on the objecting employee to show the invalidity of the regulation; the Court said that such appearance regulations are generally valid unless those regulations are so irrational that they are arbitrary. Furthermore, the regulations in question were rationally justified by either a desire to make police officers readily recognizable to the members of the public or a desire to maintain the *esprit de corps* (i.e., morale) of the organization.

Summary

Most young people entering the labor force would probably like to retain their individuality, feel free to express themselves, have a sense of being an important part of the team, and realize both extrinsic and intrinsic rewards from their work. The reality is, however, that a majority of people entering the job market will work within the structure of an organization that will not meet all of their personal needs.

We have seen that many organizations have a highly refined bureaucracy. Whether an organization will meet an employee's needs depends largely on its administrative philosophy. Therefore, the discussions in this chapter covered the structure and function of organizations and, just as important, how administrators and subordinates function within them. Also shown to be of major importance is the need for effective communication.

The point to be made above all else is that administrators must know their people. In addition to covering several prominent theories that have withstood the test of time, I pointed out some approaches that have not succeeded. One can learn much from a failed approach or even from a poor boss who failed to appreciate and understand subordinates and used improper or no motivational techniques.

Questions for Review

1. Define *organization*. What is its function and structure?
2. Explain the evolution of organizational theory, including scientific, human relations, systems, and bureaucratic management theories.
3. Define *span of control* and *unity of command*.
4. Explain the characteristics and skills of America's best leaders.
5. What did Katz say are the three most important general qualities in leaders?
6. What does *communication* mean? What is its importance in organizations? Explain cultural cues, the nature and uniqueness of police communications, and some of the major barriers to effective communication.
7. Objectively assess what kind of leader you would likely be. Is it an effective style? What are some of the possible advantages and disadvantages of that style?
8. What kind of world did the X, Y, and Next generations grow up in, and what advantages and challenges do those persons pose in the criminal justice workplace? In criminal justice, what are the policy and legal implications of the younger generations' penchant for tattoos and a generally nontraditional appearance?

Learn by Doing

1. As part of a criminal justice class project concerning government careers, you are assigned to examine bureaucracies. What would you say are some of the specific characteristics and criticisms of bureaucracies? What could happen in criminal justice if these characteristics were applied in the extreme?
2. You are contacted by a friend who belongs to a local civic club that is planning a Labor Day luncheon to recognize all workers in the community. Knowing of your background and prior study of organizational theory, she asks you to speak at this luncheon concerning the scientific management approach to organizational theory—particularly the career of Frederick W. Taylor and his contributions and primary motivations regarding management. What will you report?
3. Your prison duty shift's middle manager (a lieutenant) comes to you saying he has personally observed a number of problems concerning the manner in which communication is occurring from one duty shift to another. These problems appear to primarily involve inaccurate information being disseminated, a grapevine that seems bent on carrying incorrect, malicious information; and a diverse group of employees with language and cultural barriers. You are assigned to look at the problem as well as recommend means by which communications could be improved. How would you proceed, and what kinds of ideas might you put forth?

Related Websites

Criminal Justice Management Council
http://www.co.la-crosse.wi.us/Minutes%20and%20Agendas/HmPgsSpecial/CJMC.htm

Criminal Justice Management Institute
http://cjmi.com

Embassy of the United States: Strengthening Criminal Justice Management in Foreign Countries
http://phnompenh.usembassy.gov/ilea.html

GOVNET: Criminal Justice Management Corporate Information
http://www.govnet.co.uk/corporate/cjm.htm

JUSTINFO: The Newsletter of the National Criminal Justice Reference Service
http://www.theiacp.org

National Center for Policy Analysis
http://ncpa.org/pi/crime/crime71.html

National Institute of Justice International Center
http://www.ojp.usdoj.gov/nij

Policy Action Network
http://movingideas.org

Sourcebook of Criminal Justice Statistics
http://www.albany.edu/sourcebook

Notes

1. Steven Levy, "Working in Dilbert's World," *Newsweek* (August 12, 1996):52–57.
2. David A. Tansik and James F. Elliott, *Managing Police Organizations* (Monterey, CA: Duxbury Press, 1981), p. 1.
3. Stephen P. Robbins, *Organizational Theory: Structure, Design and Applications* (Upper Saddle River, NJ: Prentice Hall, 1987).
4. Larry K. Gaines, John L. Worrall, Mittie D. Southerland, and John E. Angell, *Police Administration,* 2nd ed. (New York: McGraw-Hill, 2002), p. 8.
5. Peter W. Blau and W. Richard Scott, *Formal Organizations* (Scranton, PA: Chandler, 1962), p. 43.
6. Gaines et al., *Police Administration,* p. 12.
7. Ronald G. Lynch, *The Police Manager: Professional Leadership Skills,* 3rd ed. (New York: Random House, 1986), p. 4.
8. Samuel C. Certo, *Principles of Modern Management: Functions and Systems,* 4th ed. (Boston: Allyn and Bacon, 1989), p. 35.
9. See Elton Mayo, *The Human Problems of an Industrial Civilization* (New York: Macmillan, 1933).
10. Paul M. Whisenand and Fred Ferguson, *The Managing of Police Organizations,* 3rd ed. (Upper Saddle River, NJ: Prentice Hall, 1989), pp. 218–219.
11. Lynch, *Police Manager,* pp. 5–6.
12. Abraham H. Maslow, *Motivation and Personality* (New York: Harper & Row, 1954).
13. Douglas McGregor, *The Human Side of Enterprise* (New York: McGraw-Hill, 1960).
14. Robert R. Blake and Jane S. Mouton, *The Managerial Grid* (Houston, TX: Gulf, 1964).
15. Lynch, *Police Manager,* pp. 7–8.
16. Max Weber, *The Theory of Social and Economic Organization,* trans. A. M. Henderson and Talcott Parsons (New York: Oxford University Press, 1947), pp. 329–330.
17. James Q. Wilson, *Varieties of Police Behavior* (Cambridge, MA: Harvard University Press, 1968), pp. 2–3.
18. Ibid., p. 3.
19. Lyndall F. Urwick, *Notes on the Theory of Organization* (New York: American Management Association, 1952).
20. Troy Lane, "Span of Control for Law Enforcement Agencies," *The Associate* (March–April 2006): 19–31.
21. Ibid.
22. Gaines et al., *Police Administration,* p. 12.
23. Leonard R. Sayles and George Strauss, *Human Behavior in Organizations* (Upper Saddle River, NJ: Prentice Hall, 1966), p. 349.
24. Charles R. Swanson, Leonard Territo, and Robert W. Taylor, *Police Administration,* 2nd ed. (New York: Macmillan, 1988), p. 308.
25. Mario Pei, *Language for Everybody: What It Is and How to Master It* (Greenwich, CT: Devin-Adair Co., 1961), pp. 4–5.
26. Louis A. Radelet, *The Police and the Community: Studies* (Beverly Hills, CA: Glencoe, 1973), p. 92.
27. Swanson et al., *Police Administration,* p. 86.
28. Institute of Government, University of Georgia, *Interpersonal Communication: A Guide for Staff Development* (Athens: Author, 1974), p. 15.
29. Wayne W. Bennett and Karen Hess, *Management and Supervision in Law Enforcement* (St. Paul, MN: West, 1992), p. 72.
30. See R. C. Huseman, quoted in ibid., pp. 21–27. Material for this section was also drawn from Swanson et al., *Police Administration,* pp. 309–311.
31. Swanson et al., *Police Administration,* pp. 312–313.
32. D. Katz and R. L. Kahn, *The Social Psychology of Organizations* (New York: Wiley, 1966), p. 239. As cited in P. V. Lewis, *Organizational Communication: The Essence of Effective Management* (Columbus, OH: Grid, 1975), p. 36.
33. Lewis, *Organizational Communication,* p. 38.
34. Swanson et al., *Police Administration,* p. 315.
35. See R. K. Allen, *Organizational Management Through Communication* (New York: Harper & Row, 1977), pp. 77–79.
36. Michael L. Birzer and Cliff Roberson, *Police Field Operations: Theory Meets Practice* (Boston: Pearson, 2008).
37. Swanson et al., *Police Administration,* p. 343.
38. Stephen W. Mastrofski, "Police Agency Accreditation: The Prospects of Reform," *American Journal of Police* 5(3) (1986):45–81.
39. Alex Markels, "Managers Aren't Always Able to Get the Right Message Across with E-Mail," *The Wall Street Journal* (August 6, 1996), p. 2.
40. Robert L. Montgomery, "Are You a Good Listener?" *Nation's Business* (October 1981):65–68.
41. Bennett and Hess, *Management and Supervision in Law Enforcement,* p. 82.
42. G. Weaver, "Law Enforcement in a Culturally Diverse Society," *FBI Law Enforcement Bulletin* (September 1992):1–10.

43. Certo, *Principles of Modern Management*, p. 103.

44. Wayne W. Bennett and Karen M. Hess, *Management and Supervision in Law Enforcement,* 4th ed. (Belmont, CA: Wadsworth, 2004), p. 52; Warren Bennis and Burt Nanus, *Leaders* (New York: Harper & Row, 1985).

45. Bennett and Hess, *Management and Supervision in Law Enforcement*, 4th ed., pp. 53–54.

46. Paul Hersey and Kenneth H. Blanchard, *Management of Organizational Behavior,* 3rd ed. (Upper Saddle River, NJ: Prentice Hall, 1977), p. 12.

47. Ibid.

48. Bennett and Hess, *Management and Supervision in Law Enforcement,* 4th ed., p. 52.

49. Ibid.

50. Roger D. Evered and James C. Selman, "Coaching and the Art of Management," *Organizational Dynamics* 18 (Autumn 1989):16.

51. Charles R. Swanson, Leonard Territo, and Robert W. Taylor, *Police Administration: Structures, Processes, and Behavior,* 6th ed. (Upper Saddle River, NJ: Prentice Hall, 2005), p. 272.

52. Richard Holden, *Modern Police Management,* 2nd ed. (Upper Saddle River, NJ: Prentice Hall, 1994), p. 47.

53. Thomas A. Mahoney, Thomas H. Jerdee, and Alan N. Nash, "Predicting Managerial Effectiveness," *Personnel Psychology* 13(2) (Summer 1960):147–163.

54. Joe Kelly, *Organizational Behavior: An Existential Systems Approach,* rev. ed. (Homewood, IL: Richard D. Irwin, 1974), p. 363.

55. Bennett and Hess, *Management and Supervision in Law Enforcement*, 4th ed., p. 57.

56. Edwin Fleishman, "Leadership Climate, Human Relations Training and Supervisory Behavior," *Personnel Psychology* 6 (1953):208–222.

57. Stephen M. Sales, "Supervisory Style and Productivity: Review and Theory," in Larry Cummings and William E. Scott (eds.), *Readings in Organizational Behavior and Human Performance* (Homewood, IL: Richard D. Irwin, 1969), p. 122.

58. Holden, *Modern Police Management,* pp. 39–40.

59. Ibid., pp. 41–42.

60. Bill George, "Truly Authentic Leadership," *U.S. News & World Report* (October 30, 2006): 52.

61. Ibid.

62. Robert L. Katz, "Skills of an Effective Administrator," *Harvard Business Review* 52 (1975):23.

63. Ibid., p. 23.

64. Dan L. Costley and Ralph Todd, *Human Relations in Organizations* (St. Paul, MN: West, 1978).

65. Ibid., p. 24.

66. James M. Higgins, *Human Relations: Concepts and Skills* (New York: Random House, 1982).

67. Ibid., p. 27.

68. Favreau and Gillespie, *Modern Police Administration,* p. 85.

69. Warren Richard Plunkett, *Supervision: The Direction of People at Work* (Dubuque, IA: Wm. C. Brown, 1983), p. 121.

70. Elton Mayo, *The Social Problems of an Industrial Civilization* (Boston: Division of Research, Graduate School of Business Administration, Harvard University, 1945), pp. 68–86.

71. Favreau and Gillespie, *Modern Police Administration,* pp. 100–101.

72. Frederick J. Roethlisberger and William J. Dickson, *Management and the Worker* (Cambridge, MA: Harvard University Press, 1939), p. 522.

73. Favreau and Gillespie, *Modern Police Administration,* p. 87.

74. Ibid.

75. Ibid., p. 88.

76. Ibid., p. 89.

77. Ibid.

78. Harry W. More and W. Fred Wegener, *Behavioral Police Management* (New York: Macmillan, 1992), pp. 163–164.

79. Frederick Herzberg, "One More Time: How Do You Motivate Employees?" in *Harvard Business Review Classic,* September–October 1987, http://www.sky-lakebios.com/2%20Herzburg%20kita.pdf (accessed July 22, 2008).

80. Randall S. Schuler, *Personnel and Human Resources Management* (St. Paul, MN: West, 1981), pp. 41–43.

81. Walter B. Newsom, "Motivate, Now!" *Personnel Journal* 14 (February 1990):51–55.

82. Plunkett, *Supervision,* pp. 131–132.

83. See, for example, Bob Harrison, "Gamers, Millennials, and Generation Next: Implications for Policing," *The Police Chief* (October 2007):150–160; Douglas Coupland, *Generation X: Tales for an Accelerated Culture* (New York: St. Martin's, 1992); Carolyn A. Martin and Bruce Tulgan, *Managing Generation Y* (Amherst, MA: HRD Press, 2001).

84. Stephen's Generation X Site, http://www.users.metro2000.net/~stabbott/genx.htm (accessed September 7, 2005).

85. Pew Research Center, "How Young People View Their Lives, Futures, and Politics: A Portrait of Generation Next," http://people-press.org/reports/pdf/300.pdf (accessed January 3, 2008).

LEARNING OBJECTIVES

After reading this chapter, the student will:

- understand why police agencies are arranged into organizations
- understand the division of labor in an organization
- be familiar with the seven elements of police organizational structure
- know how the military model can both help and hinder policing
- understand community policing and its problem-solving S.A.R.A. process
- know the underlying assumptions and functions of crime prevention through environmental design (CPTED) and situational crime prevention (SCP)
- know what is meant by an Executive Session, and how it can influence policing
- understand what experts say is needed to transform a good police organization into a great one
- know how a police organization can become accredited and the benefits of doing so
- comprehend the purposes of policies, procedures, rules, and regulations in police organizations

Good order is the foundation of all things.

—EDMUND BURKE

INTRODUCTION

To perform smoothly (at least as smoothly as society, resources, politics, and other influences permit), police agencies must be organized to enhance the accomplishment of their basic mission and goals. This chapter examines the elements of contemporary police organization and what is needed organizationally to effect the transition to a community-oriented policing and problem-solving operation

First, we consider how law enforcement agencies constitute and operate as bona fide organizations; included here are the seven elements of police organizational structure, examples of basic as well as more specialized organizational structures for police agencies, the need for grouping of activities and the division of labor, and a comment on their quasi-military nature. Next, after an overview of policies, procedures, rules, and regulations that provide guidelines for organizations, we examine what is now the dominant concept in police philosophy and operations: community-oriented policing and problem solving, or COPPS; this approach has caused many changes in the organization and administration of police agencies. In addition to defining the term and discussing the problem-solving process, under the COPPS umbrella, we look at two related aspects of crime analysis and prevention: crime prevention through environmental design (CPTED) and situational crime prevention (SCP) (in Chapter 16, we discuss another tool: CompStat). Then, we look at what experts say is needed in order to transform a good police organization into a great one. Following that is a discussion of how a police organization may become accredited and the benefits of doing so. Examples of COPPS and crime prevention are provided throughout the chapter as well.

POLICE AGENCIES AS ORGANIZATIONS

Today the policing of America is a very labor-intensive and costly undertaking, with about 1.1 million people being employed by local (about three-fourths of all employees), state (about one-tenth of employees), and federal levels of government, and having a combined annual payroll of more than $5.25 billion.[1] In this chapter section, we will look at how all of these personnel—and their collective functions—are organized for greater efficiency.

The Grouping of Activities

An **organization** is an artificial structure created to coordinate either people or groups and resources to achieve a mission or goal.[2] Certainly, police agencies fit this definition. First, the organization of these agencies includes a number of specialized units (e.g., patrol, traffic, investigation, records). The role of chief executives, middle managers, and first-line supervisors is to ensure that these units work together to reach a common goal; allowing each unit to work independently would lead to fragmentation, conflict, and competition and would subvert the entire organization's goals and purposes. Second, police agencies consist of people who interact within the organization and with external organizations.

Through mission statements, policies and procedures (discussed later), and management style, among other factors, police administrators attempt to ensure that the organization meets its overall goals of investigating and suppressing crime and that the organization works amicably with similar organizations. As the organization becomes larger, the need for people to cooperate to achieve the organizational goals increases. Formal organization charts assist in this endeavor by spelling out areas of responsibility and lines of communication and by defining the chain of command.

Police administrators modify or design the structure of their organization to fulfill their mission. An organizational structure reflects the formal organization of task and authority relationships determined to be best suited to accomplishing the police mission (organizational structures are discussed and shown later in this chapter).

The Division of Labor

The larger an agency, the greater the need for specialization and the more vertical (taller) its organizational chart becomes. Some 2,300 years ago, Plato observed that "each thing becomes . . . easier when one man, exempt from other tasks, does one thing."[3]

Specialization, or the **division of labor**, is one of the basic features of traditional organizational theory.[4] Specialization produces different groups of functional responsibilities, and the jobs allocated to meet these different responsibilities are held by people who are considered to be especially well qualified to perform those jobs. Thus, specialization is crucial to effectiveness and efficiency in large organizations.[5]

Specialization makes the organization more complex, however, by complicating communication, increasing the number of units from which cooperation must be obtained, and creating conflict among different units. Specialization creates an increased need for coordination because it adds to the hierarchy, which can lead to narrowly defined jobs that stifle the creativity and energy of those who hold them. Police administrators are aware of these potential shortcomings of specialization and attempt, through various means, to inspire their employees to the extent possible. For example, personnel can be rotated to various jobs and given additional responsibilities that challenge them. In addition, in a medium-sized department—for example, one serving a community of 100,000 or more—a police officer with 10 years of experience may have had the responsibilities of dog handler, motorcycle officer, detective, and/or traffic officer while being a member of special weapons or hostage negotiation teams.

In sum, the advantages to specialization in large police departments include the following:

- *Placement of responsibility.* The responsibility for performing given tasks can be placed on specific units or individuals. For example, the traffic division investigates all accidents and the patrol division handles all calls for service.
- *Development of expertise.* Those who have specialized responsibilities receive specialized training. Homicide investigators can be sent to forensic pathology classes; special weapons and tactics teams train regularly to deal with terrorists or hostage situations.
- *Group esprit de corps.* Groups of specially trained persons share camaraderie and depend on one another for success; this leads to cohesion and high morale.
- *Increased efficiency and effectiveness.* Specialized units have a high degree of proficiency in performing job tasks. For example, a specially trained financial crimes unit normally is more successful in handling complex fraud cases than a general detective division.[6]

ELEMENTS OF POLICE ORGANIZATIONAL STRUCTURE

According to Henryx Mintzberg, an **organizational structure** can be defined simply as the sum total of the ways in which the organization divides its labor into distinct tasks and then achieves coordination among them.[7] This definition translates into measures that are relatively easy to compute.

Supported in part by a grant from the National Institute of Justice, Maguire et al. accomplished an excellent analysis of organizations and structural change in large police agencies. Essentially, they determined that there are seven specific elements of law enforcement organizational structure; the first four are types of structural differentiation, or methods of dividing labor. These elements are (1) functional, (2) occupational, (3) spatial, and (4) vertical differentiation, and (5) centralization, (6) formalization, and (7) administrative intensity[8]:

1. **Functional differentiation** is the degree to which tasks are broken down into functionally distinct units. A police agency with a homicide unit, an accident reconstruction unit, and a juvenile division is more functionally differentiated than one that only employs patrol officers. Law enforcement organizations became more functionally differentiated throughout the twentieth century, adding new bureaus, divisions, and specialized units to perform separate functions as the need arose.[9]
2. **Occupational differentiation** measures distinctions within the staff (job titles) and the extent to which an organization relies on specially trained workers from distinct occupational groups. Civilianization has increased in policing, and today, civilian police employees represent a separate occupational group.[10]
3. **Spatial differentiation** is the extent to which an organization is spread geographically. A police agency with a headquarters and several precinct stations is more spatially differentiated than a department that operates out of a single police facility. Police agencies with a single patrol beat and a single facility are the least spatially differentiated. Those agencies that carve the jurisdiction into a large number of small beats, with functioning ministations scattered throughout the jurisdiction and district stations in different areas of the community, are the most spatially differentiated.[11]

4. **Vertical differentiation** focuses on the hierarchical nature of an organization's command structure, including its (a) segmentation, (b) concentration, and (c) height. Organizations with elaborate chains of command are more vertically differentiated than those with flatter command structures. *Segmentation* is the number of command levels in an organization, from the lowest ranking to the highest. Some agencies maintain "status" ranks that carry greater prestige and/or pay but no supervisory or command authority other than in very limited circumstances. Examples are master police officers and corporals in some agencies, who are given supervisory authority on rare occasion, such as when a sergeant is unavailable. Other rank structures are a mix of functional and hierarchical differentiation; for example, sometimes detectives may receive greater pay and prestige than other officers but have no greater supervisory or command authority. *Concentration* is the percentage of personnel located at various levels, and *height* is the social distance between the lowest- and the highest-ranking employees in the organization. Police agencies in which patrol officers can drop in routinely to chat with the chief of police or sheriff are less vertically differentiated than those in which there is significant social distance between the chief and the lowest-ranking employees.[12]

5. **Centralization** is the extent to which the decision-making capacity within an organization is concentrated in a single individual or a small, select group. Organizations in which lower-ranking employees are given the autonomy to make decisions are less centralized than those in which senior administrators make most decisions.

6. **Formalization** is the extent to which employees are governed by specific rules and policies. Some factors in law enforcement, including liability issues and accreditation, are likely to encourage increase in formalization.

7. **Administrative intensity** refers to the proportion of organizational resources committed to administration. Organizations with high levels of administrative intensity are often thought of as being more bureaucratic.[13]

EXAMPLES OF POLICE ORGANIZATION

The Basic Organizational Structure

As noted previously, an organizational structure helps departments carry out the many complex responsibilities of policing. It should be noted, however, that organizational structures vary from one jurisdiction to another and are fluid in nature. The highly decentralized nature and the different sizes of police departments in the United States, as well as the turnover in the chief executive officer (chief of police or sheriff) position, cause these structures to change. It is possible, however, to make certain general statements about all agencies to characterize a typical police organization.

The police traditionally organize along military lines, with a rank structure that normally includes the patrol officer, sergeant, lieutenant, captain, and chief. Many departments, particularly larger ones, employ additional ranks, such as corporal, major, and deputy chief, but there is a legitimate concern that these departments will become top-heavy. The military rank hierarchy allows the organization to designate authority and responsibility at each level and to maintain a chain of command. The military model also allows the organization to emphasize supervisor–subordinate relationships and to maintain discipline and control. The quasi-military style of policing is discussed later.

Every police agency, regardless of size, has a basic plan of organization. In addition, every such agency, no matter how large or small, has an organizational structure. A visitor to the police station or sheriff's office may even see this organizational structure displayed prominently on a

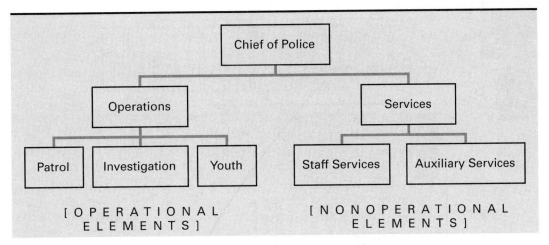

FIGURE 3.1 Basic Police Organizational Structure

wall. Even if it is not on paper, such a structure exists. A basic organizational structure for a small agency is shown in Figure 3.1.

Operational or line elements involve policing functions in the field and may be subdivided into primary and secondary line elements. The patrol function—often called the "backbone" of policing—is the primary line element because it is the major law enforcement responsibility within the police organization. Most small police agencies, in fact, can be described as patrol agencies, with the patrol forces responsible for all line activities. Such agencies provide routine patrols, conduct criminal and traffic investigations, and make arrests. These agencies are basically generalists. In a community that has only one policing employee—a city marshal, for example— he or she obviously must perform all the functions just listed. This agency's organizational chart is a simple horizontal one with little or no specialization.

Investigative and youth activities are the secondary line elements. These functions would not be needed if the police were totally successful in their patrol and crime prevention efforts— an obviously impossible goal. Time and area restrictions on the patrol officers, as well as the need for specialized training and experience, require some augmenting of the patrol activity.

The nonoperational functions and activities can become quite numerous, especially in a large community. These functions fall within two broad categories: *staff services* (also known as *administrative*) and *auxiliary* (or *technical*) *services*. Staff services are usually people oriented and include recruitment, training, promotion, planning and research, community relations, and public information services. Auxiliary services involve the types of functions that a nonpolice person rarely sees, including jail management, property and evidence handling, crime laboratory services, communications (dispatch), and records and identification. Many career opportunities exist for persons interested in police-related work who cannot or do not want to be a field officer.

Consider the organizational structure for a larger police organization, that of the Portland (Oregon) Police Bureau (PPB) (see Figure 3.2). Portland has a population of about 550,000, but the metropolitan area (consisting of five counties) has about 2 million people.[14] The PPB has about 1,350 personnel, 1,000 of whom are sworn.[15] As with all organizations, especially those that are medium or large in size, some of the PPB functions are unique to that organization.[16]

Portland's and other cities' police department organizational structures are designed to fulfill five functions: (1) apportioning the workload among members and units according to a

Portland Police Bureau
Organizational Chart

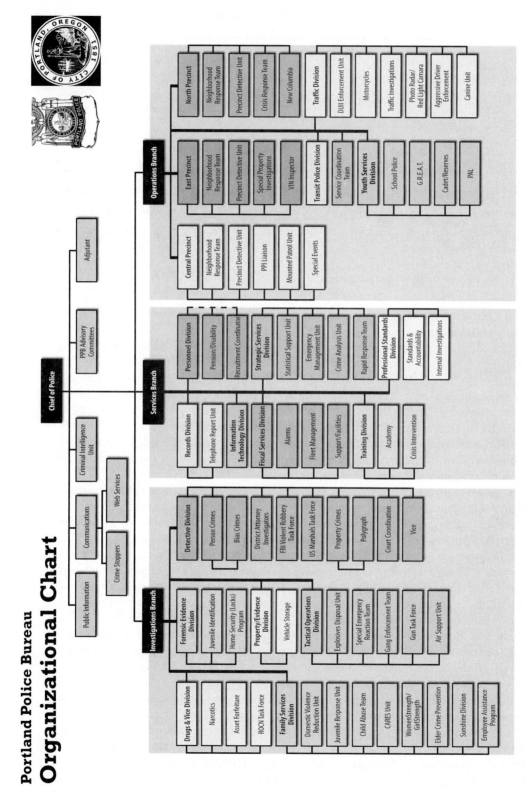

FIGURE 3.2 Portland Police Bureau Organizational Chart

logical plan; (2) ensuring that lines of authority and responsibility are as definite and direct as possible; (3) specifying unity of command throughout so that there is no question as to which orders should be followed; (4) placing responsibility and authority, and if responsibility is delegated, holding the delegator responsible; and (5) coordinating the efforts of members so that all will work harmoniously to accomplish the mission.[17] In sum, this structure establishes the chain of command and determines lines of communication and responsibility.

Commentary on the Quasi-Military Style of Policing

Police experts have long written about the quasi-military style of policing.[18] Egon Bittner, for example, felt that the adoption of the **military model** by the police—wearing uniforms, using rank designations, adopting a hierarchical command structure, acquiring legal authority (use of weapons and force)—was a reaction to the political influences over the police in the late nineteenth century that contributed to corruption[19] (e.g., payoffs for underenforcement of laws, political activity to get out the vote).

Proponents of the military style of policing uphold the model's tradition, its imposition of control and commanding authority with strict discipline,[20] respect for chain of command and rigid rank differences, the "elite warrior" self-image, and centralized command. Critics of the model, however, note that it is excessively rigid (controlled by micromanaging bureaucrats), autocratic, secretive, intellectually and creatively constraining, and highly resistant to any initiative that will allow employee participation in the decision-making processes. In other words, it is said to often discourage creativity; cultivate the "us-versus-them" and "war on crime" mentalities;[21] eschew scientific or academic approaches in favor of an "applied" focus; rely heavily on tradition, or the "we've always done it this way" approach, causing a commitment to outmoded methods of operation; and have a distinct tendency to mismatch talent with job positions.

With today's emphasis on COPPS, discussed later, many COPPS advocates believe that the quasi-military model is incompatible with this philosophy. As one police chief executive put it:

> Whereas community policing requires a policing approach that demonstrates openness, a service orientation, innovative/creative thinking, and problem solving, these characteristics are not likely to be developed in a militaristic managerial model. This is a style which at worst will tend to give rise to an operational police culture which is action oriented, cynical, suspicious, reactive and, most importantly in the context of community policing, insular and isolated from the general community.[22]

Some types of situations, such as critical incidents, will likely compel the retention of command and control in police training and tactical application. But in nonemergency situations involving a focus on crime and disorder, problem-solving policing requires personal and intellectual reasoning skills, skills that must be trained if a COPPS culture is to be developed.

ORGANIZATIONAL GUIDELINES: POLICIES, PROCEDURES, RULES, AND REGULATIONS

Policies, procedures, rules, and regulations are important for defining role expectations for all police officers. The officers are granted unusually strong power in a democratic society; because they possess such extraordinary powers, police officers pose a potential threat to individual freedom. Thus, because police agencies are service oriented in nature, they must work within well-defined, specific guidelines designed to ensure that all officers conform to behavior that will enhance public protection.[23]

Related to this need for policies, procedures, rules, and regulations is the fact that police officers possess a broad spectrum of discretionary authority in performing their duties. This fact, coupled with the danger posed by their work and the opportunities to settle problems informally, works against having narrow, inflexible job requirements.

Thus, the task for the organization's chief executive is to find the middle ground between unlimited discretion and total standardization. The police role is much too ambiguous to become totally standardized, but it is also much too serious and important to be left completely to the discretion of the patrol officer. As Robert Sheehan and Gary Cordner put it, the idea is for chief executives to "harness, but not choke, their employees."[24]

Organizational policies are more general than procedures, rules, or regulations. **Policies** are basically guides to the organization's philosophy and mission and help in interpreting their elements to the officers.[25] Policies should be committed to writing, then modified according to the changing times and circumstances of the department and community.

Procedures are more specific than policies; they serve as guides to action. A procedure is "more specific than a policy but less restrictive than a rule or regulation. It describes a method of operation while still allowing some flexibility within limits."[26]

Many organizations are awash in procedures. Police organizations have procedures that cover investigation, patrol, booking, radio communications, filing, roll call, arrest, sick leave, evidence handling, promotion, and others. Such procedures are not totally inflexible, but they do describe in rather detailed terms the preferred methods for carrying out policy.

Some procedures are mandated by the U.S. Supreme Court. A good example is the Court's 1985 decision in *Tennessee v. Garner.* This decision resulted in a new policy concerning the use of deadly force. Officers are allowed to use deadly force only when a "suspect threatens the officer with a weapon or there is probable cause to believe that [the suspect] has committed a crime involving the infliction or threatened infliction of serious physical harm."[27]

Some police executives have attempted to run their departments via flurries of memos containing new procedures. This method is often fraught with difficulty. An abundance of standardized procedures can stifle initiative and imagination, as well as complicate jobs.[28] On the positive side, procedures can decrease the time wasted in figuring out how to accomplish tasks and thereby increase productivity. As they do with policies, chief executives must seek the middle ground in drafting procedures and remember that it is next to impossible to have procedures that cover all possible exigencies.

Rules and regulations are specific managerial guidelines that leave little or no latitude for individual discretion; they require action (or, in some cases, inaction). Some require officers to wear their hats when outside their patrol vehicle, check the patrol vehicle's oil and emergency lights before going on patrol, not consume alcoholic beverages within 4 hours of going on duty, and arrive in court 30 minutes before sessions open or at roll call 15 minutes before scheduled duty time. Rules and regulations are not always popular, especially if perceived as unfair or unrelated to the job. Nonetheless, they contribute to the total police mission of community service.

Rules and regulations should obviously be kept to a minimum because of their coercive nature. If they become too numerous, they can hinder action and send the message that management believes that it cannot trust the rank and file to act responsibly on their own. Once again, the middle ground is the best. As Thomas Reddin, former Los Angeles police chief, stated:

> Certainly we must have rules, regulations and procedures, and they should be followed. But they are no substitutes for initiative and intelligence. The more a [person] is given an opportunity to make decisions and, in the process, to learn, the more rules and regulations will be followed.[29]

Next, we discuss COPPS, including some evaluation and research efforts.

COMMUNITY-ORIENTED POLICING AND PROBLEM SOLVING (COPPS)

Rationale and Definition

Community-oriented policing and problem solving—**COPPS**—has emerged as the dominant strategy of policing—*a form of police operation*. It is an approach to crime detection and prevention that provides police officers and supervisors with new tools for addressing recurrent problems that plague communities and consume a majority of police agency time and resources. The California Department of Justice provided the following definition of COPPS:

> Community-oriented policing and problem solving is a philosophy, management style, and organizational strategy that promotes proactive problem solving and police–community partnerships to address the causes of crime and fear as well as other community issues.[30]

Two principal and interrelated components emerge from this definition: community engagement (partnerships) and problem solving. With its focus on collaborative problem solving, COPPS seeks to improve the quality of policing.

The S.A.R.A. process discussed next provides the police with the tools necessary to accomplish these tasks.

The S.A.R.A. Process

S.A.R.A. (*Scanning, Analysis, Response, Assessment*) (see Figure 3.3) provides officers with a logical, step-by-step framework in which to identify, analyze, respond to, and evaluate crime, fear of crime, and neighborhood disorder. This approach, with its emphasis on in-depth analysis and collaboration, replaces officers' short-term, reactive responses with a process vested in longer-term outcomes.

SCANNING: PROBLEM IDENTIFICATION   Scanning involves problem identification. The police officer initiates the problem-solving process by conducting a preliminary inquiry to determine whether a problem really exists and whether further analysis is needed. A problem may be defined as a cluster of two or more similar or related incidents that are of substantive concern to the community and to the police. If the incidents to which the police respond do not fall within the definition of a problem, then the problem-solving process is not applicable.

Numerous resources are available to the police for identifying problems, including calls for service data (especially repeat calls), crime analysis information, police reports, and officers' experiences. Scanning helps the officer to determine whether a problem really exists before moving on to more in-depth analysis.

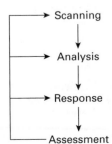

FIGURE 3.3   A Problem-Solving Process

Source: John E. Eck and William Spelman, *Problem-Solving: Problem-Oriented Policing in Newport News* (Washington, DC: U.S. Department of Justice, National Institute of Justice, 1987), p. 43.

ANALYSIS: DETERMINING THE EXTENT OF THE PROBLEM   Analysis is the heart of the problem-solving process. It is the most difficult and important step in the S.A.R.A. process. Without analysis, long-term solutions are unlikely and the problem will persist.

Here, officers gather as much information as possible from a variety of sources. A complete and thorough analysis consists of identifying the seriousness of the problem, all persons affected, and the underlying causes. Officers should also assess the effectiveness of current responses.

Many tools are available to assist analysis. Crime analysis may be useful in collecting, collating, analyzing, and disseminating data relating to crime, incidents not requiring a report, criminal offenders, victims, and locations. Mapping and geographic information systems (GIS) can identify patterns of crime and "hot spots." Police offense reports can also be analyzed for suspect characteristics, victim characteristics, and information about high-crime areas and addresses. Computer-aided dispatch (CAD) is also a reliable source of information, as it collects data on all incidents and specific locations from which an unusual number of incidents require a police response.

Generally, three elements are needed for a problem to occur: an *offender*, a *victim*, and a *location*. The problem analysis triangle, shown in Figure 3.4, helps officers to visualize the problem and understand the relationship among the three elements. The three elements must be present for a crime or harmful event to occur; removing one or more of these elements will remove the problem. Strategies for removing one of these elements are limited only by an officer's ability to develop responses and the available resources.

RESPONSE: FORMULATING TAILOR-MADE STRATEGIES   Once a problem has been clearly defined, officers may seek the most effective responses. Developing long-term solutions to problems is of paramount importance in COPPS; however, officers cannot ignore the fact that more serious situations may require immediate action. For example, in the case of an open-air drug market involving rival gang violence, police may initially increase the number of patrols in the area to arrest offenders, gain control of public space, and secure the safety of residents and officers. Once this is accomplished, long-term responses, which include the collaborative efforts of officers, residents, and other agencies, may be considered.

Administrators must bear in mind that responses to substantive problems rarely involve a single agency or tactic or a quick fix. Arrest is often viewed as the only response to a problem even though it is rarely sufficient to provide permanent solutions. More appropriate responses often involve the police and public and other appropriate actors, including businesses, private and social service organizations, and other government agencies.

Patrol officers have many options to use in responding to problems, but they should not expect to eliminate every problem they take on. With some social problems, such as gangs and homelessness, elimination is impractical and improbable.

Offender   Problem   Victim

Place

FIGURE 3.4   Problem Analysis Triangle

Source: Bureau of Justice Assistance, U.S. Department of Justice, *Comprehensive Gang Initiative: Operations Manual for Implementing Local Gang Prevention and Control Programs* (Draft, October 1993), pp. 3–10.

ASSESSMENT: EVALUATING OVERALL EFFECTIVENESS The final stage of the S.A.R.A. process is assessment. Here, officers evaluate the effectiveness of their actions and may use the results to revise their responses, collect more data, or even redefine the problem. A COPPS initiative that is not reinforced by an evaluation process may have difficulty establishing whether it succeeded and thus should continue to receive resources. Therefore, rigorous evaluation is an essential component of the COPPS initiative. Evaluations provide knowledge; key decision makers in the jurisdiction need a gauge of the strategy's impact and cost effectiveness.

Exhibit 3.1 provides an example of the S.A.R.A. process in action, in Oakland, California.

EXHIBIT 3.1

A Winning Example of S.A.R.A.: The Oakland Airport Motel Program

The Oakland Police Department (OPD) addressed a serious motel problem near its local airport; for the following efforts, the OPD won the coveted Herman Goldstein Award for Excellence in Problem-Oriented Policing, conferred at the Annual International Problem Oriented Policing Conference.

- SCANNING: Located along a major gateway to the city of Oakland, the Oakland Airport Motel is situated within a commercial area comprising lodging, restaurants, and fast food outlets; it is also situated about 2 miles from Oakland's professional baseball, football, and basketball franchises. A complainant informed an Oakland officer that, while he had been working at the motel for several weeks, prostitutes soliciting sex had approached him nightly, prostitutes "had the run of the place", there were loud parties and disturbances each night around the clock, junked vehicles littered the parking lot, and the smell of marijuana came through his window nightly.
- ANALYSIS: After consulting with the city zoning and attorneys' offices concerning applicable laws, an officer reviewed the property owner information and determined that a large corporation owned the motel, there was no policy of limiting the duration of guest stays, and a disproportionately high number of narcotics arrests had occurred over the previous 2 years. The officer made a site visit, photographing and documenting his observations, and interviewing tenants and the motel staff. He noted that a corner of the motel parking lot was used as a freelance and illegal auto repair business, that rooms were routinely rented to minors, and that prostitution activity was rampant. A review of police incidents over the past 3 years revealed that the motel had an astounding 900 percent higher number of police incidents than other comparable lodging facilities in the area.
- RESPONSE: A response plan was developed. Phase One involved working with the motel manager to clean up the property and deal with problem tenants. A policy was implemented to rent rooms only to persons 21 years of age or older, to evict problem tenants in a timely manner, to monitor the parking lot to prevent junked vehicles from being dumped there, and to fire employees caught renting out rooms "under the table" and using their passkeys. Corporate officials balked at several of these initiatives, however, so the officer sent a drug nuisance abatement notification letter to the motel. Police surveillance revealed that motel security guards were not taking steps to keep nuisances out of the parking lot, and frequent prostitution and open drug transactions continued to occur. An undercover officer rented rooms at the motel; on two occasions, motel managers changed the room locks and took the officer's property left in the rooms in order to double-rent the rooms. Given this lack of improvement, Phase Two involved meeting with the motel's corporate officials. A document

was prepared covering the criminal activity at the motel over a 3-year period, descriptions and photographs of the prostitution and violent crimes occurring at the site, and the legal consequences and costs of not complying with relevant legal, health, and safety codes. It was requested that the motel be closed for 90 days to improve its physical aspects and to retrain motel staff in their proper duties, post a $250,000 performance bond, and repay OPD for its investigative costs. Corporate officials promised swift change; again, however, there was little improvement in the conditions at the motel after 2 weeks had passed. Phase Three of the project was then launched: preparation of lawsuits and negotiations. Police continued surveillance of activities at the motel, and a drug nuisance abatement lawsuit was prepared for filing and sent to the CEO at his home in France. Finally, after 7 hours of negotiations, corporate officials agreed to post the performance bond and to pay the city $35,000 in fees and expenses incurred to date. Furthermore, barbed wire was installed along all fence lines to discourage fence climbing, area lighting was upgraded, room rates were increased by 50 percent to improve the quality of the motel's clientele, room rentals for more than 30 days were prohibited, foot and vehicle traffic was stopped for identification by security guards, a "no-rent" list was developed for banned guests, the property was cleaned and painted, rigorous background checks were performed on new employees, and problem employees were fired.

- ASSESSMENT. Seven months after these activities were launched, calls for service to the motel dropped by 59 percent. Two years later, there had been only one call for police service. Overall, crime and nuisance activity was also on par with the other five adjacent motels.

Source: Based on "The Oakland Airport Motel Program: Eliminating Criminal and Nuisance Behavior at a Motel," 2003, http://www.popcenter.org/library/awards/goldstein/2003/03-26(W).pdf (accessed August 4, 2011).

Viewing Crime Prevention by Two Additional Means

Two other approaches for viewing and addressing crime have become well known and deserve brief mention: crime prevention through environmental design (CPTED) and situational crime prevention (SCP).

The broad concept of crime prevention began in policing as a "lock it or lose it" concept, with police giving citizens advice about how to target-harden and protect their residences and businesses from potential offenders. But we now have a much better understanding of crime theories—and more sophisticated approaches to crime control—and make crime prevention the responsibility of all officers and community members. CPTED and SCP are major parts of the problem-solving process.

CPTED is defined as the "proper design and effective use of the environment that can lead to a reduction in the fear and incidence of crime, and an improvement in the quality of life."[31] At its core are three principles that support problem-solving approaches to crime:

1. *Natural access control.* Natural access control includes doors, shrubs, fences, and gates to deny admission to a crime target and to create a perception among offenders that there is a risk in selecting the target.
2. *Natural surveillance.* Natural surveillance includes the proper placement of windows, lighting, and landscaping to increase the ability of those who care to observe intruders as well as regular users, allowing them to challenge inappropriate behavior or report it to the police or the property owner.

3. **Territorial reinforcement.** Using such elements as sidewalks, landscaping, and porches helps distinguish between public and private areas and helps users exhibit signs of ownership that send "hands-off" messages to would-be offenders.

SCP is a targeted means of reducing crime, providing a framework for strategies to prevent crime by making settings less conducive to unwanted or illegal activities; it also focuses on the environment rather than the offender while making criminal activity less attractive to offenders; it examines the roots of a problem and identifies a unique solution to the problem. SCP relies on the rational choice theory of crime, which asserts that criminals choose to commit crimes based on the costs and benefits involved. Specifically, crime prevention goals are divided into five primary objectives, each of which is designed to dissuade the criminal by making the crime too hard to commit, too risky, or too small in terms of rewards to be worth the criminal's time and effort[32]:

1. **Increasing the effort needed to commit the crime.** Crimes typically happen because they are easy to commit. Casual criminals are eliminated by increasing the effort needed to commit a crime by doing the following:
   - **Target hardening:** installing physical barriers (such as locks, bolts, protective screens, and mechanical containment and antifraud devices to impede an offender's from penetrating a potential target).
   - **Access control:** installing barriers and designing walkways, paths, and roads so that unwanted users are prevented from entering vulnerable areas.
   - **Deflecting offenders:** discouraging crime by giving people alternate, legal venues for their activities (such as separating fans of rival teams after athletic events).
   - **Controlling facilitators:** facilitators are accessories that aid in the commission of crimes. Controlling them is achieved by universal measures (such as firearm permit regulations) and specific measures (such as metal detectors in community centers).
2. **Increasing the risks associated with the crime.** Following are examples for increasing the risks associated with a crime to convince potential offenders that they will be caught:
   - **Entry and exit screening:** using screening methods such as guest sign-ins or a required display of identification.
   - **Formal surveillance:** using security personnel and hardware (such as closed-circuit television [CCTV] and burglar alarms) serves as a deterrent to unwanted activities.
   - **Informal surveillance:** the presence of building attendants, concierges, maintenance workers, and attendants increases site surveillance and crime reporting.
   - **Natural surveillance:** the surveillance provided by people as they go about their daily activities, making potential offenders feel exposed and vulnerable.
3. **Reducing the rewards.** Reducing the rewards from crime makes offending not worthwhile to offenders, by such means as:
   - **Target removal:** eliminating crime purposes from public areas. Examples include a no-cash policy and keeping valuable property in a secure area overnight.
   - **Identifying property:** using indelible marks, establishing ownership, and preventing individuals from reselling the property.
   - **Removing inducements:** removing temptations in advance, such as razing dilapidated houses or fixing broken windows and light fixtures.
4. **Reducing the provocations.** The environment may provoke crime and violence; studies show that certain types of lighting improve people's mood and morale in the workplace.
5. **Removing the excuses.** Many offenders say, "I didn't know any better," so this strategy involves informing them of the law, such as posting an enforceable no-trespassing sign.

Desired Organizational Elements Under COPPS

Part of the analysis of police organizations by Maguire et al. included the extent to which these organizations changed during the 1990s, when COPPS was in full bloom. To accomplish its goals, COPPS relies on some form of structural innovation for its implementation efforts: reducing levels of vertical and functional differentiation (officers being "uniformed generalists," responsible for developing customized responses to a wide variety of situations), increasing levels of occupational differentiation (greater use of civilians in police agencies, thereby freeing up officers' time and allowing them to patrol the streets) and spatial differentiation (using more ministations and precincts to extend officers into their communities) and decreasing formalization (less reliance on and enforcement of formal written rules, policies, and procedures), centralization (shared decision making), and administrative intensity (smaller administrative components and less bureaucracy, concentrating police on the streets and not at desks).[33]

Maguire et al. determined that most large municipal organizations in the United States experienced significant decreases in centralization and administrative intensity, together with significant increases in occupational differentiation. These changes are consistent with the structural reform agendas of community policing (which call for law enforcement administrators to decrease the levels of centralization and administrative intensity within their organizations). On the other hand, the flattening of the police hierarchy did not occur, and segmentation, or the number of command levels, did not change significantly during the 1990s.[34] Hierarchy height increased significantly, and there was no change in formalization. With regard to spatial differentiation, although there was a significant increase in the number of police stations, there was also a significant increase in the use of ministations.[35]

Overall, Maguire et al. found room for optimism for community policing reformers, with police agencies being less centralized, employing a greater proportion of civilian employees, and having leaner administrative components. Spatially, they have more ministations and police stations, but their beat coverage has remained about the same. Police organizations are capable of changing in many dimensions: in culture, leadership, management, programs, and operations, although many of these changes were not reflected in Maguire et al.'s analysis.[36]

Most community policing reformers felt that it was essential for law enforcement agencies to move from the traditional organizational structures to accommodate COPPS' philosophy and operations. Although policing has been in the community policing era for a relatively short period of time, much has been written about how agencies have modified their structures, as well as their implementation and evaluation of COPPS. There are also countless examples of the resulting successes they have achieved through COPPS in dealing with crime and disorder.[37] The reader is encouraged to explore some of these resources to better understand the current era of policing.

HARVARD, NIJ, AND COPPS: THE INFLUENCE OF TWO EXECUTIVE SESSIONS

Executive Sessions Defined

In the early 1980s, Harvard University's John F. Kennedy School of Government and the National Institute of Justice (NIJ) developed a series of **Executive Sessions** with the general purpose of allowing practitioners and academics to meet, confer, and search for effective means of addressing important public problems. More specifically, these Executive Sessions brought together a core group of members to consider policy recommendations that would guide policing for the next two decades; the overarching strategy was that community policing would become the dominant paradigm for policing across the nation and around the world.[38]

Over a 3-year period beginning in 1983, the first series of five or six 3-day meetings were held in which 25–30 high-level practitioners and academics engaged in a creative dialogue with a view to redefining, and proposing solutions for, substantive policy issues.[39] Papers were published following this Session in a series called *Perspectives on Policing*; these papers would become essential reading in thousands of departments and executive offices across the country.

Now Awaited: A Second Executive Session

Of course, policing has changed tremendously since September 11. Therefore, given the impact of the first series of Executive Sessions, and to better understand how policing will change in the future, the John F. Kennedy School of Government and the NIJ are now collaborating on a second Session, which like its predecessor, has high ambitions and will result in a new series of papers—*New Perspectives in Policing*—that hopes to influence the field in the way the earlier series did.[40] Hopefully, this Executive Session on policing and public safety will be as positively received and influential as the first session was; it will examine:

- How police can manage the challenges of the coming years, including community relations, terrorism, and the rising costs of public policing.
- New challenges and opportunities made possible by fast-changing technologies.
- The impact of the growing internationalization of crime.[41]
- Police-community relations and the legitimacy of law enforcement in minority communities.
- The federal role in policing.
- The impact of international crime and terrorism.
- The changing face of technology.
- The effects of mass incarceration on relationships between police and their communities.
- The role of detectives, forensic scientists, and other police professionals.
- The media's role in driving police action and focus.
- Professional development of police officers and leaders.[42]

MOVING FROM A GOOD TO A GREAT POLICE ORGANIZATION

In 2001, Jim Collins wrote a book entitled *Good to Great: Why Some Companies Make the Leap and Others Don't*,[43] which sought to answer the compelling question: Can a good company become a great company, and if so, how? Collins and his team of assistants searched for companies that made a "leap to greatness," as defined by stock market performance and long-term success; they found 11 companies that met their criteria and spent more than 10 years studying what made them great. Following that, and acknowledging the growing interest in his book by nonbusiness entities, 4 years later, he published a monograph entitled *Good to Great and the Social Sectors*,[44] concerning how his lessons could be modified to fit government agencies. Certainly, much of the success of great police organizations has to do with their leadership.

Collins coined the term *Level 5 leader* to describe the highest level of executive capabilities (Levels 1 through 4 are highly capable individual, contributing team member, competent manager, and effective leader, respectively). Level 5 leaders are ambitious, but their ambition is directed first and foremost to the organization and its success, not to personal renown. Level 5 leaders, Collins stressed, are "fanatically driven, infected with an incurable need to produce results."[45]

Such leaders, Collins found, do not exhibit enormous egos; instead, they are self-effacing, quiet, reserved, even shy. Perhaps this has to do with the nature of their organizations. Unlike business executives, police leaders have to answer to the public; unions and civil service systems further inhibit their power. Therefore, Level 5 leadership in a police organization may involve a greater degree of legislative-type skills—relying heavily on persuasion, political currency, and shared interests to create the conditions for the right decisions to happen.[46]

Collins also likes to use a bus metaphor when talking about igniting the transformation from good to great:

> The executives who ignited the transformations . . . did not first figure out where to drive the bus and then get people to take it there. No, they *first* got the right people on the bus (and the wrong people off the bus) and *then* figured out where to drive it. (emphasis in the original)[47]

In fact, Collins wrote, "The main point is not about assembling the right team—that's nothing new." Rather, the main point is that great leaders assemble their teams *before* they decide where to go. The executive who hires the right people does not need to waste time looking for ways to manage and motivate them; the right people will be self-motivated. Good-to-great organizations, Collins found, also have a "culture of discipline" in which employees show extreme diligence and intensity in their thoughts and actions, always focusing on implementing the organization's mission, purpose, and goals.[48]

People are not an organization's most important asset; rather, the *right* people are. When police executives are appointed or promoted, they inherit nearly all of their personnel, including poor performers who are unenthusiastic about the organization's vision and philosophy. Some of these people may be near retirement (about ready to "get off the bus"). Collins states that picking the right people and getting the wrong people off the bus are critical: "By whatever means possible, personnel problems have to be confronted in an organization that aspires to greatness."[49]

This is why performance evaluations are so critical. Unfortunately, however, many police departments still have not created evaluation tools that adequately reflect the work police do. The tendency is to measure what is easy to measure: orderliness (neatness, attendance, punctuality) and conformity to organizational rules and regulations. A consultant to a Texas police agency asked how employees could be expected to act like supervisors, managers, and leaders when everyone in the organization was evaluated by an instrument that was "designed to control a 20-year old, high-testosterone male who was armed with a gun and given a fast car to drive."[50] Until police agencies invest in valid and reliable instruments for measuring the real work of policing, it will remain very difficult to move the nonperformers out of the organization.

As an illustration, when William Bratton became Police Commissioner of the New York City, he decided that he had to reach down at least two generations to get leaders who were motivated to improve the organization. Overnight, he wiped out several generations of command staff, which was unheard of in New York. He promoted Jack Maple, then a lieutenant in the Transit Police, to Deputy Commissioner for Crime Control; Maple designed CompStat (see Chapter 16). The message from a Level 5 leader is clear: It is no longer business as usual.

Perhaps the most difficult part of achieving greatness is *sustaining* that greatness. Police chiefs have notoriously short tenure in office. Therefore, in their world, some of Collins' principles may be particularly important—for example, finding Level 5 leaders who pay close attention to preparing for the next generation of leaders, giving managers authority to make key decisions, sending them to leadership academies and conferences, and encouraging them to think on their own and ask questions. This process is termed *succession planning*. This major aspect of police leadership and motivation is discussed more fully in Chapter 5.

AGENCY ACCREDITATION

In 1979, the **accreditation** of police agencies began slowly with the creation of the Commission on Accreditation for Law Enforcement Agencies (CALEA), located in Fairfax, Virginia. CALEA is a nonprofit organization that has developed and administers 459 voluntary standards for law enforcement agencies to meet. These standards cover the role and responsibilities of the agency; its organization and administration; law enforcement, traffic, and operational support; prisoner- and court-related services; and auxiliary and technical services. Accreditation, a voluntary process, is quite expensive, both in dollars and in human resources; it often takes 12–18 months for an agency to prepare for the assessment.[51] Today, there are nearly 600 agencies accredited or recognized in one of the Commission's various programs, with several hundred others working toward their first award.[52]

Once an agency believes it is ready to be accredited, an application is filed and the agency receives a self-evaluation questionnaire to determine its current status. If the self-evaluation indicates that the agency is ready to attempt accreditation, an on-site team appointed by CALEA conducts an assessment and writes a report on its findings. After becoming accredited, the agency must apply for reaccreditation after 5 years.[53]

Several unanticipated consequences of the accreditation process have emerged. First, a number of states have formed coalitions to assist police agencies in the process of accreditation. Second, some departments report decreased insurance costs as a result of accreditation. Finally, the accreditation self-assessment process provides many opportunities to institutionalize community policing. Not only do the accreditation standards help to weave community policing into an agency's internal fabric, but they also provide a way to integrate such objectives into external service delivery, such as:

- enhancing the role and authority of patrol officers,
- improving analysis and information management, and
- managing CFS.[54]

In comparing accredited and nonaccredited police agencies, Kimberly A. McCabe and Robin G. Fajardo found that accredited police agencies (1) provided more training for their officers and required higher minimum educational requirements for new officers, (2) were nearly twice as likely to require drug testing for sworn applicants, and (3) were more likely to operate special units for the enforcement of drug laws and laws against child abuse.[55]

Summary

This chapter explored the importance and elements of police organizational structure, including the bureaucratic nature of such organizations, division of labor, and the policies, procedures, rules, and regulations that are a part of such organizations. Included was an examination of the current era and the organizational paradigm of policing, community-oriented policing, and problem solving. In considering this topic, we examined two related aspects of its crime prevention function: crime prevention through environmental design and situational crime prevention. We also considered how a police organization may become great rather than merely being good, and in a related vein, we looked at how police agencies become accredited and the benefits of doing so.

Perhaps what was most clearly demonstrated in this chapter is the extent to which modern policing is changing, and how its organizational elements must also be viewed as fluid in nature and must be modified in order to adapt to and provide the foundation for today's demands on the police.

Clearly, the traditional reactive, unilateral approach to addressing crime and disorder is not suited for today's police organization and administra- tion. The manner in which the organization remains fluid as needs arise and its structures and functions are of paramount concern to police administrators.

Questions for Review

1. What is an organization, and how does a typical police agency constitute an organization? What are the key components of a basic police organizational structure, and how would it look if graphically illustrated?
2. What is a bureaucracy, and which aspects of police organizations make them bureaucracies?
3. What are the definitions of a policy, a procedure, and rules and regulations? Why are they necessary in police agencies? What are their relationship and role vis-à-vis police discretion?
4. What is meant by *community-oriented policing and problem solving,* and what are the components of the problem-solving process?
5. How would you explain what is meant by crime prevention through environmental design (CPTED) and situational crime prevention (SCP)?
6. What is needed to transform a good police organiza- tion into a great one?
7. How does a police organization become accredited, and what are the benefits of doing so?

Learn by Doing

1. Your chief law enforcement executive has become increasingly concerned about the potential for prob- lems with employee dress and appearance, particu- larly with their wanting to sport beards and tattoos. You are directed to write a new policy that prohibits beards, arm or otherwise visible tattoos, and branding and intentional scarring on the face, head, neck, hands, and exposed arms and legs. Employees who already have tattoos are to be exempt. How will your policy read?
2. A new low-income housing development in your com- munity consists of 58 apartments and has become a popular hangout for selling drugs, drinking liquor, and intimidating residents until early morning hours. Gunshots are an occasional occurrence, with 5–10 calls for service in every 24-hour period. Criminals hide guns in the thick overgrowth around the complex, and when approached, they flee through a large open field behind the complex. An adjacent convenience store has become a problem as well, particularly as a magnet for drug dealers. A nearby drug house also contributes to the problem, and a T-shaped alley behind the store provides easy ingress and egress for buyers, both on foot and in vehicles. The lighting is poor (with people frequently shooting out street lights), and pay tele- phones in the store's front are used constantly by traf- fickers. Street people in the area also engage in theft-, drug-, prostitution-, and vandalism-related activities. Additionally, these people sleep on private property, defecate and urinate on public streets, and engage in public drunkenness, graffiti, and littering. You are assigned to launch a problem-oriented policing (POP)/ SARA initiative at the location to effect long-term results. What kinds of information would you collect concerning the area and its drug problem? What kinds of responses might be considered? What type of assess- ment would you perform?
3. Your chief executive has assigned you, as head of the agency's research, planning, and analysis unit, the task of developing a comprehensive report containing recommendations for establishing intelligence-led policing. Explain what your report would contain.

Related Websites

Center for Problem-Oriented Policing
   http://www.popcenter.org
Commission on Accreditation for Law Enforcement Agencies
   http://www.calea.org

Community Policing Consortium
   http://www.communitypolicing.org
COPS Office
   http://www.cops.usdoj.gov

Law Enforcement Jobs
http://lawenforcementjobs.com

National Association of Police Organizations (NAPO)
http://www.napo.org

Police Guide
http://www.policeguide.com

SafeState: Focus on Community Policing
http://safestate.org

Texas Regional Community Policing Institute
http://www.cjcenter.org/trcpi

Notes

1. Bureau of Justice Statistics, "Justice Expenditure and Employment Extracts, 2007," Table cjee0702.csv, http://bjs.ojp.usdoj.gov/index.cfm?ty=pbdetail&iid=2315 (accessed November 22, 2010).

2. Wayne W. Bennett and Karen M. Hess, *Management and Supervision in Law Enforcement*, 4th ed. (Belmont, CA: Wadsworth, 2004), p. 2.

3. *The Republic of Plato*, trans. Allen Bloom (New York: Basic Books, 1968), p. 7.

4. Luther Gulick and L. Urwick (eds.), *Papers on the Science of Administration* (New York: Augustus M. Kelley, 1969).

5. Charles R. Swanson, Leonard Territo, and Robert W. Taylor, *Police Administration: Structures, Processes, and Behavior*, 6th ed. (Upper Saddle River, NJ: Prentice Hall, 2005), pp. 232–233.

6. Ibid., p. 233.

7. Henry Mintzberg, *The Structure of Organizations* (Upper Saddle River, NJ: Prentice Hall, 1979), p. 253.

8. Edward R. Maguire, Heunhee Shin, Zihong Zhao, and Kimberly D. Hassell, "Structural Change in Large Police Agencies During the 1990s," *Policing: An International Journal of Police Strategies & Management* 26(2) (2003):251–275.

9. Ibid., p. 255.

10. Ibid., p. 259.

11. Ibid., p. 261.

12. Ibid., pp. 266–267.

13. Ibid., pp. 268–270.

14. Portland, Oregon, population statistics from: http://www.portland.com/portland/articles/population-of-portland/ (accessed December 1, 2010).

15. "Portland Police Bureau Statistical Report 2008," http://www.portlandonline.com/police/index.cfm?a=281742&c=29863 (accessed December 1, 2010), p. 6.

16. In the Portland Police Bureau (PPB) organizational structure shown in Figure 3.2, the Sunshine Division includes personnel who work to provide food, clothing, and toys to needy families; PPI liaison is Portland Patrol, Inc., which provides armed security services to the downtown area and uses many retired PPB officers and supervisors; ROCN is the Regional Organized Crime and Narcotics task force; and WomenStrength is a program that teaches women self-defense tactics.

17. President's Commission on Law Enforcement and Administration of Justice, *Task Force Report: The Police* (Washington, DC: U.S. Government Printing Office, 1967), p. 46.

18. See, for example, Egon Bittner, "The Quasi-Military Organization of the Police," in Victor Kappeler (ed.), *Police and Society: Touchstone Readings*, 2nd ed. (Long Grove, IL: Waveland, 2003), pp. 170–181.

19. Ibid.

20. Thomas J. Cowper, "The Myth of the 'Military Model' of Leadership in Law Enforcement," in Quint C. Thurman and Jihong Zhao (eds.), *Contemporary Policing: Controversies, Challenges, and Solutions* (Los Angeles, CA: Roxbury, 2004), pp. 113–125.

21. Samuel Walker and Charles M. Katz, *The Police in America*, 5th ed. (Columbus, OH: McGraw-Hill, 2005).

22. John Murray, "Developing the 'Right' Police for Community Policing," *Platypus Magazine* 74 (March 2002): 7–13.

23. Robert Sheehan and Gary W. Cordner, *Introduction to Police Administration*, 2nd ed. (Cincinnati, OH: Anderson, 1989), pp. 446–447.

24. Ibid., p. 449.

25. Ibid.

26. O. W. Wilson and Roy C. McLaren, *Police Administration*, 3rd ed. (New York: McGraw-Hill, 1972), p. 79.

27. 471 U.S. 1 (1985).

28. Raymond O. Loen, *Manage More by Doing Less* (New York: McGraw-Hill, 1971), pp. 86–89.

29. Thomas Reddin, "Are You Oriented to Hold Them? A Searching Look at Police Management," *The Police Chief* (March 1966): 17.

LEARNING OBJECTIVES

After reading this chapter, the student will:

■ be able to describe each of Mintzberg's three main roles of the chief executive officer (CEO)

■ know the kinds of activities that can be included in an assessment center to obtain the most capable chief executive, as well as the skills the executive must possess

■ be able to define anomia and to explain whether or not it is a problem affecting today's police executives

■ understand the duties and qualifications for the office of chief of police, including their job status in the political arena

■ know the duties performed by the sheriff's office

■ know the tasks performed by middle managers (captains and lieutenants)

■ be familiar with the criteria for a first-line supervisor (patrol sergeant) position, as well as its roles and tasks

■ understand the tasks of patrol officers and be able to name the 12 qualities imperative for entry-level officers

■ be able to describe some innovative strategies for recruiting and hiring the best police personnel, as well as training them after the academy under the field training officer (FTO) and police training officer (PTO) concepts

■ know the roles and functions performed by all leadership personnel in COPPS

The police are the public and the public are the police.

—Robert Peel

INTRODUCTION

Some of the most important and challenging positions in our society are those of a police administrator, manager, or supervisor. This chapter examines the roles and functions of law enforcement chief executives (chiefs of police and county sheriffs), middle managers (typically captains and lieutenants), first-line supervisors (sergeants), and patrol officers.

First, we examine, in general terms, the roles of law enforcement chief executives, adapting Mintzberg's model of chief executive officers (CEOs) to policing in order to better understand what roles police executives play and what they actually do. Next, we review other aspects of police administration, including the use of the assessment center process to hire chief executives; the "Ten Commandments" of good police leadership; some of the critical components of the law enforcement organization that must be managed; and the question of whether or not anomia tends to exist among police executives.

Next, we explore more specifically the functions of chiefs of police and sheriffs, and then consider the roles and functions of middle managers (captains and lieutenants), supervisors (sergeants), and patrol officers. Regarding the latter, we will consider the traits that executives should look for and methods used when trying to hire quality personnel and a new training model that has been developed to assist new recruits as they make the transition from the academy to the street. Finally, we look at the roles of each of these four levels under the community-oriented policing and problem-solving strategy.

ROLES OF THE POLICE EXECUTIVE: THE MINTZBERG MODEL FOR CEOs

A CEO fills many roles. Henry Mintzberg[1] described a model that serves to delineate and define those roles. And while the **Mintzberg model for CEOs** could therefore be applied to courts and corrections administrators as well as to the police, it is most easily applied and understood when used with the latter. Therefore, following is an examination of the three primary roles of police **chief executive officers (CEOs)**—the chief of police or sheriff—as per Mintzberg: the interpersonal, the informational, and the decision-maker roles.

The Interpersonal Role

The *interpersonal* role has three components: (1) the figurehead, (2) leadership, and (3) liaison duties.

In the figurehead role, the CEO performs various ceremonial functions. He or she rides in parades and attends civic events; speaks to school and university classes and civic organizations; meets visiting officials and dignitaries; attends academy graduations, swearing-in ceremonies, and certain weddings and funerals; and visits injured officers. Like a city's mayor, whose public responsibilities include cutting ribbons and kissing babies, the police CEO performs these duties simply because of his or her title and position within the organization. Although the chiefs or sheriffs are not expected to attend the grand opening of every retail or commercial business and other such events to which they are invited, they are certainly obligated from a professional standpoint to attend many civic functions and ceremonies.

The leadership role requires the CEO to motivate and coordinate workers while achieving the mission, goals, and needs within the department and the community. A chief or sheriff may have to urge the governing board to enact a code or ordinance that, whether or not popular, is in the best interest of the jurisdiction. For example, a chief in a western state recently led a drive to pass an ordinance that prohibited parking by university students in residential neighborhoods surrounding the campus. This was a highly unpopular undertaking, but the chief was prompted by the complaints of hardships suffered by the area residents. The CEO also may provide leadership by taking stands on bond issues (seeking funds to hire more officers or build new buildings, for example) and by advising the governing body on the effects of proposed ordinances.

The liaison role is undertaken when the CEO of a police organization interacts with other organizations and coordinates work assignments. It is not uncommon for executives from a geographical area—the police chief, sheriff, ranking officer of the local highway patrol office, district attorney, campus police chief, and so on—to meet informally each month to discuss common problems and strategies. The chief executive also serves as liaison to regional law enforcement councils, narcotics units, crime labs, dispatching centers, and so on. He or she also meets with the representatives of the courts, the juvenile system, and other criminal justice agencies.

The Informational Role

Another role identified by Mintzberg's model is the *informational* one. In this capacity, the CEO engages in tasks relating to (1) monitoring/inspecting, (2) dissemination, and (3) spokesperson duties.

In the monitoring/inspecting function, the CEO constantly reviews the department's operations to ensure that it is operating smoothly (or as smoothly as police operations can be expected to be). This function is often referred to as "roaming the ship"; many CEOs who isolated themselves from their personnel and the daily operations of the agency can speak from sad experience of the need to be involved and present. Many police executives use daily staff meetings to acquire information about their jurisdictions, especially criminal and other activities during the previous 24 hours.

Dissemination tasks involve distributing information to members of the department via memoranda, special orders, general orders, and policies and procedures as described in Chapter 3. The spokesperson function is related to the dissemination task but is focused more on providing information to the news media. This is a difficult task for the chief executive; news organizations, especially television and the print media, are competitive businesses that seek to obtain the most complete news in the shortest amount of time, which often translates into wider viewership and therefore greater advertising revenues for them. From one perspective, the media must appreciate that a criminal investigation can be seriously compromised by premature or excessive coverage. From the other perspective, the public has a right to know what is occurring in the community, especially matters relating to crime. Therefore, the prudent police executive attempts to have an open and professional relationship with the media in which each side knows and understands its responsibilities. The prudent chief executive also remembers the power of the media and does not alienate them; as an old saying goes, "Never argue with someone who buys his ink by the barrel." Unfortunately, many police executives (a good number of whom left office involuntarily) can speak of the results of failing to develop an appropriate relationship with the media.

An example of the good–bad relationship that often exists between the police and the media is the Washington, D.C.-area "Beltway sniper" investigation of late 2002. Although Montgomery County, Maryland, Police Chief Charles Moose was at times very frustrated by leaks of confidential information to the media, he also used the media to communicate with the snipers, who eventually were captured after the suspects' photographs and a vehicle description were broadcast. This case is discussed more thoroughly in Chapter 5.

The Decision-Maker Role

In the decision-maker role, the CEO of a police organization serves as (1) an entrepreneur, (2) a disturbance handler, (3) a resource allocator, and (4) a negotiator.

In the capacity of entrepreneur, the CEO must sell ideas to the members of the governing board or the department—perhaps helping them to understand a new computer or communications system, the implementation of a policing strategy, or different work methods, all of which are intended to improve the organization. Sometimes roles blend, as when several police executives band together (in their entrepreneurial and liaison functions) to lobby the state attorney general and the legislature for new crime-fighting laws.

As a disturbance handler, the executive's tasks range from resolving minor disputes between staff members to dealing with major events, such as riots, continued muggings in a local park, or the cleanup of the downtown area. Sometimes, the executive must solve intradepartmental disputes, which can reach major proportions. For example, the executive must intervene when friction develops between different units, as when the patrol commanders' instruction to street officers to increase arrests for public drunkenness causes a strain on the resources of the jail division's commander.

As a resource allocator, the CEO must clearly understand the agency's budget and its priorities. The resource allocator must consider requests for funds from various groups. Personnel, for example, will ask for higher salaries, additional officers, and better equipment. Citizens may complain about speeding motorists in a specific area, which would require the allocation of additional resources to that neighborhood. In the resource-allocator role, the CEO must be able to prioritize requests and to defend his or her choices.

As a negotiator, the CEO resolves employee grievances and, through an appointed representative at the bargaining table, tries to represent the best interests of both the city and labor during collective bargaining. In this role, the CEO must consider the rank and file's request for raises and increased benefits as part of budget administration. If funds available to the jurisdiction are limited, the CEO must negotiate with the collective bargaining unit to reach an agreement. At times, contract negotiations reach an impasse or a deadlock.

I will elaborate on some of these chief executive functions later in the chapter; labor relations—including unionism and collective bargaining—are discussed more fully in Chapter 14.

LAW ENFORCEMENT EXECUTIVES, GENERALLY

Prior to examining the role and functions of contemporary police executives, I consider how such persons are selected for these positions. Given the responsibilities placed on those who occupy such positions, the means employed to test applicants for or to promote individuals to them becomes important.

Obtaining the Best: The Assessment Center

To obtain the most capable people for chief executive positions (and also for middle-management and even supervisory positions) in policing, the **assessment center** method has proved to be an efficacious means of hiring and promoting personnel. (*Note:* Sheriffs are normally elected, not hired or promoted into their position; thus, the assessment center is of little use for that position.) The assessment center method is now increasingly utilized to select people for all management or supervisory ranks. The process may include interviews; psychological tests; in-basket exercises; management tasks; group discussions; role-playing exercises, such as simulations of interviews with subordinates, the public, and news media; fact-finding exercises; oral presentation exercises; and written communications exercises.[2]

The first step is to identify behaviors important to successful performance in the position. Job descriptions listing responsibilities and skills should exist for all executive, middle management, and supervisory positions (such as chief, captain, lieutenant, sergeant, and so on). Then, each candidate's abilities and skill levels should be evaluated using several of the techniques mentioned.

Individual and group role playing are valuable hands-on exercises during the selection process. Candidates may be required to help solve simulated police–community problems (they conduct a "meeting" to hear the concerns of local minority groups), to react to a major incident (explaining what they would do and in what order in a simulated shooting or riot situation), to hold a news briefing, or to participate in other such exercises. They may be given an in-basket situation in which they receive an abundance of paperwork, policies, and problems to be prioritized and dealt with in a prescribed amount of time. Writing abilities may also be evaluated: Candidates may be given 30 minutes to develop a use-of-force policy for a hypothetical or real police agency. This type of exercise not only demonstrates candidates' written communications skills and understanding of the technical side of police work but also shows how they think cognitively and build a case.

During each exercise, several assessors or raters analyze each candidate's performance and record some type of evaluation; when the assessment center process ends, each rater submits his or her rating information to the person making the hiring or promotion decision. Typically selected because they have held the position for which candidates are now vying, assessors must not only know the types of problems and duties incumbent in the position but also should be keen observers of human behavior.

Assessment center procedures are logistically more difficult to conduct, as well as more labor-intensive and costly, than traditional interviews, but they are well worth the extra investment. Monies invested at the early stages of a hiring or promotional process can help avoid selecting the wrong person and can prevent untold problems for years to come. Good executives, middle managers, and supervisors make fewer mistakes and are probably sued less often.

Skills of Good Managers

To expand on the discussion of leadership skills in Chapter 2, note the basic management skills that the police executive must develop. First is *technical skill* which involves specialized knowledge, analytical ability, and facility in the use of the tools and techniques of the specific discipline. This is the skill most easily trained for. Examples in policing include budgeting, computer use, and fundamental knowledge of some specialized equipment, such as radar or breathalyzer machines.

Second is *human skill* the executive's ability to work effectively as a group member and build cooperation; this includes being sensitive to the needs and feelings of others, tolerating ambiguity, and being able to empathize with persons with different views and those from different cultures.

Last is *conceptual skills* involve coordinating and integrating all the activities and interests of the organization in pursuit of a common objective, in other words, being able to translate knowledge into action.[3]

These skills can be taught, just as other skills can, which proves that good administrators are not simply born. They can be trained in the classroom and by practicing the skills on the job.

The "Ten Commandments"

Following is an adaptation of the "Ten Commandments" of being a police executive—rules of personal and professional conduct that are vital to one's success—developed by Jurkanin et al.[4]

1. *Practice what you preach:* You must lead by example, remembering that actions speak louder than words. The chief executive must be a person of morality, integrity, and honor.
2. *A day's pay for a day-and-a-half of work:* The chief must put in long hours to accomplish all that needs to be done, at the expense of personal freedom. Staff meetings, phone conversations, luncheon meetings, press conferences, interviews, report reading, and labor negotiations all take place during the day, leaving the evenings for letter and report writing, budget review, reading professional journals, attending governing board meetings, and meeting with civic, church, or other groups.
3. *Maintain and promote integrity:* See the First Commandment.
4. *Develop a positive image:* The chief executive is also responsible for the morale of the employees; although law enforcement can be filled with bad news, disappointment, and failures, the chief must work to accentuate the positive. Recognition of employees' contributions and valiant actions are one way to do so, with awards ceremonies, memorandums, and so forth.
5. *Remain committed:* The chief must be committed to implementing the agency's goals, mission, and values; this might mean taking risks, which can have its dangers.

Failure must be faced immediately, and one must learn from mistakes. The chief executive can normally weather the storm by taking responsibility and being responsive.

6. *Be respectful:* Be prepared to stand up for employees who have performed admirably well while being fair, firm, concerned, and sincere. When possible, criticize in private and praise in public. Remember that there will always be some people who will vigorously oppose your views. Do not compromise yourself to try to obtain everyone's support.

7. *Accept assistance from others:* This will build a teamwork approach, although the chief remains the final authority in the agency. Two (or more) heads are always better than one. The chief also needs a confidante with whom to share thoughts, ideas, and concerns.

8. *Be eager for knowledge:* Stay abreast of technology, current events, topics that impact the community, and current management, leadership, and administration trends and issues. Be familiar with the history of the agency and the community to avoid repeating past mistakes. Know the financial aspects of the jurisdiction. Employ both formal (workshops) and informal (networking with other executives) means of training and education. Encourage employees to do likewise.

9. *Maintain a healthy lifestyle:* One who is physically fit is better able to perform and react to demands of the position. Obviously, wise choices in diet, exercise, annual checkups, and avoidance of all things harmful to one's health are keys to healthy living.

10. *Set personal goals:* Having reached the helm, one should still review short-, medium-, and long-term objectives and skills that need development, to assist in establishing a future direction for oneself as well as for the organization. Along with career goals, personal goals should be examined.

Managing the Organization's Critical Components

Successful law enforcement administration demands that chief executives successfully manage several critical components of the organization.

Human resource planning includes recruitment, training, development, evaluation, and discipline of personnel. The quality of personnel and their management are the most important factors affecting the services provided by the organization.

Remember that the two types of law enforcement executives are those who have been sued and those who are going to be sued. The level of hierarchical responsibility, the high public profile, the oversight of potentially risky activities, an increasingly litigious society, and a civil justice system with a focus on individual rights place the modern law enforcement executive squarely in the path of litigation (see Chapter 14).[5] Finally, it is critical that contemporary law enforcement executives be well grounded in the political (see later discussion), labor-relations (see Chapter 14), financial (see Chapter 15), and technological (see Chapter 16) aspects of the role.

Anomia among Police Executives

Recent research has examined another important element of the personality makeup of police administrators: **anomia**. Anomia is related to the breaking down of an individual's sense of attachment to society and to others. An anomic individual feels that community leaders are indifferent to his or her needs, that the social order is unpredictable, that he or she cannot count on anyone for support, and that life itself is meaningless.[6] Kraig Hays et al.[7] examined whether or not police chiefs are high or low in their level of anomia and found that the latter is generally the case; the majority of the 1,500 police chiefs in their study did not appear to experience high levels of social distancing from their fellow human beings.

This is important since police chiefs must be well connected with their communities, their subordinates, municipal leaders, and significant others. As leaders of policing organizations, chiefs must be well integrated into their communities, and this research found that they appeared to be. In a very real sense, the position of police chief is a networking type of job and chiefs must be well integrated with a variety of people. A severely anomic police chief or sheriff could have disastrous effects on their jurisdiction.[8]

CHIEFS OF POLICE

What do law enforcement executives do? In contrast to Mintzberg's rather sophisticated model described earlier, Ronald Lynch stated the primary tasks of these executives in simple terms:

> They listen, talk, write, confer, think, decide—about [personnel], money, materials, methods, facilities—in order to plan, organize, direct, coordinate, and control their research service, production, public relations, employee relations, and all other activities so that they may more effectively serve the citizens to whom they are responsible.[9]

Next, I look at what city officials and the community expect of police chiefs, as well as how individuals ascend to this position.

Expectations of Government and the Community

The **chief of police** (also known as the *commissioner* or *superintendent*) is generally considered to be one of the most influential and prestigious persons in local government. Indeed, people at this position often amass considerable power and influence in their jurisdiction. Mayors, city managers and administrators, members of the agency, labor organizations, citizens, special-interest groups, and the media all have differing role expectations of the chief of police that often conflict.

The mayor or city manager likely wants the chief of police to promote departmental efficiency, reduce crime, improve service, and so on. Others appreciate the chief who simply keeps morale high and citizens' complaints low.

The mayor also expects the chief to communicate with city management about police-related issues and to be part of the city management team; to communicate city management's policies to police personnel; to establish agency policies, goals, and objectives and put them in writing; to develop an administrative system for managing people, equipment, and the budget in a professional and businesslike manner; to set a good example, both personally and professionally; to administer disciplinary action consistently and fairly when required; and to select personnel whose performance will ably and professionally promote the organization's objectives.

Members of the agency also have expectations of the chief executive: to be their advocate, supporting them when necessary, and representing the agency's interests when dealing with judges and prosecutors who may be indifferent or hostile. Citizens tend to expect the chief of police to provide efficient and cost-effective police services while keeping crime and tax rates down (often an area of built-in conflict) and preventing corruption and illegal use of force. Special-interest groups expect the chief to advocate policy positions that they favor. For example, Mothers Against Drunk Driving (MADD) would desire strong anti-DUI measures by the police. Finally, the media expect the chief to cooperate fully with their efforts to obtain fast and complete information on crime.

Qualifications

Qualifications for the position of police chief vary widely, depending on the size of the agency and the region of the country. Small agencies, especially those in rural areas, may not have a minimum educational requirement for the job. In the early 1970s, the National Advisory Commission on Criminal Justice Standards and Goals surveyed police chiefs and their superiors to determine the essential qualities for the job.

Education was found to be an important consideration; today, many agencies require a college education along with several years of progressively responsible police management experience. A survey by the Police Executive Research Forum (PERF) of 358 police chiefs in jurisdictions of 50,000 or more residents found that chiefs were generally highly educated—87 percent held a bachelor's degree and 47 percent had a master's—and were more likely to be chosen from outside the agencies they headed, but they spent less than 5 years in the position.[10]

Police chief executives also need several important management skills. In 1998, the National Advisory Commission asked police chiefs and their superiors to rate, on a scale of 1 to 10, the importance of 14 desirable management skills. The ability to motivate and control personnel and to relate to the community was considered most important. A survey today would probably yield similar results.[11]

Many cities finding themselves in need of a police chief have to consider whether it would be better to promote someone from within the ranks or hire from outside (perhaps using the assessment center process described earlier). Although it is perhaps more economical and certainly less trouble to select a police chief from within the organization than to use an assessment center, both methods have advantages and disadvantages. One study of police chiefs promoted from within or hired from outside indicated only one significant difference in qualification: educational attainment. The outsiders were more highly educated. No differences were found with respect to other aspects of their background, attitudes, salary, tenure in their current position or in policing, the size of the agency or community, and their current budget.[12] Some states, however, have made it nearly impossible for an outsider to come in. California has mandated that the chief should be a graduate of its own Peace Officers Standards and Training (POST) academy; New Jersey and New York also encourage "homegrown" chiefs.[13]

Job Protection, Termination, and the Political Arena

Traditionally, the job tenure of police chiefs has been short. A federal study in the mid-1970s found that the average length in office of chiefs of police was 5.4 years.[14] Another PERF study in the mid-1980s found the average to be practically unchanged: 5.5 years. That figure has not varied much in recent times.[15] This short tenure of police chiefs has several negative consequences. It prevents long-range planning, results in frequent new policies and administrative styles, and prohibits the development of the chief's political power base and local influence.

Police chiefs would, of course, prefer to possess some type of protection against their arbitrary and unjustified removal from office by an elected or political officeholder.[16] In fact, some police chiefs have resigned and reverted to their former position of assistant or deputy chief simply to have some job protection until retirement.

In some states, statutory protections against such actions exist, or special boards or commissions have been created for the sole purpose of establishing recruitment, selection, and retention policies for chiefs of police. Other states require written notice of the basis for the proposed termination, a hearing on the charges, and a finding of cause before the dismissal can be effected. Still, police chiefs across the country are looking for job protection in local civil service codes, municipal ordinances, and such individual employment contracts as they can negotiate.[17]

Losing the job of police chief is not difficult. Although some, of course, lose their positions because of their shortcomings, others leave their post as a result of situations and conflicts outside their control. These conflicts have been termed *political arenas* and can be divided into three types based on their duration, intensity, and pervasiveness: (1) confrontation, (2) shaky alliance, and (3) a politicized organization.[18]

The first type of political arena, *confrontation*, occurs when the situational conflict is intense but brief and confined. One obvious example is the termination of a police chief in the aftermath of a major incident (e.g., a scandal or acts of racial profiling by officers).

The second type of political arena is the *shaky alliance* in which conflict is less intense but still pervasive. An example involves a former Los Angeles police chief, Willie Williams—Daryl Gates's successor and the first outsider appointed as chief in that city in more than 40 years. Williams had to deal with both external pressures (the impact of the 1991 Rodney King incident on the public) and internal pressures (the resentment of his own officers). This was a shaky alliance and Williams's contract was not renewed.

The third type of political arena, *politicized organization* features pervasive but muted conflict that is tolerable for a time. This kind of conflict is commonplace in American policing, and in this situation, the chief's survival depends on external support. Examples would be a riot resulting from allegations of police brutality or a lengthy, unsuccessful, and possibly botched homicide investigation.

The history of policing is so replete with politics that it even experienced a political "era" in the United States, roughly from the 1840s to the 1930s. Still, this is an aspect of policing that is often overlooked and has had both good and bad elements. Politics colors nearly everything, and political influence can range from major policy, personnel, and budgetary decisions to the overzealous governing board member who wishes to micromanage the police agency and even appears unexpectedly at night at a crime scene (overheard on the police scanner) to "assist" the officers.

Norm Stamper, former chief of police in Seattle, Washington, described quite well the power and influence of politics in policing. Stamper wrote that "*everything* about policing is ultimately political. Who gets which office: political. Which services are cut when there's a budget freeze: political. Who gets hired, fired, promoted: political, political, political."[19] Stamper also observed that there is both good and bad politics: "I hire my brother-in-law's cousin, a certifiable doofus, because he's got a bass boat I wouldn't mind borrowing—bad politics. I promote a drinking buddy—bad politics. I pick an individual because he or she will add value to the organization and will serve the community honorably—good politics."[20]

THE SHERIFF

The position of **sheriff** has a long tradition, rooted in the time of the Norman conquest of England (in 1066), and it played an important part in the early law enforcement activities of colonial America. Unfortunately, because of television and movie depictions, many people today view the county sheriff as a bumbling, cruel, overweight, or corrupt individual wearing a cowboy hat and sunglasses while talking with a Southern drawl (see, e.g., reruns of movies such as *Smoky and the Bandit, Mississippi Burning, The Dukes of Hazzard, Walking Tall* and many others). This image is both unfair and highly inaccurate. Next, we examine the role of today's county sheriffs.

Because of the diversity of sheriff's offices throughout the country, it is difficult to describe a typical sheriff's department; these offices run the gamut from the traditional, highly political, limited-service office to the modern, fairly nonpolitical, full-service police organization. It is possible, however, to list functions commonly associated with the sheriff's office:

1. Serving and/or implementing civil processes (divorce papers, liens, evictions, garnishments and attachments, and other civil duties, such as extradition and transportation of prisoners)
2. Collecting certain taxes and conducting real estate sales (usually for nonpayment of taxes) for the county
3. Performing routine order-maintenance duties by enforcing state statutes and county ordinances, arresting offenders, and performing traffic and criminal investigations
4. Serving as bailiff of the courts
5. Maintaining and operating the county correctional institutions[21]

Sheriffs, therefore, have a unique role in that they typically serve all three components of the justice system: (1) law enforcement (with patrol, traffic, and investigative functions), (2) the courts (as civil process servers and bailiffs), and (3) corrections (in the county jails). In many urban areas, civil process duties consume more time and resources than those involving law enforcement.[22]

Sheriffs are elected in all but two states (Rhode Island and Hawaii; note, however, that in some consolidated jurisdictions, such as Miami–Dade county, Flurida, sheriffs are also appointed); thus, they tend to be aligned with a political party. As elected officials, sheriffs are important political figures and, in many rural areas, represent the most powerful political force in the county. As a result, sheriffs are far more independent than appointed municipal police chiefs, who can be removed from office by the mayors or city managers who appoint them. However, because they are elected, sheriffs receive considerable media scrutiny and are subject to state accountability processes.

Because of this electoral system, it is possible that the only qualification for the office is the ability to get votes. In some areas of the country, the sheriff's term of office is limited to one 2-year term at a time (a sheriff cannot succeed himself or herself); thus, the office has been known to be rotated between the sheriff and undersheriff. In most counties, however, the sheriff has a 4-year term of office and can be reelected.

The sheriff enjoys no tenure guarantee, although one study found that sheriffs (averaging 6.7 years in office) had longer tenure in office than chiefs of police (5.4 years). The politicization of the office of sheriff can result in high turnover rates of personnel who do not have civil service protection. The uncertainty concerning tenure is not conducive to long-range (strategic) planning. Largely as a result of the political nature of the office, sheriffs tend to be older, less likely to have been promoted through the ranks of the agency, and less likely to be college graduates and to have specialized training than police chiefs. Research has also found that sheriffs in small agencies have more difficulty with organizational problems (field activities, budget management) and that sheriffs in large agencies find dealing with local officials and planning and evaluation to be more troublesome.[23]

MIDDLE MANAGERS: CAPTAINS AND LIEUTENANTS

Few police administration books contain information about the **middle managers** of a police department: the captains and lieutenants. This is unfortunate because they are too numerous and too powerful within police organizations to ignore. Opinions concerning these middle-management personnel vary, however, as I discuss later.

Leonhard Fuld, one of the early progressive police administration researchers, said in 1909 that the captain is one of the most important officers in the organization. Fuld believed that the position had two broad duties—policing and administration. The captain was held responsible for preserving the public peace and protecting life and property within the precinct. Fuld defined the captain's administrative duties as being of three kinds: clerical, janitorial, and supervisory.[24]

Although every ranking officer in the police department exercises some managerial skills and duties, here, we are concerned with the managers to whom first-line supervisors report, for they generally are unit commanders. In a mid-sized or large police agency, a patrol shift or watch may be commanded by a captain, who will have several lieutenants reporting to him or her. The lieutenants may assist the captain in running the shift, but when there is a shortage of sergeants as a result of vacations or retirements, the lieutenant may assume the duties of a first-line supervisor. In some respects, the lieutenant's position in some departments is a training ground for future unit commanders (the rank of captain or higher).

Perhaps the best way to understand what these shift commanders do is to examine the tasks they perform in a medium-sized police department. First, I examine the tasks generally performed by the captain, using the Lexington, Kentucky, Police Department as an example. The 15 most important tasks performed by captains are as follows:[25]

1. Issuing assignments to individuals and units within the section
2. Receiving assignments for the section/unit
3. Reviewing incoming written complaints and reports
4. Preparing routine reports
5. Reviewing the final disposition of assignments
6. Ensuring that subordinates comply with general and special orders
7. Monitoring crime and other activity statistics
8. Evaluating the work of individuals and units within the section
9. Maintaining sector facilities
10. Discussing concerns and problems with people
11. Attending various staff meetings
12. Maintaining working contacts and responding to inquiries from other sections of the division
13. Reviewing and approving overtime in the section/unit
14. Monitoring section/unit operations to evaluate performance
15. Fielding and responding to complaints against subordinates

A review of these tasks shows that captains have more administrative responsibilities than lieutenants or sergeants, with 9 of the 15 tasks being administrative in nature. Captains spend a substantial amount of time coordinating their units' activities with those of other units and overseeing the operation of their units. As an officer progresses up the chain of command, his or her responsibilities become more administrative. At the same time, captains also have supervisory responsibilities (tasks 1, 3, 5, 6, 8, and 15). Whereas a sergeant or lieutenant may be supervising individual officers, a captain is more concerned with individual tasks, unit activities, and the overall performance of the officers under his or her command.

Every commander and administrator in the department, including the police chief, possesses administrative and supervisory responsibilities to some extent. As can be seen from the previous list, the unit commander functions to some extent like a police chief. The unit commander has many of the same responsibilities as the chief but on a smaller scale. The chief performs these functions for the total department, while the unit commander is concerned with only one unit.

Next, we examine the tasks generally performed by the **lieutenant**, again using the Lexington Police Department as an example. The 15 most important responsibilities for lieutenants include the following (this list is based on the frequency with which they are performed and their urgency):[26]

1. Assisting in supervising or directing the activities of the unit
2. Performing the duties of a police officer
3. Ensuring that departmental and governmental policies are followed
4. Preparing the duty roster
5. Reviewing the work of individuals or groups in the section
6. Responding to field calls requiring an on-scene commander
7. Holding the roll call
8. Preparing various reports
9. Reviewing various reports
10. Coordinating the activities of subordinates on major investigations
11. Meeting with superiors concerning unit operations
12. Maintaining time sheets
13. Notifying the captain/bureau commander of significant calls
14. Answering inquiries from other sections/units, divisions, and outside agencies
15. Serving as the captain/bureau commander in the latter's absence

Notice that some of the tasks performed by the lieutenants are purely administrative in nature (tasks 4, 7, 8, and 12). These are administrative activities that occur in every operational unit in the police department. The lieutenants in Lexington also perform supervisory functions (tasks 1, 3, 5, 6, and 9). These functions include overseeing officers and sergeants to ensure that different tasks are completed. Here, direct supervision generally focuses on the most critical tasks or those tasks that, when performed incorrectly, can result in dire consequences. Tasks 11 and 13 through 15 are managerial in nature. These responsibilities are generally vested within a unit commander, but many lieutenants perform them, especially in the absence of the captain. Finally, lieutenants perform the duties of a police officer (task 2). With their supervisory and managerial responsibilities, they engage in a limited amount of police work. The list shows that lieutenants have a wide range of supervisory, managerial, and police duties.

One potential problem of police organizations is that they may become top-heavy, with too many administrative, management, and supervisory personnel in general or too many who are working in offices and not on the streets. Such structures can hinder the accomplishment of goals and objectives. Too often, middle managers become glorified paper pushers, especially in the present climate that requires myriad reports, budgets, grants, and so on.

The agency should determine what administrative, management, and supervisory functions are essential and how many captains, lieutenants, and sergeants are needed to perform them. Some communities, such as Kansas City, Missouri, have eliminated the rank of lieutenant; they found that this move had no negative consequences.[27]

FIRST-LINE SUPERVISORS: THE PATROL SERGEANT

Seeking the Gold Badge

Sometime during the career of a patrol officer (provided that he or she acquires the minimal number of years of experience), the opportunity for career advancement is presented—the chance to wear the sergeant's "gold badge." This is a difficult position to occupy because at this middle level, **first-line supervisors** are caught between upper management and the rank-and-file officers.

This initial opportunity to attain the rank of sergeant is normally quite attractive. It is not uncommon for 60–65 percent or more of those who are eligible to take the test for promotion; thus, competition for the sergeant openings in most departments is quite keen.

Becoming a sergeant often involves an assessment center process, discussed earlier, and departmental and civil service procedures that are intended to guarantee legitimacy and impartiality in the process. Officers are often told that it is best to rotate into different assignments before testing for sergeant to gain exposure to a variety of police functions and supervisors. The promotional system, then, favors well-rounded officers; furthermore, being skilled at test taking is often of tremendous assistance, so even if one fails the first or several tests, going through the testing process can be invaluable. As with the chief executives' hiring process, an assessment center, which includes critical-incident, problem solving, in-basket, disciplinary problems, role-playing exercises, and/or other components, will provide candidates with valuable training and testing experience. Other factors that might come into play as part of the promotional process include education and training, years of experience, supervisory ratings, psychological evaluations, and departmental commendations.

Assuming the Position: General Roles and Functions

Administrative personnel know that a good patrol officer is not automatically a good supervisor. Because supervisors are promoted from within the ranks, they are often placed in charge of their friends and peers. Longstanding relationships are put under stress when a new sergeant suddenly has official authority over former equals. Leniency or preferential treatment is often expected of new sergeants by their former peers.

When new supervisors attempt to correct deficient behavior, their previous performance may be recalled as a means of challenging the reasonableness or legitimacy of their supervisory action. Supervisors with any skeletons in their closets can expect to hear those skeletons rattling as they begin to use their new-found authority. This places a great deal of pressure on the supervisor. A new supervisor, therefore, must go through a transitional phase to learn how to exercise command and get cooperation from subordinates.

The new supervisor is no longer responsible solely for her or his behavior but also for the behavior of several other employees. The step from officer to supervisor is a big one and calls for a new set of skills and knowledge largely separate from those learned at lower levels in the organization.

Supervision is challenging not only in policing but also in corrections, where supervisors must follow federal and state laws and court decisions that concern the custody, care, and treatment of inmates. Their subordinates, however, expect them to be understanding, to protect them from prison management's potentially unreasonable expectations and arbitrary decisions, and to represent their interests.

The supervisor's role, put simply, is to get his or her subordinates to do their very best. This task involves a host of actions, including communicating, motivating, leading, team building, training, appraising, counseling, and disciplining. Getting them to do their very best includes figuring out each subordinate's strengths and weaknesses, defining good and bad performance, measuring performance, providing feedback, and making sure that subordinates' efforts coincide with the organization's mission, values, goals, and objectives.

Supervising a group of subordinates is made more difficult because of the so-called human element. People are complex and sometimes unpredictable. Rules and principles for communicating, leading, and other supervisory tasks are rarely hard and fast because different people react differently. What works for a supervisor in one situation may not work for that supervisor in another situation, much less for some other supervisor. Thus, supervisors have to learn to "read" subordinates and diagnose situations before choosing how to respond. Supervisors have to become students of human behavior and of behavioral science disciplines such as psychology and sociology.

Effective supervision is also difficult because the job is dynamic, not static. One's subordinates change over time as they age, grow, mature, and experience satisfaction and dissatisfaction in their personal and work lives. In addition, attrition is common, as personnel retire, promote, and transfer into other units within the department. When new subordinates come under the supervisor's wing, the supervisor must learn the best way to handle them and also be attuned to the new officers' effects on other subordinates and on the work group as a whole.

It is not only one's subordinates who change; the organization and its environment change over time. The organization's rules and expectations may change. The public may make new demands. Societal values evolve and change. Effective supervision over the long haul requires continuous monitoring and adaptation. The department expects the supervisor to keep up with such changes to better supervise subordinates. Subordinates, on the other hand, expect the supervisor to help them to interpret and adapt successfully to this changing environment. Table 4.1 shows the expectations that both managers and rank-and-file officers have of first-line supervisors.

TABLE 4.1 Management's and Officers' Expectations of Supervisors

MANAGEMENT'S EXPECTATIONS

- Interpret departmental policies, procedures, and rules and ensure that officers follow them
- Initiate disciplinary action when officers fail to follow policies
- Ensure that officers' paperwork and reports are accurate and filed on a timely basis
- Train officers when they are deficient or unskilled
- Complete performance evaluations
- Ensure that officers treat citizens respectfully, professionally, and impartially
- Ensure that officers' equipment and appearance are in order
- Back up officers and review their performance when officers answer calls for service
- Take charge of high-risk or potential critical-incident situations
- Make assignments to ensure that the objectives of the unit are met

OFFICERS' EXPECTATIONS

- Interpret departmental policies, procedures, and rules to meet the needs of the officers
- Handle disciplinary actions informally rather than taking direct action, especially regarding minor infractions
- Advocate for officers when they request a vacation or time off
- Support them when there is a conflict with citizens
- Provide them with support and backup at high-risk calls
- Assist them in getting better assignments and shifts
- Emphasize law enforcement activities over other activities such as providing services, community policing activities, or mundane assignments such as traffic control
- Understand that officers need to take breaks and sometimes attend to personal needs while on duty

Basic Tasks

The following nine tasks are most important for police supervisors; they are listed with the most important first:[28]

1. Supervise subordinate officers in the performance of their duties
2. Disseminate information to subordinates
3. Ensure that general and special orders are followed
4. Review and approve various reports
5. Listen to problems voiced by officers
6. Answer calls
7. Keep superiors apprised of ongoing situations
8. Provide direct supervision for potential high-risk calls or situations
9. Interpret policies and inform subordinates

Tasks 1 and 8 on this list are global supervisory tasks that incorporate both direction and control. Tasks 2 and 9 are aspects of the directing function, whereas tasks 3 through 5 are elements of control. Thus, six of these top nine sergeant's tasks involve directing and controlling. The remaining three tasks provide interesting glimpses into some of the other duties and responsibilities of police supervisors: listening to subordinates' problems, notifying superiors of problems, and directly assisting subordinates in performing their work. Police supervisors provide an important communications link in the hierarchy between workers and management, as well as a sounding board for problems and grievances. They also get involved in performing street police work from time to time.

Supervisory tasks can range from the mundane (such as typing and filing reports, operating dictation equipment) to the challenging (assigning priorities to investigations, training personnel in forced-entry procedures and barricaded-person situations). Tasks may be administrative (preparing monthly activity reports, scheduling vacation leave), operational (securing major crime scenes, assisting stranded motorists), general (maintaining an inventory of equipment, training subordinates), or specialized (conducting stakeouts, training animals for use in specialized units).

Types of Supervisors

Robin S. Engel[29] studied police supervisors and found four distinct types: traditional, innovative, supportive, and active. Each of these types can be found in any police department. A particular supervisor's style is largely dependent on his or her experiences on the job, his or her training, and the department's organizational climate.

The first type, *traditional* is law enforcement oriented. Traditional supervisors expect their subordinates to produce high levels of measurable activities, such as traffic citations and arrests. They expect officers to respond to calls for service efficiently, place a great deal of emphasis on reports and other paperwork, and provide officers with a substantial amount of instruction and oversight. To a great extent, traditional supervisors are task oriented. They tend to place greater emphasis on punishment than rewards and often believe that they do not have a great deal of power in the department. These supervisors see their primary role as controlling subordinates. Traditional supervisors often have morale and motivation problems with their subordinates.

The second type is the *innovative* supervisor, who is most closely associated with community policing. To some extent, innovative supervisors are the opposite of traditional supervisors. Innovative supervisors generally do not place a great deal of emphasis on citations or arrests. They also depend more on developing relationships with subordinates than on using power to control or motivate. Innovative supervisors usually are good mentors, and they tend to coach rather than order. They are open to new ideas and innovations. Their ultimate goal is to develop officers who can solve problems and have good relations with citizens. Innovative supervisors sometimes have problems with officers who are task oriented or who emphasize enforcement and neglect community relations.

The third type of supervisor is the *supportive* supervisor, who, like the innovative supervisor, is concerned with developing good relations with subordinates. The primary difference is that supportive supervisors are concerned with protecting officers from what are viewed as unfair management practices. They see themselves as a buffer between management and officers. They attempt to develop strong work teams and motivate officers by inspiring them. Their shortcoming is that they tend to see themselves as "one of the boys," and they sometimes neglect emphasizing departmental goals and responsibilities.

The final category of supervisors, according to Engel, is the *active* supervisor, who tends to work in the field. Active supervisors sometimes are police officers with stripes or rank. They often take charge of field situations rather than supervise them, although they are active supervisors in most situations. They are able to develop good relations with subordinates because they are perceived as being hard-working and competent. Their shortcoming is that, by being overly involved in some field situations, they do not give their subordinates the opportunity to develop.

Engel[30] found that the four types of supervision were fairly evenly distributed in the departments. The most effective supervisor was the active supervisor. Subordinates working for active supervisors performed better in a number of areas, including problem solving and community policing. This led Engel to conclude that active supervisors were able to develop a more productive work unit because of their ability to lead by example. It seems that working supervisors inspire subordinates to work and be productive.

Engel did identify one problem with active police supervisors: a higher incidence of the use of force relative to the other types. Because active supervisors are very involved in the provision of police services, efforts should be made to ensure that they follow policies and that their subordinates adhere to policies and procedures. Supervisors must not only be well trained and selected carefully but they must also receive a measure of supervision from their superiors. If the supervisor fails to make sure that employees perform correctly, the unit will not be successful, causing difficulties for the manager, the lieutenant, or the captain.

A police department is really nothing more than the sum total of all its units, and one problem unit can adversely affect other units and reduce the department's total effectiveness. This is particularly true for police organizations because there is substantial interdependence among the various units in a police department. For example, if patrol officers do a poor job of writing reports when they respond to crimes, the workload of detectives who later complete the case's follow-up investigation will increase.

THE PATROL OFFICER

Countless books and articles have been written about, and other chapters in this book deal, in part, with the beat officer. Here, we briefly discuss the nature of this position. Included is a review of their basic tasks, some traits of good officers, hiring the best personnel possible, and some basic training methods.

Basic Tasks

Many people believe that the police officer has the most difficult job in the United States. In fundamental terms, the police perform four basic functions: (1) enforcing the laws, (2) performing services (such as maintaining or assisting animal control units, reporting burned-out street lights or stolen traffic lights and signs, delivering death messages, checking the welfare of people in their homes, delivering blood), (3) preventing crime (patrolling, providing the public with information on locks and lighting to reduce the opportunity for crime), and (4) protecting the innocent (by investigating crimes, police systematically remove innocent people from consideration as crime suspects).[31]

Because police officers are solitary workers, spending much of their time on the job unsupervised, and because those officers who are hired today will become the supervisors of the future, police administrators must attempt to attract the best individuals possible. A major problem of police administration today involves personnel recruitment.

What Traits Make a Good Officer?

Although it may be difficult for the average police administrator to describe the qualities he or she looks for when recruiting, training, and generally creating a good officer, some psychological characteristics can be identified. According to psychologist Lawrence Wrightsman,[32] it is important that good officers be *incorruptible*, of high moral character. They should be *well adjusted* able to carry out the hazardous and stressful tasks of policing without cracking up, and thick-skinned enough to operate without defensiveness. They should also be *people oriented* and able to respond to situations without becoming overly emotional, impulsive, or aggressive; they need to exercise restraint. They also need *cognitive skills* to assist in their investigative work.

Dennis Nowicki[33] compiled 12 qualities that he believes are imperative for entry-level police officers:

1. *Enthusiasm.* Believes in what he or she is doing and goes about it with a vigor that is almost contagious
2. *Good communications skills.* Highly developed speaking and listening skills; ability to interact equally well with people from all socioeconomic levels
3. *Good judgment.* Wisdom and analytical ability to make good decisions based on an understanding of the problem
4. *Sense of humor.* Ability to laugh and smile, to help officers cope with the regular exposure to human pain and suffering
5. *Creativity.* Ability to use creative techniques by placing themselves in the mind of the criminal and legally accomplishing arrests
6. *Self-motivation.* Making things happen, proactively solving difficult cases, creating their own luck
7. *Knowing the job and the system.* Understanding the role of a police officer, the intricacies of the justice system, what the administration requires, and using both formal and informal channels to be effective
8. *Ego.* Believing they are good officers, having the self-confidence that enables them to solve difficult crimes
9. *Courage.* Ability to meet physical and psychological challenges, thinking clearly during times of high stress, admitting when they are wrong, and standing up for what is difficult and right
10. *Understanding discretion.* Enforcing the spirit, not the letter, of the law; not being hard-nosed, hardheaded, or hardhearted; giving people a break and showing empathy
11. *Tenacity.* Staying focused; seeing challenges, not obstacles; viewing failure not as a setback but as an experience
12. *Thirst for knowledge.* Staying current on new laws and court decisions, always learning (not only from the classroom but also via informal discussions with other officers)

Addressing a Front-End Problem: Recruiting Quality Officers

Certainly, the recruitment of quality police officers is the key to the success, values, and culture of any police organization. The current "cop crunch" is exacerbated in many cities by exploding growth, a competitive job market, natural catastrophes (e.g., Hurricane Katrina in New Orleans), and struggles to retain diversity.[34] Furthermore, this crunch comes at a time when today's police need a stronger focus on problem-solving skills, ability to collaborate with the community, and a greater capacity to use technology.[35] Adding to the problems are today's higher incidence of obesity, major debt, drug use, and criminal records that are found among potential recruits.[36]

Police recruitment issues are such a concern at present that a national meeting was recently convened to discuss these issues by the U.S. Department of Justice, the National Institute of Justice, and the RAND Corporation. This national meeting produced several recruiting measures that can be adopted, however, toward generating a satisfactory applicant pool:

- Have one leader in charge of the entire recruiting process, from marketing to testing to background investigation through academy training.
- Consider the academy dropout rate: are recruiters signing up the most promising candidates for the academy?[37]
- Publicize hiring campaigns on business cards, use department vehicles as billboards, and make the agency websites more effective by emphasizing the positive reasons for joining (rather than focusing on the challenges faced by police officers).
- Limit recruiting trips to those locations where candidates are likely to be found, such as areas with economic difficulties; out-of-town recruiting trips are generally not effective.[38]
- Look at the academy program to see if something is hindering diversity and in effect "washing out" candidates, particularly those whose native language is not English.[39]
- Make the department's recruiting efforts focus on the positives of police work, such as job security, the satisfaction of public service, and superior pay and benefits; too often they emphasize the challenges involved in becoming a police officer.[40]
- Use bonuses for officers who refer candidates to the academy.
- Include an online sample test on the agency website to give recruits an idea of the types of questions they will be facing.
- Allow other standardized tests, such as the Armed Services Vocational Aptitude Battery, to substitute for the police department's own written test; this will speed the acceptance process.[41]

The Oakland, California, Police Department may well represent the best example of a city that rebounded from hard times, as shown in Exhibit 4.1; then, Exhibit 4.2 demonstrates how police agencies are using social networking sites to perform background checks on recruits.

EXHIBIT 4.1

Oakland Rebounds: Hiring for Community Needs

The Oakland, California, Police Department (OPD), like many agencies, experienced hiring freezes—ultimately resulting in an eight percent reduction in force. Oakland voters passed legislation that provided about $19 million for community policing and other public-safety initiatives over a ten-year period; OPD was to hire more than 60 new officers. To attract new candidates, OPD launched a one million dollar advertising campaign featuring billboards and other saturation advertising; it streamlined its hiring process so that a candidate could pass the background check within three weeks—helping the department hire promising candidates who were considering other agencies. OPD sent applicants e-mails concerning the status of their applications, and accepted applications from other academies. To foster retention, OPD established a new shift schedule with seven 12-hour shifts over a two-week period, increased pay 20 percent, added a 4.5 percent increase for those officers meeting standards and training qualifications, and offered another 4.5 percent for officers with a bachelor's degree.

Source: Based on Jeremy M. Wilson and Clifford A. Grammich, *Police Recruitment and Retention in the Contemporary Urban Environment: A National Discussion of Personnel Experiences and Promising Practices from the Front Lines* (Santa Monica, CA: RAND Corporation, 2009), pp. 11–12.

EXHIBIT 4.2

Using Social Networking Sites for Background Checks

Police agencies are using social networking sites to perform background checks, requesting that candidates sign waivers allowing investigators access to their Facebook, MySpace, YouTube, Twitter and other personal Internet accounts. Some agencies also demand that applicants provide private passwords, Internet pseudonyms, text messages and e-mail logs to allow the agency even greater access to information for the hiring process. Indeed, more than one-third of police agencies now review applicants' social media activity during background checks, according to the International Association of Chiefs of Police (IACP) in a recent survey of about 100 police chiefs.

In addition to inherent privacy concerns, there are also concerns that defense attorneys could use officers' posts to undercut their credibility in court, according to the National Fraternal Order of Police.

Among the findings on social networking sites are the following:

- In Massachusetts, an agency requested electronic message logs and found a recruit's text messages revealed past threats of suicide, resulting in disqualification.
- A New Jersey agency disqualified a candidate for posting racy photographs of himself with scantily clad women.
- Inappropriate officers' postings have been found that range from sexually explicit photographs to racially charged commentary.

Source: Based on Kevin Johnson, "Cops get screened for digital dirt," USA TODAY, November 12, 2010, http://www.usatoday.com/tech/news/2010-11-12-1Afacebookcops12_ST_N.htm (accessed November 15, 2010); also see Martha Stonebrook and Rick Stubbs, "Social Networking in Law Enforcement," International Association of Chiefs of Police 2010 Annual Conference, Orlando, Florida, http://www.aele.org/los2010s&s.pdf (accessed November 15, 2010).

From Field Training Officer to Police Training Officer

A new aspect of policing that concerns rank-and-file officers and with which all police chiefs and sheriffs should be acquainted is a new method of officer training. This training concept is known as the **police training officer (PTO)** program.

The basic recruit academy is certainly a major phase of the neophyte officers' career—the starting point for their occupational socialization into the police role, providing them with essential formal training, shaping their attitudes, and developing technical occupational skills. However, once the recruits leave the academy, where their training was primarily academic, their training is still incomplete. They must then undergo a field training process while under the tutelage and supervision of a qualified **field training officer (FTO)**. The FTO program was developed in the late 1960s in San Jose, California,[42] to provide new officers and deputies with a smooth, supervised, and educational transition from the academy to the field at their respective agencies. FTO programs remain in wide use today and generally consist of several identifiable phases: introduction (with the recruit learning agency policies and local laws); training and evaluation (the recruit is introduced to more complicated tasks performed by patrol officers); and the final portion (wherein the FTO trainer may act as an observer and evaluator while the recruit performs all the functions of a patrol officer). The length of time a recruit is assigned to an FTO will vary but normally the range is from 1 to 12 weeks.[43]

However, the FTO approach has changed very little in the past 40-plus years and is devoid of contemporary approaches to training that include adult- and problem-based learning and leadership principles. The newer approach departs from traditional police training methods that emphasize mechanical repetition skills and rote memory capabilities; rather, the focus is on developing an officer's learning capacity, leadership, and problem-solving skills. Its theoretical underpinnings include adult and problem-based learning. Regarding the former, Malcolm Knowles[44] believed in self-directed learning and thought that the adults should acquire the skills necessary to live up to their potential, understand their society, and be skilled in directing social change. Furthermore, adults should learn to react to the causes, not the symptoms, of behavior. Therefore, many police executives have come to believe that the FTO approach is not relevant to the methods and challenges of community-oriented policing and problem solving (COPPS, discussed in Chapter 3). Therefore, PTO was developed to better meet the needs of those agencies.

PTO seeks to take the traditional FTO program to a higher level—one that embraces and evaluates new officers based on their understanding and application of COPPS. With $500,000 in federal assistance, a new PTO program was recently developed and initiated at six national sites, including adult- and problem-based learning principles. PTO covers two primary training areas: substantive topics (the most common activities in policing) and core competencies (the common skills that officers are required to utilize in the daily performance of their duties). New officers must master 15 core competencies, which are specific skills, knowledge, and abilities that have been identified as essential for good policing. There is a learning matrix that serves as a guide for trainees and trainers during the training period, and demonstrates the interrelationships between the core competencies and daily policing activities during the eight phases of the PTO program.[45]

It is believed that PTO provides a foundation for lifelong learning that prepares new officers for the complexities of policing today and in the future. This approach is very different from traditional police training methods that emphasize mechanical repetition skills and rote memory capabilities; rather, the PTO focus is on developing an officer's learning capacity, leadership, and problem-solving skills. While applied skills (e.g., weaponless defense, shooting, and defensive tactics) are essential, they constitute only one set of skills for contemporary policing. This approach is also highly flexible, able to be tailored to each agency's needs; furthermore, because of its flexibility, it may be adjusted to meet future police training challenges.

ROLES AND FUNCTIONS OF POLICE PERSONNEL UNDER COPPS

Earlier in this chapter, we examined the basic roles of chief executives, middle managers, and first-line supervisors. Next, we briefly examine their roles under COPPS.

The Chief Executive

The advent of community policing has brought new challenges for police chiefs, calling for new skills and attitudes and even the ability to be an entrepreneur.[46] First, the police chief executive is ultimately responsible for all facets of COPPS, from implementation to training to evaluation. Therefore, what is needed are the chief executives who are "risk takers and boat rockers within a culture where daily exposure to life-or-death situations makes officers natural conservators of the status quo."[47] For them, "standing still is not only insufficient . . . it is going backwards."[48] Therefore, police executives must be *viable change agents*. The chief executive must be both visible and credible and must create a climate conducive to change.

In sum, the chief executive's roles and responsibilities during the change to COPPS include the following:

- Articulating a clear vision to the organization
- Understanding and accepting the depth of change and the amount of time required to implement COPPS
- Assembling a management team that is committed to translating the new vision into action
- Being committed to removing bureaucratic obstacles whenever possible

Middle Managers

COPPS's emphasis on problem solving requires middle managers (captains and lieutenants) to draw on their familiarity with the bureaucracy to secure, maintain, and use authority to empower subordinates, helping officers to actively and creatively confront and resolve issues, and sometimes using unconventional approaches on a trial-and-error basis.

Middle managers must *build on the strengths* of their subordinates, capitalizing on their training and competence.[49] They must "cheerlead," encouraging supervisors and patrol officers to solve the problems they are confronting.[50] The lieutenants are the "gatekeepers" and must develop the system, resources, and support mechanisms to ensure that the officers/detectives and supervisors can achieve the best results. The officers and supervisors cannot perform without the necessary equipment, resources, and reinforcement.[51]

In sum, the roles and responsibilities of middle managers during the change to COPPS include the following:

- Assuming responsibility for strategic planning
- Eliminating red tape and bottlenecks that impede the work of officers and supervisors
- Conducting regular meetings with subordinates to discuss plans, activities, and results
- Assessing COPPS efforts in a continuous manner

First-Line Supervisors

Perhaps the most challenging aspect of changing the culture of a police agency is achieving the support of first-line supervisors. Supervisors must be convinced that COPPS makes good sense in today's environment.

The roles and responsibilities of first-line supervisors during a change to COPPS include the following:

- Understanding and practicing problem solving
- Managing time, staff, and resources

- Encouraging teamwork
- Helping officers to mobilize stakeholders
- Tracking and managing officers' problem solving
- Providing officers with ongoing feedback and support

Rank-and-File Officers

All experts on the subject of police innovation and change emphasize the importance of empowering and using the input from the street officers. The patrol officer becomes a *problem solver*. There is an emphasis on practical intelligence—the ability to quickly analyze key elements of a situation and identify possible courses of action to reach logical conclusions. In order to formulate a response, the officer must define the problem and address the motivations of the offenders.[52]

Under COPPS, the patrol officer is expected to recognize when old methods are inadequate and new and different solutions are needed. The officer is expected to display many of the skills demanded of higher-level personnel, such as detectives, including being creative, flexible, and innovative; working independently; and maintaining self-discipline. Communication skills are also vital. The officer must possess the ability to work cooperatively with others to solve problems and to listen.[53]

Summary

This chapter has described the traits and duties of today's law enforcement executive. Clearly, these individuals occupy positions of tremendous responsibility. Police executives, managers, and supervisors must decide what the best leadership method is, both inside and outside their organizations. They must be concerned with their agency's performance and standing with the community, governing board, and rank and file. Their abilities will be challenged in additional ways if the COPPS strategy is being contemplated or is already being implemented.

Questions for Review

1. What are some of a police executive's primary roles? (Use the three major categories of the Mintzberg model of CEOs in developing your response.)

2. What are the components and advantages of using the assessment center process for hiring and promoting police personnel?

3. What are some elements of the police chief's and sheriff's positions that make them attractive and unattractive? Do you think that contemporary qualifications for the positions are adequate? How do chiefs and sheriffs differ in role and background?

4. What is meant by anomia in policing, and what do studies indicate concerning whether it is a problem among police leaders?

5. What are the "Ten Commandments" of good executive leadership?

6. How do the role and function of sergeants differ from those of upper or middle managers?

7. What are the three types of political arena conflicts that can cause police chiefs to lose their jobs? What are examples of "good politics" and "bad politics?"

8. What are some of the 12 qualities said to make a good police officer, and what are some of the innovative means now in use for recruiting and hiring quality officers?

9. What are some similarities and differences between the FTO and PTO concepts?

10. What are the primary responsibilities of executive, management, and supervisory personnel under COPPS?

Learn by Doing

1. You have been the Park City police chief for 6 months, overseeing an agency of 70 sworn officers in a tourist-based community of 80,000 people. Today is July 3, and at 8:00 A.M. you briefly attend a staff meeting of detectives to plan the agency's approach to a highly publicized kidnapping. In the afternoon, you plan to deliver a news release concerning the case status. Then, you will give the graduation speech at the area police academy; your calendar shows you are then to attend a meeting of the Tri-County Regional Major Case Squad, where you will provide intelligence information concerning an identity theft problem in your jurisdiction. You then learn from Dispatch that one of your motorcycle officers has gone down, and you speed to the hospital emergency room to offer your support. You then meet with your events staff and other city officials to finalize security and traffic plans for tomorrow's huge fireworks display and parade—in which you are also scheduled to ride on a float. At day's end, you make final preparations for your July 7th presentation to the City Council concerning the need for a modern communications system, which you hope to convince the council to purchase. At 4:45 P.M., you are asked to speak at a city hall awards ceremony honoring meritorious acts by local citizens during the past year. Using Mintzberg's model for CEOs, classify each of the functions mentioned in the earlier scenario.

2. Your criminal justice professor has been hired as a consultant with an area police agency to develop and help conduct an assessment center for a sergeant's promotional examination. You are asked to assist him in doing so. What kinds of testing activities would you believe should be included at minimum, and how will you arrange to have the candidates' performance evaluated?

3. You are guest lecturing before a group of university students in a criminal justice organization and administration class. One of the students indicates confusion about the use of organizational structures in general as well as the roles of middle managers (captains and lieutenants) in specific. Provide an explanation.

Related Websites

CopSeek.com
  http://www.copseek.com

International Association of Chiefs of Police (IACP)
  http://www.theiacp.org

National Crime Prevention Council
  http://www.ncpc.org

National Sheriff's Association
  http://www.sheriffs.org

Police Executive Research Forum (PERF)
  http://www.policeforum.org

Police Foundation
  http://www.policefoundation.org

Royal Canadian Mounted Police (RCMP)
  http://www.rcmp-grc.gc.ca

Notes

1. Henry Mintzberg, "The Manager's Job: Folklore and Fact," *Harvard Business Review* 53 (July–August 1975):49–61.

2. For a comprehensive look at the assessment center process and tips for how to participate as a candidate, see John L. Coleman, *Police Assessment Testing: An Assessment Center Handbook for Law Enforcement Personnel* (Springfield, IL: Charles C Thomas, 2002).

3. Robert Katz, "Skills of an Effective Administrator," *Harvard Business Review,* http://www.harvardbusiness. com/hbsp/hbr/articles/article.jsp;jsessionid=NICF GQFFLQ1D0AKRGWDR5VQBKE0YIISW?ml_ action=get-article&articleID=74509&ml_ page=1&ml_subscriber=true (accessed July 15, 2008).

4. Thomas J. Jurkanin, Larry T. Hoover, Jerry L. Dowling, and Janice Ahmad, *Enduring, Surviving, and Thriving as a Law Enforcement Executive* (Springfield, IL: Charles C Thomas, 2001), pp. 12–29.

5. Ibid., pp. 64–65; also see, for example, Isidore Silver, *Police Civil Liability* (available through the LexisNexis Bookstore, http://www.lexisnexis.com/book-store/catalog), a resource for law enforcement officers at all levels, with looseleaf supplements that

are updated twice per year; Kenneth J. Peak, *Policing America: Methods, Issues, Challenges,* 6th ed. (Upper Saddle River, NJ: Prentice Hall, 2009), Chapter 12.

6. R. Simpson and H. Miller, "Social Status and Anomia," *Social Problems* 10(3) (1963):256–264.

7. Kraig L. Hayes, Robert M. Regoli, and John D. Hewitt, "Police Chiefs, Anomia, and Leadership," *Police Quarterly* 10(1) (2007):3–40.

8. Ibid., pp. 14–15.

9. Ronald G. Lynch, *The Police Manager,* 3rd ed. (New York: Random House, 1986), p. 1.

10. "Survey Says Big-City Chiefs Are Better-Educated Outsiders," *Law Enforcement News* (April 30, 1998):7.

11. Ibid.

12. Janice K. Penegor and Ken Peak, "Police Chief Acquisitions: A Comparison of Internal and External Selections," *American Journal of Police* 11 (1992):17–32.

13. Richard B. Weinblatt, "The Shifting Landscape of Chiefs' Jobs," *Law and Order* 47(10) (1999):50.

14. National Advisory Commission on Criminal Justice Standards and Goals, *Police Chief Executive* (Washington, DC: U.S. Government Printing Office, 1976), p. 7.

15. Weinblatt, "The Shifting Landscape of Chiefs' Jobs," p. 51.

16. For an excellent compilation of articles concerning the chief's role, see William Geller (ed.), *Police Leadership in America: Crisis and Opportunity* (New York: Praeger, 1985).

17. Janet Ferris, "Present and Potential Legal Job Protections Available to Heads of Agencies," *Florida Police Chief* 14 (1994):43–45.

18. Henry Mintzberg, *Power In and Around Organizations* (Upper Saddle River, NJ: Prentice Hall, 1983).

19. Norm Stamper, *Breaking Rank: A Top Cop's Exposé of the Dark Side of American Policing* (New York: Nation Books, 2005), p. 185.

20. Ibid.

21. Clemens Bartollas, Stuart J. Miller, and Paul B. Wice, *Participants in American Criminal Justice: The Promise and the Performance* (Englewood Cliffs, NJ: Prentice Hall, 1983), p. 35

22. Charles R. Swanson, Leonard Territo, and Robert W. Taylor, *Police Administration: Structures, Processes, and Behavior,* 6th ed. (Upper Saddle River, NJ: Prentice Hall, 2005), pp. 129–130.

23. Colin Hayes, "The Office of Sheriff in the United States," *The Prison Journal* 74(2001):50–54.

24. Leonhard F. Fuld, *Police Administration* (New York: G. P. Putnam's Sons, 1909), pp. 59–60.

25. See Kenneth J. Peak, Larry K. Gaines, and Ronald W. Glensor, *Police Supervision and Management: In an Era of Community Policing,* 2nd ed. (Upper Saddle River, NJ: Prentice Hall, 2004), pp. 33–34.

26. Ibid., p. 33.

27. Richard N. Holden, *Modern Police Management,* 2nd ed. (Upper Saddle River, NJ: Prentice Hall, 1994), pp. 294–295.

28. Peak et al., *Police Supervision and Management,* Chapter 2 generally.

29. Robin S. Engel, "Patrol Officer Supervision in the Community Policing Era," *Journal of Criminal Justice* 30(2002):51–64.

30. Robin S. Engel, "Supervisory Styles of Patrol Sergeants and Lieutenants," *Journal of Criminal Justice* 29(2001):341–355.

31. Kenneth J. Peak, *Policing America: Methods, Issues, Challenges*, 6th ed. (Upper Saddle River, NJ: Prentice Hall, 2009), p. 127.

32. Lawrence S. Wrightsman, *Psychology and the Legal System* (Monterey, CA: Brooks/Cole, 1987), pp. 85–86.

33. Based on Dennis Nowicki, "Twelve Traits of Highly Effective Police Officers," *Law and Order* (October 1999):45–46.

34. Jeremy M. Wilson and Clifford A. Grammich, Police Recruitment and Retention in the Contemporary Urban Environment: A National Discussion of Personnel Experiences and Promising Practices from the Front Lines (Santa Monica, CA: RAND Corporation, 2009), p. 5; also available at: http://www.rand.org/pubs/conf_proceedings/2009/RAND_CF261.pdf (accessed July 14, 2010).

35. Ibid., p. 2.

36. Stephanie Slahor, "RAND Study Suggests Strategies to Address Recruiting Shortage," Law and Order (December 8, 2008): 32.

37. Ibid., p. 18.

38. Ibid., pp. 18–19.

39. Ibid.

40. Slahor, "RAND Study Suggests Strategies to Address Recruiting Shortage," pp. 32–38.

41. Wilson and Grammich, Police Recruitment and Retention in the Contemporary Urban Environment, p. 33.

42. G. Kaminsky, *San Jose Field Training Model* (San Jose, CA: San Jose Police Department, 1970).

43. Roger G. Dunham and Geoffrey P. Alpert, Critical Issues in Policing: Contemporary Readings (Prospect Heights, IL: Waveland Press, 1989), pp. 111–115.

44. Malcolm Knowles, *Andragogy in Action* (San Francisco: Jossey-Bass, 1981).

45. Kenneth J. Peak, Steven Pitts, and Ronald W. Glensor, "From 'FTO' to 'PTO': A Contemporary Approach to Post-Academy Recruit Training," paper presented at the annual conference of the Academy of Criminal Justice Sciences, Seattle, Washington, March 22, 2007.

46. See, for example, Kenneth J. Peak and Ronald W. Glensor, *Community Policing and Problem Solving: Strategies and Practices,* 5th ed. (Upper Saddle River, NJ: Prentice Hall, 2008), Chapter 6, generally.

47. Mike Tharp and Dorian Friedman, "New Cops on the Block," *U.S. News and World Report* (August 2, 1993):23.

48. John Eck, quoted in ibid., p. 24.

49. William A. Geller and Guy Swanger, *Managing Innovation in Policing: The Untapped Potential of the Middle Manager* (Washington, DC: Police Executive Research Forum, 1995), p. 105.

50. Ibid., p. 109.

51. Ibid., p. 112.

52. Ibid., p. 116.

52. Ibid., pp. 119–120.

Police Issues and Practices

KEY TERMS AND CONCEPTS

Civilianization

Consolidation

Contagious shootings

Contract policing

Dress code

Dynamic resistance response model (DRRM)

Federalization

Fusion center

Intelligence-led policing

Militarization

Police–media relations

Police uniforms (legal/psychological aspects)

Predictive policing

Succession planning

Suicide by cop

Terrorism

Typology of abuse of authority

Use of force

Vehicular pursuits

Verbal and psychological abuse

LEARNING OBJECTIVES

After reading this chapter, the student will:

■ understand the definition and nature of terrorism, including bioterrorism, and the several practical and legislative responses to it.

■ be able to define and apply the concepts of intelligence-led policing (ILP), predictive policing, and fusion centers.

■ know the types of abuse of authority, and what administrators and supervisors must do to manage the use of force.

■ be able to explain what is meant by contagious shootings and suicide by cop.

■ be able to explain why some police leaders are moving away from the traditional use of force continuum, and the elements of the dynamic resistance response model (DRRM) that some are proposing be utilized in its place.

■ understand why vehicle pursuits are of great concern to police executives, managers, and supervisors, as well as related decisions of the U.S. Supreme Court.

■ determine how far women and minorities have come—and still must go—in terms of their representation in policing.

■ understand how and why police agencies are stretching and combining their resources.

■ know how the police can achieve positive media relations.

■ comprehend why succession planning is needed in order to prepare police leaders of the future.

■ understand the legal and psychological aspects of the police uniforms and dress codes.

Semper paratus—
—Latin Phrase, Meaning "*Always Prepared*"

INTRODUCTION

Other chapters of this book focused, or will focus, on some of the pressing issues and contemporary practices of law enforcement executives, specifically issues relating to police organization, operations, and personnel; later chapters, for example, will focus on ethics, liability, financial administration, and the application of new technologies.

This chapter looks at some equally challenging issues. It has been said, tongue in cheek, that in the earlier days of policing, "a size 3 hat and a size 43 jacket" were the only qualifications necessary for entering and doing the work of policing. Given the kinds of topics that are discussed in this chapter, this description could not be further from the truth today. In several ways, the police have increasingly been placed under the microscope with regard to how they deal with the public, exercise their force prerogative, guard our borders from uninvited intruders, and offer employment opportunity to all qualified Americans.

The chapter begins with an examination of **terrorism,** including definition, types, and some available practical and legislative means available for responding to this omnipresent threat. Also included are discussions of three relatively new approaches to terrorism—**ILP, predictive policing,** and fusion centers—and some concerns with what some perceive as creeping federalization and militarization of local police.

Then we consider how law enforcement executives must manage the use of force, including a typology of the abuse of authority, and how use-of-force incidents should be reported and examined; also incorporated are discussions of a model for determining the proper level(s) of police force, contagious shootings, suicide by cop, and policy- and supervisory-related aspects of vehicle pursuits. Following that, we look at the issue of women and minorities in law enforcement ranks, including the chief executive position, and what needs to be done to achieve greater diversity. We consider some ways in which agencies can, and are combining and stretching their resources. Following that is a consideration of what must be done to achieve positive police–media relations.

Then a looming "crisis stage" is discussed: the need to begin identifying, grooming, and promoting future police executives as the baby boomer generation nears retirement. We conclude the chapter with an examination of the legal and psychological aspects of police uniforms and dress codes.

TERRORISM

A 23-year-old Nigerian man purchased his $2,831 Lagos-to-Amsterdam-to-Detroit airline ticket with cash, checked no bags, had been on a security watch list for 7 months, and even his own father had reported him to the U.S. Embassy as a possible threat. Still, on Christmas Day 2009, Umar Farouk Abdulmutallab attempted to detonate a bomb on Northwest Flight 253 over Detroit. His weapon of choice was a chemical explosive sewn into his underwear, which was obtained from a bomb expert in Yemen who is associated with Al-Qaeda.[1]

This airline scare—the second attempt in a year to launch a strike on American soil—exposed a litany of security flaws in the global aviation security network and, according to Michael Duffy and Mark Thompson, provided several lessons for the United States and its allies:

1. Our methods for tracking terrorists still are not working: even with four U.S. terrorism databases, he was not prevented from flying to and out of Detroit.
2. The search-and-scan system at airports can be beat: although body scanning and searching protocols at airports have been beefed up, terrorists are determined to exploit their weak points.
3. Al-Qaeda is bigger than [the late] Osama bin Laden: although the United States maintains a strong military presence in Afghanistan, Al-Qaeda has set up terrorist training and bomb-making camps in Pakistan, Yemen, and Somalia.[2]

Definition and Types

The Federal Bureau of Investigation (FBI) defines terrorism as the "unlawful use of force against persons or property to intimidate or coerce a government, the civilian population, or any segment thereof, in furtherance of political or social objectives."[3] Furthermore, international terrorist threats are divided into the following three categories:

1. *Foreign sponsors of international terrorism.* This includes countries that have been designated as such sponsors and view terrorism as a tool of foreign policy. They fund, organize, network, and provide other support to formal terrorist groups and extremists.
2. *Formalized terrorist groups.* Autonomous organizations (such as bin Laden's Al-Qaeda, Afghanistan's Taliban, Iranian-backed Hezbollah, and Palestinian HAMAS) have their own infrastructures, personnel, finances, and training facilities.

3. *Loosely affiliated international radical extremists.* Examples are the persons who bombed the World Trade Center in 1993. They do not represent a particular nation but may pose the most urgent threat to the United States because they remain relatively unknown to law enforcement agencies.

Terrorist attacks in the United States are caused by both foreign and domestic terrorists. Examples of the former are the attacks in September 2001 with hijacked jetliners on the World Trade Center complex in New York City and the Pentagon in Virginia, with more than 3,000 people killed or missing. An example of the latter is the April 1995 bombing of the Alfred P. Murrah Building in Oklahoma City by Timothy McVeigh, killing 168 people and injuring more than 500.[5] (McVeigh was executed in June 2001.)

A Companion Threat: Bioterrorism

The United States is also vulnerable to biological weapons and bioterrorism. Smallpox, botulism, and plague also constitute major threats, and many experts feel that it is only a matter of time before biological weapons get into the wrong hands and are used like explosives were in the past.

This form of terrorism is capable of eradicating an entire civilization. All that required is a toxin that can be cultured and put into a spray form that can be weaponized and disseminated into the population. Fortunately, they *are* extremely difficult for all but specially trained individuals to make in large quantities and in the correct dosage; tricky to transport because live organisms are delicate; and must be dispersed in a proper molecule size to infect the lungs of the target. Like chemical weapons, they are also dependent on the wind and the weather and are difficult to control.[7]

Practical and Legislative Responses

Several means exist for attempting to address domestic terrorism, both practical and legislative in nature or origin. Next, we discuss several of them.

POSSE COMITATUS   First is military support of law enforcement. The Posse Comitatus Act of 1878 prohibits using the military to execute the laws domestically; the military may be called on, however, to provide personnel and equipment for certain special support activities such as domestic terrorist events involving weapons of mass destruction.[8]

NATIONAL INCIDENT MANAGEMENT SYSTEM   In Department of Homeland Security (DHS) Presidential Directive 5, *Management of Domestic Incidents*, President George W. Bush directed the DHS secretary to develop and administer a National Incident Management System (NIMS). This system provides a consistent nationwide approach for federal, state, and local governments to work effectively together to prepare for, prevent, respond to, and recover from domestic incidents. This directive requires all federal departments and agencies to adopt the NIMS and to use it—and to make its adoption and use by state and local agencies a condition for federal preparedness assistance beginning in fiscal year 2005.[9] The NIMS is a lengthy document that cannot be duplicated here in its entirety; interested persons may find the document at: http://www.fema.gov/pdf/emergency/nims/NIMS_core.pdf.

USA PATRIOT ACT   Enacted shortly after the 9/11 attacks, this act dramatically expanded the federal government's ability to investigate Americans without establishing probable cause for "intelligence purposes," and to conduct searches if there are "reasonable grounds to believe" that there may be national security threats. Federal agencies such as the FBI and others are given access to financial, mental health, medical, library, and other records. The act was reauthorized in March 2006, providing additional tools for protecting mass transportation systems and seaports from attack, taking steps to combat the methamphetamine epidemic, closing loopholes in our ability to prevent terrorist financing, and creating a National Security Division at the Department of Justice.[11]

MILITARY COMMISSIONS ACT OF 2006 The fight against terrorism was also aided and expanded in October 2006 with the enactment of Public Law 109-366, the Military Commissions Act (MCA) of 2006, which he hailed as "one of the most important pieces of legislation in the War on Terror."[12] Under the MCA, the president is authorized to establish military commissions to try unlawful enemy combatants, the commissions are authorized to sentence defendants to death, and defendants are prevented from invoking the Geneva Conventions as a source of rights during commission proceedings. The law contains a provision stripping detainees of the right to file *habeas corpus* petitions in federal court and also allows hearsay evidence to be admitted during proceedings, so long as the presiding officer determines it to be reliable.[13]

Intelligence-Led Policing, Predictive Policing, and Fusion Centers

Note that two of the following three topics of discussion—ILP and predictive policing—could well be discussed in Chapter 3, concerning community policing and problem solving, as they concern and extend the analysis phase of the problem solving process. They are included here as an essential tool to be used in conjunction with fusion centers and applied to the problem of terrorism.

ILP operates under the assumptions that a relatively small number of people were responsible for a comparatively large percentage of crimes, and that officers will have the best effect on crime by focusing on the most prevalent offenses occurring in their jurisdiction.[14] "Intelligence" is not synonymous with "information." Rather, "information plus analysis equals intelligence." Intelligence is what is produced after collected data are evaluated and analyzed by a trained intelligence professional.[15]

Many police agencies have both crime analysts and intelligence analysts. Crime analysts keep their fingers on the pulse of crime in the jurisdiction: which crime trends are up, which ones are down, where the hot spots are, what type of property is being stolen, and so on. Intelligence analysts, on the contrary, are likely to be more aware of the specific people responsible for crime in the jurisdiction–who they are, where they live, what they do, who they associate with, and so on. Integrating these two functions–crime analysis and intelligence analysis–is essential for obtaining a comprehensive grasp of the crime picture. Crime analysis allows police to understand the "who, what, when, and where," whereas intelligence analysis provides an understanding the "who"—crime networks and individuals.

As shown in Figure 5.1, the National Criminal Intelligence Sharing Plan[16] categorizes the intelligence gathering process into six steps: planning and direction, collection, processing/collation, analysis, dissemination, and reevaluation.

"Predictive policing" is another relatively new law enforcement concept that "integrates approaches such as cutting-edge crime analysis, crime-fighting technology, intelligence-led policing, and more to inform forward thinking crime prevention strategies and tactics."[17] The

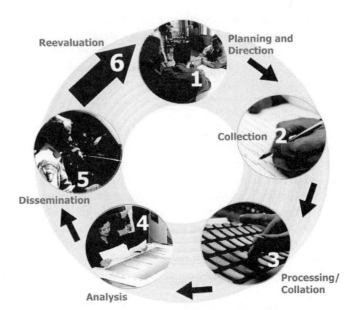

FIGURE 5.1 The Intelligence Gathering Process

Source: U.S. Department of Justice, Office of Justice Programs, *National Criminal Intelligence Sharing Plan*, p. 6; http://www.fas.org/irp/agency/doj/ncisp.pdf (accessed December 1, 2010).

police have always known, for example, that robberies surge near check-cashing businesses, that crime spikes on hot days and plummets during the rain, that residential burglaries often occur on Sunday mornings (while people are attending church services), and that Super Bowl Sunday is usually the slowest day of the year with respect to crimes occurring.[18] But officers' minds can store and remember only so much data. Therefore, when the police monitor crime data and query a computer system for historical and real-time patterns, they can predict—more systematically, over a bigger area, and across shifts and time spans—where crimes are likely to occur. More importantly, unlike police officers, the crime-analysis software does not forget details, get sick, take vacation, or transfer to a different precinct. So if commercial robberies were high in, say, March of one year, their software will predict another spike in March of the following year; the police can then look at the types of businesses that were hit, their locations, and time of day. The system can even analyze a robber's modus operandi—what was said, type of weapon used, and so on.[19]

Fusion centers have been formed by a number of cities and counties in partnership with the FBI as early warning groups for terrorism.[20] The fusion center coordinates all response and counter-terrorism elements within a community or metropolitan area. As information or intelligence is gathered by local and federal agencies, it is fed into the center and analyzed. Once analyzed, terrorist threat or activity information is generated and supplied to affected constituents. The fusion centers include medical personnel and fire department personnel as well as law enforcement personnel. The medical personnel can provide the fusion center with information about suspicious illnesses—an early warning system for a biological attack—and the firefighter personnel can provide information about suspicious fires or chemical problems. The fusion center also allows for more comprehensive planning and a better coordinated response should a terrorist event occur.

Police Reorganization Since 9/11

What has been the effect of 9/11 on police organization? Marks and Sun[21] examined the impact of the 9/11 terrorist attacks, finding organizational change in two areas. The less common area of change occurred in internal organizational structure; the most common area of change was in large metropolitan police departments. It was found that since 9/11, many larger police departments have undergone internal restructuring as a way of dealing with terrorism, primarily with the creation of a terrorism or counterterrorism units. The other, more frequent and diverse area of change was with organizational boundaries—in other words, how interactions between agencies have changed since 9/11. Marks and Sun found increased interaction between law enforcement agencies—specifically, the extent to which police departments interact with their communities, federal law enforcement agencies, and other state and local law enforcement agencies.[22]

Another specific change they observed concerned departmental procedures for sharing information and intelligence. These changes involve the ways state and local law enforcement agencies are allowed to communicate with federal law enforcement. As an example, after 9/11, the FBI implemented the State and Local Law Enforcement Executives and Elected Officials Security Clearance Initiative. This initiative allows the FBI to brief state and local officials with classified information that would or could affect their area of jurisdiction. This initiative is considered to be a significant improvement over the previous requirements for receiving intelligence information, which required that police go through the lengthy process of applying for a security clearance. Thus, it is clear that information sharing and cooperation has increased.[23]

Related Concerns: Federalization and Militarization of Police

Even discounting the above findings by Marks and Sun concerning reorganization of and heightened communication between federal, state, and local law enforcement agencies, several prominent authors have also become concerned with what they perceive as a too-chummy relationship and blurring of lines in terms of communications between and jurisdictions of federal and local law enforcement. Next, we briefly discuss those concerns.

Specifically, some people are concerned about how some residual effects of 9/11 have affected policing in terms of shifting emphases away from the local level of police work and directing available budgets to antiterrorism—rather than to solving problems of neighborhood crime and disorder. They perceive a trend whereby the local police are being coopted by federal law enforcement agencies, and the police themselves becoming more militarized in this era of community policing. A companion question they pose is whether there is room for a dual role: certainly the public appreciates having the Officer Friendly type of public servant; however, when they experience a serious problem, danger, or victimization, do they prefer that their officers forcefully and swiftly enforce the law?

Roberg et al.[24] believe a trend toward federalizing local police agencies "seems to be gaining increasing momentum," whereas Gaines and Kappeler state that:

> Municipal police are devoting more of their attention and resources to securing the conduits of capital. Whether they are controlling the nation's borders, the Internet, seaports, or enforcing immigration laws, municipal agencies are assuming a more federalized agenda. They are experiencing greater centralization, a loss of jurisdictional integrity, and local political control. Local police are beginning to play a greater role in domestic surveillance, controlling protestors, and are becoming the eyes and ears of Federal enforcement agencies.[25]

Roberg et al.[26] also argued that the trend toward **federalization** undercuts the state and local officers and agencies who are in the best position to deal with most crime, while depleting their resources and creating greater distance between law enforcers and the community—which directly conflicts with the aforementioned community era of policing.

Another observer is disturbed by what is seen as increasing federalization of criminal law:

- There has been a proliferation of federal law—now more than 4,000 federal crimes and possibly tens of thousands of jailable regulatory offenses—which means that many people do in fact get charged.
- Furthermore, federal crimes typically carry stiffer penalties, leading to alarmingly disparate results for similarly situated defendants depending on prosecutorial venue; the case is cited of a Nevada woman who faces up to 20 years in prison and up to $500,000 in fines for cutting down three trees on federal land near her Lake Tahoe home. In contrast, voluntary manslaughter carries a 10-year maximum.[27]

The federalization of national criminal policy is most disturbing, it is argued, because it leads to a concentration of police power at the national level that is democratically unhealthy and undermines the most basic principles under which the nation was founded.

In light of the above, many people believe it is time to think carefully about the risks of excessive federalization of the criminal law. According to the American Bar Association, Congress should not bring into play the federal government's investigative power, prosecutorial discretion, judicial authority, and sentencing sanctions unless there is a strong reason for making wrongful conduct a federal crime—and unless there is a distinct federal interest of some sort involved.[28]

Closely related to the above perceived trend of federalization is what many see as the concurrent **militarization** of the local police. Traditionally, the Posse Comitatus Act of 1878[29] prohibits using the military to execute the laws domestically; the military may be called upon, however, to provide personnel and equipment for certain special support activities such as domestic terrorist events involving weapons of mass destruction. Certainly, this restriction against use of military power seems warranted in view of how the control and use of military forces in foreign venues has served to enable some foreign dictators to long remain in power, control elections, stifle dissent, trample human rights, and so on.

Again, however, some authors are of the opinion that the line separating police and military jurisdictions has been blurred, and that there has been a heightened level of activity linking the military to the police. For example, in testimony before the U.S. House of Representatives Subcommittee on Crime, it was stated that: "Since the late 1980s, millions of pieces of surplus military equipment have been given to local police departments across the country: military-grade semiautomatic weapons, armored personnel vehicles, tanks, helicopters, and airplanes." It was also noted that these transfers of equipment have caused a dramatic rise in paramilitary special weapons and tactics (SWAT) teams over the last quarter century, which is felt to be troubling because paramilitary police actions are "extremely volatile, necessarily violent, overly confrontational, and leave very little margin for error."[30]

Of course, not all Americans perceive a threat or harm posed by increased collaboration between the police and the military; and, for their part, the police themselves will no doubt welcome military assistance rendered during such crises as hurricanes or terrorist attacks. State national guard units have a nearly 400-year history in the United States, being founded as militias in the earliest English colonies when the colonists organized their able-bodied male citizens for protection against Indian attack, foreign invaders, and to even win the Revolutionary War.[31]

MANAGING THE USE OF FORCE: ISSUES AND PRACTICES

Power to Be Used Judiciously

The 1991 Rodney King case and others similar to it raise the question in the public mind of how often such incidents occur that are not videotaped. They also show how wide the rift between the police and public can be and demonstrate how critical effective police administration is in this country.

Unfortunately, the King incident was not the only one to receive national attention. After this incident, Amadou Diallo, a 22-year-old unarmed West African street vendor, was shot 19 times by four New York police officers who mistook him for a serial rapist. Abner Louima, a Haitian emigré, was beaten and sodomized by four Brooklyn, New York, police officers. Such celebrated cases are comparatively rare; most instances of police brutality involve relatively minor abuse: discourtesy, name calling, racial or ethnic slurs, or a shove that leaves no injury.[32] Still, these incidents raise the collective ire of all Americans, result in public demonstrations and protests, foster calls for the firing of police executives, and even provoke widespread rioting. If any good can come from such unfortunate incidents, perhaps it is educational in nature: The public and police leadership realize that they must be aware of the potential for the use of excessive force by officers.

Americans and their judicial system bestow a tremendous amount of authority on their police officers. The police are the only element of our society (except for the military, under certain circumstances) that is allowed to use force against its citizens, up to and including lethal force. The quid pro quo, however, is that the police are given this power and authority with the expectation that they will use it judiciously, only when necessary, and as a last resort. A serious problem arises when officers deploy this force improperly.

Regardless of the type of force used, police officers must use it in a legally acceptable manner. The U.S. Supreme Court ruled that the **use of force** at arrest must be

> [o]bjectively reasonable in view of all the facts and circumstances of each particular case, including the severity of the crime at issue, whether the suspect poses an immediate threat to the safety of the officers or others, and whether he is actively resisting arrest or attempting to evade arrest by flight.[33]

However, determining what constitutes "objectively reasonable" is not an easy task.

Police officers are allowed to use only that force necessary to affect an arrest. Thus, the amount of force that a police officer uses is dependent on the amount of resistance demonstrated by the person being arrested. This concept has traditionally been taught to police officers in training academies through a use-of-force continuum, the applicability of which is now being questioned and which is discussed more later.

A Typology of Abuse of Authority

The use-of-force continuum shows the range of force that officers can employ. David Carter[34] looked at officers' conduct and provided a **typology of abuse of authority**, which includes (1) physical abuse/excessive force, (2) verbal/psychological abuse, and (3) legal abuse/violations of civil rights.

PHYSICAL ABUSE AND EXCESSIVE FORCE As noted earlier, police use of physical force often results in substantial public scrutiny. Local incidents may not receive national media coverage, but they often have the same dramatic, chilling effect in a community. All police officers are judged by the actions of one or a few officers, and history has shown that such incidents can also result in rioting by citizens.

The application of deadly force can be a form of excessive force. When a police officer deliberately kills someone, a determination is made as to whether the homicide was justified to prevent imminent death or serious bodily injury to the officer or another person. In 1985, the U.S. Supreme Court ruled that the shooting of any unarmed, nonviolent fleeing felony suspect violates the Fourth Amendment to the Constitution.[35] As a result, almost all major urban police departments enacted restrictive policies regarding deadly force.

VERBAL AND PSYCHOLOGICAL ABUSE   Police officers sometimes inflict **verbal and psychological abuse** on citizens by berating or belittling them. They antagonize citizens knowing that, as police officers, they are wrapped in the shroud of authority and that citizens must take the abuse. One of the most common methods used by police officers to verbally abuse citizens is through the use of profanity. Research indicates that profanity is used for a variety of reasons: as a source of power to control others,[36] as a weapon to degrade or insult others,[37] as a method of alienating others,[38] as a method of labeling others,[39] and as a way of defying authority.[40] Unfortunately, profanity has become a part of the police culture and of many officers' everyday speech. When profanity is used liberally in the work setting, it increases the likelihood that it will be used inappropriately.

Profane language tends to polarize a situation. A citizen will either passively submit or respond aggressively; in either case, the citizen will distrust and dislike the police. When police officers use profanity, especially in an aggressive manner, the focus shifts from the problem to the officer's language, and when it is used aggressively, profanity can easily create greater physical risks to the officer. Furthermore, even if the officer intended to resolve the situation, it may no longer be possible because of the harm caused by the language. Because it can inflame situations, profanity also increases the potential for liability and citizens' complaints; therefore, it also heightens the possibility of the officer's facing administrative action.[41]

For all of these reasons, profanity by the police toward citizens is not justified, wise, or advised. Supervisors should discourage its use and review every instance when an officer uses it with a citizen.

LEGAL ABUSE AND VIOLATIONS OF CIVIL RIGHTS   Legal abuse and civil rights violations consist of police actions that violate citizens' constitutional or statutory rights. This abuse usually involves false arrest, false imprisonment, and harassment. For example, a police officer may knowingly make an unlawful search, charge the suspect with a crime, and then lie about the nature of the search. Another situation occurs when police officers hassle a criminal to gain information or hassle a business owner to obtain some monetary gain.

Supervisors and managers play a key role in preventing legal abuse and violations of citizens' civil rights. Supervisors frequently back up officers when responding to calls and observe situations that lead to an arrest. They should ensure that officers' decisions to arrest are based on probable cause, not some lesser standard. They should also review arrest reports and question officers when arrests are not observed to ensure that the arrests meet the probable cause standard.

Officers should provide the same level of services to all citizens, and they should use consistent decision-making criteria when deciding to make an arrest regardless of race, gender, or social standing.

Reporting and Examining Use-of-Force Occurrences

To identify and monitor officers' use of force, law enforcement agencies need a comprehensive data collection strategy. At a minimum, departments should utilize use-of-force reports completed by officers involved in forceful incidents. Traditionally, agencies required reports when officers used force that was likely to cause death or serious bodily harm (e.g., firing a weapon); in recent years, however, a growing number of agencies have begun documenting *all* instances involving force, regardless of the potential for deadly force or injuries.[42]

Administrators should implement supervisors' control-of-persons reports, requiring supervisors to go to the scene of all incidents when officers use force in order to interview the officers, suspects, and witnesses and record their responses. Supervisors should also take photographs of any injuries or record complaints of injuries. These forms can also require information on demographics, level and type of force, resistance, weapons, and other information (some agencies go further, wanting information on suspects' race, ethnicity, health status, nature of treatment, impairment, and observed behavior). This kind of information should be supplemented by a detailed narrative explaining each of the parties' perspectives, allowing the supervisor to write a sequential account of all relevant actions: the original call or observation, officer's and suspect's behaviors, why suspects resisted, and levels and types of resistance. Similarly, officers' actions, including levels of force and how it was used, are documented. It is crucial that supervisors capture the stories provided by the parties and not set out to justify the officers' actions or argue with the suspects.[43]

Regardless of the data collection method used, it is important that officers receive proper training on when and how reports should be completed. Second, the nature and level of both police force and citizen resistance need to be measured; from a legal and policy perspective, the nature or degree of citizen resistance is a critical factor in determining whether the officer used legitimate and justifiable level(s) of force. Finally, the report on the use of force should account for multiple uses of both force and resistance. The best way to examine the force used by the officer is to understand the sequence of events and multiple stages of citizen resistance and officer force applied, not only the highest level used.[44]

Recently, there have been several developments involving the issue of police use of force and about which today's police chief executives should be knowledgeable: the force continuum, contagious shootings, and suicide by cop. Next, we discuss each.

Concerns with the Traditional Use-of-Force Continuum and a New Approach

Use-of-force continuums have been evolving for over three decades; graphically, their explanations range from the very simple (a staircase, wheel, or ladder) to the more elaborate. Basically, a simple linear use-of-force continuum contains the following five escalating steps: officer presence/verbal direction, touch control, empty-hand tactics and chemical agents, hand-held impact weapons, and lethal force.[45]

Today, however, more police executives and researchers are uncomfortable with the simplistic, sequential depiction of the force continuum. They feel that police use of force is not and cannot always be employed in such a sequential, stair-step fashion as this continuum implies. So the question remains: how much force is reasonable for a police officer to use against a suspect? Even when agency policies accompany the continuum (as they always should), such continuums have always been confusing to most police officers. "How far and when do I 'climb the next rung' of the ladder" sort of confusion could and did exist. Force continuums also fail to represent properly the dynamic encounter between the officer and a resistant suspect and to take into account the wide array of tools that are available to officers today; it is too difficult for a department to dictate by a continuum in what situations, say, a baton or pepper spray or Taser or other, less lethal weapons, should be used.

Instead, many agencies now require their officers to be "objectively reasonable" in their use of force and have adopted the following definition of *objectively reasonable* as developed by the International Association of Chiefs of Police (IACP): "An officer's use of force on a free person shall be objectively reasonable based upon the totality of the circumstances known or perceived by him or her at the time force was used."[46]

A new approach to determine proper use of force has recently been developed by two special agents of the FBI. It is designed to "more accurately reflect the intent of the law and the changing expectations of society" and to provide officers with "simple, clear, unambiguous, and consistent guidelines in the use of force."[47]

Known as the **DRRM**, this approach combines a use-of-force continuum with the behaviors of suspects. *Dynamic* indicates that the model is fluid, and *resistance* demonstrates that the suspect controls the interaction. In this view, a major failing of past continuums has been that the emphasis was on the officer and the amount of force used. DRRM instead emphasizes that the suspect's level of resistance determines the officer's response. The model also divides suspects into one of four categories (see Figure 5.2).

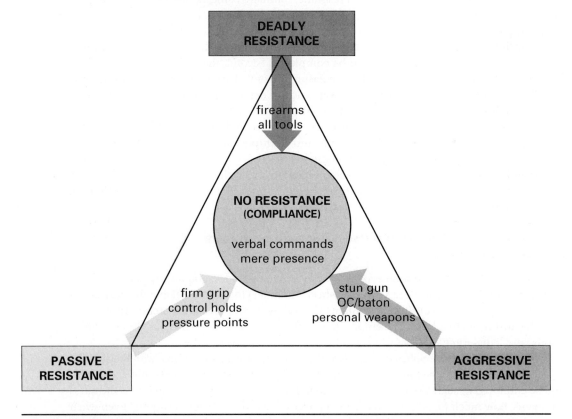

Typical configuration of the dynamic resistance response model with traditional use-of-force options

FIGURE 5.2 Dynamic Resistance Response Model

Source: From Charles Joyner and Chad Basile, "The Dynamic Resistance Response Model," *FBI Law Enforcement Bulletin,* September 2007, p. 19.

As shown in Figure 5.2, if a passively resistant suspect fails to follow commands and perhaps attempts to move away from the officer or escape, appropriate responses include using a firm grip, control holds, and pressure points to gain compliance. An aggressively resistant suspect—one who is taking offensive action by attempting to push, throw, strike, tackle, or physically harm the officer—on the contrary, would call for such responses as the use of personal weapons (hands, fists, and feet), batons, pepper spray, and a stun gun. Finally, because a deadly resistant (i.e., lethal force is being or is about to be utilized) suspect can seriously injure or kill the officer or another person, the officer is justified in using force, including deadly force, as is *objectively reasonable* to overcome the offender.

In the DRRM model, a suspect's lack of resistance (compliance) is in the center of the triangle, which is emphasized as the goal of every encounter. If a suspect's resistance level places him or her on one of the three corners of the triangle, the officer's response is intended to move the suspect's behavior to the center of the triangle and compliance. The sole purpose of the application of force is to gain compliance.

Contagious Shootings

Clearly, nothing can inflame a police executive's community and raise tensions such as police shootings. And there has been no dearth of high-profile police shooting incidents during the early twenty-first century:

- In April 2007, three New York Police Department officers were indicted for manslaughter and reckless endangerment for a shooting incident where they fired 50 rounds at a car of unarmed men leaving a bachelor party at a strip club; the groom died on his wedding day.[48] The incident heightened racial tensions and, for many people, brought to mind the 1999 New York police killing of an unarmed West African, Amadou Diallo, whom officers shot as he was reaching for his wallet, firing 41 shots and striking him 19 times.
- In July 2005, more than 30 Los Angeles officers, including its SWAT team, responded to a hostage situation and were caught in a cross-fire from the front and back of an auto sales lot; the 19-month-old daughter of the suspect was killed. The Police Commission found poor communication and a breakdown in command and control during the incident; it also found that 17 officers needed additional training. The probe involved microscopic analysis of about 130 bullets and more than 100 casings involving 13 firearms.[49]

These are what is known in police parlance as **contagious shootings**–gunfire that spreads among officers who believe that they, or their colleagues, are facing a threat. It spreads like wildfire and often leads to an outcry from community leaders or family members. Contagious shooting appears to have happened again in 2005, when eight officers fired 43 shots at an armed man in Queens, New York, killing him. In July 2005, three officers fired 26 shots at a pit bull that had bitten a chunk out of an officer's leg in a Bronx apartment building. And there have been other episodes: in 1995, in the Bronx, New York, officers fired 125 bullets during a bodega robbery, one officer firing 45 rounds.[50]

These incidents that also involve minority group members will often heighten the tension and lead to charges of racism against the entire police agency; one *Washington Post* columnist stated that "it is the police culture, more than race, that is at the crux of the problem—a mentality of brutality."[51] Such uses of police force even caused one organization, Human Rights Watch, to state in a report entitled *Shielded from Justice: Police Brutality and Accountability in the United States*[52]:

Police abuse remains one of the most serious and divisive human rights violations in the United States. The excessive use of force by police officers, including unjustified shootings, severe beatings, fatal chokings, and rough treatment, persists because overwhelming barriers to accountability make it possible for officers who commit human rights violations to escape due punishment and often to repeat their offenses.

Human Rights Watch also noted in the report that officers who repeatedly commit human rights violations tend to be a small minority but that "they are protected, routinely, by the silence of their fellow officers and by flawed systems of reporting, oversight, and accountability; by the scarcity of meaningful information about trends in abuse; data lacking regarding the police departments' response to those incidents; and their plans or actions to prevent brutality."[53]

Paradoxically, for all their severity and inflammatory nature, the extent of police shootings is largely unknown. As the *New York Times* stated:

We like to think we live in the information age. For all the careful accounting, however, there are two figures Americans do not have: the precise number of people killed by the police and the number of times police use excessive force. Despite widespread public interest and a provision in the 1994 Crime Control Act requiring the Attorney General to collect the data, statistics on police shootings and use of nondeadly force continue to be piecemeal products of spotty collection, and are dependent on the cooperation of local police departments. No comprehensive accounting for the nation's 17,000 police department exists.[54]

The *Times* suggests that this lack of accurate statistics makes it impossible to draw meaningful conclusions about deadly encounters between the police and the civilian population, and that the major reason for the vacuum is the failure of the police in many cities to keep and report accurate figures that distinguish between what the police see as justifiable shootings—those in which the suspect posed a serious threat—and incidents where an officer may have unlawfully fired at an unarmed civilian.[55]

Suicide by Cop

EXAMPLE, EXTENT, AND DEFINITION

An officer is dispatched to an apartment building in response to a woman yelling for help. Upon arriving at the location, the officer observes a woman standing on the front steps. The officer enters the apartment and she hears a man yelling, and then sees him standing in the kitchen area. When the male observes the female officer, he produces a large butcher knife and holds the blade of the knife firmly against his stomach with both hands; he appears highly intoxicated, agitated, and angry. The officer draws her service weapon and orders the man to put down the knife. The offender responds by stating, "[Expletive] you, kill me!" The officer attempts to talk with the offender, who responds by turning around and slicing himself severely on his forearm, bleeding profusely. The officer repeatedly asks him to drop the knife. The offender begins to advance toward the officer, and tells her to shoot him while still ignoring her commands to drop the knife. From a distance of approximately 12 feet, he raises the knife in a threatening manner and charges the officer; she fires her weapon, striking him in the chest and hand, killing him.[56]

Although each case of suicide by cop is different, the above account, based on an actual occurrence, describes how such an incident might unfold.

Suicide by cop represents a burgeoning area of use of force and violence both against and by the police; therefore, it is also an area of police operations about which police executives must become well informed. **Suicide by cop** has been defined as "an act motivated in whole or in part by the offender's desire to commit suicide that results in a justifiable homicide by a law enforcement officer."[57]

Presently, the extent of suicide by cop remains unknown for two reasons: first, there is a lack of both a clear definition and established reporting procedures; second, suicide attempts are immediately removed from the criminal process and placed within the mental health arena, causing the police investigation to cease and preventing an agency from identifying a potential threat to its officers. Although suicide by cop is thus difficult to measure, one study of deputy-involved shootings by a medical organization in the Los Angeles County, California, Sheriff's Department found that such incidents accounted for 11 percent of all deputy-involved shootings and 13 percent of all deputy-involved justifiable homicides. The report concluded that suicide by cop constitutes an actual form of suicide.[58]

A TWO-TIER INVESTIGATION   At minimum, for police agencies to recognize suicide by cop and to track the number of incidents, it is recommended that the following two investigative steps take place when such an incident appears to have occurred:

1. *Reporting procedure:* The reporting officer should list in detail in the initial offense report the specific elements observed at the scene, such as:
   - statements made by the offender, including the names of any witnesses to the statements;
   - the type(s) of weapon possessed by the offender;
   - the offender's specific actions that resulted in the use of deadly force;
   - offender conduct that the officer deemed bizarre or inappropriate; and
   - circumstances indicating that the offender's motivation may have been suicide

A trained individual or unit must then sift carefully through the facts and circumstances, using stringent criteria to determine whether the incident probably was motivated by the offender's *will* to commit suicide, noting such items as:
   - notes or recent correspondence left at the scene or any other place the offender frequented;
   - detailed and verbatim statements from family members, friends, and associates;
   - forensic evidence pertinent to the investigation (e.g., if the offender used a firearm, whether it was loaded with proper ammunition or capable of firing ammunition);
   - personal history of the offender, including medical and psychiatric information, credit reports, insurance policies, employment records, history of significant relationships, prior suicides of family members, prior attempted suicides; and
   - criminal history, including sentencing information, presentence reports, psychiatric evaluations, and prison records.

As an example, the follow-up investigation of the above case study would reveal the following:
   - The offender possessed a weapon capable of inflicting serious bodily injury or death.
   - He used the weapon to seriously injure himself and attacked the officer with the weapon.
   - During the attack, he demanded that the officer kill him.

Following those findings, there should also be a:

2. *Classifying procedure:* An officer or unit with expertise in the use of deadly force incidents makes the final determination of whether a suicide-by-cop incident has occurred, focusing

on the subject's motivation; this can help establish motivations and behavior patterns of the offender for later tabulation and analysis.[59]

The investigation of the above case study would thus demonstrate that the elements of a suicide-by-cop event were present, and, therefore, the case would be classified as such.

VEHICULAR PURSUITS

A High-Stakes Operation

Vehicular pursuits are also related to police use of force and pose great concern to police leadership. Civil litigation arising out of collisions involving police pursuits reveals it to be a high-stakes undertaking with serious and sometimes tragic results. Several hundred people are killed each year during police pursuits;[60] many of the resulting deaths and injuries involve innocent third parties or stem from minor traffic violations. The U.S. Supreme Court, as discussed in the next section, has strengthened most progressive chase policies, but the Court has also conferred responsibility on the police. The responsibility for ensuring that proper policies and procedures exist rests squarely with the chief executive officer (CEO) of the agency.

Vehicular pursuits involve a delicate balancing act. On the one hand is the need to show that flight from the law is no way to freedom. If a police agency completely bans high-speed pursuits, its credibility with both law-abiding citizens and law violators may suffer; public knowledge that the agency has a no-pursuit policy may encourage people to flee, decreasing the probability of apprehension.[61] Still, according to one author, because of safety and liability concerns, "A growing number of agencies have the position that if the bad guy puts the pedal to the metal, it's a 'freebie.' They will not pursue him."[62]

On the other hand, the high-speed chase threatens everyone within range of the pursuit, including suspects, their passengers, and other drivers or bystanders. One police trainer tells officers to ask themselves a simple question to determine whether to continue a pursuit: "Is this person a threat to the public safety other than the fact that the police are chasing him?" If the officer cannot objectively answer "yes," the pursuit should be terminated.[63]

The Supreme Court's View

In May 1990, two Sacramento County, California, deputies responded to a fight call. At the scene, they observed a motorcycle with two riders approaching their vehicle at high speed; turning on their red lights, they ordered the driver to stop. The motorcycle operator began to elude the officers, who initiated a pursuit reaching speeds of more than 100 miles per hour over about 1.3 miles. The pursuit ended when the motorcycle crashed; the deputies' vehicle could not stop in time and struck the bike's passenger, killing him; his family brought suit, claiming that the pursuit had violated the crash victim's due process rights under the Fourteenth Amendment.

In May 1998, the U.S. Supreme Court, in *County of Sacramento v. Lewis*,[64] ruled that the proper standard to be employed in these cases is whether the officer's conduct during the pursuit was conscience shocking; it further determined that high-speed chases with no intent to harm suspects do not give rise to liability under the Fourteenth Amendment.[65] The Court left unanswered many important questions such as whether an innocent third party can file a claim against the police for damages or whether a municipality can be held liable for its failure to train officers in pursuit issues.

Leadership Rejoinder

The following incidents demonstrate the dangerous nature of police pursuits:

- In Omaha, Nebraska, a 70-mile-per-hour pursuit through a residential neighborhood of a motorcyclist for expired license plates ended when the motorcyclist ran a stop sign, crashing into another vehicle and killing the female passenger on the motorcycle.
- A sheriff's deputy in Florida intentionally rammed a vehicle during a pursuit for an outstanding misdemeanor warrant, causing a collision and killing a backseat passenger.
- A police officer pursuing a shoplifter in Mobile, Alabama, crashed into a mall security vehicle, seriously injuring the guard.

In the past, such tragic stories were all too common; again, the onus is on law enforcement executives to develop pursuit policies that consider input from line personnel, supervisors and managers, and attorneys versed in civil liability and remain vigilant in seeing that they are enforced. Pursuit policies provide general guidelines for the officer and supervisor. The courts will evaluate these policy issues when considering whether an agency or its officers or supervisors should be held culpable for damages or injuries resulting from pursuits.

The field supervisor is responsible for ensuring that proper methods are employed by patrol officers during pursuits, whether the pursuit involves simply a primary pursuing officer and a backup or a more elaborate scenario.

Two rather elaborate methods of pursuit termination may be used. The first is *boxing:* Three police vehicles are positioned during the chase at the front, rear, and side of the suspect's vehicle; the three police vehicles slow in unison, causing the offender to slow down and eventually stop. This technique can result in damage to any or all of the vehicles involved. The second termination tactic, a *precision immobilization technique*, involves a police vehicle making contact with the suspect's vehicle. The officer gently pushes one of the rear quarter panels of the suspect vehicle to displace its forward motion, causing it to spin. This technique also involves considerable risk to the officer and the suspect.[66] Both of these methods, as well as other tactics employed during pursuits, are potentially perilous and require extensive officer training to obtain proficiency.

Oversight of pursuits enables a third, neutral party, the supervisor, to guard against what has been termed a *pursuit fixation*, wherein pursuing officers act recklessly.[67] Supervisors need to set the rules on what will be tolerated and what level of performance is expected during a pursuit. They must clearly establish that once the pursuit team is in place, other officers not directly involved should drive parallel to the pursuit, obeying all traffic laws.[68]

Supervisors depend on other officers to give them the information needed to make the decisions demanded by the courts. The supervisor needs to know the speed and direction of the fleeing suspect's vehicle; the offense, suspected offense, or status (i.e., warrants) of the suspect; the number of police units involved in the pursuit; and the suspect's actions (is he or she close to putting others in danger with his or her driving?).[69] Supervisors serve as the "safety officer" of the pursuit—a role they may not wish to take because they do not want to be unpopular with their officers, but one that is far better than attending an officer's funeral or visiting one in the hospital.

It is obvious that the liabilities associated with police pursuits should be a primary concern of every police chief executive. The courts have awarded numerous six- and seven-figure settlements to plaintiffs seeking redress for injuries, damages, or deaths resulting from police pursuits. The development of pursuit policies and officer and supervisor training can help to protect agencies against liability suits.

It is the responsibility of command personnel and supervisors to ensure that officers thoroughly understand and comply with pursuit policies. In addition to the policy issues and supervisory information identified earlier, other factors considered by the courts in evaluating pursuit liability include the following:

- **The reason for the pursuit.** Does it justify the actions taken by the officer?
- **Driving conditions.** Any factor that could hinder an officer's ability to safely conduct a pursuit should be considered sufficient reason to terminate it.
- **The use of police warning devices.** Typically, lights and siren are required by state statutes.
- **Excessive speed.** This often depends on the conditions of the environment. For example, a 30-mile-per-hour pursuit in a school zone may be considered excessive and dangerous.
- **Demonstrations of due regard in officers' actions.** Officers who choose the course of safety will create the least danger to all parties affected and maintain the highest degree of protection from liability.
- **The use of deadly force.** There are few instances in which officers can justify driving tactics that result in the death of a fleeing driver; such situations include roadblocks, boxing in (which involves police pursuit vehicles surrounding a violator's moving vehicle, and then slowing the violator's vehicle to a stop), and ramming.
- **Departmental policies and state law.** These must be obeyed; to do otherwise greatly increases the potential liability of both the officer and the department.
- **Appropriate supervision and training.** In the absence of such measures, the department will be subject to a finding of negligence, and liability will attach.[70]

Police pursuits represent an ongoing hazardous problem. Therefore, efforts must continue to develop electromagnetic field devices that officers can place on the roadway and use to interrupt the electronic ignition systems in suspects' vehicles and terminate pursuits. In the meantime, tire deflation devices, which can end chases by slowly deflating one or more tires of a suspect's vehicle, have been welcomed by the police.[71]

BRINGING DOWN THE WALLS: WOMEN AND MINORITIES WEARING THE BADGE

Over the past 30 years, the proportion of women police officers has grown steadily. During the 1970s, some formal barriers to hiring women, such as height requirements, were eliminated; in addition, subjective physical agility tests and oral interviews were modified.[72] Some job discrimination suits further expanded women's opportunities.

Women as Officers and Chief Executives

Women represent about 14.5 percent of sworn personnel in municipal agencies, 13.5 percent in county agencies, and 8.2 percent in small agencies.[73] State agencies as a whole have a much lower percentage of female officers than either local or federal law enforcement agencies: 6.8 percent.[74] Women account for 14.8 percent of all federal officers, which is a bit higher than the percentage in local agencies.[75]

Although the representation of women officers is low compared with their overall proportion in the total population, the discrepancy is even more evident in the leadership ranks, where women number only 1 percent of the police chiefs in the United States.[76] The number of women serving as chiefs has expanded considerably, however, since Penny Harrington took over as chief in Portland (becoming the first woman chief in a large agency) in 1985 and Elizabeth (Betsy) Watson assumed the helm in Houston (becoming the first woman chief in a city of more than one million population) in 1990. As examples, in early 2004, newly appointed women were serving as chiefs of police in San Francisco, Boston, Detroit, and Milwaukee, providing further evidence that today's "mayors are looking for sophisticated CEOs who can oversee large budgets, negotiate thorny management problems, and set sound department-wide policy."[77]

One survey[78] identified 157 women serving as chiefs of police and 25 who were sheriffs; 96 of these chiefs participated in a survey intended to establish a demographic profile of the women. Forty-eight (49 percent) of these chief executives were in charge of municipal police departments, whereas 40 (42 percent) led college and university police departments. Only seven of the respondents led agencies with more than 100 sworn officers (five being municipal, one a campus police agency, and one a tribal agency). Conversely, 23 (25.8 percent) were in agencies with 10 or fewer officers. These women CEOs reflect the increasing levels of education achieved by today's chiefs, with three-fourths having either a bachelor's or a master's degree. About one-third had a partner who was also in policing.[79]

A large enough proportion of women have now been employed in policing long enough to be considered for promotion. A number of researchers question the commitment of police agencies and their male administrators in promoting women and have made recommendations for changing the evaluation and promotional process.[80]

Key Issues

Peter Horne identified several key issues that need to be addressed[81]:

1. *Recruitment.* Unfocused, random recruiting is unlikely to achieve diversity. Literature such as flyers, posters, and brochures should feature female officers working in all areas of policing. Furthermore, agencies should go anywhere (local colleges, women's groups, female community leaders, gyms, and martial arts schools) and use all types of media to attract qualified applicants.[82]

2. *Preemployment physical testing.* Historically, women have been screened out disproportionately in the preemployment screening physical testing used by many agencies. Tests that include such components as scaling a 6-feet wall, bench pressing one's own weight, and throwing medicine balls are likely to discriminate against female applicants, so agencies should examine their physical tests to determine the reasons for which women are disproportionately screened out. In addition, agencies should permit all candidates to practice for the preemployment physical examination.

3. *Academy training.* Recruits must be trained in sexually integrated academy classes to ensure full integration between female and male officers. Female instructors are especially important during academy training because they are positive role models and help female rookies to develop skills and confidence. Involving female instructors in firearms and physical/self-defense training will send the message that trained, veteran female officers can effectively handle the physical aspects of policing.

4. *Field training.* Field training officers (FTOs) play a crucial role in transforming the academy graduate into a competent field officer. FTOs should be both supportive of female rookies and effective evaluators of their competence. Women should also serve as FTOs.

5. *Assignments.* Agencies should routinely review the daily assignments of all probationary officers to ensure that they have an equal opportunity to become effective patrol officers. If women are removed from patrol early in their careers (for any reason), they will miss vital

field patrol experience. The majority of supervisory positions exist in the patrol division, and departments generally believe that field supervisors must have adequate field experience to be effective and respected by subordinates.

6. *Promotions.* The so-called glass ceiling continues to restrict women's progress through the ranks. Performance evaluations and the overall promotional system utilized by agencies should be scrutinized for gender bias. For example, studies show that the more subjective the promotion process, the less likely women are to pass it. To provide more objectivity (in terms of ability to measure aptitude), the process may include more hands-on (practical, applied) tasks and the selection of board members of both genders.

7. *Harassment and discrimination.* Where they exist, sexual discrimination and harassment take a toll on the women involved—including a negative impact on their performance and careers (and probably a negative impact on the recruitment of other women into policing). A Police Foundation study found that "most women officers have experienced both sex discrimination and harassment on the job."[83] Departments need to have policies in place concerning sexual harassment and gender discrimination—and they need to enforce them.

8. *Mentoring.* The employee's experience as he or she transitions into the organization can be a deciding factor in whether the employee remains with the organization. Formal mentoring programs—which can begin even before the rookie enters the academy—have helped some agencies raise their retention rates for women; such programs can include having a veteran employee provide new hires with information concerning what to expect at the academy and beyond, during field training, and in the probationary period.

9. *Career and family.* Police work can create considerable conflict between work life and family life. Police agencies should have a leave policy covering pregnancy and maternity leave. Light- or limited-duty assignments (e.g., desk, communications, and records) can be made available to female officers when reassignment is necessary. Other issues include the availability of quality childcare and shift rotation (which can more heavily burden single parents), as well as uniforms, body armor, and firearms that fit women.

As the community-oriented policing and problem solving (examined in Chapter 3) concept continues to expand, female officers can play an increasingly vital role. Experts also maintain that the verbal skills many women possess often have a calming effect that defuses potentially explosive situations.

Still, this clearly remains an area in which law enforcement must change. For women to serve effectively as police officers, executives must see the value of utilizing and vigorously recruiting, hiring, and retaining them. A basic task for the chief executive is to consider how departmental policies impact female officers with respect to selection, training, promotion, sexual harassment, and family leave. Most important, executives must set a tone of welcoming women into the department.

Minorities as Law Enforcement Officers

The recruitment of minority officers also remains a difficult task. Probably, the greatest problem is the negative image that police officers have in the minority communities. Unfortunately, police officers have been seen as symbols of oppression and have been charged with using excessive brutality; they are often seen as an army of occupation.

Black police officers face problems similar to those of women who attempt to enter and prosper in police work. Until more black officers are promoted and can affect police policy and serve as role models, they are likely to be treated unequally and have difficulty being promoted—

a classic catch-22 situation. Blacks considering a police career may be encouraged by a survey of black officers, which found that most thought their jobs were satisfying and offered opportunities for advancement.[84]

STRETCHING RESOURCES: COMBINING AND CIVILIANIZING SERVICES

There is an old saying among criminal justice planners: "There's a lot of crime prevention in a T-bone steak." Although historically that statement was likely to be more false than true—the commission of most crimes probably being much more closely associated with *greed* rather than *need*—with today's economic unrest, there is a causal relationship between the economy and crime, greater accountability for police agencies, and a greater than ever need to tighten belts and stretch resources.

The United States has many small police agencies; in fact, of the estimated 17,000 local police departments, nearly half (45.5 percent) employ fewer than 10 sworn personnel; three-fourths employ 25 or fewer sworn personnel.[85] Many small communities find it extremely difficult, if not impossible, to maintain a 24/7 police or sheriff's department—particularly one that is trained and staffed well enough to provide a full range of policing services. Therefore, several approaches have been developed by agencies facing staffing and funding shortages for reducing and/or sharing the costs of full-enforcement operations: contracting, consolidating, and civilianizing services.

These concepts are not of recent origin. Indeed, as early as 1973, a major presidential commission on criminal justice—the National Advisory Commission on Criminal Justice Standards and Goals—recommended that

> at a minimum, police agencies that employ fewer than 10 sworn employees should consolidate for improved efficiency and effectiveness. If the most effective and efficient police service can be provided through mutual agreement or joint participation with other criminal justice agencies, the governmental entity or the police agency immediately should enter into the appropriate agreement or joint operation.[86]

Next, we discuss two means by which this can and is being done.

Contract and Consolidated Policing

There are two primary means by which police agencies can be unified. The first, and simplest, is **contract policing**. Here, smaller communities, either incorporated or unincorporated, can contract their police services with another larger agency. For example, the Los Angeles Sheriff's Department contracts with 40 separate cities to provide police service.[87] This approach is attractive if a jurisdiction finds itself unable to afford the full spectrum of policing expenditures; it might enter into a contractual agreement with another agency to share these expenses. Contract policing is, in effect, *partial* consolidation, with a unit of government maintaining its own police agency but contracting with another jurisdiction(s) for services it cannot afford. Some examples of contracted services include personnel wages and benefits, patrol vehicle and maintenance costs, uniforms, dispatchers, communications equipment, jails, forensic laboratories, mobile crime scene units, consolidated narcotics units, and even airplanes for extraditing arrestees. Pooling their human and technological resources can typically result in better services, while avoiding duplication of those services, at less expense.

Another means of unifying agencies and possibly achieving cost savings is through **consolidation**, which is the merging of two or more city and/or county governments into a single policing entity. Two jurisdictions can be completely combined into a single agency, with its sworn personnel enforcing a single set of statutes or ordinances, wearing the same uniform, driving the same type of patrol vehicle, and so on. Again, the advantage is in avoiding duplication of services and the ability to purchase equipment in larger volume, which leads to economy of scale. However, the initial cost of implementing consolidation can be high. In some states, the enabling legislation requires that, when two or more agencies combine their operations, the best salary and benefit packages that already exist must be brought into the newly consolidated organization. This "cherry-picking" can obviously be quite expensive, especially in the initial stages of consolidation—at a time when the new, consolidated agency may also be top heavy with administrative personnel. Cost savings through consolidation, therefore, may not be realized for many years, if ever, depending on how the agency is structured, how enabling legislation is written, and so on.

Civilianization

Most citizen calls for police service do not involve a crime or a sworn officer to enforce the laws. For that reason, many agencies have increasingly civilianized many functions performed traditionally by sworn personnel. This has worked particularly well for aspects of policing such as dispatching, crime analysis (forensics), crime scene investigation, report taking, and even supplemental patrol duties. And, like contract and consolidated police services, **civilianization** can be much more cost-effective by using nonsworn personnel, thus freeing sworn officers for critical police work; this is especially important when many agencies today are being asked to do more with less.

In fact, the use of civilians has become so widespread that controversy about it has arisen: how civilianized should the department become? Police unions are becoming increasingly wary of management's outsourcing traditional police tasks to a civilian body, viewing the latter as potential threats to their livelihood. Therefore, as civilianization becomes more widespread, police chief executives must be mindful of the potential for friction and poor officer morale; no one—citizens, sworn officers, or civilian personnel—will benefit by the loss of a healthy and productive work environment. Where they exist, the unions should be included in any planning and discussion of civilianization, and should help to fashion a plan that benefits the agency in ways that will be received well by the rank and file.[88]

In Chapter 15, where we address financial administration, we will discuss further the effects of, and challenges posed by the recent economic downturn on criminal justice agencies, including the police.

POLICE–MEDIA RELATIONS

The topic of **police–media relations** was mentioned briefly in Chapter 4 in the discussion of the Mintzberg model of CEOs. However, because of its importance, we discuss it here in greater detail.

As the saying goes, "Perception is reality." Although there are far fewer police programs on television today than in the past—such as in the 1970s, when 42 police programs premiered[89]—the manner in which the police are depicted there, and in films, has a strong influence on how the police are viewed by our society. Not only do people identify with the struggle between good and evil that is dramatized by the actors in such programs (and they especially like private investigators, who can be more "flexible" in their adherence to the rule of law), but they also apparently find the methods and idiosyncrasies of title figures such as *"Dirty Harry"* (Clint Eastwood), *Columbo* (Peter Falk), and *Kojak* (Telly Savales) to be as endearing as the investigations they are conducting.[90]

News dissemination is a delicate undertaking for the police CEO; news organizations, especially television and the print media, are highly competitive businesses that seek to obtain the most complete news in the shortest amount of time, which often translates into wider viewership and, therefore, greater advertising revenues for them. From one perspective, the media must appreciate that a criminal investigation can be seriously compromised by premature or excessive coverage. From another perspective, the public has a right to know what is occurring in the community, especially matters relating to crime. Therefore, the prudent police executive attempts to maintain an open, professional relationship with the media in which each side knows and understands its responsibilities. It is, therefore, of the utmost importance that either the chief executive or his/her designee—a trained public information officer—knows how to perform public speaking, and what kind and how much information to divulge to media outlets.

Unfortunately, many police executives (a good number of whom involuntarily left office) can speak of the results of failing to develop an appropriate relationship with the media. (The author is aware of one former police chief in a medium-sized Western city who sported a bumper sticker on his vehicle stating "I don't trust the liberal media." This action obviously did not endear him to the local newspaper, nor did it help him in editorials and articles when an issue concerning his involvement in a sexual harassment allegation became public, and he ultimately resigned. This chief obviously did not recognize the power of the pen; as stated in Chapter 3, "Don't argue with someone who buys his ink by the barrel!")

An example of the positive relationship that can develop between the police and the media is the one involving the 2002 Beltway Sniper case. There, media were used to communicate with the snipers—who eventually were captured after the suspects' photographs and a vehicle description were broadcast. There were three other key components. First, the police refused to engage in speculation, thereby defusing all of the "what if" scenarios posed by copy-hungry reporters. Second, media briefings were conducted on a regular basis. Finally, this high degree of media access enabled the police to build public trust, rather than have reporters engage in further and often damaging speculation as the case progressed. Reliable information flow is crucial to the success of such a major investigation. The ability to collect, analyze, and disseminate tips, lead, intelligence, and criminal histories can mean the difference between a quick apprehension and a prolonged, frustrating effort. In this case, it was also crucial that effective communication was maintained with residents, government leaders, and the media. Police executives also kept their patrol officers informed of all pertinent and current information about the investigation, and provided them with a list of questions to ask when talking to residents or conducting field interviews. The lessons learned from this case will serve as an important blueprint for similarly situated law enforcement executives in the future.[91]

A "CRISIS STAGE": SUCCESSION PLANNING FOR FUTURE LEADERS

Soon the administration, management, and supervision of police agencies could be in a crisis stage unless measures are taken in the near future to prepare for what is coming: the current aging, turnover, and retirement of baby boomers and other generational employees. Today an essential part of every chief's job is to prepare colleagues in the organization for the next advance in their careers; indeed, today the mark of a good leader is the ability to ensure a ready supply of capable leaders for the future.

Thorough preparation of successors can help a chief establish an important legacy—one that will sustain the improvements and progress that have been made, offer opportunities for mentoring, and instill the importance of the organization's history.

Chiefs need to take a long view and look at **succession planning** and leadership development as a continuous process that changes the organizational culture. To provide the ongoing supply of talent needed to meet organizational needs, chiefs should use recruitment, development tools (such as job coaching, mentoring, understudy, job rotation, lateral moves, higher-level exposure, acting assignments, and instructing), and career planning.[92]

Organizations may already have a sufficient pipeline of strong leaders—people who are competent in handling the ground-level, tactical operations but who are not trained in how to look at the big picture. Although not everyone can excel at both levels of execution, efforts must definitely be made to help prospective leaders develop a broader vision—as one author put it, prepare employees to take on broader roles and "escape the silos."[93] To develop police leaders who do not see the world in zero-sum terms but instead can appreciate the bigger picture requires people to leave their comfort zones and to offer them challenging assignments in different roles.[94]

A number of excellent police promotional academies and management institutes exist for developing chief executives, as well as middle managers and supervisors, in the kinds of skills described above as well as later in this chapter. One of these training programs is described in Exhibit 5.1.

EXHIBIT 5.1

Senior Management Institute for Police Builds Leaders

One of the experiences that helped shape my career was my attendance at the Police Executive Research Forum's Senior Management Institute for Police (SMIP), which provided the best executive leadership program for me personally. This program excels because superb instructors provide an excellent forum during the 3-week period. They use an applied, case-based curriculum and rigorously demand thinking in ways one might not be accustomed to. The combination of the intensive curriculum and spending 3 weeks working with, and learning from, a group of peers presented an excellent learning environment. As a course graduate and chief, I have witnessed others return from that program better able to accomplish tasks with higher levels of responsibility.

Source: Based on Robert McNeilly, "SMIP Builds Leaders," in Chuck Wexler, Mary Ann Wycoff, and Craig Fischer, eds., *Good to Great Policing: Application of Business Management Principles in the Public Sector* (Washington, DC: Office of Community Oriented Policing Services and Police Executive Research Forum, 2007), p. 28.

In addition, *agencies* can provide skill development opportunities by having those persons with leadership potential do things such as plan an event, write a training bulletin, update policies or procedures, conduct training and research, write a proposal or grant, counsel peers, become a mentor, write contingency plans, and so on. Meanwhile, the *individual* can lay plans for the future through activities such as doing academic coursework, participating in and leading civic events, attending voluntary conferences and training sessions, reading the relevant literature, studying national and local reports, guest lecturing in college or academy classes, engaging in research, and so on.[95]

In Chapter 3, we discussed CompStat, the crime analysis and police management process that has been widely adopted as a crime analysis management process nationwide and affords accountability at all levels of a police agency.[96] But the CompStat process provides another major, inherent opportunity as well: the development of leaders.

In its earlier stages of development—and still today in some agencies—CompStat was viewed as requiring a quasi-military, intimidating mode; at CompStat meetings, police leaders often employed demeaning, deprecating, or other offensive language, raising their voices with subordinates who were not abreast of crime issues in their sectors or were not doing enough to address them. Such an approach may well be counterproductive for developing competent leaders who will take greater initiative and solve problems more effectively. Rather, public CompStat meetings should be a time to exercise command presence and establish accountability—not a time for criticizing personnel in front of an audience of colleagues, subordinates, or members of other government agencies.

With today's leadership theory holding that law enforcement executives should adopt a participative management style, also known as *democratic leadership*, except when emergencies arise,[97] an autocratic management style that includes public criticism can cause resentment among subordinates rather than a sense of teamwork or a spirit of cooperation. This style may also inhibit the development of future leaders and undermine the cooperative leadership process. Leadership is learned behavior, and new leaders can be developed through properly designed leadership experiences.[98]

This process should begin prior to the public CompStat meeting with a pre-CompStat meeting in private and between the chief executive and the individual commander. Thus, both will understand the data and the underlying conditions in the beat sector, and then the commander can work with the staff to devise effective strategies and tactics, giving officers the latitude to be creative in their problem-solving efforts.[99]

Then, at the actual CompStat meeting, public praise and accolades should be given where justified; commanders should publicly recognize outstanding performance, explaining the analyses and tactics that resulted in successful crime reduction and problem solving. The CompStat process, when used effectively for accountability and problem solving, can be a means for developing potential leaders and promoting cooperative and creative leadership. The CompStat podium can also be a place where new and hopeful supervisors and officers aspire to stand someday.

LEGAL AND PSYCHOLOGICAL ASPECTS OF POLICE UNIFORMS

As discussed in earlier chapters, the police are paramilitary in nature; as such, in addition to being hierarchical in organization, with rank and chain of command, they are typically uniformed (unless assigned to undercover work). And, as two authors stated, "The uniform stands out as one of the most important visual representations of the law enforcement profession."[100]

From the moment a neophyte officer puts on a uniform, his or her world changes; the officer is immediately and uniquely set apart from society. For some, the uniform seems to be a target for all kinds of verbal abuse and even fists or bullets; for others, it is a welcomed as a symbol of their legal authority. In either case, the uniform along with overall appearance of police officers has several psychological and legal aspects.

For the above reasons, police chief executives need to understand the legal and psychological aspects of their officers' uniforms. Included in this discussion is the existence of a dress code–an area of police administration that is witnessing considerable change due to the increasing desire by many people today to display body art, branding, intentional scarring, and body hair.

Succinctly stated, police administrators have long been able to regulate the appearance of their officers. In *Kelley v. Johnson*,[101] 1976, the U.S. Supreme Court held that police agencies have a legitimate, "rational" interest in establishing such rules and regulations. There, the Suffolk County (New York) Police Department's hair-grooming standards applicable to male members of the police force (governing the style and length of hair, sideburns, and mustaches; also, beards and goatees were prohibited) were attacked as violating officers' First and Fourteenth Amendment rights of expression and liberty. The Supreme Court upheld such regulations, on the grounds they:

> may be based on a desire to make police officers readily recognizable to the members of the public, or a desire for the esprit de corps, which such similarity is felt to inculcate within the police force itself. Either one is a sufficiently rational justification for regulations...[102]

Therefore, police administrators can dictate how the uniform will be worn—as well as other aspects of personal appearance. Why do most agencies insist that patrol officers dress in uniforms? Certainly, the uniform conveys power and authority; it identifies a person with powers to arrest and use force and establishes order, as well as conformity within the ranks of those who wear it by suppressing individuality.[103]

Research has consistently supported suggestions about the police uniform's power and authority. In one study, individuals ranked 25 different occupational uniforms by several categories of feelings. The test subjects consistently ranked the police uniform as the one most likely to induce feelings of safety. Studies have also shown that people consistently rate models as more competent, reliable, intelligent, and helpful when pictured in a police uniform, rather than in casual clothes.[104]

Details about a police officer's uniform, such as the style of hat or the tailoring, can also influence the level of authority emanating from the officer. For example, studies show that the traditional "bus driver" garrison cap and the "Smoky the Bear" campaign hat conveyed more authority than the baseball cap or no hat at all.[105]

Instituting (and Enforcing) a Dress Code

Many, if not most, police agencies have general orders or policies constituting a dress code—how their officers will dress and their general appearance—so as to:

> promote a professional image to the community served; have uniformed officers be consistently attired to reflect their authority, respective assignment, and rank within the agency; require the wearing of agency approved uniforms; have officers be properly groomed and his/her uniform clean, pressed, and in proper condition.[106]

Such dress codes might address matters such as the length of hair and sideburns, beards and goatees (whether or not they are permitted), types of sunglasses to be worn (mirrored, for example, are often banned), and tattoos (whether or not any body art is to be permitted for officers, and if they are to be covered while on duty).

The wearing of uniforms and displaying of tattoos, bodily hair, and beards are only the tip of the iceberg, however. Regulations might also spell out, for example, when officers are to begin wearing their summer and winter uniforms (specified dates normally occurring in spring and fall) and the proper components of each uniform (the list can specify certain types of socks, shoes, turtleneck, patches, and insignia—as well as prohibitions against the displaying of items of clothing with an identifying logo, so the jurisdiction is not viewed as endorsing a particular name brand).

Imposing the will of the police administration concerning officers' appearance and attire is not always as easy as it might appear, however; today officers show little reluctance to file lawsuits if feeling that such codes violate their rights to freedom of expression:

- A northeastern Pennsylvania man sued in late 2009, claiming his rights were violated when he was not hired with the state police because he would not have his arm tattoo removed. Applicants' tattoos are subject to review by the Tattoo and Replica Review Committee, which can insist they be removed before a job will be offered. The lawsuit seeks to determine whether "the government can require you to physically alter your body in exchange for employment," and infringes on the applicant's "freedom of choice in personal matters."[107]
- The Houston City Council voted in late 2009 to spend up to $150,000 to hire outside lawyers to defend the city's no-beard policy for police. Four black officers filed a federal civil rights lawsuit against the city, claiming discrimination because shaving exacerbates a skin condition that disproportionately affects black men; officers with beards are barred from wearing the Houston Police Department uniform.[108]
- Des Moines, Iowa, police policy states that any tattoos, branding and intentional scarring on the face, head, neck, hands, and exposed arms and legs are prohibited. Employees who already have tattoos are exempted. The police union said the policy is unreasonable and filed a grievance.[109]
- Other agencies have implemented or are considering policies that would require officers to either not be tattooed or to cover the tattoos completely when on duty.[110]

As mentioned above, there are several legal and psychological issues surrounding police uniforms and dress codes. This is an area where the views of administrators toward officers' uniforms and appearance may well inherently clash with the street officers' viewpoints, as the latter tries to be more "expressive" in an era where tattoos and facial hair are more commonplace and less stigmatized. However, this is also an area of importance to the American public, and studies show that the public does not support relaxed grooming standards: one study found that 88 percent of Americans believe that public respect for police would drop if officers deviated from strict grooming standards.[111]

Summary

This chapter examined a number of issues that have challenged and will continue to challenge law enforcement administrators for years: managing the use of force; biased policing; women and minorities in law enforcement; contract, consolidated, and civilianized services; police–media relations; succession planning; and police uniforms and dress codes.

Perhaps just as important as having administrators today who understand and deal with these problems are the subordinates of tomorrow; those who will wear the mantle of leadership in the future must likewise attempt to understand how to address these issues.

Questions for Review

1. What is terrorism, and why is the prospect of bioterrorism particularly frightening?
2. What is meant by intelligence-led policing, predictive policing, and fusion centers?
3. What are some of the problems involving police use of force, and how would you explain the DRRM use-of-force continuum?
4. What is involved in contagious shootings and suicide by cop?
5. What types of issues are involved in Carter's typology of abuse of police authority?
6. What are some problems surrounding police vehicle pursuits and what has the U.S. Supreme Court stated about them? What policy and practical responsibilities do law enforcement administrators and patrol supervisors have in regard to pursuits?
7. What are contract, consolidated, and civilianized police services, and what are the advantages and limitations of each?
8. How does a police administrator establish a good system of media relations?
9. What is succession planning, and why should it begin immediately in policing?
10. What are the legal and psychological effects of police uniforms? How are times changing in these areas?

Learn by Doing

1. An investigative report by the local media has revealed an unusually high number of incidents involving inappropriate use of force by the police during the past few years. One aspect of the public reaction to this revelation is that the agency's training, policies, and procedures are now being questioned. What training topics as well as policies and procedures (refer to Chapter 3) concerning use of force do you believe should be examined (or, as necessary, added, clarified, or expanded) for the department? Defend your answers.
2. Your county sheriff has recently come out publicly in favor of consolidating all police agencies in your county. Having caught your new police chief off-guard, you—the agency's director of research, planning, and analysis—are tasked to draft a memorandum explaining all that would be involved in creating and maintaining a single county-wide police agency to include any advantages and disadvantages of doing so. How do you respond?
3. You are a new university police chief in a medium-sized city, and today is a huge football game at your university. You have just received information from a patrol sergeant that one of your male officers, Spicer, is at the football stadium working overtime and wearing an earring and sporting a new (and rather risqué) tattoo on his arm. The sergeant says both are highly visible, and that a rudimentary dress code exists in your agency but does not cover earrings. You are aware that the other officers are anxiously watching the situation to see what you do. Spicer, the recipient of many letters of reprimand and filer of many grievances, is fully aware of what he can and cannot do, and no doubt aware that there is no specific prohibition against either earrings or tattoos under the agency's dress code, and that he is merely "expressing" himself under the First Amendment. What, if any, action will you take regarding the earring? Can you legally regulate the appearance of the employees in the workplace and require a "professional" appearance? Can you use to advantage any U.S. Supreme Court decisions in response to this matter?

Related Websites

Bureau of Justice Statistics: Use of Force
   http://www.ojp.gov/bjs/abstract/ufbponld.htm
Criminal Justice Policy Review—Vehicular Pursuits
   http://cjp.sagepub.com/cgi/content/abstract/14/1/75
Globalsecurity.org
   Globalsecurity.org
Iowa City Police Media Relations Policy
   http://www.icgov.org/policefiles/genorder9.pdf

National Association of Blacks in Criminal Justice
   http://www.nabcj.org
National Center for Women and Policing
   http://www.womenandpolicing.org/aboutus.asp
National Criminal Justice Reference Service – Predictive Policing
   http://www.ncjrs.gov/pdffiles1/nij/grants/230404.pdf

National Law Enforcement and Corrections Technology Center
 http://www.nlectc.org

National Organization of Black Law Enforcement Executives (NOBLE)
 http://www.noblentl.org

Police Media Relations
 http://www.policemediarelations.com

Security Guard Officers Use of Force Continuum
 http://www.crimedoctor.com/security_guards_2.htm

Urban Institute
 http://www.urban.org/publications/410380.html

U.S. Department of Justice: Office of Justice Programs—Use of Force
 http://www.ncjrs.gov/pdffiles1/nij/176330-1.pdf

Notes

1. Michael Duffy and Mark Thompson, "The Lessons of Flight 253," *Time*, January 11, 2010, p. 26.
2. Ibid., pp. 30–31.
3. Quoted in M. K. Rehm and W. R. Rehm, "Terrorism Preparedness Calls for Proactive Approach," *Police Chief* (December 2000):38–43.
4. J. F. Lewis, Jr., "Fighting Terrorism in the 21st Century," *FBI Law Enforcement Bulletin* (March 1999):3.
5. Ibid., p. 3.
6. K. Strandberg, "Bioterrorism: A Real or Imagined Threat?" *Law Enforcement Technology* (June 2001):88–97.
7. D. Rogers, "A Nation Tested: What Is the Terrorist Threat We Face and How Can We Train for It?" *Law Enforcement Technology* (November 2001):16–21.
8. D. G. Bolgiano, "Military Support of Domestic Law Enforcement Operations: Working within Posse Comitatus," *FBI Law Enforcement Bulletin* (December 2001):16–24.
9. U.S. Department of Homeland Security, *National Incident Management System* (Washington, DC: Author, March 2004), pp. viii, ix.
10. Gary Peck and Laura Mijanovich, "Give Us Security While Retaining Freedoms," *Reno Gazette Journal,* August 28, 2003, p. 9A.
11. "House Approves Patriot Act Renewal," http://www.cnn.com/2006/POLITICS/03/07/patriot.act/ (accessed January 3, 2007).
12. Jurist: Legal News and Research, "Bush Signs Military Commissions Act," http://jurist.law.pitt.edu/paperchase/2006/10/bush-signs-military-commissions-act.php (accessed January 2, 2007).
13. Ibid.
14. U.S. Department of Justice, Office of Justice Programs, Bureau of Justice Statistics, *Intelligence-Led / Policing: The New Intelligence Architecture* (Washington, DC: Author, 2005), p. 9.
15. Ibid., p. 3.
16. See U.S. Department of Justice, Office of Justice Programs, *National Criminal Intelligence Sharing Plan*, p. 6; http://www.fas.org/irp/agency/doj/ncisp.pdf (accessed December 7, 2009).
17. U.S. Department of Justice, "Predictive Policing: A National Discussion," http://blogs.usdoj.gov/blog/archives/385 (accessed February 11, 2010); also see U.S. Department of Justice, National Institute of Justice, "Predictive Policing Symposium: Agenda," http://www.ojp.usdoj.gov/nij/topics/law-enforcement/predictive-policing/symposium/agenda.htm (accessed February 11, 2010).
18. Ellen Perlman, "Policing by the Odds," *Governing*, December 1, 2008, http://www.governing.com/article/policing-odds (accessed November 8, 2010).
19. Ibid.
20. J. Sullivan, "Terrorism Early Warning Groups: Regional Intelligence to Combat Terrorism." In eds. R. Howard, J. Forest, and J. Moore, *Homeland Security and Terrorism* (New York: McGraw-Hill, 2006), pp. 235–245.
21. Daniel E. Marks and Ivan Y. Sun, "The Impact of 9/11 on Organizational Development Among State and Local Law Enforcement Agencies," *Journal of Contemporary Criminal Justice* 23(2) (May 2007):159-173.
22. Ibid, pp. 166, 169-170.
23. Ibid., p. 166.
24. Roy Roberg, Kenneth Novak, and Gary Cordner, *Police & Society* (New York: Oxford University Press, 2009), p. 480;
25. Larry K. Gaines and Victor E. Kappeler, *Policing in America* (Cincinnati: Anderson, 2005), p. 579.
26. Roberg et. al., *Police & Society*, p. 481.
27. Samson Habte, "Guest Speaker Warns of Dangers of Federalization of Criminal Law," *Virginia Law Weekly* (March 21, 2008)), http://www.lawweekly.org/?module=displaystory&story_id=2004&edition_id=86&format=html (accessed July 6, 2009).

28. American Bar Association, "Task Force on the Federalization of Criminal Law 1998," http://www.criminaljustice.org/public.nsf/legislation/overcriminalization/$FILE/fedcrimlaw2.pdf (accessed July 6, 2009; see also The 2009 Criminal Justice Transition Coalition, "Overcriminalization of Conduct, Federalization of Criminal Law, and the Exercise of Enforcement Discretion" (November 2008), http://www.2009transition.org/criminaljustice/index.php?option=com_content&view=article&id=26&Itemid=86 (accessed July 6, 2009) Ibid.

29. Codified at 18 U.S.C. § 1385.

30. Radley Balko, "Our Militarized Police Departments," http://www.reason.com/news/show/121169.html (accessed November 8, 2010).

31. National Guard Bureau, "About the National Guard," http://www.ngb.army.mil/About/default.aspx (accessed November 8, 2010).

32. Samuel Walker, *Police Accountability: The Role of Citizen Oversight* (Belmont, CA: Wadsworth, 2001), p. 141.

33. *Graham v. Connor,* 490 U.S. 386 (1989), p. 397.

34. David Carter, "Theoretical Dimensions in the Abuse of Authority," in T. Barker and D. Carter (eds.), *Police Deviance* (Cincinnati: Anderson, 1994), pp. 269–290.

35. *Tennessee v. Garner,* 471 U.S. 1, 105 S.Ct. 1694, 85 L.Ed.2d 1 (1985).

36. G. W. Selnow, "Sex Differences in Uses and Perceptions of Profanity," *Sex Roles* 12 (1985):303–312.

37. D. L. Paletz and W. F. Harris, "Four-Letter Threats to Authority," *Journal of Politics* 37 (1975):955–979.

38. Selnow, "Sex Differences in Uses and Perceptions of Profanity," p. 306.

39. D. W. Warshay and L. H. Warshay, "Obscenity and Male Hegemony," paper presented at the annual meeting of the International Sociological Association, Detroit, Michigan, 1978.

40. Paletz and Harris, "Four-Letter Threats to Authority," p. 955.

41. Ibid.

42. William Terrill, Geoffrey P. Alpert, Roger G. Dunham, and Michael R. Smith, "A Management Tool for Evaluating Police Use of Force: An Application of the Force Factor," *Police Quarterly* 6(2) (June 2003):150–171.

43. Ibid., p. 152.

44. Ibid., pp. 153–154.

45. Based on Lorie A. Fridell, "Improving Use-of-Force Policy: Policy Enforcement and Training," in Joshua A. Ederheimer and Lorie A. Fridell (eds.), *Chief Concerns: Exploring the Challenges of Police Use of Force* (Washington, DC: Police Executive Research Form, April 2005), p. 48.

46. International Association of Chiefs of Police, "Force Continuums: Three Questions," *The Police Chief,* October 2010, http://www.policechiefmagazine.org/magazine/index.cfm?fuseaction=display_arch&article_id=791&issue_id=12006 (accessed November 8, 2010).

47. Charles Joyner and Chad Basile, "The Dynamic Resistance Response Model," *FBI Law Enforcement Bulletin* (September 2007):17.

48. Pat Milton, "Grand Jury Indicts 3 in NYPD Shooting," http://abcnews.go.com/US/wireStory?id=2957956 (accessed April 19, 2007).

49. latimes.com, "LAPD Shooting Blamed on Poor Supervision," http://www.latimes.com/news/local/los_angeles_metro/la-me-pena6dec06,0,5058221,print.story?coll=la-commun-los_angeles_metro (accessed January 12, 2007).

50. Michael Wilson, "50 Shots Fired, and the Experts Offer a Theory," http://www.nytimes.com/2006/11/27/nyregion/27fire.html?ei=5088&en=357cf73362b1de61&ex=1322283600&partner=rs&pagewanted=print (accessed January 10, 2007).

51. "L.A. Police Corruption Case Continues to Grow," *Washington Post* (February 13, 2000):1A.

52. Human Rights Watch, *Shielded from Justice: Police Brutality and Accountability in the United States* (New York: Author, 1998).

53. Ibid.

54. *New York Times,* April 29, 2001, p. A1.

55. Ibid.

56. Based on Anthony J. Pinizzotto, Edward F. Davis, and Charles E. Miller III, "Suicide by Cop: Defining a Devastating Dilemma," *FBI Law Enforcement Bulletin* 74(2) (February 2005), http://www.fbi.gov/publications/leb/2005/feb2005/feb2005.htm#page8 (accessed January 8, 2007).

57. Ibid.

58. H. Range Huston, and Diedre Anglin, "Suicide by Cop," *Annals of Emergency Medicine* 32(6) (December 1998):665–669.

59. Ibid.

60. National Highway Traffic Safety Administration, *National Highway Traffic Safety Administration Statistics* (Washington, DC: Author, 1995).

61. C. B. Eisenberg, "Pursuit Management," *Law and Order* (March 1999):73–77.

62. A. Belotto, "Supervisors Govern Pursuits," *Law and Order* (January 1999):86.

63. G. T. Williams, "When Do We Keep Pursuing? Justifying High-Speed Pursuits," *The Police Chief* (March 1997):24–27.

64. 118 S.Ct. 1708.

65. Ibid. at p. 1720.

66. Eisenberg, "Pursuit Management," p. 77.

67. E. M. Sweeney, "Vehicular Pursuit: A Serious—and Ongoing—Problem," *The Police Chief* (January 1997):16–21.

68. Belotto, "Supervisors Govern Pursuits," p. 86.

69. Williams, "When Do We Keep Pursuing?" p. 27.

70. D. N. Falcone, M. T. Charles, and E. Wells, "A Study of Pursuits in Illinois," *The Police Chief* (March 1994):59–64.

71. Ibid.

72. Barbara Raffel Price, "Sexual Integration in American Law Enforcement," in William C. Heffernan and Timothy Stroup (eds.), *Police Ethics: Hard Choices in Law Enforcement,* (New York: John Jay Press, 1985), pp. 205–214; see also Vivian B. Lord and Kenneth J. Peak, *Women in Law Enforcement Careers: A Guide for Preparing and Succeeding* (Upper Saddle River, NJ: Prentice Hall, 2005).

73. U.S. Department of Justice, Bureau of Justice Statistics, *Local Police Departments, 2003* (Washington, DC: Author, 2006), p. iii; U.S. Department of Justice, Bureau of Justice Statistics, *Sheriff's Offices, 2003* (Washington, DC: Author, 2006), p. iii.

74. National Center for Women and Policing, *Equality Denied: The Status of Women in Policing* (Washington, DC: Feminist Majority Foundation, 2001), p. 5.

75. Department of Justice, Bureau of Justice Statistics, *Federal Law Enforcement Officers, 2004* (Washington, DC: Author, July 2006), p. 1.

76. Dorothy Moses Schulz, "Women Police Chiefs: A Statistical Profile," *Police Quarterly* 6(3) (September 2003):330–345.

77. Peg Tyre, "Ms. Top Cop," *Newsweek* (April 12, 2004):49.

78. Schulz, "Women Police Chiefs, p. 333.

79. Ibid.

80. Ibid.

81. Peter Horne, "Policewomen: 2000 A.D. Redux," *Law and Order* (November 1999):53.

82. For information about successful recruiting efforts as well as the diverse kinds of assignments women now occupy in law enforcement, see Vivian B. Lord and Kenneth J. Peak, *Women in Law Enforcement Careers: A Guide for Preparing and Succeeding* (Upper Saddle River, NJ: Prentice Hall, 2005).

83. Quoted in Horne, "Policewomen," p. 59.

84. Lena Williams, "Police Officers Tell of Strains of Living as a 'Black in Blue,'" *The New York Times*, February 14, 1988, pp.1, 26.

85. U.S. Department of Justice, Bureau of Justice Statistics, Law Enforcement Management and Administrative Statistics, *Local Police Departments, 2003* (Washington, DC: Author, May 2006), p. 2.

86. National Advisory Commission on Criminal Justice Standards and Goals, *Police* (Washington, DC: U.S. Government Printing Office, 1973), p. 108.

87. Samuel Walker and Charles M. Katz, *The Police in America: An Introduction* (New York: McGraw-Hill, 2002).

88. Jerome H. Skolnick and James J. Fyfe, *Above the Law: Police and the Excessive Use of Force* (New York: Free Press, 1993).

89. The Museum of Broadcast Communications, "Police Programs," http://www.museum.tv/archives/etv/P/htmlP/policeprogra/policeprogra.htm (accessed January 4, 2007).

90. Ibid.

91. Based on Gerard R. Murphy and Chuck Wexler, *Managing a Multi-jurisdictional Case: Lessons Learned from the Sniper Investigation* (Washington, DC: Police Executive Research Forum, October 2004), p. 39; Richard B. Weinblatt, "The Police and the Press," http://www.policeone.com/media-relations/articles/118445/ (accessed January 4, 2007); Patrick Collins, "Handling the Media: The Lessons of Some Moose-terpiece Theater," *Law Enforcement News* (November 30, 2002):1.

92. Edward Davis and Ellen Hanson, "Succession Planning: Mentoring Future Leaders" (Washington, DC: Police Executive Research Forum, 2006), p. 5.

93. Douglas A. Ready, "How to Grow Leaders," *Harvard Business Review* (December 2004):93–100.

94. Ibid.

95. Rick Michelson, "Succession Planning for Police Leadership," *The Police Chief* (June 2006):16–22.

96. Jon M. Shane, "CompStat Design," *FBI Law Enforcement Bulletin* (May 2004):17–18.

97. Donald J. Schroeder, Frank Lombardo, and Jerry Strollo, *Management and Supervision of Police Personnel* (Binghamton, NY: Gould, 1995).

98. Gina Hernez-Broome and Richard L. Hughes, "Leadership Development: Past, Present, and Future," *Human Resource Planning* 27(1) (2004):25.

99. International Association of Chiefs of Police, "Police Leadership in the 21st Century: Achieving and Sustaining Executive Success," http://www.

theiacp.org/documents/pdfs/Publications/ policeleadership%2Epdf (accessed January 3, 2008).

100. Paul Tinsley and Darryl Plecas, "Studying Public Perceptions of Police Grooming Standards," *The Police Chief*, November 2003, http://policechiefmag azine.org/magazine/index.cfm?fuseaction=display_ arch&article_id=152&issue_id=112003 (accessed September 6, 2009).

101. 425 U.S. 238 (1976).

102. Ibid., at pp. 247–248.

103. Richard R. Johnson, "The Psychological Influence of the Police Uniform," *FBI Law Enforcement Bulletin*, March 2001, pp. 27–32; Tinsley and Plecas, "Studying Public Perceptions of Police Grooming Standards," p. 2.

104. Ibid., p. 29

105. Tinsley and Plecas, "Studying Public Perceptions of Police Grooming Standards," p. 3.

106. Based on the Watertown, South Dakota, Police Department General Order A-170, http://www. watertownpd.com/images/pdf_ files/a-170%20personnel%20dress%20code%20 and%20uniform%20regulations.pdf (accessed September 6, 2009).

107. "Tattooed State Police Job Applicant Sues over Policy," http://www.wpxi.com/news/20567045/detail. html (accessed September 6, 2009).

108. Gene Park, "HPD weighs tattoo cover-up," http:// www.starbulletin.com/news/20090126_hpd_weighs_ tattoo_cover_up.html (accessed September 6, 2009);

109. Des Moines Police Ban New Tattoos," http://www. foxnews.com/story/0,2933,379203,00.html(accessed September 6, 2009).

110. Park, "HPD weighs tattoo cover-up," p. 1.

111. Paul Tinsley and Darryl Plecas, "Studying Public Perceptions of Police Grooming Standards," p. 4.

PART 3

The Courts

This part consists of three chapters. Chapter 6 examines court organization and operation, Chapter 7 covers personnel roles and functions, and Chapter 8 discusses court issues and practices. The introductory section of each chapter previews the specific chapter content. Case studies in court administration appear in Appendix I.

6

Court Organization
and Operation

KEY TERMS AND CONCEPTS

Adversarial system

Court culture

Court of last resort

Court unification

Décor

Decorum

Dual court system

Federal court system

Intermediate courts of appeals (ICAs)

Judicial Conference of the United States

Jurisdiction

Policymaking

State court reform

State court system

Trial courts

LEARNING OBJECTIVES

After reading this chapter, the student will:

- be familiar with the ramifications of the adversarial system
- know the importance of citizen groups in the courtroom
- understand the organization and administration of our dual (federal and state) court systems
- comprehend the roles and functions of the Judicial Conference of the United States and the Administrative Office of the U.S. Courts
- be able to explain the kinds of jurisdiction that courts possess
- be familiar with state courts and trial courts of general and limited jurisdictions
- know the four components of court unification, how a unified court is organized, and the functional and financial advantages of court unification
- understand the importance of court decor and decorum
- know why the courts' caseloads have increased
- understand the influence of courts on policymaking

The place of justice is a hallowed place.

—Francis Bacon

Courts and camps are the only places to learn the world in.

—Earl of Chesterfield

INTRODUCTION

Courts have existed in some form for thousands of years. Indeed, the ancient trial court of Israel, and the most common tribunal throughout its biblical history, was the "court at the gate," where elders of each clan resolved controversies within the kin group. In the fourth century B.C.E., courts in Athens, Greece, dealt with all premeditated homicides and heard cases. The court system has survived the dark eras of the Inquisition and the Star Chamber (which, in England during the 1500s and 1600s, without a jury, enforced unpopular political policies and meted out severe punishment, including whipping, branding, and mutilation). The U.S. court system developed rapidly after the American Revolution and led to the establishment of law and justice on the western frontier.

This chapter opens by going inside the courts, considering their special nature in our country, as well as typical courtroom decor and decorum. Then I discuss how the courts attempt to get at truth within the controversial adversary system of justice. The nature of our dual court system, comprising federal and state-level courts, is examined next; included are discussions of two entities [the Judicial Conference of the United States and the Administrative Office of the U.S. Courts (AO)] that administer those at the federal level. The discussion of the federal court system focuses on the U.S. Supreme Court, appeals courts, and district courts; the overview of state courts includes their courts of last resort, appeals courts, and trial courts (including the major trial courts having general jurisdiction and limited-jurisdiction lower courts). Included in the discussion of state court systems is an in-depth look at the functional and financial advantages of statewide court unification. An underlying theme is that caseloads are generally burgeoning, and we consider some reasons for that trend. Finally, we discuss the role of courts as policymaking bodies.

INSIDE THE COURTS: DECOR, DECORUM, CITIZENS

Hallowed Places

Practically everything one sees and hears in an American courtroom is intended to convey the sense that the courtroom is a hallowed place in our society. Alexis de Tocqueville, in his study of the United States more than a century ago, observed the extent to which our legal system permeates our lives:

> Scarcely any political question arises in the United States that is not resolved, sooner or later, into a judicial question. Hence all parties are obliged to borrow, in their daily controversies, the ideas, and even the language, peculiar to judicial proceedings. [T]he spirit of the law, which is produced in the schools and courts of justice, gradually penetrates beyond their walls into the bosom of society, where it descends to the lowest classes, so that at last the whole people contract the habits and the tastes of the judicial magistrate.[1]

The physical **décor** one finds in the courts conveys this sense of importance. On their first visit, citizens often are struck by the court's high ceilings, ornate marble walls, and comparatively expensive furnishings.

A formal level of **decorum** is accorded to this institution. All people must stand up when the judge enters the courtroom, permission must be granted before a person can approach the elevated bench, and a general attitude of deference is granted to the judge. A vitriolic utterance that could lawfully be directed to the president of the United States could result in the individuals being jailed for contempt of court when directed to a judge.

The design of the courtroom, although generally dignified in nature, also provides a safe, functional space that is conducive to efficient and effective court proceedings. The formal arrangement of the participants and furnishings reflects society's view of the appropriate relationships between the defendant and judicial authority. The courtroom must accommodate judges, court reporters, clerks, bailiffs, witnesses, plaintiffs, defendants, attorneys, juries, and spectators, as well as police officers, social workers, probation officers, guardians ad litem, interpreters, and the press. Space must also be allotted for evidence, exhibits, recording equipment, and computers.

Judges and court staff now may require high-technology audiovisual equipment and computer terminals to access automated information systems. Chapter 16 discusses the kinds of technology that are now commonly used in the nation's courtrooms.

Justice in the Eye of the Beholder

Whether or not justice is obtained in the courtrooms depends on the interests or viewpoints of the affected or interested parties. A victim may not agree with a jury's verdict; a winner in a civil case may not believe that he or she received an adequate sum of money for the suffering or damages involved. Thus, because the definition of *justice* is not always agreed on, the courts must *appear* to provide justice. The court's responsibility is to provide a fair hearing, with rights accorded to all parties to speak or not to speak, to have the assistance of counsel, to cross-examine the other side, to produce witnesses and relevant documents, and to argue their viewpoint. This process, embodied in the due process clause, must appear to result in justice.[2]

Seeking Truth in an Adversarial Atmosphere

Ralph Waldo Emerson stated that "every violation of truth is a stab at the health of human society."[3] Certainly, most people would agree that the traditional, primary purpose of our courts is to provide a forum for seeking and—through the adversarial system of justice—obtaining the truth. Indeed, the U.S. Supreme Court declared in 1966 in *Tehan v. United States ex rel. Shott*[4] that "the basic purpose of a trial is the determination of truth."

Today, however, increasing numbers of Americans have the impression that truth is being compromised and even violated with regularity in the trial, plea bargaining, and appellate apparatus of our justice system, thereby "stabbing at the health of human society."

High on their list of impediments is the **adversarial system** itself because of cases that included jury nullification (acquitting a defendant because the jury disagrees with a law or the evidence), lawyer grandstanding, improper and racist police procedures, and a general circus atmosphere allowed by the judge and engaged in by the media. Although many people would argue that such a system is vital to a free democratic society, under this system the courtroom becomes a battleground where participants often have little regard for guilt or innocence; rather, concern centers on whether the state is able to prove guilt beyond a reasonable doubt. To many people, this philosophy contradicts what courts were intended to accomplish. In the adversary system, the desire to win can become overpowering. As one state Supreme Court justice put it, prosecutors "are proud of the notches on their gun."[5] The defense counsel enjoys winning equally. The attention can shift from the goal of finding truth to being effective game players.

Should this system be modified or replaced? That is an important and difficult question. As one law professor observed, "Lawyers are simply not appropriate to correct the defects of our adversary system. Their hearts will never be in it; it is unfair to both their clients and themselves to require them to serve two masters."[6]

It would appear, however, that the adversarial system is here to stay. Indeed, several safeguards have been put in place to enable this system to reach the truth. First, evidence is tested under this approach through cross-examination of witnesses. Second, power is lodged with several different people; each courtroom actor is granted limited powers to counteract those of the others. If, for example, the judge is biased or unfair, the jury can disregard the judge and reach a fair verdict. If the judge believes the jury has acted improperly, he or she can set aside the jury's verdict and order a new trial. Furthermore, both the prosecuting and defense attorneys have certain rights and authority under each state's constitution. This series of checks and balances is aimed at curbing misuse of the criminal courts.

A Dual Court System

In order to better understand the court system of the United States, it is important to know that this country has a **dual court system**: one national **federal court system** and 50 **state court systems** plus the system of the District of Columbia. First, we will examine the federal court system; included are discussions of the entities responsible for overseeing the federal courts' operations: the Judicial Conference of the United States, and the AO. Following that, we examine the state and local trial courts.

ORGANIZATION AND ADMINISTRATION OF FEDERAL COURTS

The U.S. Supreme Court: Its Jurists, Traditions, and Work

JUDGES AND ADVOCACY   The U.S. Supreme Court is the highest and one of the oldest courts in the nation—formed in 1790. It is composed of nine justices: one chief justice and eight associate justices. Like other federal judges appointed under Article III of the Constitution, they are nominated to their post by the president and confirmed by the Senate, and they serve for life.[7] Each new term of the Supreme Court begins, by statute, on the first Monday in October.

Not just any lawyer may advocate a cause before the high court; all who wish to do so must first secure admission to the Supreme Court bar. Applicants must submit an application form that requires, under Supreme Court Rule 5, that applicants have been admitted to practice in the highest court of their state for a period of at least 3 years (during which time they must not have been the subject of any adverse disciplinary action), and they must appear to the Court to be of good moral and professional character. Each applicant must file with the clerk a certificate from the presiding judge or clerk of that court attesting that the applicant practices there and is in good standing, as well as the statements of two sponsors affirming that he or she is of good moral and professional character. Finally, applicants must swear or affirm to act "uprightly and according to law, and support the Constitution of the United States."[8]

INSIDE THE COURT: REVERED TRADITIONS AND PRACTICES   The Supreme Court Building, constructed in 1935, has 16 marble columns at the main west entrance that support the portico; on the architrave above is incised the words "Equal Justice Under Law." The building's chamber measures 82 feet wide by 99 feet long, rising 44 feet above the dark African marble floor. Gold leaf and red adorn the ceiling recesses. Twenty-four massive columns of silver gray Italian marble line walls of ivory mined in Spain. High on the walls, four 36-foot-long marble friezes depict the great classical and Christian lawgivers. A large clock is suspended high above the bench to remind the sometimes too verbose advocate that time marches on. Behind the bench are nine high-backed chairs and a flag. The clerk's desk is at the left end of the bench, and counsel tables are in front of and below the bench. Squarely in the middle, facing the chief justice, is the lectern used by attorneys while addressing the Court. On the lectern are two lights; a white one comes on when the speaker has 5 minutes remaining and a red one is the signal to stop.[9] Millions of visitors to the U.S. Supreme Court have been struck by the sight and the power of the building and its primary occupants. Justice Robert Jackson once described the Court's uniqueness, saying, "We are not final because we are infallible, but we are infallible because we are final."[10]

In many respects, the Court is the same institution that first met in 1790. Since at least 1800, it has been traditional for justices to wear black robes while in session. White quills are placed on counsel tables each day that the Court sits, as was done at the earliest sessions of the Court. The "Conference handshake" has been a tradition since the late nineteenth century. When the justices assemble to go on the bench each day and at the beginning of the private conferences at which they discuss decisions, each justice shakes hands with each of the other eight—a reminder that differences of opinion on the Court do not preclude overall harmony of purpose. When the Court is in session, the following seating arrangement exists for each justice: The chief justice always sits in the middle, with four associate justices on either side. The justice who is senior in terms of service sits on the chief's immediate right as the justices face out; the justice who is second in seniority sits on the chief's left; thereafter, the justices are seated alternately right and left according to the amount of time served. The junior justice is always on the chief justice's extreme left.[11]

Exhibit 6.1 shows the current seating arrangement of the sitting justices of the U.S. Supreme Court.

EXHIBIT 6.1

Courtroom Seating Chart of the Current Supreme Court of the United States

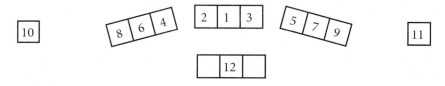

1. Chief Justice Roberts	**7.** Justice Alito
2. Justice Scalia	**8.** Justice Sotomayor
3. Justice Kennedy	**9.** Justice kagan
4. Justice Thomas	**10.** Clerk of the Court
5. Justice Ginsburg	**11.** Marshal of the Court
6. Justice Breyer	**12.** Counsel

Source: Supreme Court of the United States, "'Visitor's Guide to Oral Arguments,' p. 1, http://www.supremecourt.gov/visiting/visitorsguidetooralargument.aspx (accessed August 8, 2011).

CASELOAD AND CONFERENCES The Court does not meet continuously in formal sessions during its 9-month term. Instead, the Court divides its time into four separate but related activities. First, some time is allocated to reading through the thousands of petitions for review of cases that come annually to the Court—usually during the summer and when the Court is not sitting to hear cases. Second, the Court allocates blocks of time for oral arguments—the live discussion in which lawyers for both sides present their clients' positions to the justices. During the weeks of oral arguments the Court sets aside its third allotment of time, for private discussions of how each justice will vote on the cases they have just heard. Time is also allowed for the justices to discuss which additional cases to hear. These private discussions are usually held on Wednesday afternoons and Fridays during the weeks of oral arguments. The justices set aside a fourth block of time to work on writing their opinions.[12]

The Court has complete discretion to control the nature and number of the cases it reviews by means of the writ (order) of *certiorari*—an order from a higher court directing a lower court to send the record of a case for review. The Court considers requests for writs of certiorari according to the *rule of four*; if four justices decide to "grant cert," the Court will agree to hear the case. Several criteria are used to decide whether a case requires action: First, does the case concern an issue of constitutional or legal importance? Does it fall within the Court's jurisdiction (the Court can only hear cases that are mandated by Congress or the Constitution)? Does the party bringing the case has *standing*—a strong vested interest in the issues raised in the case and in its outcome?[13]

The Court hears only a tiny fraction of the thousands of cases it is petitioned to consider. When it declines to hear a case, the decision of the lower court stands as the final word on the case. Adding to the Court's workload is a steady growth in congressional and state legislation that requires judicial interpretation and an increasing number of constitutional and other issues that can be reviewed in the federal courts.[14]

ADMINISTRATION   The chief justice orders the business of the Supreme Court and administers the oath of office to the president and vice president upon their inauguration. According to Article 1, Section 3, of the Constitution of the United States, the chief justice is also empowered to preside over the Senate in the event that it sits as a court to try an impeachment of the president. The duties of the chief justice are described more fully in Chapter 7.

The clerk of the Court serves as the Supreme Court's chief administrative officer, supervising a staff of 30 under the guidance of the chief justice. The marshal of the Court supervises all building operations. The reporter of decisions oversees the printing and publication of the Court's decisions. Other key personnel are the librarian and the public information officer. In addition, each justice is entitled to hire four law clerks, almost always recent top graduates of law schools, many of whom have served clerkships in a lower court in the previous year.[15]

U. S. Courts of Appeals

JUDGES, JURISDICTION, CASELOADS   The courts of appeals are the intermediate courts of appeals (ICAs) for the federal court system. Eleven of the circuits are identified by number, and another is called the D.C. Circuit (see Figure 6.1). A court of appeals hears appeals from the district courts located within its circuit, as well as appeals from decisions of federal administrative agencies.

The courts of appeals are staffed with 179 judges nominated by the president and confirmed by the Senate. As with the U.S. district courts, discussed below, the number of judges in each circuit varies, from six in the First Circuit to 28 in the Ninth, depending on the volume and complexity of the caseload. Each circuit has a chief judge (chosen by seniority) who has supervisory responsibilities. Several staffers aid the judges in conducting the work of the courts of appeals. A circuit executive assists the chief judge in administering the circuit. The clerk's office maintains the records. Each judge is also allowed to hire three law clerks. In deciding cases, the courts of appeals may use rotating three-judge panels. Or, by majority vote, all the judges in the circuit may sit together to decide a case or reconsider a panel's decision. However, such *en banc* hearings are rare.[16] The caseload of the courts of appeals is about 60,375 per year[17]—about half being civil in nature, one-fourth being criminal, and the remainder originating from administrative agencies.[18]

U. S. District Courts

JUDGES, JURISDICTION, CASELOADS   Congress created 94 U.S. district courts, of which 89 are located within the 50 states. There is at least one district court in each state (some states have more, such as California, New York, and Texas, all of which have four). Congress has created 678 district court judgeships for the 94 districts. As with the other federal court judges discussed previously, the president nominates district judges, who must then be confirmed by the Senate; they then serve for life unless removed for cause. In the federal system, the U.S. district courts are the federal trial courts of original **jurisdiction** for all major violations of federal criminal law (some 500 full-time magistrate judges hear minor violations).[19]

District court judges are assisted by an elaborate supporting cast of clerks, secretaries, law clerks, court reporters, probation officers, pretrial services officers, and U.S. marshals. The larger

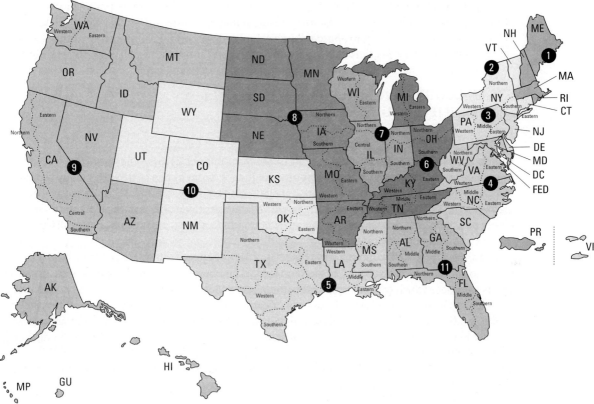

FIGURE 6.1 Geographic Boundaries of United States Courts of Appeals and United States District Courts

Source: United States Courts of Appeals and United States District Courts, www.uscourts.gov/images/circuitmap.pdf.

districts also have a public defender. Another important actor at the district court level is the U.S. attorney; there is one U.S. attorney in each district. The work of district judges is significantly assisted by 352 bankruptcy judges, who are appointed for 14-year terms by the court of appeals in the district it is located.[20] There are about 75,000 criminal cases filed per year in the U.S. district courts.[21]

Judicial Conference of the United States

The **Judicial Conference of the United States** is the administrative policymaking organization of the federal judicial system. Its membership consists of the chief justice, the chief judges of each of the courts of appeals, one district judge from each circuit, and the chief judge of the Court of International Trade. The conference meets semiannually for only 2-day sessions, but most of the work is done by about 25 committees. The Judicial Conference directs the AO, discussed below, in administering the judiciary budget and makes recommendations to Congress, concerning the creation of new judgeships, increase in judicial salaries, revising federal rules of procedure, and budgets for court operations. The Judicial Conference also plays a major role in the impeachment of federal judges.[22]

Administrative Office of the U.S. Courts

Since 1939, the day-to-day administrative tasks of the federal courts have been handled by the AO, a judicial agency. The director of the AO is appointed by the chief justice of the Supreme Court and reports to the Judicial Conference. The AO's lobbying and liaison responsibilities include presenting the annual budget request for the federal judiciary, arguing for the need for additional judgeships, and transmitting proposed changes in court rules. The AO is also the housekeeping agency of the judiciary, responsible for allotting authorized funds and supervising expenditures.[23]

STATE COURTS: LAST RESORT, APPELLATE, AND UNIFIED COURT SYSTEMS

Courts of Last Resort

Courts of last resort are usually referred to as *state supreme courts*. The specific names differ from state to state, however, as do the number of judges (from as few as five to as many as nine—see Figure 6.2). Unlike the intermediate appellate courts (discussed below), these courts do not use panels in making decisions; rather, the entire court sits to decide each case. All state supreme courts have a limited amount of original jurisdiction in dealing with matters such as disciplining lawyers and judges.[24]

In those 11 states without an intermediate court of appeals, the state supreme court has no power to choose which cases will be placed on its docket. However, the ability of most state supreme courts to choose which cases to hear makes them important policymaking bodies. Although intermediate appellate courts review thousands of cases each year, looking for errors, state supreme courts handle 100 or so cases that present the most challenging legal issues arising in that state.

Nowhere is the policymaking role of state supreme courts more apparent than in deciding death penalty cases—which, in most states, are automatically appealed to the state's highest court, thus bypassing the ICAs. The state supreme courts are also the ultimate review board for matters involving interpretation of state law.[25]

Intermediate Courts of Appeals

Like their federal counterparts, state courts have experienced a significant growth in appellate cases that threatens to overwhelm the state supreme court; therefore, to alleviate the caseload burden on courts of last resort, state officials in 39 states have responded by creating **ICAs** (the only states not having an ICA are sparsely populated ones with low volumes of appeals). There are about 1,000 such judges in the nation today. The ICAs must hear all properly filed appeals.[26]

The structure of the ICA varies; in most states, these bodies hear both civil and criminal appeals; and like their federal counterparts, these courts typically use rotating three-judge panels. Also, like the federal appellate courts, the state ICAs' workload is demanding: According to the National Center for State Courts, state ICAs hear about 270,000 cases annually.[27] ICAs engage primarily in error corrections; they review trials to make sure that the law was followed; the overall standard is one of fairness. The ICAs represent the final stage of the process for most litigants; very few cases make it to the appellate court in the first place, and of those cases, only a small proportion will be heard by the state's court of last resort.[28]

Administration

The issue of state court organization and unification is the focus of court reform and is the subject of a major discussion below. Here, suffice to say that, for court reformers, the multiplicity of courts at the state level is both inefficient, because judges cannot be shifted to meet the caseload needs of other courts, and inequitable because administration of justice is not uniform.

The advantages and cost benefits of court unification are described in the discussion below.

Supreme Court	Alabama (9), Alaska (5), Arizona (5), Arkansas (7), California (7), Connecticut (7), Delaware (5), Florida (7), Georgia (7), Hawaii (5), Idaho (5), Illinois (7), Indiana (5), Iowa (9), Kansas (7), Kentucky (7), Louisiana (8), Michigan (7), Minnesota (9), Mississippi (9), Missouri (7), Montana (7), Nebraska (7), Nevada (5), New Hampshire (5), New Jersey (7), New Mexico (5), North Carolina (7), North Dakota (5), Ohio (7), Oklahoma (9),[a] Oregon (7), Pennsylvania (7), Rhode Island (5), South Carolina (5), South Dakota (5), Tennessee (5), Texas (9),[a] Utah (5), Vermont (5), Virginia (7), Washington (9), Wisconsin (7), Wyoming (5)
Court of Appeals	District of Columbia (9), Maryland (7), New York (7)
Supreme Judicial Court	Maine (7), Massachusetts (7)
Court of Criminal Appeals	Oklahoma (3),[a] Texas (9)[a]
Supreme Court of Appeals	West Virginia (5)

[a]Two courts of last resort in these states.

FIGURE 6.2   Courts of Last Resort in U.S. States

Attempts at State Court Reform: Organization and Unification

The current status of state court systems—both courts of last resort and ICAs—is shown in Figures 6.2 and 6.3. It was shown earlier that there is widespread variation in terms of these courts' names and the number of judges for each.

Appeals Court	Massachusetts (14)
Appellate Court	Connecticut (9), Illinois (42)
Appellate Division of Superior Court	New Jersey (28)
Appellate Divisions of Superior Court	New York (48)
Appellate Terms of Supreme Court	New York (15)
Commonwealth Court	Pennsylvania (9)
Court of Appeals	Alaska (3), Arizona (21), Arkansas (6), Colorado (16), Georgia (9), Idaho (30), Indiana (5), Iowa (6), Kansas (10), Kentucky (14), Michigan (24), Minnesota (16), Missouri (32), Nebraska (6), New Mexico (10), North Carolina (12), North Dakota (3),[b] Ohio (65), Oklahoma (12),[a] Oregon (10), South Carolina (6), Tennessee (12),[a] Utah (7), Virginia (10), Washington (23), Wisconsin (15)
Court of Appeal	California (88), Louisiana (55), Texas (80)
Court of Civil Appeals	Alabama (3)
Court of Criminal Appeals	Alabama (5), Tennessee (9)
Court of Special Appeals	Maryland (13)
District Court of Appeals	Florida (57)
Intermediate Court of Appeals	Hawaii (3)
Superior Court	Pennsylvania (15)

[a]Civil only
[b]Temporary

FIGURE 6.3   Intermediate Courts of Appeals

Historically, **state court reform** has centered on implementing **court unification**. Indeed, since the beginning of the 1900s, the organization of U.S. courts has been a primary concern of court reformers who believe that the multiplicity of courts is inefficient.

A unified court system would, first and foremost, shift judicial control to centralized management. The loose network of independent judges and courts would be replaced by a hierarchy with authority concentrated in the state capital.

Other perceived benefits of court unification would include the following four general principles:[29]

1. *Simplified court structure.* Court reformers stress the need for a simple, uniform court structure for the entire state. In particular, the multiplicity of minor and specialized courts, which often have overlapping jurisdiction, would be consolidated; therefore, variations among counties would be eliminated. There would be a three-tier system: a state supreme court at the top, an intermediate court of appeal, and a single trial court.
2. *Centralized administration.* Reformers envision the state supreme court working with state and county court administrators and providing leadership for the state court system.
3. *Centralized rule making.* Reformers argue that the state supreme court should have the power to adopt uniform rules that would be followed by all courts in the state, including procedures for disciplining attorneys and setting time standards for disposing of cases. This change would shift control from legislatures to judges and lawyers.
4. *Centralized budgeting.* With unification would come centralized budgeting by the state judicial administrator, who would report to the state supreme court. A single budget would be prepared for the entire state judiciary and sent to the state legislature. The governor's power to recommend a judicial budget would be eliminated. Lower courts would be dependent on the Supreme Court for their monies.

Looking at two systems—one that is unified on a statewide basis and one that is not—may assist in better comprehending the concept of unification; to do so, we look at the states of Illinois and New York (Figure 6.4). In 1964, Illinois became the first state to become unified. All of its trial

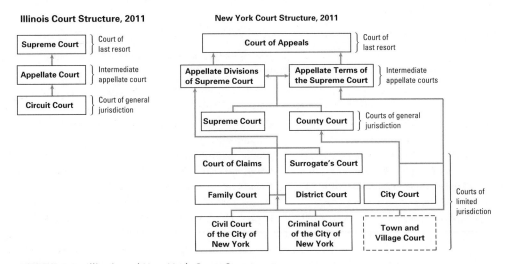

FIGURE 6.4   Illinois and New York Court Structures

courts were consolidated into a unified circuit court with one chief judge overseeing the operations and procedures in each division. Today, Illinois's state court system includes one court of last resort, one intermediate appellate court divided into five districts, and one court of general jurisdiction sectioned into 22 trial court divisions. From 1987 to 2004, most trial court expenses in Illinois were funded entirely at the state level. Counties were responsible for funding at least part of the operating and property expenses associated with the courthouse buildings in their jurisdictions.[30]

In contrast, New York's state court system, as depicted in Figure 6.4, included one court of last resort, two intermediate appellate courts, two types of general jurisdiction trial courts divided into 69 divisions, and eight types of limited jurisdiction trial courts separated into 1,695 divisions. In New York's numerous local courts, most expenses—including salaries, travel, building, and property—were funded at the county level.[31]

In February 2002, a governmental body examined the budgetary impact of trial court restructuring in New York State; first, it was observed that "no state in the nation has a more complex court system structure than New York's, which consists of 11 separate courts—the Supreme Court, the Court of Claims, the County Court, the Family Court, the Surrogate's Court, the New York City Civil and Criminal Courts, the District Courts on Long Island, the City Courts outside of New York City, and the Town and Village Justice Courts." The study noted the "numerous inefficiencies" of the arcane court structure while listing a number of benefits that would accrue to court unification—including an annual estimated net savings of $131.4 million over a 5-year period.[32]

According to the National Center for State Courts, today 10 states and the District of Columbia are identified as having unified court systems (California, Connecticut, Illinois, Iowa, Kansas, Minnesota, Missouri, North and South Dakota, and Wisconsin).[33] This change can be partly attributed to the growing caseload pressures at the trial and appellate levels, mentioned previously. Furthermore, growing numbers of state courts sought to consolidate and professionalize systems that were highly fragmented, like that of New York's. This unification movement also increased professionalism among court judicial, clerical, and administrative staff (court personnel, including administrators, are discussed in Chapter 7). Over half of all the states have mandated that their trial court judges hold law degrees and take judicial education classes while serving on the bench.[34]

TRIAL COURTS

General Jurisdiction: Major Trial Courts

Trial courts of general jurisdiction are usually referred to as the *major trial courts*. There are an estimated 2,000 major trial courts in the 50 states and Washington, D.C., staffed with more than 11,500 general-jurisdiction judges. The term *general jurisdiction* means that these courts have the legal authority to decide all matters not specifically delegated to lower courts; this division of jurisdiction is specified in law. The most common names for these courts are *district, circuit*, and *superior*.[35]

Each court has its own support staff consisting of a clerk of court, a sheriff, and others. In most states, the trial courts of general jurisdiction are also grouped into judicial districts or circuits. In rural areas, these districts or circuits encompass several adjoining counties, and the judges are true generalists who hear a wide variety of cases and literally ride the circuit; conversely, larger counties have only one circuit or district for the area, and the judges are often specialists assigned to hear only certain types of cases.[36]

The great majority of the nation's judicial business occurs at the state, not the federal, level. State courts decide primarily street crimes. The more serious criminal violations are heard

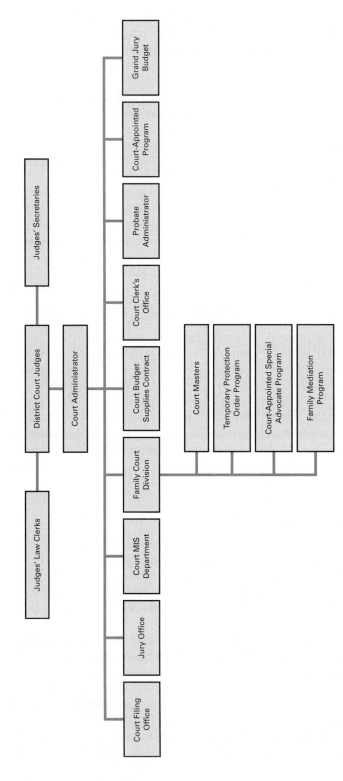

FIGURE 6.5 Organizational Structure of a District Court Serving a Population of 300,000 (MIS = Management Information Systems)

in the trial courts of general jurisdiction. State courts must also process a rising volume of drug-related offenses. Over the past 15 years, the number of criminal cases filed in general jurisdiction courts has increased by 25 percent; most criminal cases do not go to trial; thus, the dominant issue in the trial courts of general jurisdiction is not guilt or innocence, but what penalty to apply to the guilty.[37]

Figure 6.5 shows the organizational structure of a county district court serving a population of 300,000. Note the variety of functions and programs that exist in addition to the basic court role of hearing trials and rendering dispositions.

It should also be noted that within the trial courts, a number of problem-solving or specialty courts—helping offenders with drug and mental health issues, as well as military veterans experiencing problems (all of which is discussed in Chapter 8)—have also become more common.[38] Exhibit 6.2 speaks to those courts and several other aspects of court administration, looking at whether or not these courts have a culture of their own.

EXHIBIT 6.2

Is There a Legal Culture within the Trial Courts?

Do criminal trial courts have a legal culture, with distinctive norms, values, beliefs, and expectations? The National Institute of Justice funded a study that set out to answer that question. Data were obtained by surveying judges, senior court administrators, and prosecuting/defense attorneys to gauge their views concerning how their courts handled cases, managed relationships between judges and court staff, and exercised courthouse leadership.

The study determined that there were four cultural orientations that can shape the conduct and performance of U.S. state trial courts: communal, networked, autonomous, and hierarchical.

1. *Communal* courts emphasize *flexibility*; general agreement on performance goals exists, but centralized judicial and administrative staff leadership is downplayed and creativity is encouraged. As a result, alternative and acceptable ways exist for individual judges to apply court rules, policies, and procedures. Here, judges and administrators emphasize the importance of getting along and acting collectively; group involvement, mutually agreed upon goals, teamwork, and developing a humane work environment are emphasized.

2. *Networked* courts emphasize *judicial consensus.* Judicial expectations, creativity, innovation, and policymaking involve planning efforts of the entire bench. As innovators, these courts attempt to incorporate the latest thinking in specialty courts, problem-solving courts, and therapeutic justice. The networked court hopes to achieve both high solidarity and high sociability—judges, court administrators, and other court staff coordinate and work together to accomplish the work of the court.

3. *Autonomous* courts emphasize *self-management.* Limited discussion and agreement exist on the importance of court-wide performance goals. Judges and administrators emphasize the importance of allowing each judge to conduct business as he or she sees fit. Many judges in this type of court are most comfortable with the traditional adversarial model of dispute resolution, wherein the judge is relatively passive and essentially referees the cases presented by attorneys.

4. *Hierarchical* courts emphasize *clear rules.* Judges are committed to the use of case flow management (e.g., case coordination and firm trial dates), and written court rules and

procedures are emphasized and applied uniformly by judges. These courts seek to achieve the advantages of order and efficiency, and the approach is to create a structured decision-making environment.

The survey also determined that every court surveyed exhibited a combination of cultures, that is, no court is wholly one type in its cultural nature. However, in every court, a particular culture tends to dominate each work area. Although there is no "correct" culture for a particular area of work, different cultural orientations do affect how work is accomplished. In sum, the conventional wisdom that U.S. courts are generally loosely run organizations dominated by autonomous judges who resist administrative controls is not supported.

Source: Based on Brian J. Ostrom, Charles W. Ostrom, Roger A. Hanson, Matthew Kleiman, *The Mosaic of Institutional Culture and Performance: Trial Courts as Organizations*, November 2005, pp. 51–52, http://www.ncjrs.gov/pdffiles1/nij/grants/212083.pdf (accessed October 15, 2010).

Limited Jurisdiction: Lower Courts

At the lowest level of state courts are trial courts of limited jurisdiction, also known as *inferior courts* or *lower courts*. There are more than 13,500 trial courts of limited jurisdiction in the United States, staffed with about 18,000 judicial officers. The lower courts constitute 85 percent of all judicial bodies in the United States.

EXHIBIT 6.3

An Insider's View of a Lower Court

A lower court judge provided compelling realism and insight—as well as a bit of humor— on his court's website concerning the proper decorum and performance of lawyers who are about to litigate cases therein:

> We tend to be the fast-food operators of the court system—high volumes of traffic for short visits with a base of loyal repeat customers. Don't plan on having a private conversation with your client or a witness amidst the throngs of other people trying to do the same thing. Prepared attorneys can be in and out in short order. Meeting your client for the first time after calling out his name in the lobby can take longer.
>
> Patience is a virtue and communication with the bailiffs and court staff will keep everyone happy. We coordinate the court's calendar, your calendar, and opposing counsel's calendar with the availability of the witnesses. Here are a few other "do's" and "don'ts" for successfully navigating this Court:
>
> - Everyone goes through the metal detector. Having to go back to your car to stow your Leatherman, linoleum cutting knife, stun gun, giant padlock, or sword-cane (all items caught by security) can be annoying.
> - I once ruled against a very sweet elderly lady who reminded me of my own grandmother. She simply didn't have a case and I thought I had ruled fairly and gently. As she slowly walked by the front of the bench on the way out of the courtroom, she looked up and said, "Aw, go—yourself," and walked out

the door. My mouth was hanging open; I just didn't know what to do. I'm fairly sure that this is the first and last time someone will get away with this, so even if the judge rules against you, smile on the way out. You can mutter to yourself all you want on the way back to the office rather than the holding cell in the back of the courthouse.

- I once watched a gentleman in the back row feed his parrot peanuts while it was sitting on his shoulder. I assumed I had a parrot case in the pile somewhere, but after the last case was called, the parrot left without testifying. I asked the security officer why he let the man with the parrot come into court. I was told that the man had been there to watch a friend's case and that his sick parrot needed to be fed every 15 minutes. While admiring the logic of his decision, I have advised our new court security officers that unless an animal is actually a service animal, various beasts, fish, and fowl are not allowed in simply to watch court.

- Expect the unexpected. Recent interesting events include a live pipe bomb being left at the front door by a concerned citizen; a gentleman dancing on top of his motor home in the parking lot while his laundry hung from the trees and his morning coffee perked on the propane stove he had set up in the next space; and the occasional ammonia discharges into the holding cell by one of the neighboring businesses.

Source: Based on Hon. Kevin Higgins, "An Insider's View of Justice Court," *Nevada Lawyer*, August 2008, http://www.judgehiggins.com/an-insiders-view-of-the-sparks-justice-court.php (accessed August 20, 2010).

Variously called *district, justice, justice of the peace, city, magistrate,* or *municipal courts,* the lower courts decide a restricted range of cases. These courts are created and maintained by city or county governments and, therefore, are not part of the state judiciary. The caseload of the lower courts is staggering—more than 34 million criminal and civil cases filed per year, the overwhelming number of which are traffic cases (more than 41 million in any given year)—more than half of which is traffic related.[39]

The workload of the lower courts can be divided into felony criminal cases, non-felony criminal cases, and civil cases. In the felony arena, lower court jurisdiction typically includes the preliminary stages of felony cases. Therefore, after an arrest, a judge in a trial court of limited jurisdiction will hold the initial appearance, appoint counsel for indigents, and conduct the preliminary hearing. Later, the case is transferred to a trial court of general jurisdiction (discussed previously) for trial (or plea) and sentencing.[40] Note: Appendix I contains a quiz, consisting of five questions, which checks your knowledge concerning the actions and jurisdiction of federal and state courts.

THE INFLUENCE OF COURTS IN POLICYMAKING

The judicial branch has the responsibility to determine the legislative intent of the law and to provide public forums—the courts—for resolving disputes. This is accomplished by determining the facts and their legal significance in each case. If the court determines the legal significance of the facts by applying an existing rule of law, it is engaging in pure dispute resolution.[41] On the contrary, "if to resolve the dispute the court must create a new rule or modify an old one that is law creation."[42]

Determining what the law says and providing a public forum involves the courts in policymaking. **Policymaking** can be defined as choosing among alternative choices of action, particularly in the allocation of limited resources "where the chosen action affects the behavior and well being of others who are subject to the policymaker's authority."[43] The policy decisions of the courts affect virtually all of us in our daily lives. In recent decades, the courts have been asked to deal with issues that previously were within the purview of the legislative and judicial branches. Because many of the Constitution's limitations on government are couched in vague language, the judicial branch must eventually deal with potentially volatile social issues such as those involving prisons, abortion, and schools.[44]

U.S. Supreme Court decisions have dramatically changed race relations, resulted in the overhaul of juvenile courts, increased the rights of the accused, prohibited prayer and segregation in public schools, legalized abortion, and allowed for destruction of the U.S. flag. State and federal courts have together overturned minimum residency requirements for welfare recipients, equalized school expenditures, and prevented road and highway construction from damaging the environment. They have eliminated the requirement of a high school diploma for a firefighter's job and ordered increased property taxes to desegregate public schools. The only governmental area that has not witnessed judicial policymaking since the Civil War is foreign affairs. Cases in which courts make policy determinations usually involve government, the Fourteenth Amendment, and the need for equity—the remedy most often used against governmental violations of law. Recent policymaking decisions by the judicial branch have not been based on the Constitution, but rather on federal statutes concerning the rights of the disadvantaged and consumers and the environment.[45]

Perhaps nowhere have the nation's courts had more of an impact than in the prisons—from which nearly 60,000 prisoner petitions are filed each year in the U.S. district courts.[46] Among the accomplishments of judicial intervention have been extending recognized constitutional rights of free speech, religion, and due process to prisoners; abolishing the South's plantation model of prisons; accelerating the professionalization of U.S. correctional managers; encouraging a new generation of correctional administrators more amenable to reform; reinforcing the adoption of national standards for prisons; and promoting increased accountability and efficiency of prisons. The only failure of judicial intervention has been its inability to prevent the explosion in prison populations and costs.[47]

The courts have become particularly involved in administrative policy because of public interest group litigation. For example, legislation was enacted allowing citizen lawsuits when certain federal regulatory agencies, such as the Environmental Protection Agency (EPA), failed to perform certain duties as required by statute. Thus, a citizens' environmental group was allowed to sue the EPA.

It may appear that the courts are too broad in their review of issues. However, it should be remembered that judges "cannot impose their views until someone brings a case to court, often as a last resort after complaints to unresponsive legislators and executives."[48] Plaintiffs must be truly aggrieved or have *standing*. The independence of the judicial branch, particularly at the federal court level, at which judges enjoy lifetime appointments, allows the courts to champion the causes of the underclasses: those with fewer financial resources or votes (by virtue of, say, being a minority group) or without a positive public profile.[49] It is also important to note that the judiciary is the "least dangerous branch," having no enforcement powers. Moreover, the decisions of the courts can be overturned by legislative action. Even decisions based on the Constitution can be overruled by subsequent constitutional amendment. Thus, the judicial branch depends on a perception of legitimacy surrounding its decisions.[50]

Summary

This chapter reviewed the distinctive nature of the courts and their organization and some of their administration. Several areas were highlighted, including the nature of the courts in terms of the status they are accorded and their use of the adversarial system in trying to arrive at the truth; the dual system of courts in our country—the courts of last resort, appeals courts, and trial courts at the federal and state levels; and how the federal courts are administered and the growing movement toward court unification. We also discussed the role of courts in policymaking.

With regard to court unification, a need and an issue that is indicated in this chapter is that of court reform because of the often confusing way in which courts and judges are organized and utilized; many notable authorities believe changes are necessary to improve court efficiency and possibly to save large amounts of public money. It is clear, however, that until a number of political and tradition-based impediments are overcome, widespread court reform is unlikely.

Another issue raised in this chapter is the burgeoning caseloads of the courts; alternative dispute resolution, discussed in Chapter 8, is proposed as a means of helping in this area of court operation.

Questions for Review

1. In what ways are courts "hallowed" and unique in our society in terms of their décor and required decorum?
2. How is the adversarial system of justice related to the truth-seeking function of the courts?
3. What is the organization of our dual court system, and what are the primary functions of each of the major types of courts that exist within the federal and state court systems?
4. What are some of the traditions of the U.S. Supreme Court, and what functions do they provide?
5. What are some perceived benefits of unifying the state court systems, and how would a unified state court system be organized?
6. What are the types of, and reasons for, court jurisdiction?
7. How do the courts influence public policymaking?

Learn by Doing

1. You are a court administrator and have been invited to appear at a luncheon meeting of a local civic group of community and business leaders. While discussing your duties within the state court system, you are asked to explain the overall functions and interrelationship between the federal and state courts; how do you reply?
2. A county historical society has invited your criminal justice professor to speak at a meeting concerning the history and importance of the traditions within the U.S. Supreme Court. Your professor asks you, the graduate assistant, to draft an overview for this purpose. What will you write?
3. You are a teaching assistant in your university's criminal justice department and your instructor has fallen ill at the outset of the semester. As your instructor is a J.D./Ph.D., she often instructs courts courses. You are tasked to develop a 1-hour lecture on how state trial courts of general jurisdiction (i.e., the major trial courts) differ in scope and function from the higher state courts of last resort as well as appellate courts. What will you include in your lecture?

Related Websites

Administrative Offices of the United States Courts
   http://www.uscourts.gov/adminoff.html
American Arbitration Association
   http://www.adr.org/

Courts.Net
   http://www.courts.net
Court TV
   http://www.courttv.com

Court Operations and Administration
http://www.jud.state.ct.us/ystday/adminop.html

International Chamber of Commerce–Arbitration Commission
http://www.iccwbo.org/policy/arbitration/id2882/index.html

Law.Com
http://www.law.com

Law Guru
http://www.lawguru.com

National Arbitration Forum
http://www.arb-forum.com/

National Center for State Courts
http://www.ncsconline.org

U.S. Equal Opportunity Commission
http://www.eeoc.gov/mediate/index.html

Notes

1. Alexis de Tocqueville, *Democracy in America,* Vol. 1, trans. H. Reeve (New York: D. Appleton, 1904), pp. 283–284.
2. H. Ted Rubin, *The Courts: Fulcrum of the Justice System* (Santa Monica, CA: Goodyear, 1976), p. 3.
3. Stephen Whicher and R. Spiller (eds.), *The Early Lectures of Ralph Waldo Emerson* (Philadelphia: University of Pennsylvania Press, 1953), p. 112.
4. 382 U.S. 406 (1966), 416.
5. Thomas L. Steffen, "Truth as Second Fiddle: Reevaluating the Place of Truth in the Adversarial Trial Ensemble," *Utah Law Review* 4 (1988):821.
6. W. Alschuler, "The Preservation of a Client's Confidences: One Value Among Many or a Categorical Imperative?" *University of Colorado Law Review* 52 (1981):349.
7. David W. Neubauer, *America's Courts and the Criminal Justice System,* 9th ed. (Belmont, CA: Thomson Wadsworth, 2008), p. 63.
8. Supreme Court of the United States, "Instructions for Admission to the Bar," http://www.supreme courtus.gov/bar/barinstructions.pdf (accessed November 8, 2010).
9. Ibid., "Visitor's Guide to Oral Arguments," p. 1, http://www.supremecourt.gov/visiting/visitorsgui detooralargument.aspx (accessed August 8, 2011).
10. Robert H. Jackson Center, "The Flags at Nuremberg," http://www.robertjackson.org/Man/Speeches_About_Nuremberg_ Cole (accessed January 11, 2008).
11. Supreme Court of the United States, "The Court and Its Traditions," http://www.supremecourtus.gov/about/traditions.pdf (accessed August 8, 2011).
12. United States Courts, "U.S. Supreme Court Procedures," http://www.uscourts.gov/Educational Resources/ConstitutionResources/SeparationOf Powers/USSupremeCourtProcedures.aspx (accessed August 8, 2011).
13. Ibid., "Writs of Certiorari," http://www.uscourts. gov/EducationalResources/ConstitutionResources/ SeparationOfPowers/USSupremeCourtProcedures. aspx (accessed August 8, 2011).
14. See University of Missouri – Kansas City Law School, "Exploring Constitutional Conflict: The Supreme Court in the American System of Government," http://law2.umkc.edu/faculty/projects/ftrials/conlaw/ supremecourtintro.html (accessed August 8, 2011).
15. Supreme Court of the United States, "Members," http://www.supremecourt.gov/about/about_us.aspx (accessed August 8, 2011).
16. Federal Judicial Center, "The U.S. Courts of Appeals and the Federal Judiciary," http://www.fjc.gov/history/ home.nsf (accessed November 8, 2010).
17. U.S. Courts, "U.S. Courts of Appeals—Appeals Commenced, Terminated, and Pending—During the 12-Month Periods Ending March 31, 2008 and 2009," http://www.uscourts.gov/caseload2006/ contents.html (accessed November 8, 2010).
18. U.S. Courts, "Judicial Facts and Figures," http:// www.uscourts.gov/uscourts/Statistics/Judicial-FactsAndFigures/2008/alljudicialfactsfigures.pdf (accessed November 8, 2010).
19. United States Courts, "Federal Judgeships," http:// www.uscourts.gov/JudgesAndJudgeships/Federal Judgeships.aspx (accessed November 8, 2010).
20. Ibid.
21. United States Courts, "Judicial Caseload Indicators," http://www.uscourts.gov/Viewer.aspx?doc=/ uscourts/Statistics/FederalJudicialCaseload Statistics/2009/front/IndicatorsMar09.pdf (accessed November 8, 2010).
22. Neubauer, *America's Courts and the Criminal Justice System,* p. 68.
23. U.S. Courts, "The Federal Judiciary," http://www. uscourts.gov/adminoff.html (accessed November 8, 2010).
24. Neubauer, *America's Courts and the Criminal Justice System,* p. 85.
25. Ibid., p. 87.

26. U.S. Department of Justice, Bureau of Justice Statistics, *State Court Organization, 1987–2004.* (Washington, DC: Author, October 2007), p. 3.

27. National Center for State Courts, "Appellate Caseloads," http://www.ncsconline.org/d_research/csp/2007B_files/Appellate.pdf (accessed November 8, 2010).

28. Neubauer, *America's Courts and the Criminal Justice System*, p. 85.

29. Ibid., p. 90.

30. U.S. Department of Justice, Bureau of Justice Statistics, *State Court Organization*, p. 5.

31. Ibid.

32. New York State Unified Court System, "The Budgetary Impact of Trial Court Restructuring," http://www.nycourts.gov/reports/trialcourtrestructuring/ctmerger/2802.pdf (accessed January 8, 2008).

33. National Center for State Courts, "Court Unification FAQs," http://www.ncsc.org/topics/court-management/court-unification/faq.aspx#How many states have unified court systems (Accessed August 27, 2011).

34. U.S. Department of Justice, Bureau of Justice Statistics, *State Court Organization*, p. 1.

35. National Center for State Courts, "State Court Caseload Statistics," http://www.ncsconline.org/D_Research/csp/2007_files/StateCourtCaseload StatisticsFINAL.pdf (accessed November 8, 2010).

36. Neubauer, *America's Courts and the Criminal Justice System*, p. 82.

37. Ibid., pp. 82–83.

38. U.S. Department of Justice, Bureau of Justice Statistics, *State Court Organization*, p. 3.

39. See National Center for State Courts, "Trial Courts: Criminal Caseloads," http://www.ncsconline.org/D_Research/csp/2007B_files/criminal.pdf; and ibid., "Trial Courts: Criminal Caseloads," "http://www.ncsconline.org/D_Research/csp/2007B_files/civil.pdf (accessed November 8, 2010).

40. Ibid., pp. 402–403.

41. Howard Abadinsky, *Law and Justice: An Introduction to the American Legal System,* 4th ed. (Chicago: Nelson-Hall, 1999), p. 33.

42. Richard A. Posner, *The Federal Courts: Crisis and Reform* (Cambridge, MA: Harvard University Press, 1985), p. 3.

43. Harold J. Spaeth, *Supreme Court Policy Making: Explanation and Prediction* (San Francisco, CA: W. H. Freeman, 1979), p. 19.

44. Abadinsky, *Law and Justice,* p. 174.

45. Ibid., p. 170.

46. U.S. Department of Justice, *Sourcebook of Criminal Justice Statistics 2000* (Washington, DC: U.S. Government Printing Office, 2001), p. 467.

47. Malcolm M. Feeley and Edward L. Rubin, *Judicial Policy Making and the Modern State: How the Courts Reformed America's Prisons* (New York: Cambridge University Press, 1998).

48. Stephen L. Wasby, *The Supreme Court in the Federal System,* 3rd ed. (Chicago: Nelson-Hall, 1989), p. 5.

49. Abadinsky, *Law and Justice,* p. 171.

50. Ibid., p. 166.

Court Personnel Roles
and Functions

KEY TERMS AND CONCEPTS

Chief justice

Court administration

Court management

Courtroom civility

Executive appointment

Judges' use of social networking sites

Judicial administration

Judicial selection

Jury administration

Merit selection

Missouri Bar Plan

Model Code of Judicial Conduct

Nonpartisan elections

Notorious cases

Partisan elections

The National Judicial College (NJC)

LEARNING OBJECTIVES

After reading this chapter, the student will:

- be able to define and understand judicial administration and court administration
- understand the methods of judicial selection: partisan elections, nonpartisan elections, merit selection, and appointment
- understand how civility is maintained in the courtroom, the meaning of *good judging*, and a new model code of conduct for state and local judges
- be able to explain some ethical considerations surrounding judges' personal and professional use of social networking sites
- know the benefits and problems encountered by judges, including the problems faced by newly appointed judges
- be familiar with the duties of judges who serve as court managers, including the Chief Justice of the United States Supreme Court
- know the importance of court clerks
- understand the six major duties of court administrators
- know the five strategies that judges follow in determining the quality of administrators' work
- understand the components of jury administration, including special considerations during notorious cases

Four things belong to a Judge:
To hear courteously,
To answer wisely,
To consider soberly, and
To decide impartially.

—Socrates

INTRODUCTION

Chapter 6 looked at the "hallowed" nature of the courts and at how the courts and judges—with gavels, flowing robes, ornate surroundings, and other aspects of décor and decorum that are accorded their office—are enveloped in a mystique of importance and authority. This chapter expands that discussion, focusing more on judges and other key personnel who are involved in court administration.

The administration of the judicial process is probably the least understood area of justice administration and possibly all of criminal justice. This lack of understanding is compounded by the fact that, very often, even judges and court administrators are not formally trained in their roles. Furthermore, few judges would probably "like to spend all day or most of the day handling union grievances or making sure that employees know what their benefits are."[1] Opportunities to receive training and education are expanding, however, and this chapter addresses some of the means by which that can be accomplished.

This chapter opens by defining and distinguishing the terms *judicial administration* and *court administration* and then considering judges: how they ascend to the bench, benefits and problems of the position, and some thoughts on good judging and courtroom civility; included here are discussions of a revised code of conduct for state and local judges as well as some ethical considerations concerning judges' personal and professional use of social networking sites. Then, we specifically examine the judge's role as the ultimate judicial administrator. The historically important role of court clerks is then reviewed, and next, we examine the relatively new position of the specially trained court administrator, including training and duties, judges' evaluation criteria, and conflict among judicial administrators. This is followed by an overview of the problems court administrators might confront in creating and maintaining juries, especially during sequestration and notorious trials.

DEFINING JUDICIAL ADMINISTRATION

The purpose of judicial independence is to mitigate arbitrariness in judging. But what is the purpose of **judicial administration**? That is more difficult to define. Consequently, as Russell Wheeler noted, "many court administrators today find themselves under the inevitable strain of not knowing for certain what their purpose is."[2]

Most works on judicial administration point to Roscoe Pound as the founder of the study of judicial administration because of his 1906 essay "The Causes of Popular Dissatisfaction with Administration of Justice."[3] Pound's essay was a call to improve **court administration** and a preview of his theory of law. It has remained a classic statement on the need for efficient and equitable judicial administration. Pound acknowledged that some people have always been dissatisfied with the law, but he contended that the courts were archaic and did indeed need to be administered more effectively. He also noted that the adversary system often turned litigation into a game, irritating parties, jurors, and witnesses and giving the public a false notion of the purpose and end of law. Pound's lecture remains a treasure trove of ideas concerning the management of courts. Many states have also heeded Pound's advice and unified their trial courts (discussed in Chapter 6), thereby eliminating several layers of courts.[4]

However, one should properly regard as just as much a founding document a major essay by Woodrow Wilson written 19 years earlier (in 1887), entitled "The Study of Administration." Wilson stressed that the vocation of administration was a noble calling and not a task for which every person was competent.[5] He emphasized that policy and administration are two different matters and, with great foresight, wrote that judges are responsible for judging and "establishing fundamental court policy," and that a third task was for a "trained executive officer, working under the chief judge or presiding judge, [to] relieve judges generally [of] the function of handling the numerous business and administrative affairs of the courts."[6] Courts have not always regarded administration as a noble calling, but they have always defended the distinction Wilson drew between policy and administration.[7]

Wilson's essay certainly gives intellectual respectability to the field of administration. However, it also poses two troubling problems. First, although it may be accurate in the abstract to state that a wall exists between administration and policy, almost every administrator and policymaker knows, as Wheeler phrased it, that "the wall is full of many gaps and is easily scaled."[8] Policy decisions inevitably intertwine with administrative decisions. Second, trying to honor this policy–administration dichotomy would leave the administrator adrift when confronted with inevitable policy decisions. For example, today's court administrator must often set policy for dealing with issues such as celebrity cases, evidence, case scheduling, and the use of cameras in the courtroom—the kinds of issues discussed here and in Chapter 8.

The difficulty of defining judicial administration became obvious during the 1970s, when it nevertheless became an attractive vocation. Various people and commissions tried to define it but seemed capable only of listing the duties of the office. For example, the National Advisory Commission on Criminal Justice Standards and Goals stated in 1973 that "the basic purpose of court administration is to relieve judges of some administrative chores and to help them perform those they retain."[9] Furthermore, in 1974, the American Bar Association specified a variety of functions for the court administrator to perform "under the authority of the judicial council and the supervision of the chief justice."[10]

The problem of definition continued into the 1980s; one law professor who had conducted a great deal of research in the field believed in 1987 that the safest approach was "not . . . to attempt a definition" but simply "to accept that it is a sub-branch of administration—more precisely of public administration."[11]

To help solve this problem and provide more clarity, a good working definition of judicial administration was advanced by Russell Wheeler and Howard Whitcomb; this definition allows an analysis from a variety of perspectives: "The direction of and influences on the activities of those who are expected to contribute to just and efficient case processing—except legal doctrinal considerations, insofar as they dispose of the particular factual and legal claims presented in a case."[12] This definition also separates the judicial and nonjudicial functions of the court, and it implies that a *set* of people share a role norm and that judicial administration constitutes *all* of the factors that direct and influence those people.[13]

Notably, however, the term *court administration* might be conceived of loosely as the specific activities of those persons who are organizationally responsible for manipulating these various judicial administration directions and influences.[14] This term is more commonly used in this chapter because I focus on the development of the role and functions of the *individual trial court administrator*. This will become clearer as the chapter unfolds and the relationship between judge and court administrator is discussed.

THE JURISTS

Those Who Would Be Judges: Methods of Selection

To a large extent, the quality of justice Americans receive depends on the quality of the judges who dispense it. Many factors have a bearing on the quality of judicial personnel: salary, length of term, prestige, independence, and personal satisfaction with the job. The most important factor considered by court reformers is judicial selection.[15]

As noted in Chapter 6, all federal judges are nominated by the president and confirmed by the Senate; they then serve for life (unless they resign or are impeached). **Judicial selection** in the state courts is very different, as judges are likely to face an election as part of their selection process and to serve fixed terms. Judicial selection occurs to fill an unexpired term upon the death, retirement, or resignation of a judge; to select for a full term; and at the end of a special term.[16]

A variety of methods are used to select judges: partisan elections, nonpartisan elections, merit selection, or appointment. Figure 7.1 depicts regional patterns in the methods of judicial selection. It shows that partisan elections are concentrated in the South, nonpartisan elections in the West and upper Midwest, legislative elections and executive appointments in the East, and merit selection in the west of the Mississippi River. How selection is conducted determines who becomes a judge.[17]

Merit Selection (17)	Partisan Election (9)	Non-Partisan Election (17)	Gubernatorial (2) or Legislative (2) Appointment	Combined Methods (4)[1]
Alaska	Alabama	Arkansas	Maine (G)	Arizona
Colorado	Illinois	California	New Jersey (G)	Indiana
Connecticut	Louisiana	Florida	South Carolina (L)	Kansas
Delaware[2]	New York	Georgia	Virginia (L)	Missouri
District of columbia	Ohio[3]	Idaho		
Hawaii[4]	Pennsylvania	Kentucky		
Iowa	Tennessee	Michigan		
Maryland[2]	Texas	Minnesota		
Massachusetts[2]	West Virginia	Mississippi		
Nebraska		Montana		
Nevada		North Carolina		
New Hampshire[2]		North Dakota		
New Mexico		Oklahoma		
Rhode Island		Oregon		
Utah		South Dakota		
Vermont		Washington		
Wyoming		Wisconsin		

1. In these states, some judges are chosen through merit selection and some are chosen in competitive elections.
2. Merit selection is established by executive order.
3. Candidates appear on the general election ballot without party affiliation but are nominated in partisan primaries.
4. The chief justice makes appointments to the district court and family court.

FIGURE 7.1   Initial Selection of State Judges (Trial Courts of General Jurisdiction)

Source: "Initial Selection of State Judges (Trial Courts of General Jurisdiction)" from *Judicial Selection in the States: Appellate and General Jurisdiction Courts,* January 2004, p. 4. Reprinted by permission of the American Judicature Society.

Following are brief discussions of the partisan election, nonpartisan election, and merit selection methods of judicial selection (only three states use the **executive appointment** method, whereby a vacancy is filled by the governor). In some states, judges are selected using **partisan elections** (the nominee's party is listed on the ballot). In other states, judges are selected using **nonpartisan elections** (no party affiliations are listed on the ballot). Nevertheless, even in these elections, partisan influences are often present: Judicial candidates are endorsed or nominated by parties, receive party support during campaigns, and are identified with party labels. In either case, although campaigns for judgeships are normally low key and low visibility, in recent years, some contests—particularly for state supreme court seats—have been contentious and costly election battles involving millions of dollars.

The general lack of information about judges and the low levels of voter interest, however, give incumbent judges important advantages in running for reelection. The prestigious title of "judge" is often listed on the ballot in front of the judge's name or on political signs and billboards. Few sitting judges are even opposed for reelection.[18]

Merit selection has been favored by court reformers wanting to "remove the courts from politics!" They point to three problems with popular elections of judges: (1) Elections fail to encourage the ablest lawyers to seek judicial posts and discourage qualified persons who want to avoid the rigors (if not the ordeal) of a campaign; (2) elections may provide an incentive for judges to decide cases in a popular manner; and (3) the elective system is a contest in which the electorate is likely to be uninformed about the merits of the candidates. To solve these problems, reformers advocate merit selection, also known as the **Missouri Bar Plan**. Thirty-four states and the District of Columbia use the merit system, and a number of other states have considered it. Merit selection involves the creation of a nominating commission whenever a vacancy occurs for any reason; the commission is composed of lawyers and laypersons; this group suggests a list of qualified nominees (usually three) to the governor, who chooses one person as the judge. After serving a period on the bench, the new judge stands uncontested before the voters. The sole question on the ballot is: "Should Judge X be retained in office?" If the incumbent wins a majority of the votes, then he or she earns a full term of office, and each subsequent term is secured through another uncontested *retention ballot*. Most judges are returned to office by a healthy margin.[19]

The question is often raised as to which method is best for choosing judges. A key criterion is whether one system produces better judges than the others. In short, methods of judicial selection are not related to judges' personal characteristics. No evidence exists that one selection system produces better judges than another.[20]

However, many experts—both individuals and groups—strongly believe that candidates for judgeships should not have to run for election to that office. For instance, retired U.S. Supreme Court Justice Sandra Day O'Connor said in November 2007 that she would do away with such partisan elections because candidates for judgeships risk being compromised by the growing amount of campaign funds they must raise; she stated, "If I could wave a magic wand, I would wave it to secure some kind of merit selection of judges across the country."[21] After O'Connor's home state of Arizona switched from partisan elections of judges to an appointed system in the 1970s, she "watched the improvement of the judiciary in the state."[22]

Similarly, the American Judicature Society has supported limiting the role of politics in the selection of state judges, compiling comprehensive information on judicial selection processes in each of the 50 states and the District of Columbia and providing a website on the subject (at http://www.judicialselection.us/; topics covered include methods of selecting, retaining, and removing judges; successful and unsuccessful reform efforts; the roles of parties, interest groups, and professional organizations in selecting judges; and the diversity of the bench).[23]

Judicial Benefits and Problems

Judges enjoy several benefits of office, including life terms for federal positions and in some states. Ascending to the bench can be the capstone of a successful legal career for a lawyer, even though a judge's salary can be less than that of a lawyer in private practice. Judges certainly warrant a high degree of respect and prestige as well; from arrest to final disposition, the accused face judges at every juncture involving important decisions about their future: bail, pretrial motions, evidence presentation, trial, and punishment.

Although it would seem that judges are the primary decision makers in the court, such is not always the case. Judges often accept recommendations from others who are more familiar with the case—for example, bail recommendations from prosecutors, plea agreements struck by prosecuting and defense counsels, and sentence recommendations from the probation officer. These kinds of input are frequently accepted by judges in the informal courtroom network that exists. Although judges run the court, if they deviate from the consensus of the courtroom work group, they may be sanctioned: Attorneys can make court dockets go awry by requesting continuances or by not having witnesses appear on time.

EXHIBIT 7.1

Judges Must Train to Take the Bench

At the **National Judicial College (NJC)** in Reno, Nevada, classroom bells—not gavels and bailiffs—rule the day. And the underlying message rings loud: Wearing a black robe alone does not make a judge. In times when the legal profession and the courts are coming under increased scrutiny and public criticism, the weight of judicial robes can be heavy.

At the judicial college, the goal is not only to coach lawyers on how to be judges but also to teach veteran judges how to be better arbiters of justice. For many lawyers, the move to the other side of the bench is an awesome transition. "Judges aren't born judges," said former U.S. Supreme Court Justice Sandra Day O'Connor, who attended the NJC on her election as an Arizona Superior Court judge in 1974. She recalled her anxieties the first time she assumed the bench: "It was frightening, really. There was so much to think about and to learn." Justice Anthony M. Kennedy, who is on the judicial college's faculty, described the college as

> an institutional reminder of the very basic proposition that an independent judiciary is essential in any society that is going to be based on the rule of law. Judicial independence cannot exist unless you have skilled, dedicated, and principled judges. This leads to so many different areas—judicial demeanor, how to control a courtroom, basic rules of civility, how to control attorneys. These are difficult skills for judges to learn. They're not something judges innately have. Judges have to acquire these skills.

Founded in 1963, the college put on its first course the following year in Boulder, Colorado. It is the only full-time institution in the country that provides judicial training primarily for state judges. It is affiliated with the American Bar Association, which pays about 10 percent of the college's annual budget. Other money comes from an endowment fund, donations, and program tuition and fees. The NJC offers about 96 on-site courses and about 10 online each year, ranging from a few days' duration to several weeks. Regular curriculum includes courses on courtroom technology; dealing with jurors; courtroom disruptions; domestic violence; managing complex cases; death penalty issues; traffic cases; ethics; mediation; family law; forensic, medical, and scientific evidence; and opinion writing.

As legal issues become increasingly complex and courts become overloaded with cases, judicial training becomes more critical. As stated by Joseph R. Weisberger, chief justice of the Rhode Island Supreme Court and an NJC instructor for 30 years, "It is the judiciary that transforms constitutional rights and liberties from a piece of parchment and printed words into living, breathing reality."

Sources: Based on The National Judicial College, "2011 Courses at a Glance," http://www.judges.org/pdf/2011_coursesglance.pdf (Accessed August 27, 2011); information also taken from Sandra Chereb, Associated Press, "Judges Must Train to Take the Bench," *Reno Gazette-Journal*, May 28, 1996, pp. 1B, 5B.

Other problems can await a new jurist-elect or appointee. Judges who are new to the bench commonly face three general problems:

1. ***Mastering the breadth of law they must know and apply.*** New judges would be wise, at least early in their career, to depend on other court staff, lawyers who appear before them, and experienced judges for invaluable information on procedural and substantive aspects

of the law and local court procedures. Through informal discussions and formal meetings, judges learn how to deal with common problems. Judicial training schools and seminars have also been developed to ease the transition into the judiciary. For example, the National Judicial College (NJC), located on the campus of the University of Nevada, Reno, is a full-time institution offering nearly 100 educational sessions per year—including a number that are offered on the Web as well as in 10 cities across the country—for more than 3,300 state judges, including judges from around the world (see Exhibit 7.1).

2. ***Administering the court and the docket while supervising court staff.*** One of the most frustrating aspects of being a judge is the heavy caseload and corresponding administrative problems. Instead of having time to reflect on challenging legal questions or to consider the proper sentence for a convicted felon, trial judges must move cases. They can seldom act like a judge in the "grand tradition." As Abraham Blumberg noted several years ago, the working judge must be a politician, administrator, bureaucrat, and lawyer in order to cope with the crushing calendar of cases.[24] Judges are required to be competent administrators, a fact of judicial life that comes as a surprise to many new judges. One survey of 30 federal judges found that 23 (77 percent) acknowledged having major administrative difficulties on first assuming the bench. Half complained of heavy caseloads, stating that their judgeship had accumulated backlogs and that other adverse conditions compounded the problem. A federal judge maintained that it takes about 4 years to "get a full feel of a docket."[25]

   The NJC offers several courses that can assist judges in better administering their courts. The following 1-week courses are available:

   - Court Management for Judges and Court Administrators (covering topics such as managing human resources, conflict resolution, team building, budgeting, data collection, public relations)
   - Management Skills for Presiding Judges
   - Judges as Change Agents: Problem-Solving Courts

   The National Center for State Courts in Williamsburg, Virginia, also has a program designed specifically for management and leadership in the courts: the Institute for Court Management's Court Executive Development Program (CEDP).[26]

3. ***Coping with the psychological discomfort that accompanies the new position.*** Most trial judges experience psychological discomfort on assuming the bench. Seventy-seven percent of new federal judges acknowledged having psychological problems in at least one of five areas: maintaining a judicial bearing both on and off the bench, the loneliness of the judicial office, sentencing criminals, forgetting the adversary role, and local pressure. One aspect of the judicial role is that of assuming a proper mien, or "learning to act like a judge." One judge remembers his first day in court: "I'll never forget going into my courtroom for the first time with the robes and all, and the crier tells everyone to rise. You sit down and realize that it's all different, that everyone is looking at you and you're supposed to do something."[27] Like police officers and probation and parole workers, judges complain that they "can't go to the places you used to. You always have to be careful about what you talk about. When you go to a party, you have to be careful not to drink too much so you won't make a fool of yourself."[28] And the position can be a lonely one:

   > After you become a … judge some people tend to avoid you. For instance, you lose all your lawyer friends and generally have to begin to make new friends. I guess the lawyers are afraid that they will some day have a case before you and it would be awkward for them if they were on too close terms with you.[29]

Judges frequently describe sentencing criminals as the most difficult aspect of their job: "This is the hardest part of being a judge. You see so many pathetic people and you're never sure of what is a right or a fair sentence."[30]

JUDGES AND COURTROOM CIVILITY

"Good Judging"

What traits make for good judging? Obviously, judges should treat each case and all parties before them in court with absolute impartiality and dignity while providing leadership as the steward of their organization in all of the **court management** areas described in the following section. In addition to those official duties, however, other issues and suggestions have been put forth.

For example, a retired jurist with 20 years on the Wisconsin Supreme Court maintained that the following qualities define the art and craft of judging:

- Judges are keenly aware that they occupy a special place in a democratic society. They exercise their power in the most undemocratic of institutions with great restraint.
- They are aware of the necessity for intellectual humility—an awareness that what they think they know might well be incorrect.
- They do not allow the law to become their entire life; they get out of the courtroom, mingle with the public, and remain knowledgeable about current events.[31]

Other writers believe that judges should remember that the robe does not confer omniscience or omnipotence; as one trial attorney put it, "Your name is now 'Your Honor,' but you are still the same person you used to be, warts and all."[32] As if it weren't difficult enough to strive for and maintain humility, civility, and balance in their personal lives, judges must also enforce **courtroom civility**. Many persons have observed that we are becoming an increasingly uncivil society; the courts are certainly not immune to acts involving misconduct (see the discussion of courthouse violence in Chapter 8).

Personal character attacks by lawyers, directed at judges, attorneys, interested parties, clerks, jurors, and witnesses, both inside and outside the courtroom, in criminal and civil actions have increased at an alarming rate in the past 15 years.[33]

Following are some examples of the kinds of conduct involved:

- An attorney stated that opposing counsel and other attorneys were "a bunch of starving slobs," "incompetents," and "stooges."[34]
- A prosecutor argued to a jury that defense witnesses were "egg-sucking, chicken-stealing gutter trash."[35]
- The prosecutor called defense counsel "maggots" and "poor excuses for human beings." Defense counsel implied that the prosecutor was a "scumbag."[36]
- Counsel in trial and argument before a jury referred to parties as "cowardly, dirty, low-down dogs."[37]

Such invective clearly does not enhance the dignity or appearance of justice and propriety that is so important to the courts' public image and function. The Code of Judicial Conduct addresses these kinds of behaviors; Canon 3B(4) requires judges to be "patient, dignified, and courteous to litigants, jurors, witnesses, lawyers, and others with whom the judge deals in an official capacity" and requires judges to demand "similar conduct of lawyers, and of staff, court officials, and others subject to the judge's direction and control."[38]

At a minimum, judges need to attempt to prevent such vitriol and discipline offenders when it occurs. Some means that judges have at their disposal to control errant counsel include attorney disqualifications, new trials, and reporting of attorneys to disciplinary boards.[39]

Problems of Their Own: Types of Judicial Misconduct

What types of misconduct among judges themselves must the judiciary confront? Sometimes, medications may affect a judge's cognitive process or emotional temperament, causing him or her to treat parties, witnesses, jurors, lawyers, and staff poorly. Some stay on the bench too long; such judges will ideally have colleagues who can approach them, suggest retirement, and explain why this would be to their benefit. And sometimes, according to one author, judicial arrogance (sometimes termed "black robe disease" or "robe-itis") is the primary problem. This is seen when judges "do not know when to close their mouths, do not treat people with dignity and compassion, do not arrive on time, or do not issue timely decisions."[40]

Some bar associations or judicial circuits perform an anonymous survey of a sample of local attorneys who have recently argued a case before a particular judge and then share the results with the judge. Sometimes, these surveys are popularity contests, but a pattern of negative responses can have a sobering effect on the judge and encourage him or her to correct bad habits. Many judges will be reluctant to acknowledge that they have problems such as those described earlier. In such cases, the chief judge may have to scold or correct a subordinate judge. Although this is difficult, it may be imperative to do so in trying to maintain good relations with bar associations, individual lawyers, and the public. A single judge's blunders and behaviors can affect the reputation of the entire judiciary as well as the workloads of the other judges in his or her judicial district. Chief judges must therefore step forward to address such problems formally or informally.[41]

Next, we discuss what is being done formally to address problems of sexual harassment within the judiciary; Chapter 8 also includes discussion of a related matter: gender bias in the courts.

A Revised Model Code of Conduct for State and Local Judges

The American Bar Association (ABA) **Model Code of Judicial Conduct** adopted in 2007 for state and local judges spells out, for the first time, that they are to avoid "sexual advances," requests for sexual favors, and other such unwelcome behavior. The code is not binding, but it has long served as a model that individual states use in adopting rules for disciplining their judges. It covers a range of conduct, including ethical behavior for judicial candidates, when judges might accept gifts, and in what instances they should disqualify themselves from hearing cases. The ABA commission that prepared the revised code said that it adopted the language on sexual harassment after hearing from witnesses who were "emphatic about the need to single out sexual harassment for special mention, given the nature, extent, and history of the problem."[42]

Judges' Use of Social Networking Sites: Some Ethical Considerations

Although they may appear stoic and quite satisfied in their roles, much has been written concerning the social isolation and professional stress that is endured by many judges. Their inability to relax socially, the feeling that one is "entering a monastery," a shrinking circle of friends, and a general sense of "becoming anonymous" has been described in the literature.[43] Certainly, the décor and decorum generally accorded to the judiciary (discussed in Chapter 6) contribute to this transition; as a clinical psychologist observed:

> The higher status conferred on the former lawyer casts wide social ripples. The subculture of the courthouse reinforces the new identity through the powerful symbolism of the robing ceremony and constant deferential behavior. This even includes the architecture of the building and courtroom with its raised bench and solemnity.[44]

Given this widespread sense of isolation, it is probably not unusual for judges to consider using social networks for both their personal and professional lives; in fact, more than one-third of state court judges and magistrates responding to a survey said they have used social media either in their personal or professional lives; more than half (56 percent) of the judges reported using routine juror instructions that included some mention of such media use during the trial; and a small fraction of courts (7 percent) even had social media profile sites like Facebook (7 percent used microblogging sites like Twitter, while 3.2 percent used visual media sharing sites like YouTube). Importantly, the survey also found that nearly half of the judges surveyed believed that a judge—in a professional capacity—could *not* participate in social networking sites without compromising ethical codes of conduct.[45]

While judges generally are free to join Internet social networks, they should insure that such activities do not otherwise violate any code of ethics. For example, prior to joining an Internet social network, a judge should consider whether participating in the network could lead to judicial disqualification in matters pending in his or her court. Another consideration is whether using social networks gives the appearance of jeopardizing the judge's independence, integrity, or impartiality. For example, joining a group promoting the legalization of marijuana and other such sites could be fraught with controversy. Even when joining a general network group (e.g., LinkedIn or a personal profile page on Facebook), the judge should be mindful of the public aspect of these networks and adjust his or her postings accordingly, so as to not project an unethical image. Likewise, an attorney or someone else appearing in the judge's court being connected to the judge through networks like Facebook or MySpace could lead to problems. At a minimum, a judge should remove the attorney or party as a "friend" from his Facebook or MySpace list until the case is over.[46]

In sum, judges can become involved with Internet social networking, but they need to take certain precautions in doing so. As a judicial ethics advisory commission in New York observed in 2009, judges should "employ an appropriate level of prudence, discretion, and decorum in how they make use of this technology."[47]

JUDGES AS COURT MANAGERS

The Administrative Office of the U.S. Courts coordinates and administers the operations of the federal courts. In the states, judges assume three types of administrative roles: (1) statewide jurisdiction for state supreme court chief justices; (2) local jurisdiction—a trial judge is responsible for administering the operations of his or her individual court; and (3) *presiding* or *chief* judge—supervising several courts within a judicial district.

The practice of having a judge preside over several courts within a district developed as early as 1940, when Dean Roscoe Pound recommended that a chief or presiding judge of a district or a region be responsible for case and judge assignment.[48] Today, these judges assume "general administrative duties over the court and its divisions" and are typically granted authority over all judicial personnel and court officials.[49] The duties of the presiding judge are numerous and include personnel and docket management and case and judge assignments; coordination and development of all judicial budgets; the convening of *en banc* (judges meeting as a whole) court meetings; coordination of judicial schedules; creation and use of appropriate court committees to investigate problems and handle court business; interaction with outside agencies and the media; the drafting of local court rules and policies; the maintenance of the courts' facilities; and the issuing of orders for keeping, destroying, and transferring records.[50]

A basic flaw in this system is that the chief or presiding judge is actually a "first among equals" with his or her peers. The title of chief judge is often assigned by seniority; therefore, there is no guarantee that the chief judge will be interested in management or will be effective at it.[51]

From a court administrator's standpoint, the office of presiding judge and the person serving in that capacity are of the utmost importance. As one judge put it, "the single most determinative factor of the extent of the administrator's role, aside from his personal attributes, is probably the rate of turnover in the office of the presiding judge."[52]

While discussing the functions of the chief or presiding judges of this country, this is a good point at which to consider the duties of the **chief justice** of the United States; a few of those duties are listed in Exhibit 7.2.

EXHIBIT 7.2

Duties of the Chief Justice of the United States

Often incorrectly called the chief justice of the Supreme Court, the chief justice of the United States has 53 duties enumerated in the U.S. Code, the Constitution, and other sources. Following is a list of a few of those duties:

- Approve appointments and salaries of some court employees
- Direct the publication of Supreme Court opinions
- Approve rules for the Supreme Court library
- Select a company to handle the printing and binding of court opinions
- Send appeals back to lower courts, if justices cannot agree on them
- Approve appointments of employees to care for the Supreme Court building and grounds as well as regulations for their protection
- Call and preside over an annual meeting of the Judicial Conference of the United States and report to Congress the conference's recommendations for legislation (the Judicial Conference is composed of 27 federal judges who represent all the levels and regions of the federal judiciary; the conference meets twice a year to discuss common problems and needed policies and to recommend to Congress measures for improving the operation of the federal courts)
- Report to Congress on changes in the Rules of Criminal Procedure
- Report to the president if certain judges have become unable to discharge their duties
- Designate a member of the Smithsonian Institution

Source: Based on The Federal Judicial Center, "History of the Federal Judiciary," http://www.fjc.gov/history/home.nsf/page/admin_04.html (accessed July 29, 2010).

COURT CLERKS

Not to be overlooked in the administration of the courts is the **court clerk,** also referred to as a *prothonotary, registrar of deeds, circuit clerk, registrar of probate*, and even *auditor*. Most courts have de facto court administrators in these clerks, even if they have appointed administrators. These are key individuals in the administration of local court systems. They docket cases, collect fees and costs, oversee jury selection, and maintain court records. These local officials, elected in all but six states, can amass tremendous power.[53]

From the beginning of English settlement in North America, court clerks were vital members of the society. "Clerks of writs" or "clerks of the assize" existed in early Massachusetts, where people were litigious primarily about land boundaries. Hostility toward lawyers carried over from England, and the clerk was the intermediary between the litigants and the justice of the peace. During the late seventeenth century, American courts became more structured and formalized. Books were available that imposed English court practices in the colonies, and clerks, judges, and attorneys were provided proper forms that had to be used. In fact, some of the forms used by clerks 200 years ago are similar to those in use today.[54]

Clerks have traditionally competed with judges for control over local judicial administration. In fact, one study found that the majority (58.9 percent) of elected clerks perceived themselves as colleagues of and equal to the judges.[55] Court clerks have not as a rule been identified with effective management, however:

> Generally they are conservative in nature and reflect the attitudes and culture of the community. Their parochial backgrounds, coupled with their conservative orientation, in part accounts for this resistance to change. This resistance often compels judicial systems to retain archaic procedures and managerial techniques.[56]

TRAINED COURT ADMINISTRATORS

Development and Training

One of the most recent and innovative approaches to solving the courts' management problems has been the creation of the position of court administrator. This relatively new criminal justice position began to develop in earnest during the 1960s; since that time, the number of practicing trial court administrators has increased tenfold and continues to expand. Actually, this concept has its roots in early England, where, historically, judges abstained from any involvement in court administration. This fact has not been lost on contemporary court administrators and proponents of this position: "It seems to be a very valuable characteristic of the English system that the judges expect to *judge* when they are in the courthouse . . . it does not allow time for administrative distractions."[57]

The development of the position of court administrator has been sporadic. In the early 1960s, probably only 30 people in the United States worked as court administrators. By 1970, there were fewer than 50 such specially trained employees.[58] Estimates differ concerning the expansion of the administrator's role during the 1980s. One expert maintained that by 1982 between 2,000 and 3,000 people were in the ranks of court managers;[59] another argued that there were only about 500.[60] At any rate, most agree that more than twice as many of these positions were created between 1970 and 1980 than in the preceding six decades.[61]

By the 1980s, every state had a statewide court administrator, normally reporting to the state supreme court or the chief justice of the state supreme court. The three primary functions of state court administrators are preparing annual reports, summarizing caseload data, preparing budgets, and troubleshooting.[62]

Today, few, if any, metropolitan areas are without full-time court administrators[63] (the court organization chart shown in Figure 6.5 essentially demonstrates the breadth of responsibilities held by court administrators). An underlying premise and justification for this role is that by having a trained person performing the tasks of court management, judges are left free to do what they do best: decide cases. Indeed, since the first trial-court administrative positions began to appear, "there was little doubt or confusion about their exact purpose."[64] (As will be seen later, however, there has been doubt and confusion concerning their proper role and functions.)

As court reformers have called for better-trained specialists (as opposed to political appointees) for administering court processes, the qualifications for this position have come under debate. The creation of the Institute for Court Management in 1970 was a landmark in the training for this role, legitimizing its standing in the legal profession. Many judges, however, still believe that a law degree is essential, whereas others prefer a background in business administration. There will probably never be total agreement concerning the skills and background necessary for this position, but the specialized training that is offered by the Institute and a few graduate programs in judicial administration across the country would seem ideal.

Court administrators are trained specifically to provide the courts with the expertise and talent they have historically lacked. This point was powerfully made by Bernadine Meyer:

> Management—like law—is a profession today. Few judges or lawyers with severe chest pains would attempt to treat themselves. Congested dockets and long delays are symptoms that court systems need the help of professionals. Those professionals are managers. If court administration is to be effective, judicial recognition that managerial skill and knowledge are necessary to efficient performance is vital.[65]

General Duties

Trial court administrators generally perform the following six major duties:

1. *Reports.* Administrators have primary responsibility for the preparation and submission to the judges of periodic reports on the activities and state of business of the court.
2. *Personnel administration.* Court administrators serve as personnel officers for the court's nonjudicial personnel.
3. *Research and evaluation.* This function is designed to improve court business methods.
4. *Equipment management.* Administrators are engaged in procurement, allocation, inventory control, and replacement of furniture and equipment.
5. *Preparation of the court budget*
6. *Training coordination.* Court administrators provide training for nonjudicial personnel.[66]

Other duties that are assumed by the trained court administrator include jury management, case flow or calendar management, public information, and management of automated data processing operations.[67]

Evaluating Court Administrators

Judges must determine whether or not their court administrator is performing competently and effectively. According to John Greacen,[68] following are several basic strategies in determining the quality of the work performed by their administrators:

1. *The judge looks for indications of good management.* A well-managed organization will have a number of plans and procedures in place, including personnel policies, recruitment and selection procedures, an orientation program for new employees, performance evaluation procedures, a discipline and grievance process, case management policies, financial controls, and other administrative policies (such as for facilities and records management).
2. *The judge should be receiving regular information.* Critically important reports and data on the court's performance, plans, activities, and accomplishments should be provided to the judge on a routine basis. The judge should be notified of the number of case filings, terminations, and pending cases; financial information; staff performance; long- and short-range plans; and other statistical data.
3. *Judges must often ask others about the performance of the administrator.* This includes soliciting input from lawyers, other judges, and other court staff members.

JURY ADMINISTRATION

The jury system has been in the forefront of the public's mind in recent years, primarily as a result of the jury nullification concept (the right of juries to nullify or refuse to apply law in criminal cases despite facts that leave no reasonable doubt that the law was violated).[69] Here, however, I focus on the responsibilities of the court administrator in **jury administration**: ensuring that a jury is properly composed and sustained during trials. Elements of the jury system that involve court administration include jury selection, sequestration, comfort, and notorious cases.

Regarding jury selection, the court administrator is responsible for compilation of a master jury list; this is a large pool of potential jurors compiled from voter registration, driver's license, or utility customer or telephone customer lists to produce a representative cross-section of the community. From that master list, a randomly selected smaller venire (or jury pool) is drawn; a summons is mailed out to citizens, asking them to appear at the courthouse for jury duty. There, they will be asked questions and either retained or removed as jury members.

Here is where juror comfort enters in. Unfortunately, many jurors experience great frustration in the process, being made to wait long hours, possibly in uncomfortable physical surroundings, while receiving minimal compensation and generally being inconvenienced. Courts in all states now have a juror call-in system, enabling jurors to dial a phone number to learn whether their attendance is needed on a particular day; in addition, many jurisdictions have reduced the number of days a juror remains in the pool.

Some trials involving extensive media coverage require jury sequestration—jurors remain in virtual quarantine, sometimes for many weeks, and are compelled to live in a hotel together. This can be a tiring experience for jurors and poses great logistical problems for court administrators. The court administrator must also consider security issues (protecting the jury from outside interference and providing for conjugal visits, room searches, transportation, and so on) as well as jurors' personal needs (such as entertainment and medical supplies).[70]

The existence of **notorious cases**—those involving celebrities or particularly egregious crimes—has always been a part of, and caused problems in, courtrooms: the trials of celebrities such as Martha Stewart and Michael Jackson; athletes like O. J. Simpson and Mike Tyson;

mafia don John Gotti, and child star Robert Blake were clearly "notorious."[71] Court administrators and other court staff members must deal with media requests; courtroom and courthouse logistics for handling crowds, the media, and security; and the management of the court's docket of other cases. A notorious trial may also require that a larger courtroom be used and many attorneys accommodated.[72] A number of other issues must be considered: Are identification and press passes and entry screening devices needed? Do purses, briefcases, and other such items need to be searched? Perhaps the most important task in managing notorious cases is communication with the media, often by setting aside a certain time when reporters may discuss the case.[73]

Summary

Today, the functions of judges and court administrators are quite different from those of earlier times and involve policymaking as well. It is clear that, as one New York judge put it,

> Today, the functions of judges and court administrators are quite different from those of earlier times and involve policymaking as well. It is clear that, as one New York judge put it, [t]he "grand tradition" judge, the aloof brooding charismatic figure in the Old Testament tradition, is hardly a real figure."[74]

In addition, the nonlawyers who help judges to run the courts, judicial administrators, now possess a basic body of practical knowledge, a rudimentary theoretical perspective, and a concern for professional ethics.

It was also shown that there are still several obstacles to the total acceptance of court administration as an integral part of the judiciary. Court administration in many ways is still a developing field. Still, it has come far from its roots and is evolving into a bona fide element of the American justice system.

Questions for Review

1. Why is the term *judicial administration* multifaceted? What would be a good working definition for this term? For *court administration*?
2. What is meant by "good judging?"
3. Why is civility so important for the appearance of justice and propriety in our courts?
4. What are the elements of the newly revised Model Code of Judicial Conduct for state and local judges?
5. What is the "conventional wisdom" concerning whether or not judges can and should use social networking sites for their personal and professional purposes? To what extent are they being used?

6. How might judges and court administrators receive training for their roles?
7. How have court clerks traditionally assumed and performed the role of court administrator?
8. What criteria may be employed by judges to evaluate the effectiveness of their administrators?
9. What are the court administrator's duties in general? What issues must the court administrator address in composing or sequestering a jury? In dealing with notorious cases?

Learn by Doing

1. After many years of debate concerning its pros and cons, your state legislature appears to be edging closer to implementing the Missouri (or merit selection) Plan for judicial selection on the ballot. As a court administrator in your municipal court, you are asked by your local newspaper to prepare a position paper that presents both sides of the issues. What will you say are pros and cons, when compared with the current system of electing judges.

2. You are a court administrator and are currently attending a workshop that includes a section on ethical con-

siderations. You are given the following case involving actual impeachment hearings against a federal judge in Texas (see, e.g., http://www.vanityfair.com/online/daily/2009/06/a-real-case-of-judicial-misconduct.html) who had served in that position for 18 years. The judge had long lied concerning an "atrocious pattern of sexual misconduct" toward his subordinates. For years, two female staff members were assaulted by the judge, who was frequently intoxicated while on duty. After pleading guilty, the judge was convicted and sentenced to 3 years in prison. Then, he also asked that he

- might retain his salary and benefits while he serves his sentence
- be allowed to tender his resignation effective in about 1 year, so as to retain his medical insurance for a little bit longer
- be shown mercy due to alcoholism and the death of his wife a few years earlier.

Assume that you are one of the members of the panel that is considering whether or not the judge should be granted the earlier-mentioned concessions, as well as whether or not he should be impeached. How will you respond or vote, and why?

Related Websites

American Bar Association (ABA)
   http://abanet.org

American Judicature Society
   http://www.ajs.org

CrimeLynx—the Criminal Defense Practitioner's Guide Through the Internet
   http://www.crimelynx.com

Criminal Law Links
   http://findlaw.com/01topics/09criminal/

Find Law
   http://www.findlaw.com

Jury Science and Consultation
   http://www.courtroomconsultants.com/services/jury/jury.htm

Lexis ONE
   http://www.lexisone.com

National District Attorneys Association (NDAA)
   http://www.ndaa.apri.org

National Judicial College
   http://www.judges.org

U.S. Supreme Court
   http://www.supremecourtus.gov

Notes

1. Robert C. Harrall, "In Defense of Court Managers: The Critics Misconceive Our Role," *Court Management Journal* 14 (1982):52.
2. Russell Wheeler, *Judicial Administration: Its Relation to Judicial Independence* (Williamsburg, VA: National Center for State Courts, 1988), p. 19.
3. Roscoe Pound, "The Causes of Popular Dissatisfaction with the Administration of Justice," *Crime and Delinquency* 10 (1964):355–371; see also American Bar Association, 29 *A.B.A. Rep.*, pt. I, 395–417, 1906; Answers.com, http://www.answers.com/topic/the-causes-of-popular-dissatisfaction-with-the-administration-of-justice?cat=biz-fin (accessed March 10, 2008).
4. Ibid.
5. Woodrow Wilson, "The Study of Administration," *Political Science Quarterly* 2 (1887):197; reprinted in *Political Science Quarterly* 56 (1941):481.
6. Quoted in Paul Nejelski and Russell Wheeler, *Wingspread Conference on Contemporary and Future Issues in the Field of Court Management* 4 (1980), Proceedings of the July 1979 Conference of the Institute for Court Management, July 9–11, 1979, Racine, Wisconsin.
7. Wheeler, *Judicial Administration*, p. 21.
8. Ibid., p. 22.
9. National Advisory Commission on Criminal Justice Standards and Goals, *Courts* (Washington, DC: U.S. Government Printing Office, 1973), p. 171.
10. American Bar Association, Commission on Standards of Judicial Admission, *Standards Relating to Court Organization, Standard 1.41* (Chicago: Author, 1974).
11. Ian R. Scott, "Procedural Law and Judicial Administration," *Justice System Journal* 12 (1987):67–68.
12. Russell R. Wheeler and Howard R. Whitcomb, *Judicial Administration: Text and Readings* (Upper Saddle River, NJ: Prentice Hall, 1977), p. 8.

13. Ibid.

14. Ibid., p. 9.

15. David W. Neubauer, *America's Courts and the Criminal Justice System,* 9th ed. (Belmont, CA: Thomson/Wadsworth, 2008), pp. 170–176.

16. U.S. Department of Justice, Bureau of Justice Statistics, *State Court Organization, 2004* (Washington, DC: Author, October 2006), p. 23.

17. Barbara Luck Graham, "Do Judicial Selection Systems Matter? A Study of Black Representation on State Courts," *American Politics Quarterly* 18 (1990):316–336.

18. Neubauer, *America's Courts and the Criminal Justice System,* p. 172.

19. Ibid., p. 173.

20. Craig Emmert and Henry Glick, "The Selection of State Supreme Court Justices," *American Politics Quarterly* 16 (1988): 445–465.

21. Law.com, "O'Connor Says Judges Shouldn't Be Elected," http://www.law.com/jsp/law/LawArticl Friendly.jsp?id=1194429842107 (accessed January 16, 2008).

22. Ibid.

23. American Judicature Society, "Judicial Selection in the States," http://www.judicialselection.us/ (accessed January 12, 2008).

24. Abraham Blumberg, *Criminal Justice* (Chicago: Quadrangle Books, 1967).

25. Wheeler and Whitcomb, *Judicial Administration,* p. 370.

26. National Center for State Courts web-site, http:// www.ncsconline.org. (accessed January 4, 2008); also see the Institute for Court Management's website, http://www.ncsconline.org/D_ICM/icmindex. html (accessed January 4, 2008).

27. Wheeler and Whitcomb, *Judicial Administration,* p. 372.

28. Ibid.

29. Ibid.

30. Ibid., p. 373.

31. William A. Batlitch, "Reflections on the Art and Craft of Judging," *The Judges Journal* 43(4) (Fall 2003):7–8.

32. Charles E. Patterson, "The Good Judge: A Trial Lawyer's Perspective," *The Judges Journal* 43(4) (Fall 2003):14–15.

33. See, for example, Allen K. Harris, "The Professionalism Crisis—The 'Z' Words and Other Rambo Tactics: The Conference of Chief Justices' Solution," 53 S.C. L. Rev. 549, 589 (2002).

34. *In re First City Bancorp of Tex., Inc.,* 282 F.3d 864 (5th Cir. 2002).

35. *People v. Williamson,* 172 Cal. App. 3d 737, 749 (1985).

36. *Landry v. State,* 620 So. 2d 1099, 1102-03 (Fla. Dist. Ct. App. 1993).

37. *Gaddy v. Cirbo,* 293 P.2d (Colo. 1956), at 962.

38. Marla N. Greenstein, "The Craft of Ethics," *The Judges Journal* 43(4) (Fall 2003):17–18.

39. Ty Tasker, "Sticks and Stones: Judicial Handling of Invective in Advocacy," *The Judges Journal* 43(4) (Fall 2003):17–18.

40. Collins T. Fitzpatrick, "Building a Better Bench: Informally Addressing Instances of Judicial Misconduct," *The Judges Journal* 44 (Winter 2005):16–20.

41. Ibid., pp. 18–20.

42. See American Bar Association, ABA Model Code of Judicial Conduct, "Preamble," p. 39, http://www.ajs. org/ethics/pdfs/ABA2007modelcodeasapproved. pdf (accessed August 11, 2011).

43. Isaiah M. Zimmerman, "Isolation in the Judicial Career," *Court Review,* Winter 2000, http://aja.ncsc. dni.us/courtrv/cr36-4/36-4Zimmerman.pdf (accessed November 19, 2010).

44. Ibid., p. 4.

45. Conference of Court Public Information Officers, *Judges and Courts on Social Media? Report Released on New Media's Impact on the Judiciary,* August 26, 2010, http://www.ccpio.org/documents/newmedi- aproject/News-Release-8-26.pdf (accessed November 19, 2010).

46. See Adrienne Meiring, "Ethical Considerations of Using Social Networking Sites," *Indiana Courttimes,* http://indianacourts.us/times/2009/12/ethical- considerations-of-using-social-networking-sites/, December 31, 2009 (accessed November 19, 2010).

47. See "New York Advisory Opinion 08-176," January 29, 2009, at: www.nycourts.gov/ip/judicialethics/ opinions/08-176.htm) (accessed November 19, 2010).

48. Roscoe Pound, "Principles and Outlines of a Modern Unified Court Organization," *Journal of the American Judicature Society* 23 (April 1940):229.

49. See, for example, the Missouri Constitution, Article V, Sec. 15, paragraph 3.

50. Forest Hanna, "Delineating the Role of the Presiding Judge," *State Court Journal* 10 (Spring 1986):17–22.

51. Neubauer, *America's Courts and the Criminal Justice System,* p. 102.

52. Robert A. Wenke, "The Administrator in the Court," *Court Management Journal* 14 (1982):17–18, 29.

53. Marc Gertz, "Influence in the Court Systems: The Clerk as Interface," *Justice System Journal* 2 (1977):30–37.

54. Robert B. Revere, "The Court Clerk in Early American History," *Court Management Journal* 10 (1978):12–13.

55. G. Larry Mays and William Taggart, "Court Clerks, Court Administrators, and Judges: Conflict in Managing the Courts," *Journal of Criminal Justice* 14 (1986):1–7.

56. Larry Berkson, "Delay and Congestion in State Systems: An Overview," in Larry Berkson, Steven Hays, and Susan Carbon (eds.), *Managing the State Courts: Text and Readings* (St. Paul, MN: West, 1977), p. 164.

57. Ernest C. Friesen and I. R. Scott, *English Criminal Justice* (Birmingham: University of Birmingham Institute of Judicial Administration, 1977), p. 12.

58. Harvey E. Solomon, "The Training of Court Managers," in Charles R. Swanson and Susette M. Talarico (eds.), *Court Administration: Issues and Responses* (Athens: University of Georgia Press, 1987), pp. 15–20.

59. Ernest C. Friesen, "Court Managers: Magnificently Successful or Merely Surviving?" *Court Management Journal* 14 (1982):21.

60. Solomon, "The Training of Court Managers," p. 16.

61. Harrall, "In Defense of Court Managers," p. 51.

62. Neubauer, *America's Courts and the Criminal Justice System,* p. 104.

63. Ibid.

64. Geoffrey A. Mort and Michael D. Hall, "The Trial Court Administrator: Court Executive or Administrative Aide?" *Court Management Journal* 12 (1980):12–16, 30.

65. Bernadine Meyer, "Court Administration: The Newest Profession," *Duquesne Law Review* 10 (Winter 1971):220–235.

66. Mort and Hall, "The Trial Court Administrator," p. 15.

67. Ibid.

68. John M. Greacen, "Has Your Court Administrator Retired? Without Telling You?" National Association for Court Management, Conference Papers from the Second National Conference on Court Management, Managing Courts in Changing Times, Phoenix, Ariz., September 9–14, 1990, pp. 1–20.

69. Darryl Brown, "Jury Nullification within the Rule of Law," *Minnesota Law Review* 81 (1997):1149–1200.

70. Timothy R. Murphy, Genevra Kay Loveland, and G. Thomas Munsterman, *A Manual for Managing Notorious Cases* (Washington, DC: National Center for State Courts, 1992), pp. 4–6. See also Timothy R. Murphy, Paul L. Hannaford, and Kay Genevra, *Managing Notorious Trials* (Williamsburg, VA: National Center for State Courts, 1998).

71. See Murphy et al., *A Manual for Managing Notorious Cases,* pp. 53, 73, for other notable celebrity cases.

72. Ibid., p. 23.

73. Ibid., pp. 27–30.

74. Blumberg, *Criminal Justice,* p. 120.

Court Issues and Practices

KEY TERMS AND CONCEPTS

Alternative dispute resolution (ADR)

Arbitration

Case delay

Courthouse violence

Court performance standards "CSI effect"

Crime control model

Drug court

Due process model

Exclusionary rule

Individual calendar system

Jury science

Juveniles tried as adults

Litigation

Master calendar system

Media relations

Mediation

Mental health court

Nontargeted courthouse violence

Plea bargaining

Problem-solving courts

Targeted courthouse violence

Threat assessment

Veterans court

LEARNING OBJECTIVES

After reading this chapter, the student will:

- understand the differences between the due process and crime control models
- know the meaning and influence of the "CSI effect" on court operations and actors
- be knowledgeable about courthouse violence, both actual and potential, and what must be done to assess and deal with threats to court actors
- have a grasp of the growing trend toward problem-solving courts—and some concerns
- be familiar with the problems and consequences of, and solutions for, trial delays
- understand the two systems used in scheduling cases
- be able to explain the courts' role in media relations
- know the importance of alternative dispute resolution (ADR) for decreasing litigation
- be familiar with a recent major U.S. Supreme Court decision concerning federal sentencing guidelines
- be able to discuss issues such as juveniles being tried as adults, the exclusionary rule, the use of cameras in the courtroom, and plea bargaining

Threatening or intimidating our judges cannot be tolerated in this country. The rise in threats against our judges puts the men and women who serve in our justice system at risk and is a repugnant assault on our independent judiciary.

—U.S. Senator Patrick Leahy, Chairman,
Senate Judiciary Committee,
110thCongress

Justice is such a fine thing that we cannot pay too dearly for it.

—Alain Rene LeSage

INTRODUCTION

Many of the topics discussed previously, primarily in Chapter 6—such as reforming court organization and unification, use of the adversary system, and alternative dispute resolution (ADR)—could have been included in this chapter. They are challenging areas. This chapter, however, examines additional contemporary issues and practices.

It is helpful for court administrators to view court issues and practices through the lenses of the crime control and due process models of criminal justice; these models represent what might be termed the *hard-line* and *soft-line* approaches to offenders and how the justice system should deal with them. Therefore, the chapter begins with an overview of these opposing models. We then consider the so-called "CSI effect," and whether or not it has an impact on court operations and actors. Next, because history has shown that our courts—like the rest of our society— can be mean and brutish places, we review courthouse violence, its basic forms, and how to perform a threat assessment. We then discuss how problem-solving courts (particularly drug, mental health, and **veterans' courts**) are expanding and using their authority and innovative techniques to forge new responses to chronic social, human, and legal problems. Then, we examine the dilemma of delay (including its consequences, suggested solutions, and two systems of scheduling cases) and review how the spreading concept of ADR is used to decrease litigation and court backlogs. In a related vein, we look at two recent U.S. Supreme Court decisions concerning federal sentencing guidelines. Next, after a brief look at media relations and the courts, the following issues are considered: whether juveniles should be tried as adults, whether or not the exclusionary rule should be banned, the use of cameras during trial, and plea bargaining. The chapter concludes with a brief discussion of jury science.

JUSTICE FROM THE DUE PROCESS AND CRIME CONTROL PERSPECTIVES

We briefly discussed the crime control and due process models of criminal justice in Chapter 1; here, we will elaborate on the main points of these two philosophies.

In 1968, Herbert Packer presented these two now-classic competing models, which describe how criminal cases are processed. The **due process model** holds that defendants should be presumed innocent, that the courts' first priority is to protect suspects' rights, and that granting too much freedom to law enforcement officials will result in the loss of freedom and civil liberties for all Americans. Therefore, each court case must involve formal fact finding to uncover mistakes by the police and prosecutors. This view also stresses that crime is not a result of individual moral failure but rather of social influences (such as unemployment, racial discrimination, and other factors that disadvantage the poor); thus, courts that do not follow this philosophy are fundamentally unfair to these defendants. Furthermore, rehabilitation will prevent further crime.

Standing in contrast is the **crime control model**, which views crime as a breakdown of individual responsibility and places the highest importance on repressing criminal conduct, thus protecting society. Those persons who are charged are presumed guilty, and the courts should not hinder effective enforcement of the laws; rather, legal loopholes should be eliminated and offenders swiftly punished. The police and prosecutors should have a high degree of discretion. Punishment will deter crime, so there must be speed and finality in the courts to ensure crime suppression.

IS THERE A "CSI EFFECT"?

Television programs focusing on criminal investigations and forensic techniques may not only be providing viewers with entertainment but also creating certain expectations about criminal cases in general and investigations in specific. This has been labeled the potential "**CSI effect**." Of particular concern to the administration of justice is whether or not such television programming may create inaccurate expectations in the minds of jurors regarding the power and use of forensic evidence. Indeed, the creator of "CSI," Anthony E. Zuiker, observed that "'The CSI

Effect' is, in my opinion, the most amazing thing that has ever come out of the series. For the first time in American history, you're not allowed to fool the jury anymore."[1]

Anecdotal evidence indicates that some prosecutors and defense attorneys believe that the shows aid their opponents: prosecutors believe that juries want to see all evidence subjected to substantial forensic examination, whether warranted in a specific case or not, while defense attorneys have indicated that juries believe that scientific evidence is perfect and thus trustworthy in establishing guilt. Prosecutors may also use PowerPoint and video presentations more frequently, and might take pains to explain to jurors that forensic evidence is not always collectible—or at the very least use experts to explain to jurors why they did not logically collect forensic evidence in a particular case. The *voir dire* process may also be altered to ensure that those jurors who are unduly influenced by shows like *CSI* are screened from jury service. Attorneys and judges may well be more careful in the jury selection process. These adaptations could result in longer trials and an increased use of expert witnesses to aid the jury in understanding the presence or absence of physical evidence.[2]

For their own part, some police have reported that citizens who observe their investigatory techniques have attempted to correct the officers' actions based upon what the citizen has seen on television. Victims and their families may also question the extent and speed of forensic analysis.[3]

In an attempt to assess the possible impact of programs like "CSI," Hughes and Magers conducted a survey of Kentucky circuit court judges. They observed that the impact has been strong—but not in areas where one might expect. First, they observed that juries have indeed come to expect more forensic evidence: 76 percent of the respondents strongly agreed or agreed with the statement, "I have observed an increase in the jury's expectations for forensic evidence since shows like *CSI* have become popular." Furthermore, 82 percent of the judges believed that "shows like *CSI* have distorted the public's perception of time needed to obtain forensic results." In that same connection, a slight majority (53.4 percent) believed that the popularity of shows like *CSI* has made it harder to convict defendants.[4]

However, 90 percent of the judges disagreed that the *technology* shown in such programs has made it harder to convict defendants. Furthermore, the judges did not perceive an increase in the use of forensic or expert witness evidence in trials. The respondents did perceive, however, that these television shows created unrealistic representations as to the state of the forensic art in their jurisdiction, as well as to the speed of forensic testing.[5]

In sum, this study observed that these televised programs have had a negative impact on the courts but not to the extent that judges sense a need to change the manner in which their courts are administered. While judges perceived an increased demand for and distorted perception of forensic evidence due to such programs, they did not perceive an increased use of forensic evidence, that the impact required changes in the administration of the court, or that the changes are beyond their ability to remedy. It may be that the "CSI effect" is, in reality, more of a nuisance for those who are involved in administering justice, rather than a substantial factor in criminal justice processing. Or it may be that the "CSI effect" is substantial in only certain types of cases involving certain issues.[6]

COURTHOUSE VIOLENCE

Shooters in the Courthouses

It has been said that judges deal with "a segment of society that most people don't have to deal with—people who are violent, might be mentally unstable, are desperate because they don't have much more to lose."[7] That assessment is becoming increasingly true, especially when one considers some of the recent violent acts committed against the judiciary:

- a family court judge in Reno, Nevada, standing at a window in his chambers, is shot by a sniper.[8]
- a prisoner in Atlanta steals a deputy's gun and fatally shoots a judge, his court reporter, and a deputy sheriff.[9]
- A federal district court judge found her husband and mother shot dead in the basement of her Chicago home, less than a year after a white supremacist was convicted of trying to have her murdered for holding him in contempt of court.[10]

Recently, Etter and Swymeler conducted a study of courthouse shootings[11] and determined that the problem has escalated in recent years. Following are the selected findings:

- Litigants (plaintiffs, defendants, witnesses, or lawyers) were the intended targets in about 60 percent of the shooting incidents, while judges and police officers were targeted in about 40 percent.
- About 40 percent of the shooters were shot either by the court's security forces or by their own hand (with 87 percent of the shooters dying as a result).
- The majority (61 percent) of the 114 courthouse shooting incidents that were identified occurred in about the past 25 years.
- The firearms used were either brought in by the shooter (77 percent), taken from a deputy (19 percent), or smuggled into a defendant or prisoner (4 percent).
- Domestic violence or problems was the motive in one-third of the shootings, escape was the motive in one-fourth, and assassination or another reason was the motive in 35 percent.
- Victims of the shootings were judges (8 percent), police officers (about one-third); litigants or other court officials (including plaintiffs, defendants, witnesses, and lawyers (59 percent).
- In about four of 10 courthouse shooting cases, the shooter was shot either by security forces or via self-inflicted gunshot wounds; the vast majority of the shooters were captured.
- While 91 percent of the respondents indicated they have access to metal detectors, their usage varies widely; usage was often spotty or only for major trials.

General Types of Court Violence

There are two types of violence that can occur in courthouses:

- **Nontargeted courthouse violence** involves an individual who has no specific preexisting intention of engaging in violence but who, either during, at the conclusion of, or sometime shortly after the court proceeding becomes incensed and defiant at some procedure or outcome and acts out in the courtroom or public corridors. If this person also has a weapon, it might be used against the source of the grievance—a judge, attorney, witness, court employee, defendant or plaintiff, or bystander. If there are no judicial security screening devices or patrols on the premises, the person may proceed to attack people within the courthouse.
- **Targeted courthouse violence** involves an individual who expressly intends to engage in courthouse violence. These persons often simmer and stew for long periods of time, so there is often some delay in responding to real or perceived affronts and insults. During this time, these people may or may not make threats and often create plans to circumvent security measures. They deliberately focus on specific individuals or the judiciary itself.[12]

Of the two groups, the nontargeting group has been responsible for most of the violent incidents in our nation's courthouses. With proper security precautions, many of these acts can be prevented or thwarted. This is a daunting task, however; each year, nearly 100 million cases are filed in the nation's 18,000 lower courts (61 million cases) and its 2,000 major trial courts (31 million cases),[13] which are presided over by more than 11,000 judges and quasi-judicial officers (e.g., masters, magistrates).[14] Because each filed case is potentially contentious, violence is also a potential outcome.

Other disturbing behaviors can affect the courts' functions as well. For example, judges can be sent inappropriate communications containing threats. Bombings of state and local government buildings have occurred as well.[15] Concerns about such acts of violence have spurred the implementation of enhanced security measures in many of our nation's courthouses, most of which have focused on the courts' physical environment, to detect weapons. Duress alarms and video surveillance cameras have been installed and separate prisoner, court staff, and public areas created.

One problem with enhancing courthouse security is its cost. In 1997, the cost to install 35 bullet-resistant windows in a Tacoma, Washington, federal courthouse following a shooting through a judge's window was $550,000. Today, the cost is still quite high: To install bullet-resistant glass would cost over $1,500 for the window frame and $120 per square foot for the glass. Another problem is that such glass can weigh up to 224 pounds a square foot; not all buildings can handle such weight.[16]

Following the sniper shooting of the judge in Reno,[17] mentioned earlier, several U.S. senators introduced a bill, The Court Security Improvement Act of 2006, which would have provided funds for both federal and state court security measures, but the bill was not passed before Congress adjourned.[18]

Making a Threat Assessment

A good beginning point for enhancing courthouse security is the **threat assessment** approach. A good threat assessment involves three principles:

1. Targeted violence is the end result of an understandable and often discernible process of thinking and acting. Acts of targeted violence are neither impulsive nor spontaneous. Ideas about mounting an attack usually develop over time; the subject engages in planning the attack, and might collect information about the target, the setting, or other related attacks. This suggests that many incidents of targeted violence may be preventable.
2. One must distinguish between expressing a threat and posing a threat. Many people who make threats do not pose a serious risk of harm to a target; they may make idle threats for a variety of reasons. On the other hand, many who pose a serious risk of harm will not issue direct threats prior to an attack. Although all threats should be taken seriously, they are not the most reliable indicator of risk.
3. Violence is the product of an interaction among the potential attacker, his or her current situation, the target, and the setting. One might reasonably examine the development and evolution of ideas concerning the attack, preparatory behaviors, and how the individual has dealt with what he or she felt to be unbearable stress in the past. Consideration of the subject's current situation may include an assessment of what stressful events are occurring in the subject's life, how he or she is responding, and how others in the subject's environment are responding to his or her stress and potential risk. Things to be considered include the subject's degree of familiarity with the target's work and lifestyle patterns, the target's vulnerability, and the target's sophistication about the need for caution.[19]

Clearly, at a minimum, all courts should employ certain security procedures, such as the following: On arrival at a courthouse, persons are required to pass through the security control point located at the front door (this control point is equipped much like a security control point at airports) and to pass purses, briefcases, or anything else they may be carrying through an x-ray machine. They are also required to place any metal objects in the trays provided and then pass through the magnetometer (a device that indicates the presence of metal objects). If they are carrying anything that can be construed as a weapon, they can take it back to their vehicle or leave it with the security officer and pick the item up when they leave the courthouse (and, of course, are subject to arrest if found to be carrying a weapon that is illegal to carry or possess by law). If they continue to set off the magnetometer after all items are removed, the security officer will pass a hand wand around their person to determine what is continuing to set off the alarm.

PROBLEM-SOLVING COURTS

Origin, Functions, and Rationale

The 1990s saw a wave of court reform across the United States as judges and other court actors experimented with new ways to deliver justice: Drug courts (discussed later) expanded into every state, and new mental health and veterans' courts began targeting different kinds of problems in different places, all with a desire to improve the results for victims, litigants, defendants, and communities.

Although **problem-solving courts** are still very much a work in progress, according to Robert V. Wolf[20] they share five principle aspects:

1. The proactive, problem-solving orientation of the judge;
2. The integration of social services;
3. The team-based, nonadversarial approach;
4. Their interaction with the defendant/litigant; and
5. Their ongoing judicial supervision

These courts use their authority to forge new responses to chronic social, human, and legal problems, such as family dysfunction, addiction, delinquency, and domestic violence that have proven resistant to conventional solutions. Community courts, like those in New York City, target misdemeanor "quality-of-life" crimes (e.g., prostitution, shoplifting, and low-level drug possession) and have offenders pay back the community by performing service functions. Similar stories can be told about the genesis and spread of domestic violence courts, **mental health courts** (MHCs), and others.[21]

What prompted such experiments? Actually, several social and historical forces set the stage for these efforts:

- Breakdown of and loss of respect for social and community institutions (such as families and organized religion) that have traditionally addressed social problems
- A surge in the nation's incarcerated population, which forced policymakers to rethink their approach to crime
- Trends emphasizing the accountability of public institutions, along with technological innovations (discussed in Chapter 16) that have improved analysis of court outcomes
- Advances in the quality and availability of therapeutic interventions, particularly drug treatment programs
- Shifts in public policies and priorities, such as the "broken windows" theory that says that society must address low-level crimes to prevent more serious crimes later[22]

Perhaps the most important forces are rising caseloads and increasing frustration with the standard approach to case processing.[23]

Wolf noted, however, that problem-solving courts do not receive consistent support. The idea of engaging the community—such as identifying neighborhood problems, setting goals, creating work service programs, and educating stakeholders—makes some judges nervous who believe interacting with the community might indicate that they are biased; others think of the judge's role as deciding cases, not solving problems, or being a "social worker." Some prosecutors, meanwhile, are also wary of social services that appear to be "soft" on crime, and view problem solving as "social work" rather than protecting society. Also, some defense attorneys do not want judges speaking directly to offenders, and that exploring alternative sentences—like drug treatment—falls outside their responsibilities.[24]

Still, problem-solving courts seek to achieve tangible outcomes for victims, offenders, and society; they rely on the active use of judicial authority to change the behavior of litigants, with judges staying involved in each case long after adjudication.

Drug, Mental Health, and Veterans' Courts

Drug courts are now proliferating: According to the National Drug Court Institute, there are 2,459 drug courts operating in the U.S. – a 40 percent increase in the past five years.[25] Figure 8.1 depicts this rapid growth in drug courts since 1989, and Figure 8.2 shows the number of existing drug courts in each state. Drug court participants undergo long-term treatment and counseling, are given sanctions and incentives, and make frequent court appearances. Successful completion of the program results in dismissal of charges, reduced or set-aside sentences, lesser penalties, or a combination of these. Most important, graduating participants gain the necessary tools to rebuild their lives. The drug court model includes the following key components:

- Incorporating drug testing into case processing
- Creating a nonadversarial relationship between the defendant and the court
- Identifying defendants in need of treatment and referring them to treatment as soon as possible after arrest
- Providing access to a continuum of treatment and rehabilitation services
- Monitoring abstinence through frequent mandatory drug testing[26]

Year	To Date	Year	To Date
1989	1	2000	665
1990	1	2001	847
1991	5	2002	1,048
1992	10	2003	1,183
1993	19	2004	1,621
1994	40	2005	1,756
1995	75	2006	1,926
1996	139	2007	2,147
1997	230	2008	2,326
1998	347	2009	2,459
1999	472		

FIGURE 8.1 Operational Drug Courts by Year

Source: Based on C. West Huddleston III and Douglas B. Marlowe, *Painting the Current Picture: A National Report on Drug Courts and Other Problem-Solving Courts* (Alexandria, VA: National Drug Court Institute, July 2011), p. 6.

FIGURE 8.2 Operational Drug Courts in the U.S.

Source: Based on C. West Huddleston III and Douglas B. Marlowe, *Painting the Current Picture: A National Report on Drug Courts and Other Problem-Solving Courts* (Alexandria, VA: National Drug Court Institute, July 2011), p. 21.

A national study of drug courts by the U.S. Government Accounting Office (GAO) found:

- Lower percentages of drug court program participants than comparison group members were rearrested or reconvicted.
- Program participants had fewer recidivism events than those in comparison groups.
- Recidivism reductions for participants who had committed different types of offenses.
- Of the programs that provided sufficient data to estimate their cost benefits, all of them yielded positive net benefits, primarily from reductions in recidivism affecting judicial system costs and avoided costs to potential victims.[27]

MHCs are also beginning to spread as alternatives to traditional criminal court proceedings. Since the late 1990s, more than 175 have been established and dozens more are being planned. Eligible participants typically have a misdemeanor or low-level felony charge and a diagnosis of schizophrenia, bipolar disorder, or major depression. Judges hold participants accountable to take their psychotropic medications, avoid taking illegal drugs, and attend hearings. Other characteristics of MHCs, according to the Federal Bureau of Justice Assistance, are as follows:

- A specialized court docket, which employs a problem-solving approach in lieu of more traditional court procedures
- Judicially supervised, community-based treatment plans for each defendant participating in the court, designed and implemented by a team of court staff and mental health professionals
- Regular court hearings, where incentives are offered to reward adherence to court conditions and sanctions are imposed on participants who do not adhere to the conditions of participation[28]

The basic premise of these courts is that they increase public safety, facilitate participation in effective mental health and substance abuse treatment, improve the quality of life for people with mental illnesses charged with crimes, and make more effective use of limited criminal justice and mental health resources.[29] Exhibit 8.1 provides a good example of the potential for success—and financial struggles—now associated with these courts.

EXHIBIT 8.1

Will Funding Cuts Make Mental Health Courts Become Extinct?

A former corrections officer was so afflicted by bipolar disorder that he thought he was a military general whose job was to save the world. In reality, he was a homeless man, living in bus shelters, and sleeping on warm car hoods on nights when he was not in jail. Eventually, he wound up in Washoe County, Nevada's, MHC, where he regained his stable way of life and even became president of a state organization battling mental illness. But now this program—which has been designated by the Bureau of Justice Assistance as a "learning court" for others around the country to study and now involves 300 clients per year—and many others like it are in jeopardy. Budget cuts force service providers and courts administrators to decide which programs are "core" and which are "optional." Certainly, when pitted against funding for traditional mental hospitals and outpatient clinics, MHCs will not prevail. And, although the cost to incarcerate these people may well exceed the cost to fund the court, still many such programs will likely fall under the budget axe in the near future, and unfortunately, as the former corrections officer and later homeless person stated, "Jail is no place for the mentally ill."

Source: Based on Michelle Rindels, "Advocates fear funding cuts to Nevada Mental Health Court," *Associated Press*, February 20, 2011, http://www.rgj.com/article/20110219/NEWS11/110219013/Nevada-mental-health-advocates-fear-budget-cuts (accessed February 22, 2011).

In addition to the problems maintaining MHCs, as shown in Exhibit 8.1, some believe that another problem needing to be addressed with them concerns their terms of participation. Redlich et al.[30] examined whether MHCs are truly voluntary, as intended. They found that, on the one hand, the majority (more than half) of the respondents claimed it was their decision to enter the MHC and cited advantages to being in the court. However, more than half of the respondents claimed neither to have been informed prior to enrolling that enrollment was voluntary nor to have been told of the requirements of the court that the final decision (after eligibility decisions) to enroll in the court was theirs to make, and that they could stop being in the court if they so chose. The implications are clear because one controversial aspect of MHCs is whether they are indeed voluntary as intended: these individuals should have more than a basic knowledge of procedures, requirements, and consequences, particularly if there are sanctions for noncompliance. MHCs must determine what information participants should have at the time of enrollment, and what assurances can be put in place that the information is meaningfully understood.[31]

Veterans' courts are also spreading across the United States. Certainly, the wars in Iraq and Afghanistan have created a nationwide push to help veterans who have troubling reintegrating into civilian life—20 percent of whom suffer from posttraumatic stress disorder (PTSD) and traumatic brain injuries (that percentage increases with the number of tours served).[32] Even Congressional legislation has been introduced that would establish a grant program to help develop such courts across the nation.[33] These courts are diversion programs where, in exchange for a guilty plea to crimes charged, the veteran consents to regular court visits, counseling, and random drug testing. Then, if successfully completing the treatment program, the criminal record is expunged (meaning it is erased or stricken from the record). This allows for better access to employment, housing, and educational opportunities while also avoiding the pains of prison and having a criminal record.[34]

Veterans' courts have not received universal support, however. Some people worry about what they see as the courts' perpetuation of stereotypes of veterans' problems; furthermore, the American Civil Liberties Union is opposed, saying it wrongly emphasizes some criminal offenders' "status" in society; the reasoning is that, unlike drug courts or MHCs, which are for people with diagnosed conditions, veterans' courts are based on who offenders are; therefore, the ACLU believes that veterans' courts are tantamount to creating special courts for "crimes committed by police officers, teachers or politicians."[35]

THE DILEMMA OF DELAY

"Justice Delayed—"

There is no consensus on how long is too long with respect to bringing a criminal case to trial, and the test centers on the prosecutor's and defense attorney's conduct.[36] Still, a point at which Packer's due process and crime control models, discussed earlier, begin to diverge involves **case**

delay. The crime control model requires swift justice to protect society by incarcerating offenders, whereas the due process model calls for a more thoughtful and careful approach.

The principle that "justice delayed is justice denied" says much about the long-standing goal of processing court cases with due dispatch. Charles Dickens condemned the practice of slow litigation in nineteenth-century England, and Shakespeare mentioned "the law's delay" in *Hamlet*. Delay in processing cases is one of the oldest problems of U.S. courts. The public often hears of cases that have languished on court dockets for years. This can only erode public confidence in the judicial process.[37] The overload in our bloated court system has been building for years, with the most immediate source of pressure on the courts being the intensifying drug war; with increasing drug arrests, backlogs are growing.

Case backlog and trial delay affect many of our country's courts. The magnitude of the backlog and the length of the delay vary greatly, however, depending on the court involved. It is best to view delay not as a problem but as a symptom of a problem.[38] Generally, the term *delay* suggests abnormal or unacceptable time lapses in the processing of cases. Yet, some time is needed to prepare a case. What is a concern is *unnecessary* delay. However, there seems to be no agreed-on definition of unnecessary delay.

The Consequences

The consequences of delay can be severe. It can jeopardize the values and guarantees inherent in our justice system. Delay deprives defendants of their Sixth Amendment right to a speedy trial. Lengthy pretrial incarceration pressures can cause a defendant to plead guilty.[39] The reverse is also true: Delay can strengthen a defendant's bargaining position; prosecutors are more apt to accept pleas to a lesser charge when dockets are crowded. Delays cause pretrial detainees to clog the jails, police officers to appear in court on numerous occasions, and attorneys to spend unproductive time appearing on the same case.

One factor contributing to court delay is the lack of incentive to process cases speedily. Although at least 10 states require cases to be dismissed and defendants to be released if they are denied a speedy trial,[40] the U.S. Supreme Court has refused to give the rather vague concept of a "speedy trial" any precise time frame.[41] The problem with time frames, however, is twofold: First, more complex cases legitimately take a long time to prepare, and second, these time limits may be waived due to congested court dockets. In sum, there is no legally binding mechanism that works.

Suggested Solutions and Performance Standards

The best-known legislation addressing the problem is the Speedy Trial Act of 1974, amended in 1979. It provides firm time limits: 30 days from the time of arrest to indictment and 70 days from indictment to trial. Thus, federal prosecutors have a total of 100 days from the time of arrest until trial. This speedy trial law has proven effective over the years.

Unfortunately, however, laws that attempt to speed up trials at the state level have had less success than this federal law because most state laws fail to provide the courts with adequate and effective enforcement mechanisms. As a result, the time limits specified by speedy trial laws are seldom followed in practice.[42]

A number of proposals have emerged to alleviate state and local courts' logjams, ranging from judicial jury selection and limits on criminal appeals to six-person juries. The latter was actually suggested more than two decades ago as a means of relieving the congestion of court calendars and reducing court costs for jurors.[43] Thirty-three states have specifically authorized juries of fewer than 12, but most allow smaller juries only in misdemeanor cases. In federal courts, defendants are entitled to a 12-person jury unless the prosecuting and defense attorneys agree in writing to a smaller one.[44]

The National Center for State Courts (NCSC) has developed a listing of *CourTools*,[45] which together provide a set of trial court performance measures that offer court administrators a balanced perspective on court operations. Note that nearly all of the measures involve the timely disposing of cases in some way.

1. *Clearance rates:* This is the number of outgoing cases as a percentage of the number of incoming cases. Essentially, this is a measure of whether the court is keeping up with its incoming caseload and its ability to avoid a backlog of cases awaiting disposition. This measure is a single number that can be determined for any and all case types, on a monthly or yearly basis, in order to help a court pinpoint emerging problems.

2. *Time to disposition:* This is the percentage of cases disposed or otherwise resolved within established time frames. This measure, used in conjunction with the clearance rates measure above and the age of active pending caseload measure below, helps to assess the length of time it takes a court to process cases.

3. *Age of active pending caseload:* This is the number of days from filing until the time of measurement. Knowing the age of the active cases pending before the court is most useful for addressing two related questions: Does a backlog exist? Which cases pose a problem?

4. *Trial date certainty:* This involves the number of times cases are scheduled for trial—a court's ability to hold trials on the first date they are scheduled to be heard. This measure provides a tool to evaluate the effectiveness of calendaring and continuance practices.

5. *Reliability and integrity of case files:* This concerns the percentage of files that can be retrieved within established time standards. The maintenance of case records directly affects the timeliness and integrity of case processing. Courts need to know how long it takes to locate a file, whether the file's contents and case summary information coincide, and the organization and completeness of the file.

6. *Effective use of jurors:* The number of citizens selected for jury duty who are qualified and report to serve relates to the integrity of source lists, the effectiveness of jury management practices, the willingness of citizens to serve, the efficacy of excuse and postponement policies, and the number of exemptions allowed.

7. *Cost per case:* Monitoring the average cost per case, from year to year, provides a practical means to evaluate existing case processing practices and to improve court operations. Cost per case forges a direct connection between how much is spent and what is accomplished.

Figure 8.3 provides an example of how the NCSC recommends measuring trial performance standards—here, the accessibility and reliability of case files, as stated earlier.

Case Scheduling: Two Systems

A key part of addressing case delay concerns the ability of the court administrator to set a date for trial. Scheduling trials is problematic because of forces outside the administrator's control: slow or inaccurate mail delivery, which can result in notices of court appearances arriving after the scheduled hearing; an illegible address that prevents a key witness or defendant from ever being contacted about a hearing or trial; or a jailer's inadvertent failure to include a defendant on a list for transportation. If just one key person fails to appear, the matter must be rescheduled. Furthermore, judges have limited ability to control the actions of personnel from law enforcement, probation, or the court reporter's offices, all of whom have scheduling problems of their own.[46]

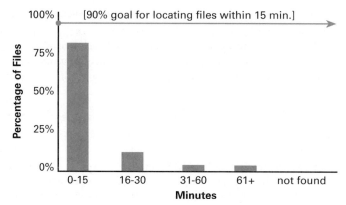

FIGURE 8.3   Measuring Accessibility and Reliability of Case Files

The two primary methods by which cases are scheduled by the courts are the individual calendar and the master calendar.

INDIVIDUAL CALENDAR SYSTEM   The simpler procedure for scheduling cases is the **individual calendar system**. A case is assigned to a single judge, who oversees all aspects of it from arraignment to pretrial motions and trial. The primary advantage is continuity; all parties to the case know that a single judge is responsible for its conclusion. There are other important advantages as well. Judge shopping (in which attorneys try to get their client's case on a particular judge's docket) is minimal, and administrative responsibility for each case is fixed. In addition, it is easier to pinpoint delays because one can easily compare judges' dockets to determine where cases are moving along and where they are not.

This system, however, is often affected by major differences in *case stacking* because judges work at different speeds. In addition, if a judge draws a difficult case, others must wait. Because most cases will be pleaded, however, case stacking is not normally a major problem unless a judge schedules too many cases for adjudication on a given day. Conversely, if a judge stacks too few cases for hearing or adjudication each day, delay will also result. If all cases settle, the judge has dead time, with a large backlog and nothing to do for the rest of the day.

MASTER CALENDAR SYSTEM   The **master calendar system** is a more recent development. Here, judges oversee (usually on a rotating basis) given stages of a case: preliminary hearings, arraignments, motions, bargaining, or trials. A judge is assigned a case from a central or master pool; once he or she has completed a specific phase of it, the case is returned to the pool. The primary advantage of this system is that judges who are good in one particular aspect of litigation (such as preliminary hearings) can be assigned to the job they do best. The disadvantage is that it is more difficult to pinpoint the location of or responsibility for delays. Judges also have less incentive to keep their docket current because when they dispose off one case, another appears. In addition, the distribution of work can be quite uneven. If, for example, three judges are responsible for preliminary hearings and one is much slower than the others, an unequal shifting of the workload will ensue; in other words, the two harder-working judges will be penalized by having to handle more cases.

WHICH SYSTEM IS BETTER?   Each calendar system has advantages and disadvantages, and a debate has developed over which is better. The answer probably depends on the nature of the court. Small courts, such as U.S. district courts, use the individual calendar system more successfully. Largely because of their complex dockets, however, metropolitan and state courts almost uniformly use the master calendar system. Research indicates that courts using the master calendar experience greater difficulty. Typical problems include the following: (1) some judges refuse to take their fair share of cases; (2) the administrative burden on the chief judge is often great; and (3) as a result of these two factors, a significant backlog of cases may develop. In those courts where the master calendar system was discontinued in favor of the individual system, delay was greatly reduced.[47]

DECREASING LITIGATION: ALTERNATIVE DISPUTE RESOLUTION

Chapter 6 included information concerning annual caseloads of some of the nation's courts. Although these lawsuits—both criminal and civil—have arguably resulted in greater safety and a better quality of life in the United States, the fact remains that the weight of this **litigation** has imposed a tremendous workload on the nation's courts.

Several methods are now being proposed to reduce the number of lawsuits in this country. One is to limit punitive damages, with only the judge being allowed to levy them. Another is to force losers to pay the winners' legal fees. The process of discovery also warrants examination. This process involves exchange of information between prosecutors and defense attorneys to ensure that the adversary system does not give one side an unfair advantage over the other. Many knowledgeable people believe that the process of discovery wastes much time and could be revamped.[48]

Another procedure that is already in relatively widespread use is **alternative dispute resolution (ADR)**. Realizing that the exploding backlog of both criminal and civil cases pushes business cases to the back of the queue, many private corporations are attempting to avoid courts and lawyers by using alternative means of resolving their legal conflicts. Some corporations have even opted out of litigation altogether; about 600 top corporations have signed pledges with other companies to consider negotiation and other forms of ADR prior to suing other corporate signers.[49]

ADR is appropriate when new law is not being created. ADR can provide the parties with a forum to reach a resolution that may benefit both sides. Litigation is adversarial; ADR can resolve disputes in a collaborative manner that allows parties' relationship to be maintained. Furthermore, ADR proceedings are normally confidential, with only the final agreement being made public. ADR is also much more expedient and less costly than a trial.[50]

The two most common forms of ADR used today are arbitration and mediation. **Arbitration** is similar to a trial, though less formal. An arbitrator is selected or appointed to a case; civil court rules generally apply. Parties are usually represented by counsel. The arbitrator listens to testimony by witnesses for both sides; then, after hearing closing remarks by counsel, the arbitrator renders a verdict. Arbitration may be mandatory and binding, meaning that the parties abandon their right to go to court once they agree to arbitrate. The arbitration award is usually appealable. Types of disputes commonly resolved through arbitration include collective bargaining agreements, construction and trademark disputes, sales contracts, warranties, and leases.[51]

Mediation is considerably less formal and more friendly than arbitration. Parties agree to negotiate with the aid of an impartial person who facilitates the settlement negotiations. A mediation session includes the mediator and both parties; each side presents his or her position and identifies the issues and areas of dispute. The mediator works with the parties until a settlement is reached or the negotiations become deadlocked; in the latter case, the matter may be continued in court. Mediation is not binding or adversarial; instead, it encourages the parties to resolve the dispute themselves. Mediation is commonly used when the parties in dispute have a continuing relationship, as in landlord–tenant disputes, long-term employment/labor disputes, and disputes between businesses.[52]

One of the oldest and leading ADR firms is Judicial Arbitration & Mediation Services, Inc. (JAMS), headquartered in Irvine, California, and started in 1979. It employs a panel of about 260 former judges. An Internet search will reveal a large number of other firms specializing in ADR as well, and there are even websites available to assist people in locating ADR firms to fit their specific needs. Fees for these private arbitration and mediation firms appear to range from $150 to $500 per hour *per party*, depending on the nature of the services provided and the mediator; this is still a huge savings given the $300 an hour that a battery of lawyers might each charge the litigants.[53]

Given the increasing number of lawsuits in this country, it appears that ADR is the wave of the future; as one law professor noted, "In the future, instead of walking into a building called a courthouse, you might walk into the Dispute Resolution Center."[54]

RECENT SUPREME COURT DECISIONS ON FEDERAL SENTENCING GUIDELINES

Two notable recent U.S. Supreme Court decisions concern federal sentencing guidelines and federal judges' sentences. First, what was termed a "blockbuster" Court decision was issued in January 2005 concerning the federal courts and the Sentencing Reform Act of 1984.[55] The act created the U.S. Sentencing Commission to establish sentencing policies and guidelines (the U.S. Sentencing Guidelines) for the federal criminal justice system. It also required federal courts to use the sentencing guidelines when determining the appropriate sentence for a crime, using an elaborate point system whereby points are assigned to various levels of offenses and the defendant's history. The purpose was to ensure that similarly situated defendants were treated more or less alike rather than depending on the judge to whom their case happened to be assigned.[56]

The Supreme Court's decision came in *U.S. v. Booker*.[57] The defendant, Booker, was found guilty by a jury of possessing at least 50 grams of crack cocaine, based on evidence that he actually had 92.5 grams. Under those facts, the Guidelines required a possible 210- to 262-month sentence. Although the jury never heard any such evidence, the judge, finding by a preponderance of the evidence that Booker possessed the much larger amount of cocaine, rendered a sentence that was almost 10 years longer than the one the Guidelines prescribed.[58]

By a five to four vote, the U.S. Supreme Court found that the U.S. Sentencing Guidelines violated the Sixth Amendment by allowing judicial, rather than jury, fact finding to form the basis for the sentence; in other words, letting in these judge-made facts is unconstitutional. The Guidelines also allowed judges to make such determinations with a lesser standard of proof than that of the jury's "beyond a reasonable doubt" and to rely on hearsay evidence that would not be admissible at trial.[59]

The Court did not discard the Guidelines entirely. The Guidelines, the Court said, are to be merely advisory and not mandatory. Thus, the Guidelines are a resource a judge can consider but may choose to ignore. Although courts still must consider the Guidelines, they need not follow them. In addition, sentences for federal crimes will become subject to appellate review for "unreasonableness," allowing appeals courts to reduce particular sentences that seem far too harsh.

Then, in late 2007, the Supreme Court went further and explained what it meant in 2005 by "advisory" and "reasonableness," deciding two cases that together restored federal judges to their traditional central role in criminal sentencing. The Court found that district court judges do not have to justify their deviations from the federal sentencing Guidelines and have broad discretion to disagree with the Guidelines and to impose what they believe are reasonable sentences—even if the Guidelines call for different sentences. Both cases—*Gall v. U.S.* and *Kimbrough v. U.S.*—were decided by the same 7-2 margin, and the Supreme Court chided federal appeals courts for failing to give district judges sufficient leeway.[60]

A related subject—the effect of the Prison Litigation Reform Act of 1996 on the filing of petitions by state prisoners—is discussed in Chapter 9.

COURTS' MEDIA RELATIONS

As with the police (see Chapter 5), good **media relations** can also be very important for the courts—particularly in high-profile cases. People often wonder why the courts act as they do with respect to public information. As an example, the lawyer defending singer Michael Jackson at his child molestation trial in 2005 caused a furor among the popular media when he asked the judge for a gag order in the case. The lawyer said he was not thinking about the First Amendment when he requested the order but rather about his client's best interests. The media, conversely, felt that the public had a right to know what was occurring in the case.

A debate between journalists and key players in high-profile legal cases occurred recently at one of many conferences sponsored by an organization that is a corollary to the National Judicial College, discussed in Chapter 7; this organization, the National Center for Courts and Media, also located in Reno, Nevada, was established to foster better communication and understanding between judges and lawyers, on the one hand, and between judges and journalists who serve the public on the other hand. The goal is to eliminate unnecessary friction between courts and the media, and bridge the gap between the two through workshops and conferences. The center helps judges to understand what a reporter is seeking and why; conversely, the workshops help journalists learn what records are open to the public, how the legal system works, who to go to for court information, how to gain access to documents, and what restrictions a judge works under.[61]

Exhibit 8.2 discusses the U.S. Supreme Court's relations with the media under new Chief Justice John Roberts.

EXHIBIT 8.2

The Roberts Court Becomes More Media-Friendly

Many Supreme Court justices prize the anonymity that comes with their lifetime appointments and camera-free courtroom. On rare occasion, a justice might consent to an interview on the C-SPAN cable network to discuss a recent book or be shown addressing a lawyers' gathering somewhere. Lately, however, some members of the court have been appearing in unusual places, including network television news programs, and talking about more than just the law; justices are talking off the bench informally to reporters, on the record, off the record, in public, on tape, and on film. Justices Antonin Scalia and Stephen Breyer recently debated their competing views of the Constitution. Breyer and retired Justice Sandra Day O'Connor have talked publicly and repeatedly about threats to judicial independence. Perhaps most noteworthy has been the media-friendly attitude adopted by Chief Justice John Roberts, who was featured on ABC News' "Nightline" discussing both his view of the court and his son's Spiderman imitation.

Source: Based on Fox News and the Associated Press, "Roberts Court: More Media-Friendly?" http://www.foxnews.com/story/0,2933,238758,00.html (accessed July 18, 2008).

OTHER ISSUES

Should Juveniles Be Tried as Adults?

During the mid-1990s, the nation's focus on crime began to shift from drugs to juvenile crime, particularly violent crime. Beginning in the mid-1980s, a juvenile crime wave that would be like none other was predicted to be on the horizon; a "superpredator" form of juvenile offender was anticipated to prey on society in large numbers, bolstered by the realization that the juvenile population would increase from 27 to 39 million by 2000. That prediction, however, never came to pass.[62]

Numerous states are responding to public perceptions that violent juvenile crime is a growing menace, however, by making it easier to transfer juveniles from the relatively "protective shroud" of juvenile court to the jurisdiction of adult courts, thus **juveniles tried as adults**. The philosophy and treatment of juveniles are quite different in the latter courts, where the process is adversarial instead of amicable and punitive rather than treatment oriented.

States are also lowering the age and increasing the list of crimes for which juveniles can be transferred. The state of Georgia, for example, enacted mandatory transfer for juveniles 13 years of age and older who have been charged with specified serious offenses (if convicted, a 13-year-old may face a minimum 10-year prison sentence). Today, at least 24 states have laws sending violent juveniles to adult courts.[63]

Concerns regarding due process include the worry that this approach carries the possibility of juveniles being incarcerated with adult offenders and possibly being raped or assaulted by older inmates. Advocates of restorative justice emphasize that juveniles are the prime example of a group where efforts at reconciliation are likely to yield more positive results than punitive measures.[64]

Should juveniles be prosecuted as adults? If so, under what conditions should they be sentenced and incarcerated? Should potential and traditional rehabilitative philosophies and functions of the juvenile court be taken into account? These questions must be addressed not only in light of the hardened nature of today's violent juvenile offenders but also in terms of what the future holds for juvenile violence.

Should the Exclusionary Rule Be Banned?

The **exclusionary rule** quickly became controversial for both crime control and due process advocates when it was adopted in 1961 by the U.S. Supreme Court in *Mapp v. Ohio*.[65] The view of the crime control model—as expressed by President Ronald Reagan in 1981—was, and is, that the rule "rests on the absurd proposition that a law enforcement error, no matter how technical, can be used to justify throwing an entire case out of court. The plain consequence is a grievous miscarriage of justice: the criminal goes free."[66]

For many legal experts who are inclined toward the due process model, however, illegal conduct by the police cannot be ignored. They believe that a court that admits tainted evidence tolerates the unconstitutional conduct that produced it and demonstrates an "insufficient commitment to the guarantee against unreasonable search and seizure."[67]

Although the exclusionary rule remains controversial, the nature of the debate has changed. Initially, critics called for complete abolition of the rule; now, they suggest modifications. Former Chief Justice Warren Burger urged an "egregious violation standard," whereby the police could be liable to civil suits when they were believed to be in error. Others support an exception for reasonable mistakes by the police. In fact, the U.S. Supreme Court recognized an "honest mistake" or "good faith" exception to the rule only in extremely narrow and limited circumstances.[68] Furthermore, the Rehnquist Court included six justices who publicly criticized *Mapp*. This majority, however, was not able to fashion a means of replacing *Mapp* while prohibiting truly bad-faith searches by the police. As a result, predicting the future of the exclusionary rule is difficult at best.

Should the exclusionary rule be abolished outright? Modified? Kept in its present form? These are compelling questions that our society and its courts may continue to ponder for many years to come.

Should Cameras Be Banned?

As the trial of actor Robert Blake (charged with murdering his wife, Bonny Lee Bakley) was being prepared in 2002, the controversy over whether cameras should be allowed in court—with a well-known actor playing himself in a real-life courtroom drama—was rekindled. The widely televised trial of O.J. Simpson clearly caused a reconsideration of this issue.

Perceptions that Simpson's lawyers played to the cameras apparently had an impact in several highly publicized cases that followed: A judge refused to allow broadcasts in the trial of Susan Smith, a South Carolina woman accused of drowning her two young sons in 1995,[69] and a California judge barred cameras in the trial of Richard Allen Davis, who kidnapped and killed Polly Klaas in 1993.

By the late 1990s, however, despite the Simpson trial backlash, opposition had cooled; a study found that four of every five television requests were approved by judges in California in 1998 and 1999.[70] Indeed, a judge allowed coverage of the trial of four police officers accused (and acquitted) of murdering Amadou Diallo in New York City in 2000.

The Blake trial once again brought to center stage all of the concerns about televising high-publicity trials. Opponents of cameras in court—including due process advocates—complain that televising trials distorts the process by encouraging participants to play to the cameras, and that by covering only sensational trials and presenting only dramatic moments of testimony, television does not portray the trial process accurately.[71] They argue that in celebrity cases, even the witnesses "exaggerate things to give themselves a bigger role."[72] Supporters of the practice, conversely, maintain that televising trials has educational value, providing the public with a firsthand view of how courts operate. Indeed, studies have found that viewers of a television trial of moderate interest became more knowledgeable about the judicial process.[73]

The question of publicizing high-profile cases is not new. Cameras or recording devices were forbidden in the courthouse following the excessive press coverage of the trial of German immigrant Bruno Hauptman, who was accused of kidnapping and murdering the son of the famous aviator Charles Lindbergh in the 1930s. This case is the reason that television stations began to hire artists to provide sketches of courtroom participants.

Restrictions on cameras in the courtroom are changing, however. The Supreme Court unanimously held that electronic media and still-photographic coverage of public judicial proceedings does not violate a defendant's right to a fair trial; states are therefore free to set their own guidelines. Only two states prohibit all forms of electronic coverage of criminal trial proceedings; 35 states allow it.[74] The remaining states are still undecided.

To prevent disruption of the proceedings and to prohibit camera operators from moving about the courtroom while the trial is in session, states have limitations on electronic coverage. Furthermore, some states require the consent of the parties, meaning that either side can veto it. In others, the news media need only receive permission from the trial judge to broadcast the proceedings.[75]

The lingering question is whether cameras are an asset or a liability in the courtroom. To answer it, one must determine whether their education and publicity value exceeds their potential liabilities.

Does Plea Bargaining Belong?

Some people within the court system believe that **plea bargaining** reduces the courthouse to something akin to a Turkish bazaar, where people barter over the price of copper jugs.[76] They see it as justice on the cheap. Others believe that plea bargaining makes the job of the judge, prosecutor, and defense attorney much easier. Primary opposition to plea bargaining involves ideological preferences. Regardless of which side of the issue one supports, however, it is ironic that both police and civil libertarians oppose plea bargaining, but for different reasons.

Police and others in the crime control camp view plea bargaining as undesirable because defendants can avoid conviction for crimes they actually committed while pleading to and receiving a sentence for lesser offenses. The police see victims at their worst and are highly upset when, for example, an accused rapist is allowed to plead guilty to a lesser charge because a prosecutor believes that evidence for a rape conviction is lacking. These advocates of crime control would much prefer to see the defendant convicted for the crime charged.

Civil libertarians and supporters of the due process model oppose plea bargaining because, when agreeing to plead to a crime(s), the accused forfeits a long list of due process protections afforded under the Bill of Rights: the presumption of innocence; the government's burden of proof; and the rights to face one's accuser, to testify and present witnesses in one's defense, to have an attorney, to appeal, and so on. Another concern is that an innocent defendant might be forced to enter a plea of guilty.

A bargained agreement on reduced charges may be the product of initial overcharging and/or of evidence problems that surface later. Furthermore, defendants who gain the most from plea bargaining are the less serious, marginal offenders in cases lacking evidence. By contrast, defendants in serious cases who have prior criminal histories do not benefit. In short, plea bargaining appears to reflect a rational rather than a coercive process.

Overall, does plea bargaining sacrifice the rights of the defendant or does justice suffer by giving too much benefit to guilty persons? These are the fundamental questions that have swirled around this concept since its inception.

JURY SCIENCE

Another issue in today's courtrooms relates to various services provided under the general designation of **jury science**. Although scientific jury selection—hiring a private consulting firm to sample a geographical area and determine what constitutes a jury of one's peers—has existed for many years, methods used and services provided by many firms today to assist trial attorneys *are* relatively new. Many private firms provide consultation concerning jury selection and focus on the thought processes of jurors to also make the jury more predictable. Using what they market as "proven scientific techniques,"[77] such firms analyze litigation issues and advise clients and attorneys on every facet of case development, providing services such as fieldwork, focus groups, jury simulations, witness preparation, mock trials, and courtroom observation. They also prepare courtroom graphics, animations, and estimates of the probability of damages based on jury research.

Summary

This chapter discussed several challenges involving the courts, generated from both internal and external sources, for today and for the future.

It is obvious that contemporary and future court issues and operations carry tremendous challenges for administrators. Those who serve as court leaders must be innovative, open to new ideas, accountable, well trained, and educated for the challenges that lie ahead. Legislators and policymakers must also become more aware of the difficulties confronting the courts and be prepared to provide additional resources for meeting the increasing caseloads, issues, and problems of the future.

Questions for Review

1. What is the "CSI effect," and how does it affect—and not affect—court operations and court actors?
2. What are the characteristics of courthouse shootings, the differences between courthouse violence that is targeted and nontargeted, and means by which a threat assessment help to determine whether someone poses a serious risk to court safety?
3. Give examples of problem-solving courts. How are they different in philosophy and function from traditional courts? What are some issues now confronting mental health courts?
4. What are the possible consequences of delay in the courts, and what are some possible solutions to this problem?
5. What are the two primary methods of case scheduling employed by the courts? What are the advantages and disadvantages of each?
6. In what ways does ADR hold promise for reducing the current avalanche of lawsuits?
7. What did the U.S. Supreme Court recently decide concerning the application of federal sentencing guidelines?
8. What are the major considerations regarding the courts' relations with the media?
9. Should juveniles be tried as adults? Why or why not?
10. Should the exclusionary rule be banned? Why or why not?
11. Should plea bargaining and courtroom cameras be kept or barred from our legal system? Why or why not?
12. What are the services provided and methods used in the field of jury science?

Learn by Doing

1. You are enrolled in a criminal justice internship with the district attorney's Victim Assistance Program. In the course of your work, you have access to all files and reports in the prosecutor's office. One current case has generated a lot of community publicity and interest and involves a child who was kidnapped and locked in a closet at the home of her captor for six months prior to her being rescued. The case is scheduled for trial next week. The defendant has a lengthy criminal history, and the community grapevine has been alive with discontentment about his being paroled only to commit this heinous crime. Through the victim's office staff, you have been able to follow the case progression closely, from the point of the initial investigation to attempts at plea negotiation between the attorneys. You are finishing some work and answering phones in the office, you receive a phone call from a newspaper reporter asking pointed questions about the case and the "rumor that a plea bargain has been struck." The reporter has also heard rumors of a planned attack against the defendant by some citizen-observers in court. How will you respond to this reporter's queries?

2. As part of a paper, you and your criminal justice professor are preparing for an approaching conference, you wish to discuss on how drug courts and MHCs focus on underlying chronic behaviors of criminal defendants. However, your professor asks you to include the kinds of problems and approaches that might be used by homeless courts and teen courts as well. What will you write?

3. Your local chapter of the League of Women Voters is planning a workshop to better understand some forthcoming political campaign issues, including the so-called "CSI effect," increasing numbers of juveniles who are remanded to adult court, use of cameras in the courtroom, and cases being plea bargained. As your criminal justice agency's legislative liaison, you are asked to assist by preparing a brief pro/con paper for two of these issues. What will you report?

Related Websites

ABA—Courthouse Violence
http://www.abanet.org/media/releases/opedcourtviolence.html

Center for Court Innovation
http://www.courtinnovation.org

Center for Therapeutic Justice
http://www.therapeuticjustice.com

Drug Court Technology
http://www.drugcourttech.org

National Association of Drug Courts and Drug Court Professionals
http://www.nadcp.org

National Center for Preventive Law
http://www.preventivelawyer.org/main/default.asp?pid=essays/town.htm

Notes

1. Brian Dakss, "The CSI Effect: Does The TV Crime Drama Influence How Jurors Think?" March 21, 2005, http://www.cbsnews.com/stories/2005/03/21/earlyshow/main681949.shtml (accessed November 16, 2010).

2. Thomas Hughes and Megan Magers, "The Perceived Impact of Crime Scene Investigation Shows on the Administration of Justice," *Journal of Criminal Justice and Popular Culture* 14(3):(2007), http://www.albany.edu/scj/jcjpc/vol14is3/HughesMagers.pdf (accessed October 17, 2010).

3. Ibid.

4. Ibid.

5. Ibid.

6. Ibid.

7. Herbert L. Packer, *The Limits of the Criminal Sanction* (Stanford, CA: Stanford University Press, 1968).

8. Lee Sinclair, "Judicial Violence: Tipping the Scales," in Gary Hengstler (ed.), *Case in Point* (Reno, NV: The National Judicial College, 2006), p. 5.

9. Gary Hengstler, "Judicial Violence: Tipping the Scales," ibid., pp. 3–5.

10. Ibid., p. 3.

11. Gregg W. Etter and Warren G. Swymeler, "Research Note: Courthouse Shootings, 1907–2007," *Homicide Studies* 14(1)(2009):90–100, http://0-hsx.sagepub.com.innopac.library.unr.edu/content/14/1/90.full.pdf+html (accessed October 15, 2010).

12. Ibid.

13. Don Hardenbergh and Neil Alan Weiner, "Preface," in Don Hardenbergh and Neil Alan Weiner (eds.), *The Annals of the American Academy of Political and Social Science, Vol. 576: Courthouse Violence: Protecting the Judicial Workplace* (Thousand Oaks, CA: Author, 2001), p. 10.

14. David W. Neubauer, *America's Courts and the Criminal Justice System,* 9th ed. (Belmont, CA: Wadsworth, 2008), p. 402.

15. Ibid., p. 82.

16. Bryan Vossekuil, Randy Borum, Robert Fein, and Marisa Reddy, "Preventing Targeted Violence Against Judicial Officials and Courts," in Hardenbergh and Weiner (eds.), *The Annals of the American Academy of Political and Social Science, Vol. 576: Courthouse Violence,* pp. 78–90.

17. Susan Voyles, "Shooting Sparks Worries about Safety," *Reno Gazette-Journal,* June 14, 2006, p. 1C.

18. See GovTrack.US, "H.R. 1751 [109th]: Court Security Improvement Act of 2006," http://www.govtrack.us/congress/bill.xpd?bill=h109-1751 (accessed February 6, 2008).

19. Vossekuil et al., "Preventing Targeted Violence Against Judicial Officials and Courts," p. 80.

20. Robert V. Wolf, "Breaking with Tradition: Introducing Problem Solving in Conventional Courts," *International Review of Law Computers & Technology* 22(1–2)(2008):77–93.

21. Greg Berman and John Feinblatt, "Problem-Solving Courts: A Brief Primer," *Law & Policy* 23(2)(2001): 125–140.

22. Ibid., p. 127.

23. Ibid., p. 128.

24. Wolf, "Breaking with Tradition: Introducing Problem Solving in Conventional Courts," p. 80.

25. West Huddleston and Douglas B. Marlowe, *Painting the Current Picture: A National Report on Drug Courts and Other Problem-Solving Court Programs in the United States* (Alexandria, VA: U.S. Department of Justice, National Drug Court Institute, 2011), p. 1.

26. U.S. Department of Justice, National Criminal Justice Reference Service, "Drug Court Resources: Facts

and Figures," http://www.ncjrs.org/drug_courts/facts.html (accessed February 17, 2005).

27. U.S. Government Accounting Office, *Adult Drug Courts: Evidence Indicates Recidivism Reductions and Mixed Results for Other Outcomes*, December 2005, http://www.gao.gov/new.items/d05219.pdf (accessed December 24, 2010).

28. U.S. Department of Justice, Bureau of Justice Assistance, *Improving Responses to People with Mental Illnesses*, 2007, p. vii, http://www.ojp.usdoj.gov/BJA/pdf/MHC_Essential_Elements.pdf (accessed December 24, 2010).

29. Ibid.

30. Allison D. Redlich, Steven Hoover, Alicia Summers, and Henry J. Steadman, "Enrollment in Mental Health Courts: Voluntariness, Knowingness, and Adjudicative Competence," *Law & Human Behavior* 34 (2010):91–104.

31. Ibid.

32. Nicholas Riccardi, "These Courts Give Wayward Veterans a Chance," *Los Angeles Times*, March 30, 2009, http://articles.latimes.com/2009/mar/10/nation/na-veterans-court10 (accessed November 19, 2010).

33. Amanda Ruggeri, "New Courts Give Troubled Veterans a Second Chance," *US News and World Report*, April 3, 2009, http://politics.usnews.com/news/national/articles/2009/04/03/new-courts-give-troubled-veterans-a-second-chance.html (accessed November 19, 2010).

34. Disabled World, "Veterans Courts: A Second Chance for Those Who Have Served," http://www.disabled-world.com/disability/legal/veterans-court.php (accessed November 19, 2010).

35. Quoted in The Pew Center on the States, "New courts tailored to war veterans," June 18, 2009, http://www.stateline.org/live/details/story?contentId=407573 (accessed November 19, 2010).

36. *Barker v. Wingo,* 407 U.S. 514 (1972).

37. Neubauer, *America's Courts and the Criminal Justice System,* pp. 112–114.

38. Ibid.

39. Ibid.

40. See *Barker v. Wingo,* 407 U.S. 514 (1972).

41. Ibid., p. 522.

42. Neubauer, *America's Courts and the Criminal Justice System,* pp. 114–116.

43. National Advisory Commission on Criminal Justice Standards and Goals, *Courts* (Washington, DC: U.S. Government Printing Office, 1973), p. 12.

44. Neubauer, *America's Courts and the Criminal Justice System* pp. 293–295.

45. Adapted from the National Center for State Courts, "CourTools: Trial Court Performance Standards," http://www.ncsconline.org/D_Research/CourTools/Images/CourToolsOnlineBrochure.pdf (accessed November 17, 2010).

46. Steven Flanders, *Case Management and Court Management in the United States District Courts* (Washington, DC: Federal Judicial Center, 1977).

47. David W. Neubauer, Maria Lipetz, Mary Luskin, and John Paul Ryan, *Managing the Pace of Justice: An Evaluation of LEAA's Court Delay Reduction Programs* (Washington, DC: U.S. Government Printing Office, 1981).

48. Bob Cohn, "The Lawsuit Cha-Cha," *Newsweek* (August 26, 1991):59.

49. Michele Galen, Alice Cuneo, and David Greising, "Guilty!" *Business Week* (April 13, 1992):63.

50. American Bar Association, *Dispute Resolution: A 60-Minute Primer* (Washington, DC: Author, 1994), pp. 1–2.

51. Ibid., p. 3.

52. Ibid., p. 4.

53. Quoted in American Bar Association, Dispute Resolution; also see Judicial Arbitration and Mediation Services, Inc., "About JAMS," http://www.jamsadr.com/aboutus_overview/(accessed August 27, 2011).

54. ABA, Dispute Resolution, p. 64.

55. 18 U.S.C. Secs. 3551–3626 and 28 U.S. C. Secs. 991–998 (October 12, 1984).

56. Mark Allenbaugh, "The Supreme Court's New Blockbuster U.S. Sentencing Guidelines Decision," http://writ.news.findlaw.com/allenbaugh/20050114.html (accessed January 17, 2005).

57. *U.S. v. Booker,* 543 U.S.125 S.Ct. 738 (2005).

58. FindLaw Legal News, "*United States v. Booker,*" http://caselaw.lp.findlaw.com/scripts/printer_friendly.pl?page=us/000/04-104.html (accessed January 17, 2005).

59. Allenbaugh, "The Supreme Court's New Blockbuster U.S. Sentencing Guidelines Decision," p. 2.

60. *San Francisco Chronicle*, SFGate.com, "High Court Gives U.S. Judges More Freedom in Sentencing," http://www.sfgate.com/cgi-bin/article.cgi?f=/c/a/2007/12/11/MNE3TRS7O.DTL (accessed December 11, 2007). See *Gall v. U.S.,* 446 F3d 884 (cert. granted 6/11/2007), and *Kimbrough v. U.S*, 174 Fed. Appx. 798 (cert. granted 6/11/2007).

61. Martha Bellisle, "Bridging the Gap: Judges, Lawyers, and Members of the Media Learn to Understand One Another," *Reno Magazine* (September–October 2006):74.

62. Kevin Johnson and Gary Fields, "Juvenile Crime 'Wave' May Be Just a Ripple," *USA Today,* December 13, 1996, p. 3.

63. Neubauer, *America's Courts and the Criminal Justice System*, p. 429.

64. Ibid., pp. 428–429.

65. 367 U.S. 643.

66. Quoted in Neubauer, *America's Courts and the Criminal Justice System*, p. 265.

67. Yale Kamisar, "Is the Exclusionary Rule an 'Illogical' or 'Unnatural' Interpretation of the Fourth Amendment?" *Judicature* 78 (1994):83–84.

68. See, for example, *U.S. v. Leon,* 486 U.S. 897 (1984), and *Illinois v. Krull,* 480 U.S. 340 (1987).

69. Jesse Holland, "Susan Smith Judge Bars TV Cameras from Murder Trial," *Times-Picayune,* June 25, 1995, p. 1A.

70. Zanto Peabody, "Blake Case Revives Issue of Cameras in Court," *Los Angeles Times,* May 27, 2002, p. 1A.

71. Paul Thaler, *The Watchful Eye: American Justice in the Age of the Television Trial* (Westport, CT: Praeger, 1994).

72. Peabody, "Blake Case Revives Issue of Cameras in Court," p. 1A.

73. S. L. Alexander, "Cameras in the Courtroom: A Case Study," *Judicature* 74 (1991):307–313; Paul Raymond, "The Impact of a Televised Trial on Individuals' Information and Attitudes," *Judicature* 57 (1992):204–209.

74. Alexander, "Cameras in the Courtroom."

75. Neubauer, *America's Courts and the Criminal Justice System*, pp. 312–313.

76. Alvin Rubin, "How We Can Improve Judicial Treatment of Individual Cases without Sacrificing Individual Rights: The Problems of the Criminal Law," *Federal Rules of Decisions* 70 (1976):176.

77. For example, for the kinds of services provided, see Trial Practices, Inc., http://www.trialpractice.com/intro.htm (accessed December 1, 2010).

PART 4

Corrections

This part includes three chapters about corrections administration. Chapter 9 examines corrections organization and operation, including prisons, jails, and probation and parole agencies. Chapter 10 covers personnel roles and functions. Chapter 11 reviews corrections issues and practices. Specific chapter content is previewed in the introductory section of each chapter. Case studies relating to this part appear in Appendix I.

Corrections Organization and Operation

KEY TERMS AND CONCEPTS

Accreditation

Central office

Custodial functions

Customer model

Direct supervision jail

Employer model

Frivolous lawsuits

Hands-off policy

Jails as organizations

Parole

Personnel model

Prisons as organizations

Prison industries

Prison Litigation Reform Act (PLRA)

Prisoners' rights

Probation

Reentry (into the community)

Treatment functions

Rehabilitation

Warden

Supermax prison

LEARNING OBJECTIVES

After reading this chapter, the student will:

- be familiar with the general features of a correctional organization in the United States, including the levels of correctional incarceration, employment, expenditures, and several factors affecting prison and jail populations
- have an idea of the personnel and divisions found in the state's central office as well as in individual prisons
- be able to describe supermax prisons, including their method of operation, alleged effects on inmates, constitutionality, and implications for corrections policy
- know what is meant by the early *hands-off era* of the courts toward prisons, and several substantive U.S. Supreme Court decisions that afforded inmates significant constitutional rights
- understand the nature and extent of litigation by prison and jail inmates, including the rationale, provisions, and impact of the **Prison Litigation Reform Act** (**PLRA**)
- know how direct supervision jails differ from the traditional model in design and functions, how jails can prepare inmates for **reentry in the community**, and general functions of jail administrators
- be familiar with the means and rationale for accreditation of corrections facilities
- know the systems theory of probation and the six categories of probation systems, including their resources, activities, and outcomes
- know the three services of parole agencies and the two models used for administering them
- know the advantages of the independent and consolidated models of parole

> *The founders of a new colony . . . recognized it among their earliest practical necessities to allot a portion of the virgin soil as a cemetery, and another portion as the site of a prison.*
> —Nathaniel Hawthorne

> *Even I / Regained my freedom with a sigh.*
> —Lord Byron

INTRODUCTION

The organization and operation of prisons, jails, and probation and parole functions in our society are largely unknown and misunderstood. Indeed, most of what the public "knows" about the inner workings of these organizations is obtained through Hollywood's eyes and depictions—*The*

Shawshank Redemption, The Green Mile, The Longest Yard, Escape from Alcatraz, and *Cool Hand Luke* are a few examples of such popular depictions that are frequently shown on television.

Unfortunately, however, because the movie industry is more concerned with box-office sales than with depicting reality, liberties are taken and the portrayal of prisons in film is generally inaccurate. Furthermore, although problems certainly can and do arise in correctional institutions, movies often accentuate and exaggerate their negative aspects. Therefore, it should be remembered that the reality of prison operations is often at considerable variance with what is projected on the big screen.

The opening of this chapter demonstrates that corrections is now a booming industry in terms of both expenditures and employment; we look at some reasons for the increase in correction populations and its general mission. Then we focus on correctional agencies as organizations, including a view of the statewide central offices overseeing prison systems and their related functions as well as individual prisons. Next is a discussion of the relatively new supermax prisons, including their unique method of operation, alleged effects on inmates, constitutionality, and implications for corrections policy. After that is a consideration of selected major federal court decisions concerning prisoners' rights under the First, Fourth, Eighth, and Fourteenth Amendments; following that is a review of prison litigation generally, including the rationale and impact of the PLRA.

Next, we examine local jails, including their organization, the unique structure and function of podular direct supervision jails, and how jails can prepare inmates for reentry into society. After briefly considering the rationale for and means of accreditation of corrections facilities, we conclude by looking at the organization of probation and parole agencies.

CORRECTIONAL ORGANIZATIONS

Inmates, Employment, and Expenditures

Today, prisons and jails at the federal, state, and local levels employ about 780,000 people (one-third of them at the local level and about 60 percent for state governments), and cost about $3 billion in annual payrolls.[1] Furthermore, as shown in Table 9.1, these prisons and jails now have about 1.6 million prisoners in custody. It is also seen that this is an increase of about 225,000 inmates from 2000 to present. Why this increase in corrections populations? There are several factors affecting prison and jail populations. First are arrests for drug use. (Of course, there is long-standing debate in this country concerning the efficacy of America's "War on Drugs," and whether some currently illegal drugs—marijuana in particular—should be legalized. For some people, the nation's drug policy is even racist—as one put it, that the "high rates of incarceration is the United States government's relentless and racist pursuit of the 'War on Drugs'."[2] Others believe that the failed lessons of Prohibition—when "crime rates shot up, corruption was unprecedented, criminal gangs were nurtured, and respect for law diminished"—should bring the repeal of laws relating to many drugs that are sold and consumed in the United States[3] This controversial subject probably reached its high-water mark in November 2010, when 3.4 million voters in California—which, along with 14 other states, has enacted laws that legalize medical marijuana—supported persons over 21 years being allowed to grow up to 25 square feet of marijuana and to possess up to an ounce for personal consumption; Proposition 19 lost, however.[4]) Controversy notwithstanding, the fact remains that more than 1.6 million adults and nearly 200,000 juveniles are arrested for drug abuse violations in the United .States each year.[5]

TABLE 9.1

TABLE 9.1 Prisoners Under the Jurisdiction of State or Federal Prisons or in the Custody of State or Federal Prisons or Local Jails. December 31, 2000 and 2008, and June 30, 2008 and 2009

Year	Prisoners under jurisdiction						Imprisonment rate[b]	Incarceration rate for inmates in custody[c]
	Total	Federal	State	Male	Female	Sentenced prisoners[a]		
2000	1,391,261	145,416	1,245,845	1,298,027	93,234	1,331,278	478	684
2001	1,404,032	156,993	1,247,039	1,311,053	92,979	1,345,217	470	685
2002	1,440,144	163,528	1,276,616	1,342,513	97,631	1,380,516	476	701
2003	1,468,601	173,059	1,295,542	1,367,755	100,846	1,408,361	482	712
2004	1,497,100	180,328	1,316,772	1,392,278	104,822	1,433,728	486	723
2005	1,527,929	187,618	1,340,311	1,420,303	107,626	1,462,866	491	737
2006	1,569,945	193,046	1,376,899	1,457,486	112,459	1,504,660	501	751
2007	1,598,245	199,618	1,398,627	1,483,740	114,505	1,532,850	506	756
2008								
June 30	1,610,542	201,142	1,409,400	1,494,662	115,880	1,541,847	509	762
December 31	1,609,759	201,280	1,408,479	1,495,110	114,649	1,547,742	504	756
2009								
June 30	1,617,478	206,577	1,410,901	1,502,499	114,979	1,551,135	504	748
Annual change								
Average annual change, 12/31/2000-12/31/2008	1.8 %	4.1 %	1.5 %	1.8 %	2.6 %	1.9 %	0.7 %	1.2 %
6/30/2008-6/30/2009	0.4	2.7	0.1	0.5	-0.8	0.6	-1.0	-1.8
6-month change								
12/31/2007-06/30/2008	0.8 %	0.8 %	0.8 %	0.7 %	1.2 %	0.6 %	0.6 %	0.8 %
12/31/2008-06/30/2009	0.5	2.6	0.2	0.5	0.3	0.2	-0.1	-0.8

Source: U.S. Department of Justice, Bureau of Justice Statistics, "Correctional Populations in the United States, 2009," p. 2 (December, 2010), http://bjs.gov/content/pub/pdf/cpus09.pdf (Accessed August 27, 2011).

[a]Includes prisoners under the jurisdiction of state or federal correctional officials with sentences of more than one year.

[b]Imprisonment rate is the number of prisoners under state or federal jurisdiction with a sentence of more than one year per 100,000 U.S. residents. Resident population estimates are from the U.S. Census Bureau for January 1 of the following year for December 31 estimates and July 1 of the current year for midyear estimates.

[c]Incarceration rate is the total number of inmates held in custody of state or federal prisons or in local jails per 100,000 U.S. residents.

Other commonly cited factors for high incarceration rates include truth-in-sentencing laws, violence on television and in the movies, and a general deterioration of morals and of the family.

Truth in sentencing for prison inmates began in 1984 in Washington State. The concept, which involves restriction or elimination of parole eligibility and good-time credits, quickly spread to other states after a determination in 1996 that prisoners were serving on average about 44 percent of their court sentence. To ensure that offenders serve larger portions of their sentence, Congress authorized funding for additional state prisons and jails if states met eligibility criteria for truth-in-sentencing programs.[6] To qualify, states had to require violent offenders to serve at least 85 percent of their prison sentence. Congress allocated to the 50 participating states nearly $11 billion in funding for the Violent Offender Incarceration/Truth-in-Sentencing program through fiscal year 2001; no funding was allocated thereafter.[7]

A philosophical shift about the purpose of incarceration also contributed to prison crowding. In response to the apparent failure of **rehabilitation** policies, the now-prevailing philosophy sees prisons as places to incarcerate and punish inmates in an effort to deter crime. This philosophy has resulted in get-tough sentencing practices (including mandatory sentencing laws), which contribute to rising prison populations. Legislators have essentially removed the word *rehabilitation* from the penal code while focusing on fixed sentences. This shift from rehabilitating inmates to what is termed *just desserts* is based on the view that offenders make free-will decisions to commit crimes and, therefore, no longer deserve compassion and correction. U.S. citizens, however, may be leaning more toward rehabilitative efforts. One survey found that about 72 percent of Americans "completely agree" or "mostly agree" that it is more important to try to rehabilitate people who are in prison than merely to punish them.[8]

Robert Martinson's well-publicized finding that "almost nothing works" in correctional treatment programs served to ignite a firestorm of debate that has lasted more than two decades.[9] Although Martinson's methodology was brought into serious question and he later attempted to recant his findings, his assessment clearly had a major impact. Legislators and corrections administrators became unwilling to fund treatment programs from dwindling budgets, whereas academics and policymakers claimed that the medical model of correctional treatment programs failed to accomplish its goals. Paul Louis and Jerry Sparger noted that "perhaps the most lasting effect of the 'nothing works' philosophy is the spread of cynicism and hopelessness" among prison administrators and staff members.[10]

An even greater widening between the rehabilitation and just-desserts approaches occurred in the 1980s. Ted Palmer[11] identified these modified positions as the "skeptical" and "sanguine" camps. The skeptics believed that relatively few prison programs work and that successful ones account for only negligible reductions in recidivism. Furthermore, they believed that rehabilitation programs had not been given an adequate chance in correctional settings because they were either poorly designed or badly implemented. The sanguine perspective is that although the existing rehabilitation programs have not been very effective to date, evidence indicates that many programs provide positive treatment for selected portions of the offender population. A reassessment of Martinson's "nothing works" statement by Palmer and others has given new hope for rehabilitation. Palmer rejected Martinson's indictment of correctional treatment modalities and demonstrated that many of the programs initially reviewed by Martinson were actually quite successful.[12] Other research has supported Palmer's position.[13] Still, the rehabilitative philosophy is not expected to see a resurgence in the foreseeable future.

Some observers, however, also believe that the just-desserts logic is defeated by a combination of demography and justice system inefficiency. Each year, a new crop of youths in their upper teens constitutes the majority of those arrested for serious crimes. As these offenders are arrested and removed from the crime scene, a new crop replaces them: "The justice system is eating its young. It imprisons them, paroles them, and rearrests them with no rehabilitation in between," according to Dale Secrest.[14]

Still, large-scale, long-term imprisonment unquestionably keeps truly serious offenders behind bars, preventing them from committing more crimes.

General Mission and Features

Correctional organizations are complex hybrid organizations that utilize two distinct yet related management subsystems to achieve their goals: One is concerned primarily with managing correctional employees and the other is concerned primarily with delivering correctional services to a designated offender population. The correctional organization, therefore, employs one group of people—correctional personnel—to work with and control another group—offenders.

The mission of corrections agencies has changed little over time. It is as follows: to protect the citizens from crime by safely and securely handling criminal offenders while providing offenders some opportunities for self-improvement and increasing the chance that they will become productive and law-abiding citizens.[15]

An interesting feature of the correctional organization is that *every* correctional employee who exercises legal authority over offenders is a supervisor, even if the person is the lowest-ranking member in the agency or institution. Another feature of the correctional organization is that—as with the police—everything a correctional supervisor does may have civil or criminal ramifications, both for himself or herself and for the agency or institution. Therefore, the legal and ethical responsibility for the correctional (and police) supervisor is greater than it is for supervisors in other types of organizations.

PRISONS AS ORGANIZATIONS

As noted earlier in this chapter, the mission of most **prisons** is to provide a safe and secure environment for staff and inmates, as well as programs for offenders that can assist them after release.[16] This section describes how prisons are organized to accomplish this mission. First, we look at the larger picture—the typical organization of the central office within the state government that oversees *all* prisons within its jurisdiction. Then we review the characteristic organization of an individual prison.

The Central Office

The state's central organization that oversees its prison system is often called the **central office**. Some of the personnel and functions typically found in a central office are discussed in the following subsections.

OFFICE OF THE DIRECTOR Each state normally has a central department of corrections that is headed by a secretary (or someone with a similar title); in turn, the secretary appoints a person to direct the operation of all of the prisons in the state. The **prison director** sets policy for all wardens to follow in terms of how the institutions should be managed and inmates treated (with regard to both custody and treatment). In addition to the director, the staff within the office of the director includes public or media affairs coordinators, legislative liaisons, legal advisers, and internal affairs representatives.

As they are one of the largest state agencies, a tremendous demand for public information is made on correctional agencies. If a policy issue or a major incident is involved, the media will contact the director for a response. The office of public affairs also oversees the preparation of standard reports, such as an annual review of the department and its status or information on a high-profile program or project. In addition, because state correctional agencies use a large percentage of the state budget, the legislature is always interested in their operations. Therefore, there is usually within the department of corrections an office of legislative affairs, which responds to legislative requests and tries to build support for resources and programs.[17]

Legal divisions, typically composed of four to six attorneys, often report to the director as well. The work of the legal division includes responding to inmate lawsuits, reviewing policy for its legal impact, and offering general advice regarding the implementation of programs in terms of past legal decisions. These attorneys will predict how the courts are likely to respond to a new program in light of legal precedents.

Finally, the director's office usually has an inspector or internal affairs division. Ethics in government is a major priority; corrections staff may be enticed to bring contraband into a prison or may be physically abusive to inmates. Whenever there is a complaint of staff misconduct by anyone, the allegation needs to be investigated.

ADMINISTRATION DIVISION   Two major areas of the administrative division of a corrections central office are budget development/auditing and new prison construction. The administrative division collects information from all of the state's prisons, other divisions, and the governor's office to create a budget that represents ongoing operations and desired programs and growth. Once it is approved by the governor's office, this division begins to explain the budget to the legislative budget committee, which reviews the request and makes a recommendation for funding to the full legislature. After a budget is approved, this division maintains accountability of funds and oversees the design and construction of new and renovated facilities.[18]

CORRECTIONAL PROGRAMS DIVISION   A central office will usually have a division that oversees the operation of correctional programs such as security, education, religious services, mental health, and unit management. It is clear that

> offenders enter prison with a variety of deficits. Some are socially or morally inept, others are intellectually or vocationally handicapped, some have emotional hangups that stem from psychological problems, still others have a mixture of varying proportions of some or even all of these.[19]

Having to deal with inmates suffering from such serious and varied problems is a daunting task for correctional organizations. Prison culture makes the environment inhospitable to programs designed to rehabilitate or reform.

A major contemporary problem among persons entering prison is drug addiction. Drug-addicted offenders are subjected to one of three types of treatment programming, which attempts to address the problem: punitive (largely involving withdrawal and punishment), medical (consisting of detoxification, rebuilding physical health, counseling, and social services), and the communal approach (using group encounters and seminars conducted by former addicts who serve as positive role models).[20] Chapter 11 discusses what prison administrators can do to interdict drugs coming into prisons and the kinds of treatment programs that are maintained in them.

MEDICAL OR HEALTH CARE DIVISION   One of the most complicated and expensive functions within a prison is health care. As a result, this division develops policy, performs quality assurance, and looks for ways to make health care more efficient for inmates and less expensive for the prison. One of the best outcomes for a corrections health care program involved HIV/AIDS. A widespread epidemic of HIV/AIDS cases was initially feared in prisons (through homosexual acts and prior drug use) but such an outbreak never happened. Today, the overall rate of confirmed AIDS cases among the nation's prison population is 0.6 percent, and it has been growing at a much slower rate than that of the overall prison population.[21]

HUMAN RESOURCE MANAGEMENT DIVISION   The usual personnel functions of recruitment, hiring, training, evaluation, and retirement are accomplished in the human resource management division. Affirmative action and labor relations (discussed in Chapter 15) may also be included. Workplace diversity is important for corrections agencies, particularly with the growing number of African American and Hispanic inmates. Most states have a unionized workforce, and negotiating and managing labor issues are time consuming. Therefore, this division has staff with expertise in labor relations.

Figure 9.1 shows the organizational structure of a central office in a state of 3 million people.

Individual Prisons

Over time, prison organizational structure (see Figure 9.2, an organizational structure for a maximum-security prison) has changed considerably to respond to external needs. Until the beginning of the twentieth century, prisons were administered by state boards of charities, boards composed of citizens, boards of inspectors, state prison commissions, or individual prison keepers. Most prisons were individual provinces; wardens, who were given absolute control over their domain, were appointed by governors through a system of political patronage. Individuals were attracted to the position of **warden** because it carried many fringe benefits such as a lavish residence, unlimited inmate servants, food and supplies from institutional farms and warehouses, furnishings, and a personal automobile. Now most wardens or superintendents are civil service employees who have earned their position through seniority and merit.[22]

Attached to the warden's office are (possibly by some other title) an institutional services inspector and the institutional investigator who deals with inmate complaints against staff. As mentioned in the earlier section on the central office, prisons also need personnel who deal with labor contracts and the media, and who collect and provide this information to the central office. A computer services manager maintains the management information systems.

Also reporting to the warden are deputy or associate wardens, each of whom supervises a department within the prison. The deputy warden for operations will normally oversee correctional security, unit management, the inmate disciplinary committee, and recreation. The deputy warden for special services will typically be responsible for functions that are more **treatment oriented**, including the library, mental health services, drug and alcohol recovery services, education, prison job assignments, religious services, and prison industries. Finally, the deputy warden for administration will manage the business office, prison maintenance, laundry, food service, medical services, prison farms, and the issuance of clothing.[23]

It is important to note that custody and treatment are not either/or in correctional organizations; rather, they are complementary. Although custody overshadows treatment in terms of operational priorities—treatment programs are unable to flourish if security is weak and staff and inmates work and live in chronic fear and danger—prisons without programming options

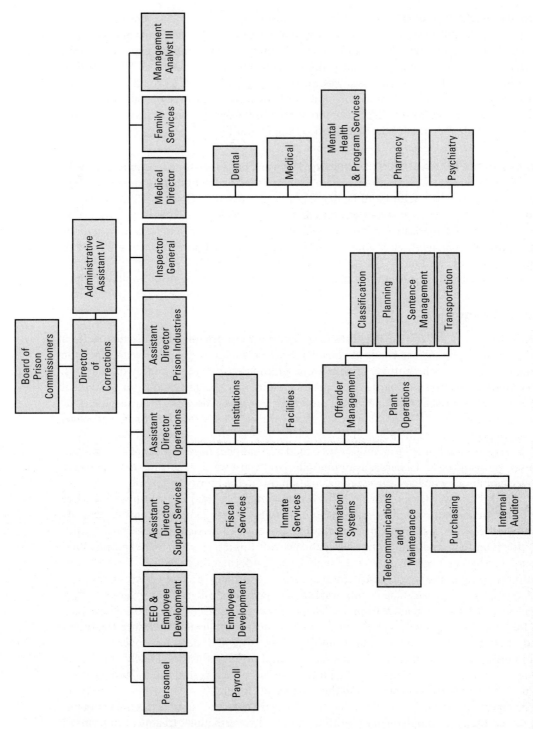

FIGURE 9.1 Organizational Structure for a Correctional Central Office (EEO = Equal Employment Opportunity)

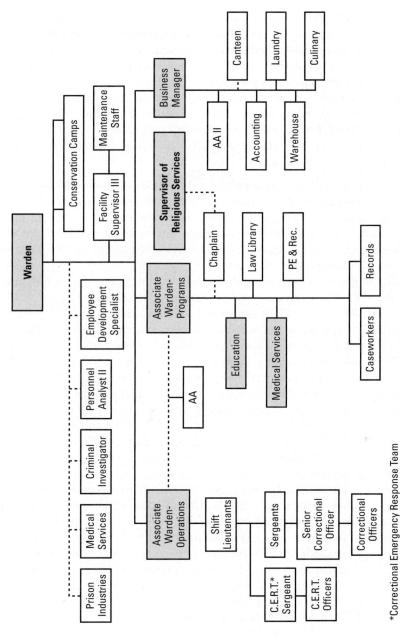

*Correctional Emergency Response Team

FIGURE 9.2 Organizational Structure for a Maximum Security Prison (AA = Administrative Aide; PE & Rec. = Physical Education and Recreation)

for offenders are nothing more than warehouses, being amenable to violence, disruption, and the continuation of criminally deviant behavior. Correctional staff, regardless of their job function, do not support such volatile conditions. Most often, the overriding concern in a prison or jail is and should be security. Security must be maintained so that programs can be implemented. Programs are generally supported by staff, especially those that address inmate deficiencies such as lack of education and job skills as well as substance abuse. Prison administrators must decide which programs they will allow to be introduced into their facility; this is not often an easy task, especially when much of the public preceives that programs only "coddle" inmates.[24]

Next, we discuss several related aspects—correctional security, unit management, education, and penal industries—in more detail.

- The correctional security department is normally the largest department in a prison, with 50 to 70 percent of all staff. It supervises all of the security activities within a prison, including any special housing units, inmate transportation, and the inmate disciplinary process. Security staff wears military-style uniforms; a captain normally runs each 8-hour shift, lieutenants often are responsible for an area of the prison, and sergeants oversee the rank-and-file correctional staff.
- The *unit management* concept originated in the federal prison system in the 1970s and now is used in nearly every state to control prisons by providing a "small, self-contained, inmate living and staff office area that operates semiautonomously within the larger institution."[25] The purpose of unit management is twofold: to decentralize the administration of the prison and to enhance communication among staff and between staff and inmates. Unit management breaks the prison into more manageable sections based on housing assignments; assignment of staff to a particular unit; and staff authority to make decisions, manage the unit, and deal directly with inmates. Units are usually composed of 200 to 300 inmates; staff are not only assigned to units, but their offices are also located in the housing area, making them more accessible to inmates and better able to monitor inmate activities and behavior. Directly reporting to the unit manager are *case managers*, or social workers, who develop the program of work and rehabilitation for each inmate and write progress reports for parole authorities, classification, or transfer to another prison. Correctional counselors also work with inmates in the units on daily issues, such as finding a prison job, working with their prison finances, and creating a visiting and telephone list.[26]
- The education department operates the academic teaching, vocational training, library services, and sometimes recreation programs for inmates. An education department is managed similarly to a conventional elementary or high school, with certified teachers for all subjects that are required by the state department of education or are part of the General Education Degree test. Vocational training can include carpentry, landscaping or horticulture, food service, and office skills.
- **Prison industries** are legislatively chartered as separate government corporations and report directly to the warden because there is often a requirement that the industry be self-supporting or operate from funds generated from the sale of products. Generally, no tax dollars are used to run the programs, and there is strict accountability of funds. A typical prison industry organizational structure is presented in Figure 9.3. Correctional administrators report that joint ventures provide meaningful, productive employment that helps to reduce inmate idleness and supplies companies with a readily available and dependable source of labor, as well as the partial return to society of inmate earnings to pay state and federal taxes, offset incarceration costs, contribute to the support of inmates'

FIGURE 9.3 Organizational Structure for a Prison Industry

Source: From Richard P. Seiter, *Correctional Administration: Integrating Theory and Practice,* p. 199. © 2002. Reprinted by permission of Pearson Education, Inc., Upper Saddle River, New Jersey.

families, and compensate victims. Different types of business relationships have been developed. In the **personnel model**, prisoners are employed by the state division of correctional industries, which in turn charges the companies a fixed rate for their labor. In the **employer model**, the company employs the inmates, and private companies own and operate their prison-based businesses, with prison officials providing the space in which the companies operate as well as a qualified labor pool from which the companies hire employees. In the **customer model**, the company contracts with the prison to provide a finished product at an agreed-on price. The correctional institution owns and operates the business that employs the inmates. These joint ventures provide challenges and problems: absenteeism and rapid turnover of employees, limited opportunities for training, and logistical concerns. Still, many inmates participate in these programs show up for their jobs on time, work hard during their shifts, and have been hired by companies after their release.[27]

RISE OF THE SUPERMAX PRISONS

Definition and Operation

There are 31 **supermax prisons** in the United States.[28] Their method of operations—and, as will be seen, the degree of controversy about them among academics—justify some discussion about them specifically. To understand what supermax prisons are and how they operate, one can look at the Administrative Maximum prison, or ADX, located in Florence, Colorado.

ADX is the only federal supermax prison in the country (the others are state prisons). It is home to a Who's Who of criminals: "Unabomber" Ted Kaczynski, "Shoe Bomber" Richard Reid; Ramzi Yousef, who plotted the 1993 World Trade Center attack; Oklahoma City bomber Terry Nichols; and Olympic Park bomber Eric Rudolph. ADX is known as the "Alcatraz of the Rockies"; 95 percent of its prisoners are the most violent, disruptive, and escape-prone inmates from other federal prisons. Upon viewing its external aspect for the first time, one immediately sees that this is not the usual prison: Large cables are strung above the basketball courts and track; they are helicopter deterrents.[29]

The supermax prison is known variously in different states as a *special management unit, security housing unit (SHU), high-security unit, intensive management unit,* or *special control unit*; its operations are quite different inside as well. Supermax inmates rarely leave their cells; in most cases, an hour a day of out-of-cell time is the norm. They eat all of their meals alone in the cells, and typically no group or social activity of any kind is permitted; they are generally denied access to vocational or educational training programs. Inmates can exist for many years separated from the natural world around them.[30]

Effects on Inmates

Given the high degree of isolation and lack of activities, a major concern voiced by critics of supermax facilities is their *social pathology* and potential effect on inmates' mental health. Although there is very little research to date concerning the effects of supermax prison confinement,[31] some authors point to previous isolation research showing that greater levels of deprivation lead to psychological, emotional, and physical problems—that as inmates face greater restrictions and social deprivations, their level of social withdrawal increases; limiting human contact, autonomy, goods, or services is detrimental to inmates' health and rehabilitative prognoses, and tends to result in depression, hostility, severe anger, sleep disturbances, and anxiety. Women living in a high-security unit have been found to experience claustrophobia, chronic rage reactions, depression, hallucinatory symptoms, withdrawal, and apathy.[32]

Constitutionality

Because of their relatively recent origin, the constitutionality of supermax prisons—whether or not the conditions of confinement constitute cruel and unusual punishment—has been tested in only a few cases. The first, *Madrid v. Gomez*,[33] in 1995, addressed conditions of confinement in California's Pelican Bay SHU. The judge pointed to the "stark sterility and unremitting monotony" of the interior of the prison and noted that its image was "hauntingly similar to that of caged felines pacing in a zoo" (p. 1229; however, the judge concluded that he lacked any constitutional basis to close the prison).

In 1999, a federal district court in *Ruiz v. Johnson*[34] looked at Texas's high-security units and concluded that prisoners there "suffer actual psychological harm from the almost total deprivation of human contact, personal property, and human dignity" (p. 913). This judge also opined that such units are virtual incubators of psychoses and that long-term supermax confinement could result in mental illness.

In the most recent case, *Jones 'El v. Berge*,[35] in 2004, a federal district court in Wisconsin concluded that "extremely isolating conditions cause SHU syndrome in relatively healthy prisoners, as well as prisoners who have never suffered a breakdown; supermax is not appropriate for seriously mentally ill inmates." The judge ordered several prisoners to be removed from the supermax facility.

A Boon to Public Safety?

Pizarro et al.[36] examined whether supermax prisons, by housing the worst of the worst inmates, actually enhance public and prison safety. This claim, Pizarro et al. argue, has not been proven; they believe that the potential long-term, negative effects of supermax institutions (as discussed above) on inmates will contribute to future violence because the inmates begin to lose touch with reality and exhibit symptoms of psychiatric decomposition. Consequently, they believe that supermax prisons potentially endanger society, beyond regular imprisonment. They also bemoan that although most supermax inmates will one day return to society or to the general prison population, only a few supermax prisons provide inmates with a transitional program (e.g., moving inmates from supermax prison into a maximum-security prison, allow inmates to participate in group activities, place inmates in institutional jobs).[37]

Policy Implications

Given the negative psychological effects of many forms of long-term supermax confinement, researchers such as Craig Haney[38] believe that there is a strong argument for limiting the use of supermax prisons:

> We should take steps to ensure that all such facilities implement the best and most humane of the available practices. Far more careful screening, monitoring, and removal policies should be implemented to ensure that psychologically vulnerable prisoners do not end up there in the first place, and that those who deteriorate once they are immediately identified and transferred. Strict time limits should be placed on the length of time that prisoners are housed in supermax. While people may decide that the harm that supermax prisons inflict is worth the benefit that they arguably beget and that the pains of such confinement are the regrettable but unavoidable… there are very serious psychological, correctional, legal, and even moral issues at the core that are worthy of serious, continued debate.

SELECTED COURT DECISIONS AFFECTING PRISONERS' RIGHTS

From Hands Off to Hands On: A Shift in Prisoners' Rights, Law, and Philosophy

Historically, the courts followed a **hands-off policy** regarding prisons and **prisoners' rights**, deeming prisoners to be "slaves of the state." The judiciary, recognizing that it was not trained in or knowledgeable about penology, allowed wardens the freedom and discretion to operate their institutions without outside interference while being fearful of undermining the structure and discipline of the prison.

All that has changed, and the hands-on policy, beginning in the mid-1960s, brought about a change of philosophy in the courts regarding prisoners' rights; prison inmates now retain all the rights of free citizens except those restrictions necessary for their orderly confinement or to provide safety in the prison community.

Below we discuss several U.S. Supreme Court decisions that spelled the demise of the hands-off era, in which it was established that no "iron curtain" was erected between the inmates and the Constitution and that they were not "wholly stripped of constitutional protections" (see the discussion of *Wolff v. McDonnell* below). These decisions improved the everyday lives of prison and jail inmates and reformed correctional administration. Specifically, basic rights extended to inmates included greater access to the courts, to appeal their convictions and conditions of confinement; greater freedom of religion expression; restricting mail censorship by prison officials; and granting them due process for the purpose of inmate disciplinary proceedings.

A "Slave of the State"

RUFFIN V. COMMONWEALTH (1871) An excellent beginning point for this overview of significant court decisions concerning inmates' rights is the 1871 case of *Ruffin v. Commonwealth*.[39] There, the Virginia Supreme Court held that a prisoner "had, as a consequence of his crime, not only forfeited his liberty, but also all his personal rights except those that the law in its humanity accords to him." The *Ruffin* court even declared inmates to be "slaves of the state," mentioned above, losing all their citizenship rights, including the right to complain about living conditions.

This view certainly does not reflect the law at present and may never have been entirely accurate. For example, in 1948, in *Price v. Johnston*,[40] the Supreme Court declared that "lawful incarceration brings about the necessary withdrawal or limitation of many privileges and rights," which indicated a much softer view than that stated in *Ruffin*; furthermore, "many" privileges indicate less than "all," and it was clear that the due process and equal protection clauses did apply to prisoners to some extent.

Prison Regulations and Laws Vis-à-vis Inmates' Constitutional Rights

TURNER V. SAFLEY[41] **(1987)**   Prison inmates brought a class action suit challenging the reasonableness of certain regulations of the Missouri Division of Corrections. Here, the Supreme Court took the opportunity to modify previous standards—such as "compelling state interest," "least restrictive means," and "rational relationship"—used to determine whether prison regulations and laws violate constitutional rights of inmates. In *Turner v. Safley*, the Court said that a prison regulation that impinges on inmates' constitutional rights is valid if it is reasonably related to *legitimate penological interests* (emphasis added). This decision gave prison authorities more power; all they must do is prove that a prison regulation is reasonably related to a legitimate penological interest in order for that regulation to be valid even if a constitutional right is infringed.

Legal Remedy and Access to the Courts

COOPER V. PATE[42] **(1964)**   One of the earliest prison cases, it is significant because the Supreme Court first recognized the use of Title 42 of the United States Code Section 1983 as a legal remedy for inmates. (Section 1983, discussed thoroughly in Chapter 13, concerns a public officer's violation of a prisoner's constitutional rights while acting "under color" of law.) Cooper, an inmate at the Illinois State Penitentiary, sued prison officials under Section 1983, alleging that he was unconstitutionally punished (i.e., placed in solitary confinement) and denied permission to purchase certain Muslim religious publications. Both the federal district court and the circuit court of appeals upheld Cooper's punishment but the Supreme Court reversed their ruling, finding that he was entitled to relief—and that he could use Section 1983.

JOHNSON V. AVERY[43] **(1969)**   This was one of the first prison decisions that involved an alleged violation of a constitutional right—here, the right of access to the courts. Johnson, a Tennessee prisoner, was disciplined for violating a prison regulation that prohibited inmates from assisting other prisoners in preparing writs. The Supreme Court acknowledged that "writ writers" like Johnson are sometimes a menace to prison discipline, and their petitions are often so unskillful as to be a burden on the courts receiving them. However, because the State of Tennessee provided no "reasonable alternative" to assist illiterate or poorly educated inmates in preparing petitions for postconviction relief, the Supreme Court held that the state could not bar inmates from furnishing such assistance to other prisoners. However, what constituted "reasonable alternatives" to writ writers was not explained.

BOUNDS V. SMITH[44] **(1977)**   This was another court-access decision, clarifying *Johnson v. Avery*. In *Bounds*—where North Carolina inmates alleged denial of reasonable access by having only one library in the prison (which was inadequate in nature)—the Court went further, saying that prisoners have a constitutional right to adequate law libraries or assistance from persons trained in the law. This case also listed several possible alternatives that prisons could use for providing inmates such access, including training inmates as paralegals to work under lawyers' supervision; using paraprofessionals and law students to advise inmates; hiring lawyers on a part-time consultant basis; and having voluntary programs through bar associations, whereby lawyers visit the prisons to consult with inmates.

First Amendment

CRUZ V. BETO[45] **(1972) (RELIGIOUS PRACTICES)** This landmark case clarified the right of inmates to exercise their religious beliefs, even if they did not belong to what are considered mainstream or traditional religions. Cruz, a Buddhist, was not allowed to use the prison chapel and was placed in solitary confinement on a diet of bread and water for sharing his religious material with other prisoners. He sued under Section 1983, alleging violations of the First Amendment right to freedom of religion. The Supreme Court held that inmates with unconventional religious beliefs must be given a reasonable opportunity to exercise those beliefs.

PROCUNIER V. MARTINEZ[46] **(1974) (MAIL CENSORSHIP)** Here, the Supreme Court invalidated prison mail censorship regulations that permitted authorities to hold back or to censor mail to and from prisoners whenever they thought that the letters "unduly complain[ed]," "express[ed] inflammatory views or beliefs," or were "defamatory" or "otherwise inappropriate." The Court based its ruling not on the rights of the prisoner but instead on the free-world recipient's right to communicate with the prisoner, either by sending or by receiving mail. The Court held that the regulation of mail must further an important interest unrelated to the suppression of expression; regulation must be shown to further the substantial interest of security, order, and rehabilitation; and it must not be utilized simply to censor opinions or other expressions. Furthermore, a prison's restriction on mail must be no greater than is necessary to the protection of the security interest involved.

Fourth Amendment

BELL V. WOLFISH[47] **(1979) (SEARCHES OF BODY CAVITIES AND CELLS, OTHER CONDITIONS OF CONFINEMENT)** This is one of the few cases decided by the Supreme Court concerning the rights of pretrial detainees housed in local jails. Here, the Court in effect said that jail officials may run their institutions the same way prisons are managed. New York City's Metropolitan Correctional Center, within a short time of opening, experienced overcrowding and began double-bunking inmates in rooms built for single occupancy (double bunking is discussed further below). Guards also conducted searches of inmates' cells in their absence, prohibited inmates from receiving hardcover books that were not mailed directly by publishers or bookstores; prohibited inmates' receipt of personal items from visitors; and employed body cavity searches of inmates following contact visits. Inmates sued and alleged several constitutional violations, but the Supreme Court held none of these practices to be unconstitutional "punishment," saying that these restrictions and practices were reasonable responses to legitimate security concerns and noting that they were of only limited duration.

(Note that in a 1981 case specifically challenging the use of double bunking, *Rhodes v. Chapman*,[48] the Court held that double bunking of prisoners does not constitute cruel and unusual punishment as long as the conditions of confinement are not bad.)

Eighth Amendment

ESTELLE V. GAMBLE[49] **(1976) (MEDICAL CARE)** Although Gamble lost in this case, it was the first major prison medical treatment case decided by the Supreme Court and set the standards by which such cases are determined. Here, the Court coined the term *deliberate indifference*, which occurs when the serious medical needs of prisoners involve the unnecessary and wanton inflic-tion of pain. Examples the Court gave are injecting penicillin with the knowledge that the pris-oner is allergic to it, refusing to administer a prescribed painkiller, and requiring a prisoner to stand despite the contrary instructions of a surgeon. Gamble, an inmate of the Texas Department of Corrections, claimed that he received cruel and unusual punishment because of inadequate treatment of a back injury sustained while he was engaged in prison work. The Court did not find a constitutional violation in his case, however, because medical personnel saw him on 17 occasions during a 3-month period, and treated his injury and other problems.

Fourteenth Amendment

WOLFF V. MCDONNELL[50] **(1974) (DUE PROCESS)**   This case is significant because, for the first time, the Supreme Court acknowledged that inmates are entitled to certain due process rights—"fundamental fairness"—during prison disciplinary proceedings. McDonnell and other inmates at a Nebraska prison alleged, among other things, that disciplinary proceedings at the prison violated their due process rights. To establish misconduct, prison officials required a preliminary conference, where the prisoner was orally informed of the charge; a conduct report was prepared and a hearing was held before the prison's disciplinary body; and the inmate could ask questions of the charging party. The Court said, now rather famously, that "There is no iron curtain drawn between the Constitution and the prisons of this country," that "a prisoner is not wholly stripped of constitutional protections," and that prisoners must be given the following due process rights:

- Advance written notice of charges no less than 24 hours before appearing before the hear-ing committee.
- A written statement by the fact finders as to the evidence relied on and reasons for the dis-ciplinary action.
- Ability to call witnesses and to present documentary evidence in the inmate's defense (if this did not jeopardize institutional safety or correctional goals).
- Use of counsel substitutes (e.g., a friend or staff member) when the inmate is illiterate or when complex issues require such assistance.
- An impartial prison disciplinary board.

INMATE LITIGATION

Increases in Litigation and Frivolous Lawsuits Prior to the Twenty-First Century

The volume of inmate litigation increased significantly following the aforementioned *Cooper v. Pate* decision in 1964. In 1980, inmates in state and federal correctional institutions filed 23,287 petitions alleging both civil and criminal violations of their rights and seeking compensatory damages, injunctions, and property claims.[51] By 1990, the number of such petitions had swollen to nearly 43,000, and more than 64,000 petitions were filed in 1996[52] (a more contemporary view of inmate filings, since passage of the PLRA of 1995, is provided below).

Prisoners sued primarily because they were either unwilling to accept their conviction or wished to harass their keepers.[53] Inmate litigants tend to fall into one of two categories. First are those who file a single suit during their entire period of incarceration (usually requiring the assistance of others to do it); one study found that 71 percent of all litigants filed only one action but accounted for about half of all litigation.[54] The other group is composed of inmates who make law a prison career—the so-called jailhouse lawyers.[55]

Although in past decades the media brought to light many abuses inside prisons, in the 1980s and 1990s media attention began turning in another direction: reports of trivial and **frivolous lawsuits** filed by inmates. Following are some examples:

- A death row inmate sued correction officials for taking away his Gameboy electronic game.
- A prisoner sued demanding L.A. Gear or Reebok "Pumps" instead of Converse.
- An inmate sued because he was served chunky instead of smooth peanut butter.
- An inmate claimed it was cruel and unusual punishment that he was forced to listen to his unit manager's country and western music.
- An inmate claimed $1 million in damages because his ice cream melted (the judge ruled that the "right to eat ice cream was clearly not within the contemplation" of our nation's forefathers).[56]

Such examples of litigation caused an uproar over frivolous civil right lawsuits brought by inmates. Furthermore, the expense of defending against such lawsuits, coupled with the fact that the United States has the world's largest and costliest prison system,[57] combined to foster public resentment against prisons and prisoners.

Of course, not all lawsuits against prison administrators concerning inmate living conditions and treatment are frivolous. For example, in August 2006, Timothy Joe Souders, a 21-year-old mentally ill young man held in the Southern Michigan Correctional Facility in Jackson, died after 5 days of horrific abuse and neglect. He was held for 5 days in isolation, naked, shackled by his arms and legs to a concrete slab in temperatures exceeding 100 degrees, forced to lie in his own urine. His family settled for $3.25 million.[58] A federal judge called Souders's death "predictable and preventable," and cited numerous documented and appalling instances of nontreatment, including an inmate who died of untreated cancer. He was found lying in excrement in his cell, after having lost 60 pounds from a "hunger strike."[59]

The Prison Litigation Reform Act

FOUR MAIN PARTS   By the late 1980s, the courts were displaying more tolerance for minor violations of prisoners' constitutional rights, as exemplified by the following three cases:

1. *Turner v. Safley* (1987),[60] discussed above, in which the Supreme Court stated that when a prison regulation impinges on inmates' constitutional rights, "the regulation is valid if it is reasonably related to legitimate penological interests."
2. *Wilson v. Seiter* (1991),[61] which stated that when an inmate claims that the conditions of his or her confinement violate the Eighth Amendment, he or she must show a culpable state of mind on the part of prison officials.
3. *Sandin v. Conner* (1995),[62] which emphasized the Supreme Court's desire to give "deference and flexibility to state officials trying to maintain a volatile environment." This decision made it "more difficult to bring constitutional suits challenging prison management."[63]

Then, in April 1996, the **PLRA** of 1995 was enacted.[64] The PLRA has been praised by proponents as necessary "to provide for appropriate remedies for prison condition lawsuits, to discourage frivolous and abusive prison lawsuits, and for other purposes."[65]

The PLRA has four main parts[66]:

- *Exhaustion of administrative remedies.* Before inmates can file a lawsuit, they must try to resolve their complaint through the prison's grievance procedure, which usually includes giving a written description of their complaint to a prison official; if the prison requires additional steps, such as appealing to the warden, then the inmate must also follow those steps.

- **Filing fees.** All prisoners must pay court filing fees in full. If they do not have the money up front, they can pay the fee over time through monthly deductions from their prison commissary account. A complex statutory formula requires the indigent prisoner to pay an initial fee of 20 percent of the greater of the prisoner's average balance or the average deposits to the account for the preceding 6 months.
- **Three-strikes provision.** Each lawsuit or appeal that an inmate files that is dismissed for being frivolous, malicious, or not stating a proper claim counts as a *strike.* After an inmate receives three strikes, he or she cannot file another lawsuit *in forma pauperis*—that is, he or she cannot file another lawsuit unless he or she pays the entire court filing fee up front (an exception is made if the inmate is at risk of suffering serious physical injury in the immediate future, described in the next point). An appeal of a dismissed action that is dismissed is a separate strike, and even dismissals that occurred prior to the effective date of the PLRA count as strikes.
- **Physical injury requirement.** An inmate cannot file a lawsuit for mental or emotional injury unless he or she can also show physical injury. (The courts differ in their evaluation of what constitutes sufficient harm to qualify as physical injury.)

HAS PLRA SERVED ITS PURPOSE?   According to data provided by the federal courts, in 1995—the year before implementation of the act—there were 63,550 total prisoner petitions; in 1997, the first year following implementation of the act, there were 62,966 petitions, or 8 percent fewer.[67] Then, in 2009, there were 10,566 such petitions—an *83 percent* decrease since 1997.[68] Clearly, prisoner petitions to the U.S. District Courts have significantly diminished in number.

JAILS AS ORGANIZATIONS

Across the United States, approximately 2,850 local jails are administered, which together will house about 785,000 inmates per year.[69] Their organization and hierarchical levels are determined by several factors: size, budget, level of crowding, local views on punishment and treatment, and even the levels of training and education of the jail administrator. An organizational structure for a jail serving a population of about 250,000 is suggested in Figure 9.4.

The administration of jails is frequently one of the major tasks of county sheriffs. Several writers have concluded that sheriffs and police personnel see themselves primarily as law enforcers first and view the responsibility of organizing and operating a jail as an unwelcome task.[70] Therefore, their approach is often said to be at odds with advanced corrections philosophy and trends.

Podular/Direct Supervision Jails

RATIONALE AND EXPANDING USE   As noted previously, in the past, the federal courts have at times become more willing to hear inmate allegations of constitutional violations ranging from inadequate heating, lighting, and ventilation to the censorship of mail. One of every five cases filed in federal courts was on behalf of prisoners,[71] and 20 percent of all jails were a party in a pending lawsuit.[72]

Over the past three decades, in response to this deluge of lawsuits and to improve conditions, many local jurisdictions constructed new podular or direct supervision jails. Court-ordered pres-

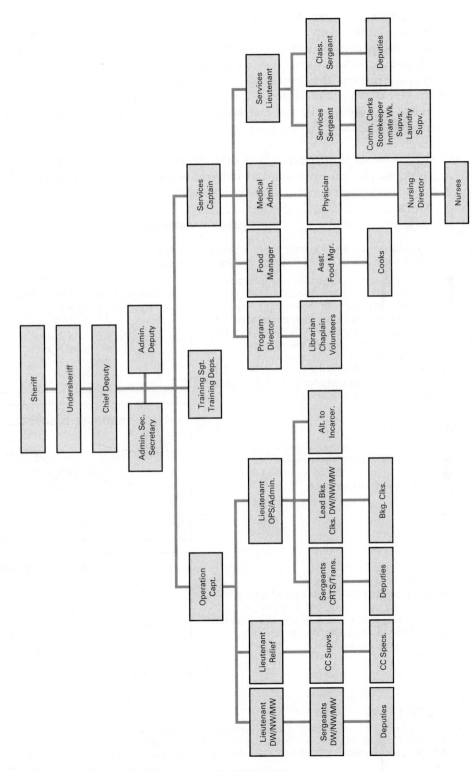

FIGURE 9.4 Organizational Structure for a Jail Serving a County of 250,000 Population (DW = day watch; NW = night watch; MW = mid-watch; CC = conservation camps; CRTS/Trans. = courts transportation; OPS/Admin. = operations/administration; Comm. Clerks = commissary clerks)

sures to improve jail conditions afforded an opportunity for administrators to explore new ideas and designs. The **direct supervision jail** (also known as "new-generation" jail) represents a comparatively new approach for addressing many of the earlier problems found in local jails.[73]

According to the National Institute of Corrections (NIC), the number of direct supervision jails increased in the United States from approximately 199 in 1995 to about 350 at present. This growing number, the NIC stated, "suggests that direct supervision continues to be adopted as a design style and management philosophy in large and small jurisdictions across the United States."[74]

DEPARTING FROM TRADITION Direct supervision jails differ from traditional jails in several ways. First, the physical environment is different (see Figure 9.5). In traditional jails, cells are arranged linearly along a corridor, with officers being separated from inmates by bars, glass, or other

---

DIRECT SUPERVISION JAILS

Jails that are not predominantly direct supervision in design or management can have an addition or section of inmate housing that uses direct supervision.

Inmates' cells are arranged around a common area, usually called a "dayroom." An officer is stationed in the pod with the inmates. The officer moves about the pod and interacts with the inmates to manage their behavior. There is no secure control booth for the supervising officer, and there are no physical barriers between the officer and the inmates. The officer may have a desk or table for paperwork, but it is in the open dayroom area.

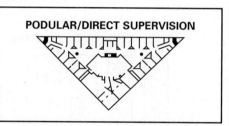

PODULAR/DIRECT SUPERVISION

Includes jails with cells arranged along the sides of a cell block. Officers come into the housing unit on scheduled rounds or as needed to interact with the inmates.

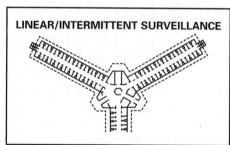

LINEAR/INTERMITTENT SURVEILLANCE

Includes jails that have a podular design with cells around a dayroom, but no officer is permanently stationed inside the pod. Indirect supervision is provided through remote monitoring at a console.

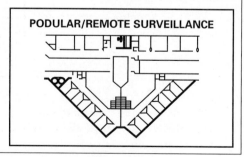

PODULAR/REMOTE SURVEILLANCE

FIGURE 9.5 Direct Supervision Jails

Source: Based on U.S. Department of Justice, National Institute of Justice, *Direct Supervision Jails: 2006 Yearbook* (Longmont, CO: National Institute of Corrections Information Center, 2006, p. vii); also available at: http://nicic.org/Downloads/PDF/Library/021968.pdf (accessed October 18, 2010).

physical barriers. Officers must patrol halls where their line of sight into each cell is severely restricted, and officers can observe what is happening inside a cell only when they are almost directly in front of it. In the direct supervision jail, inmates are separated into relatively small groups (usually 50 or less), housed in self-contained living units including several one- to two-person cells, a day room, and recreation space. These units, or "pods," usually are triangular or wedge shaped so that jail officers have a direct line of sight into all areas of the pod at all times. The furnishings in the living units also differ and generally include carpeting, porcelain lavatories, moveable furniture that may be padded or plastic, and other "soft" fixtures. The direct supervision philosophy has officers stationed within the living area with no physical barriers to separate them from inmates. In these units, officers maintain a constant physical presence, but they also interact extensively with inmates.[75]

Because of their constant physical and close presence, correctional officers (COs) in direct supervision jails must use active observation in order to gather information about what is occurring in the module, to gauge sources of conflict or tension, and to identify and react to situations before they escalate into serious problems. They must also develop a higher degree of interpersonal skills and creativity in managing inmates. Even minor conflicts and problems must be proactively addressed within the pod. The COs must also be fair with their discipline, and treat inmates with respect and dignity. Both formal and informal sanctions should be used, so that punishment meted out is commensurate with the gravity of the infraction. Inmates should also be told the reason for their punishment.[76]

Most evaluations of direct supervision jails have been encouraging. Researchers and practitioners have reported reductions in inmate–inmate violence and assaults against jail officers and staff members[77]; inmates have also reported having more positive attitudes about the officers than inmates in more traditional facilities, and direct supervision officers have reported feeling less hostile toward the inmates.[78]

Preparing Inmates for Reentry

Of the aforementioned 785,000 Americans who are housed in jails each year, most will be released through a variety of means—bail, promise to reappear, on their own recognizance, and so forth—prior to going to trial; many if not most will also be convicted for petty crimes. For these reasons, jail inmates thus spend shorter periods of time of incarceration than do prison inmates, and may well return to their local neighborhoods soon after their arrest or even following conviction. Therefore, according to Maiello and Pottorff,[79] jails have a role in serving as agents of change and in preparing inmates for reentry back into society, and should attempt to accomplish the following four goals:

1. *Purposeful intake and assessment on all new admissions:* This means that inmates must begin to prepare for reentry the moment they enter the jail—even those who will be in jail a relatively short period of time. A dedicated reception unit for new admissions can observe inmate adjustment and behavior firsthand prior to the housing unit assignment is made. The intake and assessment process can measure not only the risk to institutional security (classification) but also the risk to community (pretrial or work release eligibility) and the risk of reoffending (to help to establish rehabilitative program and treatment goals).
2. *A sound inmate classification system and follow-up housing unit assignment:* Classification systems provide an opportunity to identify, perhaps for the first time, an individual's social and health needs and public safety risks, and to develop a plan to address those needs and risks. These reentry plans need to work in conjunction with the basic institutional classification process that serves to identify individuals who might be at risk to themselves or to others and to correctly place them at the appropriate security level in the facility.

Identifying inmates who cannot be managed in the general population is critical to institutional security and treatment goals; violent or disruptive inmates are separated, in order that the general population units are more stable and can thus allow residents to focus on positive behavior change rather than safety concerns.

3. *Meaningful jail treatment programs:* The reentry of jail inmates back into society can benefit from treatment programs. Some jurisdictions have developed community-based reentry programs—including work release—that allow carefully selected portions of the jail population to live, work, and receive treatment services in the community. In these programs, participants may live in contracted halfway houses or prerelease facilities or at home under electronic monitoring surveillance. Clients are able to work and contribute to their own and their families' financial support, develop deeper ties with their families, and access community resources directly while remaining in a structured and highly accountable setting. Individualized reentry plans developed in this community setting can better match the needs of clients to the available resources in the community. These programs also contribute to reduced jail crowding and more efficient management, allowing correctional systems to allocate their most scarce and valuable resource—a secure cell—to the most dangerous and risky offenders in the jail population. However, participants can commit new criminal offenses, escape relatively easily, and—particularly for the addicted—succumb to the many temptations of the street. Therefore, such programs must be carefully designed and implemented.

4. *The jail environment:* Jails that are well-lit, clean, and that have calming colors will be more comfortable and likely safer—for the inmates in the housing units as well as for volunteers, medical personnel, counselors, and visitors. This will result in fewer incidents among inmates, reduced staff turnover, better interaction between personnel and inmates, increased visitors, and more community volunteers. This is essential for an inmate's smooth transition back into the community.

In Chapter 10, we will discuss the functions of jail administrators.

CORRECTIONS ACCREDITATION

Like police organizations, as discussed in Chapter 3, corrections organizations may become **accredited** by meeting national standards through a series of reviews, evaluations, audits, and hearings. Since 1978, the American Correctional Association (ACA) has promulgated standards generally covering administrative and fiscal controls, staff training and development, physical plant, safety and emergency procedures, sanitation, food service, and rules and discipline. The ACA utilizes a 28-member private, nonprofit body, the Commission on **Accreditation** for Corrections, to render accreditation decisions.[80]

There are 21 different sets or manuals of accreditation standards covering all types of correctional facilities and programs, including state and federal adult institutions, juvenile facilities, probation and parole agencies, and health care and electronic monitoring programs. In order for a state or federal adult corrections institution to be accredited, it must meet 100 percent of 62 mandatory standards as well as 90 percent of 468 nonmandatory standards.[81]

As with the police, there are several benefits to be realized for corrections agencies wishing to become accredited: determining the facility or program's strengths and weaknesses, identifying obtainable goals, implementing state-of-the-art policies and procedures, establishing specific guidelines for daily operations, aiding in defending against frivolous lawsuits, and ensuring a higher level of staff professionalism and morale.[82]

PROBATION AND PAROLE AGENCIES AS ORGANIZATIONS

Community corrections originated in the years following World War II, when returning veterans encountered adjustment problems as they attempted to reenter civilian life.[83] It has also been stated that community corrections is "the last bastion of discretion in the criminal justice system."[84] Community corrections are typically viewed as a humane, logical, and effective approach for working with and changing criminal offenders.[85]

Probation Systems

TYPES OF SYSTEMS Figure 9.6 depicts an organizational structure for a regional probation and parole organization. **Probation** is the most frequently used sanction; it costs offenders their privacy and self-determination and usually includes some element of the other sanctions: jail

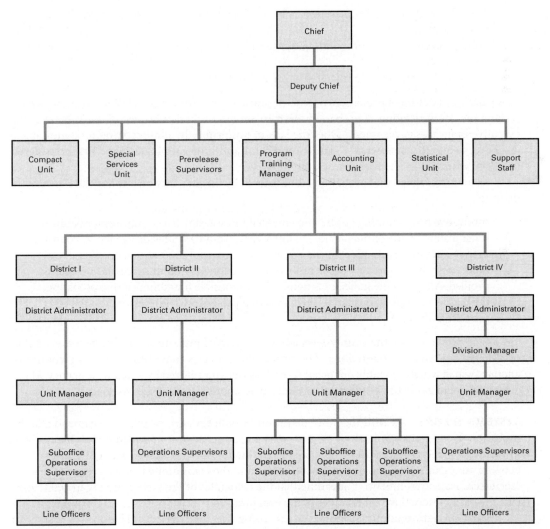

FIGURE 9.6 Organizational Structure for a Regional Adult Probation and Parole Agency

time, fines, restitution, or community service.[86] Probation in the United States is administered by more than 2,000 different agencies. Its organization is a patchwork that defies simple explanation. In about three-fourths of the states, adult probation is part of the executive branch of state government.[87] In contrast, more than half of the agencies providing juvenile probation services are administered in juvenile courts on the local level.[88]

According to Howard Abadinsky, the administration of probation systems can be separated into six categories[89]:

1. *Juvenile.* Separate probation services for juveniles are administered on a county, municipal, or state level.
2. *Municipal.* Independent probation units are administered by the lower courts under state laws and guidelines.
3. *County.* Under laws and guidelines established by the state, a county operates its own probation agency.
4. *State.* One agency administers a central probation system, which provides services throughout the state.
5. *State combined.* Probation and parole services are administered on a statewide basis by one agency.
6. *Federal.* Probation is administered as an arm of the federal courts.

This patchwork nature of probation systems has raised two central organizational questions concerning the administration of probation services: Should probation be part of the judicial or the executive branch of government? Does the lack of uniformity in administering probation make justice less equitable statewide?[90] These important and lingering issues were first considered nearly 40 years ago by the President's Commission.[91]

Abadinsky argued that probation administered by the judiciary on a county level promotes diversity:

> Innovative programming can be implemented more easily in a county agency because it has a shorter line of bureaucratic control than would a statewide agency. A county agency can more easily adapt to change, and the successful programs of one agency can more easily be adopted by other probation departments and unsuccessful programs avoided. Although the judiciary is nominally responsible for administering probation, the day-to-day operations are in the hands of a professional administrator—the chief probation officer.[92]

One problem with the county-level administration of probation services, however, is that of reduced oversight of operations. The officer/client ratios may differ from one county to another, which would probably not occur if services were monitored by a statewide agency whose personnel could easily be shifted from one county to another to equalize caseloads.

SYSTEMS THEORY As with the administration of police, court, or prison organizations, the probation department administrator's goals may affect the services provided to the client, which in turn may have an impact on the client's request for services. This systematic interaction between an organization's resources and structure and the community has been referred to as its "sociotechnical environment,"[93] meaning that the principles of the system are organized to execute the basic production technologies of the organization.

Each probation administrator needs to recognize that the organization is a system of inputs, processes, and outputs (discussed in Chapter 2). For probation, inputs are clients coming into the office for counseling and supervision (the processes); outputs are the probationer's obtaining employment, acquiring a skill, observing a curfew, and so on. This understanding of probation, using systems theory, provides a means of learning how probation departments function and interact with their environment and of examining the resources, activities, and outcomes in a way that can identify the goals, describe the day-to-day activities, and link the department's activities to resources and outcomes.

According to systems theory, probation may be conceptualized as a network of interwoven resources, activities, and outcomes.[94] According to Hardyman, resources include the probation department's funding level, goals, policies and procedures, organizational structure, and caseload; the probation staff's characteristics; the services available to probationers; and the rates of unemployment, poverty, and crime in the county. Activities are supervision techniques, rewards, leadership style, contacts, and direct and indirect services provided by the probation department. Outcomes, according to systems theory, are the number of probationers who were arrested, incarcerated, and/or cited for a technical violation during the follow-up period, as well as the needs of probationers that were considered.[95]

Parole Systems

MODELS FOR PROVIDING SERVICES The administration of **parole** is much less complex than that of probation because parole services are administered centrally on a statewide basis.[96] (It should also be noted that in about 20 states, probation officers also serve as parole officers; thus, much of the information presented in the previous section applies to parole as well.) One state agency administers the parole function on a statewide basis, except that in a number of states, parolees from a local jail come under the supervision of a county probation and parole department.[97]

A parole agency can provide three basic services: parole release, parole supervision, and executive clemency. In a number of states that have abolished parole release (such as California), parole officers continue to supervise offenders released by the prison on good time (reduction of sentence through good behavior).

The National Advisory Commission on Criminal Justice Standards and Goals delineated two basic models for administering parole services:

1. *The independent model.* A parole board is responsible for making release (parole) determinations as well as supervising persons released on parole (or good time). It is independent of any other state agency and reports directly to the governor.
2. *The consolidated model.* The parole board is a semiautonomous agency within a large department that also administers correctional institutions. Supervision of persons released on parole (or good time) is under the direction of the commissioner of corrections, not the parole board.[98]

Both models sometimes combine probation services with parole services in a single statewide agency.

The President's Commission summarized the advantages of the independent model[99]:

1. The parole board is in the best position to promote the idea of parole and to generate public support and acceptance of it. Because the board is accountable for parole failures, it should be responsible for supervising parolees.
2. The parole board that is in direct control of administering parole services can evaluate and adjust the system more effectively.

3. Supervision by the parole board and its officers properly divorces parole release and parolees from the correctional institution.

4. An independent parole board in charge of its own services is in the best position to present its own budget request to the legislature.

The advantages of including both parole services and institutions in a consolidated department of corrections were summarized by the President's Commission as follows[100]:

1. The correctional process is a continuum; all staff, both institutional and parole, are under a single administration rather than divided, which avoids competition for public funds and friction in policies.

2. A consolidated correctional department has consistent administration, including staff selection and supervision.

3. Parole boards are ineffective in performing administrative functions; their major focus should be on case decision, not on day-to-day field operations.

4. Community-based programs that fall between institutions and parole, such as work release, can best be handled by a single centralized administration.

Clearly, the trend in this country, beginning in the late 1960s, has been in the direction of consolidation.

Summary

This chapter presented an overview of corrections as a booming industry; it discussed prison and jail organization; the rise of, and controversies surrounding, supermax prisons; selected inmate rights under the First, Fourth, Eighth, and Fourteenth Amendments as set forth by the U.S. Supreme Court; inmate litigation; and the organization of probation and parole agencies.

The chapter also demonstrated how times have changed with respect to the manner in which correctional facilities are organized, while providing a glimpse into some of the issues and problems that challenge administrators, some of which are further examined in the following chapter.

Questions for Review

1. What factors contribute to the correctional populations? What impact do drug laws have on them?

2. What are some of the major administrative positions within a prison system?

3. How do supermax prisons operate differently from other prisons? What concerns have been raised concerning their alleged effects on inmates, constitutionality, and public safety?

4. What are at least five of the major U.S. Supreme Court decisions affording rights to prisoners? When and how did such decisions serve to end the hands-off doctrine?

5. What is a direct supervision jail, and how does it differ in design and function from traditional jails?

6. Why was the Prison Litigation Reform Act enacted, and has it made an impact?

7. In what major ways do jails differ from prisons in their organization and administration? Assist with inmate reentry back into the community?

8. What are the primary functions of a jail administrator?

9. What advantages accrue to a corrections facility if it is accredited?

10. What are the various types of probation systems administered in the United States? Describe each.

11. Should probation services be placed within the judicial or the executive branch of government? Defend your answer.

12. What are the two basic models of parole administration?

Learn by Doing

1. As part of a criminal justice honor society paper to be presented at a national conference, you are examining the role of local jails. Considering the diagram of the flow of the justice system process in the front matter of this book, process, as well as this chapter's discussion about jails, at which point(s) would you argue that jails become involved and contribute to the overall functions of the criminal justice system? How does the direct supervision jail concept apply to these functions?

2. Your criminal justice professor has assigned a class debate wherein class members are to determine which court decision within *each* of three amendments—the Fourth, Fifth, and Sixth—is the most important right therein granted to inmates. You are to analyze those three amendments and explain and defend your decision.

3. Your criminal justice professor is concerned because it seems that students know relatively little about the general functions and organizational attributes of probation and parole agencies. As an upper-division criminal justice student, she asks you to prepare a short presentation on that topic for the coming "Career Day" program offered each year by the faculty. What will you say?

Related Websites

American Civil Liberties Union: Prisoner's Rights
http://www.aclu.org/prison/index.html

American Jail Association
http://www.aja.org/

Corrections Connection
http://www.corrections.com

Federal Bureau of Prisons
http://www.bop.gov

Global Bibliography of Prison Systems
http://www.uncjin.org/country/GBOPS/gbops.html

Human Rights Watch
http://hrw.org/prisons

Probono.net
http://www.probono.net/prisoners/index.cfm

Notes

1. Bureau of Justice Statistics, "Justice Expenditure and Employment Extracts, 2007," Table cjee0702.csv, http://bjs.ojp.usdoj.gov/index.cfm?ty=pbdetail&iid=2315 (accessed November 22, 2010).

2. Deborah Small, "The War on Drugs Is a War on Racial Justice," *Social Research* 68(3) (Fall 2001): 896–903.

3. Steven Duke, "End the Drug War," *Social Research*, 68(3) (Fall 2001): 875–880.

4. Reuters, "Postscript to California's marijuana vote," November 5, 2010, http://blogs.reuters.com/great-debate/2010/11/05/postscript-to-californias-marijuana-vote/ (accessed November 22, 2010).

5. U.S. Department of Justice, Bureau of Justice Statistics, "Estimated arrests for drug abuse violations by age group, 1970–2007," http://bjs.ojp.usdoj.gov/content/glance/tables/drugtab.cfm (accessed November 20, 2010).

6. See the Violent Offender Incarceration and Truth-in-Sentencing Incentive Grants program, Public Law 103–322, 108 Stat. 1796 (1994).

7. U.S. Department of Justice, Bureau of Justice Assistance, *Report to Congress: Violent Offender Incarceration and Truth-In-Sentencing Incentive Formula Grant Program* (February 2005), http://www.ojp.usdoj.gov/BJA/pdf/VOITISreport.pdf (accessed July 18, 2008).

8. *Sourcebook of Criminal Justice Statistics Online*, "Attitudes Toward Whether the Criminal Justice System Should Try to Rehabilitate Criminals," http://www.ojp.usdoj.gov/bjs/correct.htm (accessed January 3, 2008), p. 139.

9. T. Paul Louis and Jerry R. Sparger, "Treatment Modalities within Prison," in John W. Murphy and Jack E. Dison (eds.), *Are Prisons Any Better? Twenty Years of Correctional Reform* (Newbury Park, CA: Sage, 1990), p. 148.

10. Ibid., p. 149.

11. Ted Palmer, "The 'Effectiveness' Issue Today: An Overview," *Federal Probation* 42 (1983):3–10.

12. Ibid.

13. See D. A. Andrews, "Program Structure and Effective Correctional Practices: A Summary of the

CAVIC Research," in Robert R. Ross and Paul Gendreau (eds.), *Effective Correctional Treatment* (Toronto: Butterworth, 1980); R. Peters, *Deviant Behavioral Contracting with Conduct Problem Youth* (Kingston, Canada: Queen's University Press, 1981).

14. Quoted in Andrews, "Program Structure and Effective Correctional Practices," p. 42.

15. Richard P. Seiter, *Correctional Administration: Integrating Theory and Practice* (Upper Saddle River, NJ: Prentice Hall, 2002), p. 11.

16. Ibid., p. 192.

17. Ibid., p. 189.

18. Ibid., pp. 190–191.

19. Robert Levinson, "Try Softer," in Robert Johnson and Hans Toch (eds.), *The Pains of Imprisonment* (Beverly Hills, CA: Sage, 1982), p. 246.

20. Louis and Sparger, "Treatment Modalities within Prison," pp. 147–162.

21. U.S. Department of Justice, Bureau of Justice Statistics, "HIV in Prisons and Jails," http://www.ojp.usdoj.gov/bjs/abstract/hivpj99.htm (accessed June 24, 2002).

22. James A. Inciardi, *Criminal Justice,* 7th ed. (Fort Worth, TX: Harcourt Brace, 2001), p. 454.

23. Ibid., p. 194.

24. Mary Ellen Mastrorilli, personal communication, September 1, 2010.

25. United States Bureau of Prisons, *Unit Management Manual* (Washington, DC: Author, 1977), p. 6.

26. Seiter, *Correctional Administration,* p. 196.

27. U.S. Department of Justice, National Institute of Justice, *Work in American Prisons: Joint Ventures with the Private Sector* (Washington, DC: U.S. Government Printing Office, 1995), pp. 2–3.

28. ABCNews.go.com, "How to Survive a Supermax Prison," http://abcnews.go.com/TheLaw/Story?id=3435989&page=1 (accessed July 18, 2008).

29. CNN.com/U.S., "Reporters Get First Look Inside Mysterious Supermax Prison," http://www.cnn.com/2007/US/09/13/supermax.btsc/index.html (accessed January 12, 2008).

30. Craig Haney, "Mental Health Issues in Long-Term Solitary and 'Supermax' Confinement," *Crime & Delinquency* 49(1) (January 2003):124–156.

31. See, however, ibid.

32. Jesenia Pizarro and Vanja M. K. Stenius, "Supermax Prisons: Their Rise, Current Practices, and Effect on Inmates," *The Prison Journal* 84(2) (June 2004): 248–264.

33. *Madrid v. Gomez,* 889 F. Supp. 1146 (1995).

34. 37 F. Supp. 1265 (1980).

35. 374 F.3d 541 (7th Cir. 2004), p. 1118.

36. Jesenia M. Pizarro, Vanja M. K. Stenius, and Travis C. Pratt, "Supermax Prisons: Myths, Realities, and the Politics of Punishment in American Society," *Criminal Justice Policy Review* 17(1) (March 2006): 6–21.

37. Ibid.

38. Haney, "Mental Health Issues in Long-Term Solitary and 'Supermax' Confinement," p. 150.

39. *Ruffin v. Commonwealth,* 62 Va. 790 (1871).

40. *Price v. Johnston,* 334 U.S. 266, 144 F.2d 260 (1948).

41. *Turner v. Safley,* 482 U.S. 78 (1987).

42. *Cooper v. Pate,* 378 U.S. 546, 384 S. Ct. 1733 (1964).

43. *Johnson v. Avery,* 393 U.S. 483, 89 S. Ct. 747 (1969).

44. *Bounds v. Smith,* 430 U.S. 817, 97 S. Ct. 1491 (1977).

45. *Cruz v. Beto,* 405 U.S. 319, 92 S. Ct. 1079 (1972).

46. *Procunier v. Martinez,* 416 U.S. 396, 94 S. Ct. 1800 (1974).

47. *Bell v. Wolfish,* 441 US 520, 99 S. Ct. 1861 (1979).

48. *Rhodes v. Chapman,* 452 U.S. 337 (1981).

49. *Estelle v. Gamble,* 429 U.S. 974, 97 S. Ct. 285 (1976).

50. *Wolff v. McDonnell,* 418 U.S. 539, 394 S. Ct. 296 (1974).

51. Timothy J. Flanagan and Kathleen Maguire (eds.), *Sourcebook of Criminal Justice Statistics 1991* (Washington, DC: U.S. Government Printing Office, 1992), p. 555.

52. Ibid. Also see Kathleen Maguire and Ann L. Pastore (eds.), *Sourcebook of Criminal Justice Statistics 1995* (Washington, DC: U.S. Government Printing Office, 1996), p. 177.

53. Jim Thomas, Kathy Harris, and Devin Keeler, "Issues and Misconceptions in Prisoner Litigation," *Criminology* 24 (1987):901–919.

54. Jim Thomas, "Repackaging the Data: The 'Reality' of Prisoner Litigation," *New England Journal of Criminal and Civil Confinement* 15 (1989):195–230.

55. Ibid., p. 50.

56. Jennifer A. Puplava, "Peanut Butter and the Prison Litigation Reform Act," http://www.law.indiana.edu/ilj.v73/no1/puplava.html (accessed November 12, 2004).

57. Francis X. Cline, "Prisons Run Out of Cells, Money and Choices," *New York Times,* May 28, 1993, p. B7.

58. Associated Press, "Lawsuit over Michigan inmate death settled for $3.25 million," http://blog.mlive.com/grpress/2008/07/lawsuit_over_michigan_inmate_d.html (accessed November 20, 2010).

59. Libby Sander, "Inmate's Death in Solitary Cell Prompts Judge to Ban Restraints," *The New York Times,* http://www.nytimes.com/2006/11/15/us/15prison.html (accessed November 20, 2010).

60. 107 S. Ct. 2254 (1987), at 2254.

61. 111 S. Ct. 2321 (1991).

62. 115 S. Ct. 2321 (1995), at 2293.

63. Linda Greenhouse, "High Court Makes It Harder for Prisoners to Sue," *New York Times,* June 20, 1995, p. A11.

64. Public Law No. 104-134, 110 Stat. 1321 [codified as amended in scattered sections of 18 U.S.C., 28 U.S.C., and 42 U.S.C.] (1996).

65. See 141 *Congressional Record* S14,413 (daily ed., September 27, 1995), Senator Robert Dole's statement in his introduction of the PLRA as a bill to the Senate. Senator Dole provided other examples of the frivolous litigation that he felt the PLRA was needed to cure: "insufficient storage locker space, a defective haircut by a prison barber, [and] the failure of prison officials to invite a prisoner to a pizza party for a departing prison employee."

66. American Civil Liberties Union, "The Prison Litigation Reform Act (PLRA)," http://www.aclu.org/ Prisons/Prisons.cfm?ID=14379&=26 (accessed September 16, 2005).

67. Office of Judges Programs, Administrative Office of the U.S. Courts, "1997 Judicial Business of the United States Courts," http://www.uscourts.gov/ judicial_business/contents.html (accessed January 9, 2008).

68. United States Courts, "Caseload Statistics, 2009," Table C3, http://www.uscourts.gov/Statistics/Federal Judicial Caseload Statistics / Federal Judicial-CaseloadStatistics2009.aspx (accessed November 21, 2010).

69. U.S. Department of Justice, Bureau of Justice Statistics, "Corrections Populations: Key Facts at a Glance," http://bjs.ojp.usdoj.gov/content/glance/ tables/corr2tab.cfm (accessed November 24, 2010).

70. For example, see James M. Moynahan and Earle K. Stewart, *The American Jail: Its Development and Growth* (Chicago: Nelson-Hall, 1980), p. 100; Clemens Bartollas, Stuart J. Miller, and Paul B. Wice, *Participants in American Criminal Justice: The Promise and the Performance* (Upper Saddle River, NJ: Prentice Hall, 1983), p. 59.

71. J. Moore, "Prison Litigation and the States: A Case Law Review," *State Legislative Report* 8 (1981):1.

72. National Sheriffs' Association, *The State of Our Nation's Jails, 1982* (Washington, DC: Author, 1982), p. 55.

73. Linda L. Zupan, *Jails: Reform and the New Generation Philosophy* (Cincinnati, OH: Anderson, 1991), p. 71.

74. U.S. Department of Justice, National Institute of Justice, *Direct Supervision Jails: 2006 Yearbook* (Longmont, CO: National Institute of Corrections Information Center, 2006), p. viii.

75. G. J. Bayens, J. J. Williams, and J. O. Smykla, "Jail Type Makes a Difference: Evaluating the Transition from a Traditional to a Podular, Direct Supervision Jail Across Ten Years," *American Jails, 11*(2) (1997): 32–39.

76. Ibid.

77. Ibid.

78. R. Yocum, J. Anderson, T. DaVigo, and S. Lee, "Direct-supervision and Remote-supervision Jails: A Comparative Study of Psychosocial Factors," *Journal of Applied Social Psychology* 36(7) (2006):1790–1812.

79. Based on Laura Maiello and April D. Pottorff, "The Jail Facility: Agent of Change in the Reentry Process," *American Jails* 23(1) (March/April 2009):29–34; also see Amy L. Solomon, Jenny W.L. Osborne, Stefan F. LoBuglio, Jeff Mellow, and Debbie A. Mukamal, *Life After Lockup: Improving Reentry from Jail to the Community*, National Criminal Justice Reference Service, May 2008, pp. 38–42, http:// www.ncjrs.gov/pdffiles1/bja/220095.pdf (accessed November 21, 2006).

80. American Correctional Association, "Standards & Accreditation," http://www.aca.org/standards.faq. asp (accessed May 29, 2008).

81. Ibid.

82. Ibid.

83. Belinda McCarthy and Bernard McCarthy, quoted in Howard Abadinsky, *Probation and Parole: Theory and Practice,* 7th ed. (Upper Saddle River, NJ: Prentice Hall, 2000), p. 196.

84. Todd R. Clear, "Punishment and Control in Community Supervision," in Clayton A. Hartjen and Edward E. Rhine (eds.), *Correctional Theory and Practice* (Chicago: Nelson-Hall, 1992), pp. 31–42.

85. See the President's Commission on Law Enforcement and Administration of Justice, *Task Force Report: Corrections* (Washington, DC: U.S. Government Printing Office, 1967), p. 7.

86. Barry J. Nidorf, "Community Corrections: Turning the Crowding Crisis into Opportunities," *Corrections Today* (October 1989):82–88.

87. Howard Abadinsky, *Probation and Parole: Theory and Practice*, 5th ed. (Englewood Cliffs, NJ: Prentice Hall, 1994), p. 104.

88. Ibid., p. 57.

89. Ibid., pp. 104–105.

90. Ibid., pp. 106–107.
91. See President's Commission, *Task Force Report,* pp. 35–37.
92. Abadinsky, *Probation and Parole,* p. 107.
93. Eric Trist, "On Socio-Technical Systems," in Kenneth Benne and Robert Chin (eds.), *The Planning of Change,* 2nd ed. (New York: Holt, Rinehart and Winston, 1969), pp. 269–281.
94. Daniel Katz and Robert I. Kahn, *The Social Psychology of Organizations* (New York: John Wiley & Sons, 1966).
95. Patricia L. Hardyman, "Management Styles in Probation: Policy Implications Derived from Systems Theory," in Hartjen and Rhine (eds.), *Correctional Theory and Practice,* p. 68.
96. Abadinsky, *Probation and Parole,* p. 223.
97. Ibid.
98. National Advisory Commission on Criminal Justice Standards and Goals, *Corrections* (Washington, DC: U.S. Government Printing Office, 1973), pp. 396–397.
99. President's Commission, *Task Force Report,* p. 71.
100. Ibid.

10

Corrections Personnel Roles and Functions

KEY TERMS AND CONCEPTS

Code of Ethics

Correctional officer

Corruption

Death penalty

Detention as a career path

Inappropriate staff–inmate relationships

Middle managers

Motivating and retaining personnel

New old penology

NIC Executive Training Program for New
  Wardens

Principles of prison and jail leadership

Probation and parole management style

Supervisors

Typology (of correctional officers)

Warden

LEARNING OBJECTIVES

After reading this chapter, the student will:

- know in general the duties of prison, jail, and probation and parole administrators and their employees.

- be familiar with the principles of good prison leadership and the training needs of new wardens for them to be successful.

- know the basic responsibilities of prison wardens in carrying out executions

- understand the responsibilities of middle managers and supervisors.

- know the duties and types of correctional officers.

- know the functions of jail administrators.

- be able to explain how jail administrators can motivate and retain jail employees.

- be familiar with probation administrators' management styles.

> *The mood and temper of the public in regard to the treatment of crime and criminals is one of the most unfailing tests of the civilization of any country.*
>
> —WINSTON CHURCHILL

INTRODUCTION

This chapter focuses on the role and functions of personnel who work within correctional institutions and in probation and parole agencies. Presented first is a profile of prison wardens including means of preparing new wardens for the position, principles of good prison leadership, and the administrator's role in carrying out death sentences. Then, we cover the roles of correctional middle managers and supervisors, and following that we examine the front-line personnel in prisons: correctional officers (COs). This section includes a typology of the types of COs in terms of their overall job performance. Then, we consider the "cousins" of prisons, the local jails: the functions of the jail administrator, motivating and retaining jail personnel, and some problems in selecting and keeping people who will want detention work to be their career. Next, we consider administrative functions and management styles as they relate to probation and parole.

Before examining these personnel who work within corrections, it is important to bear in mind that correctional facilities constitute a society within a society; as such, a wide range of personnel are employed therein. As examples, a typical prison employs food service workers, skilled tradesmen (e.g., carpenters and electricians), teachers, secretaries, chaplains, nurses, mental health clinicians, computer technicians, and recreation personnel.

Even more importantly, remember that whether or not one wears a correction officer's uniform, *everyone's* job is to be security oriented. As former corrections administrator Mary Ellen Mastrorilli puts it:

> Nurses must double and triple check their syringe counts to ensure that syringes do not end up in the hands of an inmate. Catholic priests must substitute grape juice

for wine when saying Mass, as alcohol is prohibited inside prison walls. Carpenters must carefully account for each and every one of their tools during the work day. A hacksaw in the hands of an inmate can mean a future escape or a deadly assault. Every secretary's desk is home to a pair of scissors or a letter opener, but not so in a prison. A prison chef must keep track of all kitchen utensils, especially cutlery, because metal objects can be easily fashioned into shanks (homemade prison knives).[1]

Finally, before discussing corrections administration, we need to mention two basic principles that undergird corrections administration: First, whatever the reasons for which a person is incarcerated, he or she is not to suffer pains beyond the deprivation of liberty—confinement itself is the punishment. Second, regardless of the crime, the prisoner must be treated humanely and in accordance with his or her behavior. Even the most heinous offender is to be treated with respect and dignity and given privileges if institutional behavior warrants it.[2] Our analysis of institutional management is predicated on these two principles.

PRISONS

The Warden: A Profile

Several guest corrections speakers in the author's justice administration class have stated that the job of prison **warden** is the most difficult of all in this field[3]; this assessment is probably true because the warden must take the director's general policies and put them into effect throughout the prison while being responsible for the smooth day-to-day operation of the institution. These correctional executives also oversee the fastest-growing agencies in state government; administer increasingly visible operations; and are held accountable by politicians, auditors, the press, organized labor, and numerous other stakeholders.[4] Wardens work within a field that has become more demanding, consumes an increasing share of public funds, and involves responsibility for the lives and safety of others.

Of course, both staff and inmates are sensitive to the warden's granting of what each side perceives to be a strengthened position for the other side. For example, if a policy is enacted that gives the staff more power over inmates, the inmates will be unhappy, perhaps even rebellious; conversely, if a policy is put into practice that the staff thinks affords too much additional freedom to inmates, the staff will feel sold out. Furthermore, the prison director, typically appointed by and serving at the pleasure of the state's governor, can exert on the warden all manner of political influences at any time.

A national survey by Kim et al.[5] of more than 600 male and female prison wardens at adult state prisons provided the following demographic and ideological information: Regional differences account for a great degree of gender difference; in fact, the South employed 21,862 female corrections officers, fully half of the female correctional population in the United States. Of the prison wardens, 85.9 percent were men and 14.1 percent were women. The mean age of all wardens was 47 years, about 47.6 years for men and 44.9 years for women. The majority (81.3 percent) were white, with 70.8 percent being white men; African American men made up 11.8 percent. White women made up 10.4 percent and African American women 3.0 percent. A large proportion of the respondents had experience as COs (57.6 percent) or treatment officers (62.6 percent). Almost half of the male wardens (49.1 percent) had some military experience, compared with only 7.5 percent of the female wardens. Almost half of the wardens had a graduate degree, a law degree, or some graduate work; female wardens were more likely to have done such postbaccalaureate work (61.1 percent compared with 47.8 percent of the men).

Regarding the goals of imprisonment, male wardens ranked their four preferred goals as follows: incapacitation, deterrence, rehabilitation, and retribution. Female wardens, however, ranked them thus: incapacitation, rehabilitation, deterrence, and retribution. A greater proportion of female wardens (89.9 percent) than male wardens (83.3 percent) strongly or very strongly agreed that rehabilitation programs had an important place in their institutions. A majority of the wardens thought that the following amenities should be reduced or eliminated in prisons: martial arts instruction, conjugal visitation, cosmetic surgery and dentistry, condom distribution, disability benefits, sexually oriented reading material, and nonregulation clothing. Male wardens were more likely than female wardens to support the reduction of college education, copy privileges, condom distribution, a full-time recreation director, musical instruments, and special diets. In contrast, female wardens were more likely to support reduction of organ transplants, weight lifting, boxing, and tobacco smoking. Generally, data support the findings that female wardens seem more likely to reduce amenities that can potentially promote violence in prison and are more interested than male wardens in the health conditions of inmates.

Overall, Kim et al. concluded that although the differences between male and female wardens are somewhat noticeable, the roles of corrections administrators are becoming more gender neutral.[6]

Preparing New Wardens for Success

The explosive growth of the nation's incarcerated population, discussed in Chapter 10, has increased the need for competent correctional administrators to ensure public safety, ensure that staff and inmates are safe, and spend tax dollars effectively. They must also understand and appreciate the importance of culture (the sum total of the organization's history, staff, inmates, community, and past leadership) as they begin their tenure at an institution. Today's correctional administrator must excel in more than just correctional operations and not rely on the all-powerful, autocratic working style and strong paramilitary organization of decades past.[7]

New wardens who were surveyed by McCampbell indicated that they would have been better prepared for these challenges had they had job experience or skills in business administration/fiscal management, personnel and labor relations, legislative issues, and media and public relations.[8] Unfortunately, however, a large majority (90 percent) of new wardens also reported in this survey that they did not receive any special training or orientation for their new responsibilities prior to, or just after, they received their assignment. Since 1994, there has been a training program for new wardens, as well as related publications and other resources, available from the National Institute of Corrections (NIC). Participants in this **NIC Executive Training Program for New Wardens** stated that the best advice they received on assuming the role included the following[9]:

- Do not let it go to your head, keep the job in perspective.
- Have faith in yourself.
- Do not shut out your family, maintain balance in your life.
- Be fair and consistent with inmates and staff.
- Remember that your every statement is subject to scrutiny.
- Do not beat yourself up over small things, you will have enough big stuff to worry about.

Principles of Good Prison Leadership

Throughout the nineteenth century and the early twentieth century, studies of prisons generally focused on the administrators rather than the inmates. Beginning in the 1940s, however, an ideological shift from studying prison administrators to studying inmates occurred. The central reason for the shift seems to have been that prisons were poorly managed or were what prison researcher John J. DiIulio Jr. referred to as "ineffective prisons."[10] Many writers expressed grave doubts about the efficacy of correctional administrators and stated that prison managers could do nothing to improve conditions behind bars.

It is not surprising that when contemporary researchers attempt to relate prison management practices to the quality of life behind bars, the results are normally quite negative: Prisons that are managed in a tight, authoritarian fashion are plagued with disorder and inadequate programs; those that are managed in a loose, participative fashion are equally troubled; and those with a mixture of these two styles are no better.[11]

In a 3-year study of prison management in Texas, Michigan, and California, however, DiIulio found that levels of disorder (rates of individual and collective violence and other forms of misconduct), amenities (availability of clean cells, decent food, and so on), and service (availability of work opportunities and educational programs) did not vary with any of the following factors: a higher socioeconomic class of inmates, higher per capita spending, lower levels of crowding, lower inmate/staff ratios, greater officer training, more modern plant and equipment, and more routine use of repressive measures. DiIulio concluded that "all roads, it seemed, led to the conclusion that the quality of prison life depended mainly on the quality of prison management."[12]

DiIulio also found that prisons managed by a stable team of like-minded executives, structured in a paramilitary, security-driven, bureaucratic fashion, had better order, amenities, and service than those managed in other ways *even when* the former institutions were more crowded, spent less per capita, and had higher inmate/staff ratios: "The only finding of this study that, to me at least, seems indispensable is that *prison management matters*" (emphasis in the original).[13]

Studies analyzing the causes of major prison riots found that they were the result of a breakdown in security procedures—the daily routine of numbering, counting, frisking, locking, contraband control, and cell searches—that are the heart of administration in most prisons.[14] Problems such as crowding, underfunding, festering inmate/staff relations, and racial animosities may make a riot more *likely*, but poor security management will make a riot *inevitable*.[15]

DiIulio offered six general principles of good prison leadership:[16]

1. Successful leaders focus, and inspire their subordinates to focus, on results rather than process, on performance rather than procedures, on ends rather than means. In short, managers are judged on results, not excuses.
2. Professional staff members—doctors, psychiatrists, accountants, nurses, and other nonuniformed staff—receive some basic prison training and come to think of themselves as COs first.
3. Leaders of successful institutions follow the *management by walking around* principle. These managers are not strangers to the cellblocks and are always on the scene when trouble erupts.
4. Successful leaders make close alliances with key politicians, judges, journalists, reformers, and other outsiders.
5. Successful leaders rarely innovate, but the innovations they implement are far reaching and the reasons for them are explained to staff and inmates well in advance. Line staff are notoriously sensitive to what administrators do "for inmates" versus "what they do for us." Thus, leaders must be careful not to upset the balance and erode staff loyalty.

6. Successful leaders are in office long enough to understand and, as necessary, modify the organization's internal operations and external relations. DiIulio used the terms *flies, fatalists, foot soldiers,* and *founders.* The flies come and go unnoticed and are inconsequential. Fatalists also serve brief terms, always complaining about the futility of incarceration and the hopelessness of correctional reform. The foot soldiers serve long terms, often inheriting their job from a fly or fatalist, and make consequential improvements whenever they can. Founders either create an agency or reorganize it in a major and positive way.

To summarize, to "old" penologists, prison administrators were admirable public servants, inmates were to be restricted, and any form of self-government was eschewed. To "new" penologists, prison administrators are loathsome and evil, inmates are responsible victims, and complete self-government is the ideal. DiIulio called for a **new old penology**, or a shift of attention from the society of captives to the government of keepers. He asserted that tight administrative control is more conducive than loose administrative control to decent prison conditions. This approach, he added, will "push administrators back to the bar of attention," treating them at least as well as their charges.[17]

Administering the Death Penalty

One of the major responsibilities of prison administrators, in 36 states and in federal prisons, is to carry out the **death penalty**. By law, the warden or a representative presides over the execution.

To minimize the possibility of error, executions are carried out by highly trained teams. The mechanics of the process have been broken down into several discrete tasks and are practiced repeatedly. During the actual death watch—the 24-hour period that ends with the prisoner's execution—a member of the execution team is with the prisoner at all times. During the last 5 or 6 hours, two officers are assigned to guard the prisoner. The prisoner then showers, dons a fresh set of clothes, and is placed in an empty tomb-like death cell. The warden reads the court order or death warrant. Meanwhile, official witnesses—normally 6 to 12 citizens—are prepared for their role. The steps that are taken from this point to perform the execution depend on the method of execution that is used.[18]

Lethal injection is the predominant method of execution, and is employed in all 36 states and in federal prisons; nine states authorize electrocution, four states authorize lethal gas, three states authorize hanging, and three states authorize firing squad (17 states authorize more than one method).[19]

Approximately 3,300 prisoners are now under sentence of death in the United States; 56 percent are white, 42 percent are black, and 2 percent are of other races; 47 (about 1.4 percent) are women.[20]

Recently, the U.S. Supreme Court rendered two significant decisions concerning the death penalty: In *Roper v. Simmons* (March 2005), the Court abolished the death penalty for convicted murderers who were less than 18 years of age when they committed their crimes; this decision ended a practice used in 19 states and affected about 70 death-row inmates who were juveniles when they committed murder. In *Atkins v. Virginia* (June 2002), the Court held that the execution of mentally retarded persons—which was permissible in 20 states—constituted cruel and unusual punishment.[21]

Achieving Racial Balance

The rapid growth of the inmate population, increased oversight by the federal courts, increased demands from the public, and a change in the demographic composition of the inmate population (more African American and Hispanic prisoners) all have presented wardens with a new set of challenges. As a result, half of all wardens in maximum-security prisons now have a policy on racially integrating male inmates within prison cells to try to achieve racial balance. Similarly, about 40 percent of these wardens do not allow their inmates to object to their cell assignments.[22]

Middle Managers and Supervisors

Chapter 4 examined in detail the roles of *police* supervisors and managers. It would be repetitious to dwell at length here on those roles and functions because most of them apply to *corrections* supervisors and managers as well. The reader is encouraged to review those roles and functions in Chapter 4.

Clearly, **supervisors** have one of the most demanding positions in correctional institutions. They must direct work activities, assign tasks, provide employee feedback, and serve as technical experts for the staff reporting to them. They serve as boss, adviser, counselor, mentor, coach, trainer, and motivator.

Middle managers, although not on the front lines, are also in challenging and important positions. They are responsible for organizing their departments, planning and developing goals and objectives, overseeing the efficient use of resources, and developing effective communication networks throughout the organization.

"Thy Brother's Keeper": COs

Subordinate to the institutional administrator, middle managers, and supervisors is the correctional staff itself—those who, in the words of Gordon Hawkins, are "the other prisoners."[23] Their role is particularly important, given that they provide the front-line supervision and control of inmates and constitute the level from which correctional administrators may be chosen.

In most assignments, COs can experience stimulus overload. They are assailed with the sounds of "doors clanging; inmates talking or shouting; radios and televisions playing; and food trays banging; and odors representing an institutional blend of food, urine, paint, disinfectant, and sweat."[24]

A Typology of COs

COs play an influential role in the lives of many inmates because of their direct and prolonged interaction. They are also responsible for creating and maintaining a humane environment in prisons and jails.

Mary Ann Farkas[25] categorized COs into five types—rule enforcer, hard liner, people worker, synthetic officer, and loner—based on their orientation toward rule enforcement, extent of mutual obligations with colleagues, orientation toward negotiation or exchange with inmates, and desire to incorporate human service activities into their approach. Farkas added three residual types that were identified by respondents in her study: officer friendly, lax officer, and wishy-washy. These eight types in this **CO typology** are discussed next.

Rule enforcers, about 43 percent of COs, are the most common type in Farkas's sample. They are characterized as rule bound and inflexible in discipline and have an esprit de corps with others sharing their enforcement philosophy. They are more likely than other COs to be less than 25 years old and to have a baccalaureate degree; they tend to have less work experience and to work the evening or night shift. They typically work on posts involving direct inmate contact such as the regular housing units and in maximum-security or segregation units. They are more likely to have entered corrections for extrinsic reasons, including job security, benefits, and job availability. They have a militaristic approach to inmates, expecting deference to their authority and obedience to their orders. Rule enforcers are not willing to negotiate or use exchange as a strategy to gain inmate compliance.[26]

The *hard liners* are actually a subtype and an extreme version of the rule enforcers. They are hard, aggressive, power hungry, and inflexible in applying rules and possess little interpersonal skill. These officers are also more likely to be men, with a high school education or GED, and between the ages of 26 and 36 years. They also tend to work later shifts and in maximum-security or segregation units, and they endorse militaristic values and distinction and deference to rank and the chain of command. At times, they may become abusive and aggressive toward inmates and perceive acting tough as the way a CO is supposed to act to maintain control and order.[27]

People workers (22 percent of COs) are characterized as "professionals trying to be social, responsible, and trying their very best." They have a more comfortable style with inmates, are more flexible in rule enforcement and disciplinary measures, use their own informal reward and punishment system, and believe that the way to gain inmate compliance is through interpersonal communication and personalized relations. They regard overreliance on conduct reports as an indication of one's inability to resolve difficult situations. They often discuss issues privately with inmates instead of embarrassing them in front of peers. They are concerned with conflict resolution, relying on verbal skills in defusing situations, enjoy the challenge of working with inmates, and prefer the posts with more inmate contact.[28] [Certainly COs provide informal counseling; they are trained to be fair, yet firm in rule enforcement; expected to de-escalate situations when an inmate becomes agitated; and to work in a courteous, respectful, and professional manner. Each of these expectations are examples of informal counseling and advance the notion of rehabilitation.]

The *synthetic officers* (14 percent) are essentially a synthesis of the rule enforcer and the people worker types. They are typically older (37 years of age or more), more experienced officers who work in regular inmate housing units on the day shift. Synthetic officers try to modify the formal policies and procedures to emphasize organizational directives and interpersonal skills. They follow rules and regulations closely, yet they try to consider the circumstances. They are careful not to deviate too far from procedure, however, which might cause sanctions for themselves. Strict enforcement of rules and flexibility in enforcement are juggled in their interactions with inmates.[29]

Loners (8 percent) are also similar to rule enforcers but differ in the motivation behind their policy of strict enforcement. Loners closely follow rules and regulations because they fear criticism of their performance. Farkas believes that female and black officers are more likely to be of this type. Loners are likely to be between the ages of 26 and 36 years, to be less experienced COs, and to work on solitary posts. They believe their job performance is more closely watched because of their female and/or minority status, and need to constantly prove themselves. They do not feel accepted by other officers, nor do they identify with them. They are wary of inmates. There is a basic mistrust, even fear, of working with inmates.[30]

To summarize, age and seniority are associated with officer types. Rule enforcers and hard liners tend to be younger, less experienced COs, whereas older, more experienced officers belong to the people worker or synthetic officer categories. Generally, as officers mature, they become more interested in service delivery.

Although one might assume that more educated officers are inclined toward rehabilitation and are less punitive or aggressive toward inmates, Farkas found that rule enforcers were more likely to hold baccalaureate or master's degrees; she suggested that education may not be a strong indicator of human service attitudes.[31] Considerable evidence suggests that higher education may lead to lower job satisfaction. One observer noted that "except for the somewhat disappointing finding that COs with more education are less satisfied with their jobs, the overall picture shows that education is not related to any attitudinal variable examined thus far."[32] Other studies have determined that as officers' educational level increased, so did their desire to become administrators, the less likely they were to feel a sense of accomplishment working as COs or to want to make a career of corrections, the more likely they were to express dissatisfaction with the pace of career advancement, and the more interest they had in counseling,[33] but the less willing they were to engage in rehabilitation activities.[34]

Shift and work assignment also affect COs' orientation—the more custodial types of officers work in later shifts because they are newer officers and are more likely to work on units with more difficult inmates (such as maximum security, segregation, or units for inmates with behavioral problems). Finally, the reason for becoming a CO is related to officer type: People workers are attracted to intrinsic factors of correctional work because of its interesting and challenging aspects. Rule enforcers and hard liners become officers for extrinsic reasons: job security and benefits of state employment and job availability.

These CO typologies are actually modes of accommodation or adaptation to the organizational factors of the correctional institutions, including overcrowded conditions, more troublesome inmates, and a more litigious environment.[35]

Managing Corruption

Certainly most COs are decent, hard-working people; however, as with any profession, there will be a few such persons who come into this work and who are unethical—either by "nature or nurture"—and thus cause problems. Prison and jail **corruption** differs from other forms of public corruption because of the uniqueness of the environment, function, opportunities, and patterns of relationships of correctional institutions. Prison and jail personnel must control a reluctant, resistant, and sometimes hostile inmate population whose welfare—and comfortable lifestyle, by their standards—may seem better served by corruption than by honest compliance with prison rules; a culture of manipulation and violence may ensue.

The Preamble of the American Correctional Association **Code of Ethics** states that members of the association should have "unfailing honesty, respect for the dignity and individuality of human beings, and a commitment to professionalism and compassionate service."[36] According to noted criminal justice ethicist Sam Souryal,[37] public corruption is ostensibly a learned behavior; no one is born corrupt, and assuming correctional applicants are carefully scrutinized prior to employment, the logical explanation must be that COs learn corruption in the course of performing their job. And, if this is a plausible explanation, then ensuring a work environment that is conducive to an ethical work culture is essential. Souryal described the following three general categories of prison corruption:

1. *Acts of misfeasance.* These are illegitimate acts more likely committed by high-ranking officials who knowingly allow contractual indiscretions that would undermine the public interest and benefit them personally. It can also involve outsiders—a building firm, a group of consultants, a planning and research agency, and a law firm hired to defend the agency—who are associated with the correctional facility through a political or professional appointment.

2. *Acts of malfeasance.* These are criminal acts or acts of misconduct that officials knowingly commit in violation of state laws and/or agency rules and regulations. Such violations are usually committed by officials at the lower or middle management levels. Acts that might

fall in this category include theft; embezzlement; trafficking in contraband; extortion; official oppression; and the exploitation of inmates or their families for money, goods, or services.

3. *Acts of nonfeasance.* These are acts of omission or avoidance knowingly committed by officials who are responsible for carrying out such acts. Examples would include looking the other way when narcotics are smuggled into a prison by inmates or visitors, and failure to report misconduct by other officers out of personal loyalty.[38]

To counter the existence of such acts, Souryal recommends that correctional administrators implement the following anticorruption measures:

1. *Upgrade the quality of correctional personnel.* The entry-level pay for COs must be competitive. Correctional administrators should ensure that their hiring standards are competitive enough to attract qualified applicants yet high enough to keep high-risk applicants away from employment. Psychological testing should also be used to check the character of those who are selected, and interviews should be conducted by a hiring board prior to appointment.

2. *Establish quality-based supervisory techniques.* Supervisors should realize that loyalty to moral principles is more durable than loyalty to individuals, and understand that although trivial and insignificant policy violations can be justified, serious transgressions must be earnestly reported. Quality-based supervisors are expected to possess the professional wisdom to be able to know which matter is trivial and which is serious, without being told.

3. *Strengthen fiscal controls.* Most acts of prison corruption involve the illegal acquisition of money. Therefore, establishing financial controls is an effective tool for checking corruption in correctional institutions and involves the proper conduct of preaudit and postaudit controls. Experienced internal auditors can determine whether bidding procedures are followed, expenditure ceilings are observed, and purchase vouchers are issued for the exact objects.

4. *Emphasize true ethical training.* If correctional leaders truly want their subordinates to act professionally, to pursue integrity, fidelity, and obligation and to shun corruption, they should support and increase such training. Doing otherwise would signal that the subject is unimportant.[39]

Staff–Inmate Relationships

Despite formal policies prohibiting familiarity between inmates and prison staff employees, infractions occur that range from serious (e.g., love affairs) to minor (e.g., giving or receiving candy or soft drinks to/from an inmate). Contemporary prisons are no longer sexually segregated, and female security officers work in male institutions. This situation allows different types of **inappropriate staff–inmate relationships** to occur. Worley et al.[40] found three types of "turners"—offenders identified as developing inappropriate relationships with staff members:

1. *Heartbreakers.* They seek to form an emotional bond with a staff member, which can even lead to marriage; they generally act alone and may spend several months courting a staff member.

2. *Exploiters.* They use an employee as a means of obtaining contraband or fun and excitement; they usually act with the help of other inmates, are very manipulative, and are likely to use a "lever" (intimidation) on prison employees.

3. *Hell raisers.* These inmates engage in a unique kind of psychological warfare, and simply want to cause trouble and create hell for the prison system. They often have a long history

of personal involvement and form relationships as a way to create problems or disruptions. They thrive on putting staff members in situations wherein their jobs are compromised and enjoy the notoriety that follows the exposure of their relationship. They focus on staff members (e.g., secretaries; trustees have even become involved with staff members' spouses) rather than security officers.

Worley et al. point out that such behaviors are not the norm in penal environments; nevertheless, prison administrators must understand that offenders are very persistent in initiating interactions with employees for a variety of reasons.[41]

JAIL PERSONNEL

About 785,000 individuals are incarcerated in local jails in the United States, either awaiting trial or serving a sentence;[42] furthermore, about 266,000 people are employed in local jails.[43] Jails represent the point of entry into the criminal justice system. Although prisons hold persons who have committed felonies and have been sentenced to at least 1 year in prison, jails hold persons who are arrested and booked for criminal activity or are waiting for a court appearance if they cannot arrange bail, as well as those who are serving sentences of up to 1 year for misdemeanors. Jails also temporarily hold felons whose convictions are on appeal or who are awaiting transfer to a state prison.

Perhaps one of the most neglected areas in criminal justice research concerns individuals who are employed in local jails; what limited studies have been performed generally focus on the conditions of confinement. Jail personnel—such as police and prison employees—often must work in an environment that is potentially unstable, uncertain, and unsafe. Therefore, it would be beneficial for jail administrators to become knowledgeable about why people choose to work in local jails, as well as jail employee job satisfaction and turnover, discussed below.

Jail Administrators' Functions

Because of their responsibilities, changes in structure and function, and shifts in inmate populations (as discussed in Chapter 9), today's jails warrant being recognized and operated as professional institutions—rather than an adjunct to, or an *ad hoc* appendage (most of them being administered by a county sheriff, in the sheriff's department). The jail administrator should be a full-time professional, capable of handling multiple roles internal and external to the jail. Therefore, according to a federal report, jail administrators must function as the jail's *leader*, as the *manager* of its operations and resources, and as its *supervisor*.[44] Exhibit 10.1 discusses these three roles in more depth.

EXHIBIT 10.1

The Sheriff's Roles in Effective Jail Operations

As a *leader,* the sheriff

- helps define the jail's mission and the goals that must be met to achieve that mission.
- creates a sheriff's office executive management team that includes the jail administrator as an equal member.
- builds a culture within the jail division that supports the attainment of desired outcomes.

- serves as liaison to the external environment (i.e., the local criminal justice system, special interest groups, stakeholders, the community, and the media).
- influences and develops public policy supporting the agency mission.
- creates and maintains a competent and diverse workforce.

As a *manager,* the sheriff

- mentors and coaches the jail administrator and other staff to elicit desired behaviors and develop talent.
- ensures that policies and procedures that meet professional standards are established to guide the staff and the organization in day-to-day operations.
- motivates the jail administrator and other staff to align their personal goals with those of the jail.
- provides thorough written directives and training on those directives.
- monitors activities and assesses results by collecting and analyzing performance data on a regular basis.
- manages and allocates budgets, staff, and other resources.
- manages the organization's preparation for and response to crisis situations and emergencies.

As a supervisor, the sheriff

- stays informed about day-to-day operations in the jail and is visible and available to assist when necessary.
- monitors compliance with policies, standards, and legal requirements through the establishment of a systematic internal inspection and review process.
- supports and facilitates the jail administrator's efforts to redirect underperformers and address misconduct of jail staff.
- monitors the jail administrator's performance through regular reviews and quality assessment.

Source: Based on Mark D. Martin and Paul Katsampes, *Sheriff's Guide to Effective Jail Operations* (Washington, D.C.: U.S. Department of Justice, National Institute of Corrections, 2006), pp. 5–6.

Motivating and Retaining Jail Personnel

Current economic conditions allow sheriffs and jail administrators to heave a small sigh of relief, with their staff largely remaining in their secure government positions, and the demand to fill vacancies is now subsiding. However, in addition to job satisfaction, discussed below, the emphasis has now shifted to *retaining* current staff. Today's greatest retention challenge is not how to reduce turnover, but rather to create a deep, unified commitment to the organizational vision.[45] Put another way, serious succession planning (discussed concerning police personnel, in Chapter 5) concerns how to inspire future leaders who will maintain the passion when the torch is passed to them.

A national survey of more than 2,000 line staff and nearly 600 administrators sought to determine how to best go about doing so. The results provided both good and bad news for sheriffs in terms of retention and motivation, whereas some of the findings also debunked many commonly held myths about jail employment:[46]

- Jail employment was not the job of "last resort"—only 13 percent of staff said they had no other employment options when they accepted the jail's offer.
- Most staff rated their jail as a good (45 percent) or an excellent (20 percent) place to work.

- Fifty-nine percent of jail staff described themselves as "very committed" to the agency where they work, and this finding held among various generations of employees.
- Among line staff, 77 percent would recommend their jail as a good place to work; 75 percent indicated that they are proud to work there.
- Most staff members (63 percent) and administrators (66 percent) reported that they "almost never" think about quitting.
- Nearly seven in 10 (69 percent) staff members felt appreciated by their supervisor, and believed that they are recognized when they do good work (64 percent).[47]

These findings indicate that jails as workplaces are not actually as grim as they are often portrayed. Still, the survey points to the need for jail administrators to strengthen the jail as a workplace, using some or all of the following approaches:

- Develop consistent, two-way communication up and down the chain-of-command. Particularly with the newer generations of employees in the workplace, this is nonnegotiable. Whether occurring informally or through formal (e.g., Internet/Intranet means, hardcopy newsletters, staff surveys, employee councils), it must be ongoing.
- Provide opportunities for growth and development. There are many low cost and free means by which organizations can provide opportunities for employee growth and development—which can keep good employees engaged and committed to the organization.
- Integrate employees through participatory management practices. Provide job experiences that broaden their knowledge, listen to their creative ideas, and gain their commitment. Ongoing encouragement, mentoring, and coaching are all strategies to enhance the value of employees to the organization.
- Establish quality, responsive supervision: New supervisors must meet the emerging expectations of newer-generation workers for mentors, and be involved with the employee's needs and personal career development goals.
- Publicly express personal recognition and appreciation. A staff recognition initiative demonstrates the agency's commitment to employees of all age groups. This appreciation starts with supervisors and may end with public ceremonies acknowledging the best employees and honoring the work they do.
- Inspire professional pride. Three-fourths of line staff surveyed report they are proud to work for their agency, which means that 25 percent are not. Employees must feel they are a part of a "bigger picture," and when they have positive interactions within the organization and the community they serve.
- Assure adequate compensation. Jail salaries should be reviewed to assure parity with their law enforcement counterparts. Jail work is often undervalued and tends to be undercompensated. This can contribute to employee turnover and the perception that the jail is a stepping stone to other employment.[48]

In line with these studies, Lambert and Paoline[49] examined the reasons for turnover among jail staff, allowing jail administrators to better predict employees' staying power. First, they found that longevity on the job was not related to turnover intent; the longer an individual was with the organization, the less likely he/she indicated a desire to leave. Supervisors were also less likely to express a desire to leave. Conversely, staff members with college degrees were *more* likely to express a desire to leave. Not surprisingly, job attitude, involvement, satisfaction, and organizational commitment were also strongly related to turnover intent: those persons who were more involved in their work and who liked their jobs were less likely to want to quit. As job satisfaction and organizational commitment increased, turnover intent dropped. Significantly, job attitude accounted for more than five times the amount of turnover intent than did the personal characteristics. The results indicated that jail administrators need to focus on increasing the job involvement, satisfaction, and organizational commitment of their employees, and focus on making changes in the work environment to facilitate improved job attitudes.

A Few Comments on "Jail First" Policies and Detention as a Career Path

A "jail first" policy is where sheriffs' offices require that recruits first work in the jail—often for several years—before they can become eligible for patrol duties. Such policies can result in jail administrators having considerable difficulty in recruiting and keeping people for jail duties, and can also result in high employee attrition due to low job satisfaction (deputies going elsewhere to do "real" police work out on patrol). Jail administrators may wish to re-examine this policy and try to create a culture that values detention work. In addition to thus establishing **detention as a career path**—where one can choose to remain in detention, be promoted within it, and, it is hoped, eventually retire from it—jail administrators can encourage their recruiters to emphasize the "big picture," for example, that only about 20 percent of a deputy's 20-year career would be spent working in detention, with the remaining 80 percent would be spent as a road deputy.

Employee Training

Jail administrators and employees need to be thoroughly trained in all aspects of their job. Jail workers have been criticized for being untrained and apathetic, although most are highly effective and dedicated. One observer wrote that

> personnel is still the number one problem of jails. Start paying decent salaries and developing decent training and you can start to attract bright young people to jobs in jails. If you don't do this, you'll continue to see the issue of personnel as the number one problem for the next 100 years.[50]

Training should be provided on the booking process; inmate management and security; general liability issues; policies related to AIDS; problems of inmates addicted to alcohol and other drugs; communication and security technology; and issues concerning suicide, mental health problems, and medication.

PROBATION AND PAROLE OFFICERS

Primary Duties

Probation and parole officers must possess important skills similar to those of a prison caseworker, such as good interpersonal communication, decision making, and writing skills. They operate independently, with less supervision than most prison staff. These officers are trained in the techniques for supervising offenders and then assigned a caseload. Probation and parole officers supervise inmates at the two ends of the sentencing continuum (incarceration being in the middle). Probation officers supervise offenders with a suspended sentence, monitoring their behavior in the community and their compliance with the conditions of their probation, and suspended prison sentence. Parole officers supervise inmates who have been conditionally released from prison and returned to their community. These officers report violations of the conditions of offenders' release to the body that authorized their community placement and placed conditions on their behavior (the court for probation and the parole board for parole).[51]

To Arm or Not to Arm?

Whether probation and parole officers should be armed continues to be an oft-debated topic in corrections. The debate revolves around whether a probation or parole officer can effectively perform traditional duties while armed. Traditionalists believe that carrying a firearm contributes to an atmosphere of distrust between the client and the officer; enforcement-oriented officers, conversely, view a firearm as an additional tool to protect themselves from the risk associated with violent, serious, or high-risk offenders.[52]

Officers must make home and employment visits in the neighborhoods in which offenders live; some of these areas are not safe, and officers must often inform offenders that they will be recommending their parole or probation revocation, which could result in imprisonment. Most probation and parole agencies believe that if officers carry weapons, they are perceived differently from counselors or advisers who guide offenders into treatment and self-help programs. Over the past two decades, there has been a move from casework to surveillance by officers; however, the caseloads include more dangerous offenders.

There is no standard policy for these agencies regarding weapons, and officers themselves are not in agreement about being armed. Some states classify probation and parole officers as peace officers and grant them the authority to carry a firearm both on and off duty.[53] Some authors believe that officers should not be required to carry a firearm if they are opposed to arming, and that providing an option allows for a better officer/assignment match.[54] In sum, it would seem that the administrator's decision concerning arming should focus on need, officer safety, and local laws and policies.

Probation Management Styles

Patricia Hardyman's study of probation administrators focused on their **probation management style**—this style being the fundamental determinant of the nature of the probation organization—and was instructive in describing the impact of this style on the department's operation. Few departments, even those with a hierarchical organizational structure, had a pure management style; administrators vacillated among a variety of styles, including laissez faire, democratic, and authoritarian. The degree to which administrators included the probation officers in the decision-making process and communicated with officers varied. Authoritarian administrators created emotional and physical distance between the officers and themselves. Surprisingly, the most common management style used by probation administrators was laissez faire.[55]

Hardyman found that many probation administrators simply did not participate in the day-to-day activities and supervision strategies of the staff. They remained remote but made final decisions on critical policies and procedures.[56] Hardyman also found that few probation administrators across the country operated with the democratic style. Those who did, of course, listened more to the concerns and suggestions of the line supervisors and officers. The administrator still made the final decisions, but information was generally sought from the line staff and their opinions were considered. Officers working under administrators with this style had a greater sense that their opinions mattered and that the administrator valued their input. An additional benefit of the democratic style was that the administrators had power by virtue of both their position and their charisma, which inspired teamwork and task accomplishment.[57]

Summary

This chapter examined the criminal justice employees who work in correctional institutions and probation and parole agencies, with particular emphasis placed on administrators. Certainly, as noted in this chapter, substantial pressures are now placed on these administrators by the external and internal environments. They must maintain a secure environment while attempting to offer some treatment to their clients, who should not leave incarceration or probation/parole in a much worse condition than when they entered. At the same time, another increasingly difficult challenge is that these administrators must constantly strive to maintain a competent, dedicated, noncorrupt workforce that will also uphold the primary tenets of incarceration: providing a secure environment while ensuring that inmates are treated with respect and dignity.

Questions for Review

1. What is meant by the term *new old penology*?
2. What are the different responsibilities of the warden and other prison administrators?
3. According to DiIulio, what are some major principles of successful prison administration?
4. What are some of the major problems encountered by prison or jail employees?
5. What are the types of COs, per Farkas? How do age, length of service, type of assignment, and education affect where one fits in this typology?
6. What are the means by which corrections personnel can become corrupted, and what can their administrators do to address and prevent it?
7. What are the three types of inmates who engage in inappropriate relationships with correctional staff members?
8. What are the functions of middle managers and supervisors in jails and prisons (see Chapter 3 if necessary)?
9. How would you describe the prison warden and his or her role? What kinds of training and education are necessary for a new warden to succeed?
10. What are the primary roles of the jail administrator?
11. Why are advantages and disadvantages of having, in effect, two career tracks in jails: a detention track and a patrol track? What can jail administrators do to foster careers and improve job satisfaction in the jail or detention side?

Learn by Doing

1. Most, if not all, of us has had to work in a position where we were supervised. Using DiIulio's "Six Principles of Good Prison Leadership," identify a supervisor you either worked for directly or were able to observe and discuss how this person measured up in his/her leadership skills. Also, discuss one of DiIulio's traits of leadership you would implement were you in a leadership position.
2. Your criminal justice honor society is planning a noon forum/debate concerning capital punishment. Your role will be to discuss the problems that exist with prison wardens administering the death penalty, as well as whether or not the recruitment of wardens is limited if one of their position requirements is the ability to supervise use of the death penalty.
3. You are a well-known jail consultant and have been hired by a medium-sized county to examine its jail operations. One observation you quickly make concerns its pattern of recruitment and hiring of personnel: a newly hired deputy, upon completion of required academy training, is automatically assigned to work in the jail. Then, perhaps several years later, as he or she gains seniority and a position becomes available, application may be made for a transfer to the patrol division. What would seem to be the advantages of such an arrangement? Disadvantages? What would you recommend is needed in order to establish a career path for correctional workers in the jail?
4. As part of your criminal justice department's annual "Career Day" program, you are to discuss the general roles of prison COs and jailers as well as the primary differences between probation and parole officers. What will be in your oral report?

Related Websites

American Correctional Association
http://www.aca.org

American Probation and Parole Association (APPA)
http://www.appa-net.org

Death Penalty Focus
http://www.deathpenalty.org

Death Penalty Information System (DPIC)
http://www.deathpenaltyinfo.org

National Coalition to Abolish the Death Penalty (NCADP)
http://www.ncadp.org

National Sheriffs Association
http://www.sheriffs.org/

Notes

1. Mary Ellen Mastrorilli, personal communication, September 11, 2010.
2. John J. DiIulio, Jr., *Governing Prisons: A Comparative Study of Correctional Management* (New York: Free Press, 1987), p. 167.
3. Personal communication, Ron Angelone, Director, Nevada Department of Prisons, April 27, 1992.
4. F. T. Cullen, E. J. Latessa, R. Kopache, L. X. Lombardo, and V. S. Burton, Jr., "Prison Wardens' Job Satisfaction," *The Prison Journal* 73 (1993):141–161.
5. Ahn-Shik Kim, Michael DeValve, Elizabeth Quinn DeValve, and W. Wesley Johnson, "Female Wardens: Results from a National Survey of State Correctional Executives," *The Prison Journal* 83(4) (December 2003):406–425.
6. Ibid.
7. Susan W. McCampbell, "Making Successful New Wardens," *Corrections Today* 64(6) (October 2002):130–134. Also see the National Institute of Corrections website, http://nicic.org.
8. Ibid.
9. Ibid.
10. John J. DiIulio, Jr., "Well Governed Prisons Are Possible," in George F. Cole, Marc C. Gertz, and Amy Bunger (eds.), *The Criminal Justice System: Politics and Policies,* 8th ed. (Belmont, CA: Wadsworth, 2002), pp. 411–420.
11. Ibid., p. 449.
12. DiIulio, *Governing Prisons,* p. 256.
13. Ibid.
14. Bert Useem, *States of Siege: U.S. Prison Riots, 1971–1986* (New York: Oxford University Press, 1988).
15. DiIulio, "Well Governed Prisons Are Possible," p. 413.
16. John J. DiIulio, Jr., *No Escape: The Future of American Corrections* (New York: Basic Books, 1991), Ch. 1.
17. DiIulio, "Well Governed Prisons Are Possible," p. 456.
18. See Robert Johnson, *Death Work: A Study of the Modern Execution Process,* 2nd ed. (Belmont, CA: West/Wadsworth, 1998); Robert Johnson, "This Man Has Expired," *Commonweal* (January 13, 1989):9–15.
19. Tracy L. Snell, *Capital Punishment, 2009: Statistical Tables* (U.S. Department of Justice, *Bureau of Justice Statistics* (December 2010), http://bjs.ojp.usdoj.gov/content/pub/pdf/cp09st.pdf (Accessed August 26, 2011), pp. 1-4.
20. Ibid.
21. *Roper v. Simmons,* No. 03-633 (2005); *Atkins v. Virginia,* 536 U.S. 304 (2002).
22. Barbara Sims, "Surveying the Correctional Environment: A Review of the Literature," *Corrections Management Quarterly* 5(2) (Spring 2001):1–12.
23. Gordon Hawkins, *The Prison* (Chicago: University of Chicago Press, 1976).
24. Ben M. Crouch, *The Keepers: Prison Guards and Contemporary Corrections* (Springfield, IL: Charles C Thomas, 1980), p. 73.
25. Mary Ann Farkas, "A Typology of Correctional Officers," *International Journal of Offender Therapy and Comparative Criminology* 44 (2000):431–449.
26. Ibid., pp. 438–439.
27. Ibid., pp. 439–440.
28. Ibid., pp. 440–441.
29. Ibid., p. 442.
30. Ibid., pp. 442–443.
31. Ibid.
32. Susan Philliber, "Thy Brother's Keeper: A Review of the Literature on Correctional Officers," *Justice Quarterly* 4 (1987): 9–37.
33. Robert Rogers, "The Effects of Educational Level on Correctional Officer Job Satisfaction," *Journal of Criminal Justice* 19 (1991):123–137.
34. David Robinson, Frank J. Porporino, and Linda Simourd, "The Influence of Educational Attainment on the Attitudes and Job Performance of Correctional Officers," *Crime and Delinquency* 43 (1997):60–77.
35. Ibid., pp. 445–446.

36. See the American Correctional Association, "ACA Code of Ethics," http://www.aca.org/pastpresentfuture/ethics.asp (accessed November 22, 2010).

37. Sam Souryal, "Deterring Corruption by Prison Personnel: A Principle-Based Perspective," *The Prison Journal* (89)1 (March 2009): 21–45.

38. Ibid., p. 36

39. Adapted from ibid., pp. 41–43.

40. Robert Worley, James W. Marquart, and Janet L. Mullings, "Prison Guard Predators: An Analysis of Inmates Who Established Inappropriate Relationships with Prison Staff, 1995–1998," *Deviant Behavior: An Interdisciplinary Journal* 24 (2003):175–194.

41. Ibid., p. 93.

42. U.S. Department of Justice, Bureau of Justice Statistics, "Key Facts at a Glance: Correctional Populations," http://bjs.ojp.usdoj.gov/content/glance/tables/corr2tab.cfm (accessed November 22, 2010).

43. U.S. Department of Justice, Bureau of Justice Statistics, *Justice Expenditure and Employment Abstracts* (see spreadsheet at: *C:\Documents and Settings\Ken Peak\Local Settings\Temporary Internet Files\Content.IE5\MGKYODXY\cjee07[1].zip* (accessed November 15, 2010).

44. Mark D. Martin Paul Katsampes, *Sheriff's Guide to Effective Jail Operations* (Washington, D.C.: U.S. Department of Justice, National Institute of Corrections, 2006), pp. 5–6.

45. Adapted from Jeanne B. Stinchcomb, Susan W. McCampbell, and Leslie Leip, *The Future is Now: Recruiting, Retaining, and Developing the 21st Century Jail Workforce*, Center for Innovative Public Policies, Inc., March 2009, http://www.cipp.org/pdf/21stCenturyJailWorkforceJan2010.pdf (accessed November 9, 2010); see also Jeanne B. Stinchcomb, Susan W. McCampbell, Elizabeth P. Layman, *FutureForce: A Guide to Building the 21st Century Community Corrections Workplace*, U. S. Department of Justice, National Institute of Corrections, http://nicic.org/Downloads/PDF/Library/021799.pdf (accessed November 9, 2010).

46. See Jeanne B. Stinchcomb, *The National Jail Workforce Survey: Methodological Challenges*, April 1, 2010, http://www.faqs.org/periodicals/201004/2041517401.html (accessed November 9, 2010).

47. Ibid.

48. Adapted from ibid., pp. 75–85.

49. Eric Lambert and Eugene A. Paoline III, "Take This Job and Shove It: An Exploratory Study of Turnover Intent among Jail Staff," *Journal of Criminal Justice* 38(2) (March-April 2010): 139-148.

50. Quoted in Advisory Commission on Intergovernmental Relations, *Jails: Intergovernmental Dimensions of a Local Problem* (Washington, DC: Author, 1984), p. 1.

51. Richard P. Seiter, *Correctional Administration: Integrating Theory and Practice* (Upper Saddle River, NJ: Prentice Hall, 2002), pp. 387–388.

52. Shawn E. Small and Sam Torres, "Arming Probation Officers: Enhancing Public Confidence and Officer Safety," *Federal Probation* 65(3) (2001):24–28.

53. Seiter, *Correctional Administration,* p. 387.

54. Small and Torres, "Arming Probation Officers," p. 27.

55. Patricia L. Hardyman, "Management Styles in Probation: Policy Implications Derived from Systems Theory," in Clayton A. Hartjen and Edward E. Rhine (eds.), *Correctional Theory and Practice* (Chicago: Nelson-Hall, 1992), pp. 61–81.

56. Ibid.

57. Ibid., p. 71.

11

Corrections Issues
and Practices

KEY TERMS AND CONCEPTS

Alternatives to incarceration

Boot camps

Classification

Day reporting

Drug interdiction

Electronic monitoring

Hostage taking

House arrest

Intensive supervision

Intermediate sanctions

Life without parole (LWOP)

Net widening

Pennsylvania plan

Prison Rape Elimination Act of 2003

Privatization

Riots

Sexual violence

Shock incarceration

Shock probation/parole

Three-strikes laws

Unit management

LEARNING OBJECTIVES

After reading this chapter, the student will:

- be aware of several issues and problems concerning inmate populations: sexual and physical violence, issuing condoms to inmates, hostage taking, dealing with mentally ill inmates, and the impact of, and modifications to three-strikes laws.
- know the rationale and major administrative considerations regarding inmate classification.
- understand the problem and possible solutions of drugs in prisons and jails.
- be able to discuss the pros and cons of privatizing correctional operations and programs.
- be familiar with the types and effects of intermediate sanctions that stop short of incarceration.

[Correctional administrators] undoubtedly must take into account the very real threats unrest presents to inmates and officials alike, in addition to the possible harms to inmates.

—United States Supreme Court,
in Whitley v. Albers, 475 U.S. 312 (1986), at 320–321

Boredom is beautiful.

—Former Nevada Prison Warden

INTRODUCTION

The preceding two chapters in this Part addressed some of the organizational and personnel issues and functions related to correctional institutions (i.e., prisons and jails) and community corrections (probation and parole). This chapter discusses additional issues for correctional administrators regarding their operations.

First, we briefly examine several selected issues in the institutional setting that concern certain offender populations: new developments concerning juvenile offenders and life sentences, sexual and physical violence in prisons (and the Prison Rape Elimination Act of 2003 or PREA), whether or not inmates should be issued condoms, hostage taking in detention facilities, mentally ill inmates, the effects and impact of three-strikes laws on sentences, the rationale and methods for using inmate **classification** for security and treatment, and an overview of the drug problem in prisons. The move to privatize prisons is then examined, including purported advantages, disadvantages, and evaluations of such attempts. The chapter concludes with discussions of several intermediate sanctions—punishments that are more severe than mere probation but less than prison—including intensive probation/parole, house arrest (HA), electronic monitoring (EM), shock probation and parole, shock incarceration, and day reporting; included here are some criticisms and evaluations of these approaches.

ISSUES CONCERNING INMATE POPULATIONS

Correctional administrators not only must deal with issues such as institutional population and design, budgets, politics, and the Eighth Amendment's proscription against cruel and unusual punishment but also cope with problems relating to the types of inmates who are under their supervision. Next, we consider several selected administrative issues and problems.

Should Juveniles Serve Life Without Parole Sentences?

Having ruled in 2005 that it is unconstitutional to execute a person who committed a capital crime while younger than 18 years (see *Roper v. Simmons*, 543 U.S. 551), in November 2009, the U.S. Supreme Court heard arguments concerning whether or not it is also unconstitutional to sentence teens to life without possibility of parole (LWOP) for a *noncapital* crime. The case involved a Florida youth, Terrance Graham, who at the age of 16 years robbed a restaurant with an accomplice; they beat the manager with a steel bar. Graham received probation for that crime, but a year later, he and accomplices committed a home invasion robbery. For that offense, and for violating the terms of his probation, Graham was sentenced to life in prison without possibility of parole.

In May 2010, the U.S. Supreme Court decided *Graham v. Florida*,[1] which held that the Eighth Amendment's ban on cruel and unusual punishment prohibits juveniles who commit nonhomicide crimes from being sentenced to LWOP. Although 37 states, the District of Columbia, and the federal government had laws allowing LWOP sentences for these youthful offenders, the justices stated that such sentences had been "rejected the world over," and that only the United States and perhaps Israel had imposed such punishment even for *homicides* committed by juveniles.

Sexual and Physical Violence: Facts of Prison Life

People who live and work in correctional institutions obviously do not leave their libido at the institution's front gate when they enter. Physical violence is a constant possibility, and **sexual violence**—termed "the plague that persists"[2]—must also be addressed.

Persons entering prisons and jails express their sexuality in many forms, with solitary or mutual masturbation at one end of the continuum, consensual homosexual behavior in the middle, and gang rapes at the other end. Factors that appear to increase sexual coercion rates include large population size (more than 1,000 inmates), understaffed workforces, racial conflict, barracks-type housing, inadequate security, and a high percentage of inmates incarcerated for crimes against persons.[3] Furthermore, inmates who are young, physically small or weak, suffering from mental illness, known to be "snitches," not gang affiliated, or convicted of sexual crimes are at increased risk of sexual victimization.[4]

Wolff and Shi[5] examined physical and sexual victimizations that were reported by nearly 7,000 male inmates. They found that during the period under study, nearly one-third (32 percent) of inmates had been *physically* assaulted at least once, and approximately three percent reported at least one *sexual* assault. On an average, regardless of the type of assault, the victims were typically in their early 30s, African American, had spent 2 years at their prison, had 4 to 5 years left on their current sentences, and had spent roughly 8 years in prison since turning 18. Mental health problems were more frequently reported by victims of sexual assault. The most common forms of physical assault reported were being threatened with a weapon and being hit. Inmate-on-inmate sexual assault most often involved forced, attempted, or coerced anal or oral sex. Physical assaults were most likely to occur between noon and midnight (primarily between noon and 6 P.M.) and in the inmate's cell or yard. For sexual assaults, the inmate's cell was also the most likely place of occurrence, and inmates were at greatest risk of sexual assault by other inmates between 6 P.M. and midnight.[6]

Wolff and Shi also found that inmate-on-inmate physical and sexual assault incidents most often involved attackers with a gang affiliation and with whom the victim was acquainted, and roughly half of the incidents involved the use of a weapon, typically a knife or shank. The victims typically did not know why they were attacked. Episodes of inmate-on-inmate sexual assault were more likely to be committed by a repeat perpetrator, and physical injuries were more likely from inmate-on-inmate sexual assaults; injuries typically involved bruises, cuts, and scratches. One-third of the physical and sexual assaults resulted in medical attention, and about one-fifth of the incidents involving medical attention required hospitalization outside the prison.[7]

Several policy issues arise from these findings. Wolff and Shi[8] suggest that, at a minimum, an intervention plan be employed that is selectively targeted to prison areas and times of day, and to inmates who are most at risk (e.g., those with mental illness; mental disabilities; or bisexual, transsexual, or homosexual orientations); these at-risk individuals should be placed in single cells or protective units. Prison administrators must attempt to prevent and prosecute sexual assaults, as well as increase surveillance in vulnerable areas such as transportation vans, holding tanks, shower rooms, stairways, and storage areas. New inmates should be informed of the potential for being sexually assaulted while incarcerated and be told about prevention and what medical, legal, and psychological help is available if they are targeted.[9]

The Prison Rape Elimination Act of 2003

Until recently, there were very little current data or information on the extent of sexual coercion in prisons. Fortunately, however, federal legislation has indirectly provided some enlightenment. As part of the **PREA** (L. 108-79), the U.S. Department of Justice's Bureau of Justice Statistics (BJS) was mandated to develop a new national data collection effort on the incidence and prevalence of sexual assault in correctional facilities. The law also required that public hearings be held concerning the prisons having the highest and lowest rates in order to determine what they are doing, that is, right and wrong; ultimately, a commission is to develop national standards for preventing prison rape.[10]

As seen in Table 11.1, a BJS survey of federal and state prisons and local jails found that the number of allegations of sexual violence actually *increased* by 21 percent following enactment of the PREA; some of this increase, BJS states, may be the result of new definitions being adopted as well as improved reporting by correctional authorities. Table 11.1 also shows respondents reporting about 6,500 allegations of sexual violence in prisons and jails in the most recent annual survey. Perhaps notably, Table 11.2 (showing outcomes of investigations of sexual violence) shows that 75 percent of the allegations of staff sexual misconduct and 86 percent of allegations of inmate-on-inmate nonconsensual sexual acts had outcomes of either "unsubstantiated" or "unfounded."[11]

Should Inmates Be Issued Condoms?

An issue related to the earlier discussion of sexual violence in prisons is whether or not inmates should be given condoms. On the one hand, this would seem to be a common sense issue of prisoners' rights and a means of preventing AIDS; on the other hand, it is argued that doing so would fly in the face of prison regulations against inmates engaging in sexual relations for reasons relating to security and sexual violence. The issue is very divisive and will likely not be resolved easily.

As noted above, sexual activity is common among prisoners; indeed, some inmates already use rubber gloves as makeshift condoms. Yet, recent efforts to expand behind-bars condom access have gone almost nowhere. Only one state—Vermont—and a handful of local jails

TABLE 11.1	Allegations of Sexual Violence and Rates per 1,000 Inmates, by Type of Facility, 2005 and 2006			
	National Estimate		**Rate per 1.000 Inmates**	
Facility Type	**2006**	**2005**	**2006**	**2005**
Total	6,528	6,241	2.91	2.83
Prisons				
Public-Federal[a]	242	268	1.50	1.71
Public-State	4,516	4,341	3.75	3.68
Private	200	182	1.91	1.80
Local jails				
Public	1,521	1,384	2.05	1.86
Private	12	22	0.72	1.33
Other adult facilities				
Indian country jails[b]	29	32	^	^
Military-operated	3	8	^	^
ICE-operated	5	4	^	^

^Too few cases to provide a reliable rate.

[a]Federal numbers for 2006 are not comparable to those in 2005 due to a change in reporting.

[b]Excludes facilities housing juveniles only.

(including those in Los Angeles, San Francisco, Philadelphia, and Washington, D.C.) have condom programs. The Center for Health Justice states that there have been no related security problems in these cities where condoms are being issued.[12]

But prison and jail administrators take another tack: Issuing condoms sends the wrong message it encourages consensual or coercive sex (and prison rapists might use condoms to avoid leaving DNA evidence after their assaults)—and condoms can be used to conceal drugs. In late 2007, California Governor Arnold Schwarzenegger agreed and vetoed a bill that would have provided condoms in penal institutions statewide. This issue is difficult for proponents to promote, and may or may not remain on the table for discussion. As the policy director of the Center for Health Justice says, "People don't like to think about prisoners having sex, even though everybody knows it goes on."[13]

Hostage Taking in Detention Facilities: An Overview

NATURE OF THE PROBLEM **Riots** and **hostage taking** are probably as old as corrections itself, and are the jail and prison administrator's worst nightmare. They can occur at any time; even the most safety-concerned staff cannot always avoid such crises. Inmates will be inmates, and they do not want to be where they are.[14] A corrections hostage-taking event occurs when any person—staff, visitor, or inmate—is held against his or her will by an inmate seeking to escape, gain concessions, or achieve other goals such as publicizing a particular cause. It may also be a planned or an impulsive act. When they occur, jail and prison rioting and hostage taking are potentially explosive and perilous situations from beginning to end; hostages are always directly in harm's way.[15] Following are some examples of such incidents:

- At the Morey Unit of the Lewis Prison Complex in Buckeye, Arizona, two inmates took two correctional officers (COs) hostage and seized the unit's tower, triggering a 15-day standoff—the longest prison hostage situation in the nation's history.[16]

TABLE 11.2 Outcomes of Investigations into Allegations of Sexual Violence, by Type of Facility, 2006

	All Facilities[a]		State and Federal Prisons		Local Jails		Private Prisons and Jails	
	Number	Percent[b]	Number	Percent[b]	Number	Percent[b]	Number	Percent[b]
Inmate-on-inmate nonconsensual sexual acts	2,205	100%	1,390	100%	725	100%	87	100%
Substantiated	262	14	147	13	111	17	3	4
Unsubstantiated	1,030	54	707	61	295	44	28	34
Unfounded	616	32	304	26	259	39	52	63
Investigation ongoing	297		232		60		4	
Inmate-on-inmate abusive sexual contacts	834	100%	707	100%	116	100%	11	100%
Substantiated	158	19	125	18	31	27	0	0
Unsubstantiated	491	60	426	62	54	48	9	100
Unfounded	165	21	139	20	28	25	0	0
Investigation ongoing	20		17		2		1	
Staff sexual misconduct	2,371	100%	1,677	100%	575	100%	95	100%
Substantiated	471	25	235	18	229	47	15	17
Unsubstantiated	877	47	745	58	91	19	36	41
Unfounded	535	28	309	24	166	34	37	42
Investigation ongoing	489		388		90		9	
Staff sexual harassment	1,118	100%	984	100%	105	100%	19	100%
Substantiated	70	7	47	6	15	15	0	0
Unsubstantiated	595	62	537	64	50	51	7	100
Unfounded	292	31	258	31	34	34	0	0
Investigation ongoing	161		141		6		12	

Note: Detail may not sum to total due to rounding.

[a]Includes jails in Indian country and facilities operated by the U.S. military and Immigration and Customs Enforcement (ICE).

[b]Percents based on allegations for which investigations have been completed.

- Approximately 450 prisoners rioted in the Southern Ohio Correctional Facility, in Lucasville, Ohio; nine inmates and one officer were murdered and six officers taken hostage during the 10-day siege.[17]
- Jail inmates in a Louisiana parish held the warden and two guards hostage at knifepoint, demanding a helicopter to escape to Cuba or anywhere else.[18]
- A SWAT team stormed the Bay County Jail in Florida after inmates threatened to rape and cut off the body parts of a fourth hostage, a nurse; four inmates overpowered the only officer on the floor, leading to an 11-hour standoff.[19]

Also permanently seared in the annals of corrections rioting are the horrific incidents at the Attica Correctional Facility in Attica, New York, in 1971 (39 inmates and staff killed), and at the New Mexico State Prison in Santa Fe, in 1980 (33 inmates dead), where inmates took over most of these institutions.[20]

Local jails are included in this discussion because such incidents certainly occur in them, and are even more common in jails in foreign venues. U.S. jails—such as prisons—can become quite dangerous because of their overcrowded conditions and the nature of their clientele, which will include arrestees awaiting trial for felony offenses, mentally ill persons awaiting movement to health facilities, convicted felons awaiting transport to a state or federal institution, military offenders, and many violent, often mentally unstable or sociopathic offenders with histories of substance abuse; certainly such individuals are capable of hostage taking. Indeed, four of 10 jail inmates have a violent arrest record.[21] Because 85 percent of local jails are operated by sheriff's offices or municipal police departments,[22] local sheriffs and police chiefs with lockup responsibilities must shoulder the burden of preparing for such emergencies.

ADMINISTRATIVE CONSIDERATIONS: USING FORCE AND NEGOTIATION   Before correctional administrators can begin to plan for emergencies within their facilities, the following three broad elements are especially important: command, planning, and training (described below). Successful resolution also requires a controlled, measured response, clear lines of authority, and effective communication. Unity of command—the principle that members of an organization are accountable to a single superior—is also a paramount consideration.[23] Also, staffing levels must be established—traditional crisis response teams (CRTs), armed CRTs, and tactical teams— all of which can employ less lethal intervention options and even the use of deadly force:

1. *Traditional CRTs.* The first, primary level of response is the traditional CRT, which is composed of staff from all job specialties who train in riot control formations and use of defensive equipment (e.g., batons, stun guns, chemical agents, control, and containment).
2. *Armed CRTs.* This level of response provides managers with an option for dealing with the emergency situation if it escalates to the point where staff members' or inmates' lives are in imminent danger; it involves a specially trained team that can respond with deadly force when necessary.
3. *Tactical teams.* These are the most highly trained and skilled emergency response staff. They must be trained in advanced skills such as barricade breaching; hostage rescue; and precision marksmanship with pistols, rifles, and assault rifles.[24]

Another critical element of emergency planning is a use-of-force policy. Which staff members are authorized to order the use of force, and what weapons and less lethal munitions are appropriate? The riot plan should also include contact names and phone numbers and an outline of existing agreements between agencies.[25] Training is another indispensable facet of emergency planning. It does little good to have an emergency plan if staff and supervisors are not trained to activate it;

people must clearly understand their own functions as well as those of people in other components; indeed, negotiators and personnel from tactical teams should train together regularly.[26]

The goals of hostage negotiation are to open communication lines, reduce stress and tension, build rapport, obtain intelligence, stall for time, allow hostage takers to express emotion and ventilate, and establish a problem-solving atmosphere.[27] Jail/prison records will provide valuable intelligence information on the hostage taker, including prior criminal, educational, work, psychological, and family history. Studies of hostage negotiations indicate that they tend to follow a common cycle: Initially, both parties make exaggerated demands. This is followed by a period of withdrawal and a return to negotiations with more moderate demands.

The passage of time can be a very important ally during such incidents and is a major element of the negotiator's role. Often, the preferred strategy for negotiating is to wait it out. The advantages of time's passing include that hostage takers may develop sympathy for their hostages, develop rapport with negotiators, or just get tired of doing what they are doing.[28] The question "How long is too long?" cannot be easily answered because every incident is different. Generally, negotiations may continue if no one is being injured and if no major damage or destruction to the facility is occurring.

Certain demands by hostage takers are nonnegotiable: Allowing release or escape, weapons, an exchange of hostages, and pardon or parole are not on the table. A number of other demands are open to negotiation. A maxim of negotiations is "Always get something for something." Negotiators should never cede to a demand without obtaining a concession in return.[29] Nor should they engage in trickery such as trying to drug hostage takers' food or drink (it might backfire) or have face-to-face contact (unless, as in rare instances, the decision is made that it is advantageous to do so).[30]

When negotiations deadlock, commanders may decide to employ ultimatums regarding use of force and issues. A *use-of-force ultimatum* can be given in the expectation that inmates, given a clear choice between surrender and an armed assault, will choose surrender.[31]

AFTERMATH: A RETURN TO NORMALCY   In the aftermath of hostage incidents, it is critical to learn whether or not there were contributing factors such as lax inmate search activities, contraband, contractors and visitors coming and going, inmate familiarity with staff work routines, unlocked doors or gates, or other contributing factors; if so, new policies and procedures must be enacted covering those exigencies. The administration must also consider any damages, renovations, repairs, and remodeling that need to be addressed, and continuing control of the inmates while these are attended to.[32]

Returning the facility to normal operations at the conclusion of a disturbance is also a major priority. The following issues should be addressed in the aftermath:

- Short-term responsibilities include searching for contraband, securing inmates, assessing damages, counting inmates, providing medical care to hostages and inmates, and collecting evidence for future prosecutions.
- Medium-range efforts include providing continued support and counseling to staff in coping with their experiences, repairing damage to facilities, normalizing institutional operations, and undertaking a thorough investigation of the causes of the crisis. A report may be commissioned to determine how the incident occurred.
- Long-term solutions include developing policy reflecting what was learned from the disturbance, discovering better ways to forecast and prevent problems, improve the flow of information, improve relationships with other agencies, boost morale, and meet challenges.[33]

Mentally Ill Offenders

While in solitary confinement in a Massachusetts prison, an inmate cut his legs and arms, tried to hang himself with tubing from a breathing machine, smashed the machine to get a sharp fragment to slice his neck, and ate pieces of it, hoping to cause internal bleeding; he eventually hanged himself. Such inmates, with histories of mental illness and depression, often try suicide. In fact, this was one of 18 suicides or attempted suicides since 2004; a federal lawsuit filed by advocates for inmates and the mentally ill is seeking to prevent the state from placing mentally ill inmates in such segregated cells.[34]

Several other states have faced similar lawsuits and other challenges in attempting to address the problem of mentally ill prisoners. Following are some related developments:

- In 2007, Indiana agreed to stop putting some mentally ill inmates in isolation cells.
- In California, after a record number of prison suicides—44—in 2005, a special master appointed by a federal judge reported that inmates "in overcrowded and understaffed segregation units are killing themselves in unprecedented numbers." The judge also ordered the governor to spend more than $600 million to improve mental health services.
- In New York, the legislature passed a law in 2007 to remove mentally ill inmates from solitary cells, but the governor vetoed it.[35]
- All states are struggling with what to do about inmates who are very violent, out of control, need to be segregated from other inmates, and also mentally ill. Such segregated inmates are typically locked up for 23 hours per day, allowed out only to shower or get outdoor exercise in a small caged space. A national expert in prison suicide argues that confining suicidal inmates under such circumstances only enhances their feeling of isolation and is antitherapeutic.[36]

Since the deinstitutionalization movement of the 1970s, the number of criminal offenders and inmates suffering from mental illness has been increasing. It is estimated that about 13 percent of all state prison inmates are receiving therapy and/or counseling, and about 10 percent of them are also taking psychotropic medications.[37]

In prison, these individuals pose a dual dilemma for administrators. They are often violent and may be serving a long sentence. Therefore, they require a high level of security and are housed with other offenders who have committed equally serious offenses and who are serving equally long sentences. The presence of potentially violent, mentally ill prisoners in high-security and probably overcrowded institutions is a dangerous situation. Mental illness must be treated while inmates are incarcerated.

A related problem concerns the release of mentally ill convicts back into the community. These inmates must be tracked and supervised to ensure that they receive proper case management and stay on their medications. This approach goes far beyond the traditional "$25 in gate money and a bus ticket" for the inmate, and not only protects the public but also helps to hold the prison population down. To provide these follow-up services, many states have developed written agreements between the state and local correctional agencies and between the state and local mental health services agencies. Local mental health agencies can be used to provide counseling and support to probationers.[38] The challenge for correctional administrators is to maintain a viable program to treat and control a difficult group of offenders. The treatment of this group requires resources, trained staff, and appropriate facilities.

EXHIBIT 11.1

Inmates' Cell Phones Facilitate Criminal Acts

As if prison administrators did not have enough security problems to keep them occupied, another problem to be added to the list is the proliferation of cell phones among inmates. This is certainly no minor issue that only involves inmates conversing with other people: An inmate escaped from a Kansas prison allegedly with the aid of a phone smuggled in by an accomplice.[1] In Texas, a death row inmate convicted of killing four persons allegedly used a wireless phone from within the prison to threaten a state senator and his family.[2]

As an indication of the extent of the problem, in 2010 prison officials in California seized about 11,000 cell phones from inmates—including one in the possession of violent murderer Charles Manson, who was caught texting and calling people in several states and Canada as well as receiving incoming calls from across the United States.[3] Eighteen cell phones were taken from death row inmates in Texas, and news accounts reveal that the problem has surfaced in other countries as well (in Brazil, inmates were even using pigeons to fly cell phones and related parts in and out of the institution).[4]

Cell phones may potentially represent the worst type of contraband an inmate can possess; phones can provide an ongoing connection to the inmate's life on the street, and also be used to intimidate and threaten witnesses, transmit photographs (including to their victims), plan crimes, coordinate escapes, bribe prison officials, order retaliatory acts against other inmates, send text messages to other prisoners, and gain access to the Internet.[5]

Prison officials have adopted aggressive measures for detecting cell phones, including random cell inspections and perimeter searches (some cell phones have been catapulted over perimeter fences). Metal detectors, X-ray technology, and routine searches of employees are also being used to detect cell phones. Furthermore, dogs are being trained specifically to detect wireless devices.[6]

[1]Don Thompson, "Prisons Press Fight Against Smuggled Cell Phones," CorrectionsOne.com, http://www.correctionsone.com/corrections/articles/1843896-Prisons-press-fight-against-smuggled-cell-phones/ (accessed February 15, 2011).

[2]Michael Graczyk, "Texas Prisons Locked Down After Death-Row Inmate Found with Phone," CorrectionsOne.com, http://www.correctionsone.com/corrections/articles/1747630-Texas-prisons-locked-down-after-death-row-inmate-found-with-phone/ (accessed February 15, 2011).

[3]Don Thompson, "Calif. wants to stop phones used by likes of Manson," Associated Press, February 14, 2011, http://www.sacbee.com/2011/02/14/3400703/calif-wants-to-stop-phones-used.html (accessed February 15, 2011).

[4]Tod W. Burke and Stephen S. Owen, "Cell Phones as Prison Contraband," *FBI Law Enforcement Bulletin*, July 2010, http://www.fbi.gov/stats-services/publications/law-enforcement-bulletin/july-2010/cell-phones-as-prison-contraband (accessed February 15, 2011).

[5]Ibid.

[6]Ibid.

Effects of Modifications to Three-Strikes Laws

Between 1993 and 1995, 24 states and the federal government enacted new habitual offender laws that have been termed "three-strikes"—laws that required the state courts to assign enhanced periods of incarceration to those persons who were convicted of a serious criminal offense on three or more separate occasions. Proponents of such laws predicted that the laws would curb crime and protect society by warehousing the worst offenders for a long period of time. Opponents argued that defendants facing lengthy mandatory sentences would be more likely to avoid plea bargaining and demand trials, thereby slowing the processing of cases, and that convicted offenders would serve long terms, causing prison populations to explode.[39] Certainly by any standard, the mandates of such laws affected corrections facilities by generating greater, and longer, prison sentences.

Since their inception, **three-strikes laws** have varied widely in their content. California's law—the first enacted, in 1994, and the most punitive and far reaching of such laws—initially required a sentence of 25 years to life for a third felony conviction. According to the Justice Policy Institute,[40] tens of thousands of persons have been sentenced in California under the law, whereas a fraction of that number were sentenced in other states. Under its initial rendition, California's law resulted in a variety of "third strike" offenses that could lead to the 25-year term of imprisonment, including two widely publicized cases that involved a 50 years to life sentence for a shoplifter of $153.54 worth of videotapes, and 25 years to life for a man who stole three golf clubs. As a result, the Justice Policy Institute reported that California's three-strikes law had a disproportionate impact on racial and ethnic communities: the African American incarceration rate for a third strike is 12 times higher than the third-strike incarceration rate for whites, whereas the Latino incarceration rate for a third strike is 45 percent higher.[41] The law has also had significant fiscal impacts on the state's budget: prisoners added to the prison system under three strikes in one decade have cost or will cost taxpayers an additional $8.1 billion in prison and jail expenditures.[42]

Since its inception and spread across the United States in the mid-1990s, however, the law appears to have been mitigated in its impact. As examples, according to National Conference of State Legislatures,[43] of the 24 states that enacted **three-strikes laws**, at least 16 have made major changes. Most notable, perhaps, are those states that eliminated **LWOP** penalties and replaced mandatory sentences with sentencing ranges. However, three-strikes laws in at least eight states remain as first enacted.[44] Following are some examples of such changes to the sentencing options relating to three-strikes laws:

- South Carolina's 2010 amendment eliminated mandatory three-strikes penalties; punishment for two- and three-strikes convictions can now be terms up to LWOP.
- At least 11 states have increased judicial discretion in three-strikes sentencing; at least seven states have narrowed the circumstances under which the court can impose a LWOP sentence for three-strikes offenses.
- Many states have modified sentencing options under their three-strikes laws such as changing their mandatory maximum prison terms to minimum and maximum ranges, adding several sentencing ranges (in addition to the life sentence requirements in the original law), adding three-strikes provisions to carry a minimum prison term that is double the length of the mandatory minimum, or some other options.
- California's legislature has removed the mandatory life sentence penalty (that required at least 25 years be served) for third-strike offenders, now requiring offenders to serve a prison term three times that for the underlying offense, 25 years, or the term for the underlying offense plus any sentence enhancements, whichever is the greatest of the three.[45]

Inmate Classification: Cornerstone of Security and Treatment

We humans sort and classify things constantly in an effort to better understand and deal with matters at hand. And so it is with corrections administrators for each new inmate committed by the courts to their institutions. Corrections staff must make decisions about at least two issues:

the inmate's level of physical restraint, or *security level*, and the inmate's level of supervision, or *custody grade*. These two concepts are not well understood and are often confused, but they significantly impact a prisoner's housing and program assignments[46] as well as an institution's overall security level.

The most recent development in classification is **unit management**, in which a large prison population is subdivided into several mini-institutions analogous to a city and its neighborhoods. Each unit has specified decision-making authority and is run by a staff of six, whose offices are on the living unit; this enables classification decisions to be made by personnel who are in daily contact with their inmates and know them fairly well.[47]

Robert Levinson delineated four categories into which corrections classifies new inmates: security, custody, housing, and programs[48]:

1. *Security* needs are classified in terms of the number and types of architectural barriers that must be placed between the inmates and the outside world to ensure that they will not escape and can be controlled. Most correctional systems have four security levels: supermax (highest), maximum (high), medium (low), and minimum (lowest).
2. *Custody* assignments determine the level of supervision and types of privileges an inmate will have. A basic consideration is whether or not an inmate will be allowed to go outside the facility's secure perimeter, so some systems have adopted four custody grades—two inside the fence (one more restrictive than the other) and two outside the fence (one more closely supervised than the other).
3. *Housing* needs were historically determined by an "assign to the next empty bed" system, which could place the new, weak inmate in the same cell with the most hardened inmate; a more sophisticated approach is known as *internal classification*, in which inmates are assigned to live with prisoners who are similar to themselves. This approach can involve the grouping of inmates into three broad categories: heavy—victimizers, light—victims, and moderate—neither intimidated by the first group nor abusers of the second.
4. *Program* classification involves using interview and testing data to determine where the newly arrived inmate should be placed in work, training, and treatment programs; these are designed to help the prisoner make a successful return to society.

In the past, most prison systems used a highly subjective system of classifying inmates that involved a review of records pertaining to the inmate's prior social and criminal history, test scores, school and work performance, and staff impressions developed from interviews. Today, however, administrators employ a much-preferred objective system that is more rational, efficient, and equitable. Factors used in making classification decisions are measurable and valid and are applied to all inmates in the same way. Criteria most often used are escape history, detainers, prior commitments, criminal history, prior institutional adjustment, history of violence, and length of sentence.[49]

Drug Use in Prisons: Interdiction and Treatment

More than half of all adult arrestees test positive for drug use at the time of their apprehension; their drug use prior to incarceration is typically chronic. Indeed, 50 percent of federal prisoners and 56 percent of state prison inmates used drugs during the month before the arrest for which they were incarcerated.[50] Furthermore, offenders still manage to obtain illicit drugs during their incarceration, threatening the safety of inmates and staff while undermining the authority of correctional administrators, contradicting rehabilitative goals, and reducing public confidence.[51]

Next, we discuss Pennsylvania's **drug interdiction** plan to prevent illicit drugs from coming into the state's prisons. Then, we look at what can be done to treat offenders' substance abuse problems inside the institution.

THE PENNSYLVANIA PLAN The state of Pennsylvania was compelled to acknowledge that drug use was pervasive in several of its prisons. Six inmates had died from overdoses in a 2-year period, and assaults on COs and inmates had increased. To combat the problem, the state first adopted a zero-tolerance drug policy, the so-called **Pennsylvania plan**: Inmates caught with drugs were to be criminally prosecuted, and those who tested positive (using hair testing) were to serve disciplinary custody time. Highly sensitive drug detection equipment was employed to detect drugs that visitors might try to smuggle into the prison, to inspect packages arriving in the mail, and to detect drugs that correctional staff might try to bring in. New policies were issued for inmate movement and visitation, and a new phone system was installed to randomly monitor inmates' calls.[52]

The results were impressive. The state's 24 prisons became 99 percent drug free. The number of drug finds during cell searches dropped 41 percent, assaults on staff decreased 57 percent, inmate-on-inmate assaults declined 70 percent, and the number of weapons seized during searches dropped from 220 to 76. Marijuana use dropped from 6.5 percent before interdiction to 0.3 percent, and there was a significant decline in the use of other types of drugs. Pennsylvania now believes that the foundation has been laid for inmates to abstain from drug use during service of their sentences—a necessary first step toward long-term abstinence and becoming a better citizen for their families and communities.[53]

TREATING THE PROBLEM During the past several years, a number of aggressive federal and state initiatives have been undertaken to expand substance abuse treatment within correctional settings. These initiatives have been fueled by the high rates of substance abuse among offenders and the view that intensive prison-based treatment efforts can significantly reduce postprison substance use and recidivism.[54]

Several barriers remain for correctional administrators in implementing substance abuse treatment programs, however. First, institutions tend to use limited criteria (such as any lifetime drug use, possession, drug sales, trafficking) to determine the need for treatment, leading to a lack of treatment of a large portion of the prison population that has abused substances; conversely, many inmates who legitimately need treatment may be excluded for reasons unrelated to their substance abuse problems (gang affiliation or the commission of a sexual or violent offense). Treatment staff should be involved in the selection of candidates to ensure the appropriateness of the program population.[55]

Second, it is difficult to find and recruit qualified and experienced staff in the remote areas where prisons are often located. In addition, counselors who are well suited for community-based treatment programs will not necessarily be effective in the prison setting. They often resist the rigid custody regulations that are common in institutional settings. For these reasons, limited human resources and high turnover rates for drug abuse treatment counselors make staffing an ongoing problem for prison administrators.[56]

Possible solutions to this staffing problem include offering sufficient wages and other amenities to induce counselors to move to and stay with the prison, recruiting and training "lifers" as inmate counselors and mentors, and professionalizing treatment positions for COs. With the use of counselors, certification and financial incentives would help to retain staff, as well as enhance their professional development for the treatment setting.[57]

THE MOVE TOWARD PRIVATIZATION

Emergence of the Concept

Perhaps one of the most controversial aspects of corrections has been the outsourcing or **privatization** of correctional operations and programs. Today, however, privately run prisons operate in 31 states and hold nearly 112,000 inmates—7.2 percent of the nearly 1.6 million total inmates held in those states.[58]

Private sector involvement in U.S. prisons is not new; federal and state governments have long contracted out specific services to private firms, including medical services, food preparation, vocational training, and inmate transportation. During the 1980s, however, with a burgeoning prison population, private business interests saw opportunities for expansion, and consequently private-sector involvement in prisons moved from the simple contracting of services to contracting for the complete management and operation of entire prisons.[59]

Probably the largest and best known of the private corporations attempting to operate correctional institutions is Corrections Corporation of America (CCA), formed in 1983 and headquartered in Nashville, Tennessee. CCA specializes in the design, building, and management of prisons, jails, and detention facilities in partnership with government. Its web site states that it:

- is the fifth-largest corrections system in the nation, behind only the federal government and three states;
- partners with all three federal corrections agencies—the Federal Bureau of Prisons (BOPs), the U.S. Marshals Service and Immigration and Customs Enforcementis—and nearly half of all states and more than a dozen local municipalities;
- has a total capacity of 80,000 inmates at all security levels in 65 facilities, with more than 17,000 professionals nationwide; and
- offers a variety of rehabilitation and educational programs, including addictions treatment, General Education Diploma (GED) preparation and testing, postsecondary studies, life skills, employment training, recreational options, and work opportunities.[60]

Arguments For and Against

Historically, strong arguments have been put forth, both pro and con, regarding the privatizing of prisons; and today there is no dearth of differing points of view on the matter. On the one side is the prominent free-market argument, such as that proffered by the Reason Foundation, which states that private prisons deliver significant cost savings and equal or higher levels of quality when compared with government-run correctional facilities; Reason found that private prisons outperformed, or were equal to, their government counterparts in 16 of 18 studies conducted since 1989.[61]

Conversely, there are a number of arguments against the concept; among them is that there is no guarantee that standards will be upheld, no one will maintain security if employees go on strike, the public will have regular access to the facility, there will be different inmate disciplinary procedures, the company will be able to refuse certain inmates or could go bankrupt, and the company can increase its fees to the state.[62]

One criticism of private prisons is that they do not provide adequate rehabilitative services. However, some experts on private prisons maintain that this criticism is more an indication of bad contracts than a problem with the industry. If the contracting state specifies that it wants drug treatment, employment training, vocational training, or any other service, this should be written in the contract. Experts in the field also say that there is a movement among private facilities to provide better rehabilitative services, which addresses the state's concern with what happens after an inmate leaves prison.[63]

Evaluations

To date, there has been a dearth of research and evaluation concerning the overall efficacy of private prisons vis-à-vis public prisons. The most frequent and painstaking research conducted thus far has been undertaken by the Federal BOPs, which has sought to compare private prisons and other BOP facilities. One such study found that the private prison contributed to a higher probability that inmates would be involved in overall misconduct than the BOP comparison prisons; the private prison also had the highest probability of drug misconduct. In sum, the performance of the private prison was generally less favorable than the performance of the BOP comparison prisons.[64]

Another BOP study focused on staff issues, given that the hiring and training of supervisory and line staff is probably the single most costly and important factor in both private and public sector prisons. The study found that privately operated prisons used more custody staff, had much higher separation (attrition) rates for COs, had much higher escape rates from secure institutions, and much higher random drug hit rates than the BOP facilities. Researchers suggested that the "greenness" of the workforce may have contributed to these findings. Because separation rates at private prisons were typically higher than those of the BOP and state public sector prisons, it was recommended that private companies either adopt an innovative strategy toward corrections or increase pay and/or benefits to attract and retain experienced employees. It was also concluded that less costly workers in private prisons have not produced an acceptable level of public safety or inmate care to date.[65]

ALTERNATIVES TO INCARCERATION: INTERMEDIATE SANCTIONS

The United States is not soft on crime, but because prisons are not in a position to effect great change,[66] the search for solutions must include correctional programs in the community. The demand for prison space has created a reaction throughout the corrections industry.[67] With the cost of prison construction now exceeding $250,000 per cell in maximum-security institutions, cost-saving alternatives are becoming more attractive, if not essential.

A real **alternative to incarceration** must have three elements to be effective: it must incapacitate offenders enough so that it is possible to interfere with their lives and activities to make committing a new offense extremely difficult, it must be unpleasant enough to deter offenders from wanting to commit new crimes, and it has to provide real and credible protection for the community.[68]

The aforementioned realities of prison construction and overcrowding have led to a search for intermediate punishments.[69] This, in turn, has brought about the emergence of a new generation of programs, making community-based corrections, according to Barry Nidorf, a "strong, full partner in the fight against crime and a leader in confronting the crowding crisis."[70] Economic reality dictates that cost-effective measures be developed, and this is motivating the development of **intermediate sanctions**.[71]

A recent survey by the BJS found that, of all persons being supervised outside a jail facility, 25 percent were engaged in some form of community service and 17 percent were involved in EM; fewer than 1 percent were undergoing home detention only.[72] Table 11.3 shows these findings as well as the number of persons under jail supervision and involved with other types of programs.

TABLE 11.3	Persons Under Jail Supervision, by Confinement Status and Type of Program, Midyear 2000 and 2006–2009

Confinement Status and Type of Program	Number of Persons Under Jail Supervision				
	2000	2006	2007	2008	2009
Total	687,033	826,041	848,419	858,407	837,833
Held in jail	621,149	765,819	780,174	785,556	767,620
Supervised outside of a jail facility[a]	65,884	60,222	68,245	72,852	70,213
Weekender programs	14,523	11,421	10,473	12,325	11,212
Electronic monitoring	10,782	10,999	13,121	13,539	11,834
Home detention[b]	332	807	512	498	738
Day reporting	3,969	4,841	6,163	5,758	6,492
Community service	13,592	14,667	15,327	18,475	17,738
Other pretrial supervision	6,279	6,409	11,148	12,452	12,439
Other work programs[c]	8,011	8,319	7,369	5,808	5,912
Treatment programs[d]	5,714	1,486	2,276	2,259	2,082
Other	2,682	1,273	1,857	1,739	1,766

[a]Excludes persons supervised by a probation or parole agency.
[b]Includes only persons without electronic monitoring.
[c]Includes persons in work release programs, work gangs, and other alternative work programs.
[d]Includes persons under drug, alcohol, mental health, and other medical treatment.

Intensive Probation or Parole

Intensive supervision has become the most popular program in probation and parole. Early versions were based on the premise that increased client contact would enhance rehabilitation while affording greater client control. Current programs are simply a means of easing the burden of prison overcrowding.[73]

Intensive supervision can be classified into two types: those stressing diversion and those stressing enhancement. A diversion program is commonly known as a *front door* program because its goal is to limit the number of generally low-risk offenders who enter prison. Enhancement programs generally select already sentenced probationers and parolees and subject them to closer supervision in the community than they receive under regular probation or parole.[74]

As of 1990, jurisdictions in all 50 states had instituted *intensive supervision probation* (ISP). Persons placed on ISP are supposedly those offenders who, in the absence of intensive supervision, would have been sentenced to imprisonment. In parole, intensive supervision is viewed as risk management—allowing a high-risk inmate to be paroled but under the most restrictive circumstances. In either case, intensive supervision is a response to overcrowding; although ISP is invariably more costly than regular supervision, the costs "are compared not with the costs of normal supervision but rather with the costs of incarceration."[75]

ISP is demanding for probationers and parolees and does not represent freedom; in fact, it may stress and isolate repeat offenders more than imprisonment does. Given the option of serving prison terms or participating in ISPs, many offenders have chosen prison.[76] Many offenders may prefer to serve a short prison term rather than spend five times as long a period in ISP. Consider the alternatives now facing offenders in one western state:

ISP. The offender serves 2 years under this alternative. During that time, a probation officer visits the offender two or three times per week and phones on the other days. The offender is subject to unannounced searches of his or her home for drugs and has his or her urine tested regularly for alcohol and drugs. The offender must strictly abide by other conditions set by the court: not carrying a weapon, not socializing with certain persons, performing community service, and being employed or participating in training or education. In addition, he or she is strongly encouraged to attend counseling and/or other treatment, particularly if he or she is a drug offender.

Prison. The alternative is a sentence of 2 to 4 years, of which the offender will serve only about 3 to 6 months. During this term, the offender is not required to work or to participate in any training or treatment but may do so voluntarily. Once released, the offender is placed on 2-year routine parole supervision and must visit his or her parole officer about once a month.[77]

Although compelling evidence of the effectiveness of ISP is lacking, it has been deemed a public relations success.[78] Intensive supervision is usually accomplished by greatly reducing the caseload size per probation or parole officer, leading to increased contact between officers and clients or their significant others (such as the client's spouse or parents). It is hoped that this increased contact will improve service delivery and control and thus reduce recidivism.[79]

House Arrest

Although **HA** (home detention) has become increasingly common, BJS data provided in Table 11.3 shows only 738 of more than 70,000 offenders (1 percent) who were supervised outside of a jail facility being on home detention only. It is seen that many more (11,834, or about 17 percent) are being monitored electronically—many of them being monitored in their homes. The primary motivation for using this intermediate sanction is a financial one: the conservation of scarce resources. It is also hoped, of course, that HA is more effective in preventing recidivism than traditional probation alone or incarceration.

Many people apparently feel that HA is not effective or punitive enough. Indeed, one study reported that nearly half (44 percent) of the public feels that HA is not very effective or not effective at all.[80]

Does HA work? Jeffrey Ulner[81] found that the sentencing combination associated with the least likelihood of rearrest was HA/probation. The combinations of HA/work release and HA/incarceration were also significantly associated with decreased chances of rearrest compared with traditional probation. Furthermore, whenever any other sentence option was paired with HA, that sentence combination significantly reduced the chances and frequency of rearrest.[82] Clearly, HA works when used in tandem with other forms of sentencing options.

What is it about HA that might explain its success? It puts the offender in touch with opportunities and resources for rehabilitative services (such as substance abuse or sex offender counseling, anger management classes, and so on), which supports the contention that for intermediate sanctions of any type to reduce recidivism, they must include a rehabilitative emphasis.[83]

Electronic Monitoring

The use of **EM** (electronic monitoring) is accelerating rapidly (see Table 11.3), with HA and EM programs being combined for use with new categories of offenders.[84] It is far cheaper to keep an offender at home on EM than to incarcerate him or her in prison—which runs about $62 per day compared with EM's cost of about $5.00 per day. Even a higher-level system where an e-mail is sent or a beep goes off if an offender goes past set boundaries or active monitoring (an offender's movement is tracked on a computer screen) costs only about $12 a day.[85]

Martin, et al.,[86] examined offenders' perceptions of HA/EM. The typical respondent in their survey spent approximately 1 month on HA/EM, paid $3,578.00 in fines, and provided 17 hours of community service. Respondents indicated that while being sentenced to HA was preferable to being incarcerated, it is a punitive sanction. These punitive aspects are manifested in at least two ways:

- The restrictive nature of personal freedoms: Offenders reported that this was the most troublesome aspect of their experience with EM. Although employed offenders were permitted to go to and from work, they are generally prohibited from leaving their homes to run errands or to complete outdoor tasks without permission from their probation officer.
- The degree to which this sanction causes embarrassment/shame for the offender: Respondents reported that EM had a shaming effect for them or their family members, and that the supervision associated with EM was intrusive. Wearing a visible ankle bracelet and having a device attached to their telephone caused embarrassment, as well as having to tell other people that they could not leave the house.

Despite the loss of freedom and embarrassment of serving time on EM, the survey respondents indicated that they preferred EM to incarceration. The majority (about 70 percent) of the respondents in this study indicated that they would rather be sentenced to HA than to jail.[87]

Although EM represents a significant cost savings, this sanction is not without controversy. Concerns include the potential for **net widening** (discussed below), and some people voice concerns about the level of punishment that is achieved with this sanction. Although the public is generally supportive of alternatives to incarceration, it is clear that there is an expectation that these alternatives serve as a punishment. So, although HA with EM is a less costly option than incarceration, the question remains, is it effective punishment?

Shock Probation/Parole

Shock probation is another less costly intermediate alternative to incarceration that is supported by many correctional administrators. This form of corrections combines a brief exposure to incarceration with subsequent release. It allows sentencing judges to reconsider the original sentence to prison and, upon a motion, to recall the inmate after a few months in prison and place him or her on probation under conditions deemed appropriate. The idea is that the "shock" of a short stay in prison will give the offender a taste of institutional life and will make such an indelible impression that he or she will be deterred from future crime and will avoid the negative effects of lengthy confinement.[88]

In many states, each candidate for **shock probation/parole** must obtain a community sponsor who will be responsible for the applicant's actions while in the community. The sponsor serves as an adjunct to and a resource for the probation officer. Specific activities for the sponsor can include providing transportation to work, checking on compliance with curfew and other restrictions, assisting with housing and employment problems, and maintaining contact with the probation officer. The offender may also be required to perform community service, usually physical labor.[89]

Boot Camps/Shock Incarceration

Correctional **boot camps**, also called **shock incarceration**, were first implemented as an intermediate sanction in 1983.[90] The early version of these programs placed offenders in a quasimilitary program of 3 to 6 months duration similar to a military basic training program. The goal was to reduce recidivism, prison and jail populations, and operating costs. Offenders generally served a short institutional sentence and then were put through a rigorous regimen of drills, strenuous workouts, marching, and hard physical labor. To be eligible, inmates generally had to be young, nonviolent offenders.

Unfortunately, early evaluations of boot camps generally found that participants did no better than other offenders without this experience.[91] Only boot camps that were carefully designed, targeted the right offenders, and provided rehabilitative services and aftercare were deemed likely to save the state money and reduce recidivism.[92] As a result of these findings, the number of boot camps declined; by the year 2000, only 51 prison boot camps remained.[93] Boot camps have evolved over time, however, and are now in their third generation. The first-generation camps were those just discussed, with military discipline and physical training being stressed. Second-generation camps emphasized rehabilitation by adding components such as alcohol and drug treatment and social skills training (some even including postrelease EM, HA, and random urine tests). Recently, in the third generation, some boot camps have substituted an emphasis on educational and vocational skills for the military components.[94]

A U.S. Department of Justice report, coauthored by Attorney General John Ashcroft, stated that correctional administrators and planners might learn from boot camps' failures to reduce recidivism or prison populations by considering the following[95]:

1. Building reintegration into the community into an inmate's program may improve the likelihood that he or she will not recidivate.
2. Programs that offer substantial reductions in time served to boot camp "graduates" and that choose for participation inmates with longer sentences are the most successful in reducing prison populations.
3. Chances of reducing recidivism increase when boot camps last longer and offer more intensive treatment and postrelease supervision.

Day Reporting Centers

Another intermediate sanction that has gained recent popularity among correctional administrators and policymakers is the **day reporting** center. Table 11.3 shows that nearly one in 10 (9 percent) of persons being supervised outside of jail were involved with day reporting. Such centers originated in Great Britain as a response to less serious but chronic offenders who lacked basic skills and were often dependent on drugs or alcohol. The British experience led several U.S. states to begin setting up day reporting centers in the mid-1980s. The purposes of day reporting centers are to heighten control and surveillance of offenders placed on community supervision, increase offender access to treatment programs, give officials more proportional and certain sanctions, and reduce prison or jail crowding. Offenders report to the centers frequently (usually once or twice a day), and treatment services (job training and placement, counseling, and education) are usually provided on-site either by the agency running the program or by other human services agencies.[96]

Exhibit 11.2 discusses some of the benefits a few jurisdictions have realized by opening day reporting centers—rather than by expanding their existing jails.

EXHIBIT 11.2

Day Reporting Centers: Uses and Cost Savings

Expanding jail capacity in order to prevent jail overcrowding is expensive. When the Franklin County Jail in Chambersburg, Pennsylvania, was reaching its limit, the jail director and county commissioners learned that expansion would cost $30,000 to $50,000 per bed. Instead, they decided to open a community-based day reporting center that would allow the county to build a smaller, more affordable jail, saving the county $10 million. At the center, offenders who are on pretrial release, probation, or parole are required to appear regularly. Through treatment and training, the centers provide an intermediate sanction for, and reduce recidivism by, low-risk offenders. Most people referred to the centers have drug and alcohol problems and are closely monitored as part of a 90- to

180-day program with random drug screens and breathalyzers. The centers also offer classes in anger management, substance abuse, life skills, cognitive skills, and employment and educational training. The Franklin County center, which opened in late 2006, manages up to 200 offenders.

In 2000, Sedgwick County, Kansas, added almost 600 beds to its jail at a cost of $37.5 million; however, by 2005, another expansion was needed. Rather than simply add more beds, the county opened a day reporting center in Wichita that will eventually see 350 offenders. Sedgwick County's center offers similar programs to Franklin County's, with intensive supervision, regular drug and alcohol screens and treatment, and training to match the specific needs of offenders.

Source: Based on Patrick Hyde, "Day reporting eases jail overcrowding," American City and County, http://americancityandcounty.com/mag/government_day_reporting_eases/ (accessed October 16, 2010).

"Net Widening" and Evaluations

Before leaving the subject of intermediate sanctions, it should be mentioned that such forms of punishment have been subjected to criticism, however. Some authors indicate concern that instead of being *alternatives* to prisons and probation, they often become *supplements* to our existing correctional system. This process is termed "net widening," which refers to "the tendency of penal reforms to extend control over more of the base population, rather than to provide alternative control as generally claimed in the promotion of various penal reforms."[97]

However, based on reviews of the different forms that intermediate sanctions can take, Homant and DeMercurio[98] concluded that:

> a reasonable generalization is that these approaches are able to supervise offenders at less cost than normal imprisonment without any loss of special deterrence (i.e., no increase in recidivism). Intermediate sanctions, taken as a whole, do seem to provide a useful addition to sentencing options by allowing for some cost savings, enhanced supervision, and more finely tuned matching of punishment and crime.[99]

Summary

This chapter has examined several major contemporary and future issues confronting correctional administrators. It is clear that many, if not all, of these issues do not have easy or quick solutions and will continue to pose challenges to correctional administrators for many years. Included in this discussion were several new forms of diversion termed *intermediate sanctions.*

Corrections agencies bear the brunt of the combined effects of increased crime, tough mandatory sentencing laws leading to increased incarceration of offenders, a get-tough public and justice system attitude toward crime that permeates the country, overcrowded prisons, and large probation and parole caseloads. As a result, and as this chapter has shown, they must develop new ways to deal with offenders.

Questions for Review

1. What were the Supreme Court's decisions concerning capital punishment for someone who committed a capital crime while younger than the age of 18 years? Whether or not it is constitutional for someone to serve a life sentence without possibility of parole for a nonhomicide offense? What was the court's reasoning in both?

2. What do studies show concerning the nature and extent of physical and sexual victimizations in prisons? What policy issues arise from those findings?

3. Has the Prison Rape Elimination Act of 2003 worked?
4. How would you delineate the major arguments for and against inmates being issued condoms?
5. What administrative considerations apply to the potential problem of hostage taking in detention facilities?
6. What is the overall rationale underlying the three-strikes laws, and how have those laws been amended in recent years?
7. How would you describe the importance of inmate classification, as well as the four categories into which new inmates are classified?
8. How can prison administrators interdict and treat the drug problem?
9. What are some stated advantages and disadvantages of privatization, and what do available studies report concerning their efficacy?
10. How would you define and describe the underlying philosophy of intermediate sanctions? Why are they so widely used, and what does research tell us about their efficacy?
11. How can shock probation further the goals of corrections? Boot camps/shock incarceration? What successes and problems have been found with these practices?

Learn by Doing

1. As a state criminal justice agency employee your duties include working as a legislative liaison for your agency. You have been contacted by a state senator and asked to summarize the problem of sexual assaults in correctional institutions, and specifically what the Prison Rape Elimination Act has added to our knowledge of sexual assaults—and whether it has contributed to its diminution—in correctional institutions. What will be the content of your report?
2. You are engaging in a class discussion about the potential problem of hostage taking in correctional institutions. Your criminal justice professor asks that, after reading the accounts of two such incidents in the 1970s and 1980s in which hostages were taken, you consider whether, in the long run, these tragedies had positive or negative effects for the administration of prisons. What is your response, and why?
3. While your criminal justice professor is away from campus attending a conference, you, her Teaching Assistant, are assigned to present a lecture on three-strikes laws in her introductory corrections course. You are to cover some of the rationales for these laws being adopted as well as their current overall legal status. What will you say?
4. You have been invited to appear at a luncheon meeting of a local civic group. During your luncheon speech, the topic of discussion turns to the high cost of incarceration, and then questions segue to using alternatives to incarceration. What will you say concerning the types—and the efficacy—of these intermediate sanctions?

Related Websites

Center for Policy Alternatives
http://www.stateaction.org/issues/issue.cfm/issue/JuvenileTransferReform.xml

National Institute of Corrections—Prison Rape
http://www.nicic.org/Library/019764

SafeYouth.org
http://www.safeyouth.org

Stop Prisoner Rape
http://spr.org/index.html

Suicide and Mental Health Association International
http://suicideandmentalhealthassociationinternational.org/preventionprison.html

Three Strikes Index
http://www.threestrikes.org

Washington Corrective Services
http://www.correctiveservices.wa.gov.au/M/managingdrugsinprison.aspx?uid=4060-6888-0316-8471

Notes

1. *Graham v. Florida*, No. 08-7412 (May 17, 2010); also see Adam Liptak, "Justices Limit Life Sentences for Juveniles," *The New York Times*, May 17, 2010, http://www.nytimes.com/2010/05/18/us/politics/18court.html?pagewanted=print (accessed November 24, 2010).

2. Robert W. Dumond, "Inmate Sexual Assault: The Plague That Persists," *The Prison Journal* 80 (December 2000):407–414; see also Human Rights Watch, *No Escape: Male Rape in U.S. Prisons* (New York: Author, 2001).

3. Cindy Struckman-Johnson and David Struckman-Johnson, "Sexual Coercion Rates in Seven Midwestern Prison Facilities for Men," *The Prison Journal* 80 (December 2000):379–390. See also Christopher Hensley, Robert W. Dumond, Richard Tewksbury, and Doris A. Dumond, "Possible Solutions for Preventing Inmate Sexual Assault: Examining Wardens' Beliefs," *American Journal of Criminal Justice* 27(1) (2002):19–33.

4. Dumond, "Inmate Sexual Assault," p. 408.

5. N. Wolff and J. Shi, "Contextualization of Physical and Sexual Assault in Male Prisons: Incidents and their Aftermath," *Journal of Correctional Health Care* 15(1) (2009), available at: http://www.ncbi. nlm.nih.gov/pmc/articles/PMC2811042/ (accessed October 20, 2010).

6. Ibid.

7. Ibid.

8. Ibid.

9. Leanne Fiftal Alarid, "Sexual Assault and Coercion Among Incarcerated Women Prisoners: Excerpts from Prison Letters," *The Prison Journal* 80 (December 2000):391–406.

10. U.S. Department of Justice, *Bureau of Justice Statistics Status Report, Data Collections for the Prison Rape Elimination Act of 2003* (Washington, DC: Author, 2004), pp. 1–2.

11. U.S. Department of Justice, Bureau of Justice Statistics, *Sexual Violence Reported by Correctional Authorities, 2006*, August 2007, p. 3, http://bjs.ojp. usdoj.gov/content/pub/pdf/svrca06.pdf (accessed November 24, 2010).

12. *Chicago Sun-Times*, "Condoms for Inmates? Prisons Say No," http://www.suntimes.com/news/nation/ 658008,con112007.article (accessed January 11, 2008).

13. Ibid.

14. Earnest A. Stepp, "Preparing for Chaos: Emergency Management," in Peter M. Carlson and Judith Simon Garrett (eds.), *Prison and Jail Administration: Practice and Theory* (Boston: Jones and Barlett Publishers, 2006), p. 367.

15. Thomas A. Zlaket, personal communication to Hon. Janet Napolitano, governor of Arizona, October 25, 2004, p. 2.

16. State of Arizona, Office of the Governor, *The Morey Unit Hostage Incident: Preliminary Findings and Recommendations* (Phoenix, AZ: Author, 2004), p. 1.

17. Ohio History Central, "Lucasville Prison Riot," http://www.ohiohistorycentral.org/entry.php?rec= 1634 (accessed August 4, 2007).

18. CNN.com, "Jail Hostages in Louisiana Make First Public Statements," http://archives.cnn.com/1999/ US/12/17/jail.hostages.03/ (accessed August 13, 2007).

19. *St. Petersburg Times*, "Officials: Inmates Talked of Killing Jail Hostage," http://www.sptimes.com/2004/ 09/08/State/Officials_Inmates_ta.shtml/ (accessed August 13, 2007).

20. For an excellent examination and comparison of these two extremely violent prison riots, see Sue Mahan, "An 'Orgy of Brutality' at Attica and the 'Killing Ground' at Santa Fe: A Comparison of Prison Riots," in Michael C. Braswell, Reid H. Montgomery, Jr., and Lucien X. Lombardo (eds.), *Prison Violence in America*, 2nd ed. (Cincinnati: Anderson, 1994), pp. 253–264.

21. U.S. Department of Justice, Bureau of Justice Statistics, *Profile of Jail Inmates* (Washington, DC: Author, 2004), pp. 1–4.

22. U.S. Department of Justice, Bureau of Justice Statistics, *Local Police Departments, 2003* (Washington, DC: Author, 2006), p. iii; U.S. Department of Justice, Bureau of Justice Statistics, *Sheriff's Offices, 2003* (Washington, DC: Author, 2006), p. iii.

23. U.S. Department of Justice, National Institute of Justice, *Resolution of Prison Riots* (Washington, DC: Author, October 1995), pp. 2–5.

24. Adapted from Stepp, "Preparing for Chaos: Emergency Management," pp. 367–368.

25. U.S. Department of Justice, *Resolution of Prison Riots*, pp. 2–5.

26. B. Wind, "A Guide to Crisis Negotiations," *FBI Law Enforcement Bulletin* (October 1995):1–7.

27. Gabriel Lafleur, Louis Stender, and Jim Lyons, "Hostage Situations in Correctional Facilities," in Peter M. Carlson and Judith Simon Garrett (eds.), *Prison and Jail Administration: Practice and Theory* (Boston: Jones and Bartlett, 2006), p. 376.

28. U.S. Department of Justice, *Resolution of Prison Riots*, p. 13.

29. Ibid., p. 292.

30. National Institute of Justice Information Center, *Prison Hostage Situations*, (Boulder, CO: Author, 1983), pp. 16–17.

31. U.S. Department of Justice, *Resolution of Prison Riots*, p. 14.

32. Ibid, p. 21.

33. Lafleur et al., "Hostage Situations in Correctional Facilities," pp. 373–378.

34. Pam Belluck, "Mentally Ill Inmates Are at Risk Isolated, Suit Says," *The New York Times*, March 9, 2007, p. A10.

35. Ibid.

36. Ibid.

37. Bureau of Justice Statistics, *Sourcebook of Criminal Justice Statistics Online*, http://www.albany.edu/sourcebook/index.html, p. 531 (accessed February 15, 2008).

38. Brendan Riley, "Mentally Ill Ex-Convicts to Get More Services After Sentences," Associated Press, in the *Reno Gazette-Journal*, February 24, 2008, http://news.rgj.com/apps/pbcs.dll/article?AID/20080224/NEWS/802240358/1002/NEWS&template=printart (accessed February 25, 2008).

39. James Austin, "'Three Strikes and You're Out': The Likely Consequences on the Courts, Prisons, and Crime in California and Washington State," *St. Louis University Public Law Review* 14(1) (1994).

40. Justice Policy Institute, *Still Striking Out: Ten Years of California's Three Strikes Law,* http://www.soros.org/initiatives/justice/articles_publications/publications/still_striking_20040305/threestrikes_press.pdf (accessed February 6, 2008).

41. Ibid.

42. Ibid.

43. National Conference of State Legislatures, "Three Strikes Laws: Past and Present," June 2010, http://www.ncsl.org/default.aspx?tabid=21422 (accessed November 26, 2010).

44. Ibid.

45. Ibid.

46. Robert B. Levinson, "Classification: The Cornerstone of Corrections," in Peter M. Carlson and Judith Simon Garrett (eds.), *Prison and Jail Administration: Practice and Theory* (Boston: Jones and Bartlett, 2006), pp. 261–267.

47. Ibid., p. 262.

48. Ibid., pp. 262–263.

49. James Austin and Patricia L. Hardyman, *Objective Prison Classification: A Guide for Correctional Agencies* (Washington, DC: National Institute of Corrections, July 2004); also see R. Buchanan, "National Evaluation of Objective Prison Classification Systems: The Current State of the Art," *Crime and Delinquency* 32(3) (1986):272–290.

50. U.S. Department of Justice, Bureau of Justice Statistics, *Drug Use and Dependence, State and Federal Prisoners, 2004* (October 2006), p. 3, http://www.ojp.usdoj.gov/bjs/pub/pdf/dudsfp04.pdf (accessed November 28, 2010).

51. Thomas E. Feucht and Andrew Keyser, *Reducing Drug Use in Prisons: Pennsylvania's Approach* (Washington, DC: National Institute of Justice Journal, October 1999), p. 11.

52. Ibid., pp. 11–12.

53. Ibid., pp. 14–15.

54. David Farabee, Michael Prendergast, Jerome Cartier, Harry Wexler, Kevin Knight, and M. Douglas Anglin, "Barriers to Implementing Effective Correctional Drug Treatment Programs," *The Prison Journal* 79 (June 1999):150–162.

55. Ibid., p. 152.

56. Ibid., p. 153.

57. Ibid., pp. 154–155.

58. Cybercast News Service, "States Look for Ways to Avoid Private Prisons," http://www.cnsnews.com/news/viewstory.asp?Page=/Nation/archive/200708/NAT20070807a.html (accessed January 7, 2008).

59. Thomas R. O'Connor, "The Debate Over Prison Privatization," http://faculty.ncwc.edu/TOConnor/417/417lect14.htm (accessed January 4, 2008).

60. Corrections Corporation of America, "About CCA," http://www.cca.com/about/ (accessed November 25, 2010).

61. Reason Foundation, "Studies Show Private Prisons Deliver Better Quality, Lower Costs," http://www.reason.org/corrections/ (accessed February 1, 2008).

62. O'Connor, "The Debate Over Prison Privatization," p. 1.

63. Cybercast News Service, "States Look for Ways to Avoid Private Prisons," p. 1.

64. Scott D. Camp and Dawn M. Daggett, "Quality of Operations at Private and Public Prisons: Using Trends in Inmate Misconduct to Compare Prisons," *Justice Research and Policy* (7) 1 (July 2005): 27–51, http://www.bop.gov/news/research_projects/published_reports/pub_vs_priv/camp_daggett.pdf (accessed November 26, 2010).

65. Scott D. Camp and Gerald G. Gaes, "Growth and Quality of U.S. Private Prisons: Evidence from a National Survey," U.S. Department of Justice, Federal Bureau of Prisons, http://www.bop.gov/news/research_projects/published_reports/pub_vs_priv/oreprres_note.pdf (accessed November 26, 2010).

66. John P. Conrad, "The Redefinition of Probation: Drastic Proposals to Solve an Urgent Problem," in Patrick McAnany, Doug Thomson, and David Fogel (eds.), *Probation and Justice: Reconsideration of Mission* (Cambridge, MA: Oelgeschlager, Gunn, and Hain, 1984), p. 258.

67. Peter J. Benekos, "Beyond Reintegration: Community Corrections in a Retributive Era," *Federal Probation* 54 (March 1990):53.

68. Ibid.

69. Belinda R. McCarthy, *Intermediate Punishments: Intensive Supervision, Home Confinement, and Electronic Surveillance* (Monsey, NY: Criminal Justice Press, 1987), p. 3.

70. Barry J. Nidorf, "Community Corrections: Turning the Crowding Crisis into Opportunities," *Corrections Today* (October 1989):85.

71. Benekos, "Beyond Reintegration," p. 54.

72. U.S. Department of Justice, Bureau of Justice Statistics, *Jail Inmates at Midyear 2009: Statistical Tables*, June 2010, p. 14, http://bjs.ojp.usdoj.gov/content/pub/pdf/jim09st.pdf (accessed November 24, 2010).

73. Howard Abadinsky, *Probation and Parole: Theory and Practice*, 7th ed. (Upper Saddle River, NJ: Prentice Hall, 2000), p. 410.

74. Joan Petersilia and Susan Turner, *Evaluating Intensive Supervision Probation/Parole: Results of a Nationwide Experiment* (Washington, DC: National Institute of Justice, 1993).

75. Lawrence A. Bennett, "Practice in Search of a Theory: The Case of Intensive Supervision—An Extension of an Old Practice," *American Journal of Criminal Justice* 12 (1988):293–310.

76. Ibid., p. 293.

77. This information was compiled from ISP brochures and information from the Oregon Department of Correction by Joan Petersilia.

78. Todd R. Clear and Patricia R. Hardyman, "The New Intensive Supervision Movement," *Crime and Delinquency* 36 (January 1990):42–60.

79. Ibid., p. 44.

80. Barbara A. Sims, "Questions of Corrections: Public Attitudes Toward Prison and Community-Based Programs," *Corrections Management Quarterly* 1(1) (1997):54.

81. Jeffery T. Ulmer, "Intermediate Sanctions: A Comparative Analysis of the Probability and Severity of Recidivism," *Sociological Inquiry* 71(2) (Spring 2001):164–193.

82. Ibid., p. 184.

83. Ibid., p. 185.

84. R. Gable and R. Gable, "Electronic monitoring: Positive intervention strategies," Federal Probation, 69(1) (2005):21–25; also see A. Crowe, L. Sydney, P. Bancroft, and B. Lawrence, *Offender Supervision with Electronic Technology: A User's Guide* (Washington, DC: U.S. Department of Justice, 2002).

85. Sandra Norman-Eady, "Electronic Monitoring of Probationers and Parolees," OLR Research Report, January 2007, http://www.cga.ct.gov/2007/rpt/2007-R-0096.htm (accessed October 18, 2010).

86. Jamie S. Martin, Kate Hanrahan, and James H. Bowers, Jr., "Offenders' Perceptions of House Arrest and Electronic Monitoring," *Journal of Offender Rehabilitation* 48 (2009): 547–570.

87. Ibid.

88. Jeanne B. Stinchcomb and Vernon B. Fox, *Introduction to Corrections*, 5th ed. (Upper Saddle River, NJ: Prentice Hall, 1999), p. 165.

89. Abadinsky, *Probation and Parole*, p. 434.

90. Gaylene Styve Armstrong, Angela R. Gover, and Doris Layton MacKenzie, "The Development and Diversity of Correctional Boot Camps," in Rosemary L. Gido and Ted Alleman (eds.), *Turnstile Justice: Issues in American Corrections* (Upper Saddle River, NJ: Prentice Hall, 2002), pp. 115–130.

91. Doris Layton MacKenzie, "Boot Camp Prisons and Recidivism in Eight States," *Criminology* 33(3) (1995):327–358.

92. Doris Layton MacKenzie and Alex Piquero, "The Impact of Shock Incarceration Programs on Prison Crowding," *Crime and Delinquency* 40(2) (April 1994):222–249.

93. John Ashcroft, Deborah J. Daniels, and Sarah V. Hart, *Correctional Boot Camps: Lessons from a Decade of Research* (Washington, DC: U.S. Department of Justice, Office of Justice Programs, June 2003), p. 2.

94. Ibid.

95. Ibid., p. 9.

96. Dale G. Parent, "Day Reporting Centers: An Evolving Intermediate Sanction," *Federal Probation* 60 (December 1996):51–54.

97. Thomas Blomberg and Karol Lucken, *American Penology* (New York: Aldine de Gruyter, 2000), p. 4.

98. Robert J. Homant and Mark A. DeMercurio, Intermediate Sanctions in Probation Officers' Sentencing: Recommendations: Consistency, Net Widening, and Net Repairing," *The Prison Journal* 89(4) (2009): 426–439, http://0-tpj.sagepub.com.innopac.library.unr.edu/content/89/4/426.full.pdf+html (accessed November 26, 2010).

99. In ibid., quoting D. Ikonomov, "The Evolution of Conditional Sentencing and the Potential for Developing a System of Intermediate Sanctions," *Canadian Criminal Law Review*, 9 (2005), pp. 295–315.

PART 5

Issues Spanning the Justice System
Administrative Challenges and Practices

The four chapters in this part focus on administrative problems or methods spanning the entire justice system. Chapter 12 examines ethical considerations that relate to police, courts, and corrections administration. The rights of criminal justice employees are reviewed in Chapter 13, and Chapter 14 discusses several challenges involving human resources (employee discipline, labor relations, and liability). Chapter 15 discusses financial administration and Chapter 16 reviews the latest technological hardware and software now in use in criminal justice agencies. With the exception of Chapter 16, case studies are provided in Appendix I for each chapter in this part.

12

Ethical Considerations

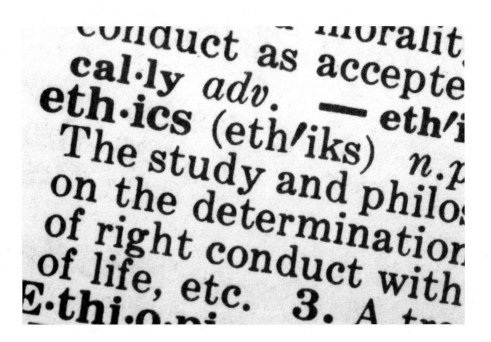

KEY TERMS AND CONCEPTS

Absolute ethics

Deontological ethics

Ethics

Gratuities

Loyalty

Model of circumstantial corruptibility

Noble cause corruption

Relative ethics

LEARNING OBJECTIVES

After reading this chapter, the student will:

- be able to distinguish between absolute and relative ethics and know the meaning of noble cause corruption

- be familiar with the utilitarian approach to ethics

- understand the issues surrounding the acceptance of gratuities and a proposed model for determining whether or not such acceptance is corrupt
- understand ethics among criminal justice employees
- be familiar with employees' role in the ethics of the court system
- understand why loyalty to one's agency superiors is problematic
- know the different tests for the justice system recruitment

> *In the fall of 1959, I spoke at one of the country's most respected law schools. The professor in charge of teaching ethics told me the big question up for discussion among his students was whether, as a lawyer, you could lie to a judge. I told the professor that I thought we had all been taught the answer to that question when we were six years old.*
>
> —ROBERT F. KENNEDY[1]

INTRODUCTION

"Character," it might be said, "is who we are when no one is watching." Unfortunately, character cannot be trained at the police or corrections academy, or in law school, or given to someone intravenously, or in a pill. Character and ethical conduct, for criminal justice personnel, mean that they would never betray their oath of office, their public trust, or their badge. Character and ethics are *sine qua non* for these persons—without those attributes, nothing else matters. These qualities constitute the foundation of their occupation and will certainly affect the manner in which they carry out their public-safety duties.

At its root, then, criminal justice administration is about people and activities; in the end, the primary responsibilities of administrators involve monitoring subordinates' activities to ensure that they act correctly relative to their tasks and responsibilities and that these duties and responsibilities are carried out in an acceptable and effective manner. Therefore, this chapter is essentially concerned with what constitutes correct behavior in the administration of criminal justice. Individuals and organizations have standards of conduct. To understand organizations, it is important to comprehend these standards and their etiology.

The chapter opens with a glimpse into the kinds of ethical situations criminal justice employees experience, providing three scenarios based on actual cases. Then, we discuss ethics in general, reviewing philosophical foundations and types of ethics.

Next, we examine ethics in policing. Because of their contact with and criticisms by the public and the unique kinds of vices, crimes, and temptations to which they are directly exposed, the police are given a high degree of attention; included here are problems such as the "slippery slope," lying and deception, the receipt of gratuities, and greed and temptation. We then also examine ethical considerations as they apply to courts and corrections organizations.

Although justice administrators are mentioned throughout the chapter, next we consider some specific challenges they face, guidelines they must issue, some ethical tests for justice professionals, and a consideration of the value of organizational loyalty.

FOOD FOR THOUGHT: THREE ETHICAL DILEMMAS

To frame the concept of ethics, I begin this chapter with three true scenarios:

Police. Seeing a vehicle weaving across the center line of the highway, Officer A stops the car, approaches the driver's door, and immediately detects a strong odor of alcohol. The motorist is removed from the car and joins Officer A and a backup, Officer B, on the roadside. Officer A decides to use a portable breath test device to confirm his suspicions of driving under the influence (DUI) of drugs or alcohol, and he gives a sterile plastic mouthpiece to the driver to blow into. The driver attempts to thwart the test by appearing (but failing) to blow into the mouthpiece. Irritated by this attempt, Officer A yanks the mouthpiece away, throws it on the ground, and arrests the driver for DUI. At trial, the driver claims that the mouthpiece was flawed (blocked), so he was unable to blow into it; Officer A testifies under oath that it was not blocked and as "evidence," he takes a mouthpiece out of his pocket, stating that it was the mouthpiece he had used for the test that night. Officer B, sitting in the room, hears this testimony and knows differently, having seen Officer A impatiently throw the mouthpiece on the ground.[2]

Courts. For several weeks, a wealthy divorcee receives menacing telephone calls that demand dates and sexual favors. The caller's voice is electronically disguised. The suspect also begins stalking the woman. After following some clues and tailing a suspect, a federal agent finally makes contact with a suspect, determining that he is the Chief Judge of the state's Supreme Court. Upon confronting him, the agent is told by the judge to "forget about it, or you'll be checking passports in a remote embassy."[3]

Corrections. A corrections officer in a minimum-security facility for young offenders is working in the night shift when a youth is admitted. The youth is frightened because this is his first time in custody, and the officer places him in isolation because the youth told the staff that he is feeling suicidal. Over the next several days, the officer develops a friendship with the youth. Looking through the youth's file, the officer learns that the boy does not wish to remain male; rather, he wants to be a female. One day while doing a routine cell search, the officer observes the youth stuffing women's panties into his pillowcase. With a terrified and pleading look, the youth explains that he prefers them to boxer shorts and begs the officer not to mention this to other staff or youths in the facility. The officer ponders what to do; surely, the boy would be severely ridiculed if others knew of the panties, and it does not seem to be important; on the contrary, if the officer does not report the action and the boy's choice of underwear is revealed later, the officer knows he will lose credibility with other staff and the administration.[4]

Each of these reality-based scenarios poses an ethical dilemma for the criminal justice employee involved. In each case, the officer or agent had to determine the best course of action. In making this determination, the employee had to draw on his or her ethical foundation and training and even on the organization's subculture.

These scenarios should be kept in mind as this chapter examines ethics and many related dilemmas.

EXHIBIT 12.1

Who Polices the Police?

In the image fueled by countless television police dramas, internal affairs divisions are peopled by self-hating cops whose incompetence on the street has led them to become veritable traitors, with few, if any, friends on the force.

Although this perspective is somewhat at odds with reality, assignment to an IA unit still carries enough of a stigma that selecting such personnel is among the most critical, even problematic, decisions made by police executives. In some major-city departments, however, serving as an internal affairs investigator is increasingly viewed as a necessary stepping stone to career advancement and often provides benefits not usually available to those in other areas of policing.

With some 80 percent of the law enforcement agencies in the United States staffed by 25 or fewer sworn officers, there is no generalization about the workings of internal affairs divisions— or perceptions held about them—that would be valid, say policing experts. In small departments, their functions may tend to be limited, whereas in big departments, such as those of New York City and Los Angeles, their quality, structure, and content can vary widely. Thus, issues such as how to attract top investigators to the unit, how long they remain there, and the message that the assignment conveys to others in the agency are all things with which law enforcement officials must grapple, say observers.

Two views have prevailed. One is that assignment to IA is a part of a career track, whereas the other suggests that those assigned to IA will subsequently require protection because of potential enemies.

In 1995, the New York City Police Department (NYPD) Mayor Rudolph Giuliani and then Commissioner William J. Bratton unveiled a number of reforms aimed at improving recruitment, training, and overall supervision within the Internal Affairs Bureau. The strategies included making assignment to the unit a 2-year hitch, which would then provide investigators with entry into the Detective Bureau, the Organized Crime Control Bureau, or other coveted divisions.

That approach exemplifies what Edwin J. Delattre, Dean of the School of Education at Boston University and author of "Character and Cops," cites as a "very old truth about human nature"—namely, that virtue has the best chance of succeeding when it is also advantageous: "Much of the time all of us have mixed motives for our actions, usually more mixed than even the most honest and self-knowledgeable of us fully recognize. Accordingly, the disposition to do "right when there is no one to make [us] do it but [ourselves]" may be strengthened by the awareness that we are not making some permanent sacrifice in behaving rightly."

The majority of departments that have paid attention to the NYPD's strategy have acknowledged that an effective way to draw the best people into IA—both by assignment and by volunteering—is by having "good places for them to land and choices of assignment in homicide, organized crime, or investigative units after IAB," said Delattre.

Source: Reprinted with permission from *Law Enforcement News,* March 31, 2000, pp. 1, 6. John Jay College of Criminal Justice (CCNY), 555 West 57th St., New York, NY 10019.

ETHICS

Philosophical Foundations

The term **ethics** is rooted in the ancient Greek idea of *character*. Ethics involves doing what is right or correct and is generally used to refer to how people should behave in a professional capacity. Many people would argue, however, that no difference should exist between one's professional and personal behavior. Ethical rules of conduct should apply to everything a person does.

A central problem with understanding ethics is the question of "whose ethics" or "which right." This becomes evident when one examines controversial issues such as the death penalty, abortion, use of deadly force, and gun control. How individuals view a particular controversy largely depends on their values, character, or ethics. Both sides on controversies such as these believe that they are morally right. These issues demonstrate that to understand behavior, the most basic values must be examined and understood.

Another area for examination is that of **deontological ethics**, which does not consider consequences, but instead examines one's duty to act. The word *deontology* comes from two Greek roots: *deos*, meaning duty, and *logos*, meaning study. Thus, deontology means the study of duty. When police officers observe a violation of law, they have a duty to act. Officers frequently use this as an excuse when they issue traffic citations that appear to have little utility and do not produce any great benefit for the rest of society. For example, when an officer writes a traffic citation for a prohibited left turn made at 2 o'clock in the morning when no traffic is around, the officer is fulfilling a departmental duty to enforce the law. From a utilitarian standpoint (where we judge an action by its consequences), however, little, if any, good was achieved. Here, duty and not good consequence was the primary motivator.

Immanuel Kant, an eighteenth-century philosopher, expanded the ethics of duty by including the idea of *good will*. People's actions must be guided by good intent. In the previous example, the officer who wrote the traffic citation for an improper left turn would be acting unethically if the ticket was a response to a quota or some irrelevant motive. On the contrary, if the citation was issued because the officer truly believed that it would result in something good, it would have been an ethical action.

Some people have expanded this argument even further. Richard Kania[5] argued that police officers should be allowed to accept gratuities because such actions would constitute the building blocks of positive social relationships between the police and the public. In this case, duty is used to justify what under normal circumstances would be considered unethical. Conversely, if officers take gratuities for self-gratification rather than to form positive community relationships, then the action would be considered unethical by many.

Types of Ethics

Ethics usually involves standards of fair and honest conduct—what we call conscience, the ability to recognize right from wrong—and actions that are good and proper. There are absolute ethics and relative ethics. **Absolute ethics** has only two sides: something is either good or bad, black or white. Some examples in police ethics would be unethical behaviors such as bribery, extortion, excessive force, and perjury, which nearly everyone would agree are unacceptable behaviors by the police.

Relative ethics is more complicated and can have a multitude of sides with varying shades of gray. What is considered ethical behavior by one person may be deemed highly unethical by someone else. Not all ethical issues are clear-cut, however, and communities *do* seem willing at times to tolerate extralegal behavior if a greater public good is served, especially in dealing with problems such as gangs and the homeless. This willingness on the part of the community can be conveyed to the police. Ethical relativism can be said to form an essential part of the community policing movement, discussed more fully later.

A community's acceptance of relative ethics as part of criminal justice may send the wrong message: that there are few boundaries placed on justice system employees' behaviors and that, at times, "anything goes" in their fight against crime. As John Kleinig[6] pointed out, giving false testimony to ensure that a public menace is "put away" or the illegal wiretapping of an organized crime figure's telephone might sometimes be viewed as necessary and justified, though illegal. Another example is that many police officers believe they are compelled to skirt the edges of the law—or even violate it—to arrest drug traffickers. The ethical problem here is that even if the action could be justified as morally proper, it remains illegal. For many persons, however, the protection of society overrides other concerns.

This viewpoint—the *principle of double effect*—holds that when one commits an act to achieve a good end and an inevitable but intended effect is negative, the act might be justified. A long-standing debate has raged about balancing the rights of individuals against the community's interest in calm and order.

These special areas of ethics can become problematic and controversial when police officers use deadly force or lie and deceive others in their work. Police can justify a whole range of activities that others may deem unethical simply because the consequences result in the greatest good for the greatest number—the *utilitarian* approach. If the ends justified the means, perjury would be ethical when committed to prevent a serial killer from being set free to prey on society. In our democratic society, however, the means are just as important as, if not more important than, the desired end.

The community—and criminal justice administrators—cannot tolerate completely unethical behavior, but they may seemingly tolerate extralegal behavior if it serves a greater public good, especially with regard to gang members and the homeless.

It is no less important today than in the past for criminal justice employees to appreciate and come to grips with ethical considerations. Indeed, ethical issues in policing have been affected by three critical factors[7]: (1) growing level of temptation stemming from illicit drug trade, (2) potentially compromising nature of the organizational culture—a culture that can exalt loyalty over integrity, with a "code of silence" that protects unethical employees, and (3) challenges posed by decentralization (flattening the organization and pushing decision making downward) through the advent of community-oriented policing and problem solving (COPPS; discussed later).

Noble Cause Corruption

BENDING THE RULES   When relative ethics and the principle of double effect, described above, are given life and practiced in overt fashion by the police, the situation is known as **noble cause corruption**—what Thomas Martinelli[8] defined as "corruption committed in the name of good ends, corruption that happens when police officers care too much about their work." This viewpoint is also known as the principle of double effect. As noted above, it holds that when an act is committed to achieve a good end (such as an illegal search) and an inevitable but intended effect is negative (the person who is searched eventually goes to prison), the act might still be justified.

Although noble cause corruption can occur anywhere in the criminal justice system, we might look at the police for examples. Officers might bend the rules, such as not reading a drunk person his rights or performing a field sobriety test; planting evidence; issuing "sewer" tickets—writing a ticket but not giving it to the person, resulting in a warrant issued for failure to appear in court; "testilying;" or "using the magic pencil," where police officers write up an incident in a way that criminalizes a suspect (this is a powerful tool for punishment). Noble cause corruption involves a different way of thinking about the police relationship with the law; here, officers operate on a standard that places personal morality above the law, become legislators *of* the law, and act as if they *are* the law.[9]

Such activities can be rationalized by some officers; however, as a Philadelphia police officer put it, "When you are shoveling society's garbage, you gotta be indulged a little bit."[10]

Nonetheless, when officers participate in such activities and believe that the ends justify the means, they corrupt their own system.

CHALLENGES FOR ADMINISTRATORS, MANAGERS, AND SUPERVISORS   Obviously, the kinds of ends-justify-means noble cause behaviors that are mentioned above often involve arrogance on the part of the police and ignore the basic constitutional guidelines their occupation demands. Administrators and middle managers must be careful to take a hard-line view that their subordinates always tell the truth and follow the law. For their part, when red flags surface, supervisors must look deep for reasons behind this sudden turn of events and make reasonable inquiries into the cause.[11] They must not fail to act, lest noble cause corruption be reinforced and entrenched; their inability to take the tough decisions that relate to subordinate misconduct can be catastrophic.

A supervisory philosophy of discipline based on due process, fairness, and equity, combined with intelligent, informed, and comprehensive decision making, is best for the department, its employees, and the community. This supervisory philosophy demonstrates the moral commitment employees look for in their leaders and the type that is expected in police service.[12]

Having defined the types of ethics and some dilemmas, we will now discuss in greater detail some of the ethical issues faced by police leaders and their subordinates.

ETHICS IN POLICING

A Primer: The Oral Interview

During oral interviews for a position in policing, applicants are often placed in a hypothetical situation that tests their ethical beliefs and character. For example, they are asked to assume the role of a police officer who is checking on foot an office supplies retail store that was found to have an unlocked door during early morning hours. On leaving the building, the officer observes another officer, Smith, removing a $100 writing pen from a display case and placing it in his uniform pocket. What should the officer do?

This kind of question commonly befuddles the applicant: "Should I rat on my fellow officer? Overlook the matter? Merely tell Smith never to do that again?" Unfortunately, applicants may do a lot of "how am I *supposed* to respond" soul-searching and second-guessing with these kinds of questions.

Bear in mind that criminal justice agencies do not wish to hire someone who possesses ethical shortcomings; it is simply too potentially dangerous and expensive, from both the perspectives of potential litigation and morality, to take the chance of bringing someone who is corrupt into an agency. That is the reason for such questioning and a thorough background investigation of applicants.

Before responding to a scenario like the one concerning Officer Smith, the applicant should consider the following issues: Is this likely to be the first time that Smith has stolen something? Don't the police arrest and jail people for this same kind of behavior?

In short, police administrators should *never* want an applicant to respond that it is acceptable for an officer to steal. Furthermore, it would be incorrect for an applicant to believe that police do not want an officer to "rat out" another officer. Applicants should never acknowledge that stealing or other such activities are to be overlooked.

Accepted and Deviant Lying

In many cases, no clear line separates acceptable and unacceptable behavior. The two are separated by an expansive gray area that comes under relative ethics. Some observers have referred to such illegal behavior as a *slippery slope*. People tread on solid or legal ground, but at some point slip beyond the acceptable into illegal or unacceptable behavior.

Criminal justice employees lie or deceive for different purposes and under varying circumstances. In some cases, their misrepresentations are accepted as an integral part of a criminal investigation; in other cases, they are viewed as violations of law. David Carter[13] examined police lying and perjury and developed a taxonomy that centered on a distinction between accepted lying and deviant lying. *Accepted lying* includes police activities intended to apprehend or entrap suspects. This type of lying is generally considered to be trickery. *Deviant lying*, on the contrary, refers to officers committing perjury to convict suspects or being deceptive about some activity that is illegal or unacceptable to the department or the public in general.

Deception has long been practiced by the police to ensnare violators and suspects. For many years, it was the principal method used by detectives and police officers to secure confessions and convictions. Accepted lying is that allowed by law and, to a great extent, is expected by the public. Gary Marx[14] identified three methods use by police to trick a suspect: (1) performing an illegal action as part of a larger, socially acceptable, and legal goal; (2) disguising the illegal action so that the suspect does not know it is illegal; and (3) morally weakening the suspect so that the suspect voluntarily becomes involved. The courts have long accepted deception as an investigative tool. For example, in *Illinois v. Perkins*,[15] the U.S. Supreme Court ruled that police undercover agents are not required to administer the *Miranda* warning to incarcerated inmates when investigating crimes. Lying, although acceptable by the courts and the public in certain circumstances, does result in an ethical dilemma. It is a dirty means to accomplish a good end; the police use untruths to gain the truth relative to some event.

In their taxonomy of lying, Barker and Carter[16] identified two types of deviant lying: lying that serves legitimate purposes and lying that conceals or promotes crimes or illegitimate ends. Lying that serves legitimate goals occurs when officers lie to secure a conviction, obtain a search warrant, or conceal omissions during an investigation. Barker[17] found that police officers believe that almost one-fourth of their agency would commit perjury to secure a conviction or to obtain a search warrant. Lying becomes an effective, routine way to sidestep legal impediments. When left unchecked by supervisors, managers, and administrators, lying can become organizationally accepted as an effective means to nullify legal entanglements and remove obstacles that stand in the way of convictions. Examples include using the services of nonexistent confidential informants to secure search warrants, concealing that an interrogator went too far, coercing a confession, or perjuring oneself to gain a conviction.

Lying to conceal or promote criminality is the most distressing form of deception. Examples range from lying by the police to conceal their use of excessive force when arresting a suspect to obscuring the commission of a criminal act.

Gratuities: A Model for Gauging Degrees of Corruption

Gratuities are commonly accepted by police officers as a part of their job. Restaurants frequently give officers free or half-price meals and drinks, and other businesses routinely give officers discounts for services or merchandise. Many police officers and departments accept these gratuities as a part of the job. Other departments prohibit such gifts and discounts, but seldom attempt to enforce any relevant policy or regulation. Finally, some departments attempt to ensure that officers do not accept free or discounted services or merchandise and routinely enforce policies or regulations against such behavior.

There are two basic arguments *against* police acceptance of gratuities. First is the slippery slope argument, discussed earlier, which proposes that gratuities are the first step in police corruption. This argument holds that once gratuities are received, police officers' ethics are subverted and they are open to additional breaches of their integrity. In addition, officers who accept minor gifts or gratuities are then obligated to provide the donors with some special service or accommodation. Furthermore, some propose that receiving a gratuity is wrong because officers are receiving rewards for services that, as a result of their employment, they are obligated to provide. That is, officers have no legitimate right to accept compensation in the form of a gratuity. If the police ever hope to be accepted as members of a full-fledged profession, then they must decide whether accepting gratuities is a professional behavior or not.

Police officers who solicit and receive free gifts were categorized by the Knapp Commission in New York City as either "grass-eaters" or "meat-eaters."[18] *Grass-eaters* are officers who freely accept gratuities and sometimes solicit minor payments and gifts. *Meat-eaters*, on the contrary, spend a significant portion of the workday aggressively seeking out situations that can be exploited for financial gain. These officers are corrupt and are involved in thefts, drugs, gambling, prostitution, and other criminal activities.

At least in some cases, it seems that taking gratuities may be the first step toward corruption. Gratuities do indeed provide a slippery slope from which officers can easily slide into corruption. The problem is that many officers fail to understand when and where to draw the line. In a different light, one writer[19] argues that retail store and restaurant owners often feel indebted to the police and that gratuities provide an avenue of repayment. Thus, gratuities result in social cohesion between the police and business owners, and the acceptance of gratuities does not necessarily lead to the solicitation of additional gratuities and gifts or corruption.

Withrow and Dailey[20] recently offered a uniquely different viewpoint on gratuities. They propose a **model of circumstantial corruptibility**, stating that the exchange of a gift is influenced by two elements: the role of the giver and the role of the receiver. The role of the giver determines the level of corruptibility; in this model, the giver is either taking a position as a

- *presenter,* who offers a gift voluntarily without any expectation of a return from the receiver;
- *contributor,* who furnishes something and expects something in return;
- *capitulator,* who involuntarily responds to the demands of the receiver.

The role of the receiver of the gift is obviously very important as well in the model; the receiver can act as

- an *acceptor,* who receives the gift humbly and without any residual feelings of reciprocity;
- an *expector,* who looks forward to the gift and regards it as likely to be given, and will be annoyed by the absence of the gift;
- a *conqueror,* who assumes total control over the exchange and influence over the giver.

The function of the model, Withrow and Dailey argue, is centered on the intersection of the giver and the receiver. For example, when the giver assumes the role of the presenter and the receiver is the acceptor, the result is a giving exchange and corruption does not occur. However, if the giver and the receiver occupy other roles, corruptibility can progress to higher levels of social harm, which they term *hierarchy of wickedness.* Bribery results when something of value is given and the giver expects something in return, while the receiver agrees to make his or her behavior conform to the desires of the giver. This model is not clear-cut, however, because the confusion of roles between givers and receivers is inevitable.[21]

Withrow and Dailey's model is distinguishable from Kania's view, discussed above, that the police should be encouraged to accept minor gratuities to foster good relations; rather, Withrow and Dailey encourage the police to consider the role of the giver as well as their own intentions when deciding whether or not to accept a gratuity. In certain circumstances, the exchange of *any* gratuity is ethical or unethical regardless of its value.[22]

Figure 12.1 is an example of a policy developed by a sheriff's office concerning gratuities.

Greed and Temptation

Fundamentally, expecting and accepting larger gratuities (setting aside for a moment the debate about whether police officers should receive free coffee or meals) and bribes or "shakedowns" are about greed. This greed is perhaps viewed by the individual officer as an entitlement because of what is perceived as an overall corrupt society, a low-paying job, the kind of work that has to be done, and so on. Mature people, however, simply do not use their position for self-indulgence.

---

1. Without the express permission of the Sheriff, members shall not solicit or accept any gift, gratuity, loan, present, or fee where there is any direct or indirect connection between this solicitation or acceptance of such gift and their employment by this office.
2. Members shall not accept, either directly or indirectly, any gift, gratuity, loan, fee or thing of value, the acceptance of which might tend to improperly influence their actions, or that of any other member, in any matter of police business, or which might tend to cast an adverse reflection on the Sheriff's Office.
3. Any unauthorized gift, gratuity, loan, fee, reward or other thing falling into any of these categories coming into the possession of any member shall be forwarded to the member's commander, together with a written report explaining the circumstances connected therewith. The commander will decide the disposition of the gift.

—Washoe County (Nevada) Sheriff's Office

FIGURE 12.1   Washoe County, Nevada, Sheriff's Office Gratuity Policy

Source: By permission of Washoe County, NV Sheriff's Office.

Consider the following account, related by Albert A. Seedman,[23] who rose from patrol officer to chief of detectives in the NYPD:

> Just before Christmas [in New York City] in 1947, Captain Ray McGuire and Officer Albert Seedman helped lug into the office dozens of cartons of toys that had been recovered from a hijacking case. There were dolls, teddy bears, and stuffed animals of all kinds. McGuire, busy overseeing the operation, saw that it was close to 3 o'clock. He said, "I was going to stop at Macy's to pick up some toys for my girls." One of the detectives mentioned that he had to do the same at Macy's. McGuire handed him a 20-dollar bill. "Pick up a pair of dolls for me, will ya?" If there were two dolls in that office, there [must have been] 2,000. Yet, I doubt it ever occurred to McGuire that a pair would never be missed or that the owner would be delighted to make them a gift.

The habit of not even considering greedy behavior, of not speculating about ways to profit from office, prevents such conduct from even occurring to most officers.[24]

(Seedman's account brings to mind one involving the author who, on a rainy, cold mid-western night, was dispatched along with two other officers to a robbery scene. An elderly couple had been beaten up, robbed, and tied to chairs in their home as a young man ransacked it, took a large amount of cash, and fled. During the offender's flight, he dropped much of the money, some of which was flowing down the curb and into the storm sewer by the time the officers arrived. In the pouring rain, the three officers hurriedly collected all the cash that could be retrieved in the yard, flowing down the curb, and—while on their bellies in the deluge out of the storm sewer. As with Seedman's story, it never even occurred to the officers to divert any of the couple's funds to their pockets; all that could be located was returned to them. Such accounts, of course, are incalculable among the police, but seldom appear in the news.)

Edward Tully[25] underscored a vast amount of temptation that confronts today's police officers and what police leaders must do to combat it:

> Socrates, Mother Teresa, or other revered individuals in our society never had to face the constant stream of ethical problems of a busy cop on the beat. One of the roles of police leaders is to create an environment that will help an officer resist the temptations that may lead to misconduct, corruption, or abuse of power. The executive cannot construct a work environment that will completely insulate the officers from the forces that lead to misconduct. The ultimate responsibility for an officer's ethical and moral welfare rests squarely with the officer.

Most citizens have no way of comprehending the amount of temptation that confronts today's police officers. They frequently find themselves alone inside retail business stores after normal business hours, clearing the building after finding an open door or window. A swing or graveyard shift officer can easily obtain considerable plunder on these occasions, acquiring everything from clothing to tires for his or her personal vehicle. At the other end of the spectrum is the potential for huge payoffs from drug traffickers or other big-money offenders who will gladly pay the officer to look away from their crimes. Some officers, of course, find this temptation impossible to overcome.

Community Policing

COPPS (examined in Chapter 3) is characterized by more frequent and closer contacts with the public, resulting, in the minds of many observers, in less accountability and, by extension, more opportunities for corruption. Is there a relationship between unethical behavior and COPPS?

Should this be a major concern? Probably not. First, only a small fraction of police officers have violated their oath of office throughout history, which includes a long tradition of using discretionary authority. Second, working more closely with the public also serves to heighten the officers' visibility and trust by the citizenry. COPPS is founded on trust and community interaction; but this is not to say that there should not be scrutiny and accountability.

A case study in Appendix I concerns ethics and community policing.

Training, Supervision, and Values

Another key element of ethics in policing is the recruitment and training of police personnel. Like people in other occupations, new officers may learn early how to steal at a burglary scene or from the body of a dead person, or they may learn how to commit perjury in court, how to cover the misdeeds of their peers, how to shake people down, or how to beat people up. Or they may be fortunate enough to work in an agency in which none of these actions is ever suggested to them.

Formal training programs in ethics can help to ensure that officers understand their department's code of ethics, elevate the importance of ethics throughout the agency, and underscore top management's support. It is imperative that police administrators see that applicants are thoroughly tested, trained, and exposed to an anticorruption environment by proper role modeling.

No supervision of police officers, no matter how thorough and conscientious, can keep bad cops from doing bad things. There are simply too many police officers and too few supervisors. If there is not enough supervision, then the bad cop will not be afraid. As Marcus Aurelius said, "A man should be upright, not be kept upright." There must be leadership at every level. Line officers are sincere and hard-working; their leaders need to ensure that core values are part of the department's operations and become the basis of the subordinates' behavior.

The organization's culture is also important in this regard. The police culture often exalts loyalty over integrity. Given the stress usually generated more from within the organization than from outside and the nature of life-and-death decisions they must make daily, even the best officers who simply want to catch criminals may become frustrated and vulnerable to bending the rules for what they view as the greater good of society.

Police agencies must also attempt to shape the standards of professional behavior. Many begin to do so by articulating their values such as "we believe in the sanctity of life" and "we believe that providing superior service to the citizens is our primary responsibility." Other rules try to guide officers' behavior such as not lying or drinking in excess in a public place.

ETHICS IN THE COURTS

Evolution of Standards of Conduct

The first call during the twentieth century for formalized standards of conduct in the legal profession came in 1906 with Roscoe Pound's speech "The Causes of Popular Dissatisfaction with the Administration of Justice,"[26] discussed in Chapter 7. The American Bar Association (ABA) quickly responded by formulating and approving the Canons of Professional Ethics in 1908 governing lawyers. No separate rules were provided for judges, however.

The first Canons of Judicial Ethics probably grew out of baseball's 1919 scandal, in which the World Series was "thrown" by the Chicago White Sox to the Cincinnati Reds. Baseball officials turned to the judiciary for leadership and hired the U.S. District Court Judge Kenesaw Mountain Landis as baseball commissioner—a position for which Landis was paid $42,500 compared with his $7,500 earnings per year as a judge. This affair prompted the 1921 ABA convention to pass a resolution of censure against the judge and appoint a committee to propose standards of judicial ethics.[27]

In 1924, the ABA approved the Canons of Judicial Ethics under the leadership of Chief Justice William Howard Taft, and in 1972 the ABA approved a new Model Code of Judicial Conduct; in 1990, the same body adopted a revised Model Code. Nearly all states and the District of Columbia have promulgated standards based on the code. In 1974, the U.S. Judicial Conference adopted a Code of Conduct for Federal Judges, and Congress has, over the years, enacted legislation regulating judicial conduct, including the Ethics Reform Act of 1989.

The Judge

Ideally, our judges are flawless. They do not allow emotion or personal biases to creep into their work, treat all cases and individual litigants with an even hand, and employ "justice tempered with mercy." The perfect judge would be like the one described by the eminent Italian legal philosopher Pierro Calamandrei:

> The good judge takes equal pains with every case, no matter how humble; he knows that important cases and unimportant cases do not exist, for injustice is not one of those poisons, which when taken in small doses may produce a salutary effect. Injustice is a dangerous poison even in doses of homeopathic proportions.[28]

Not all judges, of course, can attain this lofty status. Recognizing this fact, nearly 800 years ago, King John of England met with his barons on the field of Runnymede and, in the Magna Carta, promised that henceforth he would not "make men justices, unless they are such as know the law of the realm and are minded to observe it rightly."[29]

The subject of judicial ethics seemed to arouse little interest until relatively recently. Indeed, from 1890 to 1904, an era of trusts and political corruption, only a few articles were published on the subject of judicial ethics. In contrast, since 1975, more than 900 articles have appeared in magazines and newspapers on the topic of judges and judicial ethics.

Judges can engage in improper conduct or overstep their bounds in many ways: abuse of judicial power (against attorneys or litigants), inappropriate sanctions and dispositions (including showing favoritism or bias), not meeting the standards of impartiality and competence (discourteous behavior, gender bias and harassment, and incompetence), conflict of interest (bias, conflicting financial interests or business, social, or family relationships), and personal conduct (criminal or sexual misconduct, prejudice, or statements of opinion).[30]

Following are examples of some true-to-life ethical dilemmas involving the courts:[31]

1. A judge convinces jailers to release his son on a nonbondable offense.
2. A judge is indicted on charges that he used his office for a racketeering enterprise.
3. Two judges attend the governor's $500-per-person inaugural ball.
4. A judge's allegedly intemperate treatment of lawyers in the courtroom is spurred by a lawyer's earlier complaints against the judge.
5. A judge is accused of acting with bias in giving a convicted murderer a less severe sentence because the victims were homosexual.
6. A judge whose car bears a bumper sticker reading "I am a pro-life democrat" acquits six pro-life demonstrators of trespassing at an abortion clinic on the ground of necessity to protect human life.

These incidents do little to bolster public confidence in the justice system. People expect more from judges, who are "the most highly visible symbol of justice."[32] The quality of the judges determines the quality of justice.

Many judges recoil at the need for a code of judicial conduct or an independent commission to investigate complaints. They dislike being considered suspect and put under regulation. No one likes to be watched, but judges must heed Thomas Jefferson's admonition that everyone in public life should be answerable to someone.[33]

Unfortunately, codes of ethical conduct have not served to eradicate the problems or allay the concerns about judges' behavior. Indeed, as three professors of law put it, "The public and the bar appear at times to be more interested in judicial ethics and accountability than the judges are."[34] One judge, who teaches judicial ethics at the National Judicial College in Reno, Nevada, stated that most judges attending the college admit never having read the Code of Judicial Conduct before seeking judicial office.[35] Some judges also dismiss the need for a judicial conduct code because they believe that it governs aberrant behavior, which, they also believe, is rare among the judiciary. According to the American Judicature Society, however, during one year, 25 judges were suspended from office and more than 80 judges resigned or retired either before or after formal charges were filed against them; 120 judges also received private censure, admonition, or reprimand.[36]

The Code of Judicial Conduct strives to strike a balance between allowing judges to participate in social and public discourse and prohibiting conduct that would threaten a judge's independence. The essence of judicial independence is that judges' minds, according to John Adams, "should not be distracted with jarring interests; they should not be dependent upon any man, or body of men."[37]

Living by the code is challenging; the key to judicial ethics is to identify the troublesome issues and to sharpen one's sensitivity to them, that is, to create an "ethical alarm system" that responds.[38] Perhaps the most important tenet in the code, and the one that is most difficult to apply, is that judges should avoid the appearance of impropriety.

By adhering to ethical principles, judges can maintain their independence and follow the ancient charge Moses gave to his judges in Deuteronomy:

> Hear the causes between your brethren, and judge righteously. Ye shall not respect persons in judgment; but ye shall hear the small as well as the great; ye shall not be afraid of the face of man; for the judgment is God's; and for the cause that is too hard for you, bring it unto me, and I will hear it.[39]

EXHIBIT 12.2

Ethics Training for Federal Judges

According to the Code of Conduct for U.S. Judges, Canon 1 commentary, "Deference to the judgments and rulings of courts depends upon public confidence in the integrity and independence of judges."

To further those goals, the Federal Judicial Center—the education agency for the federal courts—works closely with the Judicial Conference to provide orientation programs for new judges. By regularly covering ethics, the goal is to heighten judges' sensitivity to ethical issues and to interpret the sources of ethical rules: statutes and the *Code of Conduct for United States Judges*.

Together they have developed curricula for in-class programs, online formats, and television programs.

An overview is provided of the seven canons of the Code of Conduct. Other specific ethical areas that are covered include conflicts of interest, relationships with a former law firm, and outside activities such as teaching, membership in legal or social organizations, fund-raising prohibitions, and political activities. Greatest attention is devoted to conflicts of interest—particularly financial conflicts—because mistakes seem to occur more commonly here. There is also a detailed discussion of how to fill out the financial-disclosure report. Examples are provided concerning judges who did not, or allegedly did not, follow the rules.

Source: Based on John S. Cooke, Judicial Ethics in the Federal Courts," *Justice System Journal* 28(3) (2007): 385–393.

Lawyers for the Defense

Defense attorneys, too, must be legally and morally bound to ethical principles as agents of the courts. Elliot Cohen[40] suggested the following moral principles for defense attorneys:

1. Treat others as ends in themselves and not as mere means to winning cases.
2. Treat clients and other professional relations in a similar fashion.
3. Do not deliberately engage in a behavior apt to deceive the court as to truth.
4. Be willing, if necessary, to make reasonable personal sacrifices of time, money, and popularity for what you believe to be a morally good cause.
5. Do not give money to, or accept money from, clients for wrongful purposes or in wrongful amounts.
6. Avoid harming others in the course of representing your client.
7. Be loyal to your client and do not betray his or her confidence.

Prosecutors

Prosecutors can also improve their ethical behavior. Contrary, perhaps, to what is popularly believed, it was decided over a half century ago that the primary duty of a prosecutor is "not that he shall win a case, but that justice shall be done."[41]

Instances of prosecutorial misconduct were reported as early as 1897[42] and are still reported today. One of the leading examples of unethical conduct by a prosecutor was *Miller v. Pate*,[43] in which the prosecutor concealed from the jury in a murder trial the fact that a pair of undershorts with red stains on it were stained not by blood but by paint.

If similar (though not so egregious) kinds of misconduct occur today, one must ask why. According to Cohen,[44] the answer is simple: misconduct works. Oral advocacy is important in the courtroom and can have a powerful effect. Another significant reason for such conduct is the *harmless error doctrine*, in which an appellate court can affirm a conviction despite the presence of serious misconduct during the trial. Only when appellate courts take a stricter, more consistent approach to this problem, will it end.[45]

Other Court Employees

Other court employees have ethical responsibilities as well. Primarily known as *confidential employees*, these are justice-system functionaries who have a special role in the court system and work closely with a judge or judges. These individuals have a special responsibility to maintain the confidentiality of the court system and, thus, have a high standard of trust. For example, an appellate court judge's secretary is asked by a good friend, who is a lawyer, whether the judge will be writing the opinion in a certain case. The lawyer may wish to attempt to influence the judge through his secretary, renegotiate with an opposing party, or engage in some other improper activity designed to alter the case outcome.[46] Bailiffs, court administrators, court reporters, courtroom clerks, and law clerks all fit into this category. The judge's secretary, of course, must use his or her own ethical standard in deciding whether to answer the lawyer's question.

It would be improper for a bailiff who is accompanying jurors back from a break in a criminal trial to mention that the judge "sure seems annoyed at the defense attorney" or for a law clerk to tell an attorney friend that the judge she works for prefers reading short bench memos.[47]

ETHICS IN CORRECTIONS

Corrections personnel confront many of the same ethical dilemmas as police personnel. Thus, prison and jail administrators, like their counterparts in the police realm, would do well to understand their occupational subculture and its effect on ethical decision making.

The strength of the corrections subculture is correlated with the security level of a correctional facility and is strongest in maximum-security institutions. Powerful forces within the correctional system have a stronger influence over the behavior of COs than the administrators of the institution, legislative decrees, or agency policies.[48] Indeed, it has been known for several decades that exposure to external danger in the workplace creates a remarkable increase in group solidarity.[49]

Some of the job-related stressors for COs are similar to those the police face: the ever-present potential for physical danger, hostility directed at officers by inmates and even by the public, unreasonable role demands, a tedious and unrewarding work environment, and dependence on one another to work effectively and safely in their environment.[50] For these reasons, several norms of corrections work have been identified: always go to the aid of an officer in distress, do not "rat," never make another officer look bad in front of inmates, always support an officer in a dispute with an inmate, always support officer sanctions against inmates, and do not wear a "white hat" (participate in behavior that suggests sympathy or identification with inmates).[51]

Security issues and the way in which COs have to rely on each other for their safety make loyalty to one another a key norm. The proscription against ratting out a colleague is strong. In one documented instance, two officers in the Corcoran, California, State Prison blew the whistle on what they considered to be unethical conduct by their colleagues: Officers were alleged to have staged a gladiator-style fight among inmates from different groups in a small exercise yard. The two officers claimed that their colleagues would even place bets on the outcome of the fights, and when the fights got out of hand, the officers would fire shots at the inmates. Since the institution had opened in 1988, eight inmates had been shot dead by officers and numerous others had been wounded. The two officers who reported these activities were labeled by colleagues as "rats" and "no-goods" and had their lives threatened; even though they were transferred to other institutions, the labels traveled with them. Four COs were indicted for their alleged involvement in these activities, and all were acquitted in a state prosecution in 2001.[52]

In another case, a female CO at a medium-security institution reported some of her colleagues for sleeping during the night shift. She had first approached them and expressed concern for her safety when they were asleep, and told them that if they did not refrain from sleeping, she would have to report them to the superintendent. They continued sleeping and she reported them. The consequences were severe: Graffiti was written about her on the walls, she received harassing phone calls and letters, her car was vandalized, and bricks were thrown through the windows of her home.[53]

It would be unfair to suggest that the kind of behavior depicted here reflects the behavior of COs in all places and at all times. The case studies do demonstrate, however, the power and loyalty of the group, and correctional administrators must be cognizant of that power. It is also noteworthy that the corrections subculture, like its police counterpart, has several positive qualities, particularly in crisis situations, including mutual support and protection, which is essential to the emotional and psychological health of the officers involved; the "family" is always there to support you.

GUIDING DECISION MAKING

One of the primary purposes of ethics is to guide decision making.[54] Ethics provides more comprehensive guidelines than law and operational procedures, and answers questions that might otherwise go unanswered. When in doubt, justice administrators and employees should be able to consider the ethical consequences of their actions or potential actions to determine how they should proceed. Guidelines must be in place to assist employees in making operational decisions. Criminal justice leaders obviously play a key role in ethics. Not only must they enforce and uphold ethical standards, they must also set an example and see that employees are instructed in the ethical conduct of police business.

Some experts in police ethics lay problems involving employees' ethics, and their lapses in good conduct, squarely at the feet of their leaders; for example, Edward Tully[55] stated the following:

> Show me an agency with a serious problem of officer misconduct and I will show you a department staffed with too many sergeants not doing their job. Leaders must recognize the vital and influential role sergeants play within an organization. They should be selected with care, given as much supervisory training as possible, and included in the decision-making process. Sergeants are the custodians of the culture, the leaders and informal disciplinarians of the department, and the individual most officers look to for advice.

Stephen Vicchio[56] added another caveat. Even in communities where all seems to be going well with respect to ethical behavior, trouble may be lurking beneath the surface:

> In departments where corruption appears to be low and citizen complaints are minimal, we assume that the officers are people of integrity. Sometimes this is a faulty assumption, particularly if the motivation to do the right thing comes from fear of punishment.

Most efforts to control justice system employees' behavior are rooted in statutes and departmental orders and policies. These written directives spell out inappropriate behavior and, in some cases, behavior or actions that are expected in specific situations. Written directives cannot address every contingency, however, and employees must often use their discretion. These discretionary decisions should be guided by ethics and values. When there is an ethics or policy failure, the resulting behavior is generally considered to be illegal or inappropriate.

ETHICS TESTS FOR JUSTICE PROFESSIONALS

Following are some tests to help guide the criminal justice employee in deciding what is and is not an ethical behavior:[57]

- *Test of common sense.* Does the act make sense or would someone look askance at it?
- *Test of publicity.* Would you be willing to see what you did highlighted on the front page of the local newspaper?
- *Test of one's best self.* Will the act fit the concept of oneself at one's best?
- *Test of one's most admired personality.* What would one's parents or minister do in this situation?
- *Test of hurting someone else.* Will it cause pain for someone?
- *Test of foresight.* What is the long-term likely result?

Other questions that the officer might ask are: Is it worth my job and career? Is my decision legal?

Another tool is that of "the bell, the book, and the candle": Do bells or warning buzzers go off as I consider my choice of actions? Does it violate any laws or codes in the statute or ordinance books? Will my decision withstand the light of day or the spotlight of publicity (the candle)?[58]

In sum, all we can do is try to make the best decisions we can and be good persons and good justice system employees, who are consistent and fair. We need to apply the law, the policy, the guidelines, or whatever it is we dispense in our occupation without bias or fear and to the best of our ability, being mindful along the way that others around us may have lost their moral compass and attempt to drag us down with them. To paraphrase Franklin Delano Roosevelt, "Be the best you can, wherever you are, with what you have."

IS WORKPLACE LOYALTY ALWAYS GOOD?

Loyalty

If you work for someone, in heaven's name, work for him!
Speak well of him and stand by the institution he represents.
Remember, an ounce of loyalty is worth a pound of cleverness.
If you must growl, condemn, and eternally find fault, resign your position.
And when you are on the outside, damn to your heart's content; but as long as you are part of the institution, do not condemn it. If you do, the first high wind that comes along will blow you away, and probably you will never know why.

—AUTHOR UNKNOWN

This quote leaves no doubt that, at least in its author's mind, **loyalty** to the organization, and to one's superior, is highly desired. But is such unequivocal loyalty always a good thing, especially in criminal justice organizations? Certainly, one would think that justice system administrators would view loyalty as a very positive attribute for their employees. There are some, however, who have serious doubts about whether loyalty is indeed an asset.

Sam S. Souryal and Deanna L. Diamond, for example, believe that criminal justice employees often suffer from a "personal loyalty syndrome," which holds them to an altogether different set of loyalty expectations. They are often compelled to offer unwavering personal loyalty to their superiors and, as a result, can violate constitutional provisions, legal requirements, or the public good. Therefore, in extreme cases, practitioners may find themselves justifying untruth, impeding justice, supporting cover-ups, and lying under oath.[59]

Souryal and Diamond argued that there are several paradoxes involving the expectation and practice of personal loyalty to superiors in criminal justice agencies:

- Despite the emotional support for the practice, there is no mention of it in agency rules and regulations. If loyalty is such a great virtue, why are agency rules and regulations silent about it?
- Superiors usually make demands for loyalty when the agency is under attack, not when the agency is stable and business is conducted "as usual."
- Personal loyalty to superiors ignores the fact that some superiors are not worthy of loyalty; hundreds of supervisors and administrators are fired or disciplined each year for violating agency rules.
- Loyalty is a one-way street (superiors need not return the loyalty).[60]

In sum, there are three types of loyalty for justice practitioners to follow and to think about before offering their loyalties unconditionally; ranked from most important to least important, they are as follows:

First is *integrated* loyalty, the highest and most virtuous level of loyalty at the workplace. It is the genuine concern of each worker for the values and ideals of the profession, honoring the ideals of accountability, rationality, fairness, and good will. This is the cornerstone of all workplace loyalties and is pursued before any institutional loyalty.

Second is *institutional* loyalty; it is the obligation of each agency member, including subordinates and superiors, to support the agency's mission. Examples include the obligation of police, court, and probation and parole officers to be loyal to agency policies, rules, and regulations. This form of loyalty is the most supportive and durable, and should be positioned ahead of loyalty to superiors.

Finally, there is *personal* loyalty, the lowest level of loyalty in the workplace because it is mechanical in nature. Examples include the obligation of deputy sheriffs to be loyal to their sheriff. This form of loyalty is the most volatile and temporal, and should never replace institutional loyalty.[61]

In the final analysis, criminal justice administrators need to educate themselves in the exercise of workplace loyalties—both as an asset and as a detriment—as it relates to ethics, public service, and public good. They must act in good faith and, at a minimum, must be certain that the loyalties of their subordinates are legally and morally justified.

Summary

This chapter has examined criminal justice employee behavior from an ethical standpoint. Ethics form the foundation for behavior. It is important that police, courts, and corrections administrators and subordinates understand ethics and the role ethics plays in the performance of their duties. It is also important that these leaders understand the incipient and dangerous nature of noble cause corruption, in which their employees (and the community) may support unethical actions if they are deemed worthwhile to accomplish a good end.

Corruption has few easy remedies. Although not discussed, given civil service regulations, union rules, and other forms of job protection, it can be very difficult to remove even the worst employees. To avoid rotten apples, criminal justice administrators need to maintain high standards for recruitment and training. And to avoid rotten structures, these kinds of agencies need leaders who will not tolerate corruption, institutional procedures for accountability, and systematic investigation of complaints and of suspicious circumstances.[62]

Questions for Review

1. How would you define *ethics*? What are examples of relative and absolute ethics?
2. What is the meaning of *noble cause corruption*, and how does it apply to policing?
3. Should police accept minor gratuities? Explain why doing so might be permitted, per Withrow and Dailey's model of circumstantial corruptibility.
4. How can community policing pose new ethical problems?
5. In what ways can judges, defense attorneys, and prosecutors engage in unethical behavior?
6. In what substantive ways do the police and corrections subcultures resemble each other?
7. How may corrections officers in prisons be unethical?
8. Which do you believe are the most difficult ethical dilemmas presented in the case studies in Appendix I? Consider the issues presented in each.

Learn by Doing

1. Your law enforcement organization's policy concerning the solicitation and acceptance of gifts reads in part that "No personnel shall accept any gift, gratuity, loan, fee, or thing of value, which might tend to improperly influence their actions in any manner." Your subordinate, Deputy Fisher, recently solved a problem involving after-hours vandalism and alcohol use at a country club. The club manager, Mr. Liu, wishes to show appreciation to the officer and has made arrangements for the officer and family to receive a 15 percent discount when eating or golfing there. Fisher is aware that Liu will be very hurt if the proffered gift is refused. Fisher approaches you for guidance—whether to accept the offer or not. What would be your response, and why?

2. You are a court administrator in County District Court, supervised by Chief Judge Williams. While walking through staff office area today, you believe you overhear a court reporter say that on two occasions that week, Judge Williams smelled like he had alcohol on his breath. They stifle their conversation when they see you walk by. Later that day, you send your administrative assistant to Judge Williams' chambers to borrow a budget sheet. When he returns, he tells you that the judge appeared to smell of alcohol. A week later, while working late, the judge summons you to his office. There he explains that he is awaiting a jury verdict, and while casually chatting, he makes himself a cocktail. In fact, he eventually consumes several of these drinks (and appears to be more than "tipsy"). When word comes that the jury has returned with its verdict, he quickly leaves his office to return to the bench.

a. What, if anything, are you ethically bound to do regarding Judge Williams?
b. Do you draw a distinction between his drinking, which occurred while he was in his office versus while he is in the court chamber and sitting on the bench?
c. Do you draw a distinction between someone merely smelling alcohol versus actually seeing him drink alcohol? The number of occasions people have smelled alcohol on his breath? Whether he only smelled of alcohol, as opposed to appearing to be intoxicated? Whether he acted inappropriately, unprofessionally, or incompetently while in the observed condition or after drinking alcohol?
d. Would you feel any differently if, instead of a judge, the same situation involved a prosecutor or defense attorney? Why or why not?

3. You are a final candidate for a staff position at a newly constructed state prison in your community. An oral board member asks you the following questions: You discover that a fellow staff member routinely accepts free food, candy, and other gifts of small value from inmates/clients. These items are not solicited from inmates, nor is special treatment given to the gift-givers. (1) How serious do you consider this behavior to be? (2) Do you believe such behavior should be prohibited under official policy in your organization? (3) What, if any, disciplinary measures do you believe to be appropriate in this case? (4) Would you report a fellow staff member to a supervisor for engaging in this behavior? How do you respond to each?

Related Websites

Amnesty International USA
http://www.amnestyusa.org/countries/usa/document.
do?id=133746465C2D34CA8025690000692D98

Human Rights Watch
http://www.hrw.org

Institute for Criminal Justice Ethics
http://www.lib.jjay.cuny.edu/cje

Notes

1. Robert F. Kennedy, *The Enemy Within: The McClellan Committee's Crusade against Jimmy Hoffa and Corrupt Labor Unions* (Jackson, Tenn.: Perseus Books, 1994), p. 324.

2. Adapted from John R. Jones and Daniel P. Carlson, *Reputable Conduct: Ethical Issues in Policing and Corrections,* 2nd ed. (Upper Saddle River, NJ: Prentice Hall, 2001), p. 14.

3. This scenario is loosely based on David Gelman, Susan Miller, and Bob Cohn, "The Strange Case of Judge Wachtler," *Newsweek* (November 23, 1992):34–35. Wachtler was later arraigned on charges of attempting to extort money from the woman and threatening her 14-year-old daughter (it was later determined that the judge had been having an affair with the woman, who had recently ended the relationship). After being placed under house arrest with an electronic monitoring bracelet, the judge resigned from the court, which he had served with distinction for two decades.

4. Adapted from Jones and Carlson, *Reputable Conduct,* pp. 162–163.

5. Richard Kania, "Police Acceptance of Gratuities," *Criminal Justice Ethics* 7 (1988):37–49.

6. John Kleinig, *The Ethics of Policing* (New York: Cambridge University Press, 1996).

7. T. J. O'Malley, "Managing for Ethics: A Mandate for Administrators," *FBI Law Enforcement Bulletin* (April 1997):20–25.

8. Thomas J. Martinelli, "Unconstitutional Policing: The Ethical Challenges in Dealing with Noble Cause Corruption," *The Police Chief* (October 2006):150.

9. John P. Crank and Michael A. Caldero, *Police Ethics: The Corruption of Noble Cause* (Cincinnati: Anderson, 2000), p. 75.

10. U.S. Department of Justice, National Institute of Justice, Office of Community Oriented Policing Services, *Police Integrity: Public Service with Honor* (Washington, DC: U.S. Government Printing Office, 1997), p. 62.

11. Ibid.

12. Ibid.

13. David Carter, "Theoretical Dimensions in the Abuse of Authority," in Thomas Barker and David Carter (eds.), *Police Deviance* (Cincinnati: Anderson, 1994), pp. 269–290; also see Thomas Barker and David Carter, "Fluffing Up the Evidence and 'Covering Your Ass': Some Conceptual Notes on Police Lying," *Deviant Behavior* 11 (1990):61–73.

14. Gary T. Marx, "Who Really Gets Stung? Some Issues Raised by the New Police Undercover Work," *Crime & Delinquency* (1982):165–193.

15. *Illinois v. Perkins,* 110 S.Ct. 2394 (1990).

16. Barker and Carter, *Police Deviance.*

17. Thomas Barker, "An Empirical Study of Police Deviance Other Than Corruption," in Barker and Carter, *Police Deviance,* pp. 123–138.

18. New York City Commission to Investigate Allegations of Police Corruption and the City's Anti-Corruption Procedures, *The Knapp Commission Report on Police Corruption* (New York: George Braziller, 1972), p. 4.

19. Kania, "Police Acceptance of Gratuities," p. 40. For an excellent analysis of how the acceptance of gratuities can become endemic to an organization and pose ethical dilemmas for new officers, see Jim Ruiz and Christine Bono, "At What Price a 'Freebie'? The Real Cost of Police Gratuities," *Criminal Justice Ethics* (Winter–Spring 2004):44–54. The authors also demonstrate through detailed calculations how the amount of gratuities accepted can reach up to 40 percent of an annual officer's income—and is therefore no minor or inconsequential infraction of rules that can be left ignored or unenforced.

20. Brian L. Withrow and Jeffrey D. Dailey, "When Strings Are Attached," in Quint C. Thurman and Jihong Zhao (eds.), *Contemporary Policing: Controversies, Challenges, and Solutions* (Los Angeles: Roxbury, 2004), pp. 319–326.

21. Ibid.

22. Ibid.

23. Albert A. Seedman and Peter Hellman, *Chief!* (New York: Avon Books, 1974), pp. 43–44.

24. Edwin J. Delattre, *Character and Cops: Ethics in Policing,* 4th ed. (Washington, DC: AEI Press, 2002), p. 41.

25. Edward Tully, "Misconduct, Corruption, Abuse of Power: What Can the Chief Do?" http://www.neiassociates.org/mis2.htm (Part I) and http://www.neiassociates.org/misconductII.htm (Part II) (accessed September 16, 2005).

26. See *Crime Delinquency* 10 (1964):355–371; American Bar Association, 29 *A.B.A. Report* 29, part I (1906): 395–417; Answers.com, http://www.answers.com/topic/the-causes-of-popular-dissatis-faction-with-the-administration-of-justice?cat=biz-fin (accessed March 10, 2008).

27. John P. MacKenzie, *The Appearance of Justice* (New York: Scribner's, 1974). See also Eliot Asimof, *Eight Men Out: The Black Sox and the 1919 World Series* (New York: Henry Holt, 1963); a movie by the same name was released in 1988.

28. Quoted in Frank Greenberg, "The Task of Judging the Judges," *Judicature* 59 (May 1976):464.

29. Ibid., p. 460; direct quote from the original.

30. For thorough discussions and examples of these areas of potential ethical shortcomings, see Jeffrey M. Shaman, Steven Lubet, and James J. Alfini, *Judicial Conduct and Ethics,* 3rd ed. (San Francisco: Matthew Bender & Co., 2000).

31. Ibid.

32. Ibid., p. vi.

33. Ibid.

34. Ibid., p. vi.

35. Tim Murphy, "Test Your Ethical Acumen," *Judges' Journal* 8 (1998):34.

36. American Judicature Society, *Judicial Conduct Reporter* 16 (1994):2–3.

37. John Adams, "On Government," quoted in Russell Wheeler, *Judicial Administration: Its Relation to Judicial Independence* (Alexandria, VA: National Center for State Courts, 1988), p. 112.

38. Shaman et al., *Judicial Conduct and Ethics,* p. viii.

39. Deut. 1:16–17.

40. Elliot D. Cohen, "Pure Legal Advocates and Moral Agents: Two Concepts of a Lawyer in an Adversary System," in Michael C. Braswell, Belinda R. McCarthy, and Bernard J. McCarthy (eds.), *Justice, Crime and Ethics,* 2nd ed. (Cincinnati: Anderson, 1996), pp. 131–167.

41. *Berger v. United States,* 295 U.S. 78 (1935).

42. See *Dunlop v. United States,* 165 U.S. 486 (1897), involving a prosecutor's inflammatory statements to the jury.

43. 386 U.S. 1 (1967). In this case, the Supreme Court overturned the defendant's conviction after determining that the prosecutor "deliberately misrepresented the truth."

44. Cohen, "Pure Legal Advocates and Moral Agents," p. 168.

45. Ibid.

46. Cynthia Kelly Conlon and Lisa L. Milord, *The Ethics Fieldbook: Tools for Trainers* (Chicago: American Judicature Society, n.d.), pp. 23–25.

47. Ibid., p. 28.

48. Elizabeth L. Grossi and Bruce L. Berg, "Stress and Job Dissatisfaction Among Correctional Officers: An Unexpected Finding," *International Journal of Offender Therapy and Comparative Criminology* 35 (1991):79.

49. Irving L. Janis, "Group Dynamics Under Conditions of External Danger," in Darwin Cartwright and Alvin Zander (eds.), *Group Dynamics: Research and Theory* (New York: Harper & Row, 1968).

50. Ibid.

51. Ibid., p. 85.

52. *CBS News,* March 30, 1977; see Jones and Carlson, *Reputable Conduct,* p. 76.

53. Jones and Carlson, *Reputable Conduct,* p. 77.

54. F. K. Fair and W. D. Pilcher, "Morality on the Line: The Role of Ethics in Police Decision-Making," *American Journal of Police* 10(2) (1991):23–38.

55. Tully, "Misconduct, Corruption, Abuse of Power.

56. Stephen J. Vicchio, "Ethics and Police Integrity," *FBI Law Enforcement Bulletin* (July 1997):8–12.

57. Kleinig, *The Ethics of Policing.*

58. Ibid.

59. Sam S. Souryal and Deanna L. Diamond, "The Rhetoric of Personal Loyalty to Superiors in Criminal Justice Agencies," *Journal of Criminal Justice* 29(2001): 543–554.

60. Ibid., p. 548.

61. Ibid., p. 549

62. Delattre, *Character and Cops,* p. 84.

13

Rights of Criminal Justice Employees

KEY TERMS AND CONCEPTS

Americans with Disabilities Act (ADA)

Affirmative action

Bona fide occupational qualifier (BFOQ)

Fair Labor Standards Act (FLSA)

Family and Medical Leave Act (FMLA)

Hatch Acts

Peace Officers Bill of Rights (POBR)

Reverse discrimination

Workplace harassment

LEARNING OBJECTIVES

After reading this chapter, the student will:

- be familiar with laws and rights affecting criminal justice employees
- understand the concept of disparate treatment

- be familiar with effective action plans
- know the elements of a due process claim under U.S. Section 1983
- understand the impact of the Fair Labor Standards Act on criminal justice employees
- understand the nature and impact of workplace harassment in criminal justice
- know the eligibility requirements for Family and Medical Leave Act benefits
- have an understanding of the Americans with Disabilities Act

Uneasy lies the head that wears the crown.
—WILLIAM SHAKESPEARE

Good orders make evil men good and bad orders make good men evil.
—JAMES HARRINGTON

INTRODUCTION

In the last few decades, the rights and obligations of criminal justice employees, like those of workers in the private sector, have changed dramatically. Changes in values, demographics, law, and technology have blurred the line dividing the manager and those who are managed in enforcement, judicial, and correctional agencies. Today's criminal justice employee is far more sophisticated about employee rights.[1] For that reason, and because of attendant liability considerations (discussed in Chapter 14), contemporary criminal justice managers must be more aware of employees' legal rights.

After an overview of the relevant employment laws, we discuss recruitment and hiring issues, age discrimination, affirmative action, discipline and discharge, pay and benefits, and safe workplace issues. Then we examine constitutional rights of criminal justice employees as determined by the courts regarding free speech, searches and seizures, self-incrimination, religious practices, sexual misconduct, residency requirements, moonlighting, misuse of firearms, alcohol and drugs in the workplace, **workplace harassment**, and the Americans with Disabilities Act.

OVERVIEW

Law and litigation affecting criminal justice employees can arise out of federal and state constitutions, statutes, administrative regulations, and judicial interpretations and rulings. Even poorly written employee handbooks or long-standing agency customs or practices may create vested rights. The ripple effect begun by improper or illegal hiring, training, discipline, or discharge can lead not only to poor agency performance and morale but also to substantial legal and economic liability. It should become apparent in the following overview and the court decisions that follow that utilizing good common sense as well as a sense of fairness will go a long way toward preventing legal problems in the employment relationship.[2]

It should also be noted that the Civil Rights Act of 1991, like its predecessors, may result in further amended versions and changes in public and private sector employment; however, it will take several years for significant decisions to wind their way through the courts for a final determination by the Supreme Court of the intent and reach of the act. Therefore, this section focuses on presenting the issues rather than on attempting to settle the law in these areas.

- *Fair Labor Standards Act (FLSA; at 29 U.S.C. 203 et seq.).* This act provides minimum salary and overtime provisions covering both public and private sector employees. Part 7(a) contains special provisions for firefighters and police officers. I discuss the FLSA more fully later.
- *Title VII of the Civil Rights Act of 1964 and its amendments (42 U.S.C. 2000e).* This broadly based act establishes a federal policy requiring fair employment practices in both the public and private sectors. It prohibits unlawful employment discrimination in the hiring process, discharge, discipline, and working conditions and the unlawful provision of benefits based on race, color, religion, sex, and national origin. Its provisions extend to "hostile work environment" claims based on sexual, racial, or religious harassment.
- *Equal Pay Act [29 U.S.C. 206(d)].* This legislation provides an alternative remedy to Title VII for sex-based discrimination in wages and benefits when men and women do similar work. It applies the simpler Fair Labor Standards Act procedures to claims. Note that the Equal Pay Act does not mean "comparable worth"—an attempt to determine wages by requiring equal pay for employees whose work is of comparable worth even if the job content is totally different.
- *The Pregnancy Discrimination Act of 1978 [42 U.S.C. Section 2000e(k)].* This act is an amendment to the scope of sexual discrimination under Title VII. It prohibits unequal treatment of women because of pregnancy or related medical conditions (e.g., nausea). The act requires that employers treat pregnant women like other temporarily disabled employees. The U.S. Supreme Court decided a major case in 1991 that limited employers' ability in excluding women who are pregnant or of childbearing years from certain jobs under a fetal protection policy.[3]
- *Age Discrimination in Employment Act (29 U.S.C. 623).* This act generally prohibits the unequal treatment of applicants or employees based on their age, if they are age 40 years or older, in regard to hiring, firing, receiving benefits, and other conditions of employment.
- *Americans with Disabilities Act of 1990 (ADA) (42 U.S.C. 12112).* The goal of this legislation is to remove barriers that might prevent otherwise qualified individuals with disabilities from enjoying the same employment opportunities as persons without disabilities. Before the ADA, the Rehabilitation Act of 1973 (see 29 U.S.C. 701) and its amendments prevented similar disability discrimination among public agencies receiving federal funds. The ADA is discussed more fully later.
- *Section 1983 (codified as Title 42, U.S. Code Section 1983).* This major piece of legislation is the instrument by which an employee may sue an employer for civil rights violations based on the deprivation of constitutional rights. It is the most versatile civil rights action and is also the most often used against criminal justice agencies. Section 1983 is discussed more in Chapter 15.

In addition to the those legislative enactments and state statutes that prohibit various acts of discrimination in employment, there are additional remedies that have tremendous impact on public sector employees. Tort actions (a tort is the infliction of a civil injury) may be brought by public sector employees against their employer for a wide variety of claims, ranging from assault and battery to defamation. Contractual claims may grow out of collective bargaining agreements, which may include procedures for assignments, seniority, due process protections (such as in the Peace Officers' Bill of Rights, discussed later), and grievance procedures. Often the source of the right defines the remedy and the procedure for obtaining that remedy. For example, statutes or legal precedents often provide for an aggrieved employee to receive back pay, compensatory damages, injunctive relief, or punitive damages.

THE EMPLOYMENT RELATIONSHIP

Recruitment and Hiring

Numerous selection methods for hiring police and corrections officers have been tried over the years. Issues in recruitment, selection, and hiring also often involve internal promotions and assignments to special units, such as a special weapons team in a police agency. Requirements concerning age (e.g., the FBI will hire no one older than 37 years), height, weight, vision, education, and possession of a valid driver's license have all been utilized over the years in criminal justice. In addition, tests are commonly used to determine intelligence, emotional suitability and stability (using psychological examinations and oral interviews), physical agility, and character (using polygraph examinations and extensive background checks).[4] More recently, drug tests have become frequently used as well (discussed more fully later).

The critical question for such tests is whether they validly test the types of skills needed for the job. A companion concern is whether the tests are used for discriminatory purposes or have an unequal impact on protected groups (e.g., minorities, the physically challenged). As a result of these considerations, a number of private companies provide valid, reliable examinations for use by the public sector.

Disparate Treatment

It should be emphasized that there is nothing in the law that states that an employer must hire or retain incompetent personnel. In effect, the law does not prohibit discrimination. Thus, it is not unlawful to refuse to hire people who have a record of driving while intoxicated for positions that require driving. What is illegal is to treat people differently because of their age, gender, sex, or other protected status, that is, disparate treatment. It is also illegal to deny equal employment opportunities to such persons; that is disparate impact.[5] Federal equal opportunity law prohibits the use of selection procedures for hiring or promotion that have a discriminatory impact on the employment opportunities of women, Hispanics, blacks, or other protected classes. An example of overt discriminatory hiring is reflected in a court decision in 1987 arising out of a situation in a sparsely populated county in Virginia. Four women sued because they were denied positions as courtroom security officer, deputy, and civil process server because of their gender. Sheriffs had refused to hire the women, justifying their decision by contending that being male was a **bona fide occupational qualifier (BFOQ)** (i.e., in certain situations it is lawful and reasonable to discriminate because of a business necessity, such as a female corrections facility maintaining at least one female staff member on duty at all times to assist inmates in toileting, showering and disrobing) for the positions and that because the positions were within the "personal staff" of the sheriff, they were exempt from the coverage of Title VII. The Fourth Circuit overturned a lower court decision, finding that the sheriff did not establish that gender was a BFOQ for the positions and that the positions were not part of the sheriff's personal staff (the positions were not high level, policymaking, or advisory in nature). Thus, the refusal to hire the women violated Title VII.[6] There may, however, be a "business justification" for a hiring policy even though it has a disparate impact. For example, in one case an employer required airline attendants to cease flying immediately on discovering they were pregnant. The court upheld the policy on the ground that pregnancy could affect one's ability to perform routine duties in an aircraft, thereby jeopardizing the safety of passengers.[7]

A classic example of an apparent neutral employment requirement that actually had a disparate impact on gender, race, and ethnicity was the once-prevalent height requirement used by most public safety agencies. Minimum height requirements of 5 feet, 10 inches or above were often advertised and effectively operated to exclude most women and many Asians and Hispanics from employment.[8] Such a requirement has gradually been superseded by a "height in proportion to weight" requirement.

Nonetheless, other existing physical agility tests serve to discriminate against women and small men with less upper-body strength. One wonders how many pushups a police officer must do on the job or be able to do to perform his or her duties adequately, or how many 6-foot walls, ditches, and attics officers must negotiate. (Occasionally, preemployment physical abilities testing becomes ludicrous. For example, I once allowed a recruiter from a major western city to recruit students in an upper-level criminal justice course. The recruiter said the city's physical test included scaling a 6-foot wall; however, he quickly pointed out that testing staff would boost all female applicants over it.)

Litigation is blossoming in this area. In a western city, a woman challenged the police department's physical abilities test as discriminatory and not job related, prompting the agency to hire a Canadian consultant who developed a job-related preemployment agility test (currently used by the Royal Canadian Mounted Police and other agencies across Canada) based on data provided by officers and later computer analyzed for incorporation into the test. In other words, recruits were soon tested in terms of the physical demands placed on police officers in that specific community (no pushups or 6-foot walls are included).[9]

Discrimination may also exist in promotions and job assignments. As an example of the former, a Nebraska female correctional center worker brought suit alleging that her employer violated her Title VII and equal protection rights by denying her a promotion. The woman was qualified for the higher-level position (assistant center manager for programming), and she also alleged that the center treated women inequitably and unprofessionally, that assertiveness in women was viewed negatively, and that women were assigned clerical duties not assigned to men. The court found that she was indeed denied a promotion because of her sex, in violation of Title VII and the equal protection clause of the Fourteenth Amendment; she was awarded back pay and front pay biweekly until a comparable position became available, general damages, and court costs.[10]

With respect to litigation in the area of job assignments, four female jail matrons who were refused assignments to correctional officer positions in Florida even though they had been trained and certified as jail officers were awarded damages. It was ruled that a state regulation prohibiting females in male areas of the jail was discriminatory without proof that gender was a BFOQ.[11] However, a particular assignment may validly exclude one gender. An assignment to work as a decoy female prostitute demonstrates a business necessity for women.[12]

How Old Is "Too Old" in Criminal Justice?

State and public agencies are not immune from age discrimination suits in which arbitrary age restrictions have been found to violate the law. In Florida, a police lieutenant with the state highway patrol with 29 years of service was forced by statute to retire at age 62. The Equal Employment Opportunity Commission (EEOC) brought suit, alleging that Florida's statute violated the Age Discrimination in Employment Act (ADEA). The court held that age should not be a BFOQ because youthfulness is not a guarantee of public safety. Rather, a physical fitness standard would better serve the purpose of ensuring the ability to perform the tasks of the position.[13]

Indeed, the U.S. Supreme Court rejected mandatory retirement plans for municipal firefighters and police officers.[14] Until 1985, the city of Baltimore had relied on a federal police officer and firefighter statute (5 U.S.C. 8335b), an exemption to the ADEA, to establish age limits for appointing and retiring its fire and police officers; the city also contended that age was a BFOQ for doing so. The U.S. Supreme Court said that although Congress had exempted federal employees from application of the ADEA, another agency cannot just adopt the same standards without showing an agency-specific need. Age is not a BFOQ for nonfederal firefighters (or, by extension, police officers). The Court also established a "reasonable federal standard" in its 1984 decision in *EEOC v. Wyoming*,[15] in which it overturned a state statute providing for the mandatory retirement of state game wardens at age 55; it held that the ADEA did not require employers to retain unfit employees, only to make individualized determinations about fitness.

Criminal Justice and Affirmative Action

Probably no single employment practice has caused as much controversy as **affirmative action**. The very words bring to mind visions of quotas and of unqualified people being given preferential hiring treatment.[16] Indeed, quotas have been at the center of legal, social, scientific, and political controversy for more than two decades.[17] However, the reality of affirmative action is substantially different from the myth; as a general rule, affirmative action plans give preferred treatment only to affected groups when all other criteria (e.g., education, skills) are equal.[18]

The legal question (and to many persons, a moral one) that arises from affirmative action is, When does preferential hiring become **reverse discrimination?** The leading case here is *Bakke v. Regents of the University of California*[19] in 1978, in which Allan Bakke was passed over for medical school admission at the University of California, Davis, partly because the school annually set aside a number of its 100 medical school admissions slots for "disadvantaged" applicants. The Supreme Court held, among other things, that race could be used as a criterion in selection decisions, but it could not be the only criterion.

In a series of cases beginning in 1986,[20] the Supreme Court considered the development and application of affirmative action plans, establishing a two-step inquiry that must be satisfied before an affirmative action plan can be put in place. A plan must have (1) a remedial purpose, to correct past inequities, and (2) there must be a manifest imbalance or significant disparity to justify the plan. The Court, however, emphasized that such plans cannot completely foreclose employment opportunities to nonminority or male candidates.

The validity of such plans is generally determined on a case-by-case basis. For example, the District of Columbia Circuit Court held in 1987 that an affirmative action plan covering the promotion of blacks to management positions in the police department was justified because only 174 of the 807 positions (22 percent) above the rank of sergeant were filled by blacks in a city where 60 percent of the labor market was black.[21] Twenty-one past and present nonminority male detectives of the Metropolitan Police Department who were passed over for promotion challenged the department's voluntary affirmative actions plan designed to place "special emphasis" on the hiring and advancement of females and minorities in those employment areas where an "obvious imbalance" in their numbers existed.[22]

The plaintiffs believed that their failure to be promoted was attributable to illegal preferential treatment of blacks and women (reverse discrimination) that violated their rights under Title VII and the due process clause of the Fifth Amendment. The court held that the nonminority and male employees of the department failed to prove that the plan was invalid; a considerable body of evidence showed racial and sexual imbalance at the time the plan was adopted. Also, the plan did not unnecessarily trammel any legitimate interests of the nonminority or male employees because it did not call for displacement or layoff and did not totally exclude them from promotion opportunities.[23]

In summary, then, whenever a criminal justice employer wishes to implement and maintain job requirements, they must be job related. Furthermore, whenever a job requirement discriminates against a protected class, it should have a strong legitimate purpose and be the least restrictive alternative. Finally, attempts to remedy past hiring inequities by such means as affirmative action programs need substantial justification to avoid reverse discrimination.[24]

Property Rights in Employment

The Fourteenth Amendment to the U.S. Constitution provides in part that

> No state shall make or enforce any law which shall abridge the privileges or immunities of citizens of the United States; nor shall any State deprive any person of life, liberty, or property without due process of law; nor deny to any person within its jurisdiction the equal protection of the law.

Furthermore, the Supreme Court has set forth four elements of a due process claim under Section 1983: (1) A person acting under color of state law (2) deprived an individual (3) of constitutionally protected property (4) without due process of law.[25]

A long line of court cases has established the legal view that public employees have a property interest in their employment. This flies in the face of the old view that employees served "at will" or until their employer, for whatever reason, no longer had need of their services. The Supreme Court has provided some general guidance on how the question of a constitutionally protected property interest is to be resolved:

> To have a property interest in a benefit, a person clearly must have more than an abstract need or desire for it. He must have more than a unilateral expectation of it. He must, instead, have a *legitimate claim of entitlement to it.* It is a purpose of the ancient institution of property to protect those claims *upon which people rely in their daily lives, reliance that must not be arbitrarily undermined* [emphasis added].[26]

The Court has also held that employees are entitled to both a pretermination and a posttermination notice,[27] as well as an opportunity to respond, and that state legislators are free to choose not to confer a property interest in public employment.

The development of a property interest in employment has an important ramification: It means that due process must be exercised by a public entity before terminating or interfering with an employee's property right. What has been established, however, is that a probationary employee has little or no property interest in employment. For example, the Ninth Circuit held that a probationary civil service employee ordinarily has no property interest and could be discharged without a hearing or even "good cause." In that same decision, however, the court held that a woman who had passed her 6-month probationary period and who had then been promoted to a new position for which there was a probationary period had the legitimate expectation of continued employment.[28]

On the contrary, an Indiana police captain was deemed to have a property interest in his position even though a state statute allowed the city manager to demote without notice. There, a captain of detectives, a Democrat, was demoted by a newly elected Republican mayor. The court determined that the dismissal of even a policymaking public employee for politically motivated reasons is forbidden unless the position inherently encompasses tasks that render political affiliation an appropriate prerequisite for effective performance.[29]

Normally, however, policy-making employees (often called exempt appointments) possess an automatic exception to the contemporary property interest view. These personnel, often elected agency heads, are generally free to hire and fire those employees who are involved in the making of important decisions and policy. Examples of this area include new sheriffs who appoint undersheriffs and wardens who appoint deputy wardens. These subordinate employees have no property interest in their positions and may be asked at any time to leave the agency or revert back to an earlier rank.

This property interest in employment is, of course, generally implied. An example of this implication is found in a Utah case in which a property interest was found to exist based on an implied contract founded on an employment manual. Due process standards were therefore violated when the police department fired an officer without showing good cause or giving him a chance to respond to the charges against him.[30] In a Pennsylvania case, a patrol officer was suspended for 30 days without pay for alleged violations of personnel policies and was not given an opportunity to file a written response to the charges. The court held that the officer's suspension resulted in a deprivation of property.[31]

The property right in one's employment does not have to involve discipline or discharge to afford an employee protections. The claim of a parole officer that he was harassed, humiliated, and interfered with in a deliberate attempt to remove him from his position established a civil rights action for deprivation of property.[32] This decision, against the Illinois Department of Corrections, resulted from allegations that the department engaged in "a deliberate and calculated effort to remove the plaintiff from his position by forcing him to resign, thereby making the protections of the personnel code unavailable to him." As a result, the plaintiff suffered anxiety and stress and eventually went on disability status at substantially reduced pay.[33]

The key questions, then, once a property right is established, are: (1) What constitutes adequate grounds for interference with that right? and (2) what is adequate process to sustain that interference?[34]

Pay and Benefits

The **Fair Labor Standards Act (FLSA)** has had a major impact on criminal justice agencies. One observer referred to the FLSA as the criminal justice administrator's "worst nightmare come true."[35] Enacted in 1938 to establish minimum wages and to require overtime compensation in the private sector, amendments were added in 1974 extending its coverage to state and local governmental employees and including special work period provisions for police and fire employees. In 1976, however, the U.S. Supreme Court ruled that the extension of the act into traditional local and state governmental functions was unconstitutional.[36] In 1985, the Court reversed itself, bringing local police employees under the coverage of the FLSA. In this major (and costly) decision, *Garcia v. San Antonio Transit Authority,*[37] the Court held, 5 to 4, that Congress could impose the requirements of the FLSA on state and local governments.

Criminal justice operations take place 24 hours per day, 7 days per week, and often require overtime and participation in off-duty activities such as court appearances and training sessions. The FLSA comes into play when overtime salaries must be paid. It provides that an employer must pay employees time and a half for all hours worked over 40 per week. Overtime must also be paid to personnel for all work in excess of 43 hours in a 7-day cycle or 171 hours in a 28-day period. Public safety employees may accrue a maximum of 240 hours of compensatory or "comp" time, which, if not utilized as leave, must be paid on separation from employment at the employee's final rate of pay or at the average pay over the last 3 years, whichever is greater.[38] Furthermore, employers usually cannot require employees to take compensatory time in lieu of cash.

A recent decision by the U.S. Supreme Court favored administrators in this regard, however. A county in Texas became concerned that after employees reached their cap on comp time accrued, it would be unable to afford to pay them for overtime worked. So, the county sought to reduce accrued comp time and implemented a policy under which the employees' supervisor set a maximum number of compensatory hours that could be accumulated. When an employee's accrued amount of comp time approached that maximum, the employee would be asked to take some compensatory time off so as to reduce his or her number of comp hours. If the employee did not do so voluntarily, the supervisor would order the employee to use his or her comp time at specified times. This policy was challenged in court by 127 deputy sheriffs. The Court held that nothing in the FLSA prohibited employers from instituting such a policy.[39]

An officer who works in the night shift must now receive pay for attending training or testifying in court during the day. Furthermore, officers who are ordered to remain at home in anticipation of emergency actions must be compensated. Notably, however, the FLSA's overtime provisions do not apply to persons employed in a bona fide executive, administrative, or professional capacity. In criminal justice, the act has generally been held to apply to detectives and sergeants but not to those of the rank of lieutenant and above.

A companion issue with respect to criminal justice pay and benefits is that of equal pay for equal work. Disparate treatment in pay and benefits can be litigated under Title VII or statutes such as the Equal Pay Act or the equal protection clause. An Ohio case involved matron/dispatchers who performed essentially the same job as jailers but were paid less. This was found to be in violation of the Equal Pay Act and, because discriminatory intent was found, Title VII.[40]

Other criminal justice employee benefits are addressed in Title VII, the ADEA, and the Pregnancy Discrimination Act (PDA). For example, it is illegal to provide less insurance coverage for a female employee who is more likely to use maternity leave or for an older employee who is more liable to use more coverage. In addition, an older person or a woman could not be forced to pay higher pension contributions because he or she might be paying in for a shorter period of time or would be expected to live longer. Regarding pregnancy, the PDA does not require an employer to discriminate in favor of a pregnancy-related condition. It demands only that the employer not treat pregnancy differently from any other temporary medical condition. For example, if an agency has a 6-month leave policy for officers who are injured or ill from off-duty circumstances (on-duty circumstances would probably be covered by workers' compensation), that agency would have to provide 6 months' leave (if needed) for a pregnancy-related condition.[41]

Criminal Justice and a Safe Workplace

It is unclear what duties are owed by public employers to their employees in providing a safe workplace. Federal, state, and local governments are exempted from the coverage of the Occupational Safety and Health Act (OSHA), in 29 U.S.C. 652. Nonetheless, criminal justice work is often dangerous, involving the use of force and often occurring in locations outside governmental control. Therefore, workplace safety issues in criminal justice are more likely to revolve around adequacy of training and supervision than physical plants.[42]

The Supreme Court has noted the unique nature and danger of public service employment. In one case, the Court specifically stated that an employee could not bring a Section 1983 civil rights action alleging a workplace so unsafe that it violated the Fourteenth Amendment's due process clause. In this matter, a sewer worker was asphyxiated while clearing a sewer line. His widow alleged that the city knew the sewer was dangerous and that the city had failed to train or supervise the decedent properly.[43]

Other federal courts, especially the federal circuits, however, have ruled inconsistently on the safe workplace issue. One federal circuit held that a constitutional violation could be brought if it was proven that the city actively engaged in conduct that was "deliberately indifferent" to the employee's constitutional rights.[44]

However, the Fifth Circuit held differently in a Louisiana case, based on a failure to comply with a court order to have three officers on duty at all times in a prison disciplinary unit.[45] Here, a prison correctional officer in Baton Rouge was the only guard on a dangerous cellblock. While attempting to transfer a handcuffed inmate, the guard got into a scuffle with the inmate and was injured, although not severely. However, he claimed that he received insufficient medical attention and that as a result he became permanently disabled and that the institution "consciously" and with wanton disregard for his personal safety conspired to have him work alone on the cellblock. He invoked 42 U.S.C. 1983 in his charges, claiming that the institution acted in an indifferent, malicious, and reckless manner toward him, and that he suffered "class-based discrimination." The court held that the guard had no cause of action (no federal or constitutional grounds for litigation).

Liability for an employee's injury, disability, or death is a critical concern for criminal justice agencies. In particular, police and correctional officers often work in circumstances involving violent actions. Although state workers' compensation coverage, disability pensions, life insurance, and survivor pensions are designed to cover such tragedies, such coverage is typically limited and only intended to be remedial. On the other hand, civil tort actions in such cases can have a devastating impact on governmental budgets. Clearly, this is a difficult and costly problem to resolve. It is also an area with moral dilemmas as well. For example, what should be done with a prison intelligence unit that has knowledge of an impending disturbance but fails to alert its officers (who are subsequently injured)? And might a police department with knowledge that its new police vehicles have defective brakes fail to take immediate action for fear that its officers will refuse to drive the vehicles, thus reducing available personnel?[46]

CONSTITUTIONAL RIGHTS OF CRIMINAL JUSTICE EMPLOYEES

Freedom of Speech and Association

Many criminal justice executives have attempted to regulate what their employees say to the public; executives develop and rely on policies and procedures designed to govern employee speech. On occasion those restrictions will be challenged; a number of court decisions have attempted to define the limits of criminal justice employees' exercise of free speech.

Although the right of freedom of speech is one of the most fundamental of all rights of Americans, the Supreme Court has indicated that "the State has interests as an employer in regulating the speech of its employees that differ significantly from those it possesses in connection with regulation of the speech of the citizenry in general."[47] Thus, the state may impose restrictions on its employees that it would not be able to impose on the citizenry at large. However, these restrictions must be reasonable.[48]

There are two basic situations in which a police regulation may be found to be an unreasonable infringement on the free speech interests of officers.[49] The first occurs when the action is overly broad. A Chicago Police Department rule prohibiting "any activity, conversation, deliberation, or discussion which is derogatory to the Department" is a good example, because such a rule obviously prohibits all criticism of the agency by its officers, even in private conversation.[50] A similar situation arose in New Orleans, where the police department had a regulation that prohibited a police officer from making statements that "unjustly criticize or ridicule, or express hatred or contempt toward, or which may be detrimental to, or cast suspicion on the reputation of, or otherwise defame, any person."[51] The regulation was revised and later ruled constitutional.[52]

The second situation in which free speech limitations may be found to be unreasonable is in the way in which the governmental action is applied. Specifically, a police department may be unable to demonstrate that the statements by an officer being disciplined actually adversely affected the operation of the department. A Baltimore regulation prohibiting public criticism of police department action was held to have been unconstitutionally applied to a police officer who was president of the police union and had stated in a television interview that the police commissioner was not leading the department effectively[53] and that "the bottom is going to fall out of this city."[54]

A related area is that of political activity. The most protected type of speech is political speech. However, governmental agencies may restrict the political behavior of their employees— and the U.S. Supreme Court has upheld the constitutionality of laws which do so.[55] Exhibit 13.1 discusses how the Hatch Act operates at the federal, state, and local levels.

EXHIBIT 13.1

Not "Politics as Usual": The Hatch Acts

All federal executive branch and civil service employees (except the president and vice president) are subject to the **Hatch Act**. Federal employees who are "further restricted"—working in several key federal law enforcement agencies—cannot run for office in a partisan election, solicit, or encourage political activity of those doing business with their agency, or use their official authority to affect the outcome of an election. In addition, political contributions may not be received from subordinates, and covered employees may not participate in political fundraising, canvass for votes, or endorse or oppose a candidate in political literature. They may, however, vote in all partisan elections and express opinions on political topics, work in nonpartisan campaigns, attend political meetings, donate money to political parties and candidates, and sign nominating petitions.

State and local agency employees are also covered by the law, often known as "Little Hatch Acts," if they perform duties connected to programs financed totally or in part by federal funds— i.e., in programs funding homeland security, training, employment, overtime, community development, emergency preparedness. Such employees may, however, run for public office in nonpartisan elections, hold office in political organizations, and actively campaign for candidates for public office (as well as engage in drafting speeches, write letters, contribute money to political organizations, and attend political fundraisers).

The Office of Special Counsel investigates alleged Hatch Act violations by federal employees, and the state or local levels of government will investigate those of their employees.

Source: Based on Michael Bulzomi, "Casting More Than Your Vote: The Hatch Act and Political Involvement for Law Enforcement Personnel," *FBI Law Enforcement Bulletin* 77(12) (2008):16–25.

Although it may appear that Supreme Court decisions have lain to rest all controversy in this area, such has not been the case. Two recent cases show lower courts opting to limit the authority of the state to restrict political activities of their employees. In Pawtucket, Rhode Island, two firefighters ran for public office (mayor and city council member), despite a city charter provision prohibiting all political activity by employees (except voting and privately expressing their opinions). The Rhode Island Supreme Court issued an injunction against enforcing the charter provision, on the ground that the provision applied only to partisan political activities.[56] In a similar Boston case, however, the court upheld the police department rule on the basis that whether the partisan–nonpartisan distinction was crucial was a matter for legislative or administrative determination.[57]

In a Michigan case, a court declared unconstitutional, for being overly broad, two city charter provisions that prohibited contributions to or solicitations for any political purpose by city employees.[58] Clearly, although the Supreme Court seems to be supportive of governmental attempts to limit the political activities of its employees, lower courts seem just as intent to limit the Supreme Court decisions to the facts of those cases.

Could a police officer be disciplined, even discharged, because of his or her political affiliations? The Supreme Court ruled on that question in a case arising out of the Sheriff's Department in Cook County, Illinois.[59] The newly elected sheriff, a Democrat, fired the chief deputy of the process division and a bailiff of the juvenile court because they were Republicans. The Court ruled that it was a violation of the employees' First Amendment rights to discharge them from nonpolicymaking positions solely on the basis of their political party affiliation.[60]

Nonpolitical associations are also protected by the First Amendment; however, it is common for police departments to prohibit officers from associating with known felons or others of questionable reputation, on the ground that "such associations may expose an officer to irresistible temptations to yield in his obligation to impartially enforce the law, and . . . may give the appearance that the police are not themselves honest and impartial enforcers of the law."[61]

However, rules against association, as with other First Amendment rights, must not be overly broad. A Detroit Police Department regulation prohibiting associating with known criminals or persons charged with crimes, except in connection with regular duties, was declared unconstitutional. The court held that it prohibited some associations that had no bearing on the officers' integrity or public confidence in the officer (e.g., an association with a fellow church member who had been arrested on one occasion years ago, or the befriending of a recently convicted person who wanted to become a productive citizen).[62]

Occasionally, a criminal justice employee will be disciplined for improper association even though it was not demonstrated that the association had a detrimental effect on the employee or the agency. For example, a Maryland court held that a fully qualified police officer who was a nudist could not be fired simply on that basis.[63] On the other hand, a court upheld the discharge of an officer who had had sexual intercourse at a party with a woman he knew to be a nude model at a local "adult theater of known disrepute."[64]

An individual has a fundamental interest in being free to enter into certain intimate or private relationships; nevertheless, freedom of association is not an absolute right. For example, a federal district court held that the dismissal of a married police officer for living with another man's wife was a violation of the officer's privacy and associational rights.[65] Other courts, however, have found that off-duty sexual activity can affect job performance. When a married city police officer allegedly had consensual, private, nonduty, heterosexual relations with single adult women other than his wife in violation of state law criminalizing adultery, the adultery was not a fundamental right. Thus, the officer's extramarital affairs were not protected and the intimate relationship affected the public's perception of the agency.[66]

In another case, a police officer became involved with a city dispatcher who was the wife of a sergeant in the same department. The adulterous officer became eligible for promotion and scored high on the exam. The chief, confirming via an investigation that the officer had in fact been involved in an adulterous relationship with the dispatcher, refused on that basis to promote the officer, as he "would not command respect and trust" from rank-and-file officers and would adversely affect the efficiency and morale of the department. The Texas Supreme Court held that the officer's private, adulterous sexual conduct was not protected by state or federal law; the U.S. Supreme Court denied the appeal.[67]

Finally, the U.S. Court of Appeals for the Sixth Circuit held that a police department could conduct an investigation into the marital sexual relations of a police officer accused of sexual harassment.[68] In this case, there were allegations that the married officer had sexually harassed coworkers and had dated a gang member's mother. The department investigated the accusations, and the officer and his wife brought a Section 1983 action, alleging that the investigation violated their constitutional rights to privacy and freedom of association. The court held that the agency's investigation was reasonable, and, furthermore, that the police department would have been derelict in not investigating the matter.

In summary, police administrators have the constitutional authority to regulate employees' off-duty associational activities, including off-duty sexual conduct that involves a supervisory/subordinate relationship and associations that impact adversely employees' ability to do their jobs or impair the effectiveness and efficiency of the organization.[69]

The First Amendment's reach also includes means of expression other than verbal utterances. The Supreme Court upheld the constitutionality of a regulation of the Suffolk County, New York, Police Department that established several grooming standards (regarding hair, sideburn, and moustache length) for its male officers. In this case, *Kelley v. Johnson,*[70] the Court believed that to make officers easily recognizable to the public and to maintain the esprit de corps within the department, the agency justified the regulations and did not violate any right guaranteed by the First Amendment.

Searches and Seizures

The Fourth Amendment to the U.S. Constitution protects "the right of the people to be secure in their persons, houses, papers, and effects, against unreasonable searches and seizures." In an important case in 1967, the Supreme Court held that the amendment also protected individuals' reasonable expectations of privacy, not just property interests.[71]

The Fourth Amendment usually applies to police officers when they are at home or off duty in the same manner as it applies to all citizens. Because of the nature of their work, however, police officers can be compelled to cooperate with investigations of their behavior when ordinary citizens would not. Examples include searches of equipment and lockers provided by the department to the officers. There, the officers have no expectation of privacy that affords or merits protection.[72] Lower courts have established limitations on searches of employees themselves. The rights of prison authorities to search their employees arose in a 1985 Iowa case in which employees were forced to sign a consent form for searches as a condition of hire; the court disagreed with such a broad policy, ruling that the consent form did not constitute a blanket waiver of all Fourth Amendment rights.[73]

Police officers may also be forced to appear in a lineup, a clear "seizure" of his or her person. Appearance in a lineup normally requires probable cause, but a federal appeals court upheld a police commissioner's ordering of 62 officers to appear in a lineup during an investigation of police brutality, holding that "the governmental interest in the particular intrusion [should be weighed] against the offense to personal dignity and integrity." Again, the court cited the nature of the work, noting that police officers do "not have the full privacy and liberty from police officials that [they] would otherwise enjoy."[74]

Self-Incrimination

The Supreme Court has also addressed questions concerning the Fifth Amendment as it applies to police officers who are under investigation. In *Garrity v. New Jersey*,[75] a police officer was ordered by the attorney general to answer questions or be discharged. The officer testified that information obtained as a result of his answers was later used to convict him of criminal charges. The Supreme Court held that the information obtained from the officer could not be used against him at his criminal trial because the Fifth Amendment forbids the use of coerced confessions.

In *Gardner v. Broderick*,[76] a police officer refused to answer questions asked by a grand jury investigating police misconduct because he believed his answers might tend to incriminate him. The officer was terminated from his position as the result. The Supreme Court ruled that the officer could not be fired for his refusal to waive his constitutional right to remain silent. The Court added, however, that the grand jury could have forced the officer to answer or be terminated for his refusal provided that the officer was informed that his answers would not be used against him later in a criminal case.

As a result of these decisions, it is proper to fire a police officer who refuses to answer questions that are related directly to the performance of his or her duties provided that the officer has been informed that any answers may not be used later in a criminal proceeding. Although there is some diversity of opinion among lower courts on the question of whether an officer may be compelled to submit to a polygraph examination, the majority of courts that have considered the question have held that an officer can be required to take the examination.[77]

Religious Practices

Criminal justice work requires that employees of police, corrections, and even some courts organizations be available and on duty 24 hours per day, 7 days a week. Although it is not always convenient or pleasant, such shift configurations require that many criminal justice employees work weekends, nights, and holidays. It is generally assumed that one who takes such a position agrees to work such hours and to abide by other such conditions (e.g., carrying a weapon, as in a policing position); it is usually the personnel with the least seniority on the job who must work the most undesirable shifts.

There are occasions when one's religious beliefs are in direct conflict with the requirements of the job. Conflicts can occur between work assignments and attendance at religious services or periods of religious observance. In these situations, the employee may be forced to choose between his or her job and religion. The author is acquainted with a midwestern state trooper whose religion posed another related cause of job–religion conflict: His religion (with which he became affiliated after being hired as a trooper) banned the carrying or use of firearms. The officer chose to give up his weapon, and thus his job. A number of people have chosen to litigate the work–religion conflict rather than accept agency demands.

Title VII of the Civil Rights Act of 1964 prohibits religious discrimination in employment. The act defines religion as including "all aspects of religious . . . practice, as well as belief, unless an employer . . . is unable to reasonably accommodate to an employee's . . . religious . . . practice without undue hardship on the conduct of the employer's business."[78] Thus, Title VII requires reasonable accommodation of religious beliefs, but not to the extent that the employee has complete freedom of religious expression.[79] For example, an Albuquerque firefighter was a Seventh Day Adventist and refused to work Friday or Saturday nights because such shifts interrupted his honoring the Sabbath. He refused to trade shifts or take leave with (as vacation) or without pay, even though existing policy permitted his doing so. Instead, he said that the *department* should make such arrangements for coverage or simply excuse him from his shifts. The department refused to do either, discharging him. The court ruled that the department's accommodations were reasonable and that no further accommodation could be made without causing an undue hardship to the department. His firing was upheld. The court emphasized, however, that future decisions would depend on the facts of the individual case.[80]

Religious practices can also conflict with state law. For example, a circuit court held that the termination of a Mormon police officer for practicing plural marriage (polygamy) in violation of state law was not a violation of his right to freely exercise his religious beliefs.[81]

Another issue relating to religious expression concerns the display of religious items on one's uniform. In a Texas case, a police veteran wished to wear a small gold cross pin on his uniform as well as on plainclothes attire "as a symbol of his evangelical Christianity." The agency forbade officers doing so unless approved by the police chief; the chief offered the plaintiff several other accommodations, such as wearing a cross ring or bracelet instead of the pin, or wearing the pin under his uniform shirt or collar. Refusing such accommodations, the plaintiff was fired for insubordination. The Fifth Circuit Court of Appeals upheld his firing, agreeing that a police uniform "is not a forum for . . . expressing one's personal beliefs," that the constitution is not violated when a department bars religious symbols, and that the plaintiff had "myriad alternative ways to manifest this tenet of his religion."[82]

Finally, policies prohibiting the wearing of beards have also been challenged on First Amendment grounds. Two devout Sunni Muslim police officers challenged the Newark, New Jersey, Police Department's banning of beards, arguing that in their religion the lack of a beard is a "major sin"; they also noted that the department had made several medical exemptions to the policy (some officers were allowed to grow beards because of a skin condition called *folliculitis barbae*, which affects up to 60 percent of African American men; this condition is exacerbated by shaving). The Third Circuit Court of Appeals accepted the plaintiff's arguments and struck down the no-beards provision as it applied to the Muslim officers. The court determined that because the department granted exemptions for nonreligious reasons, closer scrutiny was warranted; the court concluded that the policy simply could not stand up under that scrutiny.[83]

Sexual Misconduct

To be blunt, criminal justice employees have ample opportunity to become engaged in sexual affairs, incidents, trysts, dalliances, or other behavior that is clearly sexual in nature. History and news accounts have shown that wearing a uniform, occupying a high or extremely sensitive position, or being sworn to maintain an unblemished and unsullied lifestyle does not mean that all people will do so for all time. Some people are not bashful about their intentions: Several officers have told me they aspired to police work because they assumed that wearing a uniform made them sexually irresistible. On the civilian side, there are police "groupies" who chase police officers and others in uniform.

Instances of sexual impropriety in criminal justice work can range from casual flirting while on the job to becoming romantically involved with a foreign agent whose principal aim is to learn delicate matters of national security. There have been all manner of incidents between those extremes, including the discipline of female police officers who posed nude in magazines. Some major police departments have even been compelled by their mayors to recruit officers for their sexual preference (i.e., homosexuality).

This is a delicate area, one in which discipline can be and has been meted out as police managers attempt to maintain high standards of officer conduct. It has also resulted in litigation because some officers believe that their right to privacy has been intruded on.

Officers may be disciplined for impropriety involving adultery and homosexuality. Most court decisions of the 1960s and 1970s agreed that adultery, even when involving an off-duty police officer and occurring in private, could result in disciplinary action[84] because such behavior brought debilitating criticism on the agency and undermined public confidence in the police. The views of the courts in this area, however, seem to be moderating with the times. A case involving an Internal Revenue Service agent suggested that to uphold disciplinary action for adultery, the government would have to prove that the employing agency was actually discredited.[85] The U.S. Supreme Court more recently appeared to be divided on the issue of extramarital sexual activity in public employment. In 1984, the Sixth Circuit held that a Michigan police officer could not be fired simply because he was living with a woman to whom he was not married (a felony under Michigan law).[86]

The issue of homosexual activity as a ground for termination of public employees arose in an Oklahoma case in which a state law permitted the discharge of schoolteachers for engaging in "public homosexual activity."[87] A lower court held the law to be unconstitutionally restrictive, and the Supreme Court agreed.[88] Another federal court held that the firing of a bisexual guidance counselor did not deprive the counselor of her First or Fourteenth Amendment rights. The counselor's discussion of her sexual preferences with teachers was not protected by the First Amendment.[89]

Residency Requirements

In the 1970s and 1980s, interest in residency requirements for governmental employees heightened, especially in communities experiencing economic difficulties.[90] Many governmental agencies now specify that all or certain members in their employ must live within the geographical limits of their employing jurisdiction. In other words, employees must reside within the county or city of employment. Such residency requirements have often been justified by employing agencies, particularly in criminal justice, on the grounds that employees should become familiar with and be visible in the jurisdiction of employment and that they should reside where they are paid by the taxpayers to work. Perhaps the strongest rationale given by employing agencies is that criminal justice employees must live within a certain proximity of their work in order to respond quickly in the event of an emergency.

Prior to 1976, numerous challenges to residency requirements were raised, even after the Michigan Supreme Court ruled that Detroit's residency requirement for police officers was not irrational.[91] In 1976, when the U.S. Supreme Court held that Philadelphia's law requiring firefighters to live in the city did not violate the Constitution, the challenges subsided. The cases now seem to revolve around the question of what constitutes residency. Generally, the police officer must demonstrate that he or she spends a substantial amount of time at the in-city residence.[92] Strong arguments have been made, however, that in areas where housing is unavailable or is exceptionally expensive, a residency requirement is unreasonable.[93]

EXHIBIT 13.2

Residency Rule Is a Yawner: New Orleans Residents Don't Seem to Care Where Cops Live

Opponents of a New Orleans residency rule that has been on the books since the 1950s, but largely ignored until now, contend they have proof that a majority of residents do not care if their police officers live outside the city limits.

This month the New Orleans Police Foundation released a study which showed that nearly three-quarters of residents oppose the requirement. The poll of 400 city residents was conducted in September by a political analyst and assistant sociology professor at Xavier University, Silas Lee. His findings showed 73 percent agreeing that "it's OK for police officers to live in other parishes," and 55 percent who somewhat or strongly disagreed with the residency rule.

"I think the study tells us that the people of New Orleans want their city safe and they're willing to have police officers live anywhere as long as they can help achieve that goal," said Bob Stellingworth, the foundation's president. "That's their primary concern, making the city safe to live in," he told the publication New Orleans City Business.

Until 1995, when then-Mayor Marc Morial led the charge to enforce a new and more stringent residency requirement passed by the City Council, New Orleans' domicile rule was not at the top of anyone's agenda, according to local press reports. It requires anyone seeking to work for the municipal government to live within city limits. While a grandfather clause covers those who lived outside of New Orleans at the time it was enacted, they must move to the city if they want to be promoted. . . .

Opponents of the residency rule claim that it has made recruitment difficult. The police force is currently 1,600 officers strong, but officials would like to see that figure rise to 2,000. Just 6 percent of the 52 recruits as of August 25, 2004, qualified for employment on the basis of residency. In 2003, that figure was 8 percent, and in 2002, it was 13 percent. . . .

Some black supporters, however, believe that the rule will curtail incidents of profiling, harassment and police brutality. . . .

According to the findings of the police foundation's poll, 55 percent said they disagreed with the domicile policy, 41 percent said they agreed. A slim majority of 52 percent of blacks agreed with it, but just 1 in 4 white people did so. . . .

Source: Based on Law Enforcement News, November, 2004, p. 5. John Jay College of Criminal Justice (CCNY), 555 West 57th St., New York, NY 10019.

[Author's update: Obviously this survey was conducted prior to the horrific hurricane, Katrina, which decimated New Orleans in August 2005. On October 28, 2005, 51 members of the New Orleans Police Department—45 sworn officers and 6 civilian employees—were fired for abandoning their posts during the storm. Fifteen other officers resigned when placed under investigation for abandonment. *Source:* http://www.msnbc.msn.com/id/9855340/print/1/displaymode/1098 (accessed February 21, 2008)]

Moonlighting

The courts have traditionally supported criminal justice agencies placing limitations on the amount and kind of outside work their employees can perform.[94] For example, police department restrictions on moonlighting range from a complete ban on outside employment to permission to engage in certain forms of work, such as investment counseling, private security, teaching police science courses, and so on. The rationale for agency limitations is that "outside employment seriously interferes with keeping the [police and fire] departments fit and ready for action at all times."[95]

In a Louisiana case, however, firefighters successfully provided evidence that moonlighting had been a common practice for 16 years before the city banned it. No firefighters had ever needed sick leave as a result of injuries acquired while moonlighting, there had never been a problem locating off-duty firefighters to respond to an emergency, and moonlighting had never caused a level of fatigue that was serious enough to impair a firefighter's work. With this evidence, the court invalidated the city ordinance that had sought to prohibit moonlighting.[96]

Misuse of Firearms

Because of the need to defend themselves or others and be prepared for any exigency, police officers are empowered to use lethal force when justified. Although restricted by the Supreme Court's 1985 decision in *Tennessee v. Garner*[97] (deeming the killing of unarmed, nondangerous suspects as unconstitutional), the possession of, and familiarity with, firearms remains a central aspect of the contemporary officer's role and function. Some officers take this responsibility to the extreme, however, becoming overly reliant on and consumed with their firepower.

Thus, police agencies typically attempt to restrain the use of firearms through written policies and frequent training in "Shoot/Don't Shoot" scenarios. Still, a broad range of potential and actual problems remains with respect to the use and possible misuse of firearms, as the following shows.

In the face of extremely serious potential and real problems and the omnipresent specter of liability suits, police agencies generally have policies regulating the use of handguns and other firearms by their officers, both on and off duty. The courts have held that such regulations need only be reasonable and that the burden rests with the disciplined police officer to show that the regulation was arbitrary and unreasonable.[98] The courts also grant considerable latitude to administrators in determining when their firearms regulations have been violated.[99] Police firearms regulations tend to address three basic issues: (1) requirements for the safeguarding of the weapon, (2) guidelines for carrying the weapon while off duty, and (3) limitations on when the weapon may be fired.[100]

Courts and juries are becoming increasingly harsher in dealing with police officers who misuse their firearms. The current tendency is to "look behind" police shootings to determine whether the officer acted negligently or the employing agency inadequately trained and supervised the officer/employee. In one case, a federal appeals court approved a $500,000 judgment against the District of Columbia when a police officer who was not in adequate physical shape shot a man in the course of an arrest. The court noted that the District officer had received no fitness training in 4 years and was physically incapable of subduing the victim. The court noted that had the officer been physically fit and adequately trained in disarmament techniques, a gun would not have been necessary. In his condition, however, the officer posed a "foreseeable risk of harm to others."[101]

Courts have awarded damages against police officers and/or their employers for other acts involving misuse of firearms: An officer shot a person while intoxicated and off duty in a bar[102]; an officer accidentally killed an arrestee with a shotgun while handcuffing him[103]; an unstable officer shot his wife five times and then committed suicide with an off-duty weapon the department required him to carry[104]; and an officer accidentally shot and killed an innocent bystander while pursuing another man at night (the officer had had no instruction on shooting at a moving target, night shooting, or shooting in residential areas).[105]

Alcohol and Drugs in the Workplace

Alcoholism and drug abuse problems have taken on a life of their own in contemporary criminal justice; employees must be increasingly wary of the tendency to succumb to these problems, and administrative personnel must be able to recognize and attempt to counsel and treat these problems.

Indeed, in the aftermath of the early 1990s beating death of Malice Green by a group of Detroit police officers, it was reported that the Detroit Police Department had "high alcoholism rates and pervasive psychological problems connected with the stress of policing a city mired in poverty, drugs, and crime."[106] It was further revealed that although the Detroit Police Department had paid $850,000 to two drug-testing facilities, the department did not have the counseling programs many other cities offer their officers. A psychologist asserted that "There are many, many potential time bombs in that department."[107]

It is obvious, given the extant law of most jurisdictions and the nature of their work, that criminal justice employees must be able to perform their work with a clear head, unaffected by alcohol or drugs.[108] Police departments and prisons will often specify in their manual of policy and procedures that no alcoholic beverages be consumed within a specified period prior to reporting for duty.

Such regulations have been upheld uniformly because of the hazards of the work. A Louisiana court went further, upholding a regulation that prohibited police officers from consuming alcoholic beverages on or off duty to the extent that it caused the officer's behavior to become obnoxious, disruptive, or disorderly.[109] Enforcing such regulations will occasionally result in criminal justice employees being ordered to submit to drug or alcohol tests, discussed next.

DRUG TESTING The courts have had several occasions to review criminal justice agency policies requiring employees to submit to urinalysis to determine the presence of drugs or alcohol. It was held as early as 1969 that a firefighter could be ordered to submit to a blood test when the agency had reasonable grounds to believe he was intoxicated, and that it was appropriate for the firefighter to be terminated from employment if he refused to submit to the test.[110]

In March 1989, the U.S. Supreme Court issued two major decisions on drug testing of public employees in the workplace. *Skinner v. Railway Labor Executives Association*[111] and *National Treasury Employees Union v. Von Raab*[112] dealt with drug-testing plans for railroad and U.S. Customs workers, respectively. Under the Fourth Amendment, governmental workers are protected from unreasonable search and seizure, including how drug testing can be conducted. The Fifth Amendment protects federal, state, and local workers from illegal governmental conduct.

In 1983, the Federal Railway Administration promulgated regulations that required railroads to conduct urine and blood tests on their workers following major train accidents. The regulations were challenged, one side arguing that because railroads were privately owned, governmental action, including applying the Fourth Amendment, could not legally be imposed. The Supreme Court disagreed in *Skinner,* ruling that railroads must be viewed as an instrument or agent of the government.

Three of the most controversial drug-testing issues have been whether testing should be permitted when there is no indication of a drug problem in the workplace, whether the testing methods are reliable, and whether a positive test proves on-the-job impairment.[113] The *Von Raab* case addressed all three issues. The U.S. Customs Service implemented a drug-screening program that required urinalysis for employees desiring transfer or promotion to positions that were directly involved in drug interdiction, where carrying a firearm was necessary, or where classified material was handled. Only five of 3,600 employees tested positive. The Treasury Employees Union argued that such an insignificant number of positives created a "suspicionless search" argument; in other words, drug testing was unnecessary and unwarranted. The Supreme Court disagreed, ruling that although only a few employees tested positive, drug use is such a serious problem that the program could continue.

Furthermore, the Court found nothing wrong with the testing protocol. An independent contractor was used. The worker, after discarding outer garments, produced a urine specimen while being observed by a member of the same sex; the sample was signed by the employee, labeled, placed in a plastic bag, sealed and delivered to a lab for testing. The Court found no "grave potential for arbitrary and oppressive interference with the privacy and personal security of the individuals" in this method.

Proving the connection between drug testing and on-the-job impairment has been an ongoing issue. Urinalysis cannot prove when a person testing positive actually used the drug. Therefore, tests may punish and stigmatize a person for extracurricular drug use that may have no effect on the worker's on-the-job performance.[114] In *Von Raab,* the Court indicated that this dilemma is still no impediment to testing. It stated that the Customs Service had a compelling interest in having a "physically fit" employee with "unimpeachable integrity and judgment."

Together, these two cases may set a new standard for determining the reasonableness of drug testing in the criminal justice workplace. They may legalize many testing programs that formerly would have been risky. *Von Raab* presented three compelling governmental interests that could be weighed against the employee's privacy expectations: the integrity of the work force, public safety, and protection of sensitive information. *Skinner* stated that railroad workers also have diminished expectations of privacy because they are in an industry that is widely regulated to ensure safety.[115]

RIGHTS OF POLICE OFFICERS

Delineated earlier were several areas (e.g., place of residence, religious practice, freedom of speech, search, and seizure) in which criminal justice employees, particularly the police, may encounter treatment by their administrators and the federal courts that is quite different from that received by other citizens. One does give up certain constitutional rights and privileges by virtue of wearing a justice system uniform. This section looks at how, for the police at least, the pendulum has swung more in the direction of the rank and file.

In the last decade, police officers have insisted on greater procedural safeguards to protect themselves against what they perceive as arbitrary infringement on their rights. These demands have been reflected in statutes enacted in many states, generally known as the **Peace Officers' Bill of Rights (POBR)**. This legislation mandates due process rights for peace officers who are the subject of internal investigations that could lead to disciplinary action. These statutes identify the type of information that must be provided to the accused officer, the officer's responsibility to cooperate during the investigation, the officer's right to representation during the process, and the rules and procedures concerning the collection of certain types of evidence. Following are some common provisions of state POBR legislation:

> *Written notice.* The department must provide the officer with written notice of the nature of the investigation, summary of alleged misconduct, and name of the investigating officer.

> *Right to representation.* The officer may have an attorney or a representative of his or her choosing present during any phase of questioning or hearing.

> ***Polygraph examination.*** The officer may refuse to take a polygraph examination unless the complainant submits to an examination and is determined to be telling the truth. In this case, the officer may be ordered to take a polygraph examination or be subject to disciplinary action.

Officers expect to be treated fairly, honestly, and respectfully during the course of an internal investigation. In turn, the public expects that the agency will develop sound disciplinary policies and conduct thorough inquiries into allegations of misconduct.

It is imperative that administrators become thoroughly familiar with statutes, contract provisions, and existing rules between employer and employee so that procedural due process requirements can be met, particularly in disciplinary cases in which an employee's property interest might be affected.

Police officers today are also more likely to file a grievance when they believe their rights have been violated. Grievances may cover a broad range of issues, including salaries, overtime, leave, hours of work, allowances, retirement, opportunity for advancement, performance evaluations, workplace conditions, tenure, disciplinary actions, supervisory methods, and administrative practices. The preferred method for settling officers' grievances is through informal discussion: The employee explains his or her grievance to the immediate supervisor. Most complaints can be handled in this way. Those complaints that cannot be dealt with informally are usually handled through a more formal grievance process, which may involve several different levels of action.

WORKPLACE HARASSMENT

Although sexual harassment has been a major concern in the nation for several decades—and is even outlawed in the Code of Federal Regulations [see, 29 C.F.R. 1604.11(a)]—today the more contemporary approach is for agencies to have a broader policy that applies to all forms of workplace harassment. All such harassment is a form of discrimination that violates Title VII of the Civil Rights Act of 1964 and other federal laws.

Unwelcome verbal or physical conduct based on race, color, religion, sex (whether or not of a sexual nature), national origin, age (40 years and older), disability (mental or physical), sexual orientation, or retaliation constitutes harassment when:

1. The conduct is sufficiently severe to create a hostile work environment, or
2. A supervisor's harassing conduct results in a change in an employment status or benefits (such as demotion, termination, failure to promote, and so on).[116]

Hostile work environment occurs when unwelcome comments or conduct based on sex, race, or other legally protected characteristics unreasonably interferes with an employee's work performance or creates an offensive work environment. Examples of such actions can include:

- Leering in a sexually suggestive manner
- Making offensive remarks about looks, clothing, body parts
- Touching in a way that makes an employee uncomfortable, such as patting, pinching, brushing against another's body
- Sending or telling suggestive letters or notes, or telling sexual or lewd jokes
- Using racially derogatory words, phrases, epithets

A claim of harassment generally requires that the complaining party be a member of a statutorily protected class; was subjected to unwelcome verbal or physical conduct; the unwelcome conduct complained of was based on his or her membership in that protected class; and the unwelcome conduct affected a term or condition of employment and unreasonably interfered with his or her work performance. Any employee wishing to initiate an Equal Employment Complaint (EEO) arising out of the prohibited conduct described earlier must contact an EEO official within 45 days of the incident.

Still, however, sexually related improprieties can and do occur (see Exhibit 13.3); police supervisors and managers must be vigilant of such inappropriate behaviors, seven types of which have been identified[117]:

1. *Nonsexual Contacts That Are Sexually Motivated.* An officer will stop another citizen without legal justification to obtain information or get a closer look at the citizen.
2. *Voyeuristic Contacts.* Police officers attempt to observe partially clad or nude citizens. They observe apartment buildings or college dormitories. In other cases, they roust citizens parked on lovers' lanes.
3. *Contacts with Crime Victims.* Crime victims generally are emotionally distraught or upset and particularly vulnerable to sexual overtures from officers. In these instances, officers may make several return visits and calls with the intention of seducing the victim.
4. *Contacts with Offenders.* In these cases, officers may conduct body searches, frisks, and patdown searches. In some cases, officers may demand sexual favors. Offenders' complaints of sexual harassment will not be investigated by a department without corroborating evidence, which seldom exists.
5. *Contacts with Juvenile Offenders.* In some cases, officers have exhibited some of the same behaviors with juveniles that they have with adults, such as patdowns, frisks, and sexual favors. There have also been cases in which officers assigned as juvenile or school liaison officers have taken advantage of their assignment to seduce juveniles.
6. *Sexual Shakedowns.* Police officers demand sexual services from prostitutes, homosexuals, and others engaged in criminal activity as a form of protection.
7. *Citizen-Initiated Sexual Contacts.* Some citizens are attracted to police officers and attempt to seduce them. They may be attracted to the uniform, authority, or the prospect of a "safe" sexual encounter. In other cases, the citizen may be lonely or may want a "break" when caught violating the law.

EXHIBIT 13.3

Men Filing More Claims of Sexual Harassment

Although women still file the overwhelming majority of sexual harassment claims with the Equal Employment Opportunity Commission (EEOC) and state and local agencies, from 1990 to 2009, the percentage of sexual harassment claims filed by men doubled, from 8 percent to 16 percent of all claims (compared with about 12 percent of all cases a decade earlier); more than 2,000 such claims were filed in 2009 out of about 12,700 cases. Furthermore, in 2009, the percentage of lawsuits the EEOC filed on behalf of male victims hit an all-time high, making up 14 percent of all cases. Experts say, however, that the increases may actually be due to the fact that more men are simply coming forward and complaining.

While some cases allege harassment by female supervisors or coworkers, most charges involve men harassing other men. Sometimes it's unwelcome romantic advances. Other times,

(Continued)

men are picked on because they are gay, perceived as being gay or not considered masculine enough for the work setting.

Source: Based on Sam Hananel, "More Men File Workplace Sexual Harassment Claims," Associated Press, March 4, 2010, http://abcnews.go.com/Politics/wireStory?id=10006341 (accessed November 15, 2010).

FAMILY AND MEDICAL LEAVE ACT

Eligibility Requirements

The **Family and Medical Leave Act (FMLA)**, enacted by Public Law 103-3, became effective in August 1993 and is administered and enforced by the U.S. Department of Labor's Wage and Hour Division. FMLA applies to all public agencies, including state, local, and federal employers; local schools; and private sector employers with 50 or more employees in 20 or more workweeks and who are engaged in commerce. FMLA entitles eligible employees to take up to 12 weeks of unpaid, job-protected leave in a 12-month period for specified family and medical reasons.

To be eligible for FMLA benefits, an employee must:

- work for a covered employer
- have worked for a covered employer for at least 12 months (and have worked at least 1,250 hours during that time)

A covered employer must grant an eligible employee unpaid leave for one or more of the following reasons:

- For the birth and care of a newborn child of the employee
- For placement with the employee of a child for adoption or child care
- To care for an immediate family member with a serious health condition
- To take medical leave when the employee is unable to work because of a serious health condition

A serious health condition means an illness, injury, impairment, or physical or mental condition that involves either any period of incapacitation or treatment, or continuing treatment by a health care provider; this can include any period of inability to work, attend school, or perform regular daily activities.

Recent Amendments

The 2009 and 2010 amendments to the Family and Medical Leave Act (FMLA)[118] addressed hardships being placed on military families. Two new categories of leave were created in the amendments—qualifying exigency leave and military caregiver leave—are designed to ease the strains.

Qualifying exigency leave is designed to allow family members of deployed regular Armed Forces personnel to take time away from work to provide for the exigencies that arise out of a military deployment (the 2008 NDAA only allowed exigency leave to members of the National Guard or Reserves). Such leave is triggered only when the deployed military member is the employee's spouse, son, daughter, or parent. Military caregiver leave is triggered when a family member must help a wounded soldier in his return home; it also imposes new obligations on employers. An eligible employee—including a spouse, son, daughter, parent, or next-of-kin—of a covered service member—is entitled to this type of leave in order to care for a member of the Armed Forces as well as National Guard or Reserves who has a serious injury or illness that was incurred in the line of duty on active duty and requires ongoing medical treatment, recuperation, or therapy.[119]

Also, in June 2010, President Obama expanded the rights of gay workers by allowing them to take family and medical leave to care for sick or newborn children of same-sex partners. The policy was set forth in a ruling issued by the Department of Labor. The new ruling indicates that an employee in a same-sex relationship can qualify for leave to care for the child of his or her partner, even if the worker has not legally adopted the child.[120]

THE AMERICANS WITH DISABILITIES ACT (ADA)

The **Americans with Disabilities Act (ADA)** was signed into law in 1990. Although certain agencies in the federal government, such as the Federal Bureau of Investigation, are exempt from the ADA, state and local governments and their agencies are covered by the law. It is critical for administrators to develop written policies and procedures consistent with the ADA and have them in place before a problem arises.[121]

Under the law, criminal justice agencies may not discriminate against qualified individuals with disabilities. A person has a disability under the law if he or she has a mental or physical impairment that substantially limits a major life activity, such as walking, talking, breathing, sitting, standing, or learning.[122] Title I of the ADA makes it illegal to discriminate against persons with disabilities. This mandate applies to the agency's recruitment, hiring, and promotion practices. ADA is not an affirmative action law, so persons with disabilities are not entitled to preference in hiring.

Employers are to provide reasonable accommodation to disabled persons. A reasonable accommodation can include modifying existing facilities to make them accessible, job restructuring, part-time or modified work schedules, acquiring or modifying equipment, and changing policies.[123] Hiring decisions must be based on whether an applicant meets the established prerequisites of the position (e.g., experience or education) and is able to perform the essential functions of the job. Under the law, blanket exclusions of individuals with a particular disability (such as diabetes) are, in most cases, impermissible.

Corrections agencies—jails, prisons, and detention facilities—are also covered by the ADA; programs offered to inmates must be accessible. For example, if a hearing-impaired inmate wished to attend Alcoholics Anonymous meetings, the corrections facility would need to make reasonable accommodation to allow him or her to do so, through such means as providing a sign language interpreter or writing notes as needed.[124]

Summary

After providing an overview of related legislation, this chapter examined several areas of criminal justice employee rights, including the issues of drug testing, privacy, hiring and firing, sexual harassment, disabilities, and peace officers' rights. Criminal justice employers' responsibilities were also discussed.

Being an administrator in the field of criminal justice has never been easy. Unfortunately, the issues facing today's justice administrators have probably never been more difficult or complex.

This chapter clearly demonstrated that these are challenging and, occasionally, litigious times for the justice system; one act of negligence can mean financial disaster for an individual or a supervisor.

Questions for Review

1. What are criminal justice employees' rights in the workplace according to federal statutes?
2. What is the general employee–employer relationship in criminal justice regarding recruitment and hiring and affirmative action?
3. It has been stated that criminal justice employees have a "property interest" in their jobs as well as a right to a safe workplace. What does this mean?
4. What constitutional rights are implicated for criminal justice employees on the job? (In your response, address whether rights are held regarding freedom of speech, searches and seizures, self-incrimination, and religion.)
5. In what regard is a greater standard of conduct expected of criminal justice employees? (In your response, include discussions of sexual behavior, residency, moonlighting, use of firearms, and alcohol/drug abuse.)
6. How would you explain kinds of behaviors can lead to charges of workplace harassment in a criminal justice agency?
7. What are the protections afforded criminal justice employees under the Family and Medical Leave Act (including its amendments) and the Americans with Disabilities Act.

Learn by Doing

1. As an administrator in your probation and parole office, you have long been supportive of your subordinates and appreciate their hard work. Lately, however, the effects of budget cutbacks have taken a serious toll on your organization, with no new hiring occurring and positions being frozen when someone retires or resigns. Your officers have sent you a letter stating that they are very upset with the work environment now that there are too few employees, resulting in their having to be on-call for prolonged amounts of time, caseloads being extremely high, their paperwork being excessive, and their home visits with clients now seemingly much more dangerous-particularly when someone's probation or parole is revoked and they must be arrested and taken to jail. Clearly they perceive that the workplace is unsafe and their morale is low. How will you attempt to address their concerns?

2. You are a mid-manager in a campus police organization. During the fall semester, you and your personnel are quite challenged with special events-students returning to campus, football games, concerts, and other activities-that require officers to work a lot of overtime. A sergeant comes to you with a problem: two of his day-shift officers are refusing to work overtime for evening and weekend events. Their reason: they are very busy (and making a lot of extra money) moonlighting, one for a private security firm, the other installing fencing for a home developer. This is causing a major problem in terms of filling required overtime needs at special events on campus. How will you address this problem?

Related Websites

Affirmative Action Homepage
  http://www.civilrights.org/issues/affirmative

Americans with Disabilities Act Homepage
  http://www.usdoj.gov/crt/ada/adahom1.htm

Backstop: the Criminal Justice Specialists
  http://www.backstop.org.uk/index.php

Department of Labor
  http://www.dol.gov/esa/whd/fmla

Office of National Drug Control Policy
  http://www.whitehousedrugpolicy.gov

RAND Drug Policy Research Center
  http://www.rand.org/multi/dprc

Notes

1. Robert H. Chaires and Susan A. Lentz, "Criminal Justice Employee Rights: An Overview," *American Journal of Criminal Justice* 13 (April 1995):259.
2. *Ibid.*
3. *United Autoworkers v. Johnson Controls,* 111 S.Ct. 1196 (1991).

4. Kenneth J. Peak, *Policing America: Challenges and Best Practices,* 7th ed. (Upper Saddle River, NJ: Prentice Hall, 2012), Chapter 4, generally.

5. Chaires and Lentz, "Criminal Justice Employee Rights," p. 260.

6. *U.S. v. Gregory,* 818 F.2d 114 (4th Cir. 1987).

7. *Harris v. Pan American,* 649 F.2d 670 (9th Cir. 1988).

8. Chaires and Lentz, "Criminal Justice Employee Rights," p. 267.

9. Ken Peak, Douglas W. Farenholtz, and George Coxey, "Physical Abilities Testing for Police Officers: A Flexible, Job-Related Approach," *The Police Chief* 59 (January 1992): 52–56.

10. *Shaw v. Nebraska Department of Corrections,* 666 F.Supp. 1330 (ND Feb. 1987).

11. *Garrett v. Oskaloosa County,* 734 F.2d 621 (11th Cir. 1984).

12. Chaires and Lentz, "Criminal Justice Employee Rights," p. 268.

13. *EEOC v. State Department of Highway Safety,* 660 F.Supp. 1104 (ND Fla.: 1986).

14. *Johnson v. Mayor and City Council of Baltimore* (105 S.Ct. 2717, 1985).

15. 460 U.S. 226, 103 S.Ct. 1054, 75 L.Ed.2d 18 (1983).

16. Chaires and Lentz, "Criminal Justice Employee Rights," p. 269.

17. Paul J. Spiegelman, "Court-Ordered Hiring Quotas after *Stotts:* A Narrative on the Role of the Moralities of the Web and the Ladder in Employment Discrimination Doctrine," *Harvard Civil Rights–Civil Liberties Law Review* 20 (1985):72.

18. Chaires and Lentz, "Criminal Justice Employee Rights," p. 269.

19. *Regents of the University of California v. Bakke,* 98 S.Ct. 2733, 438 U.S. 265, 57 L.Ed.2d (1978).

20. *Wygant v. Jackson Board of Education,* 106 S.Ct. 1842 (1986).

21. Chaires and Lentz, "Criminal Justice Employee Rights," p. 269.

22. *Ledoux v. District of Columbia,* 820 F.2d 1293 (D.C. Cir. 1987), at 1294.

23. *Ibid.*

24. Chaires and Lentz, "Criminal Justice Employee Rights," p. 270.

25. *Parratt v. Taylor,* 451 U.S. 527, 536–537, 101 S.Ct. 1908, 1913–1914, 68 L.Ed.2d 420 (1981).

26. *Board of Regents v. Roth,* 408 U.S. at 577, 92 S.Ct. at 2709.

27. *Cleveland Board of Education v. Loudermill,* 470 U.S. 532, 541 (1985).

28. *McGraw v. City of Huntington Beach,* 882 F.2d 384 (9th Cir. 1989).

29. *Lohorn v. Michael,* 913 F.2d 327 (7th Cir. 1990).

30. *Palmer v. City of Monticello,* 731 F.Supp. 1503 (D. Utah, 1990).

31. *Young v. Municipality of Bethel Park,* 646 F.Supp. 539 (WD Pa.: 1986).

32. *McAdoo v. Lane,* 564 F.Supp. 1215 (ND Ill., 1983).

33. *Ibid.,* at 1217.

34. Chaires and Lentz, "Criminal Justice Employee Rights," p. 273.

35. Lynn Lund, "The 'Ten Commandments' of Risk Management for Jail Administrators," *Detention Reporter* 4 (June 1991):4.

36. *National League of Cities v. Usery,* 426 U.S. 833 (1976).

37. 105 S.Ct. 1005 (1985).

38. Charles R. Swanson, Leonard Territo, and Robert W. Taylor, *Police Administration: Structures, Processes, and Behavior,* 6th ed. (Upper Saddle River, NJ: Prentice Hall, 2005), p. 599.

39. *Christiansen v. Harris County,* 529 U.S. 576, 120 S. Ct. 1655, 146 L.Ed.2d 621 (2000).

40. *Jurich v. Mahoning County,* 31 Fair Emp. Prac. 1275 (BNA) (ND Ohio,1983).

41. Chaires and Lentz, "Criminal Justice Employee Rights," p. 280.

42. *Ibid.*

43. *Collins v. City of Harker Heights,* 112 S.Ct. 1061 (1992).

44. *Ruge v. City of Bellevue,* 892 F.2d 738 (1989).

45. *Galloway v. State of Louisiana,* 817 F.2d 1154 (5th Cir. 1987).

46. Chaires and Lentz, "Criminal Justice Employee Rights," pp. 280–283.

47. *Pickering v. Board of Education,* 391 U.S. 563 (1968), p. 568.

48. *Keyishian v. Board of Regents,* 385 U.S. 589 (1967).

49. Swanson, Territo, and Taylor, *Police Administration,* p. 394.

50. *Muller v. Conlisk,* 429 F.2d 901 (7th Cir. 1970).

51. *Flynn v. Giarusso,* 321 F.Supp. 1295 (ED La.: 1971), at p. 1299.

52. *Magri v. Giarusso,* 379 F.Supp. 353 (ED La.: 1974).

53. Swanson, Territo, and Taylor, *Police Administration,* p. 395.

54. *Brukiewa v. Police Commissioner of Baltimore,* 263 A.2d 210 (MD: 1970).

55. See Hatch Reform Act Amendments of 1993, Pub. L. No. 103-94, 107 Stat. 1001 (1993) (codified at 5 U.S.C. Secs. 1501-1503); also see *United Public Workers v. Mitchell,* 330 U.S. 75 (1947).

56. *Magill v. Lynch,* 400 F.Supp. 84 (R.I. 1975).
57. *Boston Police Patrolmen's Association, Inc. v. City of Boston,* 326 N.E.2d 314 (MA: 1975).
58. *Phillips v. City of Flint,* 225 N.W.2d 780 (MI: 1975).
59. *Elrod v. Burns,* 427 U.S. 347 (1976); see also *Ramey v. Harber,* 431 F.Supp 657 (WD Va., 1977) and *Branti v. Finkel,* 445 U.S. 507 (1980).
60. *Connick v. Myers,* 461 U.S. 138 (1983); *Jones v. Dodson,* 727 F.2d 1329 (4th Cir. 1984).
61. Swanson, Territo, and Taylor, *Police Administration,* p. 397.
62. *Sponick v. City of Detroit Police Department,* 211 N.W.2d 674 (MI: 1973), p. 681; but see *Wilson v. Taylor,* 733 F.2d 1539 (11th Cir. 1984).
63. *Bruns v. Pomerleau,* 319 F.Supp. 58 (D. Md. 1970); see also *McMullen v. Carson,* 754 F.2d 936 (11th Cir. 1985), where it was held that a Ku Klux Klansman could not be fired from his position as a records clerk in the sheriff's department simply because he was a Klansman. The court did uphold the dismissal because his active KKK participation threatened to negatively affect the agency's ability to perform its public duties.
64. *Civil Service Commission of Tucson v. Livingston,* 525 P.2d 949 (Ariz. 1974).
65. *Briggs v. North Muskegon Police Department,* 563 F.Supp. 585 (WD Mich., 1983), affd. 746 F.2d 1475 (6th Cir. 1984).
66. *Oliverson v. West Valley City,* 875 F.Supp. 1465 (D. Utah, 1995).
67. *Henery v. City of Sherman,* 116 S.Ct. 1098 (1997).
68. *Hughes v. City of North Olmsted,* 93 F.3d 238 (6th Cir., 1996).
69. Michael J. Bulzomi, "Constitutional Authority to Regulate Off-Duty Relationships: Recent Court Decisions," *FBI Law Enforcement Bulletin* (April 1999):26–32.
70. 425 U.S. 238 (1976).
71. *Katz v. United States,* 389 U.S. 347 (1967).
72. *People v. Tidwell,* 266 N.E.2d 787 (IL: 1971).
73. *McDonell v. Hunter,* 611 F.Supp. 1122 (SD Iowa, 1985), affd. as mod., 809 F.2d 1302 (8th Cir., 1987).
74. *Biehunik v. Felicetta,* 441 F.2d 228 (1971), p. 230.
75. 385 U.S. 483 (1967).
76. 392 U.S. 273 (1968).
77. *Gabrilowitz v. Newman,* 582 F.2d 100 (1st Cir. 1978). Cases upholding the department's authority to order a polygraph examination for police officers include *Eshelman v. Blubaum,* 560 P.2d 1283 (Ariz.: 1977); *Dolan v. Kelly,* 348 N.Y.S.2d 478 (1973); *Richardson v. City of Pasadena,* 500 S.W.2d 175 (Tex.: 1973); *Seattle Police Officer's Guild v. City of Seattle,* 494 P.2d 485 (Wash.: 1972); *Roux v. New Orleans Police Department,* 223 So.2d 905 (La.: 1969); and *Farmer v. City of Fort Lauderdale,* 427 So.2d 187 (Fla.: 1983), cert. den., 104 S.Ct. 74 (1984).
78. 42 U.S.C. 200e(j).
79. *United States v. City of Albuquerque,* 12 EPD 11, 244 (10th Cir. 1976); see also *Trans World Airlines v. Hardison,* 97 S.Ct. 2264 (1977).
80. *United States v. Albuquerque,* 545 F.2d 110 (10th Cir. 1977).
81. *Potter v. Murray City,* 760 F.2d 1065 (10th Cir. 1985).
82. *Daniels v. City of Arlington, Texas,* 246 F.3d 500 (5th Cir. 2001), *cert. denied,* 122 S. Ct. 347 (2001).
83. *Fraternal Order of Police Newark Lodge No. 12 v. City of Newark,* 170 F.3d 359 (3rd Cir. 1999), *cert. denied,* 120 S. Ct. 56 (1999).
84. *Faust v. Police Civil Service Commission,* 347 A.2d 765 (Pa. 1975); *Stewart v. Leary,* 293 N.Y.S.2d 573 (1968); *Brewer v. City of Ashland,* 86 S.W.2d 669 (Ky. 1935); *Fabio v. Civil Service Commission of Philadelphia,* 373 A.2d 751 (Penn.: 1977).
85. *Major v. Hampton,* 413 F.Supp. 66 (1976).
86. *Briggs v. City of North Muskegon Police Department,* 563 F.Supp. 585 (6th Cir. 1984).
87. *National Gay Task Force v. Bd. of Ed. of Oklahoma City,* 729 F.2d 1270 (10th Cir. 1984).
88. *Board of Education v. National Gay Task Force,* 53 U.S.L.W. 4408, No. 83-2030 (1985).
89. *Rowland v. Mad. River Sch. Dist.,* 730 F.2d 444 (6th Cir. 1984).
90. David J. Schall, *An Investigation into the Relationship between Municipal Police Residency Requirements, Professionalism, Economic Conditions, and Equal Employment Goals,* Unpublished dissertation, University of Wisconsin–Milwaukee, 1996.
91. *Detroit Police Officers Association v. City of Detroit,* 190 N.W.2d 97 (1971), appeal denied, 405 U.S. 950 (1972).
92. *Miller v. Police Board of City of Chicago,* 349 N.E.2d 544 (Ill.: 1976); *Williamson v. Village of Baskin,* 339 So.2d 474 (La.: 1976); *Nigro v. Board of Trustees of Alden,* 395 N.Y.S.2d 544 (1977).
93. *State, County, and Municipal Employees Local 339 v. City of Highland Park,* 108 N.W.2d 898 (1961).
94. See, for example, *Cox v. McNamara,* 493 P.2d 54 (Ore.: 1972); *Brenckle v. Township of Shaler,* 281 A.2d 920 (Penn.: 1972); *Hopwood v. City of Paducah,* 424 S.W.2d 134 (Ken.: 1968); *Flood v. Kennedy,* 239 N.Y.S.2d 665 (1963).

95. Richard N. Williams, *Legal Aspects of Discipline by Police Administrators* (Traffic Institute Publication 2705) (Evanston, Ill.: Northwestern University, 1975), p. 4.

96. *City of Crowley Firemen v. City of Crowley,* 264 So.2d 368 (La.: 1972).

97. 471 U.S. 1, 105 S.Ct. 1694, 85 L.Ed.2d 1 (1985).

98. *Lally v. Department of Police,* 306 So.2d 65 (La. 1974).

99. See, for example, *Peters v. Civil Service Commission of Tucson,* 539 P.2d 698 (Ariz. 1977); *Abeyta v. Town of Taos,* 499 F.2d 323 (10th Cir. 1974); *Baumgartner v. Leary,* 311 N.Y.S.2d 468 (1970); *City of Vancouver v. Jarvis,* 455 P.2d 591 (Wash.: 1969).

100. Swanson, Territo, and Taylor, *Police Administration,* p. 433.

101. *Parker v. District of Columbia,* 850 F.2d 708 (1988), at 713, 714.

102. *Marusa v. District of Columbia,* 484 F.2d 828 (1973).

103. *Sager v. City of Woodlawn Park,* 543 F.Supp. 282 (D. Colo.: 1982).

104. *Bonsignore v. City of New York,* 521 F.Supp. 394 (1981).

105. *Popow v. City of Margate,* 476 F.Supp. 1237 (1979).

106. Eloise Salholz and Frank Washington, "Detroit's Brutal Lessons," *Newsweek* (November 30, 1992):45.

107. *Ibid.*

108. *Krolick v. Lowery,* 302 N.Y.S.2d 109 (1969), p. 115; *Hester v. Milledgeville,* 598 F.Supp. 1456, 1457 (MD Ga.: 1984).

109. *McCracken v. Department of Police,* 337 So.2d 595 (La.: 1976).

110. *Krolick v. Lowery.*

111. 489 U.S. 602 (1989).

112. 489 U.S. 656 (1989).

113. Robert J. Alberts and Harvey W. Rubin, "Court's Rulings on Testing Crack Down on Drug Abuse," *Risk Management* 38 (March 1991):36–41.

114. *Ibid.,* p. 38.

115. *Ibid.,* p. 40.

116. Federal Communications Commission, "Understanding Workplace Harassment," http://www.fcc. gov/owd/understandin-harassment.html (Accessed January 18, 2008).

117. Allen D. Sapp, "Sexual Misconduct by Police Officers," in eds. T. Barker and D. Carter, *Police Deviance* (Cincinnati: Anderson, 1994), pp. 187–200.

118. The amendments were contained in the National Defense Authorization Act for Fiscal Year 2008 (2008 NDAA), which became effective on January 16, 2009; the 2009 amendments were expanded again by amendments contained in the National Defense Authorization Act for Fiscal Year 2010 (2010 NDAA); see Public Law 110-181 and Public Law 111-84, respectively.

119. See Richard G. Schott, "Family and Medical Leave Act Amendments: New Military Leave Entitlements," *FBI Law Enforcement Bulletin* 79(6) (June 2010), http://www.fbi.gov/stats-services/publications/law-enforcement-bulletin/june-2010/family-and-medical-leave-act-amendments (accessed October 16, 2010).

120. Robert Pear, "Gay Workers Will Get Time to Care for Partner's Sick Child," *The New York Times,* June 21, 2010, http://www.nytimes.com/2010/06/22/us/politics/22rights.html (accessed November 7, 2010).

121. Paula N. Rubin and Susan W. McCampbell, "The Americans with Disabilities Act and Criminal Justice: Providing Inmate Services," *U.S. Department of Justice, National Institute of Justice Research in Action* (July 1994):2.

122. Paula N. Rubin, "The Americans with Disabilities Act and Criminal Justice: An Overview," *U.S. Department of Justice, National Institute of Justice Research in Action* (September 1993):1.

123. "Health and Criminal Justice: Strengthening the Relationship,"*U.S. Department of Justice, National Institute of Justice Journal, Research in Action,* (November 1994):40.

124. *Ibid.,* p. 41.

Special Challenges
Labor Relations, Liability, and Discipline

KEY TERMS AND CONCEPTS

Appeals process

Arbitration

Automated records system

Binding arbitration

Collective bargaining

Duty of care

Early warning system (EWS)

Esprit de corps

Fact finding

Failure to protect

Grievance

Job action

Mediation

Meet and confer

Negligence

Negotiation

Personnel complaint

Positive discipline

Proximate cause

Title 18, U.S. Code, Section 242

Title 42, U.S. Code, Section 1983

Tort

Vehicular pursuits

LEARNING OBJECTIVES

After reading this chapter, the student will:

- be familiar with collective bargaining and labor negotiations generally, as well as the recent political backlash in several states against collective bargaining and workers' wage and benefits packages
- know three models used in collective bargaining
- understand the four types of job actions employees can use to express their displeasure with working conditions
- know the nature of civil liability, the kinds of actions that can lead to a determination of negligence, and different types of lawsuits filed against criminal justice practitioners
- be familiar with the due process requirements concerning the discharge of public employees
- know the kinds of disciplinary actions that may be used by agencies in an investigation of a criminal justice employee
- know the steps taken when a citizen's complaint is filed
- understand the grievance process

Discipline must be maintained.

—CHARLES DICKENS

No man is fit to command another that cannot command himself.

—WILLIAM PENN

INTRODUCTION

Those who administer criminal justice agencies are confronted with, and must successfully address, countless challenges in the course of performing their daily duties. Therefore, because they provide criminal justice administrators with nearly endless challenges—as well as trials, tribulations, and often constitute a very large proportion of their workload—we discuss three broad topics concerning personnel.

This chapter opens by discussing labor relations/collective bargaining. In the past 50 years, probably no factor has had a greater impact on the administration of criminal justice agencies, with the possible exception of civil liability, which is also discussed in this chapter. Indeed, the decade of the 2010s witnessed unprecedented battles between politicians (who are trying to address huge budget deficits, union powers, and what they perceive to be runaway wages and benefits packages) and labor unions (who are trying to protect their members' wages and benefits—and their sphere of influence). This chapter section discusses those recent battles, including how the unionization movement developed in criminal justice, contemporary collective bargaining practices, and a primer on "navigating the waters" of unionization.

Next, we examine criminal justice employees vis-à-vis potential civil liability. This discussion includes several legal concepts (such as negligence and torts), court decisions, and legislation that serve to hold criminal justice practitioners accountable, both civilly and criminally, for acts of misconduct and negligence. Finally, we look at employee discipline, including: the tradition of problems in policing; due process requirements that must be afforded such employees; what is being done to identify and deal with problem officers, how the agency might employ positive discipline, and some proper means of dealing with citizen complaints.

COLLECTIVE BARGAINING, GENERALLY: NATURE, EXTENT—AND RECENT POLITICAL BACKLASH

What Wisconsin Hath Wrought . . .

Today there are 21.6 million government workers—the majority, or 19.4 million, being employed at the state and local levels. About half of them work in education, and the remainder is mostly in public safety (police, firefighting, prisons, and so on), social work, and nursing.[1] And, according to the federal Bureau of Labor Statistics, nearly 8 million (36.2 percent) of these workers belong to a labor union (compared with 6.9 percent of workers in the private sector).[2]

Are these government workers too well compensated in salaries and benefits for what they do, especially when compared to workers in the private sector? And are the unions representing them now too powerful and obstructive to good governance? Those of course are the major questions of the day, and certainly nothing could better depict the emotions that swirl around **collective bargaining** than the events that occurred in Wisconsin and other states in early 2011.

After Wisconsin's governor announced a plan to eliminate collective bargaining rights for public employees—and to increase their health care and pension payments—14 state senate Democrats fled Wisconsin to avoid having to vote on the measure.[3] Eight days later, state troopers were dispatched to these legislators' homes in efforts to pressure them to return to the legislature, and the state capitol saw 70,000 prounion protestors gather for a rally. At least 10 other states either quickly developed similar proposals or had throngs of protestors come out in opposition to such proposals to weaken union powers and extract more money from government employees. Indeed, only a few days after the Democrats fled Wisconsin, legislators in Indiana followed suit and refused to show up at the statehouse for a vote on a labor bill.[4]

Many state politicians, facing billions of dollars in budget deficits due to the recession, promised to cut spending and to help businesses. Consequently, they began scrutinizing their employees' performance as well as their wage and benefits packages—many of which are quite lucrative and were won after tough collective bargaining by education, police, fire, prison, office, and other workers. But to try to reduce the power of public employee unions is very difficult. Therefore, following the expressed intentions of Wisconsin and other states, public and private unions announced plans to spend up to $30 million to stop antilabor measures by lobbying public officials, organizing public rallies, working phone banks, and buying media ads to swing public opinion. This confrontation also comes at a time when organized labor has been losing membership and affords an opportunity for them to flex their muscles and unite current members, while bringing on new members.[5]

Meanwhile, a USA TODAY/Gallup Poll found that a clear majority (61 percent) of Americans opposed laws such as that proposed in Wisconsin which would take away collective bargaining power, while 33 percent said they favored such a law.[6]

Certainly the collective-bargaining battle promises to be a long, emotional, and hard-fought one for those on both sides of the issue. Unions have the strength of numbers and—because of their political contributions and voting record—a history of support from liberal, prounion politicians. Perhaps in the end, the best outcomes might include: a greater balancing of pension and health care benefits for public employees so as to become more in line with the their private-sector counterparts; greater use of objective and subjective performance data and measures, so that government employees are paid more in line with meaningful job outcomes; and a greater appreciation of government workers in general—who tend to be a bit older and better educated than those in the private sector.[7]

The Nature and Principles of Shared Governance

THREE MODELS   Each state is free to decide whether and which public sector employees will have collective bargaining rights and under what terms; therefore, there is considerable variety in collective bargaining arrangements across the nation. In states with comprehensive public sector bargaining laws, the administration of the statute is the responsibility of a state agency such as a public employee relations board (PERB) or a public employee relations commission (PERC). There are three basic models used in the states: **binding arbitration**, **meet and confer**, and bargaining-not-required.[8] Table 14.1 shows the use of these models in the various states.

The *binding arbitration* model is used in 24 states and the District of Columbia. Public employees are given the right to bargain with their employers. If the bargaining reaches an impasse, the matter is submitted to a neutral arbitrator, who decides what the terms and conditions of the new collective bargaining agreement will be.[9]

Only three states use the *meet-and-confer* model, which grants very few rights to public employees. As with the binding arbitration model, criminal justice employees in meet-and-confer states have the right to organize and to select their own bargaining representatives.[10] When an impasse is reached, however, employees are at a distinct disadvantage. Their only legal choices are to accept the employer's best offer, try to influence the offer through political tactics (such as appeals for public support), or take some permissible job action.[11]

The 22 states that follow the *bargaining-not-required* model either do not statutorily require or do not allow collective bargaining by public employees.[12] In the majority of these states, laws permitting public employees to engage in collective bargaining have not been passed.

States with collective bargaining must also address the issue of whether an individual employee must be a member of a union that represents his or her class of employees in a particular organization. In a "closed shop," employees must be dues-paying members or they will be terminated by the employer. "Open" shops, conversely, allow employees a choice of whether to join, even though the union has an obligation to represent them.

Organizing for Collective Bargaining

If collective bargaining is legally established, the process of setting up a bargaining relationship is as follows: First, a union will begin an organizing drive seeking to get a majority of the class(es) of employees it wants to represent to sign authorization cards. At this point, agency administrators may attempt to convince employees that they are better off without the union. Questions may also arise, such as whether certain employees (e.g., police or prison lieutenants) are part of management and therefore ineligible for union representation.

| TABLE 14.1 | State Collective Bargaining Laws Governing Law Enforcement Officers |

State	Binding Arbitration Model	Meet and Confer Model	Bargaining Not Required Model
Alabama			X
Alaska	X		
Arizona			X
Arkansas			X
California	X		
Colorado			X
Connecticut	X		
Delaware	X		
District of Columbia	X		
Florida		X	
Georgia			X
Hawaii	X		
Idaho			X
Illinois	X		
Indiana			X
Iowa	X		
Kansas	X		
Kentucky			X
Louisiana			X
Maine	X		
Maryland			X
Massachusetts		X	
Michigan	X		
Minnesota	X		
Mississippi			X
Missouri			X
Montana	X		
Nebraska			X
Nevada	X		
New Hampshire	X		
New Jersey	X		
New Mexico	X		
New York	X		
North Carolina			X
North Dakota			X

TABLE 14.1	(Continued)		
State	**Binding Arbitration Model**	**Meet and Confer Model**	**Bargaining Not Required Model**
Ohio	X		
Oklahoma	X		
Oregon	X		
Pennsylvania	X		
Rhode Island			X
South Carolina			X
South Dakota			X
Tennessee			X
Texas			X
Utah			X
Vermont			X
Virginia			X
Washington			X
West Virginia			X
Wisconsin			X
Wyoming			X

Source: From Will Aitchison, *The Rights of Law Enforcement Officers,* 5th ed. © 2004 Will Aitchison. Reprinted by permission.

Once a majority ("50 percent plus one" of the eligible employees) have signed cards, the union notifies the criminal justice agency. If management believes that the union has obtained a majority legitimately, it will recognize the union as the bargaining agent of the employees it has sought to represent. Once recognized by the employer, the union will petition the PERB or other body responsible for administering the legislation for certification.

Negotiating

Figure 14.1 depicts a typical configuration of the union and management bargaining teams. Positions shown in the broken-line boxes typically serve in a support role and may or may not actually partake in the bargaining. Management's labor relations manager (lead negotiator) is often an attorney assigned to the human resources department, reporting to the city manager or assistant city manager and representing the city in grievances and arbitration matters; management's chief negotiator may also be the director of labor relations or human resources director for the unit of government involved or a professional labor relations specialist. Similarly, the union's chief negotiator normally is not a member of the organization involved; rather, he or she will be a specialist who is brought in to represent the union's position and to provide greater experience, expertise, objectivity, and autonomy. The union's chief negotiator may be accompanied by some people who have conducted surveys on wages and benefits, trends in the consumer price index, and so on.[13]

In the minds of many chief executives, the agency administrator should NOT appear at the bargaining table; it is difficult for the chief executive to represent management one day and then

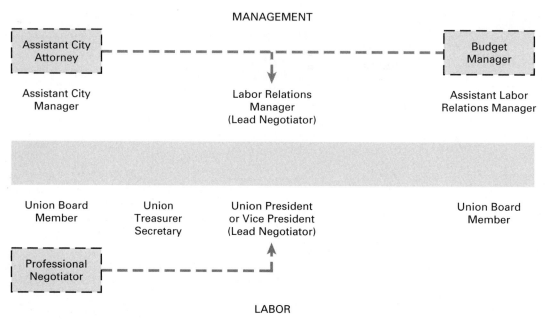

FIGURE 14.1 Union and Management Collective Bargaining Teams

Source: By permission of Jerry Hoover, Chief of Police, Reno, Nevada.

return to work among the employees the next. Rather, management is represented by a key member of the command staff having the executive's confidence.

The issues, and the way in which they are presented, will impact how the negotiations will go. The purpose of bargaining is to produce a bilateral written agreement that will bind both parties during the lifetime of the agreement. Management normally prefers a narrow scope of negotiations because it means less shared power; conversely, the union will opt for the widest possible scope. The number of negotiating sessions may run from one to several dozen, lasting from a few minutes to 10 or more hours, depending on how close or far apart union and management are when they begin to meet face to face.

In the initial session, the chief negotiator for each party will make an opening statement. Management's representative will often go first, touching on general themes such as the need for patience and the obligation to bargain in good faith. The union's negotiator will generally follow, outlining what the union seeks to achieve under the terms of the new contract. Ground rules for the bargaining may then be reviewed, modified, or developed. The attention then shifts to the terms of the contract that the union is proposing. Both sides need to understand what it is they are attempting to commit each other to. Ultimately, unless a total impasse is reached, agreement will be obtained on the terms of a new contract. The union's membership will vote on the contract as whole. If approved by the membership, the contract then goes before the necessary government officials and bodies for approval.[14]

In the Event of an Impasse . . .

Even parties bargaining in good faith may not be able to resolve their differences by themselves, and an impasse may result. In such cases, a neutral third party may be introduced to facilitate, suggest, or compel an agreement. Three major forms of impasse resolution are mediation, fact finding, and arbitration.

- **Mediation** occurs when a third party, called the mediator, comes in to help the adversaries with the negotiations.[15] This person may be a professional mediator or someone else in whom both parties have confidence. In most states, mediation may be requested by either labor or management. The mediator's task is to build agreement about the issues involved by reopening communications between the two sides. The mediator cannot compel an agreement, so an advantage of the process is that it preserves collective bargaining by maintaining the decision-making power in the hands of the involved parties.[16]

- **Fact finding** primarily involves the interpretation of facts and the determination of what weight to attach to them. Appointed in the same way as mediators, fact finders also do not have the means to impose a settlement of the dispute. Fact finders may sit alone or as part of a panel normally consisting of three people. The fact-finding hearing is quasi-judicial, although less strict rules of evidence are applied. Both labor and management may be represented by legal counsel, and verbatim transcripts are commonly made. In a majority of cases, the fact finder's recommendations will be made public at some point.[17]

- **Arbitration** is similar to fact finding but differs in that the "end product of arbitration is a final and binding decision that sets the terms of the settlement and with which the parties are legally required to comply."[18] Arbitration may be voluntary or compulsory. It is compulsory when mandated by state law and is binding on the parties even if one of them is unwilling to comply. It is voluntary when the parties undertake of their own volition to use the procedure. Even when entered into voluntarily, arbitration is compulsory and binding on the parties who have agreed to it.

The establishment of a working agreement between labor and management can also become the basis for strife. Questions can arise concerning the interpretation and application of the document and its various clauses, and grievances (discussed earlier) may arise. The sequence of grievance steps will be spelled out in the collective bargaining agreement and typically include the following five steps: (1) The employee presents the grievance to the immediate supervisor; and, if satisfaction is not achieved, (2) a written grievance is presented to the division commander, then (3) to the chief executive officer, then (4) to the city or county manager, and, finally, (5) to an arbiter, selected according to the rules of the American Arbitration Association.[19]

The burden of proof is on the grieving party, except in disciplinary cases, when it is always on the employer. The parties may be represented by counsel at the hearing, and the format will include opening statements by each side, examination and cross-examination of any witnesses, and closing arguments in the reverse order of which opening arguments were made.[20]

Job Actions

A **job action** is an activity by employees to express their dissatisfaction with a particular person, event, or condition or to attempt to influence the outcome of some matter pending before decision makers. Employees seek to create pressure that may shift the course of events to a position more favorable or acceptable to them.[21] Job actions are of four types: the vote of confidence, work slowdowns, work speedups, and work stoppages.

- *Vote of confidence.* This job action is used sparingly; a vote of no confidence signals employees' collective displeasure with the chief administrator of the agency. Although such votes have no legal standing, they may have high impact as a result of the resulting publicity.

- *Work slowdowns.* Employees continue to work during a slowdown, but they do so at a leisurely pace, causing productivity to fall. As productivity declines, the unit of government is pressured to resume normal work production; for example, a police department may urge officers to issue more citations so revenues are not lost. Citizens may complain to politicians to "get this thing settled."[22]
- *Work speedups.* These involve accelerated activity in the level of services and can foster considerable public resentment. For example, a police department may conduct a "ticket blizzard" to protest a low pay increase, pressure governmental leaders to make more concessions at the bargaining table, or abandon some policy change that affects their working conditions.
- *Work stoppages.* These constitute the most severe job action. The ultimate work stoppage is the strike, or withholding of all employees' services. This tactic is most often used by labor to force management back to the bargaining table when negotiations have reached an impasse. Criminal justice employee strikes are now rare, however. Short of a strike by all employees are briefer work stoppages, known in policing as "blue flu," that last only a few days.

LABOR RELATIONS IN CRIMINAL JUSTICE

In 1971, Tucson police legal advisor John H. Burpo authored a book entitled *The Police Labor Movement: Problems and Perspectives*,[23] In the book's Preface, Burpo stated that, "Police labor problems, of which unionization is but one facet, will be the major administrative headache facing the police service during the next decade."[24]

Burpo was certainly correct in that assessment. However, many of today's police, courts, and corrections administrators would argue that he was off by nearly a half century in his view of unionization as posing an "administrative headache" for a decade. Unions obviously are here to stay—and have become involved in all manner of issues, including not only wages and benefits but also working conditions, promotions, staffing levels, bans on smoking in public, even the kinds of vehicles officers drive. And they have contributed much to the rights and privileges that criminal justice employees enjoy and were discussed in Chapter 13.

In this chapter section, we discuss the history, nature, and principles of collective bargaining in criminal justice organizations. Included is a discussion of how criminal justice administrators must "navigate the waters" of unionization in order to coexist with them in today's criminal-justice environment.

The Movement Begins: Policing Then and Now

EARLY CAMPAIGNS   The first campaign to organize the police started shortly after World War I, when the American Federation of Labor (AFL) reversed a long-standing policy and issued charters to police unions in Boston, Washington, DC, and about 30 other cities. Many police officers were suffering from the rapid inflation following the outbreak of the war and believed that unions could obtain long-overdue pay raises for them. Capitalizing on their sentiments, the fledgling unions signed up about 60 percent of all officers in Washington, DC, 75 percent in Boston, and a similar proportion in other cities.[25]

The unions' success was short-lived, however. The Boston police commissioner refused to recognize the union, forbade officers to join it, and filed charges against several union officials. Shortly thereafter, on September 9, 1919, the Boston police initiated their now-famous 3-day strike, leading to major riots and a furor against the police all across the nation; 9 rioters were killed and 23 were seriously injured. During the strike, Massachusetts Governor Calvin Coolidge stated, "There is no right to strike against the public safety by anybody, anywhere, anytime."

During World War II, however, the unionization effort was reignited. Unions issued charters to a few dozen locals all over the country and sent in organizers to help enlist the rank and file. Most police chiefs continued speaking out against unionization, but their subordinates were moved by the thousands to join, sensing the advantage in having unions press for higher wages and benefits.[26] In a series of rulings, however, the courts upheld the right of police authorities to ban police unions.

The unions were survived in the early 1950s by many benevolent and fraternal organizations of police. Some were patrolmen's benevolent associations (PBAs), like those formed in New York City, Chicago, and Washington, DC; others were fraternal orders of police (FOPs). During the late 1950s and early 1960s, a new group of rank-and-file association leaders came into power that was more vocal in articulating their demands. Soon, a majority of the rank-and-file vocally supported higher salaries and pensions, free legal aid, low-cost insurance, and other services and benefits. Beginning with the granting of public-sector collective bargaining rights in Wisconsin in 1959, rank-and-file organizations were legally able to insist that their administrators sit down at the bargaining table.[27]

Today labor relations remain a critical topic in policing, and these relations have a significant impact on the administration of police departments and individual units. A virtual maze of affiliations dots the police labor landscape, with the two largest unions—the Fraternal Order of Police and the National Association of Police Organizations—reporting a combined membership of nearly 570,000 sworn officers.[28] Police unions are strongest in the Northeast, Midwest, and West and tend to play a greater role in larger departments. Unions in larger departments tend to have larger staffs working full-time to advance union causes; they often have lobbyists who work the political system for union purposes; and they frequently are politically active, often supporting particular candidates and contributing to campaigns. Thus, police unions in many jurisdictions are a formidable force with which to be reckoned.

Once unions are recognized in a jurisdiction, the relationship between the department and the governmental entity is codified in a contract or memorandum of understanding. The contract specifies the rights and privileges of employees, and it places restrictions on the political entity and police administrators. In effect, the contract has the force of law. The contract can only be changed via renegotiations, which occur generally on a 3-year cycle or by mutual agreement on the part of the union and police management. When there is a dispute over the interpretation of the contract or its administration, the question is sorted out by an arbitrator or sometimes in the courts.[29]

Unions can obviously have a major impact on police departments. Their activities and the contract not only affect police administrators but also place limitations or restrictions on supervisors and managers. Thus, it is important for supervisors and managers to understand the collective bargaining process, the implications of the contract, and how supervisors and managers negotiate tasks and responsibilities within the confines of the contract.

Corrections Follows the Precedent

Correctional officers (COs) were probably the last group of public workers to organize. After authorization of collective bargaining in the 1960s and 1970s, correctional administrators feared that unionization would diminish management authority and undermine staff discipline and prison security. Over the years that collective bargaining has been in place for correctional agencies, however, the early fears have not materialized, and the benefits of shared governance by line staff and management have led to better decisions and higher morale. As with the police, **negotiations** usually involve pay and benefits for correctional employees, including seniority rights, how staff members are selected for overtime, the type of clothing provided to staff by the agency, educational programs, and so on. After a contract is negotiated, each prison or community corrections office must implement and administer it. When disputes about the true meaning of a contract arise, management can make a decision, and the union can file a grievance to argue against it.[30]

Collective bargaining is now well entrenched in prison and other correctional agency operations, and it will continue to have an impact on policy and practice. There remains some disagreement, however, concerning its implications. Some argue that sharing of power in a correctional setting benefits all parties, and that unions are a powerful voice to the legislature for increases in staffing and budgets. Others maintain that collective bargaining has resulted in a clear distinction between line staff and management, with managers no longer looking out for subordinates because union leadership promotes an adversarial relationship. As James Jacobs and Norma Crotty suggested, collective bargaining "has redefined the prison organization in adversary terms so that wardens are bosses and complaints are grievances."[31]

A major issue with corrections unions involves the right to strike. One can only imagine the chaos that would occur if COs strike. Such unlawful strikes have occurred. The most infamous strike action was in New York State in 1979, when 7,000 correctional workers simultaneously struck the state's 33 prisons. A court found the union in violation of the law, heavily fined the union for the failure of its members to return to work, and jailed union leaders for contempt of court.[32] The strike ended 17 days after it began; the corrections officers gained very few concessions, and the salary gains did not offset the fines imposed on the strikers.[33]

Finally, another concern regarding collective bargaining is its impact on rehabilitation. Some argue that prison unions, stressing staff safety issues, may impede the institution's efforts toward rehabilitation, while also pointing out that rehabilitative programs that improve inmate morale, reduce idleness, and enhance security result in benefits to the staff who work in prison.[34]

Overall, much like the unionization of the police, it is the attitude of agency administrators and union leaders and the relationships that develop that set the direction of the impact. If both parties communicate with and listen to each other, show mutual respect, and are reasonable in their positions, collective bargaining can benefit corrections. If, however, the parties let issues get personal and become overly adversarial, corrections and collective bargaining will experience many negative outcomes.[35]

Unionization in the Courts

The movement to exercise the right to bargain collectively, especially when compared with law enforcement and corrections, has been rare in the courts, occurring on a random, localized basis; however, unified court systems exist in which court personnel are organized statewide, as in Hawaii. Many states adhere generally to model legislation on public employee relation commissions, which provide mediation and fact-finding services and make determinations of unfair labor practices. On occasion, these commissions make decisions that greatly affect the management authority of the judiciary over its personnel.

When a collective bargaining unit exists in a court system, the process has all the basic elements found in other systems: (1) recognition (the employing court recognizes that henceforth employees will be represented by their chosen agent); (2) negotiation (there are established methods for arriving at collective bargaining agreements, breaking deadlocks, ratifying contracts, and so on); and (3) contract administration (the day-to-day management of a court is accomplished within the framework of the labor contract).[36]

IN SUM: "NAVIGATING THE WATERS" OF UNIONIZATION

It should now be evident from the foregoing discussions that collective bargaining is now under close scrutiny and that there is inherent conflict between labor and management. Government officials expect management to represent its interests well; conversely, there is an expectation by labor that the union will be a strong advocate for its membership. However, when their relationship becomes antagonistic, everyone suffers; the challenge is to keep that conflict within a healthy range.[37] Therefore, the four principles of collective bargaining—communication, cooperation, trust, and respect—are of utmost importance. As a general rule, administrators who actively engage the union will accomplish far more than those who employ hostile isolation.[38] Furthermore, it is generally *not* fruitful for the following to occur:

- Meetings being held in the administrator's office, with management sitting at the head of the table. Rather, informal settings—or, at the very least, a generic conference room setting—communicates a great deal.
- "Secret deals" being struck. Perhaps such an arrangement might occasionally be struck, but it certainly should be done very carefully, and only rarely.
- Blending issues concerning economics with agency management. Management should not be involved in negotiations that concern limits on wages and benefits. Management's position should simply be a neutral one, that "My employees deserve as much money as the jurisdiction can possibly afford to give them." Management needs to excuse themselves when the management team caucuses on economic issues.[39]

Following are some other potential pitfalls to avoid, especially when conflicts, crises, or controversies occur, per Ronald G. DeLord:[40]

1. *Assuming traditional labor-management roles:* Management should avoid entering every contract negotiation fighting to gain control over discipline and working conditions; nor should the union seek only higher pay and benefits. Rather, they should develop a shared vision of community safety—and then realize that the methods used to gain that vision are negotiable.

2. *Rushing to judgment:* If an employee is, say, being investigated for an alleged brutality complaint caught on video, both sides should be patient and let the criminal and internal affairs investigators complete their jobs. The media always wants an immediate response from management and the union. There is no requirement that either party respond to questions quickly; sometimes a "no comment until all the facts are in" statement will suffice.

3. *Ignoring or not recognizing the pressures on management or union leaders during a crisis or controversy:* During a high-profile incident, there may be pressure from union members to take certain public positions that may appear confrontational to management, or vice versa. Although some statements or actions are required as a part of the role each has to play, communication, cooperation, respect, and trust become valuable to avoiding unnecessary conflicts.

4. *Defending the indefensible:* Assume that a high-ranking criminal justice official is caught drinking while driving and the agency administrator deems a minor suspension to be

appropriate. Or, an employee is arrested for the same offense and the union defends his or her actions as caused by "stress of the job." When such occurrences arise, union and management must be truthful—and be aware that the public might see such "discipline" as too lenient and preferential.

5. *Forgetting that elected officials do not like to make waves, and all battles are won and lost in the court of public opinion:* Just about everything that happens in a criminal justice agency is open to the public, and any conflict between management and the union during a crisis or controversy will be played out the media. Information leaks occur during high-profile incidents, and management and unions need to realize that all of their words and actions will be brought to light. Efforts by management and the union to resolve conflicts before they escalate will go a long way toward preventing a public collision.

6. *Making an end run:* When management goes around the union to communicate with or to encourage the rank-and-file to support or oppose an issue, a union backlash is sure to come. The union has a role to play, and its leadership was elected to speak for the members on labor-related issues. The same holds true for the union when it decides to make an end run to the city manager or to elected officials.

CIVIL LIABILITY: A PRIMER

Definitions and Legal Foundation

Criminal justice administrators—particularly those working in law enforcement and corrections—certainly understand, and quite possibly have learned from actual experience about, the specter of civil liability that looms over their every workday. These administrators very likely reflect their experiences and concerns with litigation in their training, policies and procedures, general orders, and so on.

They also understand that, with the possible exception of professionals working in the medical field, no group of workers is more susceptible to litigation and liability than police and corrections employees. Frequently thrust into confrontational situations, and given the complex nature of their work and its requisite training needs, they will from time to time act in a manner that evokes public scrutiny and complaints. As we will see, the price of failure among public servants can be quite high in both human and financial terms. In addition, some police officers and COs are overzealous and even brutal in their work; they may intentionally or otherwise violate the rights of the citizens they are sworn to protect, detain, or supervise. For these inappropriate actions, the public has become quick to file suit for damages for what are perceived to be egregious actions.

Next, we examine the kinds of inappropriate and negligent behaviors that can lead to civil liability and even incarceration for police and corrections personnel in the justice system; included is a discussion of a major legislative tool that citizens used to seek redress when such activities occur: Title 42, U.S. Code, Section 1983.

Torts and Negligence

It is important to have a basic understanding of tort liability. A **tort** is the infliction of some injury on one person by another. Three categories of torts generally cover most of the lawsuits filed against criminal justice practitioners: negligence, intentional torts, and constitutional torts.

Negligence can arise when a criminal justice employee's conduct creates a danger to others. In other words, the employee did not conduct his or her affairs in a manner that avoids subjecting others to a risk of harm and may be held liable for the injuries caused to others.[41]

Intentional torts occur when an employee engages in a voluntary act that is quite likely to result in injury to another; examples are assault and battery, false arrest and imprisonment, malicious prosecution, and abuse of process.

Constitutional torts involve employees' duty to recognize and uphold the constitutional rights, privileges, and immunities of others; violations of these guarantees may subject the employee to a civil suit, most frequently brought in federal court under 42 U.S. Code Section 1983, discussed below.[42]

Assault, battery, false imprisonment, false arrest, invasion of privacy, negligence, defamation, and malicious prosecution are examples of torts that are commonly brought against police officers.[43] False arrest is the arrest of a person without probable cause. False imprisonment is the intentional illegal detention of a person not only in jail but also in any confinement to a specified area. For example, the police may fail to release an arrested person after a proper bail or bond has been posted, may delay the arraignment of an arrested person unreasonably, or may fail to release a prisoner after they no longer have authority to hold him or her.[44]

A single act may also be a crime as well as a tort. If Officer Smith, in an unprovoked attack, injures Jones, the state will attempt to punish Smith in a *criminal* action by sending him to jail or prison, fining him, or both. The state would have the burden of proof at a criminal trial, having to prove Smith guilty "beyond a reasonable doubt." Furthermore, Jones may sue Smith for money damages in a *civil* action for the personal injury he suffered. In this civil suit, Jones would have the burden of proving that Smith's acts were tortious by a "preponderance of the evidence"— a lower standard than that in a criminal court and thus easier to satisfy.

Section 1983 Legislation

Following the Civil War and in reaction to the activities of the Ku Klux Klan, Congress enacted the Ku Klux Klan Act of 1871, later codified as **Title 42, U.S. Code, Section 1983**. It states:

> Every person who, under color of any statute, ordinance, regulation, custom, or usage of any State or Territory, subjects, or causes to be subjected, any citizen of the United States or any other person within the jurisdiction thereof to the deprivation of any rights, privileges, or immunities secured by the Constitution and laws, shall be liable to the party injured in an action at law, suit in equity, or other proper proceeding for redress.

This legislation was intended to provide civil rights protection to all "persons" protected under the act when a defendant acted "under color of law" (misused power of office) and provided an avenue to the federal courts for relief of alleged civil rights violations. We will see how Section 1983 can be used against the police.

Lawsuits against the Police Generally

A police executive once commented to the author that "The decision-making process is not directed so much by the question 'Is it right or wrong?' but rather 'How much will it cost us if we're sued?'"

While that may be a bit overstated, the specter of lawsuits certainly looms large over police executives, their supervisors and officers, and their unit of government. Next, we focus on this omnipresent facet of contemporary police administration.

The police are not irrationally paranoid when it comes to their being sued: between 1980 and 2005, federal court decisions involving lawsuits against the police nearly tripled; and, according to one study, the police are currently faced with more than 30,000 civil actions annually.[45]

The cost of civil suits against police can be quite high. For example, according to one study, from 1990 to 1999, the City of Los Angeles paid more than $67.8 million in judgments and settlements in 80 lawsuits involving the use of excessive force and police officer involvement in sexual assault, sexual abuse, molestation, and domestic violence; this amount does not include the millions of dollars the city spent in defending against these civil suits, nor does it cover lawsuits stemming from the Rampart Division scandal of the late 1990s[46] (where a former LAPD officer testified that he and other officers routinely lied in court, stole and resold drugs, beat handcuffed suspects in the police station, and killed unarmed people and then planted guns and drugs on them; dozens of lawsuits were filed).[47] Facing potential judgments amounting to millions of dollars, municipalities are forced to secure liability insurance to protect against civil litigation—insurance that is very expensive. But such expenditures are necessary; the cost of an average jury award of liability against a municipality is reported to be about $2 million.[48] To prevent such large judgments, many cities and their insurers attempt to settle many claims of police misconduct out of court, as opposed to having a jury give the plaintiff(s) a large award.

Such litigation—although costly in terms of both money and police morale—may have beneficial effects, however. Proponents of civil liabilities argue that these lawsuits keep the police accountable, give real meaning to citizens' rights, foster better police training, and force the police agencies to correct any deficiencies and review all policies, practices, and customs.[49]

Liability of Police Leadership

Another trend is for such litigants to cast a wide net in their lawsuits, suing not only the principal actors in the incident but also agency administrators and supervisors as well; this breadth of suing represents the notion of *vicarious liability* or the doctrine of *respondeat superior,* an old legal maxim meaning "let the master answer." In sum, an employer can be found liable in certain instances for wrongful acts of the employee.

Using Section 1983, litigants often allege inadequate hiring and/or training of personnel by police leadership, or that they knew, or should have known, of the misconduct of their officers yet failed to take corrective action and prevent future harm. An example is the case of *Brandon v. Allen,*[50] in which two teenagers parked in a lovers' lane were approached by an off-duty police officer, Allen, who showed his police identification and demanded that the male exit the car. Allen struck the young man with his fist, stabbed him with a knife, and then attempted to break into the car where the young woman was seated. The young man was able to reenter the car and manage an escape. As the two teenagers sped off, Allen fired a shot at them with his revolver. The shattered windshield glass severely injured the youths to the point that they required plastic surgery. Allen was convicted of criminal charges, and the police chief was also sued under Section 1983. The plaintiffs charged that the chief and others knew of Allen's reputation as an unstable officer; none of the other police officers wished to ride in a patrol car with him. At least two formal charges of misconduct had been filed previously, yet the chief failed to take any remedial action or even to review the disciplinary records of officers when he became chief. The court called this behavior "unjustified inaction," held the police department liable, and allowed the plaintiffs damages. The U.S. Supreme Court upheld this judgment.[51]

Police supervisors have also been found liable for injuries arising out of an official policy or custom of their department. Injuries resulting from a chief's verbal or written support of heavy-handed behavior resulting in the use of excessive force by officers have resulted in such liability.[52]

Whereas Section 1983 is a civil action, **Title 18, U.S. Code, Section 242**, makes it a *criminal* offense for any person acting under color of law to violate another's civil rights. Section 242 not only applies to police officers but also to the misconduct of public officials and to the prosecution of judges, bail bond agents, public defenders, and even prosecutors. An example of the use of Section 242 with law enforcement officers is the murder of a drug courier by two U.S. customs agents while the agents were assigned to the San Juan International Airport. The courier flew to Puerto Rico to deposit approximately $700,000 in cash and checks. He was last seen being interviewed by the two customs agents in the airport; 10 days later, his body was discovered in a Puerto Rican rain forest. An investigation revealed that the agents had lured the victim away from the airport and had murdered him for his money, later disposing of the body. They were convicted under Section 242 and related federal statutes, and each agent was sentenced to a prison term of 120 years.[53]

Duty of Care and Failure to Protect

The *public duty doctrine* is derived from common law and holds that police have a duty to protect the general public where they have a "special relationship"; this exists, for example, where the officer knows or has reason to know the likelihood of harm to someone if he or she fails to do his or her duty, and is thus defined by the circumstances surrounding an injury or damage. A special relationship can be based on:

1. whether the officer could have foreseen that he or she was expected to take action in a given situation to prevent injury[54] (such as where a police officer released from his custody an intoxicated pedestrian near a busy highway)
2. departmental policy or guidelines that prohibit a certain course of action[55] (such as a case where an officer released a drunk driver who then killed another driver, and the police department had a standard operating procedure manual that mandated that an intoxicated individual likely to do physical injury to himself or others "*will* be taken into protective custody")
3. the spatial and temporal proximity of the defendant–officer behavior to the injury damage[56] (an example is where an individual was arrested for drunk driving, taken into custody, and found to have a high blood alcohol level, was released 3 hours later, and then had a fatal car accident)

Under the general heading of **duty of care** are three related concepts: **proximate cause**, persons in custody, and safe facilities.

a. *Proximate cause* is established by asking the question "But for the officer's conduct, would the plaintiff have sustained the injury or damage?" If the answer to this question is no, then proximate cause is established, and the officer can be held liable for the damage or injury. An example is where an officer is involved in a high-speed chase and the offending driver strikes an innocent third party. Generally, if the officer was not acting in a negligent fashion and did not cause the injury, there would be no liability on the officer's part.[57] Proximate cause may also be found in such cases as one where an officer leaves the scene of an accident aware of dangerous conditions (e.g., spilled oil, smoke, vehicle debris, stray animals) without giving proper warning to motorists.[58]

b. Courts generally confer on police executives a duty of care for *persons in their custody*[59] to ensure that reasonable precautions are taken to keep detainees free from harm, to render medical assistance when necessary, and to treat detainees humanely.[60] A duty is also owed to persons in custody and while outside a jail setting, such as when arresting or transporting prisoners and mental patients, as well as in booking or interrogation areas.[61] Courts have also held that if a prisoner's suicide is "reasonably foreseeable," the jailer owes the prisoner a duty of care to help prevent that suicide.

c. A related area concerns administrators' *need to provide safe facilities.* For example, a Detroit jail's holding cell was constructed so that it did not allow officers to observe detainees' movements; there were no electronic monitoring devices for observing detainees or detoxification cells, as required under state policy. Therefore, following a suicide in this facility, the court concluded that these conditions constituted building defects and were the proximate cause of the decedent's death.[62]

Failure to protect as a form of negligence may occur if a police officer fails to protect a person from a known and foreseeable danger. These claims most often involve battered women, but other circumstances can also create a duty to protect people from crime. Informants, witnesses, and other people who are dependent on the police can be a source of police liability if officers fail to take reasonable action to prevent victimization. The officer's conduct cannot place a person in peril or demonstrate deliberate indifference to his or her safety. In one case, for example, a man became seriously ill on his porch and two police officers arrived, cancelled the request for paramedics, broke the lock and door jam on the front door of his residence, moved him inside the house, locked the door, and left. The next day, family members found the man dead inside the house as a result of respiratory failure. His mother sued under Section 1983, and the court found that the officers' conduct clearly had placed him in a more dangerous position than the one in which they found him.[63] Another example is where the Green Bay, Wisconsin, police department released the tape of a phone call from an informant, which led to the informant's death.[64]

Vehicle Pursuits

Basically, with regard to operation of their vehicles, officers are afforded *no* special privileges or immunities.[65] While driving in nonemergency situations, officers do not have immunity for their negligence or recklessness and are held to the same standard of conduct as private citizens. When responding to emergency situations, however, officers are governed by statutes covering emergency vehicles.[66] In such circumstances, most jurisdictions afford the police limited immunity for violations of traffic laws; in other words, they are accorded some protections and privileges not given to private citizens, and are permitted to take greater risks that would amount to negligence if taken by citizens.[67]

In 2007, the U.S. Supreme Court issued a major decision concerning the proper amount of force the police may use during high-speed vehicle pursuits. The fundamental question was whether or not the serious danger created by the fleeing motorist justifies the use of deadly force to eliminate the threat; in other words, was the level of force used proportionate to the threat of reckless and dangerous driving? The incident involved Harris, a 19-year-old Georgia youth driving at speeds of up to 90 miles per hour and covering 9 miles in 6 minutes with a deputy sheriff in pursuit. The chase ended in a violent crash that left the youth a quadriplegic; his lawyers argued that the Fourth Amendment protects against the use of such excessive force and high-speed drivers having their cars rammed by police (by intentionally stopping a fleeing vehicle in such a manner, a "seizure" occurs for Fourth Amendment purposes). Conversely, the deputy sheriff's lawyers argued that such drivers pose an escalating danger to the public and must be stopped to defuse the danger (the deputy's supervisor had authorized the use of the Precision Immobilization Technique [PIT], whereby the officer uses the patrol vehicle to cause the speeder's car to spin out; PIT was not used in the Harris chase, however). The Court's 8–1 opinion, authored by Justice Antonin Scalia, held that "A police officer's attempt to terminate a dangerous high-speed car chase that threatens the lives of innocent bystanders does not violate the Fourth Amendment, even when it places the fleeing motorist at risk of serious injury or death."[68]

Liability of Corrections Personnel

The liability of corrections workers often centers on their lack of due care for persons in their custody. This responsibility concerns primarily police officers and civilians responsible for inmates in local jails.

When an inmate commits suicide while in custody, police agencies are frequently—and often successfully—sued in state court under negligence and wrongful death claims. The standard used by the courts is whether the agency's act or failure to act created an unusual risk to an inmate. A "special duty" of care exists for police officers to protect inmates suffering from mental disorders and those who are impaired by drugs or alcohol. Foreseeability—the reasonable anticipation that injury or damage may occur—may be found when inmates make statements of intent to commit suicide, have a history of mental illness, are in a vulnerable emotional state, or are at a high level of intoxication or drug dependence.[69]

Suicides are not uncommon among jail inmates; each year, more than 300 jail inmates take their own lives.[70] Inmate suicide rates have also been found to be higher in small jails and highest in small jails with lower population densities.[71] State courts generally recognize that police officials have a duty of care for persons in their custody.[72] Thus, jail administrators are ultimately responsible for taking reasonable precautions to ensure the health and safety of persons in their custody; they must protect inmates from harm, render medical assistance when necessary, and treat inmates humanely.[73]

Several court decisions have helped to establish the duties and guidelines for jail employees concerning the care of their charges. An intoxicated inmate in possession of cigarettes and matches started a fire that resulted in his death; the court stated that "the prisoner may have been voluntarily drunk, but he was not in the cell voluntarily . . . [he] was helpless and the officer knew there was a means of harm on his person." The court concluded that the police administration owed a greater duty of care to such an arrestee.[74] Emotionally disturbed arrestees can also create a greater duty for jail personnel. In an Alaskan case, a woman had been arrested for intoxication in a hotel and had trouble talking, standing, and walking; her blood alcohol content was 0.26 percent. Two and a half hours after her incarceration, officers found her hanging by her sweater from mesh wiring in the cell. The Alaska Supreme Court said that the officers knew she was depressed and that in the past few months, one of her sons had been burned to death, another son had been stabbed to death, and her mother had died. Thus, the court believed that the officers should have anticipated her suicide.[75]

In New Mexico, a 17-year-old boy was arrested for armed robbery; he later told his mother that he would kill himself rather than go to prison and subsequently tried to cut his wrists with an aluminum can top. The assistant chief executive ordered the officers to watch him, but he was found dead by hanging the following morning. The state supreme court held that the knowledge officers possess is an important factor in determining liability and negligence in such cases.[76] In a New Jersey case in which a young man arrested for intoxication was put in a holding cell but officers failed to remove the leather belt that he used to take his life, the court found that the officers' conduct could have been a "substantial" factor in his death.[77]

As mentioned earlier, courts have also found the design of detention facilities to be a source of negligence—where a Detroit holding cell limited officers' ability to observe inmates' movements, and no detoxification cell or electronic monitoring devices were used; a suicide in such circumstances may constitute a "building defect" and a finding of proximate cause.[78] In another incident, an intoxicated college student was placed in a holding cell at the school's public safety building. Forty minutes later, officers found him hanging from an overhead heating device by a noose fashioned from his socks and belt. The court found the university liable for operating a defective building and awarded his parents $650,000.[79]

The behavior of jail personnel *after* a suicide or attempted suicide may also indicate a breach of duty. Officers are expected to give all possible aid to an inmate who is injured or has attempted suicide. Thus, when officers found an inmate slumped in a chair with his belt around his neck and left him in that position instead of trying to revive him or call for medical assistance, the court ruled that this behavior established a causal link between the officers' inaction and the boy's death.[80]

It is clear that correctional administrators must ensure that their organizations are cognizant of their legal responsibilities and their expanded custodial role in dealing with their detainees.

DISCIPLINARY POLICIES AND PRACTICES

Maintaining the Public Trust

The public's trust and respect are precious commodities and can be quickly lost with improper behavior by criminal justice employees and the improper handling of an allegation of misconduct. Serving communities professionally and with integrity should be the goal of every agency and its employees to ensure that trust and respect are maintained. The public expects that criminal justice agencies will make every effort to identify and correct problems and respond to citizens' complaints in a judicious, consistent, fair, and equitable manner.

One of the most important responsibilities of criminal justice agencies is implementing sound disciplinary policies and practices and responding to employee misconduct or performance problems at an early stage.

Employee misconduct and violations of departmental policy are the two principal areas in which discipline is involved.[81] Employee misconduct includes those acts that harm the public, including corruption, harassment, brutality, and civil rights violations. Violations of policy may involve a broad range of issues, including substance abuse and insubordination, as well as minor violations of dress and lack of punctuality.

Due Process Requirements

The well-established, minimum due process requirements for discharging public employees include that employees must:

1. be afforded a public hearing
2. be present during the presentation of evidence against them and have an opportunity to cross-examine their superiors
3. have an opportunity to present witnesses and other evidence concerning their side of the controversy
4. be permitted to be represented by counsel
5. have an impartial referee or hearing officer presiding
6. have a decision made based on the weight of the evidence introduced during the hearing

Such protections apply to any disciplinary action that can significantly affect a criminal justice employee's reputation and/or future chances for special assignment or promotion. A disciplinary hearing that might result in only a reprimand or short suspension may involve fewer procedural protections than one that could result in more severe sanctions.[82]

When a particular disciplinary action does not include termination or suspension, however, it may still be subject to due process considerations. An example is a Chicago case involving a police officer who was transferred from the Neighborhood Relations Division to less desirable working conditions in the patrol division, with no loss in pay or benefits. The court found that the officer's First Amendment free speech rights were violated because his de facto demotion was in retaliation for his political activities (inviting political opponents of the mayor to a civic function and in retaliation for a speech given there that criticized the police department) and that he was thus entitled to civil damages. The court stated that "Certainly a demotion can be as detrimental to an employee as denial of a promotion."[83]

On the contrary, no due process protection may be required when the property interest (one's job) was fraudulently obtained. Thus, a deputy sheriff was not deprived of due process when he was summarily discharged for lying on his application about a juvenile felony charge, which would have barred him from employment in the first place.[84]

In sum, agency rules and policies should state which due process procedures will be utilized under certain disciplinary situations; the key questions regarding due process are whether the employer follows established agency guidelines and, if not, whether the employer has a compelling reason not to do so.

At times, the administrator will determine that an employee must be disciplined or terminated. What are adequate grounds for discipline or discharge? Grounds can vary widely from agency to agency. Certainly, the agency's formal policies and procedures should specify and control what constitutes proper and improper behavior. Normally, agency practice and custom enter into these decisions. Sometimes administrators will "wink" at the formal policies and procedures, overlooking or only occasionally enforcing certain provisions contained in them. But the failure of the agency to enforce a rule or policy for a long period of time may provide "implied consent" by the employer that such behavior, although officially prohibited, is permissible. (In other words, don't allow an employee to violate the agency's lateness policy for 3 months and then decide one day to summarily fire him.) Attempts to fire employees for behavior that has been ignored or enforced only infrequently at best may give rise to a defense by the employee.

Hiring minority employees to meet state hiring goals and then attempting to terminate them as quickly and often as possible violates the employees' Title VII rights. Such a situation occurred in an Indiana case in which it was alleged that black prison COs were hired to fulfill an affirmative action program, only to be fired for disciplinary reasons for which white officers were not discharged.[85]

Generally, violations of an employee's rights in discharge and discipline occur (1) in violation of a protected interest, (2) in retaliation for the exercise of protected conduct, (3) with a discriminatory motive, and (4) with malice.[86]

A Tradition of Problems in Policing

Throughout its history, policing has experienced problems involving misconduct and corruption. As discussed in Chapter 5, a number of events during the 1990s demonstrated that the problem still exists and requires the attention of police officials. Incidents such as the beating of Rodney King in Los Angeles and of Abner Louima in New York City by officers, as well as major corruption scandals in several big-city police departments, have led many people to believe that police misbehavior is greater today than ever before.

Without question, police administrators need to pay close attention to signs of police misconduct, respond quickly, and enact policies to guide supervisors in handling disciplinary issues. Such policies should ensure that there is certainty, swiftness, fairness, and consistency of punishment when it is warranted.

Automated Records Systems

There have been many advances in the use of technology in police discipline. In 1991, the Fresno, California, Police Department automated its disciplinary process in an effort to establish a better system for tracking and sanctioning personnel for various offenses.[87] The principal objectives of this **automated records system** are to assist the chief of police in administering the department in a more equitable fashion and to improve the department's ability to defend its personnel actions. Within minutes, the database provides supervisors with 5 years of history about standards of discipline for any category of violation. A variety of reports can be produced, showing patterns of incidents for the supervisor.

Determining the Level and Nature of Action

When an investigation against an employee is sustained, the sanctions and level of discipline must be decided. Management must be careful when recommending and imposing discipline because of its impact on the morale of the agency's employees. If the recommended discipline is viewed by employees as too lenient, it may send the wrong message that the misconduct was insignificant. On the other hand, discipline that is viewed as too harsh may have a demoralizing effect on the officer(s) involved and other agency employees and result in allegations that the leadership is unfair. This alone can have significant impact on the **esprit de corps** or morale of the agency.

In addition to having a disciplinary process that is viewed by employees as fair and consistent, it is important that discipline be progressive and that more serious sanctions be invoked when repeated violations occur. For example, a third substantiated instance of rude behavior may result in a recommendation for a 1-day suspension without pay, but a first offense may be handled by documented oral counseling or a letter of reprimand. The following list shows disciplinary actions commonly used by agencies in increasing order of severity.

Counseling. This is usually a conversation between the supervisor and employee about a specific aspect of the employee's performance or conduct; it is warranted when an employee has committed a relatively minor infraction or the nature of the offense is such that oral counseling is all that is necessary. For example, an officer who is usually punctual but arrives at a briefing 10 minutes late 2 days in a row may require nothing more than a reminder and a warning to correct the problem.

Documented oral counseling. This is usually the first step in a progressive disciplinary process and is intended to address relatively minor infractions. It occurs when there are no previous reprimands or more severe disciplinary action of the same or a similar nature.

Letter of reprimand. This is a formal written notice regarding significant misconduct, more serious performance violations, or repeated offenses. It is usually the second step in the formal disciplinary process and is intended to provide the employee and agency with a written record of the violation of behavior; it identifies what specific corrective action must be taken to avoid subsequent, more serious disciplinary steps.

Suspension. This is a severe disciplinary action that results in an employee being relieved of duty, often without pay. It is usually administered when an employee commits a serious violation of established rules or after written reprimands have been given and no change in behavior or performance has resulted.

Demotion. In this situation, an employee is placed in a position of lower responsibility and pay. It is normally used when an otherwise capable employee is unable to meet the standards required for the higher position, or when the employee has committed a serious act requiring that he or she be removed from a position of management or supervision.

Transfer. Many agencies use the disciplinary transfer to deal with problem officers; officers can be transferred to a different location or assignment, and this action is often seen as an effective disciplinary tool.

Termination. This is the most severe disciplinary action that can be taken. It usually occurs when previous serious discipline has been imposed and there has been inadequate or no improvement in behavior or performance. It may also occur when an employee commits an offense so serious that continued employment would be inappropriate.

Positive and Negative Discipline

When policies and procedures are violated, positive or negative disciplinary measures may be imposed. Although different in their philosophy, both seek to accomplish the same purpose: to correct negative behavior and promote the employee's voluntary compliance with departmental policies and procedures.

A positive discipline program (also known as *positive counseling*) attempts to change employee behavior without invoking punishment. An example of positive discipline or counseling is when an employee ("John") has been nonproductive and nonpunctual, has caused interpersonal problems with coworkers, and/or has other problems on the job. To this point, John has been in control of the situation—on the offensive, one might say—whereas the supervisor ("Jane") and his coworkers have been on the defensive. John is jeopardizing the morale and productivity of the workplace, but the preferred approach is to try to salvage him because of the agency's investment in time, funds, and training.

Finally, Jane calls John into her office. She might begin with a compliment to him (if indeed she can find one) and then proceed to outline all of his workplace shortcomings; this demonstrates to John that Jane "has his number" and is aware of his various problems. Jane explains to him why it is important that he improve (for reasons related to productivity, morale, and so on) and the benefits he might realize from improvement (promotions, pay raises, bonuses). She also outlines what can happen if he does *not* show adequate improvement (demotion, transfer, termination). Now having gained John's attention, she gives him a certain time period (say, 30, 60, or 90 days) in which to improve; she emphasizes, however, that she will be constantly monitoring his progress. She might even ask John to sign a counseling statement form that sets forth all they have discussed, indicating that John has received counseling and understands the situation.

Note that Jane is now on the offensive, thereby putting John on the defensive and in control of his destiny; if he fails to perform, Jane would probably give him a warning, and if the situation continues, he will be terminated. If he sues or files a grievance, Jane has proof that every effort was made to allow John to salvage his position. This is an effective means of giving subordinates an incentive to improve their behavior while at the same time making the department less vulnerable to successful lawsuits.

Negative discipline is punishment. It is generally used when positive efforts fail or the violation is so serious that punishment is required. Negative discipline varies in its severity and involves documented oral counseling, a letter of reprimand, demotion, days off without pay, or even termination.

Dealing with Complaints

COMPLAINT ORIGIN   A **personnel complaint** is an allegation of misconduct or illegal behavior against an employee by anyone inside or outside the organization. Internal complaints may come from supervisors who observe officer misconduct, officers who complain about supervisors, supervisors who complain about other supervisors, civilian personnel who complain about officers, and so on. External complaints originate from sources outside the organization and usually involve the public.

Complaints may be received from primary, secondary, and anonymous sources. A victim is a primary source. A secondary source is someone who makes the complaint on behalf of the victim, such as an attorney, a school counselor, or a parent of a juvenile. An anonymous source complaint derives from an unknown source and may be delivered to the police station via a telephone call or an unsigned letter.

Every complaint, regardless of the source, must be accepted and investigated in accordance with established policies and procedures. Anonymous complaints are the most difficult to investigate because there is no opportunity to obtain further information or question the complainant about the allegation. Such complaints can have a negative impact on employee morale because officers may view them as unjust and frivolous.

TYPES AND CAUSES   Complaints may be handled informally or formally, depending on the seriousness of the allegation and the preference of the complainant. A formal complaint occurs when a written and signed and/or tape-recorded statement of the allegation is made and the complainant asks to be informed of the investigation's disposition. Figure 14.2 provides an example of a complaint form used to initiate a personnel investigation.

An informal complaint is an allegation of minor misconduct made for informational purposes that can usually be resolved without the need for more formal processes. When a citizen calls the watch commander to complain about the rude behavior of a dispatcher but does not wish to make a formal complaint, the supervisor may simply discuss the incident with the dispatcher and resolve it through informal counseling as long as more serious problems are not discovered and the dispatcher does not have a history of similar complaints.

Few complaints involve acts of physical violence, excessive force, or corruption. Rojek et al.[88] found that complaints against officers also fall under the general categories of verbal abuse, discourtesy, harassment, improper attitude, and ethnic slurs.[89] Another study[90] found that 42 percent of complaints involved the "verbal conduct" of officers; verbal conduct also accounted for 47 percent of all sustained complaints. The majority of repeated offenses also fell into this category. It is clear that officers' verbal actions generate a significant number of complaints. Finally, minority citizens, and those with less power and fewer resources, are more likely than persons with greater power and more resources to file complaints of misconduct and to allege more serious forms of misconduct.[91]

RECEIPT AND REFERRAL   Administrators should have in place a process for receiving complaints that is clearly delineated by departmental policy and procedures. Generally, a complaint will be made at a police facility and referred to a senior officer in charge to determine its seriousness and the need for immediate intervention.

****

Control Number_____

Date & Time Reported	Location of Interview	Interview

_____   _____   _____Verbal _____Written _____Taped

Type of Complaint: ____Force ____Procedural ____Conduct
____Other (Specify)

Source of Complaint: ____In Person ____Mail ____Telephone
____Other (Specify)

Complaint originally ____Supervisor ____On Duty Watch Commander ____Chief
Received by: ____IAU ____Other (Specify)

Notifications made: _____Division Commander _____Chief of Police
Received by: _____On-Call Command Personnel
_____Watch Commander _____Other (Specify)

Copy of formal personnel complaint given to complainant? ____Yes ____No

****

Complainant's name: Address:
_____ _____ Zip_____

Residence Phone: Business Phone:
_____ _____ ____

DOB: Race: Sex: Occupation:
_____ _____ _____ _____

****

Location of Occurrence: Date & Time of Occurrence:
_____ _____

Member(s) Involved: Member(s) Involved:
(1) _____ (2)_____
(3) _____ (4)_____

Witness(es) Involved: Witness(es) Involved:
(1) _____ (2)_____
(3) _____ (4)_____

****

(1) _____ Complainant wishes to make a formal statement and has requested an investigation into the matter with a report back to him/her on the findings and actions.

(2) _____ Complainant wishes to advise the Police Department of a problem, understand that some type of action will be taken, but does not request a report back to him/her on the findings and actions.

****

CITIZEN ADVISEMENTS

(1) If you have not yet provided the department with a signed written statement or a tape-recorded statement, one may be required in order to pursue the investigation of this matter.

(2) The complainant(s) and/or witness(es) may be required to take a polygraph examination in order to determine the credibility concerning the allegations made.

(3) Should the allegations prove to be false, the complainant(s) and/or witness(es) may be liable for criminal and/or civil prosecution.

_____ _____
Signature of Complainant   Date & Time

_____
Signature of Member Receiving Complaint

FIGURE 14.2 Police Department Formal Personnel Complaint Report Form

In most cases, the senior officer will determine the nature of the complaint and the employee involved; the matter will be referred to the employee's supervisor to conduct an initial investigation. The supervisor completes the investigation, recommends any discipline, and sends the matter to the Internal Affairs Unit (IAU) and the agency head for finalization of the disciplinary process. This method of review ensures that consistent and fair standards of discipline are applied.

THE INVESTIGATIVE PROCESS D. W. Perez[92] indicated that all but a small percentage of the 17,000 police agencies in the United States have a process for investigation of police misconduct. Generally, the employee's supervisor will conduct a preliminary inquiry of the complaint, commonly known as **fact finding**. Once it is determined that further investigation is necessary, the supervisor may conduct additional questioning of employees and witnesses, obtain written statements from those persons immediately involved in the incident, and gather any evidence that may be necessary for the case, including photographs. Care must be taken to ensure that the accused employee's rights are not violated. The initial investigation is sent to an appropriate division commander and forwarded to IAU for review.

Making a Determination and Disposition

CATEGORIES Once an investigation is completed, the supervisor or IAU officer must make a determination as to the culpability of the accused employee and report this to the administrator. Each allegation should receive a separate adjudication. Following are the categories of dispositions that are commonly used:

- *Unfounded.* The alleged act(s) did not occur.
- *Exonerated.* The act occurred, but it is lawful, proper, justified, and/or in accordance with departmental policies, procedures, rules, and regulations.
- *Not sustained.* There is insufficient evidence to prove or disprove the allegations made.
- *Misconduct not based on the complaint.* Sustainable misconduct was determined but is not a part of the original complaint. For example, a supervisor investigating an allegation of excessive force against an officer may find that the force used was within departmental policy but that the officer made an unlawful arrest.
- *Closed.* An investigation may be halted if the complainant fails to cooperate or if it is determined that the action does not fall within the administrative jurisdiction of the police agency.
- *Sustained.* The act did occur, and it was a violation of departmental rules and procedures. Sustained allegations include misconduct that falls within the broad outlines of the original allegation(s).

Once a determination of culpability has been made, the complainant should be notified of the department's findings. Details of the investigation or recommended punishment will not be included in the correspondence. As shown in Figure 14.3, the complainant will normally receive only information concerning the outcome of the complaint, including a short explanation of the finding along with an invitation to call the agency if further information is needed.

GRIEVANCES Police officers may complain about contractual or other matters about which they are upset or concerned. Following is an overview of the **grievance** process.

Grievance procedures establish a fair and expeditious process for handling employee disputes that are not disciplinary in nature. Grievance procedures involve collective bargaining issues, conditions of employment, and employer–employee relations. More specifically, grievances

```
                        Police Department
                         3300 Main Street
                         Downtown Plaza
                       Anywhere, USA. 99999
                          June 20, 2000

Mr. John Doe
2200 Main Avenue
Anywhere, USA.

Re: Internal affairs #000666-98
  Case Closure

Dear Mr. Doe:

Our investigation into your allegations against Officer Smith has been completed. It
has been determined that your complaint is SUSTAINED and the appropriate
disciplinary action has been taken.

Our department appreciates your bringing this matter to our attention. It is our
position that when a problem is identified, it should be corrected as soon as possible. It
is our goal to be responsive to the concerns expressed by citizens so as to provide more
efficient and effective services.

Your information regarding this incident was helpful and of value in our efforts to
attain that goal. Should you have any further questions about this matter, please
contact Sergeant Jane Alexander, Internal Affairs, at 555-9999.

Sincerely,



I.M. Boss
Lieutenant
Internal Affairs Unit
```

FIGURE 14.3 Citizens' Notification-of-Discipline Letter

may cover a broad range of issues, including salaries, overtime, leave, hours of work, allowances, retirement, opportunity for advancement, performance evaluations, workplace conditions, tenure, disciplinary actions, supervisory methods, and administrative practices. Grievance procedures are often established as a part of the collective bargaining process.

The preferred method for settling officers' grievances is through informal discussion, in which the employee explains his or her grievance to the immediate supervisor. Most complaints can be handled through this process. Complaints that cannot be dealt with informally are usually handled through a more formal grievance process, as described next. A formal grievance begins with the employee submitting the grievance in writing to the immediate supervisor, as illustrated in Figure 14.4.

The process for formally handling grievances will vary among agencies and may involve as many as three to six different levels of action. Following is an example of how a grievance may proceed:

Level I. An employee's grievance is submitted in writing to a supervisor. The supervisor will be given 5 days to respond. If the employee is dissatisfied with the response, the grievance moves to the next level.

Police Department
Formal Grievance Form

Grievance #_____

Employee Name: _____ Work Phone: _____
Department Assigned: _____
Date of Occurrence: _____
Location of Occurrence: _____

Name of: 1.   Department Head:_____

           2.   Division Head:_____

           3.   Immediate Supervisor:_____

Statement of Grievance: _____
_____
_____
_____

Witnesses:_____
_____
_____

What article(s) and or section(s) of the labor agreement of rules and regulations do
you believe have been violated? _____
_____
_____
_____

What remedy are you requesting?_____
_____
_____

_____   _____
Employee signature   Signature of labor representative

FIGURE 14.4   Employee Grievance Form

Level II. At this level, the grievance proceeds to the chief executive, who will be given a specified time (usually 5 days) to render a decision.

Level III. If the employee is not satisfied with the chief's decision, the grievance may proceed to the city or county manager, as appropriate. The manager will usually meet with the employee and/or representatives from the bargaining association and attempt to resolve the matter. An additional 5–10 days are usually allowed for the manager to render a decision.

Level IV. If the grievance is still not resolved, either party may request that the matter be submitted to arbitration. Arbitration involves a neutral outside person, often selected from a list of arbitrators from the Federal Mediation and Conciliation Service. An arbitrator will conduct a hearing, listen to both parties, and usually render a decision within 20–30 days.

The decision of the arbitrator can be final and binding. This does not prohibit the employee from appealing the decision to a state court.

Failure to act on grievances quickly may result in serious morale problems within an agency.

APPEALING DISCIPLINARY MEASURES Appeals processes—frequently outlined in civil service rules and regulations, labor agreements, and departmental policies and procedures—normally follow an officer's chain of command. For example, if an officer disagrees with a supervisor's recommendation for discipline, the first step of an **appeal** may involve a hearing before the division commander, usually of the rank of captain or deputy chief. The accused employee may be allowed labor representation or an attorney to assist in asking questions of the investigating supervisor, clarifying issues, and presenting new or mitigating evidence. The division commander has 5 days to review the recommendation and respond in writing to the employee.

If the employee is still not satisfied, an appeal hearing before the chief executive is granted. This is usually the final step in appeals within the agency. The chief or sheriff communicates a decision in writing to the employee within 5 to 10 days. Depending on labor agreements and civil service rules and regulations, some agencies extend their appeals of discipline beyond the department. For example, employees may bring their issue before the civil service commission or city or county manager for a final review. Employees may also have the right to an independent arbitrator's review of the discipline. The arbitrator's decision is usually binding.

THE EARLY WARNING SYSTEM Early identification of and intervention in employee misconduct or performance problems are vital to preventing ongoing and repeated incidents. An **early warning system (EWS)** is designed to identify officers whose behavior is problematic (involving citizen complaints or improper use of force) and provide a form of intervention. The system alerts the department to these individuals and warns the officers while providing counseling or training to help them change their problematic behavior. Most EWSs require three complaints in a given time frame (normally a 12-month period) before intervention is initiated. The EWS thus helps agencies to respond proactively to patterns of behavior that may lead to more serious problems. The EWS may require that the officer's supervisor intervene with early prevention methods such as counseling or training.

In some cases, repeated incidents of violent behavior may require that officers attend anger training or verbal judo sessions to learn how to deescalate confrontational situations. Some preventive measures, such as counseling, remedial training, or temporary change of assignment, may also be used. A referral to an employee assistance program (EAP) to deal with more serious psychological or substance abuse problems is another possible outcome.

Summary

This chapter has examined three aspects of criminal justice administration that pose exceptionally serious challenges for them: discipline, liability, and labor relations. It is clear from this triad of issues that administrators need to understand the current and developing laws that serve to make criminal justice practitioners legally accountable; this need cannot be overstated. It is far better to learn the proper means of discipline, areas of liability, and effective collective bargaining methods through education and training than to learn about these issues by virtue of serving in the role of a defendant in a lawsuit. Better to learn "in house," rather than to learn "in the courthouse."

Criminal justice executives need to be proactive and learn as well as follow appropriate laws and guidelines as they recruit, hire, train, supervise, and negotiate with their subordinates in order to avoid legal difficulties; for administrators not to do so could place them and their jurisdiction at serious financial, legal, and moral risk. As Edmund Burke observed in the eighteenth century, "Example is the school of mankind," and the many examples provided in this chapter lay bare that kinds of outcomes that can arise when discipline, liability, and labor relations laws are not adhered to. There is certainly merit in looking at what some agencies have done to address these complex problems.

Questions for Review

1. How and why did unionization begin, what is its contemporary status in policing, and how does it influence courts and corrections organizations?
2. What are the three models of collective bargaining, as well as the process that comes into play when an impasse is reached?
3. What are some of the primary suggestions concerning how an administrator should "navigate the waters" of unionization?
4. What are the seven forms of disciplinary action that may be taken against police officers?
5. How would you define the following: *tort, Section 1983*, and *respondeat superior*?
6. How can the doctrines of duty of care and failure to protect, as well as laws covering vehicular pursuits, lead to police liability?
7. For what kinds of actions (and lack of action) can corrections agencies be held liable?
8. How would you delineate the minimum due process requirements for discharging public employees?
9. What are the benefits and functions of an early warning system (EWS) for identifying problem officers?
10. How would you explain the differences between positive and negative discipline?
11. What are the categories of dispositions that are commonly used with complaints?
12. What is an example of how a grievance may proceed through its various levels?

Learn by Doing

1. You are enrolled in an internship with a small county sheriff's office, and after several weeks you begin to develop close friendships with some of the deputies. Eventually you learn that nearly all of the deputies are very disgruntled—and some are even irate—due to what they perceive as a lack of parity with other intracounty offices and intercounty sheriff's offices in wages and benefits, and general apathy by the county commission. They perceive a danger exists because low salaries lead to high turnover, which causes too few deputies—and too many inexperienced ones—to normally be on duty per shift. One deputy asks you if it is legally possible in your state for them to align themselves with a labor union, as well as your overall opinion concerning the pros and cons of collective bargaining and whether or not a "peaceful protest" by sheriff's personnel and their families and supporters at the county commission offices might help. What is your response?

2. Donna King has been a correctional officer in your jail for 6 years, and one of your subordinates for 2 years. Her productivity, both in terms of quality and quantity, as well as interactions with the staff and inmates, has generally been at or above standard; her performance evaluations are normally above average. In recent weeks, however, there have been rumors concerning her work; although no formal complaints have been filed, there are rumors concerning abusive treatment of inmates, not responding in a timely manner to calls by other jail staff for assistance, general lack of compliance with policies and procedures, and other matters. Today another CO contacts you to complain about her rough treatment of an inmate during an inmate booking. You decide it is time to call her into your office to discuss these matters. How will you address this situation?

3. Sergeant Tom Gresham is newly promoted and assigned to patrol on the graveyard shift; he knows each officer on his shift and several of them are his close friends. Gresham was an excellent patrol officer and prides himself on his reputation as a "cop's cop" and his ability to get along with his peers; in fact, he frequently socializes with them after work. He believes his officers perform very well, particularly as they generate the highest number of arrest and citation statistics in the entire department. Unfortunately, his shift is also generating

the highest number of citizen complaints for abusive language and improper use of force, and you—his shift lieutenant—have learned in conversations with the city attorney's office that some citizens are contemplating legal action. When questioned, Gresham tells you that such complaints are "the price of doing business." You outline for him several examples of use-of-force complaints lodged against his officers during the past few weeks while he was away on vacation. Gresham still fails to grasp the seriousness of the complaints and how his supervisory style may have contributed to them.

a. What do you believe are some of Sergeant Gresham's problems as a new supervisor? Could anything have been done *before* he assumed his new position to help him understand his role better?
b. As Gresham's superior officer, what advice would you give to him? Are there any other supervisory or command officers who you should ask to be involved in dealing with the situation?
c. What corrective action(s), if any, might Sergeant Gresham immediately take with his shift of officers?

Related Websites

Americans for Effective Law Enforcement (civil liability workshops)
http://www.aele.org/wkscivil.html

California Correctional Peace Officers Association (considered one of the largest and most powerful in the world)
http://www.ccpoa.org/

Fraternal Order of Police
http://www.grandlodgefop.org/

National Association of Police Organizations
http://www.napo.org/

Office of National Drug Control Policy
http://www.whitehousedrugpolicy.gov/

Notes

1. Amanda Ripley, "Meet Your Government Workers," *Time*, March 7, 2011, p. 42.
2. U.S. Department of Labor, Bureau of Labor Statistics, "Economic News Release: Union Members Summary," http://www.bls.gov/news.release/union2.nr0.htm (accessed March 1, 2011).
3. Tom Davies, "Dems leave Indiana House, stalling GOP labor," Associate Press, February 22, 2011, http://www.washingtonpost.com/wp-dyn/content/article/2011/02/22/AR2011022204427.html (accessed February 22, 2011); also see Scott Bauer, "Wisconsin Democrats could stay away for weeks," February 18, 2011, http://news.yahoo.com/s/ap/20110218/ap_on_re_us/us_wisconsin_budget_unions_59http://www.cbsnews.com/stories/2011/02/17/ap/politics/main20032689.shtml (accessed February 22, 2011).
4. Tom Davies, "Dems leave Indiana House, stalling GOP labor," Associate Press, February 22, 2011, http://www.washingtonpost.com/wp-dyn/content/article/2011/02/22/AR2011022204427.html (accessed February 22, 2011).
5. See David A. Lieb and Sam Hananel, "Republicans challenging unions in state capitols," Associated Press, February 18, 2011, http://hosted2.ap.org/APDEFAULT/gungrey/Article_2011-02-18-Broken%20Budgets%20Union%20Fights/id-39132cd0edef491fb137c3edc6357d68 (accessed February 22, 2011).
6. Dennis Cauchon, "Poll: Americans favor collective bargaining rights," *USA TODAY*, February 23, 2011, http://www.usatoday.com/news/nation/2011-02-22-poll-public-unions-wisconsin_N.htm (accessed March 1, 2011).
7. Ripley, "Meet Your Government Workers," p. 42; Joe Klein, "As Goes Wisconsin . . . So Goes the Nation," *Time*, March 7, 2011, pp. 36–39.
8. Will Aitchison, *The Rights of Police Officers,* 3rd ed. (Portland, OR: Labor Relations Information System, 1996), p. 7.
9. Ibid.
10. Ibid.
11. Ibid., p. 8.
12. Ibid., p. 9.
13. Charles R. Swanson, Leonard Territo, and Robert W. Taylor, *Police Administration: Structures, Processes, and Behavior,* 6th ed. (Upper Saddle River, NJ: Prentice Hall, 2005), p. 517.
14. Ibid., p. 522.
15. Arnold Zack, *Understanding Fact-Finding and Arbitration in the Public Sector* (Washington, D.C.: U.S. Government Printing Office, 1974), p. 1.

16. Thomas P. Gilroy and Anthony V. Sinicropi, "Impasse Resolution in Public Employment," *Industrial and Labor Relations Review* 25 (July 1971–1972):499.

17. Robert G. Howlett, "Fact Finding: Its Values and Limitations—Comment, Arbitration and the Expanded Role of Neutrals," in *Proceedings of the Twenty-Third Annual Meeting of the National Academy of Arbitrators* (Washington, DC: Bureau of National Affairs, 1970), p. 156.

18. Zack, *Understanding Fact-Finding,* p. 1.

19. Swanson, Territo, and Taylor, *Police Administration,* p. 530.

20. Ibid.

21. Ibid., p. 532.

22. Ibid., p. 534.

23. John H. Burpo, *The Police Labor Movement: Problems and Perspectives* (Springfield, IL: Charles C Thomas, 1971).

24. Ibid., p. xi.

25. W. Clinton Terry III, *Policing Society: An Occupational View* (New York: Wiley, 1985), p. 168.

26. Ibid., p. 168.

27. Ibid., pp. 170–171.

28. See Fraternal Order of Police, "Frequently Asked Questions," http://www.fop.net/about/faq/index.shtml http://www.napo.org/ (accessed November 7, 2010); National Association of Police Organizations, "Welcome to NAPO," http://www.napo.org/ (accessed November 7, 2010).

29. Kenneth J. Peak, Larry K. Gaines, and Ronald W. Glensor, *Police Supervision and Management: In an Era of Community Policing,* 3rd ed. (Upper Saddle River, NJ: Prentice Hall, 2010), p. 282.

30. Richard P. Seiter, *Correctional Administration: Integrating Theory and Practice* (Upper Saddle River, NJ: Prentice Hall, 2002), pp. 333–334.

31. James B. Jacobs and Norma Meacham Crotty, *Guard Unions and the Future of Prisons* (Ithaca, NY: Institute of Public Employment, 1978), p. 41.

32. James B. Jacobs, *New Perspectives on Prisons and Imprisonment* (Ithaca, NY: Cornell University Press, 1983), p. 153.

33. Ibid., pp. 154–155.

34. Seiter, *Correctional Administration,* p. 337.

35. Ibid.

36. U.S. Department of Justice, National Institute of Law Enforcement and Criminal Justice, *Trial Court Management Series, Personnel Management* (Washington, DC: U.S. Government Printing Office, 1979), pp. 42–47.

37. Larry T. Hoover, Jerry L. Dowling, and Gene Blair, "Management and Labor in Community Policing: Charting a Course," in U.S. Department of Justice, Office of Community Oriented Policing Services, *Police Labor-Management Relations (Vol. I): Perspectives and Practical Solutions for Implementing Change Making Reforms, and Handling Crises for Managers and Union Leaders,* August 2006, pp. 19–20, http://www.cops.usdoj.gov/files/ric/Publications/e07063417.pdf (accessed September 29, 2010).

38. Ibid., p. 20.

39. Ibid., p. 21.

40. Based on Ronald G. DeLord, "Ten Things that Law Enforcement Unions and Managers Do to Run Aground," in U.S. Department of Justice, Office of Community Oriented Policing Services, *Police Labor-Management Relations (Vol. I): Perspectives and Practical Solutions for Implementing Change Making Reforms, and Handling Crises for Managers and Union Leaders,* August 2006, pp. 153–157, http://www.cops.usdoj.gov/files/ric/Publications/e07063417.pdf (accessed September 29, 2010).

41. H. E. Barrineau III, *Civil Liability in Criminal Justice* (Cincinnati, OH: Pilgrimage, 1987), p. 58.

42. Ibid., p. 5.

43. Swanson et al., *Police Administration,* p. 549.

44. Ibid.

45. Isidore Silver, *Police Civil Liability* (New York: Matthew Bender, 2005), p. 4.

46. The Feminist Majority Foundation and The National Center for Women and Policing, "Gender Differences in the Cost of Police Brutality and Misconduct: A Content Analysis of LAPD Civil Liability Cases: 1990–1999," http://www.womenandpolicing.org/ExcessiveForce.asp?id=4516 (accessed April 4, 2007).

47. CNN.com, "LAPD Officers Take Stand in Rampart Scandal Trial," http://archives.cnn.com/2000/LAW/10/16/lapd.corruption.tria/ (accessed April 4, 2007).

48. Victor E. Kappeler, *Critical Issues in Police Civil Liability,* 4th ed. (Long Grove, IL: Waveland, 2005), p. 4.

49. G. P. Alpert, R. G. Dunham, and M. S. Stroshine, *Policing: Continuity and Change* (Long Grove, IL: Waveland, 2006).

50. 516 F.Supp. 1355 (W.D. Tenn., 1981).

51. *Brandon v. Holt,* 469 U.S. 464, 105 S.Ct. 873 (1985).

52. See, for example, *Black v. Stephens,* 662 F.2d 181 (1991).

53. On appeal, the Section 242 convictions were vacated, as the victim was not an inhabitant of Puerto Rico; therefore, he enjoyed no protection under the U.S.

Constitution. On resentencing, in January 1991, the agents each received 50 years in prison for convictions of several other federal crimes under Title 18.

54. *Irwin v. Ware*, 467 N.E.2d 1292 (1984).

55. *Fudge v. City of Kansas City*, 239 Kan. 369, 720 P.2d 1093 (1986), at 373.

56. *Kendrick v. City of Lake Charles*, 500 So.2d 866 (La. App. 1 Cir. 1986).

57. *Fielder v. Jenkins*, 833 A.2d 906 (N.J. Super. A.D. 1993).

58. Silver, *Police Civil Liability*, p. 4; also see *Coco v. State*, 474 N.Y.S.2d 397 (Ct.Cl. 1984).; *Duvernay v. State* 433 So.2d 254 (La.App. 1983).

59. *Joseph v. State of Alaska*, 26 P.3d 459 (2001).

60. *Thomas v. Williams*, 124 S.E.2d 409 (Ga. App. 1962).

61. *Morris v. Blake*, 552 A.2d 844 (Del. Super. 1988).

62. *Davis v. City of Detroit*, 386 N.W.2d 169 (Mich. App. 1986).

63. *Penilla v. City of Huntington Park*, 115 F.3d 707 (9th Cir., 1997).

64. *Monfils v. Taylor*, 165 F.3d 511 (7th Cir. 1998), cert. denied, 528 U.S. 810 (1999).

65. *Seide v. State of Rhode Island*, 875 A.2d 1259 (2005).

66. Silver, *Police Civil Liability*, p. 8.

67. *Seide v. State of Rhode Island*, 875 A.2d 1259 (2005).

68. *Scott v. Harris*, 550 U.S._(2007), Docket #05-1631, at p. 13.

69. Kappeler, *Critical Issues in Police Civil Liability*, pp. 177–178.

70. U.S. Department of Justice, Bureau of Justice Statistics, "Jail Suicide Rates 64 Percent Lower Than in Early 1980s," http://www.ojp.usdoj.gov/bjs/pub/press/shspljpr.htm (accessed September 28, 2005).

71. Ibid., p. 9.

72. Victor E. Kappeler and Rolando V. del Carmen, "Avoiding Police Liability for Negligent Failure to Prevent Suicide," *The Police Chief* (August 1991):53–59.

73. Ibid., p. 53.

74. *Thomas v. Williams,* 124 S.E.2d 409 (Ga. App. 1962).

75. *Kanayurak v. North Slope Borough,* 677 P.2d 892 (Alaska 1984).

76. *City of Belen v. Harrell,* 603 P.2d 711 (NM: 1979).

77. *Hake v. Manchester Township,* 486 A.2d 836 (NJ: 1985).

78. *Davis v. City of Detroit,* 386 N.W.2d 169 (Mich. App. 1986).

79. *Hickey v. Zezulka,* 443 N.W.2d 180 (Mich. App. 1989).

80. *Hake v. Manchester Township,* 486 A.2d 836 (NJ: 1985).

81. V. McLaughlin and R. Bing, "Law Enforcement Personnel Selection," *Journal of Police Science and Administration* 15 (1987):271–276.

82. Ibid.

83. *McNamara v. City of Chicago,* 700 F.Supp. 917 (ND Ill., 1988), at 919.

84. *White v. Thomas,* 660 F.2d 680 (5th Cir. 1981).

85. *Yarber v. Indiana State Prison,* 713 F.Supp. 271 (ND Ind., 1988).

86. Robert H. Chaires and Susan A. Lentz, "Criminal Justice Employee Rights: An Overview," *American Journal of Criminal Justice* 13 (April 1995):273–274.

87. M. Guthrie, "Using Automation to Apply Discipline Fairly," *FBI Law Enforcement Bulletin* 5 (1996):18–21.

88. Jeff Rojek, Allen E. Wagner, and Scott H. Decker, "Evaluating Citizen Complaints Against the Police," in R. G. Dunham and G. P. Alpert (eds.), *Critical Issues in Policing: Contemporary Readings,* 4th ed. (Prospect Heights, IL: Waveland, 2001), pp. 317–337.

89. Ibid., p. 318.

90. J. R. Dugan and D. R. Breda, "Complaints About Police Officers: A Comparison Among Types and Agencies," *Journal of Criminal Justice* 19 (1991): 165–171.

91. Kim Michelle Lersch, "Police Misconduct and Malpractice: A Critical Analysis of Citizens' Complaints," *Policing* 21 (1998):80–96.

92. D. W. Perez, *Police Review Systems* (Washington, DC: Management Information Service, 1992).

Financial Administration

KEY TERMS AND CONCEPTS

Budget

Budget audit

Budget cycle

Budget execution

Budget formulation

Corrections reform

Exigency

Expenditures

Financial accountability

Line-item budgeting

Management accountability

Program accountability

Revenue augmentation

LEARNING OBJECTIVES

After reading this chapter, the student will:

■ know a number of specific ways in which the recent financial crisis affected police, courts, and corrections agencies' operations

- be able to define the term *budget*
- understand the concepts of the budget cycle's four steps
- be familiar with the budgeting procedures in the police, courts, and corrections systems
- have examples of different ways in which monies may be acquired
- be able to distinguish among the three different budget formats and know the advantages and disadvantages of each
- understand why and how criminal justice policymakers are reforming sentencing laws to reduce corrections expenditures

> *How pleasant it is to have money, heigh ho! How pleasant it is to have money.*
>
> —ARTHUR HUGH CLOUGH

> *It's a recession when your neighbor loses his job; it's a depression when you lose yours.*
>
> —HARRY S. TRUMAN

INTRODUCTION

The importance of financial administration for criminal justice administrators is unquestioned. Money is the key to just about everything these agencies do, and the ability to obtain and expend necessary financial resources is key to an organization's short- and long-term success. Indeed, if unlimited funds were available, planning would not be needed. As Frederick Mosher observed, "Not least among the qualifications of an administrator is one's ability as a tactician and gladiator in the budget process."[1]

Certainly the recent decline in the nation's economy created many problems and challenges for contemporary criminal justice administrators. As will be seen, unprecedented actions have been taken within criminal justice agencies—long considered to be the stalwart of job security and stable revenues. This chapter examines some of those challenges.

The primary purpose of this chapter, however, is to convey the fundamental elements of controlling fiscal resources through formulating and executing a budget. And although this chapter is not intended to prepare the reader to be an expert on the more intricate aspects of financial administration, it will provide a foundation for, and insight concerning some of its basic methods and issues.

After looking at various ways in which the recent economic downturn affected criminal justice in general, we then look at the broader issue of financial *stewardship* (a word that generally refers to the responsibility of taking care of something that is owned by someone else). Of the four components of financial administration—budgeting, auditing, accounting, and purchasing—budgeting is the primary focus here. Included are discussions of budget definitions and uses; the influence of politics and fiscal realities in budgeting, which often lead to budget cuts for the organization; the several elements of the budget process, including formulation, approval, execution, and audit; and budget formats. Also presented is an examination of some of the budget pitfalls and waste problems that units of government are now experiencing, and what some criminal justice policymakers are doing to reform sentencing laws to reduce corrections expenditures.

AS BAD AS IT CAN GET: CONFRONTING FINANCIAL CRISIS

Effects on Policing

These are unprecedented times for the police, with layoffs of sworn officers being rampant in what has long been a job-security enclave for its employees. As an extreme example, in 2011 Camden, New Jersey—the poorest city in the state and one of the most crime-ridden cities in the nation—laid off nearly half (167) of its officers after attempts failed to raise property taxes and to get the union to make contract concessions.[2] In addition, a 2009 survey of police agencies by the Police Executive Research Forum (PERF) found the following (these figures were probably even more drastic in nature by the end of 2010):

- 53 percent had implemented a hiring freeze for nonsworn personnel, and 27 percent had done so for sworn positions;
- 62 percent said they had cut overtime spending, affecting their minimum staffing levels;
- 49 percent said they had cut back or eliminated plans to acquire technology;
- 47 percent had reduced or discontinued various types of officer training;
- 34 percent had discontinued, reduced in size, or delayed classes for new police recruits;
- 24 percent were reducing police employment levels through attrition;
- 12 percent said they were considering laying off police employees or forcing retirements;
- 10 percent said they used unpaid furloughs of employees to reduce spending.[3]

Furthermore, another 2010 PERF survey found that nearly 70 percent of agencies cut back or eliminated training programs,[4] while police around the nation were telling their citizens to file their own reports for home burglaries and other lesser crimes; indeed, many agencies were forced to quit responding to any property crimes, focus their resources instead on crimes of violence.[5]

Another way in which the budgetary cutbacks affected policing was in the patrol function. The escalating costs of gasoline that began in mid-2008—climbing to $4 per gallon in some areas—caused police agencies to rethink their vehicle patrol methods. Following are some of the changes that were put into effect:

- Many officers lost the right to take their patrol cars home or were forced to pay for the privilege.
- Officers in some communities were told to turn off their ignition whenever they were stopped and idling for more than a minute.[6]
- Some departments switched to lower octane gasoline and installed global positioning system receivers in patrol cars to make dispatching more efficient.[7]
- Some state troopers began sitting and monitoring traffic rather than cruising the highways, and increased their use of single-engine airplanes to look for speeders.[8]

Effects on the Courts

Certainly, the courts have felt the brunt of budget cutbacks as well. In fact, the National Center for State Courts' (NCSC) Center on Budget and Policy Priorities estimates that in coming fiscal years, states will face budget shortfalls as big as or bigger as they experienced in 2010—around $180 billion. To help the nation's courts weather the current economic storm and prepare for an uncertain financial future, the NCSC either has worked with or currently is working with nearly 40 states to re-engineer their court systems; this can involve evaluating and adjusting a court's structure as well as its use of technology and its processes.[9]

Table 15.1 shows the various effects on state courts budgets by fiscal exigencies, including hiring and salary freezes, cutting salaries, furloughing and laying off staff members, closing courts completely, and raising filing fees.

Of course, budget cuts affect other aspects of the courts as well, including their safety. As examples, cuts in state and local budgets have many courts facing the tough decision of whether to reduce court services or reduce their security—with many courts doing away with their metal detectors because they can no longer pay for personnel to operate them. Also, in Birmingham,

---

TABLE 15.1   Listing of Current Budget Impacts on State Courts

The following list is a compilation of states which have experienced specific economic impacts on their court systems up to October 4, 2010.

Hiring Freeze (23)	Frozen Salaries (12)	Pay Cut (9)	Furloughs (15)
Alabama	Arizona	Delaware	California
Arizona	California	Florida	Connecticut
California	Georgia	Idaho	Iowa
Colorado	Indiana	Iowa	Kansas
Connecticut	Kentucky	Kansas	Michigan
Delaware	Massachusetts	Kentucky	Minnesota
Florida	Nevada	Maine	Nevada
Georgia	Ohio	North Carolina	New Hampshire
Idaho	Oklahoma	Washington	New Jersey
Indiana	Oregon		North Carolina
Iowa	Pennsylvania		Oregon
Kansas	Wisconsin		South Dakota
Kentucky			Vermont
Maine			Washington
Massachusetts			Wisconsin
Minnesota			
New Hampshire			
Oklahoma			
Pennsylvania			
Rhode Island			
South Carolina			
Utah			
Wisconsin			

Court Closures (5)	Layoffs (6)	Early Retirement (6)	Raised Filing Fees (5)
California	Arizona	Alabama	Arizona
Iowa	California	Connecticut	Iowa
Massachusetts	Iowa	Massachusetts	Nevada
Minnesota	Kentucky	New Hampshire	Oregon
Vermont	Michigan	New Jersey	Washington
	Washington	South Dakota	

Source: National Center for State Courts, "Listing of Current Budget Impacts," http://www.ncsc.org/information-and-resources/budget-resource-center/~/media/Files/PDF/Information%20and%20Resources/Budget%20Resource%20Center/Cost%20Savings%20Measures%2010%204%2010.ashx (Accessed September 2, 2011). Used with permission.

Alabama, a female judge keeps a silver .38 caliber pistol under her bench after the county let go her two courtroom deputy sheriffs because of budget cuts.[10]

Effects on Corrections

Like the other two components of criminal justice, corrections also felt the brunt of the economic downturn. By the end of 2009, at least 26 states had slashed prison funding (seven by more than 10 percent), causing widespread job losses, wage freezes, changes in food offerings for inmates, and cutbacks community-based reentry programs.[11] Some states were also struggling with having to cut costs and furloughing correctional workers without sacrificing safety and security of inmates and staff (see Exhibit 15.1).

EXHIBIT 15.1

Can Prison Workers be Furloughed Without Sacrificing Safety and Security?

Nevada's prison director was given 1 month to find ways to give correctional officers and other staff members furloughs as mandated by the state legislature (lawmakers mandated that state workers take 1 day off each month without pay—amounting to a 4.6 percent pay cut and a savings of $165 million per year). Director Howard Skolnik requested more time to ensure that public safety is not threatened, and he was given a month to produce a staffing plan showing which of the 1,800 staff members could or could not be furloughed. "We cannot just ask the inmates to behave overnight and leave them alone," Skolnik said in asking for the extra planning time. He added that possible ways of saving staff time could include mothballing security towers and relying on guards in vehicles for patrolling prison perimeters. Other options could include inmate lockdowns, visiting room closures, and fewer medical staff hours. The state's attorney general indicated concern about potential lawsuits if security problems developed.

Source: Based on Brendan Riley, "Nevada prisons boss gets staff furlough leeway," *Las Vegas Review-Journal*, July 14, 2009, http://www.lvrj.com/news/breaking_news/50777632.html (accessed October 11, 2010).

The financial crisis also had an impact on prison time served, forcing probation and parole agencies in at least a handful of states—with others taking the plan under consideration—to reduce or outright drop prison time for thousands of offenders who had violated the conditions of their release. As examples, Kansas began allowing probation and parole officers to decide whether those violators should be returned to prison, Tennessee's governor implemented accelerated releases for probation and parole violators, and Arizona legislators approved a measure that allowed thousands of probationers to end their terms early.[12]

THE BUDGET

A Working Definition

The word **budget** is derived from the old French word *bougette*, meaning a small leather bag or wallet. Initially, it referred to the leather bag in which the Chancellor of the Exchequer carried documents stating the government's needs and resources given to the English Parliament.[13] Later, it came to mean the documents themselves. More recently, *budget* has been defined as a plan stated in financial terms, an estimate of future expenditures, an asking price, a policy statement, the translation of financial resources into human purposes, and a contract between those who appropriate the funds and those who spend them.[14] To some extent, all of these definitions are valid.

In addition, the budget is a management tool, a process, and a political instrument. It is a

comprehensive plan, expressed in financial terms, by which a program is operated for a given period. It includes (1) the services, activities, and projects comprising the program; (2) the resultant expenditure requirements; and (3) the resources available for their support.[15]

It is "a plan or schedule adjusting expenses during a certain period to the estimated income for that period."[16] Lester Bittel added:

A budget is, literally, a financial standard for a particular operation, activity, program, or department. Its data are presented in numerical form, mainly in dollars—to be spent for a particular purpose—over a specified period of time. Budgets are derived from planning goals and forecasts.[17]

Although these descriptions are certainly apt, one writer warns that budgets involve an inherently irrational process: "Budgets are based on little more than the past and some guesses."[18]

Financial management of governmental agencies is clearly political. Anything the government does entails the expenditure of public funds.[19] Thus, the most important political statement that any unit of government makes in a given year is its budget. Essentially, the budget causes administrators to follow the gambler's adage and "put their money where their mouth is."[20] When demands placed on government increase while funds are stable or decline, the competition for funds is keener than usual, forcing justice agencies to make the best case for their budgets. The heads of all departments, if they are doing their jobs well, are also vying for appropriations. Special-interest groups, the media, politicians, and the public, with their own views and priorities, often engage in arm twisting during the budgeting process.

ELEMENTS OF A BUDGET

The Budget Cycle

Administrators must think in terms of a **budget cycle**, which in government (and, therefore, all public criminal justice agencies) is typically on a fiscal year basis. Some states have a biennial budget cycle; their legislatures, such as those in Kentucky and Nevada, budget for a 2-year period. Normally, however, the fiscal year is a 12-month period that may coincide with a calendar year or, more commonly, will run from July 1 through June 30 of the following year. The federal government's fiscal year is October 1 through September 30. The budget cycle is important because it drives the development of the budget and determines when new monies become available.

The budget cycle consists of four sequential steps, repeated every year at about the same point in time: (1) budget formulation, (2) budget approval, (3) budget execution, and (4) budget audit.

Budget Formulation

Depending on the size and complexity of the organization and the financial condition of the jurisdiction, **budget formulation** can be a relatively simple or an exceedingly difficult task; in either case, it is likely to be the most complicated stage of the budgeting process. The administrator must anticipate all types of **expenditures** (e.g., overtime, gasoline, postage, and maintenance contracts) and predicts expenses related to major incidents or events that might arise. Certain assumptions based on the previous year's budget can be made, but they are not necessarily accurate. One observer noted that "every expense you budget should be fully supported with the proper and most logical assumptions you can develop. Avoid simply estimating, which is the least supportable form of budgeting."[21] Another criminal justice administrator, discussing budget formulation, added:

> The most important ingredient for any budgeting process is planning. Administrators should approach the budget process from the planning standpoint of "How can I best reconcile the [criminal justice] needs of the community with the ability of my jurisdiction to finance them, and then relate those plans in a convincing manner to my governing body for proper financing and execution of programs?" After all, as budget review occurs, the document is taken apart and scrutinized piece by piece or line by line. This fragmentation approach contributes significantly to our inability to defend interrelated programs in an overall budget package.[22]

To illustrate, let us assume that a police department budget is being prepared in a city having a manager form of government. Long before a criminal justice agency (or any other unit of local government) begins to prepare its annual budget, the city manager and/or the staff of the city have made revenue forecasts, considered how much (if any) of the current operating budget will be carried over into the next fiscal year, analyzed how the population of the jurisdiction will grow or shift (affecting demand for public services), and examined other priorities for the coming year. The city manager may also appear before the governing board to obtain information about its fiscal priorities, spending levels, pay raises, new positions, programs, and so on. The city manager may then send department heads a memorandum outlining the general fiscal guidelines to be followed in preparing their budgets.

On receipt of the city's guidelines for preparing its budget, the heads of functional areas, such as the chief of police, have a planning and research unit (assuming a city large enough to have this level of specialization) prepare an internal budget calendar and an internal fiscal policy memorandum (Table 15.2 shows an internal budget calendar for a large municipal police department). This memo may include input from unions and lower supervisory personnel. Each bureau is then given the responsibility for preparing its individual budget request.

In small police departments with little or no functional specialization, the chief may prepare the budget alone or with input from other officers or the city finance officer. In some small agencies, chiefs and sheriffs may not even see their budget or assist in its preparation. Because of tradition, politics, or even laziness, the administrator may have abdicated control over the budget. This puts the agency in a precarious position indeed; it will have difficulty engaging in long-term planning and spending money productively for personnel and programs when the executive has to get prior approval from the governing body to buy items such as office supplies.

The planning and research unit then reviews the bureau's budget request for compliance with the budgeting instructions and the chief's and city manager's priorities. Eventually, a consolidated budget is developed for the entire police department and submitted to the chief, who may meet with the planning and research unit and bureau commanders to discuss it. Personalities, politics, priorities, personal agendas, and other issues may need to be addressed; the chief may have to mediate disagreements concerning these matters, sometimes rewarding the loyal

TABLE 15.2	Budget Preparation Calendar for a Large Police Department	
What Should Be Done	**By Whom**	**On This Date**
Issue budget instructions and applicable forms	City administrator	November 1
Prepare and issue budget message, with instructions and applicable forms, to unit commanders	Chief of police	November 15
Develop unit budgets with appropriate justification and forward recommended budgets to planning and research unit	Unit commanders	February 1
Review unit budget	Planning and research staff with unit commanders	March 1
Consolidate unit budgets for presentation to chief of police	Planning and research unit	March 15
Review consolidated recommended budget	Chief of police, planning and research staff, and unit commanders	March 30
Obtain department approval of budget	Chief of police	April 15
Forward recommended budget to city administrator	Chief of police	April 20
Review recommended budget by administration	City administrator and chief of police	April 30
Approve revised budget	City administrator	May 5
Forward budget document to city council	City administrator	May 10
Review budget	Budget officer of city council	May 20
Present to council	City administrator and chief of police	June 1
Report back to city administrator	City council	June 5
Review and resubmit to city council	City administrator and chief of police	June 10
Take final action on police budget	City council	June 20

Source: U.S. Department of Justice, National Advisory Commission on Criminal Justice Standards and Goals, *Police* (Washington, DC: U.S. Government Printing Office, 1973), p. 137.

and sometimes reducing allotments to the disloyal.[23] Requests for programs, equipment, travel expenses, personnel, or anything else in the draft budget may be deleted, reduced, or enhanced.

The budget is then presented to the city manager. At this point, the chief executive's reputation as a budget framer becomes a factor. If the chief is known to pad the budget heavily, the city manager is far more likely to cut the department's request than if the chief is known to be reasonable in making budget requests, engages in innovative planning, and has a flexible approach to budget negotiations.

The city manager consolidates the police budget request with those from other municipal department heads and then meets with them individually to discuss their requests further. The city manager directs the city finance officer to make any necessary additions or cuts and then to prepare a budget proposal for presentation to the governing body.

The general steps in budget development are shown in Exhibit 15.2.

The courts have a similar budgetary process. In a large court, the process may include five major procedures: (1) developing an internal budgetary policy, (2) reviewing budget submissions, (3) developing a financial strategy, (4) presenting the budget, and (5) monitoring the budget. Figure 15.1 illustrates the relationship of the steps in the judicial budget process.

EXHIBIT 15.2

Steps in Budget Development

Following is a description of how the $1.98 billion budget for the California Highway Patrol (CHP) is typically developed. According to the budget section, "It is an all-year and year-on-year process" that begins at the level of the eight divisions and 118 area offices/dispatch centers, where budget requests originate. The requests are dealt with one of three ways: (1) funded within the department's base budget, (2) disapproved, or (3) carried forward for review by CHP personnel.

At the division level, managers review the area requests, make needed adjustments, and submit a consolidated request to the budget section at headquarters. This section passes input from the field to individual section management staff (e.g., planning and analysis, personnel, training, and communications) for review. Budget section staff meet with individual section management staff. Within 2 or 3 months, the budget section identifies proposals for new funding that have department-wide impact and passes them on to the executive level.

The commissioner and aides review the figures along with those from other state departments and agree on a budget to submit to the governor. The governor submits this budget to the legislature, which acts on it and returns it to the governor for signature.

Source: Based on Hal Rubin, "Working Out a Budget," *Law and Order*, May 1989, 27–28. Reprinted by permission of Hendon Publishing Company. (The adjusted budget figure of $1.98 billion shown is for 2010-2011; see http://www.ebudget.ca.gov/StateAgencyBudgets/2000/2720/spr.html (accessed November 5, 2010.)

Budget Approval

With the city manager's proposed budget request in hand, the governing board begins its deliberations on the citywide budget. The city manager may appear before the board to answer questions concerning the budget; individual department heads also may be asked to appear. Suggestions for getting monies approved and appropriated include the following:

1. Have a carefully justified budget.
2. Anticipate the environment of the budget hearing by reading news reports and understanding the priorities of the council members. Know what types of questions elected officials are likely to ask.
3. Determine which "public" will be at the police department's budget hearing and prepare accordingly. Public issues change from time to time; citizens who were outraged over one issue 1 year may be incensed by another the next.

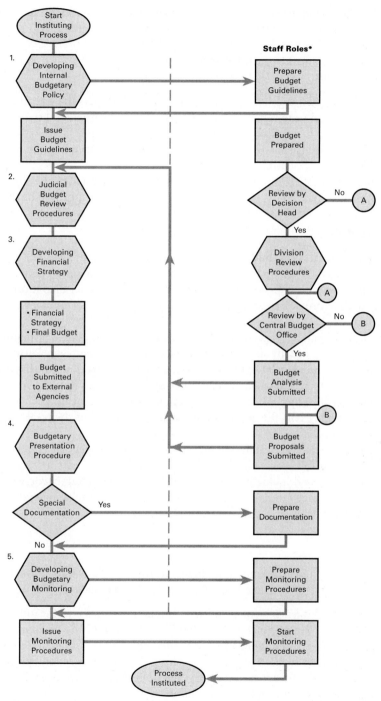

FIGURE 15.1 Steps in Judicial Budgetary Process

4. Make good use of graphics in the form of pie charts and histograms, but be selective and do not go overboard. Short case studies of successes are normal and add to the impact of graphics.
5. Rehearse and critique the presentation many times.
6. Be a political realist.[24]

After everyone scheduled has spoken, the city council directs the city manager to make further cuts in the budget or to reinstate funds or programs cut earlier, and so on. The budget is then approved. It is fair to say that at this stage, budgeting is largely a legislative function that requires some legal action, as a special ordinance or resolution approving the budget is passed each year by the governing board.

The columns in Table 15.3 indicate the budget amount requested by the chief of police, the amount recommended by the city manager, and the amount finally approved by the city council.

Budget Execution

The third stage of the process, **budget execution**, has several objectives: (1) to carry out the organization's budgeted objectives for the fiscal year in an orderly manner, (2) to ensure that the department undertakes no financial obligations or commitments other than those funded by the city council, and (3) to provide a periodic accounting of the administrator's stewardship over the department's funds.[25]

Supervision of the budget execution phase is an executive function that requires some type of fiscal control system, usually directed by the city or county manager. Periodic reports on accounts are an important element of budget control; they serve to reduce the likelihood of overspending by identifying areas in which deficits are likely to occur as a result of change in gasoline prices, extensive overtime, natural disasters, and unplanned emergencies (such as riots). A periodic budget status report tells the administrator what percentage of the total budget has been expended to date (Table 15.4).

Prudent administrators normally attempt to manage the budget conservatively for the first 8 or 9 months of the budget year, holding the line on spending until most fiscal crises have been averted. Because unplanned incidents and natural disasters can wreak havoc with any budget, this conservatism is normally the best course. Then the administrator can plan the most efficient way to allocate funds if emergency funds have not been spent.

The Audit

The word *audit* means "to verify something independently."[26] The basic rationale for a **budget audit** has been described by the controller general of the United States as follows:

> Governments and agencies entrusted with public resources and the authority for applying them have a responsibility to render a full accounting of their activities. This accountability is inherent in the governmental process and is not always specifically identified by legislative provision. This governmental accountability should identify not only the object for which the public resources have been devoted but also the manner and effect of their application.[27]

After the close of each budget year, the year's expenditures are audited to ensure that the agency spent its funds properly. Budget audits are designed to investigate three broad areas of accountability: **financial accountability** (focusing on proper fiscal operations and reports of the

TABLE 15.3 Police Operating Budget ($) in a Community of 100,000 Population

Description	FY 2010–2011 Expenses	FY 2011–2012 Expenses	FY 2012–2013 Police Request	City Manager	City Council
Salaries/wages					
Regular salaries	14,315,764	14,392,639	16,221,148	16,221,148	16,221,148
Overtime	988,165	782,421	951,875	951,875	711,875
Severance pay	36,194	226,465	82,000	-0-	-0-
Holiday pay	395,952	591,158	698,958	698,958	698,958
Callback pay	45,499	49,833	49,555	49,555	49,555
Subtotals	15,781,574	16,042,516	18,003,536	17,921,536	17,681,536
Employee benefits					
Retirement	3,345,566	3,485,888	4,069,521	4,069,521	4,069,521
Group insurance	1,256,663	1,467,406	1,752,718	1,752,718	1,752,718
Life insurance	43,797	53,164	117,590	117,396	117,396
Disability insurance	726,885	794,686	1,346,909	1,346,038	1,024,398
Uniform allowance	188,079	193,827	196,750	196,750	196,750
Medicare	77,730	80,868	100,058	99,739	99,739
Long-term disability	11,583	21,974	48,517	48,517	48,517
Subtotals	5,650,303	6,097,813	7,583,546	7,630,679	7,309,039
Services and supplies					
Office supplies	62,357	49,292	51,485	51,485	51,485
Operating supplies	227,563	148,569	270,661	270,661	270,661
Repair/maintenance	248,922	195,941	233,118	233,118	233,118

367

TABLE 15.3 (*Continued*)

Description	FY 2010–2011 Expenses	FY 2011–2012 Expenses	FY 2012–2013 Police Request	City Manager	City Council
Small tools	49,508	788	12,175	12,175	12,175
Professional services	337,263	290,359	334,765	334,765	334,765
Communications	287,757	223,200	392,906	392,906	392,906
Services and supplies					
Public utilities	111,935	116,773	121,008	121,008	121,008
Rentals	81,840	96,294	113,071	113,071	113,071
Vehicle rentals	834,416	1,193,926	1,363,278	1,363,278	1,169,278
Extradition	20,955	22,411	20,000	20,000	20,000
Other travel	4,649	5,123	23,500	23,500	23,500
Advertising	2,662	2,570	4,100	4,100	4,100
Insurance	328,360	595,257	942,921	942,921	942,921
Books/manuals	16,285	12,813	12,404	12,404	12,404
Employee training	47,029	30,851	-0-	-0-	-0-
Aircraft expenses	-0-	-0-	15,000	15,000	15,000
Special inventory	11,527	13,465	15,000	15,000	15,000
Other services and supplies	1,386,201	1,039,651	1,386,201	1,386,201	1,386,201
Subtotals	4,059,229	4,037,283	5,311,593	5,311,593	5,117,593
Capital outlay					
Machinery and equipment	572,301	102,964	-0-	-0-	-0-
Totals	26,063,407	26,280,576	30,898,675	30,863,808	30,108,168

TABLE 15.4 A Police Department's Budget Status Report ($)

Line Item	Amount Budgeted	Expenses to Date	Amount Encumbered	Balance to Date	Percentage Used
Salaries	16,221,148	8,427,062.00	-0-	7,794,086.00	52.0
Professional services	334,765	187,219.61	8,014.22	139,531.17	58.3
Office supplies	51,485	16,942.22	3,476.19	31,066.59	39.7
Repair/maintenance	49,317	20,962.53	1,111.13	27,243.34	44.8
Communications	392,906	212,099.11	1,560.03	179,246.86	54.4
Utilities	121,008	50,006.15	10,952.42	60,049.43	51.4
Vehicle rentals	1,169,278	492,616.22	103,066.19	573,595.59	51.9
Travel	23,500	6,119.22	2,044.63	15,336.15	34.7
Extraditions	20,000	12,042.19	262.22	7,695.59	61.5
Printing/binding	36,765	15,114.14	2,662.67	18,988.19	48.4
Books/manuals	12,404	5,444.11	614.11	6,345.78	48.8
Training/education	35,695	19,661.54	119.14	15,914.32	55.4
Aircraft expenses	15,000	8,112.15	579.22	6,308.63	57.9
Special investigations	15,000	6,115.75	960.50	7,922.75	47.2
Machinery	1,000	275.27	27.50	697.23	30.3
Advertising	4,100	1,119.17	142.50	2,838.33	30.8

justice agency), **management accountability** (determining whether funds were utilized efficiently and economically), and **program accountability** (determining whether the city council's goals and objectives were accomplished).[28]

Financial audits determine whether funds were spent legally, the budgeted amount was exceeded, and the financial process proceeded in a legal manner. For example, auditors investigate whether funds transferred between accounts were authorized, grant funds were used properly, computations were made accurately, disbursements were documented, financial transactions followed established procedures, and established competitive bidding procedures were employed.[29]

Justice administrators should welcome auditors' help to identify weaknesses and deficiencies and correct them.

BUDGET FORMATS

The three types of budgets primarily in use today are the line-item (or object-of-expenditure) budget, the performance budget, and the program (or results or outcomes) budget. Two additional types, the planning–programming–budgeting system (PPBS) and the zero-based budget (ZBB), are also discussed in the literature but are used to a lesser extent.

The Line-Item Budget

Line-item budgeting (or *item budgeting*) is the most commonly used budget format. It is the basic system on which all other systems rely because it affords control. It is so named because it breaks down the budget into the major categories commonly used in government (e.g., personnel, equipment, contractual services, commodities, and capital outlay items); every amount of money requested, recommended, appropriated, and expended is associated with a particular item or class of items.[30] In addition, large budget categories are broken down into smaller line-item budgets (in a police department, examples include patrol, investigation, communications, and jail function). The line-item format fosters budgetary control because no item escapes scrutiny.[31] Table 15.3, shown earlier, demonstrates a line-item budget for police, as do Tables 15.5 for a court, 15.6 for probation and parole, and 15.7 for a state prison organization. Each demonstrates the range of activities and funding needs of each agency. Note in Tables 15.3, 15.6, and 15.7 how a recession affected budgets and requests from year to year in many categories, resulting in severe cuts and even total elimination of items previously funded. Also note some of the ways in which administrators deviated from their usual practices to save money (e.g., the police budget shows that the department found it to be less expensive to lease patrol vehicles than to buy a huge fleet).

The line-item budget has several strengths and weaknesses. Its strengths include ease of control, development, comprehension (especially by elected and other executive branch officials), and administration. Weaknesses are its neglect of long-range planning and its limited ability to evaluate performance. Furthermore, the line-item budget tends to maintain the status quo; ongoing programs are seldom challenged. Line-item budgets are based on history: This year's allocation is based on last year's. Although that allows an inexperienced manager to prepare a budget more easily, it often precludes the reform-minded chief's careful deliberation and planning for the future.

The line-item budget provides ease of control because it clearly indicates the amount budgeted for each item, the amount expended as of a specific date, and the amount still available at that date (see, e.g., Table 15.4).

TABLE 15.5	Operating Budget for a District Court in a County of 100,000 Population

Category	Amount ($)
Salaries and wages	
Regular salaries	2,180,792
Part-time temporary	9,749
Incentive/longevity	50,850
Subtotal	2,241,391
Employee benefits	
Group insurance	170,100
Worker compensation	8,470
Unemployment compensation	3,220
Retirement	412,211
Social security	605
Medicare	13,503
Subtotal	608,109
Services and supplies	
Computers and office equipment	22,865
Service contracts	2,000
Minor furniture/equipment	1,000
Computer supplies	10,000
Continuous forms	4,000
Office supplies	36,066
Advertising	50
Copy machine expenses	40,000
Dues and registration	4,000
Printing	24,000
Telephone	16,000
Training	2,000
Court reporter/transcript	235,000
Court reporter per diem	265,000
Law books/supplements	9,000
Jury trials	75,000
Medical examinations	80,000
Computerized legal research	20,000
Travel	1,500
Subtotal	847,481
Child support	
Attorneys and other personnel	66,480
Court-appointed attorneys	656,000
Grand juries	18,600
Family court services	762,841
Total	5,200,902

TABLE 15.6 Probation and Parole Budget ($) for a State Serving 1 Million Population

Description	FY 2010–2011 Actual	FY 2011–2012 Agency Request	FY 2012–2013 Governor's Recommendation	Legislature Approved
Personnel	13,741,104	14,290,523	13,620,991	13,540,222
Travel	412,588	412,588	412,588	401,689
Operating expenses	1,307,020	1,395,484	1,307,020	1,256,787
Equipment	10,569	4,379	4,379	4,379
Loans to parolees	4,500	4,500	4,500	4,500
Training	9,073	9,073	9,073	9,073
Extraditions	200,000	200,000	200,000	185,000
Client drug tests	112,962	112,962	112,962	112,962
Home arrest fees	114,005	114,005	114,005	114,005
Community programs	50,000	50,000	50,000	47,500
Residential confinement	496,709	500,709	496,709	487,663
Utilities (paid by building lessors) Totals	16,458,530	17,094,223	16,332,227	16,163,780

TABLE 15.7 Operating Budget ($) for a State Medium Security Prison with 500 Inmates

Description	FY 2010–2011 Actual	FY 2011–2012 Agency Request	FY 2012–2013 Governor's Recommendation	Legislature Approved
Personnel				
Salaries	5,051,095	5,370,979	5,186,421	5,105,533
Worker's compensation	184,362	143,462	201,198	198,016
Retirement	1,142,010	1,174,968	1,215,674	1,196,028
Recruit tests	49,447	51,528	45,692	44,972
Insurance	474,330	488,250	513,000	500,175
Retirement insurance	30,963	31,872	35,917	35,349
Unemployment compensation	6,003	6,383	6,162	6,065
Overtime	165,856	-0-	-0-	-0-
Holiday pay	150,519	158,500	154,643	151,936
Medicare	39,965	45,140	42,225	40,948
Shift differential	95,925	101,011	98,553	96,828
Standby pay	6,465	6,807	6,641	6,526
Longevity pay	18,095	18,095	18,095	18,095
Subtotals	7,415,035	7,596,995	7,524,221	7,400,471
Services and supplies				
Operating supplies	180,672	277,495	180,647	214,859
Communications/freight	4,877	5,314	5,023	5,023
Printing/copying	20,900	47,222	19,016	21,527
Equipment repair	14,385	13,542	14,817	14,817
Vehicle operation	20,405	21,601	21,016	21,016

373

TABLE 15.7 (*Continued*)

Description	FY 2010–2011 Actual	FY 2011–2012 Agency Request	FY 2012–2013 Governor's Recommendation	Legislature Approved
Uniforms—custody	118,122	105,976	103,237	113,856
Inmate clothing	72,436	184,790	72,430	86,167
Equipment issued	20,403	13,236	15,451	17,086
Inmate wages	36,645	52,815	35,572	42,309
Food	895,897	1,299,838	895,759	1,065,403
Postage	7,738	8,793	7,036	7,738
Telephone	24,808	23,802	22,130	24,808
Subscriptions	382	401	725	401
Hand tools	110	286	113	113
Subtotals	1,417,780	2,055,111	1,392,972	1,635,123
Special equipment				
Grounds maintenance	116,863	34,088	12,557	13,661
Inmate law library	150,098	209,003	138,560	185,843
Special projects	18,564	20,115	16,419	21,836
Gas and power	53,237	8,887	8,887	8,887
Water	554,478	586,604	505,823	604,335
Garbage	60,390	69,377	52,266	67,171
Canine unit	80,035	101,240	82,436	82,436
	13,936	2,521	4,260	2,543
Total	9,880,416	10,683,941	9,738,401	10,022,306

Virtually all criminal justice agencies are automated to some extent, whether the financial officer prepares his or her budget using a computerized spreadsheet or a clerk enters information into a database that will be uploaded to a state's mainframe computer. Some justice agencies use an automated budgeting system that can store budget figures, make all necessary calculations for generating a budget request, monitor expenditures from budgets (similar to that shown in Table 15.7), and even generate some reports.

The Performance Budget

The key characteristic of a performance budget is that it relates the volume of work to be done to the amount of money spent.[32] It is input–output oriented, and it increases the responsibility and accountability of the manager for output as opposed to input.[33] This format specifies an organization's activities, using a format similar to that of the line-item budget. It normally measures activities that are easily quantified such as the number of traffic citations issued, crimes solved, property recovered, cases heard in the courtroom, and caseloads of probation officers. These activities are then compared with those of the unit that performs at the highest level. The ranking according to activity attempts to allocate funds fairly. Following is an example from a police department: The commander of the traffic accident investigation unit requests an additional three investigators, which the chief approves. Later, the chief might compare the unit's output and costs to these measures before the three investigators were added to determine how this change affected productivity.[34] An example of a police performance budget is provided in Table 15.8.

The performance budget format could be used in other justice system components as well. The courts could use performance measures such as filing cases, writing opinions, disposing of cases, and accuracy of presentence investigations.

Advantages of the performance budget include a consideration of outputs, the establishment of the costs of various justice agency efforts, improved evaluation of programs and managers, an emphasis on efficiency, increased availability of information for decision making, and the enhancement of budget justification and explanation.[35] The performance budget works best for an assembly line or other organization where work is easily quantifiable, such as paving streets. Its disadvantages include its expense to develop, implement, and operate because of the extensive use of cost accounting techniques and the need for additional staff (Figure 15.2 illustrates the elements used to determine the cost of providing police services); the controversy surrounding attempts to determine appropriate workload and unit cost measures (in criminal justice, although many functions are quantifiable, such reduction of duties to numbers often translates into quotas, which are anathema to many people); its emphasis on efficiency rather than effectiveness; and the failure to lend itself to long-range planning.[36]

Determining which functions in criminal justice are more important (and should receive more financial support) is difficult. Therefore, in terms of criminal justice agency budgets, the selection of meaningful work units is difficult and sometimes irrational. How can a justice agency measure its successes? How can it count what does not happen?

The Program Budget

The best-known type of budget for monitoring the activities of an organization is the *program budget*, developed by the RAND Corporation for the U.S. Department of Defense. This format examines cost units as units of activity rather than as units and subunits within the organization. This budget becomes a planning tool; it demands justification for expenditures for new programs and for deleting old ones that have not met their objectives.

TABLE 15.8	Example of a Police Performance Budget		
Category			**Amount**
Units/activities			
Administration (chief)		Subtotal	$
Strategic planning			$
Normative planning			$
Policies and procedures formulation			$
Etc.			
Patrol		Subtotal	$
Calls for service			$
Citizen contacts			$
Special details			$
Etc.			
Criminal investigation		Subtotal	$
Suspect apprehension			$
Recovery of stolen property			$
Transportation of fugitives			$
Etc.			
Traffic services		Subtotal	$
Accident investigation			$
Issuance of citations			$
Public safety speeches			$
Etc.			
Juvenile services		Subtotal	$
Locate runaways/missing juveniles			$
Arrest of offenders			$
Referrals and liaison			$
Etc.			
Research and development		Subtotal	$
Perform crime analysis			$
Prepare annual budget			$
Prepare annual reports			$
Etc.			

Police agencies probably have greater opportunities for creating new community-based programs than do the courts or corrections agencies. Some of these include crime prevention and investigation, drug abuse education, home security, selective enforcement (e.g., drunk driving) programs, and career development for personnel. Each of these endeavors requires instructional materials or special equipment, all of which must be budgeted. For example, traffic crash investigations (TCI) may be a cost area. The program budget emphasizes output measures. Outputs for TCI include the number of accidents handled and enforcement measures taken (such as citations issued, driving under the influence of alcohol and/or drugs (DUI) and other types of arrests made, and public safety speeches given). If the budget for these programs were divided by the units of output, the administrator could

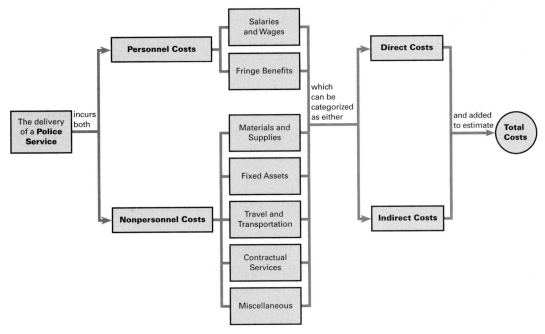

FIGURE 15.2 Elements in the Total Costs for Police Services

Source: U.S. Department of Justice, National Institute of Justice, *Measuring the Costs of Police Services* (Washington, DC: 1982), p. 20.

determine the relative cost for each unit of output or productivity. The cost of TCI, however, entails more than just the TCI unit; patrol and other support units also engage in this program.

Thus, the program budget is an extremely difficult form to execute and administer because it requires tracking the time of all personnel by activity as well as figuring in the cost of all support services and supplies. For this reason, criminal justice agencies rarely use the program budget.[37] Some advantages of the program budget, however, include its emphasis on the social utility of programs conducted by the agency; its clear relationship between policy objectives and expenditures; its ability to provide justification for and explanation of the budget; its establishment of a high degree of accountability; and its format and the wide involvement in formulating objectives, which lead employees at all levels of the organization to understand more thoroughly the importance of their roles and actions.[38]

Examples of police and court program budgets are presented in Tables 15.9 and 15.10, respectively.

PPBS and ZBB Formats

General Motors used the PPBS as early as in 1924,[39] and the RAND Corporation contributed to its development in a series of studies dating from 1949.[40] By the mid-1950s, several states were using it, and Secretary Robert McNamara introduced PPBS into the Defense Department in the mid-1960s.[41] By 1971, a survey revealed, however, that only 28 percent of the cities and 21 percent of the counties contacted had implemented PPBS or significant elements of it,[42] and, in 1971, the federal government announced that it was discontinuing its use.

PPBS treated the three basic budget processes—planning, management, and control—as coequals. It was predicated on the primacy of planning.[43] This future orientation transformed budgeting from an annual ritual into a "formulation of future goals and policies."[44] The PPBS

TABLE 15.9	Example of a Police Program Budget	
Program Area		**Amount**
Crime prevention	Subtotal	$
Salaries and benefits		$
Operating expenses		$
Capital outlay		$
Miscellaneous		$
Traffic crash investigation	Subtotal	$
Salaries and benefits		$
Operating expenses		$
Capital outlay		$
Miscellaneous		$
Traffic crash prevention	Subtotal	$
Salaries and benefits		$
Operating expenses		$
Capital outlay		$
Miscellaneous		$
Criminal investigation	Subtotal	$
Salaries and benefits		$
Operating expenses		$
Capital outlay		$
Miscellaneous		$
Juvenile delinquency prevention	Subtotal	$
Salaries and benefits		$
Operating expenses		$
Capital outlay		$
Miscellaneous		$
Special investigations	Subtotal	$
Salaries and benefits		$
Operating expenses		$
Capital outlay		$
Miscellaneous		$
Etc.		

budget featured a program structure, ZBB, the use of cost-budget analysis to distinguish among alternatives, and a budgetary horizon, often 5 years.[45]

Associated with PPBS, the zero-based planning and budgeting process requires managers to justify their entire budget request in detail rather than simply to refer to budget amounts established in previous years.[46] That is, each year, all budgets begin at zero and must justify any

TABLE 15.10	Example of a Court's Program Budget	

Program Area		Amount
Adjudicate criminal cases	Subtotal	$
Adjudicate felony cases	Total	$
Adjudicate misdemeanor appeals	Total	$
Adjudicate civil cases	Subtotal	$
Adjudicate major civil cases	Total	$
Adjudicate minor civil cases	Total	$
Adjudicate domestic relations cases	Total	$
Adjudicate juvenile cases	Subtotal	$
Adjudicate delinquency and dependent and neglect cases	Total	$
Adjudicate crimes against juveniles	Total	$
Provide alternatives to adjudication	Subtotal	$
Divert adult offenders	Total	$
Divert juvenile offenders	Total	$
Provide security	Subtotal	$
Handle prisoner transport	Total	$
Provide courtroom security Etc.	Total	$

Source: U.S. Department of Justice, National Institute of Law Enforcement and Criminal Justice, *Financial Management* (Washington, DC: The American University, 1979), p. 41.1.

funding. Following Peter Phyrr's use of ZBB at Texas Instruments, Governor Jimmy Carter adopted it in Georgia in the early 1970s and then as president implemented it in the federal government for fiscal year 1979. An analysis of this experience at the Department of Agriculture indicates that although its use saved $200,000 in the department's budget, it costs at least 180,000 labor hours of effort to develop.[47]

It is important to note that few organizations have budgets that are purely one format or another; therefore, it is not unusual to find that because of time, tradition, and personal preferences, a combination of several formats is used.

POTENTIAL PITFALLS IN BUDGETING

The Need for Budgeting Flexibility

Ancient Greek mythology tells of a highwayman named Procrustes who had an iron bedstead. He measured all who fell into his hands on the bed. If they were too long, their legs were lopped off to fit it. If they were too short, they were stretched to fit the bed. Few criminal justice administrators have not seen their monies and programs laid out on the Procrustean bed of a state or municipal budget officer and lopped off.

It, therefore, becomes imperative to build as much flexibility into the planned program and budget as possible. One technique is to make up three budgets: an optimistic one, reflecting the ideal level of service to the jurisdiction and organization; an expected one, giving the most likely level of service that will be funded; and finally, one that will provide a minimum level of service.[48]

To maximize the benefits of using budgets, managers must be able to avoid major pitfalls, which, according to Samuel Certo,[49] include the following:

1. Placing too much emphasis on relatively insignificant organizational expenses. In preparing and implementing a budget, managers should allocate more time to deal with significant organizational expenses and less time for relatively insignificant ones. For example, the amount of time spent on developing and implementing a budget for labor costs typically should be more than the amount of time spent on developing and implementing a budget for office supplies.
2. Increasing budgeted expenses year after year without adequate information. Perhaps the best-known method developed to overcome this potential pitfall is ZBB.[50]
3. Ignoring the fact that budgets must be changed periodically. Administrators must recognize that factors such as the cost of materials, new technology, and demands for services are constantly changing and that budgets should reflect that by being reviewed and modified periodically. The performance budget (discussed earlier) is designed to assist in determining the level of resources to be allocated for each organizational activity.

Common Cost and Waste Problems

To manage costs, administrators must be able to identify areas where waste and costs might be controlled. Louise Tagliaferri[51] identified 14 common cost factors that can be found in most organizations. Note that some costs are uncontrollable, but others can be reduced or at least maintained within a reasonable range:

absenteeism and turnover

accident loss

direct and indirect labor

energy

maintenance

materials and supplies

overtime

paperwork

planning and scheduling

product quality

productivity

tools and equipment

transportation

waste

Tagliaferri also noted that "literally billions of dollars are lost to industry (and criminal justice!) each year through carelessness, inattention, inefficiency, and other cost problems."[52]

POLICY AND BUDGET REFORM: STRATEGIES TO CONSIDER

As indicated above, today it is virtually impossible to watch a newscast or read a newspaper without seeing some mention of myriad fiscal and social problems that beset our nation's cities. Virtually every state, county, and city faces the dilemma of what to do about crime, the homeless, and the growing substance-abusing population (who are also frequently mentally ill)—as well as other social problems—with limited financial resources. This is the challenge for all policymakers, governing boards, and administrators, and several states have convened economic summits to seek ways to deal with these problems.

Clearly, something must be done to curb the burgeoning cost of criminal justice activities. In addition to the many ways in which costs are being cut in the police and courts components, discussed above, an area of criminal justice that has been given a lot of attention with regard to cost cutting is **corrections reform**, particularly prisons, inmates, and systems of offender sentencing. A report by the Justice Policy Institute outlined a series of issues that policymakers can consider as they make budget decisions:[53]

A. *Reform sentencing and drug laws.* Many people feel that the budget woes discussed previously will force lawmakers to consider revising some of the tough mandatory criminal penalties that are packing states' overburdened prisons. The engine behind the commitment of so many nonviolent offenders was the mandatory sentencing reforms of the 1990s. These policies took away discretion in sentencing from judges. If convicted, an individual was required to serve a set sentence, without regard for mitigating factors. These sentencing laws are the driving force behind the exponential growth of the prison system and largely affect nonviolent drug offenders, many of them women. Many states have enacted reforms of these laws, and others are considering reducing sentences for some drug and nonviolent offenses and eliminating mandatory minimum sentences for nonviolent crimes. Such reforms can save millions of dollars.

Given that the majority of mandatory minimum sentences are applied for drug offenses, if nonviolent drug offenders were instead diverted into intensive outpatient drug treatment programs, the savings could be tremendous. Some states have enacted laws to ease the burden of low-level drug offenders on the system. For example, Arizona voters passed Proposition 200, which diverts drug offenders into treatment rather than prison. Such programs save the state millions of dollars per year.

Another possible approach is to establish a sentencing commission to review the state's existing sentencing structure, laws, policies, and practices and recommend to the state supreme court and legislature changes regarding the criminal code, rules of criminal procedure, and other appropriate policies and procedures.

B. *Look at nonviolent prisoners and special populations.* There are large numbers of people serving time in prisons for nonviolent and first-time offenses. In addition, there are specific populations that pose little risk to the public and cost the state enormous amounts of money to house and care for, such as elderly prisoners, chronically ill or dying prisoners, and women. The costs of incarcerating women are considerable. They often require more extensive health care services and have children, many of whom are thrown into the child welfare system when their mothers are imprisoned. In addition, research has shown that children of incarcerated parents are at high risk for becoming incarcerated themselves. In effect, in continuing to rely on incarceration for these women, we are ensuring future increased prison costs.

Elderly prisoners represent another population that poses little risk to the public, yet costs a great deal to incarcerate. Because of their higher health care costs, these inmates cost three times more to incarcerate than younger prisoners. Truth in sentencing laws and the abolishment of parole will ensure that more and more people will grow old behind bars. Virginia has passed legislation allowing early release of inmates older than the age of 65 years who have served a minimum of 5 years or those older than 60 years who have served at least 10 years. Similarly, Texas has passed a bill to ease overcrowding by allowing supervised release for chronically ill prisoners to more appropriate facilities. The cost of care for chronically and terminally ill inmates is staggering, and such individuals pose a negligible risk to public safety.

C. *Consider parole reforms.* Research has shown that the public supports prevention and rehabilitation efforts as responses to crime. Parole and "good time" have been shown to be effective ways to control prison population levels. Confronted with the costs of more prison construction, some states have decided to use their release powers more effectively by identifying more potential candidates for parole. In addition, parole officers have used more alternatives to revocation for minor violations of the conditions of parole.

Summary

This chapter focused on the very important area of financial administration, primarily budgeting, and included its elements, formats, and potential pitfalls. Emphases were placed on the effects of the recent economic catastrophes besetting all states, as well as the need for administrators to develop skill in budget formulation and execution.

This chapter also discussed the budget process and different types of budgets. No single budgeting format is best; through tradition and personal preference, a hybrid format normally evolves in an organization. Nor should an administrator, under normal circumstances, surrender control of the organization's budget to another individual or body; the budget is integral to planning, organizing, and directing programs and operations.

Finally, it was shown that particularly hard times have befallen state and local units of government since 9/11 and the recession of 2008 and later. In these times of fiscal **exigency**, the justice administrator should attempt to become knowledgeable about, and recommend, sound means for reducing expenditures through changes in policy.

Questions for Review

1. In what major ways did the recent financial crisis that blanketed this country affect many police agencies? Courts? Corrections organizations?
2. What is a budget? How is it used?
3. What is a budget cycle? What is its importance in budgeting?
4. What is involved in formulating a budget? In its approval and execution?

5. List four budget formats used in the past. Which type is used most frequently? What are its major advantages and component parts?
6. What are some criminal justice policymakers doing to reform sentencing laws to reduce corrections expenditures?

Learn by Doing

1. You are a supervisor in your county sheriff's department and are joining an old friend for lunch; she is a newly hired in a municipal planning and budget office. During the meal, she indicates that a major part of her new assignment is to examine all agency budgets to determine where costs might be reduced. She asks for some general ideas concerning where expenses might be trimmed in the city police department's patrol division. In which specific areas would you advise her to look for cost savings and reductions in discretionary spending?

2. Historically, a major challenge in the administration of government agencies has concerned the need to pay for unfunded legislative mandates. You are a court administrator in a state where new judicial training standards have been implemented for all personnel. Unfortunately, the current economic downturn, as well as travel and tuition expenses, makes all but impossible your ability to send court employees out-of-state to obtain this required training. Furthermore, increasing caseloads and workloads combine to make it very difficult for employees to leave the court for any length of time. Your quandary: How to meet the legislative mandate while seeing that employees receive the education? You begin to consider arranging for online courses, broadcasts, videoconferencing, Webinars, podcasts, and regional and local training sessions.

Next, however, you begin to look at your budget (see examples in this chapter, particularly Table 15.5) to see where you might request permission from the chief judge to transfer funds from one line item to another. From which line item(s) will you recommend to the judge that funds be found and used for this training?

3. You are an assistant sheriff and thus jail administrator in a county that has only raised the tax rate in recent years to pay for jail improvements required by state and federal authorities. However, your county now finds itself in dire financial straits, primarily because the fragile "no new taxes" and as well as a "lock 'em up" mentality have finally combined to make fiscal matters extremely tenuous. Your judges are generally sympathetic, using a Jail Alternatives Program (intensive probation, a drug court and other options) for misdemeanants to the extent possible in order to save the cost of incarcerating and transporting jail inmates. It is estimated that these programs have reduced your jail population by more than 200 people. Now, however, one of the local judges seems bent on sentencing to jail anyone who is behind on child support payments—which accounts for around 150 people in the program. It becomes clear that this policy will soon cause the jail population to explode and soon break the county's jail budget. You know the judge personally. What will you do to save the county's jail budget?

Related Websites

American Correctional Association
http://www.aca.org/

International City/County Management Association
http://icma.org/main/sc.asp?t=0

National Association of State Budget Officers
http://www.nasbo.org/publications.php

Police Executive Research Forum
http://www.policeforum.org/

National Center for State Courts
http://www.ncsc.org/

Worldwidelearn (online fiscal accounting training)
http://www.worldwidelearn.com/business-course/accounting-courses.htm

Notes

1. Quoted in Charles R. Swanson, Leonard Territo, and Robert W. Taylor, *Police Administration: Structures, Processes, and Behavior,* 6th ed. (Upper Saddle River, NJ: Prentice Hall, 2005), p. 682.

2. Martha T. Moore, "Police layoffs make crime-plagued Camden all the worse," *USA TODAY,* http://www.usatoday.com/news/nation/2011-02-14-camden-cops_N.htm (accessed February 15, 2011).

3. Police Executive Research Forum, "63 Percent of Local Police Departments are Facing Cuts in their Total Funding, Survey Shows," http://www.police forum.org/upload/perf%20survey%20on%20polic ing%20&%20economy_908860847_222009153254. pdf (accessed October 11, 2010).

4. Police Executive Research Forum, "Survey Reveals Extent of Police Budget Cuts," September 30, 2010, http://policeforum.org/upload/Impact%20of%20 economic%20crisis%20on%20policing%20Sept%20 2010_391382430_1052010112054.pdf (accessed October 11, 2010).

5. Kevin Johnson, "Police response cut with budgets," August 25, 2010, http://www.usatoday.com/news/ nation/2010-08-25-1Anresponsecops25_ST_N.htm (accessed October 11, 2010).

6. Jeffrey Collins, "High gas prices force cops to walk the beat more," Associated Press (May 22, 2008), http://www.usatoday.com/news/nation/2008-05-22-3194321967_x.htm

7. Shaila Dewan, "As Gas Prices Rise, Police Turn to Foot Patrols," *The New York Times* (July 20, 2008), http://www.nytimes.com/2008/07/20/us/20patrol. html (accessed June 29, 2009).

8. Ibid.

9. National Center for State Courts, "As budget woes persist, NCSC helps courts redesign to save money," at: http://www.ncsc.org/services-and-experts/court-reengineering.aspx (accessed October 11, 2010).

10. Denise Lavoie, "Budget woes force touch choices for judges, courts," Associated Press, January 10, 2010, h t t p : / / a b c n e w s . g o . c o m / B u s i n e s s / wireStory?id=9524856 (accessed October 11, 2010).

11. B. Diane Williams, "Budget Cuts Must Lead to Innovation in Corrections," Corrections Today, December 1, 2009, http://www.allbusiness.com/ government/government-bodies-offices-regional/14060636-1.html (accessed October 11, 2010).

12. Kevin Johnson, "Budget crunch impacts prison time," National Center for Policy Analysis, February 19, 2009, http://www.ncpa.org/sub/dpd/index. php?Article_ID=17600 (accessed October 11, 2010).

13. James C. Snyder, "Financial Management and Planning in Local Government," *Atlanta Economic Review* (November–December 1973):43–47.

14. Aaron Wildavsky, *The Politics of the Budgetary Process,* 2nd ed. (Boston: Little, Brown, 1974), pp. 1–4.

15. Orin K. Cope, "Operation Analysis—The Basis for Performance Budgeting," in *Performance Budgeting and Unit Cost Accounting for Governmental Units* (Chicago: Municipal Finance Officers Association, 1954), p. 8.

16. Lester R. Bittel, *The McGraw-Hill 36-Hour Management Course* (New York: McGraw-Hill, 1989).

17. Ibid., p. 187.

18. Robert Townsend, *Further Up the Organization: How to Stop Management from Stifling People and Strangling Productivity* (New York: Alfred A. Knopf, 1984), p. 2.

19. Roland N. McKean, *Public Spending* (New York: McGraw-Hill, 1968), p. 1.

20. S. Kenneth Howard, *Changing State Budgeting* (Lexington, KY: Council of State Governments, 1973), p. 13.

21. Michael C. Thomsett, *The Little Black Book of Budgets and Forecasts* (New York: AMACOM, American Management Association, 1988), p. 38.

22. Quoted in V. A. Leonard and Harry W. More, *Police Organization and Management,* 7th ed. (Mineola, NY: Foundation Press, 1987), p. 212.

23. Swanson et al., *Police Administration,* p. 693.

24. Adapted, with some changes, from Wildavsky, *Politics of the Budgetary Process,* pp. 63–123.

25. Lennox L. Moak and Kathryn W. Killian, *A Manual of Techniques for the Preparation, Consideration, Adoption, and Administration of Operating Budgets* (Chicago: Municipal Finance Officers Association, 1973), p. 5, with changes.

26. Lennis M. Knighton, "Four Keys to Audit Effectiveness," *Governmental Finance* 8 (September 1979):3.

27. The Comptroller General of the United States, *Standards for Audit of Governmental Organizations, Programs, Activities, and Functions* (Washington, DC: General Accounting Office, 1972), p. 1.

28. Ibid.

29. Peter F. Rousmaniere, ed., *Local Government Auditing* (New York: Council on Municipal Performance, 1979), Tables 1 and 2, pp. 10, 14.

30. Swanson et al., *Police Administration,* p. 707.

31. Allen Schick, *Budget Innovation in the States* (Washington, DC: Brookings Institution, 1971), pp. 14–15. Schick offers 10 ways in which the line-item budget fosters control.

32. Malchus L. Watlington and Susan G. Dankel, "New Approaches to Budgeting: Are They Worth the Cost?" *Popular Government* 43 (Spring 1978):1.

33. Jesse Burkhead, *Government Budgeting* (New York: Wiley, 1956), p. 11.

34. Larry K. Gaines, John L. Worrall, Mittie D. Southerland, and John E. Angell, *Police Administration,* 2nd ed. (New York: McGraw-Hill, 2003), p. 519.

35. Swanson et al., *Police Administration,* p. 710.
36. Ibid, p. 711.
37. Gaines et al., *Police Administration,* p. 519.
38. Ibid.
39. David Novick, ed., *Program Budgeting* (New York: Holt, Rinehart and Winston, 1969), p. xxvi.
40. Ibid., p. xxiv.
41. Council of State Governments, *State Reports on Five-Five-Five* (Chicago: Author, 1968).
42. International City Management Association, *Local Government Budgeting, Program Planning and Evaluation* (Washington, DC: Author, 1972):7.
43. Allen Schick, "The Road to PPBS: The Stages of Budget Reform," *Public Administration Review* 26 (December 1966):244.
44. Ibid.
45. Swanson et al., *Police Administration,* p. 712.
46. Peter A. Phyrr, "Zero-Base Budgeting," *Harvard Business Review* (November– December 1970): 111–121; see also E. A. Kurbis, "The Case for Zero-Base Budgeting," *CA Magazine* (April 1986):104–105.
47. Joseph S. Wholey, *Zero-Base Budgeting and Program Evaluation* (Lexington, MA: Lexington Books, 1978), p. 8.
48. Donald F. Facteau and Joseph E. Gillespie, *Modern Police Administration* (Upper Saddle River, NJ: Prentice Hall, 1978), p. 204.
49. Samuel C. Certo, *Principles of Modern Management: Functions and Systems,* 4th ed. (Boston: Allyn & Bacon, 1989), pp. 484–485.
50. George S. Minmier, "Zero-Base Budgeting: A New Budgeting Technique for Discretionary Costs," *Mid-South Quarterly Business Review* 14 (October 1976):2–8.
51. Louise E. Tagliaferri, *Creative Cost Improvement for Managers* (New York: Wiley, 1981), p. 7.
52. Ibid., p. 8.
53. American Friends Service Committee, "Alternative Budget Suggestions for the State of Arizona Relative to Criminal Justice," March 2002, http://www.afsc.org/az/altbudg.htm (accessed February 15, 2005).

16

Technologies Now and for the Future

KEY TERMS AND CONCEPTS

ARJIS

Augmented reality (AR)

Automated License Plate Recognition (ALPR)

Biometrics

Blogs

CODIS

CompStat

Courtroom 21 Project

Crime mapping

DNA

Gang intelligence system

Global Positioning System (GPS)

Less-lethal weapons

MySpace

N-DEx

Offender management

Paper on demand

Postconviction testing

Pursuit management

Real-time Court Reporting

Robotics

TASER ECD

Traffic collision investigation

Unmanned aerial vehicles (UAVs)

Virtual visits

Voice-translation devices

YouTube

LEARNING OBJECTIVES

After reading this chapter, the student will:

- be aware of uses of new application of police technologies
- understand the latest major developments in the use of DNA
- know what the FBI and other agencies are doing in the fields of criminal justice information systems (i.e., N-DEx, and biometrics) and what they promise for the future
- be familiar with new developments for police less-lethal tools
- be able to explain recent legal considerations regarding the use of DNA and Global Positioning System (GPS) tracking
- understand the kinds of hardware, Web-based tools, and databases that are assisting law enforcement as well as those that are in development
- understand the benefits of using **CompStat**, crime mapping, and gang intelligence systems
- know what applications augmented reality (AR) and unmanned aerial vehicles (UAVs) bode for the future
- be able to explain the goal of paper on demand and other developing court technologies
- be familiar with the modern features of the Courtroom 21 Project and those of The National Judicial College
- know what is being done with respect to real-time court reporting and telephonic court appearances
- be aware of technologies used in correctional facilities for inmate riots and the use of GPS for inmate management

Men are only so good as their technical developments
allows them to be.

—George Orwell

However far modern science and technics have fallen short of
their inherent possibilities, they have taught mankind at least
one lesson: Nothing is impossible.

—Lewis Mumford

INTRODUCTION

Technology consists primarily to make people more productive. These tools also provide criminal justice administrators with opportunities to reshape the future with increased effectiveness and productivity.

Leadership is crucial to the development of new technologies. First, as will be seen, some technologies have legal (i.e., privacy) and policy issues that must first be addressed prior to their marketing and application. Second, without a leader championing these innovations, it is unlikely that the impetus needed for the cultural changes that technology requires will exist. These technologies and the accompanying policy must be consistent with the agency's overall goals and philosophy. The way in which administrators prepare for and address these administrative issues will largely determine the level of success enjoyed by any new technology project. Finally, another combination of challenges that accompanies the topic of new technologies for criminal justice organizations is their cost—and obtaining the necessary revenues for obtaining and using them.

Because the police component is where the bulk of technological research and development—and use—has occurred in criminal justice, we largely focus there and begin by examining many developments in this field. Included is a discussion of new developments with DNA and developments with less-lethal tools, as well as several Web-based technologies and methods (e.g., those involving robotics, **CompStat**, crime mapping, traffic and crime-scene functions, and gangs) and some fascinating tools that are either increasingly in use or are in development (e.g., augmented reality and unmanned aerial vehicles).

Next we review several major types of court technologies, looking at the overarching goal of going paperless, the Courtroom 21 Project, telephonic court appearances, real-time court reporting, several other tools that are emerging, and the challenges of implementing court technologies. The field of corrections is then examined, including what is being done technologically in institutions (prisons and jails) to manage inmates and "virtual visits" to hospitals and courtrooms. The chapter concludes with a brief discussion of the rapidly expanding field of biometrics. Eight exhibits in this chapter will highlight several new or developing technologies.

LAW ENFORCEMENT TOOLS AND METHODS

Applications in the Field: Some Examples

Following are some examples of new uses of technologies by police agencies. Note that some of them are still in the early stages of development, controversial and as yet unproven for scientific accuracy, and/or quite expensive to obtain. Nonetheless, these vignettes demonstrate the unlimited potential for applying computer technologies for policing:

1. A fast-food worker in Chicago was robbed at knifepoint, and responding officers had the restaurant's surveillance video enhanced by a Regional Computer Forensics Laboratory; a clearer picture of the suspect was compared against the Illinois drivers' license database, resulting in a match and arrest of the suspect.[1]
2. Multimedia phones are rapidly catching up with mobile phones in police application. Officers can: run queries from motor vehicle and criminal databases, send and receive information from other officers or dispatchers, obtain information about speeders or drunk drivers; the greatest advantage is e-mail capability, with officers on patrol no longer needing to go to a laptop and log on.[2]

3. Community policing has expanded its horizons with the police use of Twitter, by which they can send out "tweets" to a large segment of the population that might not read the news or watch it on television. This method of engaging the community is a positive complement to police agencies' use of other Web tools and social media sites such as Facebook and MySpace.[3]

4. Handheld **voice-translation devices** are being tested by several police agencies. The units contain interchangeable computer chips loaded with more than one thousand phrases from different languages, including Spanish, Arabic, Vietnamese, Cantonese, and Mandarin. The translators offer a menu from which users select a phrase and language with a stylus, and the device then speaks in the chosen language.[4]

5. With a wireless video networking system, officers in several states can literally watch each other's back from anywhere in the city and receive real-time video either in the field or in the office. In Oklahoma City, with nearly 500 cameras covering 555 square miles, the system streams video to laptops in the city's 700 patrol cars; when an event occurs, commanding officers take control the cameras in the area and provide the video to officers at the scene.[5]

6. A geographic information system (GIS) in New York City studies patterns of domestic violence and allows police to analyze the effectiveness of domestic violence outreach programs and to develop presentations to city agencies and nonprofit organizations. The number and time of occurrence of domestic violence reports filed and geographic information—data on streets, boundaries, congressional districts—are obtained and help the mayor's domestic violence office plan its activities.[6]

7. A tool for voice-stress analysis is in use with suspects and in prisons. At least 1,500 agencies are using such software that is loaded into a laptop when questioning subjects. During an interrogation, the subject talks into a microphone and the words are translated on screen into graphs that measure speech with algorithms and formulas, showing patterns indicative of confusion and cognitive dissonance. Critics, however, point to several anecdotal accounts where persons being questioned made false confessions and argue that such people confess because they are afraid of the analyzer. More studies will be performed to determine whether voice-stress analysis is, as one writer stated, "good science, or just bunk."[7]

8. The Department of Homeland Security has completed installation of next-generation biometrics to assess entries at 104 land border ports, as mandated by Congress. The program verifies each visitor's identity and compares his or her biometric and biographical information against watch lists of terrorists, criminals, and immigration violators. Federal penitentiary escapees, convicted rapists, drug traffickers, and others have also been nabbed at the borders using biometrics.[8]

Next, we discuss an array of new technological advances that are enabling the police to be more efficient and society more safe.

Developments in DNA: CODIS and Postconviction Testing

A recent **DNA** innovation is **CODIS**, for Combined DNA Index System. CODIS contains DNA profiles obtained from subjects convicted of homicide, sexual assault, and other serious felonies. Investigators can compare evidence from their individual cases with the system's extensive national file of DNA genetic markers.[9] CODIS provides software and support services so that state and local laboratories can establish databases of convicted offenders, unsolved crime scenes, and missing persons. It allows these forensic laboratories to exchange and compare DNA profiles electronically, thereby linking serial violent crimes, especially sexual assaults, to each other, and to identify suspects by matching DNA from crime scenes to convicted offenders.[10]

An issue in the DNA field is **postconviction testing**. Because the speed and accuracy of testing have improved, and because of the growing number of cases of convicted people later being exonerated because of DNA tests, many inmates now want to be tested if there is any evidence from which DNA can be extracted. They have everything to gain and nothing to lose.

Each state has its own procedural rules for postconviction relief. These rules set the grounds upon which a new trial is available and the threshold that must be met in order to merit a new trial. In most states, the rules of criminal procedure require new evidence to be brought before the court within 6 months of the conviction. This potentially excludes offenders who were convicted before DNA testing was available but for whom such testing may now provide important evidence relevant to their case. The potential for DNA to exonerate as well as convict offenders has led to specific state statutes to allow for postconviction DNA testing under certain circumstances, even after the convicted person has exhausted all of his or her appeals. The motions allowed and the processes being created under these new laws allow judges broader authority to order or admit DNA evidence in such cases. To date, 31 states have laws in place to provide for motions for postconviction DNA testing.[11]

A New Criminal Justice Information System

In March 2008, the FBI announced the first phase of a three-phase initiative that will provide police agencies with a powerful investigative tool to search, link, analyze, and share criminal justice information. **N-DEx** will provide nationwide connectivity to local, state, and federal agencies that will allow them to detect relationships between people, places, things, and crime characteristics—to "connect the dots" between apparently unrelated data.[12] Here is an example of how it works. Suppose John Doe fails to surrender in Denver, Colorado, to begin serving a 7-year prison sentence for money laundering, and police enter an arrest warrant into the National Crime Information Center (NCIC). Officers then search N-DEx for people connected to Doe derived from the information contained in incident and other types of reports (e.g., arrest, probation, incarceration) previously entered; N-DEx locates the names, addresses, and other identifiers of more than 100 associates of Doe and asks N-DEx to display the results on a map. Jane Doe, the fugitive's mother, who visited him every month of his incarceration in jail for a misdemeanor, is found to be living on an Indian reservation near Santa Fe, New Mexico. Officers in Denver contact the reservation's tribal police, who speak with Jane; they learn that she has been in contact with John and agrees to make an effort to convince him to surrender.[13]

Recent Developments in Less-Lethal Weapons

Police departments nationwide continue to look to new techniques for obtaining offender compliance using **less-lethal weapons** as an alternative "intermediate" weapon between the voice and the gun. Many less-lethal alternatives are relatively inexpensive for agencies to adopt and can significantly reduce a department's liability.[14]

Certainly the use by police of the TASER electronic control device (ECD) is expanding as the units have become easier to carry (now as small as 6 inch by 3 inch in size and 7 ounce in weight) and more effective to use (including a range of up to 35 feet; data port storage of date, time, and duration of deployment; a red-dot laser light; and enhanced accountability). Indeed, it is now estimated that nearly 14,500 law enforcement and military agencies now deploy **TASER ECD** technology in more than 40 countries, and more than 5,580 agencies deploy them to all of their patrol officers.[15]

Although the TASER® X26™ is the standard less-lethal TASER ECD device that is so popular and typically carried by patrol officers, research and development is ongoing at TASER International, Inc., and several new developments have been announced recently. First, the new TASER CAM™ was introduced, which offers increased protection for officers because the suspect's behavior prior to the TASER's ECD's deployment can be recorded with full audio and video, even in zero light conditions. Also new is the TASER® X3™, a multi-shot ECD that can engage multiple targets and display Warning Arcs™ while loaded. Finally, the TASER® X12™ Less Lethal Shotgun (LLS) by Mossberg® utilizes a re-engineered pump-action shotgun that fires a less-lethal, self-contained, wireless ECD (termed the XREP) that delivers a similar neuro-muscular effect as the handheld X26 ECD, but can also be delivered to a maximum effective range of 100 feet and combines a blunt impact force (the TASER® X12™ is bright yellow in color—a warning to users that it is less-lethal only; furthermore, the weapon will not accept standard shotgun rounds.)[16]

A major and promising study was announced by the Wake Forest University School of Medicine in late 2007 that was touted as "the first large, independent study to review every Taser deployment and to reliably assess the overall risk and severity of injuries in real world condition"; the study reported that 99.7 percent of nearly 1,000 cases of Taser use resulted in only mild injuries, such as scrapes and bruises, or no injuries at all; only three subjects (0.3 percent) suffered injuries severe enough to need hospitalization.[17]

The Less Than Lethal program of the National Institute of Justice coordinates research on such weapons, ensuring that they are technically feasible and also practical for police officers. In addition to the WebShot gun, the program recently provided funding for research on the following technologies:[18]

- The Laser Dazzler, a flashlight device designed to disorient or distract suspects with a green laser light
- The Sticky Shocker, a wireless projectile fired from a gas gun that sticks to the subject with glue or a barb, attaches to clothing, and delivers an electric shock
- The Ring Airfoil Projectile, a doughnut-shaped hard-rubber weapon that is under redesign to also disperse a cloud of pepper powder on impact

Pepper spray, or oleoresin capsicumoc (OC), is now used by an estimated 90 percent of police agencies, according to the National Institute of Justice.[19] This spray inflames the mucous membranes of the eyes, nose, and mouth, causing a severe burning sensation for 20 minutes or less.[20] The spray is highly effective in subduing suspects without causing undue harm or long-term effects.[21] Another relatively new less-lethal tool is a compressed-air gun that fires small pellets filled with OC or other gases.[22]

Robotics

Recent advances in robots (*bots* in tech-speak) have allowed policing—and soldiering—to become safer. Robots are now fitted with video capability, including night vision; a camera (also useful for photographing crime scenes); a Taser; and even the ability to engage in two-way communications.[23] **Robotics** researchers at Carnegie Mellon University recently developed a small, throwable, remote-controlled prototype robot with a top speed of 20 miles per hour designed for surveillance in urban settings that can see around corners and deliver information from locations where human access is dangerous.[24]

Although bomb-handling robots have been in use for several years, recently the military employed a robot that can sniff explosive devices; such robots—with 7-foot arms to scan the inside and undercarriage of vehicles for bombs, lights, video cameras that zoom and swivel, obstacle-hurling flippers, and jointed arms with hand-like grippers to disable or destroy bombs—were sent to Iraq in early 2007, to give soldiers the ability to better detect and deal with roadside bombs.[25] Their use in policing cannot be far behind and would be very helpful if programmed to sniff for methamphetamine ingredients.

A major constraint for police use of robotics is its cost. The bomb-sniffing robot described earlier costs $165,000, and one with elongated, tracked wheels that can act like legs to climb over obstacles, making it useful for search-and-rescue activities, can run more than $100,000. Even a robot that is used only for under-vehicle inspections can cost up to $15,000.[26] Many jurisdictions will have to go without or wait until the price of robots declines before they can be deployed.

CompStat

A relatively new technologically driven crime management tool used in the problem solving process (discussed in Chapter 3) is **CompStat**, a strategic control system designed for the collection and feedback of information on crime and related quality-of-life issues. CompStat has been summarized as follows: "Collect, analyze, and map crime data and other essential police performance measures on a regular basis, and hold police managers accountable for their performance as measured by these data."[27]

Since the CompStat process was introduced by the New York City Police Department (NYPD) in 1994, it has been widely adopted. It is obviously imperative that police supervisors and managers understand the basics of this approach. The key elements of CompStat are as follows:

- Specific objectives
- Accurate and timely intelligence
- Effective tactics
- Rapid deployment of personnel and resources
- Relentless follow-up and assessment[28]

CompStat pushes all precincts to generate weekly crime activity reports so that they can be held accountable for the achievement of several objectives. Crime data are readily available, offering up-to-date information that is then compared at citywide, patrol, and precinct levels. Therefore, commanders must stop simply responding to crime and have begun proactively thinking about ways to deal with it in terms of suppression, intervention, and prevention. Commanders must explain what tactics they have employed to address crime patterns, what resources they have and need, and with whom they have collaborated. Brainstorming problem-solving sessions ensue about proactively responding to crime problems and suggestions for strategies are made at subsequent meetings, with relentless follow-up by top brass to further ensure accountability.[29]

Crime Mapping

Computerized **crime mapping** has been termed "policing's latest hot topic."[30] For officers on the street, mapping puts street crime into an entirely new perspective; for administrators, it provides a way to involve the community in addressing its own problems by observing trends in neighborhood criminal activity. Crime mapping also offers crime analysts graphic representations of crime-related issues. Furthermore, detectives can use maps to better understand the hunting patterns of serial offenders and to hypothesize where these offenders might live.[31]

Computerized crime mapping combines geographic information from global positioning satellites with crime statistics gathered by a department's computer-aided dispatching (CAD) system and demographic data provided by private companies or the U.S. Census Bureau (some agencies acquire information from the Census Bureau's Internet home page). The result is a picture that combines disparate sets of data to provide a new perspective on crime. For example, a map of crimes can be overlaid with maps or layers of causative data: unemployment rates in the areas of high crime, locations of abandoned houses, population density, reports of drug activity, or geographical features (such as alleys, canals, or open fields) that might be contributing factors.[32] The hardware and software are available to nearly all police agencies and cost just a few thousand dollars. Following are instances of successful outcomes using crime mapping:

- When an armored car was robbed in Toronto, dispatchers helped officers chase the suspects through a sprawling golf course using the mapping feature of the CAD system.
- The Illinois State Police map fatal accidents throughout the state and show which districts have specific problems. They can correlate those data with data on citations written, seatbelt use, and other types of enforcement information.
- The Salinas, California, Police Department maps gang territories and correlates socioeconomic factors with crime-related incidents. Murders are down 61 percent, drive-by shootings 31 percent, and gang-related assaults 23 percent.[33]

The NIJ's Crime Mapping Research Center, established in 1997, provides information concerning research, evaluation, and training programs through its Web site.[34]

Exhibit 16.1 discusses the use of interactive crime mapping on the Internet in San Diego, California, and provides an example of a crime-analysis map that citizens can access.

EXHIBIT 16.1

Interactive Crime Mapping on the Internet

San Diego County's Automated Regional Justice Information System (ARJIS) was the first multiagency interactive crime-mapping Web site in the nation, making interactive crime maps available to the public on the Internet. These systems not only enable citizens to obtain much more information than was previously available but also free crime analysts to devote more time to analyzing crime instead of providing reports to the public. Now, anyone in the world can query and view certain crime, arrest, call, and traffic data for the county. Searches can be geographical (by street, neighborhood, police beat, or city), as well as by time of day or day of week.

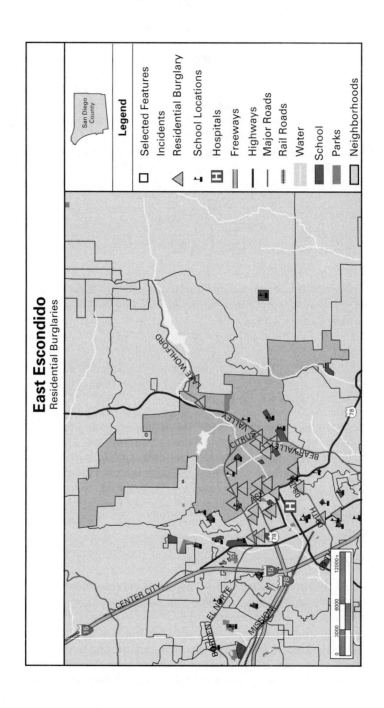

East Escondido
Residential Burglaries

Legend

	Selected Features
□	Incidents
△	Residential Burglary
⌐	School Locations
H	Hospitals
	Freeways
	Highways
	Major Roads
	Rail Roads
	Water
	School
	Parks
	Neighborhoods

San Diego County

As an example, above is a map showing citizens of East Escondido the locations of residential burglaries during a recent 1-month time frame.

Source: Based on San Diego County, Regional Crime Maps, http://mapping.arjis.org/main.aspx (accessed December 1, 2010); used with permission.

Traffic Functions

A multicar accident can turn a street or highway into a parking lot for many hours, sometimes days. The police need to collect evidence relating to the collision, including measurements and sketches of the scene and vehicle and body positions, skid marks, street or highway elevations, intersections, and curves. These tasks typically involve a measuring wheel, steel tape, pad, and pencil.

Some police agencies have begun using GPS to determine such details as vehicle location and damage, elevation, grade, radii of curves, and critical speed. A transmitter takes a series of "shots" to gain the exact location and measurements of collision details such as skid marks, area of impact, and debris. That information is then downloaded into the system, and the coordinates are plotted on an aerial shot of the intersection or roadway. With the aid of computer technology, the details are then superimposed on the aerial shot, thus re-creating the collision scene to scale. Finally, digital photos of the collision are incorporated into the final product, resulting in a highly accurate depiction of the collision. With a fatal or major injury accident, what once required several officers up to 18 hours' time is reduced to mere minutes.[35]

Another traffic-related problem is that of high-speed pursuits, which carry tremendous potential for injury, property damage, and liability resulting from high-speed chases by police (discussed in Chapters 5 and 14); indeed, this is such a concern that some agency administrators have developed **pursuit management** policies that completely prohibit such activities by officers.

Tire spikes can be deployed when a fleeing vehicle is approaching and then retracted so that other vehicles and police cars can pass safely. Tire spikes often do not work, however, or result in the suspect losing control of the vehicle (although some spike devices are designed to prevent this by breaking off in the tires and thus deflating them slowly).[36] One device has been developed using a short pulse of electrical current to disrupt electronic devices that are critical to the continued operation of the vehicle's ignition system. Once pulsed, the vehicle rolls to a controlled stop, similar to the effect of running out of fuel, and will not restart until the affected parts are replaced.[37]

Exhibit 16.2 describes another relatively new traffic-related technology: the automated license plate recognition system.

EXHIBIT 16.2

License Plate Recognition Systems: Boon or Bane?

License plate recognition systems have long been in use for traffic enforcement; cameras, either mounted on a mobile tripod or permanently fixed on a pole, trigger a flash camera when a vehicle is exceeding the speed limit. Today, however, cameras are being mounted on police patrol cars or in fixed locations and used for many more purposes, such as searching for stolen cars. In the event of a "hit" on a license plate in a stolen vehicle database, an alarm alerts the officer of the match. The officer can then contact dispatch to see if the information is correct. The cameras can also help in more serious investigations, such as where a partial license plate number is obtained from a witness to a hit-and-run. Furthermore, if a bank robbery occurs during noon hour, the personnel operating the plate reader can pass along the plates that were read at that location at that time as possible suspects. Or, if a serious crime is committed in an area, detectives can search the system to see if they have data on the cars that were parked there.[1] In late 2009, Tiburon, California, perhaps became the first U.S. city to permanently install six cameras that recognize license plate characters at two roads that basically line its borders, essentially to accomplish the earlier objectives.[2] Such applications have, of course, drawn criticism from privacy rights advocates as well as from citizens concerned with how the cameras are used to track people's movements, and what is done with the data they produce. Others, however, believe the cameras reduce the need for agencies to hire more officers, and are the "future of law enforcement."[3]

Sources: [1]Based on Jim McKay, "Freeze Frame," *Government Technology* (April 2008), http://www.gov tech.com/gt/articles/282014?printall (July 3, 2009); [2]Demian Bulwa, "Tiburon to record every car coming and going," *San Francisco Chronicle*, November 20, 2009, http://www.sfgate.com/cgi-bin/article. cgi?f=/c/a/2009/11/19/BAP71ANBF4.DTL&tsp=1 (accessed November 25, 2009); [3]McKay, "Freeze Frame."

Crime Scenes

Several technologies exist or are being developed relating to crime scene investigations. Three-dimensional computer-aided drafting (3D CAD) software is available for a few hundred dollars. By working in 3D, CAD users can create scenes that can be viewed from any angle. Technical evidence can be visualized by nontechnical observers. Juries can "view" crime scenes and see the location of evidence; they can also view just what the witness says he or she saw. Police input the exact dimensions and get a scaled drawing. A 5-day, 40-hour course in 3D CAD is available for police investigators, traffic accident reconstructionists, and evidence technicians.[38]

Crime scene evidence is often too sketchy to yield an obvious explanation of what happened. New software called Maya has been developed for this field, called *forensic animation;* this software helps experts to determine what probably occurred. Maya is so packed with scientific calculations that it can create a virtual house from old police photos and replicate the effects of several types of force, including gravity: how a fall could or could not have produced massive injuries, how flames spread in a house fire, and the way smoke cuts a pilot's visibility in a plane crash.[39]

The Federal Department of Energy is also testing a prototype laptop computer equipped with digital video and still cameras, laser range finders, and a Global Positioning System. A detective using it can beam information from a crime scene back to a laboratory to get input from experts. Researchers are also working on a chip that would give police the ability to process more evidence, including DNA samples, at the crime scene, eliminating the risk of contamination en route to the lab.[40]

Gang Intelligence Systems

The escalating problem of street gangs has prompted many police departments to search for a tool that can help them to deal with the problem. Several agencies now use a **gang intelligence**

system to collect information in a database, allowing officers to enter and access key pieces of data such as names of gangs as well as individual members, vehicles, weapons, suspected associates, and incident dates. Even if an officer has a small piece of information to work with, such as a nickname or partial license plate number of a suspect's car, the system's cross-referencing function connects that information to additional information in the database about gang members, their activities, addresses, descriptions, and photos. Officers can even access the database in their patrol cars by using laptops. The system also allows photographs to be stored and linked with other information about suspects. A statewide gang intelligence system, California's CAL/GANG, is a relational database that holds and categorizes everything from nicknames to tattoos on suspected or known gang members. This system, which has been credited with solving a number of high-visibility gang crimes, is now being considered by other states, including Florida, that have a significant gang problem.[41]

Other Technologies Increasingly in Use

GLOBAL POSITIONING SYSTEM (GPS)   More and more, police agencies are finding uses for the **Global Positioning System (GPS)**, which plots locations of vehicles and even people with remarkable accuracy. For example, GPS devices allow police agencies to efficiently, accurately, and safely track the movement of vehicles. GPS has even been adapted to the problem of knowing exactly where search-and-rescue dogs are and how effective their search efforts have been. In addition, as noted earlier, agencies have begun using GPS for traffic collision investigations, to determine such details as vehicle location and damage, debris, elevation, grade, radii of curves, skid marks, and critical speed.

As shown in Exhibit 16.3, however, the application of GPS for police work can also involve important Fourth Amendment considerations that are critical for the police to know and bear in mind.[42]

EXHIBIT 16.3

Legal Considerations in Using GPS with Tracking Vehicles

Fourth Amendment considerations apply to the installation and monitoring of GPS devices. Specifically, the Fourth Amendment is implicated if officers need to intrude into an area where people have a reasonable expectation of privacy. Consider the following hypothetical example:

> Jones has been indicted by a federal grand jury for firearms and drug trafficking offenses. Several government witnesses, subpoenaed to testify against Jones, begin to report that they have been harassed and threatened, with their vehicles being vandalized and homes shot at. Four close associates of Jones have emerged as suspects: Adamson, Boyd, Charleston, and Davidson. Police surveillances of each have been unsuccessful due to limited resources, so the decision is made to use GPS tracking devices to compare the times and locations of specific witness-tampering events with the movement of the suspects' vehicles.
>
> Adamson lives in a suburban development and parks his automobile on the street; Boyd resides in a gated community and parks his car in his driveway; Charleston regularly keeps his vehicle in the garage at his home; and Davidson owns a

sports car and stays in a variety of apartments. Technicians can accomplish the GPS installations for Adamson, Boyd, and Charleston without intruding into the vehicles; Davidson's sports car is built in such a way, however, that the device cannot be placed on its exterior without being discovered. Agents must therefore enter the vehicle to hide the equipment.

Adamson's living in a residential neighborhood and parking his vehicle in a public place makes it easy for technicians to approach his car. Adamson has an expectation of privacy in the interior of his vehicle, but he does not have it for the car's exterior. *Boyd's* living in a gated community makes his situation a little different, but the Fourth Amendment's view is not likely to be altered; no expectation of privacy exists for those persons who leave their vehicles in parking lots or on streets in gated communities. The fact that Boyd parks his automobile in his driveway can make a warrantless installation more legally tenuous, however. Although federal court decisions support the position that one does not have an expectation of privacy in the typical residential driveway, this determination will ultimately depend on the driveway's length and what measures the homeowner has taken to restrict the driveway from public view and access. Obtaining a warrant or waiting for the vehicle to move to a public place might be a better option for Boyd's vehicle. *Charleston's* vehicle presents a greater challenge because of its being parked in his garage—an area where he has an expectation of privacy. Therefore, unless the officers can locate his automobile in a public place to install an external device, they will need a warrant.

Finally, where *Davidson* parks his sports car is of no importance; the agents will need a warrant because they must enter the vehicle to install the device in the passenger compartment, in the trunk, or under the hood to access its wiring or power sources.

Assume that the four GPS devices are installed according to plan. First, because the agents will attempt to track the four men's vehicles while moving only on public roads and highways, a warrant is not needed to do the tracking. If later analysis of captured GPS data revealed that on several occasions, vehicles belonging to any of the men were in the exact locations and within a small window of time when acts of witness tampering and violent acts were perpetrated, this evidence could easily lead to their arrest.

In December 2006, Rule 41 of the Federal Rules of Criminal Procedure was modified and sets forth procedures for federal agents to obtain, process, and return warrants for installing and using tracking devices; federal magistrates may issue warrants authorizing the installation of such devices.

Source: Based on Keith Hodges, "Tracking 'Bad Guys': Legal Considerations in Using GPS" by Keith Hodges, *FBI Law Enforcement Bulletin,* July 2007.

YOUTUBE AND MYSPACE   The Internet is in a constant state of development, and there are certain sites that provide fun and relaxation and have become part of our pop culture. For example, there are 20 million visitors to the **YouTube** Web site each month, which lets users upload, view, and share video clips. Someone who is interested in people can find just about anything there; virtually any subject that can be videotaped is available. The police could not have created a tool this good and informative if they had tried, as it is probably the largest compilation of video intelligence ever assembled.[43]

MySpace is a social networking site where **blogs** are common, as are lists of "friends" or associations. By mid-2007, this Web site had more than 100 million user accounts and was growing at the rate of more than 250,000 accounts per day. Like YouTube, it is a gold mine of intelligence, with a massive, never-ending, ever-growing source of information.[44]

Police agencies that are able to take advantage of Web sites like YouTube and MySpace will be aided in researching criminal activity, performing investigations of all kinds (including background investigations), and understanding their communities.[45]

COMING ATTRACTIONS? AUGMENTED REALITY, UNMANNED AERIAL VEHICLES, AND "PREDICT-O-CAMS"

Three technologies that are in the early stages of development and may have an impact in the future are **augmented reality (AR)**, **unmanned aerial vehicles (UAVs)**, and the ability to predict and prevent crimes using software.

AR combines the real and the virtual, displaying information in real time.[46] AR is already here: In television broadcasts, yellow first-down lines are superimposed on a football field, and driver and speed information is tagged to race cars as they speed around a track. At a more advanced level, today's military fighter pilots can observe critical information superimposed on the cockpit canopy.[47]

Fundamentally, an AR system consists of a wearable computer, a head-mounted display, and tracking and sensing devices along with advanced software and virtual three-dimensional applications. AR has many possible uses in the future of policing, such as the following:

- Real-time language translation, along with data on cultural customs and traditions
- Real-time intelligence about crimes and criminals in the patrol area
- Facial, voiceprint, and other biometric recognition data on known criminals
- Integration of chemical, biological, and explosives sensors that detect local contamination
- Accessibility of scalable, three-dimensional maps (with building floor plans, utilities systems, and so forth),[48] including the ability of police SWAT officers to use advanced optics to zoom and use thermal and infrared imaging to locate fleeing criminals, as well as distinguish friend from foe and reduce or eliminate friendly fire casualties
- Speaker-recognition technology for investigative personnel to accurately match voices against those of known criminals and lip-read from a distance
- Thermal imaging to improve interrogations by indicating the truthfulness of suspects' statements to police and corrections personnel
- Video feeds for supervisors from personnel on the street or prison so that they can determine what their personnel are seeing in real time and monitor the physical status of their personnel during critical incidents[49]

A number of issues would accompany the planned adoption of AR. Would AR bring us dangerously close to a real-life "Robo-Cop" scenario in the future? The answer to that question is in the eye of the beholder. It cannot be doubted, however, that AR technology and the aforementioned uses will soon be available and could provide the criminal justice system with a degree of efficiency and effectiveness never seen before.

Another technology that warrants being followed closely is UAVs—powered aerial vehicles that do not carry human operators. They use aerodynamic forces to provide air vehicle lift, and are designed to carry less-lethal payloads for missions such as reconnaissance, command and control, and deception. UAVs are directed by a ground or airborne controller and come in a variety of designs and sizes, ranging from those that can mimic a hummingbird (with a 6-inch wingspan and is outfitted with video and audio equipment) to one with a longer wingspan than a Boeing 747. More than two dozen companies in the United States are involved in production or prototyping of UAV products.[50]

Although UAV research and development is now almost totally in the military domain, its potential uses for law enforcement are limitless. As examples, a low-flying UAV could patrol a given stretch of road, looking for high-speed offenders; images could be sent to a monitor in a patrol car along with the vehicle's rate of speed, direction of travel, and GPS coordinates, which can be map overlaid for the officer on the ground.[51] UAVs could also provide real-time reconnaissance, surveillance, and target spotting in a variety of situations.[52]

Other technologies that are being explored by the military and private research laboratories in certain situations include the following:

- A portable, battery-powered sonic rifle that fires "bullets" of earsplitting noise (as high as 140 decibels), creating the equivalent of an instant migraine headache
- A sprayable slime that makes walkways and other surfaces as slippery as ice
- The world's foulest odor, termed a "souped-up version of human waste"

Each of these projects focuses on exploiting the body's senses.[53]

Finally, in Chapter 5 we discussed predictive policing, a relatively new approach to crime-fighting wherein police monitor crime data and query a computer system for historical and real-time patterns to better predict where crimes are likely to occur. In that connection, a new "smart camera" is now being tested that sends caution alerts on a flat-screen monitor that are triggered by sensors strategically located across the city. Operators scan live video feeds to search for signs of suspicious behavior that might predict a crime in progress, and can then rapidly dispatch the nearest available patrol officer to the scene to catch the offender in real time. In order to become smarter, the system also records and stores in its database such behavior patterns as loitering, groups chasing cars, or a car slowly creeping around a corner near a pedestrian.[54]

Although violent crime in the test site of East Orange, New Jersey—where 10 such cameras are in use—has dropped by two-thirds, there are skeptics. One academic believes it is a "nice idea," but that there is "no reason to believe it will work."[55] Another asks, "Can you generate probable cause?" while cautioning that while our society does not wish to stifle innovation, "you want to structure it so that it has scientific, ethical, and legal control over technology."[56]

COURT TECHNOLOGIES

Overarching Goals: Achieving Paper on Demand and Other New Tools

Certainly a major goal for all courts in the United States is to go "**paper-on-demand**" (POD)—a term used by court administrators and judges to denote an environment in which the routine use of paper no longer exists in general; rather, paper may be used for court business only rarely, and as a last resort. The ultimate goal is that there are no more lost files, receipts could be issued electronically, all police citations are issued electronically, all filing formats and forms were standardized, all judges use POD, and there are no more folders in the courtroom.[57]

Although it may be a long time before the POD goal is attained, today an increasing proportion of administrative, civil, and even criminal cases are being presented with technology. Many people would agree that the use of technologies allows for better presentation of information and permits courtroom options not otherwise possible. Examples would include videoconferencing, which allows remote witness testimony as well as remote foreign language and American Sign Language interpretation. The most basic form of courtroom presentation technology—a document camera and a projector—can be purchased for less than $3,000. Adding a laptop computer to the system gives counsel even greater opportunities. Relatively inexpensive programs such as PowerPoint (www.microsoft.com), Presentations, Acrobat, and even Word and WordPerfect can be used for case presentations.[58]

Thomas M. Clarke, Vice President for Research and Technology of the National Center for State Courts, recently threw down the gauntlet for judges and court administrators in terms of escalating and expanding their application of court technologies. Clarke noted that courts have been improving service via technology for decades, but that the time has come for courts to use technology to a far greater extent, to reengineer their operations. While most courts have made modest improvements in their use of automated case management systems that enhance record-keeping, case scheduling, and management reporting, many of them have simply automated existing court business processes.[59]

Reengineering their court's systems, Clarke argues, involves using technologies to dramatically change business processes and create efficiencies. Doing so can be achieved only if technology projects are designed and implemented for such broad purposes as:

- how the litigants and attorneys will access the courts
- how records of court events will be kept and made accessible to the public
- how judges will access documents needed to write their decisions
- how hearings will be conducted and how the record will be made and retained[60]

Emerging Technologies

Following are several areas in which technologies are emerging:

The Electronic File. Through electronic case filing, courts can realize dramatic increases in efficiency and reductions in related costs—in clerical staff alone. Electronic filing also enables some court services—such as the payment of fines and fees, collection of fines and penalties, providing case information and documents to the public, and jury management—to be centralized or regionalized for improved efficiency and service. In addition, an electronic case file enables a court to better distribute its workload across the system.

Digital Recording. Significant savings can be realized by replacing court stenographers with digital audio- or video-recording equipment. Many states have used digital recording extensively, and some states have used digital recording exclusively for many years without experiencing significant issues. Budgetary issues have caused a number of states to take the step to dramatically reduce their use of court reporters, and that trend is expected to continue.

Conducting Hearings via Videoconferencing. Videoconferencing has rapidly improved in both cost and quality over the last few years. Prices for basic capabilities have been reduced considerably, while the quality of the networks has steadily improved. Now much of the emphasis is being devoted to how to best design rooms that serve as videoconferencing facilities—with the goal of reproducing the experience of actually talking to a person.

Challenges of Implementing Technology

Clark noted, however, that there are several challenges to the courts becoming fully reengineered:

Current Court Capabilities and Resources. Each court is in a different place on the long journey to implement all of the technology capabilities that a modern court wants. Full implementation requires human and monetary resources that will be difficult for some courts to develop and obtain.

The Importance of Effective Project Management. Although it is definitely possible to implement some or all of these technology capabilities in ways that will reap the intended efficiencies, there are risks involved, particularly where courts are inexperienced in managing or staffing such projects. Therefore, proper attention to project management and risk mitigation is required.

The Importance of Effective Change Management. Most daunting is that these technologies necessarily require significant cultural changes on a court and its staff. Such organizational change is never easy or painless; one can easily imagine the difficulty, say, in transitioning to digital recording from the longstanding system of court reporters who are in court in person. As with any organization, courts can only absorb so much change at one time.

Impact on Access to the Courts. Some citizens still do not have Internet access at their home, and some may even have difficulty accessing it at a public facility. Therefore, their taking care of court business online may be difficult if not impossible. Furthermore, centralizing or regionalizing court functions may require in-person, over-the-counter, or courtroom interactions may impose travel requirements that limit access to justice.[61]

Exhibit 16.4 is a very good example of the strategic plans, goals, and objectives that are being established by some courts in order to become more high-tech while ensuring that their citizens are receiving the best possible services given the extant technology.

EXHIBIT 16.4

Court Technology Strategic Plan for Nebraska

To demonstrate the types of planning as well as the extent to which work is being done to expand court technologies, following are selected portions of Nebraska Supreme Court's Strategic Plan, as amended in 2009:

MISSION STATEMENT

To proactively represent the computing, communications, and information technology concerns of the judicial branch and legal community in visioning, policy setting, and strategic planning. To provide timely input, advice, and feedback to the Chief Justice on policy, proposals, implementation projects, and other information technology related issues. To be a catalyst within the judicial branch in adapting technology to meet the mission of the judiciary and the needs of the people of the State of Nebraska.

- Identify and define court technology improvements.
  - Utilize digital recorders to replace analog tape recorders in county courts
  - Initiate electronic filing services in the trial courts

- Establish the use of the E-Citation in more jurisdictions and accept credit card payments for paying fines and fees
- Establish the minimum hardware requirements for evidence presentation in trial courts
- Implement electronic or credit card payment in courts
- Participate in planning for network and technology services in new or remodeled courtrooms
- Plan for and participate in the implementation of video arraignment technology in trial courts.
- Participate and plan for the use of Remote Video Interpreter services
- Create and define technology training for court staff
  - Provide appropriate software (word processing, spreadsheet, presentation, and e-mail) for trial court staff
  - Provide computer or Web-based technology training to court staff
  - Participate in Court Improvement Project (CIP) funding for juvenile court projects
- Create centralized and uniform Web site information standards and guidelines for trial courts
  - Plan and deploy standardized trial court Web pages on the Supreme Court Web site
- Identify appropriate communications bandwidth services for all courts.
  - Work to ensure the appropriate amount of bandwidth is available to all courts to engage in judicial proceedings
  - Anticipate and plan for increased technical capabilities in courts, including use of the Internet, digital video, audio recordings, remote access to a court
- Plan for the "Pro Se" filer to use technology through public access.
  - Plan for the "Pro Se" client when developing technical applications. Anticipate how the general public will communicate with the courts when deploying new technology
- Provide rural courts the same technical functionality as urban courts
  - Provide additional personal computer hardware for trial court staff.
  - Ensure an equal distribution of technology assets and functionality between rural and urban courts
- Plan and assist Specialty Courts use of technology
  - Work closely with all state specialty courts to appropriately invest in new technology that meets the needs of the courts

Source: Based on Nebraska Supreme Court Technology Committee, *Nebraska Supreme Court Technology Committee Strategic Plan 2006–2011*, pp. 31–32, available at: http://www.supremecourt.ne.gov/court-information-tech/court-information-tech.shtml (accessed October 20, 2010).

Telephonic Court Appearances

Each day throughout the United States, thousands of lawyers travel to courts to make brief appearances that may not require their physical presence in the courtroom. At today's high hourly rates, even 30 minutes of lawyers' travel time that can be avoided—through telephonic court appearances—can mean substantial savings. Prior attempts at telephonic appearances often failed because courts did not utilize appropriate technology. Using the wrong speakerphone equipment usually results in "voice clipping" and inconsistent call quality. Appropriate full-duplex speakerphone equipment properly placed in the courtroom is essential. Amplified audio conferencing equipment with port capacity to permit multiple callers and multiple cases to be routed simultaneously is also desirable. Furthermore, each judge should maintain full authority over which types of proceedings can and will be suitable for telephonic appearances. And for the program to flourish, it must be voluntary and permit attorneys to have full discretion as to when to use it.[62]

Center for Legal and Court Technology

In 1993, the College of William and Mary Law School and the National Center for State Courts unveiled the **Courtroom 21 Project**—now known as the Center for Legal and Court Technology (CLCT)—in Williamsburg, Virginia; at that time, it was the most technologically advanced courtroom in the United States, although some of its original features are not in use today. Today this project—with its abundance of courses, publications, and consulting and other services—appears to remain the preeminent "go-to" site for learning about the world of courtroom technologies.[63]

Now termed the "dream technology court" and the "world's center for experimental work,"[64] CLCT has approximately 25 affiliates worldwide, each using Courtroom 21 technologies in actual court proceedings.[65] The hub of the project, and its experimental center, is the McGlothlin Courtroom at William and Mary's law school.[66] A retrofitted courtroom in which the latest technology has been installed, it is the most technologically advanced trial and appellate courtroom in the world. The facility is capable of carrying out almost anything that needs to be done in a courtroom, including electronic filing; Internet-based case docketing; sophisticated electronic case management; presenting electronic motions, briefs, and arguments; multiple concurrent appearances by judges, lawyers, parties, and witnesses; technology-based evidence presentation; immediate Web-published court records; connectivity at the counsel table for lawyers; technology-aided foreign language interpretation; jury box computers for information display (for documents, real evidence, live or recorded videos, transcription, and the usual graphics—charts, diagrams, pictures); and LEXIS legal research. Judges and counsel are provided immediate access to legal resources through the LEXIS online legal database. If an unanticipated legal question arises during a trial, judges and counsel can use the computers to consult the database and do much more.

A well-known aspect of Courtroom 21 is its annual one-day "Lab Trial," involving a simulated case that affords an opportunity for CLCT tech staff to field-test how court technologies can be helpful as well as how they might create challenges (such as their ability to provide equal courtroom access to judges, lawyers, witnesses, and jurors with a variety of disabilities). By experiencing the uses of technologies in a lab situation, they can be better adapted to use in real trials.[67]

Exhibit 16.5 discusses another state-of-the-art courtroom, located at The National Judicial College in Reno, Nevada.

EXHIBIT 16.5

Teaching High-Tech: Model Courtroom Technologies at The National Judicial College

The National Judicial College in Reno, Nevada, like the Courtroom 21 Project in Virginia, has a state-of-the-art model courtroom, with a top-notch digital audio–video system, an evidence presentation system, and a convenient cable management system, and serves as a blueprint for other courtrooms. Created with technology donated by several vendors, the 2,700-square-foot courtroom is entirely American Disabilities Act accessible. It has a false floor with an 8-inch space above the concrete sub-floor, allowing for a computer lab and hidden wires within. The audio–video system enables Web conferencing and records everything going on in the courtroom; the system includes five cameras and a tape back-up system, which eliminates the need for a court report. The system is voice-activated. Evidence can be digitally displayed to jurors so that the evidence can be viewed more closely without having to be passed around. As a safety feature, the judge's bench is fully armored; it not only deflects bullets, it *catches* them, protecting everyone against bullet ricochets. Teleconferencing ability saves the attorneys and the court money; if a trial is not in session and the judge is deciding motions, attorneys can be in court without physically driving there. The courtroom is used for mock and actual trials, role-playing, sentencing exercises, and technology demonstrations.

Source: Based on Heather Singer, "Court Technology Partners," *Case in Point,* Winter/Spring 2005. Reprinted with permission from The National Judicial College. Copyright protected. www.judges.org.

Real-Time Court Reporting

Many people assume that court reporters would be opposed to reporting technology, as it would replace them altogether. But the fact is that court reporters have been at the forefront of applying digital technology to their work. Computer-aided transcription, real-time translation, and video-text integration have enhanced the functioning of the judicial system.[68]

Traditionally, a record of court proceedings has been taken manually (using a stenotype machine). A transcript of the record must then be made and delivered—sometimes weeks after the proceeding ends. Some court reporters now offer **real-time court reporting**, however, which allows the reporter to publish live testimony to a laptop and then connect the attorneys' laptops to the court reporting network. While the proceeding is in progress, a transcript of it is electronically transmitted to the laptop.

During the trial, judges and attorneys can also review and mark portions of testimony and make notes within their copies on their computer screens without interrupting the proceedings. They can also perform searches for specific words, phrases, roots of words, and other, more complicated information instantaneously. During the trial, judges can thus be signing orders and taking care of routine matters, and when there is an objection, all they need do is look at the monitor and have the exact testimony, questions, and objection for them to make a correct ruling.

At the end of the proceeding, the reporter can give the attorneys an uncertified rough draft transcript, with the official copy following sometimes just a few hours later. Reporters can also e-mail transcripts to attorneys or file them electronically with the court, protecting the record by applying a digital signature that ensures the integrity of the record.

EXHIBIT 16.6

Using Wi-Fi to Improve Jury Attendance

Many people would rather ignore their jury summons than have to miss a day's pay by leaving work. Harris County, Texas, which encompasses Houston, is hoping that a new free-to-use Wi-Fi network installed for the county's 700-seat jury assembly room will increase the rate of people who show up when summoned—which has been a dismal 20 percent. This low turnout limits the pool for jury selection and also forces the county to pay for mailings of reminder notices and new summonses—amounting to hundreds of thousands of dollars.

The county is now using a free, filtered Wi-Fi network that will enable telecommuting for those citizens waiting in the jury assembly room in downtown Houston. If this method of communicating with potential jurors improves the jury turnout by just five percent, it would save the government $100,000 in mailings.

Source: Based on Matt Williams, "Free Wi-Fi Could Boost Jury Duty Attendance, Cuts Costs in Houston's Harris County," *Government Technology,* July 9, 2009, http://www.govtech.com/e-government/Free-Wi-Fi-Could-Boost-Jury-Duty.html (accessed November 4, 2010).

INSTITUTIONAL CORRECTIONS

Putting Down a Riot

With America's prison population growing (see Chapter 9), the need for COs to develop tactics and equipment to handle outbreaks of violence has also risen. Although full-scale riots are rare in American prisons, potentially violent situations (such as inmates' refusing to leave their cells) can occur almost daily.

Today there are wall-climbing reconnaissance robots and futuristic "sound cannons" designed to sweep rioters into a corner or stun them with a blast of noise. There is a Hydro-Force fogger (a cross between a fire extinguisher and a can of Mace). A rolling barrier with wheels and side shields prevents officers from being struck by thrown objects.[69] A "stinger" grenade that explodes and emits dozens of hard rubber pellets is particularly useful in a cafeteria or yard riot.

COs often train with such devices in full view of the inmates to show the kinds of tools that can be employed. According to one prison administrator, what separates prison professionals from inmates is constant training and measured, unflappable control.[70]

EXHIBIT 16.7

"Heating Up" Jail Inmates

If a fight breaks out inside one Los Angeles County jail, inmates might get shot with a tiny wave from a device that penetrates the skin to heat up nerves. The Assault Intervention Device (AID) is a 7.5-foot-tall nonlethal weapon that transmits a focused, invisible beam at a specified target, causing an unbearable burning sensation. The device was unveiled in August 2010 in a 6-month experiment to see if the tool will help stop or lessen the severity of inmate assaults. When inmates fight in a dormitory, dining room, or exercise yard, deputies typically must wait for backup before they can intervene. AID would allow them to act sooner, potentially reducing injuries and curbing violence.

As with many police technologies, the AID has its roots in the military, which is testing larger versions for battlefield use. Using a joystick and computer monitor, deputies operate the apparatus, which emits an invisible beam with a range of about 80 to 100 feet. The millimeter wave travels at light speed and penetrates the skin up to 1/64 of an inch and warms up the nervous system's heat receptors. The inmate who is hit by the heat wave instinctively moves out of the beam, which makes the pain go away. The sensation is described as being similar to touching a hot stove or feeling a sudden blast of heat from the oven.

The device is not intended to become the weapon of choice in the jail; rather, it is one of many less-lethal jail tools, including tear gas, rubber bullets, and batons. The evaluation of AID, conducted in cooperation with the National Institute of Justice and Pennsylvania State University, is to examine whether the technology will impact overall patterns of jail violence.

Source: Based on Russell Nichols, "Los Angeles County Jail to Heat Up Misbehaving Inmates with Target Wave Technology," *Government Technology*, August 25, 2010, http://www.govtech.com/dc/articles/768970 (accessed November 4, 2010).

Offender Management

Technology is changing the methods of **offender management** as administrators increasingly adopt Web-based systems to manage the flow of information. New Web-based technology is now used to educate prisoners, treat prisoners who are addicted to drugs or are sex offenders, and provide vocational training. Prison administrators now keep accurate records of inmates' purchases for items in the prison store, payments to victims and their families, and other reasons for which money flows in and out of prisoners' bank accounts.[71] Automated systems control access gates and doors, individual cell doors, and the climate in cells and other areas of the prison. Corrections agencies have also used computers to conduct investigations of presence, supervise offenders in the community, and train correctional personnel. With computer assistance, jail administrators receive daily reports on court schedules, inmate rosters, time served, statistical reports, maintenance costs, and other data.

Exhibits 16.8 describes how serious adult and juvenile offenders are now being tracked using GPS bracelets.

EXHIBIT 16.8
Using GPS Bracelets to Track Offenders

In an experiment, prisoners in Nevada are required to wear global positioning devices on their wrists to track their locations at all times. Following are some of the anticipated benefits:

- An alarm will sound if an inmate enters an off-limits area or tries to escape
- In the case of a prison brawl, the devices will show the corrections staff who was in the area where the fight occurred
- If an inmate claims to have been assaulted by a prison guard, there will be a record of whether the inmate was at the correctional officer's post

It is also expected that the devices (which cost $375 each) will substantially increase the level of control without increasing staff.[1]

In Multnomah County, Oregon, the Department of Community Justice is using ankle bracelets to track juvenile gang members in real time. Anti-gang funds were appropriated for a 5-month pilot program in order to try to prevent crime and gang activity. These monitoring systems typically consist of a GPS receiver/portable tracking device, radio frequency transmitter, stationary charging unit, cell phone, and computer software to review GPS data.

Some civil libertarians and youth advocates have concerns about the bracelets, however, because the technology is far from flawless. In many jurisdictions, false alarms have strained personnel and called the effectiveness of the tracking tool into question. One state found more than 35,000 false alerts by 140 subjects wearing the GPS-monitoring devices. Another concern is that the tool could be used as evidence against juveniles who are not involved in crimes. However, supporters say the program represents one piece of a broader crime-prevention strategy that includes a bike patrol to monitor gang hot spots and funding to support people who want to escape gang life.

[1] Based on Associated Press, "Prison Inmates to Wear GPS Tracking Bracelets," *Reno Gazette Journal,* June 13, 2006, p. C6.

[2] Based on "GPS Bracelets to Track Juveniles in Multnomah County, Ore.," *Government Technology,* October 11, 2010, http://www.govtech.com/geospatial/GPS-Bracelets-Multnomah-County-Ore.html# (accessed October 17, 2010).

Automated Direct Supervision in Jails

Direct-supervision jails are springing up across the country, without the typical jail cells with steel bars. Some of these facilities are replacing the bars with bar-coded wristbands and state-of-the-art computerized information management systems. As one data communications engineer stated, "Everything from the toilets to the telephones is fully computerized" in these facilities.[72]

The information technology package used in these kinds of facilities includes live-scan fingerprinting, an automated fingerprint identification system, digitized mug shots, and computerized inmate and records management. Each inmate's wristband is keyed into the central computer system, which contains his or her name, physical description, picture, and prisoner number; the system is used to track each inmate's location, visitors, library use, medical treatment, and court appointments. The system is expected to reduce costs, provide a new level of records integrity, and increase the safety of both officers and inmates by allowing the administrators to develop a completely cashless inmate society. Without cash and with limits set on how much an inmate can spend each week, COs hope to curtail contraband problems. This cashless system virtually eliminates the illicit transactions that once were common because the administration can now regulate and monitor the flow of goods and services.[73]

"Virtual Visits" to Hospitals and Courtrooms

Prison and jail inmates make frequent visits to hospitals and courtrooms, which creates public safety concerns. In Ohio alone, 40,000 inmate trips to and from medical facilities were eliminated because videoconferencing technology—**virtual visits**—made medical consultations available from within the institution. An onsite prison physician or nurse assists with the physical part of the examination, taking cues from the offsite specialist via video and relaying information such as electrocardiogram and blood pressure data.[74]

Increasingly, prisons are using video not only for medical visits but also for arraignments, parole violation hearings, and distance learning.

A BODY OF EVIDENCE: BIOMETRICS

In 2008, the FBI awarded a 10-year contract to significantly expand the amount and kinds of biometric data it receives, embarking on a $1 billion effort to build the world's largest computer database of people's physical characteristics. Digital images of faces, fingerprints, and palm patterns are already flowing into FBI systems, and in the coming years, law enforcement agencies around the world will be able to rely on iris patterns, face-shape data, scars, and perhaps even the ways people walk and talk, to solve crimes and identify criminals and terrorists. If all goes as planned, a police officer making a traffic stop or border check could run a check on a suspect and within seconds know if the person is in a database of the most wanted criminals and terrorists.[75]

The project, operated by the FBI's Criminal Justice Information Services Division, has already been expanding in the federal government in recent years. More than 1.5 million database images of fingerprints, irises, and faces have been stored of Iraqi and Afghan detainees, Iraqi citizens, and foreigners who need access to U.S. military bases. The Department of Homeland Security has been using iris scans at some airports to verify travelers' identities.[76]

The increasing use of **biometrics** for identification is raising questions about the ability of Americans to avoid unwanted scrutiny. It is drawing criticism from those who worry that people's bodies will become their national identification cards. Furthermore, skeptics say that such projects are proceeding before there is evidence that they reliably match suspects against a huge database. But government officials counter by saying that accuracy improves as techniques are combined; to safeguard privacy, audit trails are kept on everyone who has access to records in the databases; people may request copies of their records; and the FBI audits all agencies that have access to the database.[77]

Summary

This chapter examined the exciting technological advances that are in use by, or are being developed for, law enforcement, courts, and corrections organizations. This is an exciting time for criminal justice administrators and their subordinates; more new technologies than ever before are being made available to aid them. This chapter has shown the breadth of research and development that is underway.

The rapid expansion in computer technology, while certainly a strong advantage for society overall, bodes ill as well. The first problem lies in adapting computer technologies to the needs of criminal justice. Another consideration is that modern-day crooks and hackers can adapt and employ a variety of high-technology crimes and threaten the lives of all of us.

Obviously, many challenges remain. For example, we must continue to seek a weapon with less-lethal stopping power that can be employed effectively and safely by the police. We must also strive to enhance courts and corrections effectiveness and efficiency through electronic means. The challenges remain.

As has been noted, "It is not enough to shovel faster. Criminal justice must enter the Information Age by incorporating technology as a tool to make the system run efficiently and effectively."[78]

Questions for Review

1. What are some of the latest applications of technologies in policing, including developments in DNA, less-lethal weapons, and CompStat?
2. What are the uses of technologies as they involve crime mapping? Traffic and crime scene functions? Gang problems?
3. What does the field of robotics promise for the police?
4. How will augmented reality (AR) and unmanned aerial vehicles (UAVs) function, and how might they be used in law enforcement?
5. What are the major technological capabilities in use in the nation's courts, and what are some technological tools now emerging—particularly those seen in the Courtroom 21 Project and The National Judicial College?
6. What can technologies offer to correctional institutions for putting down a riot? Managing inmates?
7. What is meant by *biometrics,* and what are its potential advantages and problems?

Learn by Doing

1. Assume you are in the research, planning, and development unit of your police organization. Your chief executive officer has tasked you to "bring the agency into the new decade" by making recommendations concerning technologies that the department should acquire. Using information and descriptions of the technologies presented in this chapter, select and prioritize five new technologies (either extant or in development) that you believe your agency should obtain, and write a justification for each in terms of its crime-fighting capabilities.

2. You occasionally consult on justice system planning and operations, and have been contacted by a nearby county to examine its court functions. Apparently the former court administrator (Jameson) was popular and considered to be efficient because he always operated within his rather meager budget. You discover, however, that those low operating costs are due to his failure to incorporate any new court technologies. The court staff is largely untrained and using outdated, manual means of performing the court's functions. Jameson believed the county could well "survive without gimmicks" and did not wish to invest in technologies that he felt were not necessary. Recently, the county—and, by extension, the court—has witnessed considerable growth due to the influx of retiring baby boomers. With Jameson retired, the county manager is now learning how antiquated the court's functions really are, supports a major upgrade, and thus contacts you to learn of the available technologies. What will you report?

3. You are scheduled to deliver a lecture next week at the county sheriff's basic academy—where both police and jail personnel are attending recruit training—on the subject of technologies. One of the academy instructors calls you today and says those recruits who are going on road patrol appear to be very interested in the potential future applications of unmanned aerial vehicles and less-lethal weapons, while those who will work in the jail are quite interested in robots. Prepare a response.

Related Websites

Center for Legal and Court Technology
   http://www.legaltechcenter.net/about.html

Computer and Internet Security Resources
   http://virturallibrarian.com/legal

Criminal Justice Technologies
   http://www.crimjustech.com

International Encyclopedia of Justice Studies
   http://www.iejs.com/TechnologyandCrime/Law_
   Enforcement_Technology/less_than_lethal_weapons.htm

JUSTNET: Justice Technology Information Network
   http://www.nlectc.org/

National Defense Magazine
   http://www.nationaldefensemagazine.org/issues/2005/
   Jun/researchers_fill.htm

National Institute of Justice Technology Publications
   http://www.ojp.usdoj.gov/nij/sciencetech/publications.
   htm

Police Science and Technology
   http://www.homeoffice.gov.uk/science-research/using-
   science/police-science-tech/

Technology and Privacy (Home Page of Gary T. Marx)
   http://web.mit.edu/gtmarx/www/garyhome.html

Notes

1. See RCFL National Program Office, "About RCFLs," http://www.rcfl.gov/index.cfm?fuseAction=Public.P_about, and http://www.rcfl.gov/index.cfm?fuseAction=Public.P_locations (accessed July 3, 2009).

2. Hilton Collins, "The Computer in your Hand," Government Technology (March 2009), http://www.govtech.com/gt/624307 (accessed July 3, 2009).

3. Jim McKay, "Cops on the Tweet to Solve Crimes and Educate the Public," http://www.govtech.com/gt/717300 (accessed November 24, 2009).

4. Jim McKay, "Lost in Translation," Government Technology (July 2005): 56.

5. Jim McKay, "Getting the Picture," Government Technology (January 2009), pp. 22–24.

6. Merrill Douglas, "Putting Violence on the Map," Government Technology (June 2006): 50.

7. Jim McKay, "Good Science or Just Bunk," Government Technology (June 2006): 46–48.

8. "DHS Completes Foundation of Biometric Entry System," http://www.govtech.net/magazine/channel_story.php/97728 (accessed January 6, 2007).

9. Terry L. Knowles, "Meeting the Challenges of the 21st Century," *The Police Chief* (June 1997):39–43.

10. Federal Bureau of Investigation, *Combined DNA Index System (CODIS),* http://www.fbi.gov/hq/lab/org/systems.htm (accessed March 3, 2007).

11. National Conference of State Legislatures, "Postconviction DNA Motions," http://www.ncsl.org/programs/health/genetics/dnamotions.htm (accessed March 3, 2007).

12. U.S. Department of Justice, Federal Bureau of Investigation, "FBI Announces Contract Award in Information Sharing Program," http://www.fbi.gov/pressrel/pressrel07/ndex021607.htm (accessed April 23, 2008).

13. U.S. Department of Justice, Federal Bureau of Investigation, "N-DEx: Entity Correlation—Scenario 1," http://www.fbi.gov/hq/cjisd/ndex/ndex_overview.htm (accessed April 23, 2008).

14. "Rethinking Stopping Power," *Law Enforcement News* (November 15, 1999):1, 9.

15. Personal communication, Hilary Gibeaut, TASER International, Inc., September 14, 2009.

16. Ibid.

17. *Medical News Today,* "Study Suggests Taser Use by U.S. Police Is Safe," October 9, 2007, http://www.medicalnewstoday.com/articles/84955.php (accessed November 16, 2007).

18. Ibid.

19. "Rethinking Stopping Power," *Law Enforcement News* (November 15, 1999):5.

20. "Effectiveness Times Three," *Law Enforcement News* (May 15, 1993):1.

21. Ibid., p. 6.

22. "Rethinking Stopping Power," p. 5.

23. Brian Huber, "Wisconsin Police Get Robo-Cop's Help," PoliceOne.com, http://www.policeone.com/police-technology/robots/articles/1190983/ (accessed April 2, 2007).

24. PoliceOne.com, "Remote-controlled Throwable Robot Developed by Carnegie Mellon with Marines Sent to Iraq for Testing," http://www.policeone.com/police-technology/robots/articles/91534/ (accessed April 2, 2007).

25. James Hannah, "New Robot Line Will Improve Bomb Detection," Associated Press, April 2, 2007, http://www.dailybreeze.com/business/articles/6807622.html (accessed April 2, 2007).

26. Ibid.

27. Daniel DeLorenzi, Jon M. Shane, and Karen L. Amendola, "The CompStat Process: Managing Performance on the Pathway to Leadership." *The Police Chief*, http://policechiefmagazine.org/magazine/index.cfm?fuseaction=display_arch&article_id=998&issue_id=92006 (accessed November 17, 2010).

28. Heath B. Grant and Karen J. Terry, *Law Enforcement in the 21st Century* (Boston: Allyn & Bacon, 2005).

29. Ibid.

30. Lois Pilant, "Computerized Crime Mapping," *The Police Chief* (December 1997):58.

31. Dan Sadler, *Exploring Crime Mapping* (Washington, DC: U.S. Department of Justice, National Institute of Justice, Crime Mapping Research Center, 1999), p. 1.

32. Pilant, "Computerized Crime Mapping," p. 58.

33. Ibid., pp. 66–67.

34. National Institute of Justice, Crime Mapping Research Center, http://www.ojp.usdoj.gov/cmrc (accessed September 19, 2005).

35. Alison Bath, "Accident Scene Investigation Is High Tech," *Reno Gazette Journal* [Sparks Today section], November 18, 2003, p. 4.

36. Ibid.

37. http://www.jaycor.com/jaycor_main/web-content/eme_ltl_auto.html (accessed September 20, 2005).

38. Tod Newcombe, "Adding a New Dimension to Crime Reconstruction," *Government Technology* 9 (August 1996):32.

39. John McCormick, "Scene of the Crime," *Newsweek* (February 28, 2000):60.

40. Joan Raymond, "Forget the Pipe, Sherlock: Gear for Tomorrow's Detectives," *Newsweek* (June 22, 1998):12.

41. Raymond Dussault, "CAL/GANG Brings Dividends," *Government Technology* (December 1998):124.

42. For an excellent analysis of whether or not the mere attaching of GPS to a vehicle is a "search," see Andre A. Moenssens, "Attaching a GPS Locator System to a Car: Is It a 'Search'?" Forensic-Evidence.com, http://www.forensic-evidence.com/site/Police/GPS_onCar.html (Accessed September 2, 2011).

43. Thomas M. Manson, "Emerging Technologies for Law Enforcement," Commission on Accreditation for Law Enforcement Agencies, CALEA Update 94 (June 2007):1, 12–14.

44. Ibid., p. 13.

45. Ibid., p. 14.

46. Thomas Cowper, "Improving the View of the World: Law Enforcement and Augmented Reality Technology," *FBI Law Enforcement Bulletin* (January 2004):13.

47. Ibid., p. 15.

48. Ibid., p. 16.

49. Chris Forsythe, "The Future of Simulation Technology for Law Enforcement: Diverse Experience with Realistic Simulated Humans," *FBI Law Enforcement Bulletin* (January 2004):19–21.

50. See Julie Watson, Tiny spy planes could mimic birds, insects," Associated Press, February 28, 2011, http://news.yahoo.com/s/ap/20110228/ap_on_re_us/us_hummingbird_drone (accessed March 1, 2011); also see Brian P. Tice, "Unmanned Aerial Vehicles: The Force Multiplier of the 1990s," http://www.airpower.maxwell.af.mil/airchronicles/apj/4spr91.html (accessed January 17, 2004).

51. "UAV One—The Unmanned Aerial Vehicle Source," http://www.uav1.com/ (accessed January 17, 2004).

52. Tice, "Unmanned Aerial Vehicles."

53. Seth Hettena, "Military Developing Non-Lethal Weapons," Associated Press (March 24, 2002).

54. Russell Nichols, "Smarty Cams," *Government Technology,* November 2010, pp. 28–30.

55. Dennis Kenny, quoted in Ibid., p. 28.

56. Peter Scharf, quoted in ibid., p. 30

57. Fredric I. Lederer, Tom O'Connor, and Timothy A. Piganelli, "Courtroom Technology," http://www.abanet.org/genpractice/magazine/2008/jun/courtroomtech.html (accessed October 20, 2010).

58. National Center for State Courts, "Future Trends in State Courts 2010: Technology Reengineering," http://www.ncsconline.org/D_KIS/Trends/index.html (accessed October 20, 2010).

59. Ibid.

60. Ibid.

61. Based on Ibid.

62. Robert V. Alvarado, Jr., and Mark Wapnick, "Telephonic Court Appearances: An Easy Way to Reduce Litigation Costs," *Case in Point,* Winter/Spring 2006. Reprinted with permission from The National Judicial College. Copyright protected. www.judges.org.

63. Center for Legal and Court Technology, "About the Center for Legal and Court Technology: Introduction," http://www.legaltechcenter.net/about.html (accessed July 22, 2008).

64. Jim McKay, "Technology on Trial," *Government Technology* (December 2002):83.

65. Ibid.

66. Fredric I. Lederer, "The Courtroom 21 Project: Creating the Courtroom of the Twenty-First Century," *Judges' Journal* 43(1)(Winter 2004):39–40.

67. See Center for Legal and Court Technology, "Experiments and Lab Trials," http://www.legaltechcenter.net/aspx/Experiments%20and%20Lab%20Trials.aspx (accessed February 8, 2011).

68. "Real-time Court Reporting: Taking Technology to a New Level," *Case in Point* (Reno, NV: The National Judicial College, Fall–Winter 2003):10–11.

69. Thomas Hayden, "Putting Down a Riot," *U.S. News and World Report* (June 14, 2004):72–73.

70. Ibid.

71. Shane Peterson, "The Internet Moves Behind Bars," *Government Technology* (Supplement: *Crime and the Tech Effect*) (April 2001):18.

72. Raymond Dussault, "Direct Supervision and Records Automation," *Government Technology* 8 (August 1995):36.

73. Ibid., p. 37.

74. Jim McKay, "Virtual Visits," *Government Technology* (October 2001):46.

75. Federal Bureau of Investigation, "FBI Announces Contract Award for Next Generation Identification System," http://www.fbi.gov/pressrel/pressrel108/ngicontract021208.htm (accessed February 12, 2008).

76. Ellen Nakashima, "FBI Prepares Vast Biometrics Database," *The Washington Post,* http://www.msnbc.msn.com/id/22366208/ (accessed December 22, 2007).

77. Ibid.

78. George Nicholson and Jeffrey Hogge, "Retooling Criminal Justice: Inter branch Cooperation Needed," *Government Technology* 9 (February 1996):32.

APPENDIX I

Case Studies

PART 1   JUSTICE ADMINISTRATION: AN INTRODUCTION

Chapter 2   Organization and Administration: Principles and Practices

I. Targeting Tattoos

You are a police chief in a medium-sized city and have just received information from a captain that one of your officers, Newton, has recently had a swastika tattooed on one arm and a naked woman on the other. The captain says that both tattoos are visible in the summer uniform and, as news is spreading about these adornments, an increasing number of officers are becoming offended and some are even saying that they will refuse to respond to any calls for service with Newton. Based on this information, you believe that the tattoo may violate the city's policy against workplace harassment and quickly call Newton into your office. He admits having the tattoos but rather sarcastically states that he has a "liberty" interest under the Fourteenth Amendment and a right to "expression" under the First Amendment.

He adds that for you to try to control such activity would constitute a "hostile" work environment. You know that there is currently no policy that prohibits the displaying of any tattoos, let alone any that are offensive.

Questions for Discussion

1. Can you take any action in response to the complaint?
2. Do you have the right to reasonably regulate the appearance of employees and require a professional appearance?
3. If you implement a policy against such tattoos, does the rule impermissibly discriminate against Newton?
4. Can you use to advantage any U.S. Supreme Court decisions in response to this matter?

PART 2   THE POLICE

Chapter 3   Police Organization and Operation

I. Malfunction Junction

Junction City, a rapidly growing community of 150,000 residents, is an agriculturally based area located in the center of the state, about 20 miles from the ocean. The city gains a population of 10,000 to 20,000 visitors a day during the summer months, when ocean recreation is a popular activity. Owing to local growth in the meat-packing industry, the city's demographics are changing rapidly, especially its blue-collar population. The

downtown area of the city has slowly deteriorated over the past few years, resulting in increased crime and disorder. A property tax cap has resulted in reduced revenues to local jurisdictions, and the recent recession has taken a substantial toll on the city's budget; the result has been significant reductions in staffing. The police department now has 100 sworn and 35 nonsworn personnel, and has experienced its share of budget cuts and staff

413

reductions. The chief of police of 10 years' duration retired recently, leaving an agency that is still very traditional in nature and has a growing number of desk-bound administrative personnel and degree of rank structure (corporal, sergeant, lieutenant, captain, deputy chief, commander, and chief). The morale of the department is poor because of the increases in workload resulting from tourism and agricultural expansion. You have been hired as the new police chief. As a result of the current situation, the city manager and council are calling for an emergency meeting with you to discuss the future of the department. They explain that at a recent council retreat, they heard a consultant's presentation on the implementation and operation of community policing and problem solving. They are now seeking your views on this strategy, its potential for Junction City, and how you might approach its implementation. (*Note:* They emphasize that you have to explain how you might reorganize the police department to move away from its current traditional organization, with only one police facility and its administration- and rank-laden status.)

Questions for Discussion

1. Do you envision any problems with traditional-thinking officers and supervisors still working in the organization? If so, how will you handle their concerns?
2. Using the seven elements of police organizational structure described in this chapter, where does it appear that you would need to reorganize the agency, especially to accommodate Community Oriented Policing and Problem Solving (COPPS)?
3. Would you anticipate that the officers' workload would be reduced or increased under the COPPS strategy?
4. What types of information would you use to evaluate the progress of your community policing initiative?

II. Sins and the City

Officers assigned to your district have been responding to a number of noise complaints, reckless driving incidents, and fight calls in the area of 7500 Commercial Row. This area contains a number of restaurants, bars, and several strip malls that attract juveniles and young adults. Within the past week, there have also been three gang-related drive-by shootings and seven gas drive-offs. A majority of the underage adults are attracted to the area by a dance club located in one of the strip mall centers and two all-night fast food restaurants. All three locations attract large crowds that loiter and drink alcohol in their parking lots. The owners of the shopping centers and restaurants have also complained about thousands of dollars in vandalism caused by the loitering youths.

Question for Discussion

1. How would you use the S.A.R.A. (scanning, analysis, response, and assessment) process to address this problem?

Chapter 4   Police Personnel Roles and Functions

I. Intruding Ima and the Falsified Report

An 8-year employee of your police agency, Officer Ima Goodenough, is a patrol officer who often serves as a field training officer. Goodenough is generally capable and experienced in both the patrol and detective divisions. She takes pride in being of the "old school" and has developed a clique of approximately 10 people with whom she gets along while mostly shunning other officers. As an officer of the old school, she typically handles calls for service without requesting cover units or backup. She has had six complaints of brutality lodged against her during the last 3 years. For Ima and her peers, officers who call for backup are "wimps." She has recently been involved in two high-speed pursuits during which her vehicle was damaged when she attempted to run the offender off the road. Ima will notify a supervisor only when dealing with a major situation. She is borderline insubordinate when dealing with new supervisors. She believes that, generally speaking, the administration exists only to "screw around with us." You, her shift commander, have been angry about her deteriorating attitude and reckless performance for some time and have been wondering whether you will soon have occasion to take some form of disciplinary action against her. You have also learned that Ima has a reputation among her supervisors as being a "hot dog." Some of her past and present supervisors have even commented that she is a "walking time bomb" who is unpredictable and could "blow" at any time.

One day, while bored on patrol, Ima decides to go outside her jurisdiction, responding to a shooting call that is just across the city limit and in the county. She radios the dispatcher that she is out "assisting," then walks into the home where paramedics are frantically working on a man with a head wound lying on the floor. Nearby on the floor is a large foreign-made revolver; Ima holds and waves the revolver in the air, examining it. A paramedic yells at

her, "Hey! Put that down, this may be an attempted homicide case!" Ima puts the revolver back on the floor. Meanwhile, you have been attempting to contact Ima via radio to get her back into her jurisdiction. Later, when the sheriff's office complains to you about her actions at their crime scene, you require her to write a report of her actions. She completes a report describing her observations at the scene but denies touching or picking up anything. Looking at Ima's personnel file, you determine that her performance evaluations for the past 8 years are "standard"—average to above average. She has never received a suspension from duty for her actions. Although verbally expressing their unhappiness with her for many years, Ima's supervisors have not expressed that attitude in writing.

Questions for Discussion

1. What are the primary issues involved in this situation?
2. Do you believe that there are sufficient grounds for bringing disciplinary action against Goodenough? If so, what would be the specific charges? What is the appropriate punishment?
3. Do you believe that this is a good opportunity to terminate Ima's employment? Do grounds for termination exist?
4. Does the fact that Ima's supervisors have rated her performance as standard have any bearing on this matter or create difficulties in bringing a case for termination? If so, how?

Chapter 5   Police Issues and Practices

I. Bias-Based Policing or Good Police Work?

Officer James and Sergeant Drummond are on surveillance in a strip mall. A detective received an anonymous tip that a credit union might be robbed at 3:00 P.M. The detective also told the patrol division that the person providing the tip is a known

drug addict and not at all reliable, but as there has been a string of credit union robberies during the past 2 months, Drummond decides to surveil the area with Officer James. The main suspects in the robberies are Asians, and the officers have stopped and talked with several Asian people in the area, taking their names and other identifying information. At approximately 2:45 P.M., Drummond and James are notified by Communications that a security officer reported hearing a gunshot in the parking lot of a nearby grocery store where he was working. Because they are nearby and there might be a connection to the credit union robberies, Drummond and James decide to take the call. On arrival at the scene, the security officer meets the two officers and informs them that he "might have" heard a small-caliber pistol shot in the parking lot; he also believes that a young black man who walked into the grocery store a few minutes ago might be carrying a gun under his coat. About 10 minutes later, a 30-year-old black man comes walking out of the store. The officers draw their guns and order him to get down on the asphalt and to their vehicle. At that time, an Asian woman carrying a child approaches the officers, yelling at them that the man is her husband and demanding to know what they are doing to him. The officers order her to go her car, whereupon she faints while suffering an epileptic seizure. The black man, seeing his wife and child on the ground, now becomes very agi-tated; as a result, the officers use considerable force to subdue and handcuff him. He is arrested for resisting arrest and a host of other offenses; later, he sues for violation of his civil rights.

Questions for Discussion

1. Did the officers have just cause to be engaged in the initial (credit union) surveillance? To question Asian people in the area? Defend your answer.
2. Did the officers violate the black man's civil rights? Why or why not? If you answer "yes," would you support (as the chief of police) some form of disciplinary action against them?
3. Should the woman be entitled to collect damages? Why or why not?
4. In which (if any) aspects of this scenario do you believe the officers are guilty of engaging in racial profiling? Explain your answer.
5. Assume that this case led to a public outcry for a citizen review board to examine questionable police activities and recommend disciplinary and policy actions. Would you support the creation of such a board? Why or why not?

II. Adapting to the Responsibilities of the Role

Sergeant Tom Gresham was newly promoted and assigned to patrol on the graveyard shift; he knew each officer on his shift, and several were close friends. Gresham was an excellent patrol officer, and prided himself on his reputation and his ability to get along with his peers. He also believed this trait would benefit him as a supervisor. From the beginning, Gresham believed that he could get more work from his officers by relating to them at their level. He made an effort to socialize with them after work and took pride in giving his team the liberty of referring to him by his first name. Gresham also believed that it was a supervisor's job to not get in the way of good police work. In his view, his team responded magnificently, generating the highest number of arrest and citation statistics in the entire department. Unfortunately, his shift also generated the highest number of citizen complaints for abusive language and improper use of force, but few complaints were sustained by Internal Affairs. It was Gresham's opinion that complaints are the product of good, aggressive police work. He had quickly developed the reputation among subordinates of being "a cop's cop."

One Monday morning, Gresham is surprised when called in to see you, his patrol captain. The Internal Affairs lieutenant is also present. You show Gresham a number of use-of-force complaints against his team over the past week, while Gresham was on vacation. Despite your efforts to describe the gravity of the situation, Gresham fails to grasp the seriousness of the complaints and how his supervisory style may have contributed to them.

Questions for Discussion

1. What do you believe are some of Sergeant Gresham's problems as a new supervisor?
2. As his captain, what advice would you give Gresham?
3. What corrective action must Gresham take immediately with his team of officers?

PART 3   THE COURTS

Chapter 6   Court Organization and Operation

I. Chief Judge Cortez's Embattled Court

You have just been hired as the new court administrator for a medium-sized court with approximately 90 employees. Once on the job, you discover that you have been preceded by two heavy-handed court administrators who together lasted less than 1 year on the job because of their inability to handle employee conflicts and to achieve a minimal level of productivity. They were more or less forced to resign because of a lack of employee cooperation and increasing talk of unionization. There is general turmoil and distrust throughout the organization. Employees do not trust each other, and as a group, they do not trust management. The courthouse runs on gossip and inertia. There is very little official communication throughout the organization. Prior court administrators made no attempt to solicit employees' opinions or ideas. The judges are all aware of the problem, but they have formed no clear consensus on how to respond to it. In fact, there is turmoil and conflict among the judges themselves. They engage in "turf protection" with operating funds and the court's cases and often take sides in office squabbles. As a result, they are unable to achieve a clear consensus or to provide the court administrator with any guidance. The chief judge, Dolores Cortez, has served in that capacity for 10 years and is known to be exceedingly fair, compassionate, and competent; however, she is approaching retirement (in 6 months) and appears unwilling to take a firm stand on, or a strong interest in, addressing intraoffice disputes and difficulties. In fact, she is not altogether convinced that there is a problem. Furthermore, in past years, she has been quite reluctant to intervene in arguments between individual judges.

Questions for Discussion

1. As the "new kid on the block," how would you respond to this organizational problem? What is the first issue you would address, and how would you address it? What additional problems require your attention?
2. As court administrator, how would you respond to the inability of the judges to develop a consensus? How could the decision-making process be improved?
3. What techniques could be employed to improve communication throughout the organization, lessen tension and strife, and generally create a more harmonious work environment?
4. What would be your general approach to Judge Cortez? To her successor?

II. What action, which court? A quiz[1]

1. Melvin entered a federally insured bank and robbed money from the safe. In which level of court will this case most likely be filed?

   Your Answer: federal   state   either

2. Two weeks later, Melvin robbed a man who had just taken money out of an ATM machine in a grocery store. Where will this case most likely be filed?

   Your Answer: federal   state   either

3. Mary works for a local criminal justice agency; she claims that her supervisor refused to promote her because she is related to his ex-wife. Where will Mary file this case?

   Your Answer: federal   state   either

4. True or false? There are two kinds of courts in the federal court system: the trial court and the Supreme Court.

   Your Answer: True   False

5. True or false? A person accused of a crime is generally charged in a formal accusation. The name of this accusation for a misdemeanor is called an indictment.

   Your Answer: True   False

Answers

1. The correct answer is "federal." Because this crime was committed within the bank and is a theft of the bank's money, which is insured by the federal government, it is a federal crime and would be filed in federal court.

2. The correct answer is "state." Because the money had already come out of the ATM machine and was in the man's possession, the victim was the man and not the bank. Thus, it is a state crime and it would be tried in state court.

3. The correct answer is "either." Both federal and state laws prohibit gender discrimination, and plaintiffs in employment discrimination cases may sue in either federal or state court.

4. The correct answer is "false." The federal system is composed of trial courts and appellate courts. The Supreme Court is the highest appellate court but not the only appeals court.

5. The correct answer is "false." The document charging a person with a misdemeanor is called an information. An indictment is used for felonies or serious crimes.

[1]Adapted from the Federal Judicial Center, "Inside the Federal Courts: What the Federal Courts Do," http://www.fjc.gov/federal/courts.nsf/autoframe!openform&nav=menu1&page=/federal/courts.nsf/page/172 (accessed October 25, 2010).

Chapter 7   Court Personnel Roles and Functions

I. The Court Administrator and the Prudent Police Chief

You are the court administrator in a system that has the following procedure for handling traffic matters:

1. All persons who are given a traffic citation are to appear in court at 9:00 A.M. either on Monday or Wednesday within 2 weeks of their citation date. They are given a specific date to appear.

2. Persons cited are not required to appear; they have the option of staying home and simply forfeiting their bond, which has been posted in advance of their initial appearance.

3. At the initial appearance, the arresting agency is represented by a court officer who has previously filed copies of all the citations with the clerk of the court.

4. The clerk, prior to the return date on the citation, prepares a file for each citation.

5. The clerk calls each case, and those persons appearing are requested by the court to enter a plea; if the plea is "not guilty," the matter is set for trial at a future date.

6. One case is scheduled per hour. On the trial date, the prosecutor and arresting officer are required to appear, ready for trial.

7. Statistics show that 75 percent of those persons pleading not guilty in this jurisdiction fail to appear for trial.

The chief of police in the court's jurisdiction is concerned about overtime for officers. He communicates with you, the court administrator, about this issue and explains that all police officers who appear in court for trial are entitled to the minimum 2 hours of overtime when they are not appearing during their regular shift. He views this as a tremendous and unnecessary expense to the city in view of the fact that most of the officers are not needed because the defendants do not appear and wishes to devise some system to save the city this high overtime cost.

Questions for Discussion

1. What system would you propose for solving the problem—within the existing law, with no changes in statutes or ordinances?

2. After you have finished designing a system, including how you would obtain the cooperation of the judges, prosecuting and defense attorneys, clerk's office, and other law enforcement agencies, discuss any proposed changes in the law that you think might improve the system further.

3. How would you go about making other significant, ongoing changes to improve the procedures and operation of this system?

Chapter 8   Court Issues and Practices

I. Carol's Construct for Court Chaos

Carol Smith, a divorced mother of one, employed as an assistant manager at a large discount center, was denied custody of her 10-year-old son following a bitter divorce (in which her husband accused her of neglect and inattentive behavior toward the child). In July, she filed several actions against the county and other parties, alleging violations of her civil rights. When these petitions were denied, she petitioned the state Supreme Court, writing a letter about her case that stated in part, "This county's courts and social services do not have a bit of compassion for anyone, and cared nothing about protecting my rights or administering due process to me. I should not have to be paying all of these lawyer's fees and losing so much sleep about getting my son back. No one should have to turn to such actions as the World Trade Center to get some proper attention, but that is the only thing some people will listen to." Smith later told former coworkers at a grocery store that if the state Supreme Court would not hear her case, she would go to the state capital "and shoot up the place." Then, when that court did decline to review her case, she became distraught. A number of her neighbors were very alarmed as she kept ranting about her violent intentions. One day she left her home and traveled to the state capital, where she went to the Supreme Court building. While there, she called a relative back home and stated that she had "found her purpose in life" that she "planned to shoot the top judge" and had bought a gun. The relative contacted the police, who arrested her for making threats against the judge's life.

Questions for Discussion

Looking at this case from a threat perspective:
1. What potential motives for her behavior first brought Carol Smith to official attention?
2. What events represented significant losses to her, which she found quite stressful?

3. What elements of the case point to her having a reasonable level of cognitive ability that would allow her to formulate and execute a plan if she chose to do so?
4. What communications and arrangements did she make that indicated that she planned to carry out her threat?
5. What events might have increased or decreased the likelihood of an attack?
6. Taken together, which events suggest that she was on a path toward a violent attack?

II. An Unmanageable Case-Management Quandary

You are the administrator for a court with 50 employees. This court, which used to dispose of about 700 cases per month, now hears an average of 100 criminal and 400 civil cases per month. Case filings have doubled in the past 7 years. The present "hybrid" combination of the individual and master case-management systems has evolved over a long period of time through tradition and expediency. A growing caseload and increasing difficulties in avoiding a backlog, however, have prompted the judges to rethink their present system. Criminal cases that formerly reached final disposition in 1 month now require 2 to 3 months. The situation shows no signs of improving in the foreseeable future. Again, the court has a mixed calendar system. Two judges are assigned to hear criminal cases and motions for a 1-month period, whereas the remaining four judges hear all manner of civil cases on a random basis on the filing of civil complaints. The judges are responsible for the management of these cases until final disposition. At the end of the 1-month period, the two judges hearing criminal cases return to the civil division and two other judges rotate onto the criminal bench; any pending criminal cases or motions are then heard by these two incoming criminal judges. One of the judges hears all juvenile-related cases in addition to any assignment in the criminal and civil divisions. The court collects statistics on the number of court filings and motions filed in each division on a month-to-month basis.

Questions for Discussion

1. In a general way, discuss both the merits and difficulties of this case-management approach. What are the general advantages and disadvantages of the individual and master calendar systems?
2. What specific problems could arise in the criminal division? Why?
3. What specific problems could be created by the permanent assignment of a judge to the juvenile division? What advantages might there be?
4. What changes would you recommend with regard to the court's statistical report? Are other data needed for management purposes? If so, what kind?

PART 4   CORRECTIONS

Chapter 9   Corrections Organization and Operation

I. As Bad as It Can Get

You are the deputy warden for operations in a comparatively small (500 inmates) maximum-security prison for adults. As is typical, you oversee correctional security, unit management, the inmate disciplinary committee, and recreation. One Wednesday at about 2:00 A.M., an inmate who is a minority group member with a history of mental health problems and violent behavior begins destroying his cell and injures himself by ramming into the walls. The supervisor in charge collects a group of four correctional officers with the intention of removing the inmate from his cell and isolating, medicating, and checking him for injuries. The group of four—all fairly new on the job, untrained in cell extraction or self-defense, and with no specialized extraction equipment—prepares to enter the cell. When the officers open the cell door, the inmate charges them, knocking two of them down. They finally wrestle the inmate to the floor, although he is still struggling. One officer attempts to subdue him by wrapping his arm around the inmate's neck, pressing on his carotid artery. Finally, the inmate quiets down and is restrained and removed to another, larger cell.

After 15 minutes, however, the inmate has failed to regain consciousness. A medical staff person rushes to the cell, sees the inmate in an unconscious state, and has him taken to a local hospital. After the inmate has remained comatose for 2 months and has been classified as brain dead, the family decides to remove the life-support system that has sustained him.

Questions for Discussion

1. What, if any, inmate rights are involved in this case?
2. Which, if any, of the inmate's rights were violated?
3. To what extent does the prison system's central office become involved? What kinds of policies need to be developed to cover similar occurrences in the future?
4. As deputy warden, what disciplinary action would you consider against the officers? Did the officers intend to harm the inmate?
5. What needs and problems require new policies? Facilities for mentally ill inmates? Officer training? Equipment?

II. When Politics Trumps Policy

For 2 years, you have been director of a prison system for adults in a medium-sized state. As a result of revenue shortfalls for several years, it has been a constant struggle to keep a full labor force in your state's 10 prisons and to lure professional staff members to work and live in the more rural areas where they are located. During the past 6 months, however, you have managed to assemble a fine staff of wardens and other subordinates in the prisons and have implemented a number of policies that provide for educational, vocational, and treat-

ment opportunities, which have been gaining national attention for their effectiveness. Recidivism has been reduced to 30 percent, and your policies are beginning to be accepted by staff and citizens alike. Running a "Take Back the Streets" anticrime campaign, a politically inexperienced person (formerly a popular college quarterback playing at a state university) was recently elected governor. The new governor has just sent you a letter stating in effect that your institution is not the "Ritz" and demanding that all "frivolous, namby-pamby programs teaching the ABCs and where cons learn how to hammer nails" cease immediately. He asks for your written response, a plan for tightening security, and the implementation of tougher inmate programs within 1 month.

Questions for Discussion

1. How would you respond? Would you just capitulate and end some or all of these programs? Explain your answer.
2. Is there any room to negotiate with the governor? As a trade-off, would you offer to put in place some programs that are known to be tough on inmates? If so, what kind?
3. Before dismantling your policies and programs, would you attempt to see how much internal and external support you have for them? If yes, whom would you contact and how?
4. How might you go about demonstrating how successful your policies have been?

III. "Out-of-Town Brown" and the Besieged Probation Supervisor

Joan Casey is a career probation officer. She majored in criminal justice as an undergraduate, holds memberships in several national correctional organizations, attends training conferences, and does a lot of reading on her own time to stay current in the field. Casey began working for the Collier County Probation Department soon after she graduated from college and was promoted to a supervisory position, where she supervises an adult probation unit consisting of eight seasoned probation officers. The unit is responsible for investigating approximately 80 offenders a month and preparing presentence investigation (PSI) reports on them. Collier County's Probation Department made the front page of the local newspapers twice in the past month. Both times it was a nightmare for the chief probation officer, Jack Brown, and the entire agency. "Northside Stalker Gets Probation!" screamed the first headline, and then, just a week later, "Collier County Soft on Crime!" Brown called a management team meeting: "Better PSIs," he said, "or heads are gonna roll!" Everybody got the point. This week Brown is on annual leave and Casey is the designated officer in charge. One of Casey's probation officers has recommended intermediate sanctions for a 23-year-old man who murdered his stepfa-

ther with a knife after suffering many years of physical and mental abuse. The young man had no prior record and had been an incest victim since he was 5 years old; he is considered an otherwise nonviolent person, a low recidivism risk. Casey is aware of the probation officer's recommendation and agrees with it. However, she receives a call from a well-known veteran local television anchor—a strong crusader in the local war against crime. He knows the young man will be sentenced tomorrow.

Questions for Discussion

1. What should Casey's response be to the reporter (other than hanging up or telling him to call back) concerning the agency's recommendation?
2. If Casey elects to discuss her officer's recommendation for some form of intermediate sanction, how can she justify such sanctions in general and in this case specifically?
3. Do you feel that the probation officer's recommendation based on these facts is correct? Why or why not?
4. Which form of intermediate sanction would appear to hold the most promise for the offender in this case?

Chapter 10   Corrections Personnel Roles and Functions

I. The Wright Way

Lieutenant Bea Wright has been in her current position in the state prison for 1 year and is the shift supervisor on the swing (evening) shift, which consists of 20 officers. There is also a recreation and development lieutenant who oversees the yard, commissary, and other high-use areas during the shift. Wright begins at 4:00 P.M. by holding a roll call for officers, briefing them on the activities of the day, any unusual inmate problems or tensions in progress, and special functions (such as Bible study groups) that will be happening during the evening. Soon after roll call, Wright has the staff conduct the very important evening count—important because inmates have not been counted since the morning. At about 5:00 P.M., Wright determines that there are only four COs in the dining room with 1,000 inmates, so she contacts other units (such as education, library, and recreation) and asks them to send available staff to the dining hall for support. After dinner, Wright finds a memo from the warden asking her to recommend ways of improving procedures for having violent inmates in the Special Housing Unit (SHU) taken to the recreation area in the evening. Wright asks two of her top COs who work in the SHU to provide her with some preliminary information concerning the system in place and any recommendations they might have. While walking the yard, Wright observes what appears to be an unusual amount of clustering and whispering by inmates by race; she asks a sergeant to quietly survey the COs to determine whether there have also been unusual periods of loud music or large amounts of long-lasting foodstuffs purchased in the commissary (together, these activities by inmates might indicate that a race war is brewing or an escape plan is being developed). Furthermore, as she is on the way to her office, an inmate stops her, saying that a group of inmates is pressuring him to arrange to have drugs brought into the prison and he fears for his safety. Wright arranges for him to be called out of the general population the next day under the guise of being transported to a prison law library, at which time he can meet privately with an investigator and thus not draw suspicion to himself for talking to the staff. At about 9:00 P.M., Anderson, a CO, comes to her office to report that he overheard another CO, Jones, making disparaging remarks to other staff members concerning Anderson's desire to go to graduate school and to become a warden some day. Anderson acknowledges that he does not get along with Jones and is tired of his "sniping," and he asks Wright to intercede. She also knows that Jones has been argumentative with other staff members and inmates of late and makes a mental note to visit with him later in the shift to see if he is having personal problems.

Questions for Discussion

1. Does it appear that Lieutenant Wright, although fairly new in her position, has a firm grasp of her role and performs well in it?
2. In what ways is it shown that Wright seeks input from her subordinates?
3. How does she delegate to and empower her subordinates?
4. Is there any indication that Wright is interested in her COs' training and professional development?
5. In which instances does Wright engage in mediation? In management by walking around?

II. "Cheerless Chuck" and the Parole Officer's Orientation Day

"So, you are the new parole officer with a criminal justice degree from the university? Well, I hope you last longer than the last recruit I had. She meant well, but I guess her idealistic ideas about the job of parole officer could not handle the realities of the work. In a way, I understand what she went through. Same thing happened to me 12 years ago when I started this job. There, I was fresh out of college with a brand new diploma. It did not take me long to realize that the real world was different from what I had learned in college. The crises we deal with here make it darned difficult to do the work we all see needs to be done. Years ago, when I first started with the parole department, things were a lot better than they are now. Caseloads were lower, fewer people were getting parole who did not deserve it, and the rest of the criminal justice system was in a lot better shape, which made our jobs a lot easier to do.

Think about it. We vote in politicians who promise the public that they are going to 'get tough' on crime, and the first thing they do is allot more money for law enforcement stuff: beat cops, car computers, helicopters, and so on. These things are great, but all they do is add more people to a system that is already overloaded. No one gets elected by promising to build more courts or add jail and prison space or hire more probation and parole officers. Eventually, these added police officers arrest more people than the system can handle. The courts back up, which in turn messes up the prisons and the jails. The inmates stuck in these crowded places get tired of living like sardines, so they sue the prisons and jails. Remember, the Constitution prohibits cruel and unusual punishment. A lot of times inmates' complaints are legitimate, and they win. The judge orders the prison to lower its population to a reasonable level, which forces the parole board to consider more inmates for early release. Nobody mentions giving the parole department more officers or a bigger budget for added administrative help. No, the bucks go to the flashy, visible things such as cops and cars.

Meanwhile, in the past 10 years, our average caseload for a parole officer has increased 75 percent. We have more people who need supervision, and we are doing it on a budget that has not kept pace with the remainder of the criminal justice system. This would not be so bad if the system was at least adding things to other areas such as the jail or the courts. The problem here is that we depend on the jail to hold our parolees who have violated their conditions. We catch some of them using booze or drugs, and we are supposed to bring them into the county jail to wait for a hearing to decide whether they are going back to prison or back on the street. But the jail has its own set of problems. A couple of years ago, the U.S. district court slapped a population cap on our jail. If it goes over that population, the jail will not accept our violators. So we send them home. If they get into more serious trouble, we call it a new crime, the police arrest them, and the jail has to take them. Then, they have to sit and wait for the court to catch up because the courts are not in much better shape than the jail. I guess the job would be easier if the prisons were doing their jobs, too. I cannot really blame them because the prisons are funded in much the same way that parole is. We are not 'glamorous' places to send your tax dollars, but if the prisons were getting more money, they might be able to improve the quality of inmate they send to us. Maybe a little more vocational training and substance abuse counseling, so that they could stay off the booze and drugs. Possibly then fewer of these parolees would wind up back behind bars a few years later.

The worst part about the job is the caseload. We presently have so many on parole that I am lucky if I can get a phone call to each of them once a week and maybe a home visit once a month. The sad part about it is that with the proper budget and staff, we could really make a difference. We spend so much time bailing water out of the boat that we do not realize that there is no one steering and we are just drifting in circles.

By the way, my name is Charlie Matthews, but everyone calls me Chuck. I am a supervisor here as well as the designated new-employee orientation specialist and all-round public relations person. Welcome aboard."

Questions for Discussion

1. Should Chuck be retained as orientation coordinator? Why or why not?
2. How would changes in politics affect the parole system directly and indirectly?

3. How does an old criminal justice planning adage that "you cannot rock one end of the boat" seem to be applicable to what Chuck says about new police positions and the subsequent impact on the courts and corrections components?

4. What administrative problems and practices might be responsible for this agency's situation?

5. Why do crowded jails and prisons make the job of parole officers more difficult?

6. How could practices of the jails and prisons change the success of the parole system?

Chapter 11   Corrections Issues and Practices

I. Double, Double, Toil, and Trouble

There seems to be trouble brewing in a nearby medium-level adult prison. Inmate informers have noted several conditions indicating that a riot may be imminent: Inmates are stocking up on long-term items (e.g., canned goods) in the commissary and banding together more throughout the institution by racial groupings; furthermore, inmates are seen standing in or near doorways, as if preparing for a quick exit. Over the past several months, the inmates have become increasingly unhappy with their conditions of confinement—not only with the usual bland food, but also with the increasing number of assaults and gang attacks—and many are either very young, nonviolent offenders or very old and frail. The staff has also become increasingly unhappy, particularly, with their low salaries and benefits, perceived unsafe working conditions and attacks on officers, institutional overcrowding, the increasing number of sexual attacks among inmates, and greater amounts of drugs and other forms of contraband found in the cellblocks. They demand that the prison administration ask the courts to give more consideration to house arrest and other intermediate sanctions. They also want the legislature to consider privatization of the prison.

You are the state's prison system director. The governor's office has asked that you prepare an immediate position paper for the chief executive setting forth a plan for dealing with this prison's current situation.

Questions for Discussion

1. What are the critical issues that should be dealt with immediately?

2. How would you proceed to defuse the potential for a riot?

3. What would be your response to the suggestions for prison privatization and the use of intermediate sanctions?

4. What, if anything, might be done to address the concerns of the inmates? The staff?

II. A Corrections Futures Forum

Assume that your jurisdiction is planning a new weeklong futures-oriented program, "Leadership Forum for 2015," which will bring together professionals from the business and governmental sectors. Topics to be discussed at the forum include a wide array of area issues, challenges, methods, and concerns. Assume further that you are a prison or probation/parole administrator. After applying for and being selected to attend this program, you are advised that you are to make a 60-minute presentation concerning your profession generally, as well as the future challenges facing your local corrections organization.

Questions for Discussion

1. Using some of the materials discussed in this book, how would you briefly explain your role as a chief executive of your agency to this group?
2. What are some of the important *current* themes and issues that you would take to the

forum concerning a corrections administrator's job to indicate its complexities and challenges?
3. How would you describe the changing nature of the corrections administrator's role and the *future* issues and challenges of this position?

PART 5   ISSUES SPANNING THE JUSTICE SYSTEM

Chapter 12   Ethical Considerations

I. Setting Up Mr. Smith

Assume that the police have multiple leads that implicate Smith as a pedophile, but they have failed in every attempt to obtain a warrant to search Smith's car and home, where evidence might be present. Officer Jones feels frustrated and, early one morning, takes his baton and breaks a rear taillight on Smith's car. The next day he stops Smith for operating his vehicle with a broken taillight; he impounds and inventories the vehicle and finds evidence leading to Smith's conviction on 25 counts of child molestation and possession of pornography. Jones receives accolades for the apprehension.

Questions for Discussion

1. Do Officer Jones's ends justify the means?
2. What if he believes he is justified in "taking bad guys off the streets?"
3. What if he argues that he is correct in using this approach because he was molested as a child?
4. What constitutional issues are involved?

II. Burns Goes Ballistic

Officer Burns is known to have extreme difficulty relating to persons of color and others who are socially different from himself. This officer never received any sensitivity or diversity training at the police academy or within the department. His supervisor fails to understand the magnitude of the problem and has little patience with Burns. So, to correct the problem, the supervisor decides to assign Burns to a minority section of town so that he will improve his ability to relate to diverse groups. Within a week, Burns responds to a disturbance at a housing project where residents are partying noisily. He immediately begins yelling at the residents to quiet down; they fail to respond, so Burns draws his baton and begins poking residents and ordering them to obey his orders. The crowd immediately turns against Burns, who then has to radio for backup assistance. After the other officers arrive, a fight ensues between them and the residents. Several members of both sides are injured, and numerous arrests are made.

Questions for Discussion

1. How could the supervisor have dealt better with Burns's lack of sensitivity?
2. What should the supervisor/administration do with Burns?
3. Are any liability or negligence issues present in this situation?

III. Justice in Jeopardy?

A municipal court judge borrows money from court employees, publicly endorses and campaigns for a candidate for judicial office, conducts personal business from chambers (displaying and selling antiques), directs other court employees to perform personal errands for him during court hours, suggests that persons appearing before him contribute to certain charities in lieu of paying fines, and requires court employees to act as translators for his mother's nursery business.

Questions for Discussion

1. Which, if any, of these activities is unethical? Why?
2. Taken together, would these activities warrant the judge's being disciplined? Removed from office?

IV. Malice over Manners

You have been employed for 2 months as a corrections officer at a detention center with about 15 young offenders, most of whom have psychological problems. You are beginning to fit in well and to be invited to other staff members' social functions. During today's lunchtime, you are in the dining room and notice eight of the youths sitting at one table. One of them is an immature 18 years old whose table manners are disgusting. Today, he decides to pour mounds of ketchup over his meal, swirling it around his plate and then slurping it into his mouth. He then eats with his mouth open and spits the food across the table while talking. You, the other officers, and even other inmates are sickened by his behavior. A fellow officer, Tom, gets up and tugs the boy away from the table by his shirt collar. The officer sets the boy's tray of food on the floor and orders him to get down on all fours next to it. "Your manners are disgusting," Tom says. "If you are going to eat like a dog, you may as well get down on all fours like a dog; get down there and lick the food off the plate till it is clean." Tom later tells you that he acted out of frustration and the desire to use a "shock tactic" to change the boy's behavior.

Questions for Discussion

1. What, if anything, should you do in this situation?
2. Did Tom act professionally? Ethically?
3. Should you have intervened on the boy's behalf?
4. What would you do about this incident if you were the superintendent of this institution and it was reported to you?

Chapter 13   Rights of Criminal Justice Employees

I. A Neanderthal Lives!

You are an administrator in a small minimum-security facility where the day shift is composed of four veteran male officers and one new female officer. The woman is a member of a minority, has a college degree from a reputable out-of-state university, and is married to a member of the armed forces. There have been recent reports from your supervisors of obscene and racially offensive remarks and drawings turning up in the female officer's mailbox, but you have not seen any such materials, nor has the woman complained to you about such occurrences. Today, however, your day shift sergeant storms into your office with a piece of paper he says was just removed from a locker room wall. It shows a "stick figure" woman and contains several racial slurs and comments to the effect that "women do not belong in this man's business, and you should go back where you came from." The woman saw this material, and the sergeant says she is now in the conference room, crying, and distraught.

Questions for Discussion

1. What would you do about this situation? Should you ignore it? Call the female officer to your office?
2. If you bring her in and she says that you should just leave the matter alone, should you pursue it?
3. If you determine which officer is responsible for these materials, what disciplinary action (if any) would you deem warranted? On what grounds?

II. At the Heart of the Matter

A police sergeant suffers a heart attack and undergoes a triple bypass operation. Now 4 years later, he takes and passes the written and oral examinations for lieutenant but is denied promotion solely because of his heart attack. The agency claims that because lieutenants can be assigned as shift commanders, they must be able to apprehend suspects and engage in high-speed pursuits. In truth, middle managers in the agency are rarely involved in situations requiring high levels of physical stress. The officer has exercised regularly and has had a strong performance record prior to and after his heart attack. Medical opinion is that his health is normal for someone of his age. The agency has adopted community policing, providing the opportunity for a manager to be assigned to one of several lieutenant positions that do not entail physical exertion.

The sergeant sues the agency for violating provisions of the ADA.

Questions for Discussion

1. Is the sergeant "handicapped" within the meaning of the law?
2. Is the sergeant otherwise qualified for the position of lieutenant?
3. Was the sergeant excluded from the position solely on the basis of a handicap? Explain your answer.
4. Should the sergeant prevail in the suit? If so, on what grounds?[i]

[i]This case study is based on *Kuntz v. City of New Haven,* No. N-90–480 (JGM), March 3, 1993. Kuntz prevailed, was promoted, and won back pay, demonstrating to the court that his possible assignment to field duties would not be dangerous to him, to other officers, or to the public.

Chapter 14   Special Challenges: Labor Relations, Liability, and Discipline

I. Lost Love—and a Lost Laborer?

A police officer, Blake, is dispatched to a domestic violence call; on his arrival, a woman runs out of the house screaming, "Help me! He is going to kill me!" Her right eye is swollen. She also tells the officer, "I have had it with his drinking and womanizing and told him to pack up his things and go. That is when he began beating me."

You, a lieutenant, heard the call go out to Blake from Communications, but at shift's end you cannot find any offense report concerning the matter submitted by Blake. You ask Blake about the report, and he tells you that on entering the home he observed another officer, Carter, who works in your agency, who commented, "Thanks for coming out here, but things are cool now. She slapped me once, and I dealt with it. I admit I got a little out of hand, but it is under control. She is nothing but a cheating, money-grubbing louse." Blake admits that he purposely avoided completing a report, deciding to consider it "like an offsetting penalty in football" and to overlook the matter.

Questions for Discussion

1. What would you, as the lieutenant and shift commander, do about this situation?

2. Should you call the female victim, or Officer Carter, into your office for an interview?
3. What action should you take if you do bring them both in, separately, and they deny that the incident occurred?
4. Suppose that you bring the woman in and she indicates that she wants to drop the matter because "it has happened before"; do you pursue it?
5. If you determine that Blake is in fact culpable for not reporting the incident, what actions (if any) should you take? On what grounds?

II. Bicycle Blues in Baskerville

Baskerville has a population of about 100,000, with an ethnic composition of 52 percent Anglo, 38 percent African American, and 10 percent Latino. The police force, however, composed of 200 sworn officers, has only about 20 percent women and minority officers. The city's central business district has deteriorated since the opening of a new shopping mall on the outskirts of the city, and the chief of police is receiving pressure from the mayor and the governing board to reduce crime in the central business district—where the largest percentage of minorities and lower-income residents in the city resides. The chief of police receives a federal grant to implement a bicycle patrol unit composed of one sergeant and five patrol officers in the central business district. The Baskerville Police Association (BPA) is the certified collective bargaining agent for all police officers and police sergeants. The collective bargaining agreement has a seniority bidding clause for all shifts and certain designated job assignments, but the agreement does not include a bike unit. Therefore, the city attorney has advised the chief of police that he can select the five officers and one sergeant without complying with the collective bargaining agreement. The chief—under pressure

from the city manager, mayor, and council to ensure that women and minority officers are given preference for these new assignments—knows that if he follows the collective bargaining agreement, only the most senior officers and sergeants, all older white males, have a chance of getting the assignments. The chief posts a notice stating that officers can apply for the new bike patrol unit but he will ultimately make the selection without regard to seniority. Several senior officers and sergeants then file a grievance with the BPA alleging that the chief has violated the agreement's seniority bidding provisions. Next, several female and minority officers approach the BPA president and say that the association betrayed them by not upholding their right to gain these high-profile assignments. The local newspaper editorializes that the chief has made the right decision, if not legally, at least morally. If the dispute heightens, the chief of police knows that his job might be in jeopardy; conversely, the BPA president may face a recall election if he is perceived as letting the chief get away with violating the agreement—and also faces a divided membership if the BPA is perceived as fighting only for its older white male members.

Questions for Discussion

1. What are the key issues in this case?
2. What steps should be taken by the police chief and union leadership in response to this crisis?
3. Who are the key stakeholders in the situation, and what are their interests?
4. What options are available to the police leadership?

Chapter 15   Financial Administration

I. The Emptying Horn of Plenty

The chief of police in a small (20,000 population) city has seen nearly one-third of the agency's officers leave in the last year. Budget cuts, attrition, and better salaries in other regional agencies have been the impetus for the departures. Furthermore, the city council is proposing a 15 percent cut in the police budget for the coming year. Citizens are already complaining about delays in police responses and about having to drive to the police department to make complaints or to file reports. The county sheriff has offered in the local newspaper to provide backup for the city when needed, but the chief of police believes the sheriff to be power hungry and primarily motivated by a desire to absorb the city's police force into his agency. Severe cutbacks have already been made in the Drug Abuse and Resistance Education and gang prevention programs, and other nonessential services have been terminated. A number of concerts, political rallies, and outdoor events—all of which are normally peaceful—will be held soon during the summer months, requiring considerable overtime; the chief's view is that "It is better to have us there and not be needed than vice versa." Federal grants have run out.

One of the chief's staff suggests that the chief propose to the city council a drastic reduction in the city's parks, streets, or fire department budget, those monies being transferred to the police budget. The council, in turn, already wants to explore the possibility of hiring private security services for some events. Exacerbating the situation is the fact that violent crimes are increasing in the jurisdiction.

Questions for Discussion

1. What measures could the chief implement or propose to the council to slow or eliminate the resignations of sworn personnel?
2. How might the chief obtain more revenues or, alternatively, realize some savings for the department?
3. Should the chief go public with the idea of reducing budgets in the parks or other city departments?
4. How should the chief deal with the local sheriff's offer?

II. The Tourist Trap

You are a veteran in a medium-sized police department, with the rank of major, and are often asked to consult with and assist in writing grants for smaller police agencies that are experiencing problems. The City of White Springs is a rural community of about 3,000 year-round residents. However, given that it is both a prime skiing and shopping location, during the summertime and Christmas holidays, the tourist population easily doubles that number on any given day. Normally, there are few crime or traffic problems, but during the past few years the growing number of local beer taverns and nightclubs has increased the incidence of alcohol-related problems—fighting, domestic violence, drunk driving, and so on. A small military base about 40 miles away has increasingly contributed to these problems. Your force of seven full-time and four part-time reserve officers is becoming strained and burned out during these peak times. More and more time is also spent with false burglar alarms, starting dead batteries, unlocking vehicles, and so on. There is no more money in the budget for additional hires, and the department's $50,000 overtime budget has been exceeded the past 2 years, causing unhappy council members to dip into other municipal budgets to bail you out. The town's charter requires that all members of the police force be graduates of the state police academy or trained by the department (for reserve officers).

Questions for Discussion

1. What are the major issues involved?
2. What are some possible solutions to the problems?

APPENDIX II

Writings of Confucius, Machiavelli, and Lao-Tzu

The writings of certain major figures have stood the test of time. The analects of Confucius (551–479 B.C.E.) and the teachings of Machiavelli (1469–1527) are still quite popular today. Many graduate and undergraduate students in a variety of academic disciplines analyze the writings of both, especially Machiavelli's *The Prince*. Both men tend to agree on many points regarding the means of governance, as the following will demonstrate. After presenting some comments from each philosopher, I will consider their application to justice administration.

Confucius often emphasized the connection between morality and leadership, saying, for example:

> He who rules by moral force is like the pole star, which remains in its place while all the lesser stars do homage to it. Govern the people by regulations, keep order among them by chastisements, and they will flee from you, and lose all self-respect. Govern them by moral force, keep order among them and they will come to you of their own accord. If the ruler is upright, all will go well even though he does not give orders. But if he himself is not upright, even though he gives orders, they will not be obeyed.[1]

Confucius also commented on the leader's treatment of subordinates: "Promote those who are worthy, train those who are incompetent; that is the best form of encouragement."[2] He also felt that leaders should learn from and emulate good administrators:

> In the presence of a good man, think all the time how you may learn to equal him. In the presence of a bad man, turn your gaze within! Even when I am walking in a party of no more than three I can always be certain of learning from those I am with. There will be good qualities that I can select for imitation and bad ones that will teach me what requires correction in myself.[3]

Unlike Confucius, Machiavelli is often maligned for being cruel; the "end justifies the means" philosophy imputed to him has cast a pall over his writings. However, although he often seems as biting as the "point of a stiletto"[4] and at times ruthless ("Men ought either to be caressed or destroyed, since they will seek revenge for minor hurts but will not be able to revenge major ones,"[5] and "If you have to make a choice, to be feared is much safer than to be loved"[6]), he, like Confucius, often spoke of the leader's need to possess character and compassion. For all of his blunt, management-oriented notions of administration, Machiavelli was prudent and pragmatic.

Like Confucius, Machiavelli felt that administrators would do well to follow examples set by other great leaders:

> Men almost always prefer to walk in paths marked out by others and pattern their actions through imitation. A prudent man should always follow the footsteps of the great and imitate those who have been supreme. A prince should read history and reflect on the actions of great men.[7]

Machiavelli's counsel also agreed with that of Confucius with regard to the need for leaders to surround themselves with persons both knowledgeable and devoted: "The first notion one gets of a prince's intelligence comes from the men around him."[8]

But, again, like Confucius, Machiavelli believed that administrators should be careful of their subordinates' ambition and greed:

> A new prince must always harm those over whom he assumes authority. You cannot stay friends with those who put you in power, because you can never satisfy them as they expected. The man who

makes another powerful ruins himself. The reason is that he gets power either by shrewdness or by strength, and both qualities are suspect to the man who has been given the power.[9]

On the need for developing and maintaining good relations with subordinates, he wrote:

> If a prince puts his trust in the people, knows how to command, is a man of courage and doesn't lose his head in adversity, and can rouse his people to action by his own example and orders, he will never find himself betrayed, and his foundations will prove to have been well laid. The best fortress of all consists in not being hated by your people. Every prince should prefer to be considered merciful rather than cruel. The prince must have people well disposed toward him; otherwise in times of adversity there's no hope.[10]

In this era of collective bargaining and a rapidly changing workforce, contemporary criminal justice administrators might do well to heed the comments of Confucius and Machiavelli.

Perhaps a leader, in the purest sense, also influences others by example. This characteristic of leadership was recognized in the sixth century B.C.E. by Lao-Tzu, who wrote:

The superior leader gets things done

With very little motion.

He imparts instruction not through many words

But through a few deeds.

He keeps informed about everything

But interferes hardly at all.

He is a catalyst.

And although things wouldn't get done as well

If he weren't there.

When they succeed he takes no credit.

And because he takes no credit

Credit never leaves him.[11]

Notes

1. Confucius, *The Analects of Confucius,* Arthur Waley (trans.) (London: George Allen and Unwin, 1938), pp. 88, 173.
2. Ibid., p. 92.
3. Ibid., pp. 105, 127.
4. Niccolo Machiavelli, *The Prince,* Robert M. Adams (trans.) (New York: W. W. Norton, 1992), p. xvii.
5. Ibid., p. 7.
6. Ibid., p. 46.
7. Ibid., pp. 15, 41.
8. Ibid., p. 63.
9. Ibid., pp. 5, 11.
10. Ibid., pp. 29, 60.
11. Quoted in Wayne W. Bennett and Karen M. Hess, *Management and Supervision in Law Enforcement,* 3rd ed. (Belmont, CA: Wadsworth, 2001), p. 63.

INDEX